MAXWELL MACMILLAN CHESS SERIES

Play the Caro-Kann
Second Edition

Maxwell Macmillan Chess Openings

Executive Editor: PAUL LAMFORD
Technical Editor: JIMMY ADAMS
Russian Series Editor: KEN NEAT

Play the Caro-Kann
Second Edition

by
Egon Varnusz

MAXWELL MACMILLAN CHESS

MAXWELL MACMILLAN INTERNATIONAL PUBLISHING GROUP

UK/EUROPE/
MIDDLE EAST / AFRICA

Maxwell Macmillan International Europe,
Purnell Distribution Centre, Paulton, Bristol BS18 5LQ, UK.
Tel: (0) 761 413301.   Fax: (0) 761 419308.   Telex: 44713.

USA/CANADA/
LATIN AMERICA/
JAPAN

Macmillan Distribution Center,
Front & Brown Streets, Riverside, New Jersey 08075, USA.
Tel: (609) 461-6500.   Fax: (609) 764-9122.

AUSTRALIA/
NEW ZEALAND

Maxwell Macmillan Publishing Pty Ltd,
Lakes Business Park,
2a Lord Street, Botany, NSW 2019, Australia
Tel: (02) 316-9444.   Fax: (02) 316-9485.

PACIFIC RIM
(EXCEPT JAPAN)

Maxwell Macmillan Publishing Singapore Pte Ltd,
72 Hillview Avenue, No 03-00 Tacam House, Singapore 2366.
Tel: (65) 769-6000.   Fax: (65) 769-3731.

Copyright © 1991 Egon Varnusz

Second Edition 1991

Library of Congress Cataloging-in-Publication Data
(applied for)

British Library Cataloguing in Publication Data
A CIP catalogue record for this book is available
from the British Library

ISBN 1 85744 0137

Cover by Pintail Design
Printed in Great Britain by BPCC Wheatons Ltd, Exeter
Typesetting by A-Type, Ripponden

Contents

Preface

The present volume is a thoroughly revised version of the English edition of 1982. In 1982, my friend IGM Murray Chandler did an excellent job when updating my Hungarian book. The most recent illustrative games then had dated from 1981 whereas now the latest one was played in 1991. For this edition, I would like to thank Chris Dunworth for his help in editing the manuscript.

The world, and the Caro-Kann along with it, has changed significantly since 1981. A number of formerly irrelevant variations have become the focus of attention — let us just mention the 1 e4 c6 2 d4 d5 3 ♘c3 dxe4 4 ♘xe4 ♘d7 line, followed by the stunning 5 ♘g5!? which was practically unknown ten years ago. There are, of course, examples as it were of a reverse progress, most notably the fashionable Two Knights' variation of the sixties can hardly be seen in today's tournaments. The popularity of flexible, easily accessible lines has definitely increased. The author, in his infinite vanity, hopes that his work has also contributed to the popularity of the opening. *Play the Caro-Kann* has now been published in four languages and I most sincerely hope that this edition will again meet public interest.

EGON VARNUSZ
Budapest, 1991

Symbols

=	the position is even
∞	the position is unclear
±	White stands slightly better
∓	Black stands slightly better
±	White is better
∓	Black is better
+−	White is winning
−+	Black is winning
!	a good move
!!	an excellent move
?	an error
??	a gross blunder
!?	interesting, appears to be good
?!	risky, appears to be dubious
+	check

Introduction

BRIEF NOTES ON THE NAME, HISTORY AND CHARACTER OF THE OPENING

Two German players, Horatius Caro and Marcus Kann, introduced this defence into competitive practice during the second half of the nineteenth century. Romantic gambits were popular among players of the time, so it is hardly surprising that this defence was regarded as being dry and boring. Its popularity only began to grow after the discovery and general acceptance of the basic positional principles. Early in this century several masters recognized the advantages that it offered, and even a world champion, in the person of Capablanca, had it in his armoury. The great Cuban is acknowledged to have been an outstanding positional player, and later adherents of the defence were to be competitors of similar inclination (Flohr, Botvinnik, Smyslov, Petrosian, Karpov, etc.).

Black's first move (1 . . . c6 in response to 1 e4) is aimed at obtaining a foothold in the centre by way of d7-d5. The concept is strongly reminiscent of the French Defence, but the development of Black's queen's bishop is, as a rule, smoother. Admittedly it does have the inherent disadvantage, as compared to the French, that after 2 d4 d5 3 ♘c3 (3 ♘d2) Black, in the absence of any other useful move, has to part with his centre pawn by 3 . . . dxe4 — thus relaxing the tension in the centre.

The middlegames which develop from the Caro-Kann are generally sound and of a rather positional character. Direct attacks against the king are rare in the early stages of the game. Flexibility is one of the chief advantages; Black remains uncommitted to any particular pawn structure. None of his pieces have any sort of development difficulty that might influence the whole opening (remember the problems that the queen's bishop has in the Queen's Gambit Declined). The Caro-Kann Defence is clear, relatively easy to learn, and therefore an eminently practical system. You can usually find your bearings without being completely familiar with the theory. Only a few particularly sharp variations require theoretical knowledge. The fact that

Black is able to avoid the pitfalls of the dangerous gambits was evidently considered to be one of the Caro-Kann's advantages in the last century.

However, the disadvantages should not be swept under the carpet. The initiative rests principally with White, while in a number of variations Black can only achieve equality in positions of a simplified and drawn character. Yet it must also be said that the game does not proceed inexorably towards a quick draw, the reason being that the pawn structures are asymmetrical and there is no mutually open file that would lend itself to the early exchange of major pieces.

White frequently acquires a space advantage, due mostly to the absence of the centre pawn. Luckily, this is a type of advantage which is most difficult to capitalize on. Moreover, the danger of White overextending himself and throwing caution to the winds is always present.

Which variation should White choose?   We do not know which of the alternatives is the most dangerous. The choice also depends a lot on fashion. One master may prefer one particular variation, another a different one. Lesser players tend to follow suit. The variation 2 ♘c3 and 3 ♘f3 was very popular for twenty years, but is practically an extinct species in today's competition practice. 2 d3, on the other hand, is a move which not so long ago was hardly ever contemplated, and then only by reckless eccentrics. Nowadays it presents serious problems to those using the Caro-Kann.

The Panov Variation, which resembles the Queen's Gambit, has for decades been the critical test of the Caro-Kann Defence. This is the sharpest of the variations, and the complications arising frequently surpass those of the King's Gambit.

Instead the natural continuation 2 d4 d5 3 ♘c3 has proved its worth and has been popular right up to the present day. After 3 . . . dxe4 4 ♘xe4 the continuations 4 . . . ♗f5, or 4 . . . ♘d7 and 4 . . . ♘f6 are equally popular. If there is a main variation in the Caro-Kann, then this is it.

Finally it should be added that the continuation 2 d4 d5 3 exd5 cxd5 4 ♗d3 has also had its devotees at various times (Fischer!), though it has never been a main variation.

How should this book be used?   This volume, like so many other works dealing with opening theory, throws a vast number of variations at the reader. However, the memorizing of the whole material is neither necessary nor intended, so the reader should not lose heart. It is important, though, to learn those moves (generally of a sharp and combinative character) which are essential for a proper understanding of the variation. This does not, however, make up the major part of the material, which consists of examples showing the possibilities hidden in a given position. The reader will tend to forget them after playing them over, but he will still grasp the salient point. It will gradually become second nature to him.

The material used here is particularly suitable for this purpose. At a time when chess books more and more resemble logarithmic tables, the illustrative games in particular offer relief. The reader will have fun learning from them, he will understand the connections between the opening and the middlegame and sometimes even the endgame.

The author has endeavoured to sift out and evaluate everything that is essentially new in competition practice. It is up to the reader to judge how far he has succeeded in achieving this aim. It is this aim of the author's that also explains why some of the variations and evaluations in this volume differ from the material contents of earlier works.

Like all chess writers, the author of this book has borrowed many variations from the works of predecessors. The work of the German chess writer Rolf Schwarz, the Yugoslav *Encyclopaedia* and the theoretical articles of Alexander Konstantinopolsky, to mention but a few, have been particularly fertile sources. To them, and my fellow masters and friends, I would like to express my gratitude for their invaluable help.

1
Nimzowitsch (Smyslov) Variation: 4 . . . ♞d7

1 e4 c6 2 d4 d5 3 ♘c3 dxe4 4 ♘xe4 ♘d7

One of the most solid variations of the Caro-Kann. Black prepares for ♘gf6 without risking the break-up of his pawn structure, as in the next two chapters. White now has two major alternatives.

In **A** he develops normally with 5 ♘f3, when after 5 ... ♘gf6 he either retreats (6 ♘g3) or can choose the sharp 6 ♘xf6+ ♘xf6 7 ♘e5! after which Black must tread warily.

IN **B**, with 5 ♗c4 ♘gf6 6 ♘g5 White uses a blunt assault on f7 and e6 to slightly disrupt Black's normal development — continuing 6 . . . e6 7 ♕e2 (7 . . . ♗e7? 8 ♘xf7). With circumspect play, however, Black's

resources should be sufficient for equality in both lines. The main fault of the Smyslov tends to be that after Black has repulsed any assault, the level positions obtained make it difficult to play for a win.

Variation **C** (5 ♘g5) demonstrates that brand new ideas at the early stage of an opening can be found even today.

A: 5 ♘f3
B: 5 ♗c4
C: 5 ♘g5

Though less frequent, alternatives are not totally innocuous:

a) **5 ♕e2 e6** *(5 . . . ♘gf6?? 6 ♘d6 mate has happened!)* **6 ♗f4 ♘df6 7 0-0-0 ♘xe4 8 ♕xe4 ♘f6 9 ♕f3 ♕a5** = Dementiev–Kholmov, USSR 1970.

b) **5 ♗d3** transposes to **C**.

c) **5 ♘e2 ♘gf6 6 ♘2g3 g6** *(6 ... e6!? planning c5)* **7 ♗c4 ♗g7 8 c3 0-0 9 0-0 ♘d5?!** *(Better is 9 ... ♘b6.)* **10 ♖e1 e5 11 ♗g5 f6?** *(11 ... ♕b6 12 dxe5 ♘xe5 13 ♗xd5 cxd5 14 ♕xd5 ♗e6 ∞)* **12 ♗d2 exd4 13 cxd4 ♘7b6 14 ♗b3 ♔h8**

1

15 ♕c1 a5 16 a3 ♘c7?! 17 ♘c5! ±
Romanishin–Petrosian, USSR 1979 as
on 17... ♕xd4 18 ♗e3 ♕h4 19 ♘xb7.

A

5 ♘f3   ♘gf6

The logical follow-up to Black's
fourth move. Instead 5... ♘df6 looks
artificial:

a) **6 ♘g3** ♗g4 7 c3 e6 8 ♗e2 ♗d6
9 0-0 ♕c7 10 ♘e5 ♗xe2 11 ♕xe2 ♘e7
12 ♗g5 h6 13 ♗d2 c5 = Bivshev–
Reshko, USSR 1960.

b) **6 ♘c3** ♗g4! 7 ♗e2 e6 8 h3 ♗xf3
9 ♗xf3 ♗d6 10 ♕d2 ♘e7 11 ♘e4 ♘f5
12 c3 ♘h4 = Shishov–Kasparian,
USSR 1956.

c) **6 ♘c5** e6 7 ♘d3 ♗d6 8 ♘de5
♘e7 9 ♗d3 ♘g6 10 ♕e2 ± Karaklaić–
Mondaini, 1951.

d) **6 ♘eg5** ♗g4 *(6... h6? 7 ♘xf7! or
6... ♗f5 7 ♘e5 ♘h6 8 ♗c4 e6 9 f3 ±)*
7 ♗e2 ♗xf3 8 ♘xf3 e6 9 0-0 ♗d6 10
♗g5 ♘e7 11 c4 ♘g6 12 d5 cxd5 13
cxd5 ± Gligorić–Rabar, Yugoslavia
1948.

Here we divide with:

A1: 6 ♘g3
A2: 6 ♘xf6+

Others:

a) **6 ♗d3** ♘xe4 7 ♗xe4 ♘f6 8 ♗d3
♗g4 9 c3 e6 10 h3 ♗h5 11 ♗e2 ♗d6
12 ♘e5 ♗xe2 13 ♕xe2 ♕c7 14 f4 0-0
15 0-0 c5 ∓ H. Steiner–Flohr, Moscow
1946.

b) **6 ♘c3** ♘b6 *(6... ♕c7 7 ♗d3 e6
8 0-0 ♗d6 9 ♖e1 0-0 10 ♕e2 ♗f4 11
♘e4 ♗xc1 12 ♖axc1 b6 13 ♘e5 ∓
Smyslov–Füstér, Moscow 1949 or 6...
e6 7 ♗d3 c5 8 ♕e2 cxd4 9 ♘xd4 ♗c5
10 ♘b3 ♗d6 11 ♗g5 a6 12 0-0-0 ♕c7
13 ♔b1 0-0 14 ♘e4 ± Tal–
Shamkovich, USSR 1972)* 7 ♗f4 ♗f5
8 ♗d3 ♗xd3 9 ♕xd3 e6 10 0-0 ♗e7 11
♖fe1 0-0 12 ♘g5!? h6 13 ♘5e4 ♘bd5
= Antoshin–Flohr, USSR 1955.

c) **6 ♘ed2** e6 *(better 6... ♘b6 7 c3
♗f5! or 7... ♗g4! equalizing)* 7 g3! b6
8 ♗g2 ♗a6?! 9 c4 ♗b7 10 ♕e2 ♗e7
11 0-0 0-0 12 ♖e1 ♖e8 13 ♘e5 ±
Kavalek–Böhm, Amsterdam 1975.

A1

6 ♘g3   e6

Alternatives are inferior:

a) **6... g6** 7 ♗e2 ♗g7 8 0-0 0-0
9 ♖e1 b6 10 ♗f4 ♗b7 11 c4 ♖e8 12
♘e5 c5 13 ♗f3 ♕c8 14 d5 ± Geller–
Rogoff, Biel (izt) 1976 – fianchettoing
both bishops is too passive.

b) **6 . . . h5** *(rather artificial)* **7 ♗d3!**
e6 8 ♕e2 c5 9 ♗g5 ♕a5+ 10 ♗d2 ♕b6
11 0-0-0 cxd4 12 ♖he1 ♗c5 13 c3!
dxc3 14 ♗xc3 ♗xf2? 15 ♘f5! ♔f8 16
♘g5 ♗xe1 17 ♖xe1 ± Gurgenidze-
Kopilov, USSR 1958 while **7 ♗g5 ♕b6
8 ♗e2!? ♕xb2 9** 0-0 ♘d5 10 ♗c4 g6?
11 ♗xd5 cxd5 12 ♕d3 e6 13 ♖ae1
was very strong in Noordijk–Franken,
1951.

c) **6 . . . c5!?** is worth considering −
7 ♗c4 *(7 d5? ♘b6 8 ♗b5+ ♗d7
9 ♗xd7+ ♕xd7 10 c4 ♘xc4 11 0-0 g6 ∓
Tal–Savon, USSR 1970; 7 ♗d3 cxd4
8 0-0 g6 9 ♘xd4 ♗g7 10 ♖e1 0-0 11 c3
♘c5 12 ♗c2 ♗g4! ∓ Zapata-
Spiridonov, Moscow 1989; 7 c3 e6
8 ♗c4 cxd4 9 ♘xd4 ♘e5 10 ♗b3 ♗c5
11 0-0 0-0 12 ♕e2 ± Liberzon–Gelfer,
Beer Sheva 1984) 7 . . . b5 (7 . . . cxd4!?)
8 ♗e2 ♗b7 9 0-0 c4?! (9 . . . a6 10 a4
bxa4 ±) 10 a4 a6 11 b3 ♗d5 12 ♘e5 ±*
Timoshchenko–Razuvaev, USSR 1972.

7 ♗d3   . . .

a) **7 ♗e2 c5** *(7 . . . b6!?)* **8** 0-0 cxd4
9 ♕xd4 ♗e7 10 ♗f4 0-0 11 c4 b6 12
♘e4 ♗b7 13 ♘c3 (Westerinen-
Christiansen, Wijk aan Zee 1976) 13
. . . ♘c5 =.

b) **7 c3 c5 8 ♗d3 cxd4 9 ♘xd4 ♗e7**
10 0-0 ♘c5 11 ♗c2 ♗d7 = Bronstein-
Petrosian, Moscow 1967.

c) **7 ♗c4 ♘b6** *(7 . . . ♗d6 8 0-0 0-0
9 ♕e2 ♕c7 10 ♘e4 ♗f4 11 ♘xf6+
♘xf6 12 ♗xf4 ♕xf4 13 ♖ad1 b6 14
♘e5 ± Boleslavsky–Zaitsev, USSR
1969 and 7 . . . c5 8 dxc5 ♗xc5 9 0-0 0-0*

*10 ♕e2 b6 11 ♘e4 ♗e7 12 ♖d1 ♕c7 13
♘eg5 ♘c5 14 ♘e5 − ± Boleslavsky −
are both weaker than the text, analysis
by Filip)* **8 ♗b3 c5 9 c3** *(9 ♕e2 cxd4 10
0-0 d3 =)* **9 . . . ♕c7** *(9 . . . cxd4 10 ♘xd4
♗e7 11 0-0 0-0 12 ♕f3! ♕c7 13 ♖e1 ±)*
10 dxc5 ♘bd7 *(10 . . . ♗xc5 11 0-0 0-0
12 ♕e2 ♗d7 13 ♗g5 ±)* **11 ♕e2 ♘xc5
12 ♗c2 ♗e7 13 ♘e5** 0-0 14 0-0 b6 with
a reasonable game.

Now Black must decide: castle
quickly or strike back in the centre
straight away:

A1.1: **7 . . . ♗e7**
A1.2: **7 . . . c5!?**

A1.1

**7 . . .   ♗e7
8 0-0   . . .**

8 ♕e2 0-0 9 ♗g5 c5 10 0-0-0 cxd4 11
♔b1 ♕a5!? is another suggestion of
Filip's; 11 . . . ♘c5?! 12 ♘xd4 ♘xd3 13
♖xd3 ± Jovčić–Čirić, Yugoslavia 1971.

8 ...   0-0

After 8 . . . c5 9 c4! cxd4 10 ♘xd4 ♘e5 11 ♗e2 0-0 bad is **12 b3?** ♛b6! with 13 . . . ♖d8 to follow, but **12 ♗f4!** ♘g6 13 ♗e3 a6 14 a3! ♛c7 15 b4 favours White, Spassky-Yanofsky, Winnipeg 1967.

Now we come to:

A1.11: 9 b3
A1.12: 9 ♛e2

Harmless is 9 c3 c5 10 ♘e5 cxd4 11 cxd4 ♘b6 12 ♗g5 ♘bd5 13 ♖c1 ♗d7 Becker-Döry, Vienna 1918, while 9 c4 c5 10 b3 transposes back to 9 b3.

A1.11

9	b3	b6
10	♗b2	♗b7
11	♛e2	c5
12	♖ad1	♛c7
13	c4	♖fe8
14	♗b1	...

On 14 ♘e5 Schwarz gives 14 . . . ♖ad8 15 ♘h5 ♘f8 =.

(See diagram) The critical stage of the variation beginning with 7 . . . ♗e7. In a Radviir-Flohr game, Pärnu 1947, Black now continued **14 . . . ♛c6?** and White reciprocated with **15 ♘e1?** ♖ad8 16 f4? cxd4 17 ♗xd4 e5! 18 ♘f5? exd4! 19 ♛xe7 g6! 20 ♘h6+ ♔g7 21 ♛xf7+ ♔xh6 22 ♖d3! ♘h5! 23 ♖h3 ♘df6 and Black won. Panov

found the refutation two years later: **15 d5!** exd5 16 cxd5 ♛c7 *(16 . . . ♘xd5? 17 ♖xd5! ♛xd5 18 ♗e4 ±)* 17 ♗f5 with a winning advantage, Panov-Flohr, USSR 1949.

Clearly, though, this line is over-ambitious and Black's position is quite solid even though there is no question of him taking the initiative for a good while, e.g. 14 : . . ♖ad8 *(Also reasonable is 14 . . . ♘f8 15 dxc5 ♗xc5 16 ♘e5 ♘g6 17 ♘e4 ♘xe4 = Spassky-Čirič, Sochi 1955)* 15 dxc5 ♛xc5 16 ♘e4 ♛c7 17 h3 ♘xe4 = Matanović-Petrosian, Biel (izt) 1976.

A1.12

9 ♛e2   ...

A sharper continuation than 9 b3.

9 ...   c5

9 . . . b6? 10 ♗f4! ♗b7 11 ♖ad1 c5? 12 dxc5 ♗xc5 13 ♘e5 ± Filip.

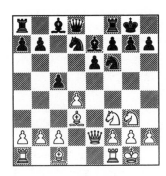

A1.121: 10 c3
A1.122: 10 ♖d1

A1.121

10 c3   ...

White bolsters d4 to secure an outpost for his knight on e5. Other possibilities:

a) **10 ♖e1 ♖e8** *(10 . . . ♕c7!? when 11 ♘f5? fails to 11 . . . exf5! 12 ♕xe7 ♖e8!; 10 . . . cxd4 11 ♘xd4 ♘c5 12 ♖d1! ♘xd3 13 ♖xd3 ♕c7 14 b3! ♘d5 15 c4 ♘f4 16 ♗xf4 ♕xf4 17 ♖ad1 ♕c7 18 ♘b5 ♕c6 19 ♘d6 b6? 20 ♘gf5! ♗f6 21 ♕e5!! ± Lilienthal)* **11 c3 ♕c7 12 ♘e5 b6?** *(12 . . . cxd4! 13 ♘xf7? ♔xf7 14 ♕xe6+ ♔f8 15 ♗c4 ♘e5!! 16 ♕xe5 ♗d8!! ∓ Lilienthal)* **13 ♘e4 ♘xe4 14 ♗xe4 ♗b7 15 ♗xh7+!** +− Lilienthal-Randviir, Pärnu 1947.

b) **10 dxc5** is another Filip suggestion, 10 . . . ♘xc5 *(10 . . . ♗xc5 11 ♗f4 b6 12 ♖ad1 ♕e7 13 c3 a5 14 ♘e4 ±)* **11 ♗c4 b6 12 ♖d1 ♕c7 13 ♘e5 ♗b7 14 ♗f4 ♖fe8?** *(14 . . . ♕c8 ±)* **15 ♘f5!**

exf5 16 ♗xf7+ ♔f8 17 ♗xe8 ♔xe8 18 ♘g6 winning (Filip).

10 . . .   b6

Now correct is **11 ♖e1 ♗b7 12 ♘e5 cxd4 13 cxd4 ♘d5** = Kashdan-Flohr, USA v USSR 1946. Instead **11 ♘e5?! ♗b7 12 f4?** *(12 ♖d1 or 12 ♖e1 were necessary)* **12 . . . cxd4 13 cxd4 ♘xe5!** *(not 13 . . . ♖e8? 14 ♗e3 a6 15 f5! ± as happened in an earlier Flohr game)* **14 dxe5** *(14 ♕xe5 ♘g4! −+)* **14 . . . ♘g4!** was a strong pawn sacrifice in Efseev-Flohr, Odessa 1949 − see illustrative games for the complete moves.

A1.122

10 ♖d1   ♕c7

10 . . . cxd4 11 ♘xd4 ♖e8 12 b3 ♕b6 13 ♗b2 ♘f8 14 ♘f3 ♗d7 15 ♘e5 ± Tal-Filip, Moscow 1967.

11 c4   ...

11 ♗g5 b6? *(11 . . . h6 =)* 12 d5! ♘xd5 13 ♗xe7 ♘xe7 14 ♗xh7+ ♔xh7 15 ♘g5+ ♔g8 16 ♖xd7! ♕xd7 17 ♕h5 ♖d8 18 ♕xf7+ ♔h8 19 h4 ♕e8 20 ♘h5! +− Capablanca-Ribeiras, 1935.

11 . . .   cxd4

Others:
a) 11 . . . ♖e8 12 dxc5?! ♘xc5 *(12 . . .*

♗xc5 13 ♘e4 ♘xe4 14 ♗xe4 ♘f6 15 ♗c2 e5 = L. Steiner-Flohr, Saltsjöbaden (izt) 1948) 13 ♗c2 ♘cd7 14 ♘e4 b6 15 ♗a4 ♖d8 16 ♘xf6+ ♗xf6 17 ♗g5 ♗b7 = Tal-Čirič, Budva 1967.
b) 11 . . . b6? 12 d5 exd5 13 ♕xe7 ♖e8 14 ♗xh7+ +−.

12 ♘xd4   a6

12 . . . b6 *(12 . . . ♕e5? 13 ♕f3 ±)* 13 ♘b5 ♕c6 14 ♗g5 ♗b7 *(14 . . . h6?! 15 ♗e4 ♘xe4 16 ♗xe7 ♘xg3 17 fxg3 ♖e8 18 ♗d6 ♖d8 19 ♘c7 ♖b8 20 ♘xe6 ♖e8 21 ♘d4 ±; 14 . . . a6 15 ♘e4 ♗b7 16 ♘d4 ♕c8 17 ♖ac1 ±)* 15 ♘e4 ±.

13 b3

Others:
a) 13 ♗g5 *(13 ♗c2 ±)* 13 . . . h6 14 ♗xh6. gxh6 15 ♘xe6 fxe6 16 ♕xe6+ ♖f7 17 ♗g6 ♘e5 18 ♗xf7+ ♔f8 −+.
b) 13 ♘df5? exf5 14 ♕xe7 ♖e8 15 ♕b4 ♘e5 ∓.
c) 13 ♘e4 ♘xe4 14 ♕xe4 ♘f6 15 ♗f4 ♕xc4! 16 ♘f5 ♕xe4 17 ♘xe7+ ♔h8 18 ♗xe4 ♘xe4 19 ♖ac1 ♘f6 =.
d) 13 a3!? b6 14 b4 ♗b7 15 ♗b2 ±.

13 . . .   ♖e8

13 . . . b6? 14 ♗b2 ♗b7 15 ♘df5!

14 ♗b2   b6
15 ♘h5!   ♗b7
16 ♘xe6!?

a) 16 ♘xg7?! ♔xg7 17 ♕xe6 ♕xh2+! 18 ♔xh2 fxe6 19 ♘xe6+ ♔f7 ∓.
b) 16 ♖ac1!? ♖ac8 17 c5!? bxc5 18 ♘xe6 ♕c6! 19 ♘ef4 ±.

16 . . .   fxe6
17 ♕xe6+   ♔f8

17 . . . ♔h8 18 ♕f7 ♘xh5 *(18 . . . ♖g8 19 ♘xf6!)* 19 ♕xh5 ♘f8 20 ♕f7 ±.

18 ♗xh7   ∞

Kasparov-Karpov, Amsterdam 1988 (Karpov, Zaitsev).

A1.2

7 . . .   c5!?
8 0-0   . . .

Nothing is gained by 8 dxc5 ♘xc5 9 ♗b5+ ♗d7 10 ♗xd7+ ♕xd7 11 ♕xd7+ ♘cxd7 12 ♗e3 *(12 c4 ♗b4+ 13 ♔e2 a5 14 ♗d2 ♔e7 15 ♖hd1 ♖hc8 16 b3 ♖a6 = Kostić-Nimzowitsch, Bled 1931)* 12 . . . ♘d5 13 ♗d4 ♘b4 14 ♔d2 0-0-0 15 c3 ♘c6 etc. Beni-Barcza, 1962.

8 . . .   cxd4

8 . . . ♗e7 transposes to A1.1 while 8 . . . ♕c7 9 c4 ♗d6 10 b3 0-0 11 ♗b2 b6 12 ♘e4 ♗e7 13 ♘xf6+ ♗xf6 14 ♕c2 h6 15 ♗h7+ ♔h8 16 ♗e4 ♗b7 17 ♖ad1 ♖ad8 18 h3 led to a space advantage for White in Adorján-

Eperjesi, Hungary (ch) 1976.

9 ♘xd4   ♗c5

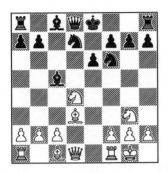

Or:

a) **9 . . . ♗e7?!** 10 b3 0-0 11 ♗b2
*(11 c4 ♕c7 12 ♗b2 ♖d8 13 ♕e2 ♘f8
14 ♘e4 ± Ivkov-Berger, Amsterdam
(izt) 1964)* 11 . . . ♘c5 12 ♗c4! ♗d7 13
♕e2 ♕b6 14 ♖ad1 ♖fe8 15 ♘f3 ±
Bradvarevic-Trifunovic, Yugoslavia
(ch) 1964.

b) **9 . . . ♘c5** 10 ♗b5+?! *(10 ♗c4!
♗e7 11 b3!)* 10 . . . ♗d7 11 b4 ♗xb5
12 ♘xb5 a6 13 ♘d4 ♘cd7 14 a3
(Spassky-Smyslov, Amsterdam (izt)
1964) 14 . . . ♘b6! =.

10 ♘f3   . . .

The most frequent move. Other
possible variations are:

a) **10 ♗e3?!** 0-0 11 ♕e2 ♘d5! 12
♖ad1 ♘xe3 13 fxe3 g6! 14 ♘e4 ♗e7∓
Cherepkov-Petrosian, USSR (ch)
1960.

b) **10 ♘b3!?** *(on 10 c3 ♗xd4! 11*

cxd4 0-0 = Filip) 10 . . . ♗b6?! *(10 . . .
♗e7 11 ♖e1 0-0 12 ♕f3! ♖e8 was a
possibility. Here, too, White can try to
freeze Black's kingside with c3-c4, ♗f4
etc., but the manœuvre is not simple
because 13 ♗f4 can be met by 13 . . .
♘d5 and 13 c4 by 13 . . . ♕c7 14 ♗f4
♗d6) 11 ♕e2 (also promising is
11 ♖e1 and 12 ♕f3! when it is not clear
whether Black can solve the development problem of his c8 bishop; for this
reason inferior is 11 ♘h5? ♘xh5 12
♕xh5 ♘f6 13 ♕h4 ♗d7) 11 . . . 0-0 12
♗d2! ♕c7 13 c4 seems good, for
instance 13 . . . ♕e5 14 ♕f3! ♕xb2 15
♗c3! ♕a3 16 ♖ad1 ♖e8 17 ♘h5! ±*
Velikov-Hansen, Groningen 1972.

10 . . .   0-0
11 ♕e2   . . .

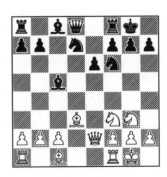

Giving nothing or less are **11 b3** b6
12 ♗b2 ♗b7 13 ♕e2 ♕c7 14 ♘e4
♘xe4 = Spassky-Filip, Nice (ol) 1974
and **11 a3?!** b6 12 ♕e2 *(12 b4?! ♗e7
13 ♗b2 Lengyel-Varnusz, Budapest*

1975, 13 . . . a5! ∓) 12 . . . ♗b7 13 b4
♗xf3! 14 gxf3 ∓ Geszosz–Flesch,
Hungary (ch) 1975.

11 . . .   b6

11 . . . ♕c7 12 ♘e4 ♗e7 13 ♗g5 b6
14 ♖ad1 ± Filip.

12 ♗f4   ♗b7

On 12 . . . ♘d5!? Schwarz gives 13
♗g5 ♕c7 14 ♕e4 ♘5f6 15 ♕xa8 ♗b7
16 ♕xa7 ♖a8 unclear.

13 ♖ad1   . . .

If 13 c4 ♕c8! and 14 . . . ♕c6. After
the text the game Tal–Vasyukov,
USSR (ch) Tallinn 1965 continued 13
. . . ♘d5? *(Filip recommends 13 . . . ♕c8
14 ♔h1?! a6)* 14 ♗g5 ♕c7 15 ♘h5!
and Black began to miss his knight in
the defence of his kingside — see
illustrative games for the continuation of the attack and instructive
endgame that followed.

A2

6 ♘xf6+   ♘xf6
7 ♘e5!   . . .

A particularly dangerous move for
Black to meet and one which nearly
caused Hort to "give up the variation
4 . . . ♘d7 almost for ever" (q.v. the
Karpov–Hort reference following!).
Instead 7 ♗c4 is discussed in

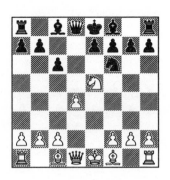

variation **B** while neutral moves
which allow the healthy development
of the c8 bishop are perfectly safe, e.g.
*7 c3 ♗g4 8 h3 (8 ♗e2 e6 9 0-0 ♗e7 10
♗f4 0-0 11 ♖e1 ♘d5 = Boleslavsky-
Kotov, Saltsjöbaden (izt) 1948, or 9 h3
♗h5 10 ♘e5 ♗xe2 11 ♕xe2 ♗d6 12
♗g5 ♕c7 13 0-0-0 ♘d7 = Pilnik-
Petrosian, Amsterdam (c) 1956) 8 . . .
♗xf3 9 ♕xf3 ♕d5 (9 . . . e6 10 ♗c4
♗e7 11 0-0 ♘d5 12 ♗e3 ♕b6 13 ♕e2
0-0 14 ♖ad1 ♗d6 15 ♗b3 ♘xe3 16
fxe3 c5 17 ♖f3 ♖ae8 ∞ Kasparov-
Karpov, Seville (m) 1987) 10 ♗e2 e6
11 0-0 ♗d6 12 ♕d3 ♗c7 13 ♗f3 ♕d7
14 ♖d1 0-0 15 c4 ♖ad8 16 ♕b3 ♕e7
17 g3 ♗b8 =* Kasparov–Karpov,
Seville (m) 1987.

A2.1: 7 . . . ♗e6!?
A2.2: 7 . . . ♘d7

A2.1

7 . . .   ♗e6!?

The Modern Variation.

The alternatives are:

a) **7 . . . ♗f5** (On f5 the bishop is exposed to harassment and this move has been virtually refuted) **8 c3 e6** *(8 . . . ♘d7 allows 9 ♘xf7! ♔xf7 10 ♕f3 e6 11 g4 ♕f6 12 gxf5 ♕xf5 13 ♕e3 c5 14 ♗h3 cxd4 15 cxd4 ♗b4+ 16 ♔f1 ♕b5+ 17 ♔g1 ♖he8 18 ♕b3 ♕b6 19 ♗e3 ♘f8 20 ♗g2 ± Kavalek-Barcza, Caracas 1971, or 13 ♕xf5+ exf5 14 ♗c4+ ♔f6 15 ♖g1 ♖e8+ 16 ♔f1 h6 17 h4 g6 18 ♗f4 ♖e4 19 ♗g3 ± Filip. 8 . . . ♗g6 is also questionable — 9 h4 ♘d7 10 ♘xg6 hxg6 11 ♗g5 ♘f6?! 12 ♕c2 e6 13 0-0-0 ± Levy-Livieros, Haifa 1971, or 10 ♘c4 h5 11 ♗g5 f6 12 ♗f4 b5 13 ♗d3 ± Karpov-Spassky, Bad Kissingen 1980)* **9 g4! ♗g6 10 h4 ♗d6** *(10 . . . h5?! 11 g5 ♘d5 12 ♘xg6 fxg6 13 ♕c2 ♔f7 14 ♖h3! ♘e7 15 ♗c4 ♘f5 16 ♖f3 ♕d7 17 ♖xf5+! gxf5 18 ♕xf5+ ♔e7 19 ♕e4 ± ♖e8 20 ♗f4 ♔d8 21 ♕e5 ♖g8 22 0-0-0 g6 23 ♖e1 ♗g7 24 ♕b8+ ♔e7 25 ♖xe6+! 1-0 was the Karpov-Hort, Bugojno 1978 game referred to above)* **11 ♕e2! c5** *(11 . . . ♗xe5 12 dxe5 ♕d5 13 ♖h3 ♘xg4 14 ♕xg4 ♗f5 15 ♕f3 ± Jansa-Flesch, Sombor 1971)* **12 ♗g2!** *(An improvement on Karpov-A. Zaitsev, Kuibyshev 1970, where after 12 h5? ♗e4! 13 f3 cxd4 14 ♕b5+ ♘d7 15 ♘xf7 ♗g3+ 16 ♔e2 d3+ 17 ♔e3 ♕f6 18 ♔xe4 ♕xf7! 19 ♖h3 a6 20 ♕g5 Black could have won with 20 . . . e5! 21 ♖xg3 ♘c5+) 12 . . . cxd4 (12 . . . ♗xe5 13 dxe5 ♗d3 14 ♕d1 ♘e4 15 f3 ♘g3 16 ♖h3 ♘e2 17 ♗e3 threatening 18 ♗f1 +−) 13 h5 dxc3 14 ♕b5+ ♔f8 15 hxg6* winning (Čirić).

b) **7 . . . e6** (Passive) **8 ♗d3 ♗e7 9 0-0 0-0 10 b3 ♕c7 11 ♗b2 b6 12 ♕f3 ♗b7 13 ♕h3** with a strong attack in Letio-Tóth, 1951.

c) **7 . . . g6 8 ♗c4 ♘d5 9 0-0 ♗g7 10 ♕e2 0-0 11 ♗b3 a5 12 a3 ♕b6 13 ♖d1 ♗e6 14 ♗a2 ±** Sakharov-Flesch, Varna 1958.

8 ♗e2 . . .

8 c4 is riskier due to the possible weakening of the pawn centre, viz. **8 . . . g6! 9 ♗e2** *(9 d5?! cxd5 10 cxd5 ♕xd5 11 ♕a4+ ♘d7 ∓)* **9 . . . ♗g7 10 0-0 0-0 11 ♗e3 ♕c7** *(11 . . . ♕c8 12 ♗f3 ♖d8 13 ♕e2 ♘d7 14 ♘g4 ♗xg4! 15 ♗xg4 ♕c7 16 ♖ad1 ♘f6 as in Browne-Rogoff, USA 1975 is also good)* **12 h3 ♖fd8 13 ♘f3 b5 14 b3** *(14 cxb5 cxb5 15 ♗xb5 ♕b7 16 ♕a4 ♗d5 ∞)* **14 . . . bxc4 15 bxc4 c5 16 d5 ♗f5 ∓** Gufeld-Razuvaev, USSR (ch) 1972. **8 c3 g6 9 ♗d3** also got White nowhere in Timoschenko-Razuvaev, USSR 1971 after **9 . . . ♗g7 10 0-0 0-0**

11 ♕e2 c5 12 dxc5 ♕c7 13 c6 bxc6 (=).

8 . . .   g6
9 0-0   ♗g7
10 c4

Others:
a) **10 a4** 0-0 11 a5! a6?! *(11 . . . ♖c8)*
12 ♖e1 ♘e8 13 c3 ♗xe5!? *(13 . . .
♘d6? 14 ♘d3! ♗c4 15 ♘c5 ±
Donchev–Kholmov, Varna 1987)* 14
dxe5 ±.
b) **10 c3** 0-0 11 ♖e1 *(11 ♗d3 c5 12
♘f3 cxd4 =)* 11 . . . ♖c8 *(11 . . . ♘d7?!
12 ♘d3 ♗f5 13 ♗g5 ♖e8 14 ♗f1 h6 15
♗h4 a5 ± Sax–Bleiman, Buenos Aires
1978; 11 . . . ♕a5 12 ♘d3 ♖ae8 13 ♗f4
♗f5 14 ♗e5 ♘d7 15 ♗xg7 ♔xg7
Kavalek–Mecking, Manila 1975, 16
♗f1! ±)* 12 ♘d3 b6 13 ♕a4 a5 14 ♗f4
c5! *(14 . . . ♘d5 15 ♗e5 ♗xe5 16 ♘xe5
♕c7 17 ♗f3 b5 ∞ Vasyukov–
Petursson, Reykjavik 1980)* 15 ♗e5
cxd4 16 ♕xd4 ♕xd4 = Arnason–
Sosonko, Malta (ol) 1980.

10 . . .   0-0
11 ♗e3   ♘e4!?

a) 11 . . . ♘d7 12 ♘f3! ♘f6 13 h3
♘e4 14 ♕c1 b5!? 15 cxb5 cxb5 16
♗xb5 ♗d5 = Belyavsky–Korchnoi,
Montpellier 1985.
b) 11 . . . ♘e8 12 ♕b3 ♘d6 13 ♖ad1
♕c8 14 ♕c3 ♖d8 15 h3 f6 16 ♘f3 ♕d7
17 ♖fe1 ± Grünfeld–Lein, New York
1985.

12 ♕c2

12 f4 f6 *(12 . . . f5! =)* 13 ♘f3 ♗f7 14
♕c2 ♘d6 15 ♗d3 b5 ± Psakhis–
Tukmakov, USSR 1987.

12 . . .   ♘d6
13 b3   c5!

Less energetic is 13 . . . ♘f5 14 ♕e4
♘xe3 15 fxe3 ±.

14 ♖ad1   ♘f5
15 d5   . . .

15 dxc5?! ♘xe3 16 fxe3 ♕a5 17
♘d3 ♗f5 =.

15 . . .   ♗xe5
16 dxe6   ♕c7
17 exf7+   ♖xf7
18 g3   ♖af8

Black has an excellent game,
Sokolov–Karpov, Linares (c) 1987.

A2.2

7 . . .   ♘d7

A solid defensive move.

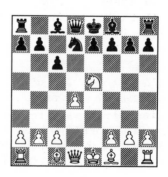

8 ♗e3!?

a) **8 ♗f4** ♘xe5 **9 ♗xe5 ♗f5!** *(9 . . .*
♕*b6? 10 ♗d3! f6 11 ♗g3 ♗e6 12 ♕e2*
± *Larsen–Rogoff, Lone Pine 1978; 9 . . .*
♕*d5 10 ♕d3 f6 11 ♗g3 ♗f5 12 c4*
♗*xd3 13 cxd5 ♗xf1 14 ♖xf1 0-0-0! =*
Ivkov–Barcza, Caracas 1971) 10 ♗c4
e6 11 0-0 ♗d6 12 ♕e2 0-0 13 ♖ad1
♕e7 = (Suetin).

b) **8 ♘d3** g6 *(8 . . . ♘f6 9 c3 g6 10*
♗*e2 ♗g7 11 0-0 0-0 12 ♗f3 ♗f5 ∞)*
9 ♗e3 *(9 c3 ♗g7 10 ♗f4 ♕a5 11 ♕d2*
0-0 12 ♗e2 e5 13 dxe5 ♘xe5 14 ♘xe5
♗*xe5 15 ♗g5 ♗e6 16 0-0 ♗g7 =*
Karpov–Sosonko, Amsterdam 1980)
9 . . . ♗g7 10 ♕d2 ♘b6!? *(10 . . . e5*
11 ♗h6!) 11 ♘e5 ♗e6 12 ♗e2 0-0 13
0-0-0 f6 14 ♘d3 ♘c4 15 ♕c3 ♘xe3 16
fxe3 ♗d5 17 ♘f4 ♗h6 = Timman–
Korchnoi, Montpellier 1985.

8 . . .	**♘xe5**
9 dxe5	**♗f5**

9 . . . ♕a5+ 10 ♕d2 ♕xe5? *(10 . . .*
♕*xd2+!)* 11 0-0-0! ±.

10 **♕xd8+**	**♖xd8**
11 **♗xa7**	**♗xc2**
12 **♗b6**	**♖a8**
13 **♗c4**	**e6**
14 **f3**	**♖a4**
15 **b3**	**♗b4+**
16 **♔e2**	**♖a3**
17 **♗d4**	**0-0**

The position is absolutely level.
Sokolov–Karpov, Linares (c) 1987.

B

5 ♗c4   **. . .**

On the whole a more aggressive
continuation than 5 ♘f3.

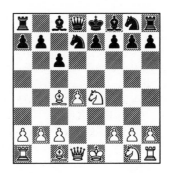

5 . . .   **♘gf6**

Once more **5 . . . ♘df6** is rather
artificial: 6 ♘g5 ♘h6 *(6 . . . ♘d5*
7 ♘1f3 ♗f5 8 g4! ♗xg4 9 ♘xf7! or 8 . . .
♗*g6 9 ♘e5 ±)* 7 c3 *(also 7 ♘1f3 ♗g4*
8 c3 e6 9 h3 ♗xf3 10 ♕xf3 ♘d5 11 ♗d2
♕*f6 12 ♕e2 ♘f4 13 ♕e4 ± Vasyukov–*
Livshin, USSR 1956) 7 . . . g6 8 ♘f3
♗g7 9 h3 0-0 10 g4 b5 11 ♗b3 ♘d5 12
♕e2 a5 13 a3 ♕b6 14 ♗d2 ♖a7 15 0-0
e6 16 ♘e4 ♔h8 17 ♘c5 f6 18 a4 ±
Shamkovich–Livshin, USSR 1961.
Also inferior is **5 . . . ♘b6** 6 ♗b3 ♗f5
7 ♘g3 ♗g6 8 h4 h6 9 ♘f3 e6 10 ♘e5
♗h7 11 ♕e2 ♕e7 12 ♗d2 ±
Liberzon–Karashev, USSR 1970.
After the text we branch out with:

B1: 6 ♘g5
B2: 6 ♘xf6+

B1

6 ♘g5   e6

To avoid hemming in the c8 bishop **6 ... ♘d5** was often played here in the early sixties, although White has several paths to the initiative, e.g.:

a) 7 ♘e2 ♘7f6 8 ♗b3 h6 9 ♘f3 ♗f5 10 ♘g3 ♗g4 11 h3 ♗xf3 12 ♕xf3 e6 13 0-0 ♗d6 14 c4 ♘e7 15 ♘e4 ♘xe4 16 ♕xe4 ♕d7 ± Honfi–Zita, 1960.

b) 7 ♗b3 h6 8 ♘5f3 ♘7f6 9 ♘e2 *(9 ♘e5!?)* 9 ... ♗f5 10 ♘g3 ♗h7 11 0-0 e6 12 c4 ♘b6 13 ♗f4 ♗e7 14 ♕e2 ± Honfi–Reshko, Budapest 1961.

c) 7 ♘1f3 h6 *(7 ... g6 8 ♕e2 h6 9 ♘e4 ♕c7 10 ♗xd5 cxd5 11 ♘c3 ♕c4 12 ♕xc4 dxc4 13 ♘d5 ± Schmidt–Hönlinger, West Germany 1955)* 8 ♘e4 ♘7b6 9 ♗b3 ♗f5 10 ♘g3 *(10 ♕e2 e6 11 0-0 ♗e7 12 ♘e5 0-0 13 ♗d2 ♘d7 14 ♘g3 ♗h7 15 ♖ad1 ± Dückstein–Bouwmeester, Switzerland 1962)* 10 ... ♗h7 11 0-0 e6 12 ♘e5 ♘d7 *(12 ... ♕c7 13 c4 ♘f6 14 ♗f4 g5 15 ♗e3 0-0-0 16 ♕e2 ♖g8 17 f4 ± Lukin–Reshko, USSR 1973)* 13 c4 ♘5f6 14 ♗f4 ♘xe5 15 ♗xe5 ♗d6 was Fischer–Portisch, Stockholm (izt) 1962, and now best is 16 ♕f3! ±.

d) 7 ♕h5 g6 8 ♕e2 ♗g7 9 ♘1f3 0-0 10 0-0 h6 11 ♘e4 ♕c7 12 ♗b3 ♘7f6 13 ♘xf6+ ± Duckstein–Kramer, 1956.

And here:

B1.1: 7 ♕e2
B1.2: 7 ♘e2

B1.1

7 ♕e2   ♘b6

Black cannot simply develop normally with **7 ... ♗e7?** due to 8 ♘xf7! Also unsatisfactory is **7 ... ♘d5** 8 ♘1f3 ♗e7 9 0-0 with ♗b3 ± to follow.

White has two ways to deal with his attacked bishop:

B1.11: 8 ♗d3
B1.12: 8 ♗b3

At present 8 ♗d3 is increasing in popularity, though theory is undecided as to which is the better move.

B1.11

8 ♗d3   h6

Pawn grabbing with 8 ... ♕xd4? costs too dearly in development after 9 ♘1f3 ♕d5 *(or else 10 ♘e5!)* 10 0-0 ±.

9 ♘5f3 c5

Black must lose no time in finding counterplay. Passive play would be met by White castling long and then launching his kingside attack with g2–g4.

B1.111: 10 ♗e3
B1.112: 10 dxc5

B1.111

10 ♗e3 . . .

This developing move is quite frequently played.
Others:
a) 10 ♗f4 ♘bd5 11 ♗e5 cxd4 12 0-0-0 ♕a5 13 ♗c4 ♘c3! 14 bxc3 ♕a3+ 15 ♔b1 dxc3 16 ♗b5+ ♘d7 17 ♗xc3 ♕xc3 18 ♘e5 ♗a3 19 ♘c4 ♕b4+ 20 ♔a1 ♕c3+ 21 ♔b1 ♕b4+ 22 ♔a1 a6!? 23 ♗xd7+ ♗xd7 24 ♕d3 ♗b5 ∓ Gipslis–Marovic, Tallinn 1975.
b) 10 c3 ♗e7 11 ♗e3 ♘bd5 12 ♘e5 ♘xe3 13 fxe3 0-0 14 ♘gf3 ♕c7 15 g4 ♘d7 16 0-0-0 ♘xe5 17 ♘xe5 ♗f6 18 ♘f3 cxd4 19 ♘xd4 b6 = Tseshkovsky–Chernin, Irkutsk 1983.

10 . . . a6!?

Maintaining the pressure on White's d-pawn and thus delaying the development of his knights by ♘e5 and ♘1f3.
a) 10 . . . ♘bd5 11 ♘e5 ♘xe3 *(11 . . . a6 12 ♘gf3 ♕c7 13 0-0 ♗d6 14 c3 b6 15*

♖ad1 0-0 16 ♗c1 ♗b7 17 ♖fe1 ♖fd8 18 ♗b1 b5 19 a3 ♖ac8 20 h3 ♗a8 21 ♘h4 cxd4 22 cxd4 ♗f8 23 ♕d3 ♕b7 24 ♘g4 ± Karpov–Balashov, Tilburg 1977) 12 fxe3 a6 *(12 . . . ♗d6? 13 ♘gf3 ♗xe5 14 ♘xe5 cxd4 15 ♗b5+ ± Shamkovich–Donner, Amsterdam 1968)* 13 ♘gf3 ♕c7 14 0-0-0 b5 15 c3 ♗d6 16 ♖hf1 ♗b7 = (Filip).
b) 10 . . . ♕c7 11 ♘e5 ♗d7 *(11 . . . a6 12 ♘gf3 ♘bd5 ± Liberzon–Rogoff, Biel (izt) 1976)* 12 ♘gf3 ♖c8 13 c3 c4 14 ♘xd7 (Korensky–Kholmov, Sochi 1973) 14 . . . ♘bxd7! 15 ♗c2 b5 =.

11 c3! . . .

11 0-0-0 c4! 12 ♗xc4 ♘xc4 13 ♕xc4 b5 14 ♕c6+ *(14 ♕f1!? ♗b7 15 ♘e2 ♖c8 16 ♔b1 ♕c7 17 ♖c1 ♗d6 18 ♘d2 0-0 ∞ Tseshkovsky–Razuvaev, USSR 1977)* 14 . . . ♗d7 15 ♕b7 ♖b8 16 ♕xa6 ♖a8 = Tompa–Navarovsky, Budapest 1976.

11 . . . ♘bd5
12 ♘e5 ♕c7
13 ♘gf3 b6
14 0-0 ♗d6
15 ♗d2! ±

15 ♖ac1?! ♗b7?! *(15 . . . ♘xe3! see 10 . . . ♘bd5)* 16 ♗d2! 0-0 17 ♗b1 cxd4 18 cxd4 ♕e7 ± Hellers–Adorjan, Thessaloniki (ol) 1988.

B1.112

10 dxc5 . . .

B1.1121: 10 . . . ♗xc5
B1.1122: 10 . . . ♘bd7!?

B1.1121

10 . . .   ♗xc5
11 ♘e5   . . .

As Boleslavsky says, the queen's knight's progress in this variation is a wonder to behold.

Another continuation applied quite frequently is 11 ♗d2:

a) **11 . . . ♘bd5** 12 0-0-0 a6 13 ♘h3 *(13 ♘e5 b5 14 f4 ♕b6 15 ♘1f3 ♗e3 16 g3 ♗xd2+ 17 ♖xd2 0-0 18 c3 ♗b7 19 ♕f2 ± Sax-Benkö, New York 1986)* 13 . . . b5 14 ♘f4 *(15 ♘e5 ♕b6 16 g4 ♘d7 16 ♗e4 ♘xe5 17 ♗xd5 exd5! 18 ♕xe5+ ♗e6 19 f4 − 19 ♕xg7 ♗d4! 20 ♗a5 = Kholmov − 19 . . . ♗d4!? 20 ♕e1?! − 20 ♕e2 or 20 ♕h5 ∞ − 20 . . . 0-0 21 f5 ♗d7 22 ♘f4 ♖fe8 ∓ Kremenecky-Kholmov, USSR 1987)* 14 . . . ♕b6 15 ♘xd5 ♘xd5 16 ♘e5 0-0 17 g4 ♗xf2 18 g5 hxg5 (Klovans-Lokomar, USSR 1987) 19 ♕h5! f5 20 ♘g6 ∞ (Klovans).

b) **11 . . . ♕c7** 12 0-0-0 *(12 ♘e5? ♗xf2+! 13 ♔xf2 ♕xe5!)* 12 . . . 0-0 *(12 . . . ♘bd7 13 ♘h3 g5 14 ♘hg1 ♖g8 15 c4 b6 16 ♗c3 ♗b7 and Black's prospects are slightly better. Boleslavsky)* 13 ♘e5 ♘bd7 14 f4 b6 15 ♘gf3 ♗b7 16 ♖hf1 (Chiburdanidze-Ioseliani, (m) 1988) 16 . . . ♗d6 17 ♘xd7 ♘xd7 18 ♘d4 a6 =.

c) **11 . . . ♘bd7** 12 0-0-0 ♕c7 *(12 . . . 0-0? 13 ♘h3 ♕c7 14 g4! ♘xg4 15 ♖hg1*

♘df6 16 ♗c3 ♗d6 17 ♘d4 ± *Fyodorov-Voltshok, USSR 1981)* **13 h4** a6 14 ♘h3 ♗d6 15 ♗c3 ♘c5 16 g4 ♗d7?! 17 g5 hxg5 18 hxg5 ♘h5 19 ♘e5 ♗c6 20 ♘xc6 ♕xc6 21 g6 (Karafiáth-Katona, (corr) 1987) 21 . . . f6! ∞. Maybe better is 13 ♘h3 g5 *(13 . . . a6)* 14 ♘e1 ♕e5!? 15 ♕f1! ♘e4 *(15 . . . ♘d5?! 16 ♔b1 ♕c7 17 f4 g4 18 ♘f2 h5 19 ♘e4 ♗e7 20 h3! ±* A. Rodriguez-Garcia, (c) Amsterdam 1989) 16 ♗xe4 ♕xe4 17 ♘d3 ± (Rodriguez).

d) **11 . . . a6!?** 12 ♘e5 ♘bd5 13 ♘gf3 ♕c7 *(13 . . . b5? 14 ♗xb5+!)* 14 0-0-0 b5 15 g4 *(15 ♖he1!? ♗b7 16 ♘xf7!? ♕xf7 17 ♘e5 ♕c7 18 ♗g6+ − 18 ♘g6 0-0-0! − 18 . . . ♔f8 19 ♘f7 ♖g8 20 ♕xe6 ♕d7! 21 ♕e2 ∞ Adorján)* 15 . . . ♗b7 16 g5 ♘h5 17 gxh6 *(17 ♘g6?! 0-0-0! 18 ♘xh8 ♘df4! ∓; 17 ♖hg1!? 0-0-0 18 ♖g4! ∞ Adorján)* 17 . . . 0-0-0! 18 hxg7! *(18 ♕e1? gxh6 19 ♔b1 f6! 20 ♘g6 ♖he8 ∓ Hellers-Adorján, Esbjerg 1988)* 18 . . . ♘df4 19 ♗xf4 ♘xf4 20 ♕d2 ♘xd3+ 21 ♘xd3 ♖hg8 22 ♕e2 ♗e7 23 ♖hg1 ♗f6 ∞ (Adorján).

11 . . .   ♘bd7
12 ♘gf3   . . .

(See diagram)

12 . . .   ♘xe5!?

The beginning of an extra-ordinarily sharp tactical line. More solid and safer is **12 . . . ♕c7** 13 0-0 *(not 13 ♗d2? ♘xe5 14 ♘xe5 ♗xf2+! 15*

♔xf2 ♛xe5 ∓ *Suetin-Kholmov,*
Budapest 1976; 13 ♗*f4?!* ♗*b4+! 14*
♔*f1 — 14* ♘*d2* ♗*xd2+ 15* ♔*xd2 0-0* ∞
— 14 ... ♗*d6 15* ♗*g3 0-0 16* ♖*d1* ♘*xe5*
17 ♘*xe5* ♖*d8! 18* ♘*c4* ♗*xg3 19 hxg3 —*
Timman-Karpov, Amsterdam 1988 —
19 . . . *b5!?* ∓*) 13* . . . *0-0 14* ♗*f4 (14*
♗*d2* ♗*d6 15* ♘*xd7* ♗*xd7 16* ♖*ae1*
♖*fd8! 17* ♘*e5* ♗*b5! 18* ♗*xb5* ♗*xe5 19*
♛*xe5* ♛*xe5 20* ♖*xe5* ♖*xd2 =*
Sokolov-Karpov, Linares (c) 1987) 14
. . . ♗*d6 15* ♘*xd7 (15* ♖*fe1 b6 16*
♘*xd7* ♗*xd7 17* ♗*xd6* ♛*xd6 18* ♘*e5*
♖*fd8 19* ♖*ad1* ♛*c7 20* ♘*xd7* ♖*xd7 =*
Korchnoi-Kholmov, Moscow 1975) 15
. . . ♗*xd7 16* ♗*xd6* ♛*xd6 17* ♘*e5*
♖*fd8 18* ♖*ad1* ♛*b6 19 c3 (for 19*
♘*xd7 see the illustrative game Jansa-*
Kholmov) 19 . . . ♗*e8 20* ♖*d2* ♖*d5 =*
Adorjan-Navarovsky, Budapest 1977.

13 ♘xe5   **0-0**
14 ♗d2

Another popular continuation is 14
0-0 b6 *(14* . . . ♗*d6 15 f4 and* ♗*d2,*
♖*ae1* ±*)* ;

a) **15** ♖**d1** ♛e7 16 b4 *(16* ♗*f4* ♗*b7*
17 ♗*g3* ♖*fd8 = Matanovic-Pfleger,*
Amsterdam (ol) 1964) 16 . . . ♗d6 17
♗b2 ♗b7 18 a3 ♖fd8 19 c4 a5 ∓
(Filip).

b) **15** ♗**f4** ♗**b7** 16 ♖ad1 ♛e7 17 c3
♖fd8 18 ♖d2 ♗d6 *(18* ... *a6 19* ♖*fd1*
b5 = Prandstetter-Speelman, Taxco
(izt) 1985) 19 ♖fd1 ♖ac8 20 ♗a6
♗xa6 21 ♛xa6 ♘e4 22 ♖d4 ♛f6! 23
♘d3 ♗xf4 24 ♘xf4 e5! = Mecking-
Hort, Las Palmas 1975.

c) **15** ♗**xh6!?** gxh6 16 ♛f3 ♘d5! 17
c4 ♛g5 18 ♖ae1 ♗b4 19 ♖e4 f5 20
♖e2 ♘f4 21 ♛xa8 ♘xe2+ 22 ♗xe2
♛g7 23 ♘f3 ♛xb2 24 ♗d3 ♖d8 25
♛c6 ♛g7 ∞ (Suetin).

d) **15** ♛**f3** ♛**c7!** *(15* ... ♖*b8? 16* ♗*f4*
♗*b7 17* ♛*h3! ±)* 16 ♖e1 ♗d6 17 ♛g3
♘d7 18 ♗f4 ♗b7 19 ♖e3 ♘xe5 =
Jansa-A. Zaitsev, Sochi 1965.

e) **15 b4** ♗**d6!** *(15* . . . ♗*xb4?! 16*
♛*f3* ♗*d7 17* ♗*xh6 gxh6 18* ♘*xd7*
♘*xd7 19* ♛*e4* ±*)* 16 ♗b2 ♗b7 17
♖ad1 *(17 a3* ♛*e7 18* ♖*fe1 a5 19* ♘*c4*
♗*c7 20 b5 a4!* ∓ *de Firmian-Dlugy,*
Tunis (izt) 1985) 17 . . . ♛c7! *(17* . . .
♛*e7 18 b5* ±*)* 18 a3 a5 ∞ Perényi-
Watson, Saint John 1988.

14 . . .   **♛d5**

B1.11211: 15 0-0-0!?
B1.11212: 15 0-0

B1.11211

15 0-0-0!?   **. . .**

Sacrificing the a-pawn for an attack. Less testing for Black was 15 f4 b5! 16 ♗e3 ♗xe3 17 ♕xe3 ♗b7 18 ♕f3 ♕xf3 19 ♘xf3 ♘h5! 20 0-0 ♘xf4 21 ♗xb5 ♖ab8 22 ♗c4 g5 ∓ Mecking-Larsen, Manila 1975.

| 15 ... | ♕xa2 |
| 16 c3 | b5!? |

16 ... ♗a3!? merits thorough examination. 17 ♗e3 *(there is perpetual check if the piece is taken)* 17 ... ♕a1+ 18 ♗b1 ♗e7 **19 ♖d4?!** ♕a5 20 ♗d2 ♖d8 21 ♖xd8+ ♕xd8 22 ♖d1 ♕e8 23 g4 ♗d7 24 g5 hxg5 25 ♗xg5 ♗b5 26 ♕f3 ♗c6 etc. was Trois-Savis, Sao Paulo 1977, but superior is the untested **19 g4!?** (Gaprindashvili, Ubilava). Clearly inferior is **16 ...** ♕a1+ 17 ♔c2 ♕a4+ 18 ♔b1 ♖b8 19 ♗c2 ♕a6 20 ♕f3! b5 21 ♗xh6 b4 22 ♗xg7 b3 23 ♗d3 ♕a2+ 24 ♔c1 ♗a3 25 ♘c4 with a winning position, Gaprindashvili-Zaitseva, USSR 1979.

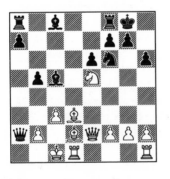

17 ♗b1 ...

17 ♗xh6 and now:

a) **17 ... b4** *(17 ... gxh6 18 ♘g4!)* 18 ♘g4 ♘e8 19 ♗xg7! f5 20 ♗xf8 ♗xf8 21 ♗c4 ♕a1+ 22 ♔c2 ♕a4+ 23 ♗b3 ♕c6 24 ♖d8 +− Radulov-Atanasov, Bulgaria (ch) 1976.

b) **17 ... ♗b7!?** 18 ♘d7! *(not 18 ♘g4? ♕a1+! 19 ♗b1 ♘e4!)* 18 ... ♘xd7 *(18 ... ♕a1+ 19 ♗b1 ♘e4 20 ♗xg7! ♔xg7 21 ♘xc5 ♘xc5 22 ♕g4+ ♔f6 23 ♕h4+!)* 19 ♕g4 ♕a1+ 20 ♗b1 g6 21 ♖xd7 ♗a3 ∞ as in Adorján-Flesch, Hungary (ch) 1975.

| 17 ... | ♕a4 |
| 18 ♕f3!? | |

18 ♕d3 ♕h4! 19 h3 ♗b7 20 ♘d7 ♖fd8 21 ♘xf6+ ♕xf6 = Reiman-Oll, USSR 1986.

18 ...	♘d5
19 ♕g3	♔h8
20 ♖he1	♗b7

20 ... ♘f6? 21 ♗xh6! gxh6 22 ♖d8! +− Diaz-Siero, Camaguey 1987.

21 ♕d3	♘f6
22 g4	♖ad8
23 ♕h3	...

The struggle is double-edged (analysis).

B1.11212

| 15 0-0 | ♗d4 |

15 ... b5!? 16 ♔h1 *(16 ♗xb5!?;*

16 ♘g4!?) 16 . . . ♗b7 17 f4 a6 18 a4 ±
Chandler–Speelman, Great Britain
1986.

16 ♗f4

16 ♘f3 *(16 ♘c4 ♗d7 17 ♘e3 ♕e5 =
Hennings–Filip, Havana 1967)* 16 . . .
♗xb2 17 ♖ab1 ♗a3 18 ♗c3 *(18 ♖fd1
♕h5 ∞ Popovic–Christiansen, Ljub-
ljana/Portoroz 1985)* 18 . . . ♗e7 19
♖fd1 ♕c5 *(19 . . . ♕h5? 20 ♖b5 ♘d5
21 ♖xd5! +–)* 20 ♗a1 ♖fd8 = de
Firmian–Dlugy, USA 1985.

16 . . .   ♗xb2
17 ♖ab1   . . .

17 ♖ad1 ♕c5! *(17 . . . ♕xa2 18 c3
♕a4 unclear; 17 . . . ♗xe5? 18 ♗xe5
♕a5 19 f4! ♘d7?! – 19 . . . ♘e8 20 ♔h1
∞ – 20 ♗xg7! ♔xg7 21 ♕g4+ ♔h8 22
♕h4 ♔g7 23 ♖f3 ♖h8   24 f5! ±
London–Dlugy, Brooklyn 1985)* 18 c4
(18 ♘c4 e5!) 18 . . . ♗d4 19 ♗b1 b6 20
♖d3 ♗b7 21 ♖g3 ♖ad8 22 h3 ♖fe8 ∓
Khalifman–Tukmakov, USSR (ch)
1987.

17 . . .   ♗d4

17 . . . ♗xe5 18 ♗xe5 ♘d7 19 ♖b5
♕c6 20 ♗xg7! ∞.

18 c4   ♕d8

18 . . . ♕c5!? (Sterengas, Solo-
zenkin).

19 ♖fd1   ♕e7

20 ♗c2   ♗b6
21 ♕f3   ♗c7
22 ♕h3 ±

22 . . . a6?! *(22 . . . ♖d8!?)* Sterengas–
Sokolin, USSR 1987; 23 ♖d3! ±.

B1.1122

10 . . .   ♘bd7!?

A popular and sharp continuation.

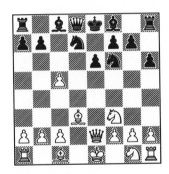

B1.11221: 11 c6
B1.11222: 11 b4?!

B1.11221

11 c6   . . .

A simple positional method, weakening Black's pawn formation.
11 ♘e5 ♘xe5 *(11 . . . ♘xc5?! 12
♗b5+!)* 12 ♕xe5 ♕a5+ *(12 . . . ♘d7
13 ♕e2 ♘xc5 14 ♗b5+ ♗d7 15 ♗d2
♗xb5 16 ♕xb5+ ♕d7 17 ♕e2 was
Radulov–Onat, Nice (ol) 1974; 17 . . .*

♕*d5! ∞)* 13 ♗d2 ♕xc5 14 ♘f3
(14 ♕e2 ♗d6 15 ♘f3 ♗d7 =) 14 . . .
♕xe5 *(14 . . . ♗d6?! 15 ♕e2 b6 16 0-0-0
♗b7 17 ♗e3 ♕c7 18 ♗b5+ ±)*
15 ♘xe5 ♗c5 *(15 . . . ♗d6 16 ♘c4 ♗c5
17 f4 b6 18 0-0-0 0-0 19 ♖he1 ♖d8 20
♘e5 ♗b7 = Radulov–Filip, Skopje (ol)
1972)* 16 ♗e2 *(16 ♗b5+ ♔e7 17 ♗e2
♘e4 18 ♘d3 ♗d6 19 ♗e3 ♗d7 20 ♗d4
f6 21 ♗f3 ♗c6 ∓ Parma–Smyslov,
Lugano (ol) 1968)* 16 . . . ♘e4 17 ♘d3
♗d6 18 ♗e3 ♗d7 = (Filip).

11 . . .	bxc6
12 ♗d2	. . .

12 ♘d2 *(12 ♗f4?! ♘d5 and 13 . . .
♕f6 ∓)* 12 . . . ♘d5 13 ♘b3 *(13 ♘e4
♘e5 14 ♘f3 ♘xd3+ 15 ♕xd3 ♕c7 16
0-0 ♗e7 17 c4 ♘f6 18 ♗d2 c5 19
♘xf6+♗xf6 20 ♗c3 − Haág–
Pachman, Solingen 1968 − 20 . . . ♗b7!
=)* 13 . . . ♘b4 14 ♗c4 ♘b6 15 a3 ♘xc4
16 ♕xc4 ♗a6 17 ♕e4 *(17 ♕c3 ♕h4!?)*
17 . . . ♕d5! 18 ♕xd5 ♘xd5 ∓ Typek–
Sapis, Poland 1987.

12 . . .	♕b6!
13 b3	♗a3!
14 ♗e3	. . .

14 ♘h3 g5! (Sapis).

14 . . .	♕a5+
15 ♗d2 =	

Przewoznik–Sapis, Poland 1988.

B1.11222

11 b4?!

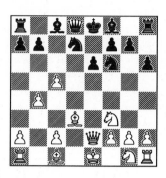

11 . . .   ♘d5

The alternatives are:

a) 11 . . . a5!? 12 c3 ♗e7 13 ♘d4
*(13 a3 ♘d5 14 ♗d2 axb4 15 cxb4 ♗f6
16 ♖a2 ♘c3 17 ♗xc3 ♗xc3+ 18 ♔f1
∞ And. Martin)* 13 . . . 0-0 14 ♘gf3
*(14 ♘h3? axb4 15 cxb4 ♘xc5 ∓; 14
♗b2 axb4 15 cxb4 e5! 16 ♘f5 b6 17
♗xe5 ♘xe5 18 ♕xe5 ♗xf5 19 ♕xf5
bxc5 20 ♘e2 ♖a3 =)* 14 . . . e5 15 ♘f5
*(15 ♘xe5? ♘xe5 16 ♕xe5 axb4 17
cxb4 ♘g4 ∓)* 15 . . . e4 16 ♘xe7+
*(16 ♗xe4 ♘xe4 17 ♕xe4 ♗xc5! 18 0-0
♘f6 ∓)* 16 . . . ♕xe7 17 ♗c4 axb4 18
cxb4 b6 *(18 . . . ♖e8 19 ♘d4 ♘e5 20 h3
b6 ∞)* 19 ♗f4 ♘h5 20 ♗d6 ♕f6 21
♘d4 (And. Martin–Meduna, Bad
Wörishofen 1988) 21 . . . bxc5! ∓.

b) 11 . . . b6 12 ♘d4 *(12 ♗e4 ♘xe4
13 ♕xe4 ♗a6 14 cxb6 axb6 15 ♘e2
♖c8 ∓ − Filip)* 12 . . . ♘d5 *(12 . . . bxc5?
13 ♘c6! ♕c7 14 ♕xe6+! 1-0 Perenyi–*

Eperjesi, Hungary 1974; 12 . . . ♘xc5 13
♗b5+ ♘cd7 14 a3! ♗b7 15 ♘gf3 ♗e7
16 ♗b2 a6 17 ♗c4 b5 18 ♗xe6!? fxe6
19 ♘xe6 ♛b6 20 ♘xg7+ ♔f7 21 0-0-0
♖hd8 − 21 . . . ♘d5 22 ♘h5 ♖he8 23
♛d3 ♛g6 24 ♛xg6+ ♔xg6 25 ♖xd5!
− 22 ♖he1 ♘e4 23 ♖xd7 ♖xd7 24
♘e5+ ♔g8 25 ♘xd7 +− Sideif-Sade −
Ivanov, Moscow 1979) 13 ♗b2 (13
♘xe6 fxe6 14 ♗g6+ ♔e7) 13 . . . ♘xb4
14 ♗e4 (14 c6! ♘xd3+ 15 ♛xd3 ♘c5
16 ♛f3 ♘a4 17 0-0-0 ♘xb2 18 ♔xb2
♛c7 19 ♛e4!? a6 20 ♘gf3 ♗e7 21 ♘e5
0-0 22 f4 ± Reinert-Kristiansson,
Aarhus 1981) 14 . . . ♗a6 15 ♛f3
♘xc5!? 16 ♘c6! (16 ♗xa8 ♘xc2+! 17
♘xc2 ♘d3+ van der Wiel-Balashov,
Malta (ol) 1980, 18 ♛xd3! ∞) 16 . . .
♘xe4 17 ♘xd8 (17 ♛xe4? ♛d5!) 17
. . . ♘xc2+ 18 ♔d1 ♖xd8+ 19 ♔xc2
♖c8+ 20 ♔d1 ♖d8+ and the game is
drawish.

12	♗d2	♛f6
13	♖b1	a5
14	a3	g5
15	♗e4	♘c3
16	♗xc3	♛xc3+
17	♛d2	♛xa3
18	♛d4	e5!?

18 . . . ♖g8?! 19 ♖a1 axb4 20
♖xa3 bxa3 21 ♘e2 a2 22 ♔d2 ♗g7 23
♛b4! ± Rodriguez-Tal, Subotica (izt)
1987.

19	♘xe5	♗g7
20	♖a1	axb4
21	♖xa3	bxa3 ∞

Mestel-K. Arkell, Great Britain (ch)
1988.

B1.12

8	♗b3	h6
9	♘5f3	

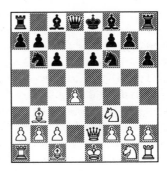

Black now has the plans 9 . . . c5 and
9 . . . a5 at his disposal.

Other possibilities are:

a) **9 . . . ♗d6** 10 ♘e5 ♛e7 11 ♘gf3
c5 *(11 . . . ♗d7 12 ♗d2 c5 13 dxc5
♗xc5 14 0-0 a6 15 a3 ♖c8 16 c4 ±
Suetin)* 12 ♗e3 0-0 13 g4 ♘fd5 14 ♗d2
cxd4 15 g5 ± Yurkov-Chistiakov,
USSR 1962.

b) **9 . . . ♗e7** 10 ♗d2 *(10 ♘h3 g5!)*
10 . . . a5 *(10 . . . 0-0?! 11 0-0-0 followed
by ♘e5 and g4 ±)* 11 c4 0-0 12 ♘h3 c5
13 dxc5 ♗xc5 14 0-0-0 ♛e7 15 ♘e5
♘bd7 16 f4 ± Khasin-Livshin, USSR
1958.

B1.121: 9 . . . c5
B1.122: 9 . . . a5?!

B1.121

9 . . .   c5

B1.1211: 10 ♗f4
B1.1212: 10 ♗e3

B1.1211

10 ♗f4

a) **10 c3** ♕c7 11 ♗e3 ♗d6?! *(11 . . .
♘bd5 ∞)* 12 dxc5 ♗xc5 13 ♗xc5
♕xc5 14 ♘e5 ± (Suetin).
  b) **10 dxc5** ♘bd7 *(10 . . . ♗xc5?! 11
♗d2 0-0 − 11 . . . ♕c7!? − 12 ♘e5
♘bd5 13 ♘gf3 b6 14 0-0-0 ♕e7 15 g4!
± Trapl–Perez, Oberhausen 1961)* 11
c6!? bxc6 12 ♘h3 ♗e7 *(12 . . . ♗d6 13
♗e3 ♕c7 14 0-0-0 0-0 15 g4 ♘xg4 16
♖hg1 ♘df6 17 ♔b1 e5 18 ♗c1 ±
Ciocaltea–Barcza, Debrecen 1961)* 13
0-0 ♕b6 14 ♘f4 ♗a6 15 c4 c5 16 ♘d3
0-0 17 ♘de5 ♖fd8 18 ♗c2 ♗b7 19 b3
♘f8 = Suetin–Petrosian, Moscow
1959.

10 . . .   ♘bd5!?

10 . . . a6 and now:
  a) **11 dxc5** ♗xc5 12 ♖d1 ♘bd7 13
♘e5 ♕a5+ 14 ♔f1 ♘xe5 15 ♗xe5
♗d7 16 ♘f3 (A. Rodriguez–Spiridonov, Belgrade 1988) 16 . . . ♗e7 =.
  b) **11 0-0-0?!** c4! 12 ♗xc4 ♘xc4 13
♕xc4 ♘d5 14 ♗d2 b5 15 ♕e2 *(15
♕d3 ♗b7 ∞ Ivanchuk–Savchenko,
USSR 1987)* 15 . . . ♗b7 16 ♘e5 ♘f6 17
♘gf3 ♖c8 18 ♔b1 ♗e4 19 ♖c1 ♕d5

20 ♖he1 ♗e7 21 g4 0-0 22 g5 ±
Kupreichik–Spiridonov, Palma de
Mallorca 1989.
  c) **11 ♖d1** c4! 12 ♗xc4 ♘xc4 13
♕xc4 b5 14 ♕b3 ♗b7 15 c4 ♖c8! 16
cxb5 *(16 c5?! g5! 17 ♗e5 g4 ∓
Minasyan–Savchenko, USSR 1987)* 16
. . . ♗d5 *(16 . . . ♕a5+ 17 ♗d2 ♕xb5
=)* 17 ♕a4 axb5 18 ♕xb5+ ♗c6 19
♕b3 ♗d5 = Savchenko.
  d) **11 c4!?** cxd4 12 0-0-0 ♗c5 13
♘xd4 ♕e7 *(13 . . . ♗xd4?! 14 ♘f3
♗xb2+ 15 ♕xb2 ♗d7 16 ♘e5 ∞±)* 14
♘gf3 0-0 15 ♖hg1!? *(15 g4 ♘xg4 16
♖hg1 e5 ∞)* 15 . . . ♖d8 ± Watson–
Spiridonov, Palma de Mallorca 1989.

11 ♗e5   ♕a5+
12 ♘d2   . . .

12 c3? ♘xc3 13 ♕d2 ♘fe4 winning.

12 . . .   b5!?

12 . . . cxd4 13 ♘f3 *(13 0-0-0?! b5! 14
♘gf3 ♘c3!)* 13 . . . ♗e7 14 0-0 0-0 15
♘xd4 ♗d7 16 a3 *(16 f4 ±)* 16 . . . ♕c5!
17 c4 ♘f4 18 ♗xf4 ♕xd4 = Suetin–
Filip, Sochi 1978.

13 c4!?

13 dxc5 ♗xc5 14 ♘gf3 0-0 15 0-0
♗a6 16 ♗xd5 ♘xd5 17 ♘b3 ♕b6
18 ♘xc5 ♕xc5 19 ♗d4 = Nunn–
Speelman, Reykjavik 1988.

13 . . .   bxc4
14 ♗xc4   ♘b6

15 b4!   ...

15 ♗d3 c4!

15 ...   ♕xb4

15 . . . cxb4?! 16 ♘b3 ♕a3 ±.

16 ♖b1	♕a5
17 ♗b5+	♗d7
18 ♗xf6	gxf6 ±

The game Short–Speelman (Hastings 1988/89) continued 19 ♘gf3 cxd4 20 0-0 ♖d8! 21 ♘e4! ♗e7 22 ♘xd4 ♔f8 23 ♖fd1 f5 ∞.

B1.1212

10 ♗e3   ...

10 ...   ♕c7

10 . . . a6?! 11 dxc5! ♘bd7 12 c6! bxc6 13 0-0-0 *(13 ♘h3 ♗d6 14 0-0-0 ♕c7 Pintér–Csom, Budapest 1976, 15 g4! ±)* 13 . . . ♕c7 14 ♘h3 ♗d6 15

♘d2! ± Jansa–Pacl, Czechoslovakia 1984.

11 ♘e5   a6

The following lines are also possible:

a) **11 . . . a5?!** 12 a3 a4 13 ♗a2 ♗d6 14 ♘gf3 ♘bd7 15 ♗f4 0-0 16 ♖d1 b6 17 ♗c4 ♘d5 18 ♗g3 ♗b7 19 ♗b5 ♘7f6 20 dxc5 bxc5 21 c4 ♘e7 22 ♖xd6! ± Kavalek–Bukic, 1979.

b) **11 . . . ♗d6** 12 ♘gf3 0-0 13 0-0 a5 *(13 . . . ♘bd5 14 c3 b6 15 ♖ad1 ♗b7 =* Spassky–Benkö, Amsterdam (izt) 1964) 14 c4 ♘bd7 15 ♘xd7 ♗xd7 = Stein–Smyslov, USSR 1964.

c) **11 . . . ♗d7** 12 ♘gf3 ♖c8 13 c4 cxd4 14 ♗xd4 ♗b4+ 15 ♔f1 ♗c5 16 ♗e3 ♗c6 17 ♘xc6 ♕xc6 18 ♘e5 (Kupreichik–Petrosian, USSR (ch) 1969) 18 . . . ♕c7! =.

d) **11 . . . cxd4** 12 ♗xd4 ♗c5 13 ♘gf3 0-0 14 0-0-0 a5 15 a3 a4 16 ♗a2 ± Spassky–Pfleger, Tallinn 1973.

12 ♘gf3	♘bd5
13 0-0	♘xe3

13 . . . ♗d6 14 ♘c4 ♗e7 15 dxc5 ♗xc5 16 ♗xc5 ♕xc5 = Gheorghiu–Filip, Tel Aviv (ol) 1964.

14 fxe3	♗d6
15 c3	0-0
16 ♗c2	♘d7

Planning 17 ♕d3 f5 = (Pintér–Flesch, Budapest 1975).

B1.122

9 . . .   a5?!

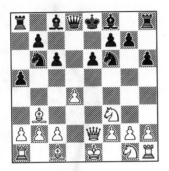

B1.1221: 10 a4!?
B1.1222: 10 a3

B1.1221

**10 a4!?   c5
11 ♗f4   ♗d6
12 ♗g3   . . .**

a) 12 ♗e5 0-0 13 0-0-0?! c4 14 ♗xc4 ♘xa4 15 ♘h3 ♘b6 16 g4 a4! 17 g5 hxg5 18 ♘hxg5 a3 19 b3 ♗b4! ∓ Tal-Petrosian, USSR (ch) 1973.
b) 12 ♘e5!? cxd4 13 0-0-0 0-0 14 ♘gf3 ♘bd5 15 ♗g3 b5! 16 ♘c6 ♕c7 17 axb5 a4 18 ♗xd5 ♘xd5 19 ♘fxd4 a3 20 c4 a2 21 ♔c2 e5! 22 cxd5 exd4 23 b3 ♗d7 ∞(±) Short-Speelman, Hastings 1987/88.

12 . . .   0-0

12 . . . ♕c7 13 dxc5 *(13 ♕b5+!? ♘fd7*

14 dxc5!? ♕xc5 15 ♕xc5 ♗xc5 ±) 13 . . . ♕xc5 14 0-0-0 ♗xg3 15 hxg3 ♗d7 16 ♖h4 ♗c6 17 ♘d4 *(17 ♘e5 ♗d5 18 ♗xd5 ♘fxd5 19 ♘gf3 ♖c8 = L. A. Schneider-Sapis, Gothenburg 1989)* 17 . . . ♗d5 18 ♘gf3 ♖c8 19 ♘e5 0-0 20 ♘g4 ± (Sapis).

13 ♖d1!

13 dxc5 ♗xg3 14 hxg3 ♘bd7 15 ♘e5 ♘xe5 16 ♕xe5 ♘d7 17 ♕d6! ♖a6 ∞ Abramovic-Watson, Brüssels 1986.

13 . . .   ♘bd5

13 . . . ♕c7? 14 dxc5! wins.

14 ♘e5   . . .

14 dxc5 ♗xc5 15 c4 ♕b6 ∞.

**14 . . .   cxd4
15 ♘gf3   ♗b4+
16 ♔f1   ♘d7**

16 . . . ♗d7!? is an interesting try here.

**17 ♘xd4   ♘xe5
18 ♗xe5   ♗d7
19 h4! ±**

M. Tseitlin-Lutz, Budapest 1989 (M. Tseitlin).

B1.1222

10 a3

10 . . .   a4

a) **10 . . . g6** 11 ♗d2! ♗g7 12 0-0-0
0-0 13 h4! ♕c7 14 ♘h3 ♘bd5 15 c4 c5
16 cxd5 cxd4+ 17 ♔b1 ♕b6 *(17 . . .
♘xd5 18 ♗xd5 ±)* 18 ♔a2! a4 19 ♗c2
♘xd5 *(19 . . . ♘e4!?)* 20 ♘f4! ♕c7 21
♘xd5 ♕xc2 22 ♘e7+ ♔h8 23 ♕b5! ±
Kupreichik–Tukmakov, USSR (ch)
1987.
b) **10 . . . ♗e7** 11 ♗d2! ♘bd5?!
(11 . . . c5!?) 12 c4 ♘c7 13 ♗c2 0-0?
*(13 . . . b5 14 ♘e5 ♗b7 15 c5 ♘cd5 16
♘gf3 ±)* 14 ♘e5! ♕xd4 15 ♗c3 ♕d8
16 ♘gf3 *(16 ♖d1 ♕e8 17 ♕d3)* 16 . . .
♘ce8 17 g4! ± Tal–Speelman,
Subotica (izt) 1987.

11 ♗a2   c5
12 c3   . . .

a) **12 dxc5** ♗xc5 13 ♘e5 0-0 14
♘gf3 ♘bd7 15 0-0 ♘xe5 16 ♘xe5 b6

17 ♕f3 ♗a6 18 ♖e1 ♕d4 19 c3 ♕h4
20 ♗e3 = Tukmakov–Zaitsev, USSR
(ch) 1969.
b) **12 ♗e3** ♘bd5 13 c3 ♕c7 *(13 . . .
♗e7 14 ♘e5 0-0 15 ♘gf3 ♕c7 16 ♗c4
b6 17 0-0 ♗b7 was Liberzon–Smyslov,
Biel (izt) 1976)* 14 ♘e5 ♗d6 15 ♘gf3
0-0 16 ♗d2 (Karpov–Kavalek, Turin
1982) 16 . . . b6! =.

12 . . .   ♗d7

12 . . . ♖a5 13 ♗e3 ♘bd5 14 ♘e5
cxd4 15 cxd4 ♗d7 16 ♘xd7 ♕xd7 ∞.

13 ♘e5   cxd4
14 cxd4   ♗e7
15 ♘gf3 ±
Karpov–Petrosian, Tilburg 1982.

B1.2

7 ♘e2   . . .

With this move White avoids any
early simplification. By not following
up so aggressively, however, his sixth

move may turn out to be a tempo wasted.

7 ...　　　　h6

Somewhat better than 7 ... ♘b6 8 ♗b3 c5 9 c3 ♗e7 10 0-0 0-0 *(10...c4 11 ♗c2 ♗d7 12 ♘f4 g6 13 ♖e1 ♗c6 14 b3 ♘fd5 15 ♘gxe6 ± Simagin-Korchnoi, USSR 1960)* 11 ♖e1 ♘bd5 12 dxc5 ♗xc5 13 ♘d4 ♕b6 14 ♘gf3 ♖d8 15 ♗g5 ± Spassky-Lein, Sochi 1965.

8 ♘f3　　　　♗d6

8 ... b5 is a touch premature after 9 ♗d3! *(9 ♗b3 c5 10 dxc5 ♗xc5 = Gulko-Razuvaev, Dubna 1970)* 9 ... ♗b7 10 c3 ♕b6 11 a4 a6 12 axb5 cxb5 13 ♘g3 ♗d6 14 ♕e2 0-0 15 ♘e5 ♖fd8 16 f4 ± Bronstein-Vasyukov, USSR (ch) 1965.

9 0-0　　　　♕c7
10 ♖e1　　　　...

10 ♘c3?! encourages Black to expand on the queenside with 10 ... b5 11 ♗d3 b4 as in Simagin-Smyslov, Moscow 1974, with excellent prospects for the initiative (see illustrative games for the complete moves).

10 ...　　　　0-0
11 ♘c3　　　　b5!

Filip's suggestion in *ECO* which he

continues 12 ♗d3 ♗b7 13 ♘e4 ♘xe4 14 ♗xe4 c5 =. Alternatives are less satisfactory:

a) **11 ... ♘d5?!** 12 ♘e4 ♗f4 13 ♗xf4 ♕xf4 14 ♘g3! *(14 ♗f1 b6 15 g3 ♕c7 16 ♗g2 ♗b7 17 c4 ♘5f6 18 ♘xf6+ ♘xf6 = Stein-Pfleger, Tel Aviv (ol) 1964)* 14 ... b6 15 ♘e5 ♘xe5 16 ♖xe5 ♕h4 17 ♕d2 ♗b7 18 ♖ae1 ± Boleslavsky.

b) **11 ... a6** 12 ♘e4 b5 13 ♘xd6 ♕xd6 14 ♗f1 c5 15 dxc5 ♕xd1 16 ♖xd1 ♘xc5 17 ♗e3 ± Geller-Smyslov, USSR 1964.

B2

6 ♘xf6+　　　　♘xf6

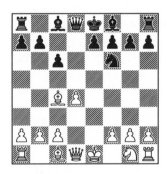

7 ♘f3　　　　...

7 c3, temporarily hindering Black's QB development, deserves attention. He can then choose from:

a) **7 ... b5?!** *(both 7 ... ♗f5 and 7 ... ♗g4? fail to 8 ♕b3! +−)* 8 ♗d3 ♗g4 9 ♘e2 e6 10 ♕c2 ♗xe2?! *(10 ... ♗e7*

11 h3 ♗h5 12 ♘f4 ±) 11 ♕xe2 ♗e7 12 0-0 0-0 13 ♗f4 ♘d5 14 ♗d2 ♖e8 15 a4 ± Ubilava-Kholmov, Tbilisi 1976.

b) **7 . . . e6** 8 ♘f3 ♗e7 9 0-0 0-0 10 ♕e2 b5 11 ♗d3 ♗b7 12 ♗f4! ♕b6 13 ♘e5 ♖ad8 14 a4 a6 15 a5 ± Stein-Vasyukov, USSR (ch) 1964.

c) **7 . . . g6** 8 ♘f3 ♗g7 9 0-0 0-0 10 h3 ♘d5?! *(10 . . . ♗f5 planning . . . ♗e4)* 11 ♖e1 h6 12 ♕e2 e6 13 ♗b3 ♕d6 14 c4 ♘e7 15 ♕e4 ± Hulak-Bertok, Vinkovci 1976.

d) **7 . . . ♕c7** (Looks best. Protecting b7 enables the queen's bishop to move) 8 ♘f3 *(8 ♕b3 e6 9 ♘f3 ♗d6 10 0-0 h6 11 ♖e1 0-0 = Wade-Richter, Trenčianske Teplice 1949; 8 ♕e2!? ♗g4 9 f3 ♗f5 10 g4! ♗g6 11 f4 ♗e4! 12 ♘f3 e6 13 0-0 ♗xf3 14 ♕xf3 ♗d6 15 a4 ± Kostyra-Sapis, Poland 1990)* 8 . . . ♗g4 9 h3 ♗h5 *(9 . . . ♗xf3 10 ♕xf3 e6 11 0-0 ♗d6 12 ♗g5 ♘d5 13 ♖fe1 ± Gheorghiu-Pachman, Havana (ol) 1966)* 10 g4 ♗g6 11 ♘e5 e6 *(11 . . . ♘d7 12 ♗f4 ♘xe5 13 ♗xe5 ± Stein-Filip, Erevan 1965)* 12 ♗f4 ♗d6 with chances for both sides (Filip).

7 . . .   ♗f5

The most natural move. **7 . . . g6** leads to the Hulak-Bertok game quoted above, and **7 . . . e6** is passive: 8 ♗g5 ♕a5+ 9 c3 ♘e4 10 ♗f4 ♗d6 11 ♗e5! ♗xe5 12 ♘xe5 ♘f6 13 0-0 0-0 14 ♕e2 ♕c7 15 ♖ad1 ♘d5 16 ♖fe1 f6 17 ♘d3 ♗d7 18 ♗b3 ♖ae8 19 ♕e4 ♕d6 20 h4! ± Keres-Barcza, 1961.

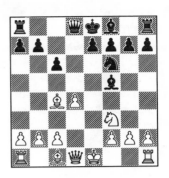

8 ♘e5   . . .

There are several playable alternatives:

a) **8 0-0** This leads to the slight space advantage characteristic of this variation of the Caro-Kann, e.g: 8 . . . e6 and then perhaps 9 ♗g5 ♗e7 10 ♕e2 ♗g4 11 ♖ad1 0-0 12 h3 ♗xf3 13 ♕xf3 ♘d5 14 ♗e3! ± *(14 ♗c1 ♗g5 15 ♗e3 ♕f6 = Larsen-Filip, Palma de Mallorca (izt) 1970)*, or alternatively 9 ♖e1 ♗g4 10 c3 ♗e7 *(10 . . . ♗d6 11 ♗e2 — 11 h3!? — 11 . . . ♕c7 12 ♘e5!? ♗xe2 13 ♕xe2 0-0 14 ♗f4 ♘d5 15 ♗g3 ♘e7!? ∞ Lidberg-Podgaec, Haifa 1989)* 11 h3 ♗xf3 12 ♕xf3 0-0 13 g3! ± Ehlvest-Kharitonov, USSR (ch) 1988.

b) **8 ♕e2** (also promising) 8 . . . e6 9 ♗g5 ♗e7 10 0-0-0!? ♗g4 *(10 . . . h6 11 ♗h4 ♘e4 12 g4! ♗h7 13 ♗g3 ♘xg3 14 fxg3 ♕c7 15 ♘e5 ♗d6 16 h4 ± Tal-Füstér, Portorož 1958)* 11 h3 ♗xf3 12 ♕xf3 ♘d5 13 ♗xe7 ♕xe7 14 ♔b1 *(14 ♖he1 0-0 15 ♔b1 ♖ad8 ± Matanović-Petrosian, Yugoslavia v USSR 1969)* 14 . . . ♖d8 15 ♕e4 b5 16 ♗d3 a5 17 c3

♕d6 18 g3 b4 19 c4 ± Fischer–Petrosian, Bled 1961.

c) **8 c3** e6 9 ♕e2 ♗g4 10 h3 ♗xf3 11 ♕xf3 ♕c7 12 0-0 ♗e7 = is playable; one last example is **8 ♗f4** e6 9 0-0 ♗e7 10 c3 0-0 11 ♕b3?! ♕b6 12 ♕xb6 axb6 13 ♗b3 b5 ∓ Pietzsch–Smyslov, Moscow 1963.

8 ...	**e6**
9 0-0	...

White can also chase the f5 bishop with **9 g4?!** ♗g6! *(9 ... ♗e4? is dubious although 10 f3 ♗d5 11 ♗d3 ♗d6 12 c4 ♗xe5 13 dxe5 ♘xg4 14 ♗f4 g5 15 cxd5 gxf4 16 fxg4 ♕xd5 17 0-0 0-0-0 18 ♖f3 ♖hg8 favoured Black in Rauser–Veresov, USSR 1934. The improved version is 11 ♗e2! b5 12 a4 ♗d6 13 axb5 ♗xe5 14 dxe5 ♘xg4 15 ♗f4 ± Stein–Ivkov, Amsterdam 1970)* 10 ♗f4! *(10 h4 ♘d7 11 ♗f4 ♘xe5 12 ♗xe5 h5 ∓)* 10 ... ♘d7 11 ♘xg6 hxg6 12 c3 ♘b6 13 ♗b3 ♗d6 14 ♗g3 ♗xg3 15 fxg3 ♕g5 16 ♕f3 0-0-0 17 0-0 = Rauser–Veresov, USSR 1934.

Also to be considered are **9 ♗b3** ♗d6 10 ♕e2 ♘d7 11 ♗d2 *(11 ♘xf7? ♔xf7 12 g4 ♘f6! 13 gxf5 ♕a5+ Schwarz)* 11 ... ♗xe5! *(not 11 ... a5? 12 ♘xf7! ♔xf7 13 g4 ♕f6 14 gxf5 ♕xf5 15 0-0-0 a4 16 ♗c4 ± Gligorić–Petrosian, 1957)* 12 dxe5 ♕c7 ± and **9 c3** ♗d6 10 ♕e2 ♕c7 11 ♗g5 h5! 12 0-0-0 ♘d5 13 ♗d2 f6 14 ♘d3 0-0-0 15 ♗b3 e5 Shiyanovsky–Berezhnoi, USSR 1964.

9 ...   ♗d6

Also satisfactory are:

a) **9 ... ♘d7** 10 ♗f4 ♘xe5 11 ♗xe5 ♗d6! = Filip.

b) **9 ... ♗e7** 10 ♖e1 *(10 ♗b3 a5 11 c4 0-0 12 ♗f4 c5 13 dxc5 ♗xc5 14 ♕e2 ♕d4 ∓ Gligorić–Smyslov, Moscow 1963)* 10 ... ♘d7 *(10 ... ♗e4 11 ♗g5 ♗d5 12 ♗d3 ±)* 11 ♗f4 ♘xe5 12 ♗xe5 0-0 13 c3 b5 14 ♗b3 c5 = Matanović–Filip, Erevan 1965.

10 ♕e2	**0-0**
11 ♗g5	**♕c7**
12 ♖ad1	**b5**

13 ♗d3 ♘d5 14 ♘f3 ♗xd3 15 ♕xd3 c5 = Spassky–Ilivitsky, Sochi 1965.

C

5 ♘g5   ...

Developed from the peripheral 5 ♗d3 ♘gf6 6 ♘g5, this line came into fashion in 1986. It aims to exert

pressure on f7 and, should Black be able to parry this, put Black in a permanent bind. At first White achieved various crushing victories, but since then Black has developed quite a few methods to counter White's attack.

C1: 5 . . . ♘gf6
C2: 5 . . . ♘b6
C3: 5 . . . ♘df6

C1

5 . . .   ♘gf6

Sober, but the QB becomes hard to develop in this line. Resignatory attempts include:
a) **5 . . . e6** 6 ♗d3 c5?! 7 ♘1f3 cxd4 8 0-0 ♗e7 (Nunn–Speelman, Brussels 1988) 9 ♗xh7! ±.
b) **5 . . . h6?!** 6 ♘e6 ♕a5+ 7 ♗d2 ♕b6 8 ♗d3 fxe6? *(8 . . . ♘gf6 9 ♘xf8 ♘xf8 10 ♘e2 or 10 ♘f3 ±)* 9 ♕h5+ ♔d8 10 ♗a5 1-0 Nunn–Kir. Georgiev, Linares 1988.

6 ♗d3   e6

Other major alternatives include:
a) **6 . . . h6** 7 ♘e6 ♕a5+ 8 ♗d2 ♕b6 9 ♘f3 fxe6 10 ♗g6+ ♔d8 11 0-0 c5? *(11 . . . ♕c7 ∞)* 12 c4 cxd4 13 ♘xd4 e5 14 c5! ♘xc5 15 ♗a5 +– Tal–Oll, USSR 1986.
b) **6 . . . ♕b6?!** 7 a4 h6 8 a5 ♕c7 9 ♘5f3 c5 10 ♘e2 c4 11 ♗f4 ♕c6 12 ♗f5 e6 13 ♗h3 gives White the edge, according to Bikhovsky.
c) **6 . . . c5** 7 ♘1f3 cxd4 8 0-0 h6 9 ♘e6 ♕b6 10 ♖e1 ♘c5 *(10 . . . fxe6 11 ♗g6+ ♔d8 12 ♘xd4 e5 13 ♖xe5 e6 14 ♘xe6+ +–)* 11 ♘xc5 ♕xc5 12 ♘xd4 a6 13 c3 e6 14 ♗f4 ♗e7 15 ♗c2 ♗d7 16 ♘f5 ♗c6 17 ♖e5 ♕b6 18 ♘xg7+ ♔f8 19 ♘f5 (Tseshkovsky–Khalifman, Tashkent 1987) 19 . . . ♖d8! ∞.
d) **6 . . . ♘b6** 7 ♘1f3 h6 *(7 . . . ♗g4 8 h3 ♗xf3 9 ♘xf3 ± Tivyakov–Abramov, USSR 1988)* 8 ♘e4 *(8 ♘xf7!? ♔xf7 9 ♘e5+ ♔g8 10 ♗g6 ♗e6 11 0-0 ♘c4 12 f4 ♘d6 13 f5 ± Abramov)* 8 . . . ♘xe4 9 ♗xe4 ♗g4 10 0-0 e6 11 h3 ♗xf3 12 ♕xf3 ♗e7 *(12 . . . ♗d6!?)* 13 c3 ♘d5 14 ♖e1 0-0 15 ♗c2 ♖e8 16 ♕d3 ♘f6 17 ♗f4 ♗d6 18 ♗e5 ± Havelko–Tomaszewski, Poland 1987.
e) **6 . . . g6** 7 ♘1f3 *(7 ♗c4!? ♘d5 8 ♘1f3 ♗g7 9 0-0 0-0 10 ♖e1 ♘7f6 11 ♘e5! ♘e8 12 ♘gf3 ±; 7 . . . e6 8 ♕e2 ♘b6 9 ♗b3 ∞)* 7 . . . ♗g7 8 0-0 0-0 9 ♖e1 h6 10 ♘e4 ♘xe4 11 ♗xe4 c5 12 c3 cxd4 13 ♘xd4 *(13 cxd4!?)* 13 . . . ♘c5 14 ♗c2 e5 15 ♘b3 ♕c7 16 ♘xc5

♕xc5 17 ♗e3 ♕c7 = Sokolov–Spraggett, St. John (c) 1988.

f) 6 ... ♕*c7 7* ♘*e2 (7* ♘*1f3 h6 8* ♘*e6 fxe6 9* ♗*g6+* ♔*d8 10 0-0* ♕*d6 – 10 ... b6?! 11 g3!* ♗*b7 12* ♗*f4* ± *– 11 c4* ± *de Firmian; 7* ♕*e2 h6 8* ♘*5f3 e6 9* ♘*e5* ♘*xe5 10 dxe5* ♘*d7 11* ♘*f3* ♘*c5 = Bikhovsky) 7 ...* e6 **8 c4** ♗b4+ **9** ♗d2 *(9* ♘*c3 0-0 10 0-0 e5 = Gelfand–Dreev, Vilnius 1988) 9 ...* ♗xd2+ **10** ♕xd2 h6 **11** ♘f3 0-0 **12** 0-0 e5 **13** dxe5 ♘xe5 **14** ♘xe5 ♕xe5 **15** ♘g3 ♗e6 = Ulybin–Georgadze, USSR 1988. Better is **8** ♗**f4!** ♗*d6 9* ♗*xd6 (9* ♕*d2 e5!) 9 ...* ♕xd6 **10** ♕d2 0-0! *(10 ... e5?! 11 0-0-0 h6 12* ♘*xf7!* ♔*xf7 13 dxe5* ♕*xe5 14* ♘*f4!* ± *Khuzman–Khelnicki, Herson 1989)* **11** 0-0-0 b6 ±.

7   ♘1f3   ...

7 ♘e2 h6 **8** ♘f3 c5 **9** 0-0 ♗e7 **10** ♗f4 a6 **11** c4 b6 **12** ♘e5 ♗b7 **13** ♕a4 0-0 **14** ♖ad1 ♕c8 **15** ♕b3 cxd4 **16** ♘xd4 ♘xe5 **17** ♗xe5 ♘d7 **18** ♗g3 ♖d8 was level in Arnasson–Burger, Reykjavik 1986.

C1.1: 7 ... h6
C1.2: 7 ... ♗e7
C1.3: 7 ... ♗d6

C1.1

7 ...   h6

7 ... ♕c7 **8** ♕e2 h6 **9** ♗g6! hxg5 **10** ♗xf7+ ♔d8 **11** ♘xg5 ♘b6 (van der Wiel–Karpov, Amsterdam 1987) **12** g3! ♗d7 **13** ♗xe6 ♗e8 **14** ♗f5 ♗f7 **15** ♗f4 ♕e7 **16** ♕xe7+ ♔xe7 **17** 0-0 ♗g8 **18** b3 ± (van der Wiel).

8   ♘xe6   ...

8 ♘e4 ♘xe4 **9** ♗xe4 ♘f6 **10** ♗d3 c5 **11** dxc5 ♗xc5 **12** 0-0 0-0 **13** ♕e2 b6 **14** ♗f4 ♗b7 **15** ♖ad1 ♕e7 **16** ♘e5 a6 **17** ♗g3 ♖fd8 **18** c3 b5 **19** ♗h4 ♖d5 **20** ♗c2 ♖xd1 **21** ♖xd1 g5 **22** ♗g3 ♖d8 = Gufeld–Speelman, Hastings 1986/87.

8 ...	♕e7
9 0-0	fxe6
10 ♗g6+	♔d8
11 ♗f4	♘d5!

11 ... ♕*b4 (11 ... b6 12 c4* ♗*b7 13* ♖*e1* ±*)* 12 a3 ♕xb2 **13** ♕e2 ♘d5 **14** ♗d2 ♗d6 (Geller–Meduna, Sochi 1986) 15 c4! ♕b6 16 cxd5 +– (Geller).

12 ♗g3	♕b4
13 ♖e1	♗e7

Not 13 ... ♘e7? because of 14 ♕d3 (±), when Black's pieces are becoming increasingly tied-up.

14 ♕e2   ♗f6
15 c4   ♘e7

After 15 ... ♘5b6? 16 c5 ♘d5 17 a3 ♕b3 18 ♕xe6 ♘xc5 19 ♕f7 Black is lost.

16 a3   ♕b3
17 ♗d3   ♘f8!

17 ... ♘f5? 18 ♗xf5 ± Chandler-Hübner, Biel 1987.

18 ♖ad1   ♗d7
19 ♘e5   ♗e8

Analysis – this position is double-edged – Black has managed to co-ordinate his minor pieces to stave off any immediate assault on his position.

C1.2

7 ...   ♗e7

(see diagram)

8 ♕e2   ...

a) **8 0-0** h6 9 ♘e4 ♘xe4 10 ♗xe4 ♘f6 11 ♗d3 0-0 12 ♗f4! *(12 ♘e5 c5 13 dxc5 ♗xc5 14 ♖e1 ♘d7 = Ulybin-Dautov, USSR 1989)* 12 ... ♘d5 *(12 ... c5 13 dxc5 ♗xc5 14 ♕e2 ±)* 13 ♗d2 c5

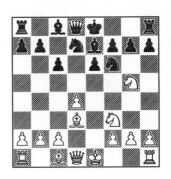

14 dxc5 ♗xc5 15 ♕e2 ♕c7 *(15 ... b6?! 16 ♕e4! f5 17 ♕e2 ±)* 16 ♕e4! (Khalifman-K. Arkell, Leningrad 1989) 16 ... f5 17 ♕e2 ♗d7 18 ♘e5 ±.

b) **8 ♘xf7** ♔xf7 9 ♘g5+ ♔g8 10 ♘xe6 ♗b4+ 11 ♔f1 *(11 c3 ♕e7 12 ♕e2 – Forchek-Voinovic, Novi Sad 1987 – 12 ... ♘b6! 13 ♗f5 ♗d6 14 0-0 ♗d7 15 ♖e1 ♖e8 ∓)* 11 ... ♕e7 12 ♘c7 ♘b6 13 ♘xa8 ♘xa8 14 c3 ♗d6 ∞ (Bikhovsky).

8 ...   0-0

8 ... h6 9 ♘e4 ♘xe4 10 ♕xe4 c5 11 0-0 cxd4 12 ♘xd4 ♘c5 = Sokolov-Spraggett, St. John (c) 1988.

9 h4   ...

9 ♘e5 h6 10 ♘gf3 ± (Bikhovsky) is also playable.

9 ...   c5
10 ♗e3   b6

10 ... a6 11 0-0-0 ♕a5 12 ♔b1 b5 13

dxc5 ♕c7 14 ♘xh7 ♘xh7 15 ♗xh7+ ♔xh7 16 ♘g5+ ♔g8 17 ♖xd7! 1-0 Shirazi–Neamtu, Biel 1987.

11 0-0-0   ♕c7
12 ♔b1 ± (Bikhovsky).

C1.3

7 ...   ♗d6

The safest line in the 5 . . . ♘gf6 variation.

8 ♕e2   ...

a) **8 c3** h6 9 ♘e4 ♘xe4 10 ♗xe4 0-0 11 0-0 e5 *(11 . . . c5 12 ♗c2 b6?! 13 dxc5! ♘xc5 14 b4 ±; 12 . . . ♘f6 ± Khalifman)* 12 ♗c2 ♖e8 13 ♖e1 exd4 14 ♖xe8+ ♕xe8 15 ♕xd4 ♕e7 16 ♗f4 ♗xf4 17 ♕xf4 ♘f8 18 ♖e1 ♗e6 19 ♘d4 ♖e8 *(19 . . . ♖d8 = see (b))* 20 g3 *(20 ♘xe6! ♘xe6 21 ♕e4 ±)* 20 . . . ♕d8 21 ♘xe6 *(21 ♖d1?! ♗h3! = Smirin–Khalifman, Moscow 1989)* 21 . . . ♖xe6 22 ♖xe6 ♘xe6 23 ♕e3 ± (Khalifman).

b) **8 0-0** h6 9 ♘e4 ♘xe4 10 ♗xe4 0-0 *(10... ♘f6!?)* 11 c3 e5 12 ♗c2 ♖e8 13 ♖e1 exd4 14 ♖xe8+ ♕xe8 15 ♕xd4 ♕e7 16 ♗f4 ♗xf4 17 ♕xf4 ♘f8 18 ♖e1 ♗e6 19 ♘d4 ♖d8 *(19... ♖e8 see Smirin–Khalifman)* 20 h4! ♕c5 21 ♖e3 ♕d6 22 ♘xe6 ± Kasparov-Karpov, Amsterdam 1988.

8 ...   h6
9 ♘e4   ♘xe4

10 ♕xe4   ...

If 10 ♗xe4, then . . . 0-0 and . . . c5, or . . . e5.

10 ...   ♘f6

10 . . . c5 11 ♗d2 *(11 ♕g4 ♕f6 ∞)* 11 . . . ♘f6 *(11 . . . cxd4 12 ♕xd4 ♘f6 13 0-0-0 ±)* 12 ♗b5+ ♗d7 13 ♕xb7 ♖b8 14 ♗xd7+ ♘xd7 15 ♕a6 ± Psakhis-Meduna, Trnava 1988.

11 ♕e2   ...

11 ♕h4 ♘d5 12 ♕xd8+ ♔xd8 13 c3 ♔e7 is level.

11 ...   c5

The alternatives are:

a) **11 . . . ♕c7** 12 ♗d2 b6 13 0-0-0 ♗b7 14 ♘e5!? *(14 ♔b1 0-0-0 15 ♗a6 b5!? 16 ♗xb7+ ♔xb7 17 c4 bxc4 18 ♖c1 ♖b8 19 ♖xc4 ♔a8 20 ♖hc1 ♖hc8 ± Chandler–Speelman, Hastings 1988/89)* 14 . . . 0-0-0 15 f4 c5 16 dxc5 ♗xc5 17 ♔b1 ♔b8 18 ♖he1 h5 19 h3 h4 20 ♗a6 ♗xa6 21 ♕xa6 ♗f2 22 ♖f1 ♗g3 23 ♕a4 ± de Firmian-Spiridonov, Lugano 1989.

b) **11 . . . ♕b6** 12 0-0 0-0 13 a3?! ♕c7 14 c4 b6 15 b4 c5 ∞ Smirin–Dreyev, Vilnius 1988.

c) **11 . . . b6** 12 ♗d2 ♗b7 13 0-0-0 ♕c7 14 ♖he1 *(14 ♘e5 0-0-0 15 ♖he1 ♔b8 16 ♔b1 ♖he8 – 16 . . . c5 17 dxc5 ♗xc5 18 f4 ± – 17 f3 – Gelfand-Adams, Adelaide 1988 – 17 . . . c5! 18*

*dxc5 ♗xc5 =; 14 ♔b1 0-0-0 15 c4 c5 16
♗c3 ♖he8 17 ♖he1 ♔b8 18 g3 ♔a8 19
♗c2 a6 20 dxc5 ♗xc5 21 ♘e5 ♖c8 22
♖d2 ♖ed8 23 ♖ed1* ± *Sokolov-
Spraggett, St. John (c) 1988)* 14 . . .
0-0-0 15 ♗a6 ♗xa6 16 ♕xa6+ ♔b8 17
♕e2 ♘d5 *(17 . . . b5!?)* 18 c4 ♘f4 19
♕f1 ♘g6 20 g3 ♗e7 21 h4 ± Sokolov-
Karpov, Belfort 1988.

d) **11 . . . 0-0** 12 ♗d2 c5 13 dxc5
♗xc5 14 0-0-0 ± (Bikhovsky).

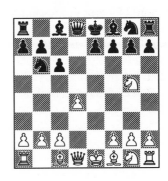

12 dxc5	**♕a5+**

12 . . . ♗xc5 13 ♗d2 0-0 14 0-0-0
♕c7 15 g4 e5 16 g5 hxg5 17 ♗xg5 e4
18 ♗xe4 ♖e8 19 ♗xf6 ♕f4+ 20 ♘d2
♕xf6 21 ♕h5 ♗d4 22 c3 ♖xe4 23
♘xe4 ♕f4+ 24 ♘d2 ♗g4 = Smirin-
Kharitonov, Sverdlovsk 1987.

13 ♗d2	**♕xc5**

'Unclear' according to Bikhovsky,
but White seems to nurture a slight
advantage in his control of the central
complex.

C2

5 . . .	**♘b6**

Black leaves the diagonal of his c8
bishop open and fianchettoes his
other bishop.

(see diagram)

6 ♘1f3	**g6**

7 c3	**. . .**

7 ♗d3!?, retaining White's slight
edge, certainly also seems playable.

7 . . .	**♗g7**
8 ♕b3	

8 ♗d3 ♘h6 9 0-0 ± (Bikhovsky).

8 . . .	**♘h6**

8 . . . ♕d5 9 c4 ♕a5+ 10 ♗d2 ♕a4 is
a suggestion of Miles.

9 ♗e2	**0-0**
10 0-0	**♘f5**
11 ♖d1	**. . .**

11 ♗f4?! ♘d5 12 ♗d2 ♘d6 13 c4
♘c7 ∓ (Miles).

11 . . .	**♕c7**
12 g3	**. . .**

12 ♘e4 ♗e6 13 ♕c2 ♘d6 is slightly
better for Black, as his minor pieces

have a greater grip in the centre.

| 12 ... | ♞d6 |
| 13 c4 | ... |

13 ♞e5 c5 ∓ van der Wiel–Karpov, Amsterdam 1988.

| 13 ... | h6 |

13 ... ♞bxc4 14 ♗xc4 h6 15 ♞xf7 ♞xf7 ∞ is one interesting possibility.

| 14 c5 | hxg5 |
| 15 ♗xg5 | ♞d5 |

15 ... ♗e6 ±.

| 16 cxd6 | exd6 |
| 17 ♗f1 | ... |

... with equal chances (Karpov, Zaitsev).

C3

| 5 ... | ♞df6 |

With its diagonal open, Black's QB will be active in the opening.

C3.1: 6 ♗d3
C3.2: 6 ♗c4
C3.3: 6 ♞1f3

C3.1

| 6 ♗d3 | ♗g4 |

6 ... h6?! 7 ♞xf7 ♚xf7 8 ♞f3 g5 9 h4 g4 10 ♞e5+ ♚g7 11 c3 h5? *(11 ... ♗e6 ∞)* 12 ♛d2 ♞h7 13 ♗xh7 ♖xh7 14 ♛g5+ ♚h8 15 ♞g6+ ± Shirazi–Burger, USA 1988.

| 7 ♞1f3 | ♗h5 |

7 ... e6 *(7 ... h6? 8 ♞xf7! ♗xf3 9 ♗g6! wins)* 8 h3 *(8 ♞xf7? ♗xf3 9 ♞xd8 ♗xd1 10 ♞xe6 ♚e7 11 ♞xf8 ♗h5 12 ♞xh7 ♞xh7 ∓)* 8 ... ♗xf3 *(8 ... ♗h5!?)* 9 ♞xf3 ♗d6 10 0-0 ♛c7 11 ♛e2 ♗f4 12 ♗xf4 ♛xf4 13 ♖ad1 ♞e7 14 ♞e5 ♖d8 15 c3 ± Nunn–Christiansen, Szirak (izt) 1987.

| 8 c3 | ... |

8 h3 h6 9 ♞e4 *(9 g4 hxg5 10 gxh5 ♖xh5 ∓)* 9 ... ♞xe4 10 ♗xe4 ♞f6 11 ♗d3 ♗xf3 12 ♛xf3 ♛xd4 ∓.

| 8 ... | ♛c7 |

8 ... e6 9 ♛b3 ♛c7 *(9 ... h6? 10 ♛xb7 hxg5 11 ♛xc6+ ♞d7 12 ♞e5 ♖c8 13 ♛a4 ± van der Wiel)* 10 ♞e5

♗d6 11 ♘c4?! *(11 f4!? ♘e7 12 0-0 ∞*
van der Wiel) 11 . . . ♗e7 12 ♘e5 ♘d7
(12 . . . ♗d6) 13 ♘xd7 ♕xd7 14 0-0
♘f6 15 ♖e1 ♖d8 16 ♘e4 = van der
Wiel-Karpov, Amsterdam 1988.

9 ♕c2   . . .

9 h3 h6 10 ♘e4 ♘xe4 11 ♗xe4 ♘f6
12 ♗d3 ♗xf3 13 ♕xf3 e6 =.

9 . . .   h6
10 ♘e6   . . .

10 ♘e4 ♗xf3 11 gxf3 ♘d5 ∓.

10 . . .   ♕d6

10 . . . fxe6? 11 ♗g6+ ♗xg6 12
♕xg6+ ♔d8 13 ♘e5 ♔c8 14 ♕f7! +−.

11 ♘xf8   . . .

11 ♘c5!? is also possible.

11 . . .	♗xf3
12 ♘g6	♗xg2
13 ♖g1	♕xh2
14 ♖xg2	♕xg2
15 ♘xh8	♕h1+
16 ♔e2	♕h5+
17 ♔e1	♕h1+

Drawn (Bikhovsky).

C3.2

6 ♗c4   . . .

6 . . .   e6

6 . . . ♘d5 *(6 . . . ♘h6?!)* 7 ♘1f3 g6
(7 . . . ♗f5) 8 0-0 ♗g7 9 ♖e1 h6 10 ♘e4
♗g4 11 a4 ♘gf6 12 ♘xf6+ ♗xf6 13
♖a3 ♔f8 14 h3 ♗xf3 15 ♖xf3 ♔g7 16
c3 ± Spassky-Karpov, Belfort 1988.

7 ♘1f3

7 ♘e2 ♗d6 8 0-0 h6 9 ♘f3 ♕c7 10
♘g3?! *(10 ♗d3 ±)* 10 . . . ♘e7 11 ♖e1
0-0 = Sokolov-Spraggett, St. John (c)
1988, or 7 . . . c5 8 0-0 h6 9 ♘f3 a6 10 a4
cxd4 11 ♘exd4 ♗d6 12 ♕e2 ♘e7 13
♘e5 *(13 b3 ♕c7 14 ♖e1 0-0 15 ♗b2*
♘ed5 ∞) 13 . . . ♕c7 14 ♘df3 0-0 15 b3
(15 ♗f4 ♘ed5 16 ♗g3 b6 =; 15 a5!?
♘ed5 16 c3 b5 = Karpov) 15 . . . b6 16
♗b2 ♗b7 = de Firmian-Karpov, Biel
1990.

7 . . .   h6

8 ♘h3	♗d6
9 ♕e2	♘e7
10 ♗d2	♕c7
11 0-0-0	b5
12 ♗d3	a6
13 ♖he1	♗b7
14 g3	c5
15 dxc5	♕xc5
16 ♘e5 =	. . .

. . . was Hübner–Karpov, Belfort 1988, though 16 ♗f4! instead would have nurtured White's slight advantage.

C3.3

6 ♘1f3   . . .

C3.31: 6 . . . e6?!
C3.32: 6 . . . ♗g4!

C3.31

6 . . .   e6?!

Inconsistent!

'Also rans' include:
a) **6 . . . h6?** 7 ♘xf7! ♔xf7 8 ♘e5+ ♔e8 *(8 . . . ♔e6 9 ♗c4+ ♘d5 10 ♕g4+ ♔d6 11 ♘f7+ ♔c7 12 ♕g3+ winning)* 9 ♗d3 ±

b) **6 . . . ♘h6** 7 c3 g6 8 ♗c4 ♗g7 9 0-0 0-0 10 ♖e1 ♘f5 11 ♘e5 ♘d5 12 ♘gf3 ♕c7 13 ♗b3 e6?! *(13 . . . b6!?)* 14 c4 ♘f6 15 g4 ± (Bikhovsky).

7 ♘e5   . . .

7 ♕d3 *(7 ♗d3 ♗d6 8 ♘e5? ♗xe5 9 dxe5 ♕a5+)* 7 . . . ♗d6 8 ♘e5 ♘h6 *(9 . . . ♗xe5 9 dxe5 ♕a5+ 10 ♔d1! ♕xe5? 11 ♕d8+!)* 9 ♗d2 a5 10 ♘e4! *(10 a3?! ♕c7 11 ♘c4?! − 11 ♘gf3 ± − 11 . . . ♗e7 12 g3 ♘f5 13 ♗g2 h6 = Sokolov–Spraggett, St John (c) 1988)* 10 . . . ♘e4 11 ♕xe4 ♘f5 12 0-0-0 ± (Yurkov).

7 . . .	♘h6
8 ♗d3	♗d6

8 . . . ♕xd4 9 ♘gxf7 ♘xf7 10 ♘xf7 ♗b4+ *(10 . . . ♘g4 11 0-0 ♗c5 12 ♘xh8 ♘xf2 13 ♗g6+ hxg6 14 ♕xd4 ♗xd4 15 ♖xf2 +−)* 11 c3 ♗xc3+ *(11 . . . ♖f8 12 0-0 ♕d5 13 cxb4 ♖xf7 14 ♕e2 ±)* 12 bxc3 ♕xc3+ 13 ♗d2 ♕xd3 14 ♘xh8 ♕e4+ 15 ♕e2 ♗d7 16 ♕xe4 ♘xe4 17 ♗e3 +− (Analysis by Nunn).

9 c3   ♕c7

9 . . . 0-0 10 ♕c2 ♘f5 11 g4 ♗xe5 12 gxf5 ♗d6 13 fxe6 ±.

10 ♕e2   c5

10 . . . 0-0?! 11 ♞gf3 ♞f5 12 g4 ♞e7
13 h4 ±; **10 . . . a6!?**, preventing the
bishop check, is a potential improvement.

11 ♗b5+   ♚e7

11 . . . ♗d7 12 ♞xd7 ♞xd7 13 dxc5
♗xc5 *(13 . . . ♕xc5 14 ♞e4 ♕c7 15
♞xd6+ ♕xd6 16 ♗xh6 gxh6 17 ♖d1
+−)* 14 ♞xe6 fxe6 15 ♕xe6+ ♚d8 16
♗g5+ ♚c8 17 0-0-0 is also conclusive.

12 0-0   cxd4

12 . . . a6 13 ♗d3 b6 14 f4 ±.

13 cxd4   ♞f5
14 ♗e3!   ♞xe3

14 . . . ♗xe5 15 dxe5 ♕xe5 16 ♗xa7
♕xe2 17 ♗c5+ ♞d6 18 ♗xe2 ± due to
the weakness of the d6 (pin) and f7
squares.

15 ♕xe3!   . . .

15 fxe3? ♗xe5 16 dxe5 ♕xe5 17
♕d3 ± Nunn–Tal, Brussels 1988.

15 . . .   ♞d5
16 ♕g3   f6
17 ♞e4!   ♖g8
18 ♕h4   . . .

. . . and then:
a) **18 . . . ♚f8?** 19 ♖ac1 ♕e7

20 f4! +−.
b) **18 . . . ♗xe5** 19 dxe5 ♕xe5 20
♕xh7 ± (Nunn).

C3.32

6 . . .   ♗g4!

7 ♗c4   . . .

7 ♞xf7 ♗xf3 8 ♞xd8 ♗xd1 9 ♞e6
♗h5 10 ♞c7+ ♚d7 ∞.

7 . . .   e6
8 ♞xf7?!   ♗xf3
9 ♞xd8   ♗xd1
10 ♞xe6   ♗xc2

10 . . . ♗g4 11 ♞c7+ ♚d7 12 ♞xa8
♗d6 ∓.

11 ♞c7+   ♚d7
12 ♞xa8   ♗d6

Black is a little better — Bikhovsky.

ILLUSTRATIVE GAMES

1   EFSEEV–FLOHR
Odessa 1949

1 e4 c6 2 d4 d5 3 ♘c3 dxe4 4 ♘xe4 ♘d7 5 ♘f3 ♘f6 6 ♘g3 e6 7 ♗d3 ♗e7 8 0-0 0-0 9 ♕e2!? c5 10 c3 b6 11 ♘e5?! ♗b7 12 f4? cxd4 13 cxd4 ♘xe5! 14 dxe5 ♘g4! 15 ♗xh7+ (White may as well accept the pawn sacrifice since 15 ♗e4 ♗c5+ 16 ♔h1 ♕h4 or 15 ♘e4 ♕d4+ 16 ♔h1 ♖fd8 are equally bad) 15 . . . ♔xh7 16 ♕xg4 ♕d4+ 17 ♔h1 ♖ac8 18 ♘h5 (18 ♕e2 ♕c4 19 ♕f2 ♕d3! threatening 20 . . . ♖c2) 18 . . . g6 19 ♕h3 ♖h8! (19 . . . gxh5 would lead to a draw, but now Black can utilize the h-file in his attack. The double-check is harmless) 20 ♘f6++ ♔g7 21 ♕e3? (21 ♕b3 offers somewhat more resistance; 21 . . . ♖h4 22 ♗e3 ♖ch8 23 ♗g1 ♗c5! 24 ♕g3 ♕xb2) 21 . . . ♖c2!! (An impressive finale! 22 ♕xd4 loses to 22 . . . ♖xg2 and 22 ♖g1 is decisively answered by 22 . . . ♕d1! 23 ♘e4 ♗xe4 24 ♕xe4 ♕h5!) 22 ♕g3 ♕d3! 23 ♕xd3 ♖xg2 24 ♘g4 ♖gxh2+! White resigned.

2   TAL–VASYUKOV
USSR Championship 1965

1 e4 c6 2 d4 d5 3 ♘c3 dxe4 4 ♘xe4 ♘d7 5 ♘f3 ♘gf6 6 ♘g3 e6 7 ♗d3 c5!? 8 0-0 cxd4 9 ♘xd4 ♗c5 10 ♘f3 0-0 11 ♕e2 b6 12 ♗f4 ♗b7 13 ♖ad1 ♘d5? 14 ♗g5 ♕c7 15 ♘h5! ♔h8! 16 ♗e4 (16 ♖fe1 ♖ae8 17 ♗e4 f5! 18 ♗xd5 ♗xd5 19 ♖xd5 exd5 20 ♕xe8 ♖xe8 21 ♖xe8+ ♘f8!) 16 . . . f6 17 ♗h4

(17 ♗f4? ♘xf4 18 ♘xf4 ♕xf4 19 ♗xb7 ♖ad8 20 ♕xe6 ♘e5!) 17 . . . ♗d6 18 c4 ♗a6! (Relatively best; the idea is 19 ♗d3 ♘f4 20 ♘xf4 ♗xf4 21 ♕xe6 ♘c5) 19 ♘xg7! (Tal is always ready for such a possibility. White recoups his piece with good play) 19 . . . ♔xg7 (19 . . . ♘f4 20 ♕d2!) 20 ♘d4! ♘c5 21 ♕g4+ ♔h8 22 ♘xe6 ♘xe6 23 ♕xe6 ♖ae8 24 ♕xd5 ♗xh2+ 25 ♔h1 ♕f4 (25 . . . ♕xc4 26 ♕xc4 ♗xc4 27 ♖fe1 was slightly better) 26 ♕h5! ♕xe4 (Perhaps Black had previously overlooked 26 . . . ♖xe4 27 ♖d7) 27 ♖fe1 (27 ♖de1!) 27 . . . ♕g6 28 ♕xg6! (28 ♗xf6+ ♕xf6 29 ♖xe8 ♗d6 30 ♖xf8+ ♕xf8 31 ♖e1 ♕xf2!) 28 . . . hxg6 29 ♗xf6+ ♔g8 30 ♖xe8 ♖xe8 31 ♔xh2 ♗xc4 32 ♖d7 ♖e6 33 ♗c3 ♗xa2 34 ♖xa7 ♗c4 (End-games of this type are only drawn if there are no rooks on the board. As it is, the defending bishop cannot oppose the attacking one, and White slowly penetrates on the black squares. An almost identical winning technique was used in the seventh match game of Portisch–Larsen, Rotterdam 1977, for those interested in similar end-games) 35 ♔g3 ♗d5 36 f3! ♔f8 37 ♗d4 b5 38 ♔f4 ♗c4 39 ♔g5 ♔e8 40 ♖a8+ ♔f7 41 ♖a7+ ♔e8 42 b4 ♗d5 43 ♖a3! (Preparing to advance the pawns) 43 . . . ♔f7 44 g4 ♖e2 45 ♗c5 ♖e5+ 46 ♔h6 ♖e6 (The king's penetration cannot be halted. Black must soon contend with a mating attack!) 47 ♖d3 ♗c6 48 ♖d8 ♖e8 49 ♖d4! ♖e6 50 f4 ♔e8 51 ♔g7 ♗e4 52

♗b6! ♗f3 53 ♖d8+ ♔e7 54 ♖d3 ♗e2 (54 . . . ♗xg4 55 ♗d8+ ♔e8 56 ♗g5 +−) 55 ♗d8+ ♔e8 56 ♖d2! ♖e3 57 ♗g5 ♗d3 58 f5 Black resigned.

3 JANSA–KHOLMOV
Budapest 1976

1 e4 c6 2 d4 d5 3 ♘d2 dxe4 4 ♘xe4 ♘d7 5 ♗c4 ♘gf6 6 ♘g5 e6 7 ♕e2 ♘b6 8 ♗d3 h6 9 ♘5f3 c5 10 dxc5 ♗xc5 11 ♘e5 ♘bd7 12 ♘gf3 ♕c7 13 0-0 0-0 14 ♗f4 ♗d6 15 ♘xd7 (? − queen and knight cooperate better than queen and bishop in an open position) 15 . . . ♗xd7 16 ♗xd6 ♕xd6 17 ♘e5 ♖fd8 18 ♖ad1 ♕b6 19 ♘xd7 ♖xd7 20 c3 ♖ad8 21 ♗c2 g6 22 ♗a4 ♖d6 23 ♖xd6 ♖xd6 24 ♖d1 (Otherwise . . . ♕d8 and . . . ♖d2) 24 . . . a6 25 g3 ♔g7 26 ♖xd6 ♕xd6 27 ♕d1 ♕c5 28 ♕d2 ♘e4 (The knight heads for its best square, d6. Black's strategy is to advance his kingside pawns to attack Jansa's king) 29 ♕e2 ♘d6 30 ♗b3 e5 31 ♔g2 e4 (Plan: . . . ♕e5, . . . f5, . . . g5 and . . . f4) 32 ♕d2 ♕e5 33 h4 g5 34 hxg5 hxg5 35 ♕e3 (Black's advanced king and pawns give him good winning chances if queens are exchanged) 35 . . . b5! 36 ♕a7 a5! 37 a3 (On 37 ♕xa5 e3 38 fxe3 ♘f5 etc. but perhaps better is 37 a4 bxa4 38 ♗xa4 ♕d5 39 ♔h2) 37 . . . a4 38 ♗a2 ♕f6 39 ♕e3 ♔h6 40 ♔f1 (Time trouble) ♘f5 41 ♕a7 e3 42 ♕b8 ♘d6 White resigned. An instructive positional win with 4 . . . ♘d7.

4 TAL–PETROSIAN
USSRChampionship 1973

1 e4 c6 2 d4 d5 3 ♘c3 dxe4 4 ♘xe4 ♘d7 5 ♗c4 ♘gf6 6 ♘g5 e6 7 ♕e2 ♘b6 8 ♗b3 a5 9 a4?! h6 (9 . . . ♕xd4?! 10 ♘f3 ♗b4+ 11 c3 ♗xc3+ 12 ♔f1! ♕b4 13 ♕d1) 10 ♘5f3 c5 11 ♗f4 (11 ♗e3!?) 11 . . . ♗d6 12 ♗e5 0-0 13 0-0-0?! (13 ♘h3 is more subtle) 13 . . . c4! 14 ♗xc4 ♘xa4 (With the exchanges, Black has both released the pressure down the d-file and made the advance of his a-pawn possible) 15 ♘h3 ♘b6 16 g4! (The only chance!) 16 . . . a4 17 g5 hxg5 18 ♘hxg5 (18 ♘fxg5!?) 18 . . . a3 19 b3 (The a-pawn will now be a constant irritant, but opening the king's position was simply not on) 19 . . . ♗b4! 20 ♖hg1! a2 (20 . . . ♗c3?! 21 d5!) 21 ♔b2 ♘xc4+? (A grave error. 21 . . . ♘bd5! when 22 ♗xd5? ♘xd5 23 ♕d3 ♗c3+ 24 ♕xc3 ♘xc3 25 ♘xe6 ♘xd1+ 26 ♔a1 f6! wins or 22 ♘e4! ♕a5! 23 ♕d3 ♘g4! threatens 24 . . . f5! taking control of c3! e.g. 24 ♗xg7 f5! 25 ♗xf8 ♔xf8! 26 ♗xd5 fxe4! 27 ♗xe4 ♘xf2 28 ♕e2 ♘xd1+ 29 ♖xd1 a1=♕+) 22 ♕xc4! ♘d5? (Presumably both players were hard pressed by the clock as now White has 23 ♘xe6! followed by ♖xg7+ leading to a draw, and neither 23 . . . ♗c3+ 24 ♕xc3! nor 23 . . . a1=♕+ 24 ♖xa1 helps) 23 ♘e4? f6 24 ♗f4? (24 ♗g3 f5 25 ♗e5 ♖f7 ∓) 24 . . . ♗a3+ 25 ♔a1 ♘xf4 26 h4 ♖f7 27 ♖g4 ♕a5 White resigned.

5   TAL-SPEELMAN
Subotica (izt) 1987

1 e4 c6 2 d4 d5 3 ♘d2 dxe4 4 ♘xe4 ♘d7 5 ♗c4 ♘gf6 6 ♘g5 e6 7 ♕e2 ♘b6 8 ♗b3 h6 9 ♘5f3 a5 10 a3 ♗e7 (A new idea at this time) 11 ♗d2! ♘bd5?! (Far superior was 11 ... c5!) 12 c4 ♘c7 13 ♗c2 0-0? 14 ♘e5! ♕xd4 15 ♗c3 (15 0-0-0? ♗xa3!) 15 ... ♕d8 16 ♘gf3 (Better was 16 ♖d1! ♕e8 17 ♕d3 with the idea of ♘g4) 16 ... ♘ce8 17 g4! b5 18 g5! hxg5 19 ♘xg5 ♖a6 20 ♕f3 b4 21 ♕h3 g6 22 ♗xg6! (An excellent move. After this sacrifice White has a very strong attack) 22 ... bxc3 (22 ... fxg6 23 ♘xg6 ♔g7 24 ♕h7 mate!) 23 ♘exf7 ♕d2+ 24 ♔f1 ♖xf7 25 ♗xf7+! (25 ♘xf7? ♔f8 26 ♕h8+ ♘g8 27 ♗h7 ♘f6 28 ♖g1 ♗c5!) 25 ... ♔g7 26 ♖g1 (with the idea 26 ♘f3+ ♔f8 27 ♕h8+ ♔xf7 28 ♘e5 mate) 26 ... ♕xg5 (26 ... cxb2 27 ♘f3+ ♘g4 28 ♕xg4+ ♗g5 29 ♖b1 ♕d3+ 30 ♔g2 +−) 27 ♖xg5+ ♔xf7 28 bxc3! (28 ♕xc3 ♘e4 29 ♕f3+ ♘8f6 28 ... e5 **Black resigned.**

6   SIMAGIN-SMYSLOV
Moscow 1963

1 e4 c6 2 d4 d5 3 ♘c3 dxe4 4 ♘xe4 ♘d7 5 ♗c4 ♘gf6 6 ♘g5 e6 7 ♘e2 h6 8 ♘f3 ♗d6 9 0-0 ♕c7 10 ♘c3?! b5 11 ♗d3 b4 12 ♘e4 ♘xe4 13 ♗xe4 ♘f6 14 ♗d3 0-0 15 ♕e2 (15 ♖e1!?) 15 ... ♗b7 16 ♗d2 c5 (Soon White will have to fight for equality. He has the lack of a healthy pawn centre to blame for this) 17 dxc5 ♕xc5! (17 ... ♗xc5? 18 ♘e5!) 18 h3? (White was worried about 18 ... ♕h5, but the tempo loss is more

damaging. According to Dr Euwe the ensuing advance should be checked by 18 ♖fe1 as on 18 ... ♕h5 19 ♘e5 or 18 ... e5 19 ♗e3 ♕a5 20 ♘d2 ♕d5 21 f3. Also superior is 18 ♗e3 ♕h5 19 h3 ♗xf3 20 ♕xf3, when the bishop pair compensates for the doubled pawns and 20 ... ♕e5 21 ♖fd1 ♕xb2 is dangerous due to 22 ♗d4) 18 ... e5! 19 ♗e3 ♕a5 20 ♗c4 ♖ac8 21 ♖fd1 ♗b8 (21 ... ♗xf3 22 ♕xf3 ♖xc4 23 ♖xd6 ♖xc2 24 ♖xf6! However, 22 ... ♗xf3! is threatened now) 22 ♘d2 ♕c7 23 ♗b3 ♕c6 24 f3 e4! 25 fxe4 (After this threats on both wings give Black a decisive advantage. 25 ♘xe4 is also bad: 25 ... ♘xe4 26 ♗d5 ♘g3! 27 ♗xc6 ♘xe2+ 28 ♔f2 ♖xc6 29 ♔xe2 ♖xc2. 25 f4 closing the long diagonal is called for when 25 ... ♘d5?! 26 ♗xd5 ♕xd5 27 ♘b3 followed by ♘d4; best is 25 ... ♖fd8! when Black still has pressure) 25 ... ♘xe4 26 ♘f1 ♘f6 27 ♖d4 a5 (With designs on the b3 bishop and the c2 pawn) 28 ♖ad1?! (28 ♖c4 ♕b5! 29 ♖e1 ♗a6 is slightly better) 28 ... ♗a6! 29 ♕f3 (Otherwise 29 ... a4) 29 ... ♕xf3 30 gxf3 ♗e2 31 ♖e1 ♗xf3 32 ♗a4?! (An oversight but it was already too late) 32 ... ♗e5 33 ♖d2 ♗xb2 34 ♖f2 ♗c6 35 ♗xc6 ♖xc6 36 ♘g3 ♖e8 37 ♘f5 ♔h7 38 ♖ef1 ♖xe3! 39 ♘xe3 ♗d4 40 ♖e1 ♖e6 **White resigned.**

7   NUNN-TAL
Brussels 1988

1 e4 c6 2 d4 d5 3 ♘d2 dxe4 4 ♘xe4 ♘d7 5 ♘g5 ♘df6 6 ♘1f3 e6?! 7 ♘e5

♘h6 8 ♗d3 ♗d6 9 c3 ♕c7 10 ♕e2 c5 ("After 10 . . . 0-0 11 ♘gf3 ♘f5 12 g4 ♘e7 13 h4 White has an automatic K-side attack while Black's counterplay hasn't started yet") **11 ♗b5+** ("Tal said after the game that he was more frightened by 11 ♗d2, but I preferred to fix the king in the centre") **11 . . . ♔e7 12 0-0 cxd4 13 cxd4 ♘f5 14 ♗e3!** ("The simplest") **14 . . . ♘xe3 15 fxe3?!** ("The correct continuation is 15 ♕xe3!") **15 . . . ♗xe5 16 dxe5 ♕xe5 17 ♕d3!** ("The point of 15 fxe3: the threat of ♕a3+ is very hard to meet")

17 . . . ♕xg5? (A blunder leading to immediate loss. The alternatives are: a) 17 . . . ♖d8? 18 ♕xd8+!; b) 17 . . . b6 18 ♖ac1; c) 17 . . . ♗d7 18 ♕a3+ ♕d6 19 ♕xd6+ ♔xd6 20 ♖ad1+ ♔e7 21 ♖xd7+! d) 17 . . . ♖f8 18 ♖ad1 ♘d5 19 ♘e4! ♕xb2 20 ♖b1 ♕xa2 21 ♖a1 ♕b2 22 ♖fb1 and finally ♕a3+; e) 17 . . . a6! 18 ♕a3+! ♕d6 19 ♕xd6+♔xd6 20 ♘xf7+ ♔e7 21 ♘xh8 axb5 22 g4 ♗d7 23 g5 ♖xh8 24 gxf6+ gxf6 ±) **18 ♕a3+ ♔d8 19 ♖ad1+ ♗d7 20 ♗xd7 Black resigned** (Nunn).

2
The Original Caro: 5 . . . exf6 and Earlier Deviations

1 e4 c6 2 d4 d5 3 ♘c3 dxe4 4 ♘xe4 ♘f6

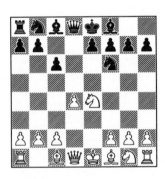

For a long time the Original Caro of 5 . . . exf6 was largely rejected by "theory" on the grounds that it gives White a straight queenside majority, supposedly without counterchances. Any pure pawn ending, as in the exchange Ruy Lopez, would be lost for Black.

However, this is not the whole picture. Simplification is as yet a remote prospect and meanwhile Black is relieved of development difficulties. The cluster of kingside pawns considerably strengthens the defence of Black's king. Indeed, as demonstrated by Viktor Korchnoi (who also utilized this line in his 1978 match v Karpov) these same pawns can sometimes be used in a kingside storm against the white position.

In variation B we examine a white attempt to sidestep the complications of 5 . . . exf6 or 5 . . . gxf6. However, Black should have few serious problems against this tamer alternative.

A: 5 ♘xf6+
B: 5 ♘g3

Quite harmless is 5 ♗d3 ♘xe4 6 ♗xe4 ♗f5! with equality.

A

5 ♘xf6+   exf6

Recapturing by 5 . . . gxf6 is examined in the next chapter. Now the various divisions, arranged in descending order of popularity, are:

40

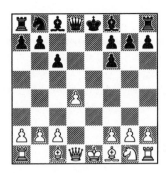

A1: 6 ♗c4
A2: 6 c3
A3: 6 ♘f3
A4: 6 g3

A couple of rare sidelines are 6 ♗e2 ♗d6 7 ♘f3 0-0 8 0-0 transposing to Karpov–Hort, Tilburg 1979, reached via the Two Knights' move order, which continued 8 . . . ♖e8 9 ♖e1 ♗f5 10 ♗e3 ♘d7 11 h3 ♗e4 = and 6 ♘e2 ♗d6 7 ♘g3 0-0 8 ♗e3 f5 9 ♕f3 ♕c7 (9 . . . ♗e6) 10 ♘h5 g6 11 ♗f4! ♗xf4 12 ♘xf4 ♖e8+ 13 ♗e2 (*Romanovsky v Ilyin-Zhenevsky, USSR 1920*) when now best is 13 . . . ♕a5+! 14 c3 ♘d7 15 0-0 ♘f6 16 ♗c4 ♗d7 =. A third alternative is 6 ♗e3, but after 6 . . . ♗f5 7 ♗d3 ♗d6! 8 ♘f3 0-0 9 ♗xf5 ♕a5+ 10 ♕d2 ♕xf5 11 0-0 c5 12 c4 ♖d8! 13 ♖fd1 ♘c6 Black has attained equality, as in Ivanovic–Matulovic, Yugoslavia (m) 1985.

A1

6 ♗c4   . . .

White's most frequent choice. Now 6 . . . ♗e6?! 7 ♗xe6 fxe6 8 ♕h5+ g6 9 ♕e2 would leave Black no compensation for the e-pawn stranded on the open file, and the various choices are:

A1.1: 6 . . . ♗e7
A1.2: 6 . . . ♗d6
A1.3: 6 . . . ♕e7+

One further interesting idea is **6 . . . ♘d7!?** 7 ♘e2 ♗d6 (*7 . . . ♘b6 8 ♗b3 ♗d6 9 c4 ♗c7 10 ♗f4 0-0 11 ♗xc7 ♕xc7 12 c5 ♘d7 13 0-0 b6 14 cxb6 axb6 15 ♖e1 ♗b7 16 ♘g3 ♖fe8 17 ♗xf7+! ♔xf7 18 ♕h5+ g6 19 ♕xh7+ ♔f8 20 h4!! 1-0 Spassky–Pfleger, Munich 1979*) 8 0-0 0-0 9 ♗f4 ♘b6 10 ♗d3. This position arose in Karpov–Korchnoi game 20 of their match in Baguio 1978. It is interesting to note that the world champion rejected the obvious ♗b3 in favour of the text. Play continued 10 . . . ♗e6 11 c3 ♘d5 12 ♗xd6 ♕xd6 13 ♕d2 ♖ad8 14 ♖fe1 g6 15 ♖ad1 ♔g7 16 ♗e4! (a sensitive diagonal for Black — he must shift the bishop) 16 . . . ♘c7 17 b3 ♖fe8 18 ♗b1 (*if 18 ♗f3 h5! 19 h3 ♗c8 planning . . . ♘e6–g5 with active play*) 18 . . . ♗g4 19 h3 ♗xe2 20 ♖xe2 ♖xe2 21 ♕xe2 ♘d5 22 ♕d2 and now instead of **22 . . . ♘f4?** 23 ♗e4 f5 24 ♗f3 ± correct was **22 . . . f5!** with counterchances.

Also interesting is **6 ... ♕d6!?** 7 c3 ♗e6 8 ♗xe6 fxe6 9 ♘f3 *(9 ♕b3 ♕d5! 10 ♕xb7?! − 10 ♕xd5 = − 10 ... ♕xg2 11 ♕xa8 ♗d6 12 ♕xa7 0-0! 13 ♗e3 ♕xh1 14 0-0-0 ♗xh2 ∓)* 9 ... ♘a6! 10 0-0 0-0-0 11 ♕e2 ♘c7 12 a4 g5 ∞ Abramovic–Mirkovic, Yugoslavia 1989.

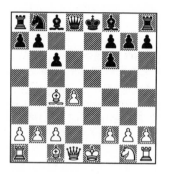

A1.1

6 ...   ♗e7
7 ♕h5   ...

As this queen excursion leads to little, White might consider:

a) 7 ♘f3 0-0 8 0-0 ♕c7 *(8 ... ♘d7 or 8 ... ♗g4 9 ♗f4 ♗d6 10 ♗g3 ♗xf3 11 ♕xf3 ♕xd4 came into consideration)* 9 h3 c5! 10 ♕e2 ♘c6 11 c3 cxd4 12 cxd4 ♗f5 13 ♗e3 ♖ad8 14 ♖ac1 ♕b8 = Smyslov–Chekhover, USSR 1945.

b) 7 ♘e2!? 0-0 *(7 ... ♘d7 8 ♘f4 0-0 9 ♗e3 f5 10 ♕d3 ♘f6 11 ♗b3 ♗d6 12 0-0-0 ♕c7 13 g3 a5 14 a3 b5 15 d5 c5! ∓ Westerinen–Lein, New York (GHI) 1977 or 8 0-0 ♘b6 9 ♗b3 0-0 10 ♗e3*

♘d5 11 ♗d2 Levenfish–Chekhover, USSR (ch) 1937 when now 11 ... b5 is ± but **10 ... ♗e6!** may be an improvement)* 8 0-0 ♘d7 9 c3 *(9 ♗f4 ♘b6 10 ♗b3 ♘d5 11 ♗g3 b5! = or 9 ♘g3 ♘b6 10 ♗b3 ♕c7 11 ♖e1 ♗d6 12 ♕h5 ♘d5 13 ♘e4 ♗d7 14 c4 ♗b4 15 ♖d1 f5 16 ♘g3 ♘f6 = Goldenov–Sokolsky, USSR 1963. But maintaining the initiative may be 9 ♗b3 ♖e8?! 10 ♘f4 ♘f8 11 ♖e1 ♗d6 12 ♖xe8 ♕xe8 13 ♗e3 ♕e4 14 ♕d2 ♘g6 ± − if 9 ... ♘b6 10 c4 ♗e6 11 ♕d3 ±)* 9 ... ♘b6 10 ♗d3 ♖e8 11 ♕c2 g6 12 ♗h6 ♘d5 13 ♖fe1 ± Bronstein–Hodos, USSR 1968.

7 ...   0-0

Instead, Najdorf–Stahlberg, Buenos Aires 1941, continued 7 ... g6 8 ♕d1 0-0 9 ♘f3 ♘d7 10 0-0 ♘b6 11 ♗b3 ♖e8 12 h3! ±.

8 ♘e2   c5

But 8 ... g6 may be O.K. now: 9 ♕h6 *(9 ♕f3 ♗e6!)* 9 ... ♗f5! 10 ♗b3 c5! 11 ♗e3 ♘c6 12 0-0-0 c4! 13 ♗xc4 ♘b4 14 ♗b3 ♖c8 *(14 ... a5!)* 15 ♘c3 ♕a5 16 ♔b1? *(correct is 16 ♗d2)* 16 ... ♖xc3! 17 bxc3 ♗xc2+ 0-1 Mnatsakanian–Simagin, USSR 1965.

9 ♗e3   ♕a5+
10 c3   ...

Also leading to equality is 10 ♗d2 ♕c7 11 ♗f4 ♕a5+ 12 c3 g6 13 ♕h4 cxd4 14 ♘xd4 ♕c5 =

(Konstantinopolsky). We have been following the game Bronstein-Boleslavsky, USSR Teams (ch) 1952, which continued 10 . . . ♘c6 11 ♗d3 *(11 dxc5 ♘e5)* 11 . . . g6 12 ♕h4 f5 13 ♕g3 cxd4 14 ♘xd4 ♗f6 with equal chances.

A1.2

| 6 . . . | ♗d6 |
| 7 ♕e2+! | . . . |

This dangerous move poses Black difficult problems. Either he must now lose tempi by retreating his bishop, accept an endgame with the inferior pawn structure, or lose the right to castle.

Alternatives are less critical: 7 ♕h5!? 0-0 8 ♘e2 ♘d7 9 0-0 c5 10 dxc5 ♗xc5 11 ♗f4 g6 12 ♕h4 ♘b6 13 ♗b3 ♗e6 14 ♗h6 ♖e8 = Gheorghiu-Donner, Hamburg 1965; 7 ♘e2 ♕c7! 8 ♗e3 0-0 9 ♕d2 ♘d7 *(9 . . . ♖e8 10 0-0-0 — Majeric-Mirkovic, Yugoslavia 1988 — 10 . . . ♘d7! =)* 10 ♗b3? *(10*

♗f4!) 10 . . . b5 11 ♘g3 a5 12 c3 ♘b6 13 ♘e4 a4 14 ♗c2 ♘c4 ∓ Tarrasch-Tartakower, Teplitz-Schönau 1922.

A1.21: 7 . . . ♕e7
A1.22: 7 . . . ♗e7

Instead 7 . . . ♔f8 hardly looks inspiring, although White still has a job to press home his advantage *(Black intends to develop with . . . h5, g6 and ♔g7)*:

a) 8 ♘f3 h5 9 ♗e3 *(9 ♗d2 g6 10 0-0-0 ♘d7?! 11 ♖he1 ♘b6 12 ♗a5!? ♔g7 13 ♔b1 ♕c7 14 h3 ♗d7 15 ♘d2 ♖ae8 ± Petrovikis-Varnusz, Athens 1976)* 9 . . . g6 10 0-0-0 b5 *(10 . . . ♘d7 and 11 . . . ♘b6 is steadier)* 11 ♗b3 a5 12 a4 ♗a6 13 ♕d2 bxa4 14 ♗xa4 ♔g7 15 d5 c5 16 ♗f4 and White stands better, Fink-Zhdanov (corr) 1961.

b) 8 ♕h5! Thwarting Black's plan. White stands much better after 8 . . . ♕c7 9 ♘e2 ♗e6 10 ♗b3 a5 11 0-0 a4 12 ♗xe6 fxe6 13 ♗d2 ± Ilyin-Zhenevsky v Silich, 1931 or 8 . . . ♕e7+ 9 ♘e2 ♗e6 *(9 . . . ♗xh2? 10 ♕xh2! ♕b4+ 11 ♗d2 ♕xc4 12 ♕c7 ♕e6 13 ♕d8+ +−)* 10 ♗b3 *(10 ♗xe6 ♕xe6 11 ♗e3 ♘a6 =)* 10 . . . ♗xb3 11 axb3 ±.

c) 8 ♗e3 (also good) 8 . . . h5 9 0-0-0 b5 10 ♗b3 a5 11 a3 ♗a6 12 ♕f3 ♕c7 13 g4 hxg4 14 ♕xg4 ± Matulović-Johansson, Halle 1967.

A1.21

| 7 . . . | ♕e7 |

Black falls in with White's basic idea although, as practice shows, his position is probably tenable, if only with drawing chances. In general this is a continuation that should only be used against tactical players.

8 ♕xe7+   ♚xe7
9 ♘e2   . . .

To control f4. Less colourful are **9 ♘f3 ♗e6 10 ♗d3 ♘d7 11 ♘d2 c5 12 dxc5 ♘xc5 13 ♗e2 ♗f5 =** Antoshin–Flohr, Moscow 1951, and **9 ♗e3 ♗e6 10 ♗d3 ♘d7 11 ♘e2** (Stein–Čirić, 1965) **11 . . . c5 =.**

9 . . .   ♗e6

Now White must retreat his bishop to maintain chances:

a) **10 ♗b3 ♘d7** *(according to Konstantinopolsky, 10 . . . a5 11 c3 a4 12 ♗c2 ♘d7 is more active)* **11 0-0 ♖he8 12 ♖e1 ♚f8** *(Zaitsev recommends moving the king to c7)* **13 ♗f4 ♗xf4 14 ♘xf4 ♗xb3 15 axb3 f5 16 f3 ♖xe1+ 17 ♖xe1 ♖e8** *(since White also has doubled pawns on the queenside the exchange is permissible)* **18 ♖a1 a6 19 ♚f2** etc, with only a minimal advantage for White, Kurajica–Kholmov, Yugoslavia v USSR 1969.

b) **10 ♗d3 ♘d7** *(10 . . . ♖d8 11 0-0 a5 12 ♖e1 ♘a6 13 a3 h6 14 ♗d2 ♘c7 15 ♘f4 ♗xf4 16 ♗xf4 ♘b5 = Matanović–Bronstein, Portorož (izt) 1958)* **11 ♗f4 ♖he8!** *(11 . . . ♘b6? 12*

♗xd6+ ♚xd6 13 b3! ♚c7 14 c4 ♖ad8 15 ♚d2! ♖he8 16 ♖ae1 ♘c8 17 ♚c3 ± Matulović–Smyslov, Siegen (ol) 1970) **12 0-0-0 f5 13 ♖he1 ♘f6 14 ♗xd6+ ♚xd6 15 ♘f4 ♗d7 16 ♗c4 ♖e4! 17 ♘d3** *(17 ♖xe4 ♘xe4 18 f3 ♘g5)* **17 . . . ♖xd4 18 ♗xf7 ♖f8** with even chances, Klovan–Kholmov, USSR 1966.

A1.22

7 . . .   ♗e7

A variation similar to the 6 . . . ♗e7 line (A1.1) has arisen with the exception that the white queen now ocupies e2. This extra tempo is not totally in White's favour as it precludes the move ♘e2. White can now just try and sit on his queenside pawn majority but there are also attacking possibilities on the kingside and Black must tread warily.

8 ♘f3   . . .

8 ♕h5 transposes to A1.1 while

8 ♕d3 0-0 **9 ♘e2 ♗d6** 10 0-0 ♕c7
*(10 . . . ♘d7 11 ♗f4 ♘b6 12 ♗b3 ♗g4
13 ♗xd6 ♗xe2 14 ♕xe2 ± Klovan-
Zheleznev, USSR 1966)* 11 g3 b5 12
♗b3 c5 13 ♗d5 ♘c6!? 14 dxc5 ♗xc5
15 ♕xb5 ♘b4 16 ♗xa8 ♗a6 gives an
equal and unclear position according
to Boleslavsky.

8 . . .   0-0

For 8 . . . ♗g4? (premature) 9 c3
♘d7 10 h3! *(10 0-0?! is illustrative
game 8 Blümich-Alekhine)* 10 . . . ♗h5
11 g4 ♗g6 12 ♘h4 ± see Bogolyubov-
Alekhine in illustrative games.

9 0-0   ♖e8

Alternatively:
a) 9 . . . ♗b6 10 ♖e1 ♗g4 *(on 10 . . .
♕c7 11 h3! or 10 . . . b5 11 ♗d3 ♘a6 12
a4 ♘b4 13 axb5 ♘xd3 14 ♕xd3 cxb5
15 ♕xb5 ♕c7 16 ♕d3 ♗b7 17 c4! ±
Konstantinopolsky)* 11 ♕e4! ♗h5!?
*(11 . . . f5?! 12 ♕d3 ♗xf3 13 ♕xf3 ♕h4
14 ♕xf5! ♕h2+ 15 ♔f1 ♕h4 16 ♗e3
c5 17 g3 ± Novopashin-Kuvaldin,
USSR 1966; 14 g3 ♕xd4 15 ♗d3 ♕g4 is
slightly better for White as well.
Relatively best is 11 . . . ♗xf3 but this
early development of the QB seems on
the whole unfavourable for Black)*
12 ♘h4! ♘d7 13 ♕f5! ± Ragozin-
Boleslavsky, Sverdlovsk 1942.
b) 9 . . . ♗g4 10 c3 ♘d7 11 ♖e1 ♗d6
12 h3 *(12 ♕e4)* 12 . . . ♗h5 13 ♗d3?!
♘b6 14 ♗d2 ♕d7 15 ♕e4 ♗g6 16
♕e2 ♗h5 led to a draw in an

Andersson-Rytov game but, as in the
illustrative game of the previous
example, more ambitious would be
13 g4 ♗g6 14 ♘h4.

10	♖e1	♘d7
11	c3	♘f8
12	♗f4	. . .

Also possible is 12 ♗e3 ♗e6 *(12 . . .
♗g4!)* 13 ♖ad1 ♗d5?! *(13 . . .
♕d7)* 14 b3 ♘g6 15 ♗xd5! ♕xd5
16 c4 ♕h5 17 ♗c1 ♔f8 18 ♘e5!
± Akhsharumova-Zaitseva, USSR
1976.

12 . . .	♗e6
13 ♗b3	. . .

On 13 ♗d3 Black might try ♗d5
followed by ♕d7. Along the lines of
Akhsharumova-Zaitseva above, 13
♖ad1 could be considered since now
Black can neutralize White's majority
on the queen's wing.

13 . . .	♗xb3
14 axb3	a5!

The chances are now balanced, as
after 15 ♕c2 ♘e6 16 ♗d2 ♗d6 17
♖e2 ♕b6 18 ♖ae1 ♖ed8 19 ♖e4 ♗f8
20 ♗e3 ♕c7 = Konstantinopolsky-
Simagin, USSR 1965.

A1.3

6 . . .   ♕e7+!?

The more up-to-date version of the line 6 . . . ♗d6 7 ♕e2+ ♕e7 (A1.21). Black is confident that the end-game can be held in spite of his inferior pawn structure. 7 ♘e2 or 7 ♗e3 would now be gross blunders on account of 7 . . . ♕b4+.

7 ♕e2   ♗e6

Also playable is 7 . . . ♗g4 8 ♕xe7+ *(8 f3 ♗e6 9 ♗xe6 ♕xe6 10 ♗f4 and now 10 . . . ♗e7 11 ♕xe6 fxe6 12 ♗xb8 = Dely-Ribli, Kecskemét 1972 or 10 . . . ♘a6 11 0-0-0 0-0-0 12 ♕xe6+ fxe6 13 ♘e2 ♗d6 14 ♗xd6 ♖xd6 15 c3 ½-½ Parma-Andersson, Dortmund 1973)* 8 . . . ♗xe7 9 ♘e2 ♘d7 10 ♘f4 *(10 ♗d3 ♘b6 11 c4 0-0-0 12 f3 ♗e6 13 b3 ♖he8 14 ♗b2 f5 15 ♔f2 ♗f6 16 ♖ab1 ♔c7 17 ♖hd1 ♗c8 18 a4 g6 19 ♗c2 ♗g5 20 ♗c1 ♗xc1 21 ♖bxc1 a5 = Matanović-Markland, Bath 1973)* 10

. . . ♘b6 11 ♗e2 ♗xe2 12 ♔xe2 0-0-0 13 ♖d1 ♖he8 14 ♔f1 c5 15 ♘e2 f5 16 ♗f4 *(Stein-Andersson, Las Palmas 1972)* and now 16 . . . ♗f6! 17 c3 *(17 dxc5 ♘a4!)* 17 . . . cxd4 18 cxd4 ♔d7! is suggested by Andersson. Black's well-posted pieces neutralize White's passed pawn.

8 ♗b3!   . . .

Offering the best prospects. Others are:

a) **8 ♗xe6 ♕xe6 9 ♘h3** *(9 ♗f4 ♘a6 10 c3 0-0-0 11 ♕xe6+ fxe6 = Gaprindashvili-Andersson, Dortmund 1978, or 10 0-0-0 0-0-0 11 c4 ♕xe2 12 ♘xe2 ♗d6 13 ♗e3 ♖he8 14 ♘c3 ♘c7 15 d5 cxd5 16 ♘xd5 b6 = Dzevlan-Despotovic, Yugoslavia 1987)* 9 . . . g5 *(preventing ♘f4, but 9 . . . ♘d7 10 ♘f4 ♕xe2+ 11 ♘xe2 0-0-0 12 ♗e3 ♘b6 = Matulović-Radulov, Yugoslavia 1977 is also quite acceptable for both sides)* 10 f4 g4 11 ♘f2 f5 12 h3 g3 13 ♘d3 ♘d7 14 b3 0-0-0 15 ♕xe6 fxe6 16 ♗b2 ♘f6 17 ♔e2 ♖g8 18 ♔f3 ♘e4= Matanović-Wade, Skopje (ol) 1972.

b) **8 ♗d3 c5!** *(8 . . . ♕c7 9 ♕f3 ♗d6 10 ♘e2 0-0 11 ♘g3 ♖e8 12 0-0 ♘d7 13 ♗d2 c5?! — 13 . . . ♗d5! ∞ Hort — 14 c3 ♖ad8 15 ♖fe1 ♘b6? 16 ♘h5! ♗e7 17 ♖xe6! Lechtinsky-Novak, Czechoslovakia 1972)* 9 ♘f3 c4 10 ♗e4 f5 11 ♗g5 ♕c7 12 ♗xf5 ♕a5+ 13 c3 ♕xf5 14 d5 ♕xd5 15 ♖d1 ♕a5 16 ♖d8+ ♕xd8 17 ♗xd8 ♔xd8 18 0-0 ♗c5 ∓ Trabance-Novarro, 1971.

8 . . .   ♘d7

Instead **8 . . . ♗xb3** 9 axb3 ♕xe2+
10 ♘xe2 ♗d6 11 ♗f4 ♗xf4 12 ♘xf4
♘a6 13 c3 0-0-0 14 b4?! *(14 0-0!)* 14 . . .
♔b8 15 ♔d2 ♘xb4!? 16 cxb4 ♖xd4+
17 ♘d3 ♖hd8 18 ♖a3 ♖xb4 = is
Kuijpers–Lechtinsky, Nice (ol) 1974
but to be seriously considered is
Black's improvement five years later:
8 . . . ♘a6! 9 ♗e3 ♗xb3 10 axb3 ♕e6
11 ♘f3 ♗d6 12 0-0 0-0 13 ♖fd1 ♖fe8
14 ♕d2 ♘b4! 15 c4 *(?! 15 c3 may be
preferable)* 16 . . . a5! 16 d5? *(16 ♘e1)*
16 . . . cxd5 17 cxd5 ♕f5 18 ♗b6 ♖a6!
(18 ♗f4 ♗e3 = Lechtinsky) 19 ♗xa5?
♖ae8 20 ♗xb4 ♖xa1 21 ♗xd6
♖xd1+ 22 ♕xd1 ♕xd5! 0-1, Sznapik–
Lechtinsky, Děčín 1979. A more
recent development is **8 . . . a5!?** 9 ♘f3
a4 10 ♗xe6 ♕xe6 11 ♗e3 ♗e7 12 0-0
0-0 13 c4 ♘a6 14 ♖fd1 ♖fd8 15 ♖ac1
♗f8 16 h3 h6 17 a3 ♘c7 = E. Geller–
King, Bern 1987.

9 ♗f4   ♘b6
10 0-0-0   ♘d5

And here:
a) **11 ♗g3?!** g6!? 12 ♘f3?! *(12 c4 ∞)*
12 . . . ♗h6+ 13 ♔b1 0-0 14 ♖he1
♖fe8 15 ♕e4 ♕d7 16 ♕h4 ♗g7 17 h3
a5 18 a3 b5 ∓ Carleton–Keene,
London 1978.
b) **11 ♗d2** b5!? *(safeguarding the
centralized knight from attack – 11 . . .
0-0-0 is also possible)* 12 ♘f3 ♕d7
13 ♘e1! ♗e7 14 ♘d3. Now Tal–
Bronstein, USSR (ch) 1974, continued

14 . . . 0-0 15 ♗a5! with the better
chances for White (see illustrative
game number 12). But instead **14 . . .
a5** would have kept the black
queenside mobile, an as yet untested
position.

A2

6 c3   . . .

A2.1: 6 . . . ♗d6
A2.2: 6 . . . ♗e6

A2.1

6 . . .   ♗d6

To be considered is **6 . . . ♕e7+** and
if 7 ♕e2?! ♗e6. Dubious, however, is
6 . . . ♗f5?! 7 ♘e2! ♗d6 8 ♘g3 ♗g6?
9 ♗c4 0-0 *(9 . . . ♕c7 10 0-0-0 0-0 11 f4 ±
Nunn)* 10 0-0 ♖e8?! *(10 . . . ♗xg3 11
hxg3 ♘d7 ± Nunn)* 11 f4 b5 *(11 . . .
♕d7 12 f5 ♗xg3 13 fxg6 +–; 11 . . . h6
12 f5 ♗h7 13 ♘h5 ± Nunn)* 12 ♗b3
♗e4 13 ♕h5! +– Nunn–K. Arkell,
London 1987. **8 . . . ♕e7+!** 9 ♗e3 ♗g6
10 ♗d3 0-0 11 ♘f5 ♗xf5 12 ♗xf5 g6
13 ♗d3 ♗f4 14 ♕f3 ♗xe3 15 fxe3 f5 =
de Firmian–Hort, Biel 1990.

7 ♗d3   0-0

Now on **7 . . . ♕e7+** 8 ♘e2. Also
dubious is **7 . . . ♕c7?!** 8 ♘e2 ♗g4?!
9 ♗e3 ♘d7 10 ♕d2 ♗xe2 11 ♕xe2 ±
as in Karpov–Smyslov, Tilburg 1979.

8 ♕c2   ...

White follows up the basic idea of 6 c3 — to induce a weakness in the black king position. Alternatives are:

a) **8 ♘e2 ♕c7?!** *(8 ... ♘d7?! 9 ♕c2 h6 10 ♗f4! ♗xf4 11 ♘xf4 c5 12 0-0-0 ♕a5 13 ♔b1 ♘b6 14 d5! ± Hort-Pfleger, London 1979 is also dubious. Instead 8 ... ♖e8 9 ♕c2 leads to the main line, though 9 0-0 is an exception: 9 ... ♕c7 10 ♘g3! ♗e6? 11 f4 c5 12 d5! ♗d7 13 c4 ♘a6 14 ♕f3 ♕b6 15 b3 ♗f8 16 ♗b2 ♘c7 17 ♗f5 ± Khalifman-Seirawan, Wijk aan Zee 1991)* **9 ♕c2 g6 10 h4 ♗e6 11 h5 f5 12 ♗h6 ♖e8 13 0-0-0 ♘d7 14 hxg6 fxg6 15 g4 ♘f8 16 gxf5 ♗xf5 17 ♗xf5 ±** Suetin-Andersson, Sochi 1973.

b) **8 ♕h5** when now **8 ... g6 9 ♕h4 c5** *(9 ... ♘d7 10 ♘e2 c5 11 0-0 ♕b6 12 ♗c4 cxd4 13 cxd4 f5 14 ♘c3 ♕b4 15 ♗b3 ♗e7 16 ♗g5 ± Medina-Donner, Beverwijk 1965)* **10 ♘e2 ♘c6 11 ♗h6 ♖e8** *(11 ... f5? 12 ♗g5 ♕b6 13 0-0 cxd4 14 cxd4 ♖e8 15 ♗c4 ± Pilnik-Najdorf, Mar del Plata 1942)* **12 dxc5 ♗xc5 =** or **8 ... ♖e8+ 9 ♘e2 g6 10 ♕h4 c5 11 0-0 ♘c6 12 ♗e3 cxd4 13 ♘xd4 ♘e5 14 ♗b5 ♗d7 15 ♗xd7 ♕xd7 16 ♕xf6** *(16 h3 f5 17 ♖ad1 ♗e7 18 ♕g3 ♗f6 and 16 ♖ad1 ♗e7 17 ♕e4 ♗f8!)* **16 ... ♘g4** etc., Konstantinopolsky.

8 ...   **♖e8+**

One advantage of this move is that f8 is cleared for the possible defensive

ploy ♘d7-f8. An abrupt lesson of the dangers Black's king may face came in the game Bronstein-Rytov, Tallinn 1978, which went **8 ... g6 9 ♘e2 ♕c7 10 h4 ♘d7 11 h5 f5 12 hxg6 hxg6 13 ♗g5 c5 14 ♗xf5 f6 15 ♗e6+ 1-0.**

9 ♘e2   ...

Playable is **9 ♗e3 h6** *(9 ... ♗f4?! 10 ♗xh7+ ♔h8 11 ♗d3 ♗xe3 12 fxe3 ♖xe3+ 13 ♘e2 ± Christiansen)* **10 ♘e2 ♘a6!?** *(10 ... ♘d7)* **11 0-0 ♘c7** *(11 ... b5!?)* **12 c4 ♗d7** *(12 ... ♘e6!?; 12 ... ♗g4!?)* **13 ♘g3 ♘e6 14 ♖ad1 ♕a5** *(14 ... ♕c7)* **15 ♕b3** *(15 d5 cxd5 16 ♗h7+ ♔h8 17 ♖xd5 ♕c7 18 ♖fd1 ♗xg3 19 ♖xd7 ♗xh2+ 20 ♔h1 ♕e5 21 ♖1d5 ♕b8 22 ♖xf7 ♗f4 ∞ Christiansen)* **15 ... ♕c7 16 ♗b1** (Chandler-Christiansen, West Germany 1988) **16 ... ♖ad8 ∞.**

9 ...   **g6**

Clearly this is an important juncture, and two other moves come under serious consideration:

a) **9 . . . h6 10 ♗e3 ♘d7** *(on 10 . . . ♗e6 11 0-0 ♕c7 12 h3 ♘d7 13 c4 ♘f8 14 ♘c3 ♖ad8 15 ♖fd1 ♗f4 was equal in Kramer-Golombek, 1951, but 11 ♕d2! with attack is sharper)* **11 ♕d2** *(11 0-0-0 ♕a5 ∞)* **11 . . . ♕c7 12 ♘g3 ♗f4 13 0-0 ♗xe3 14 fxe3 ♘f8 15 ♖f2 ♕e7 16 e4** Asztalos-Nimzovitch, Bled 1931 and now **16 . . . c5! =** *(17 d5? ♘g6 ∓)*. Better for White is **10 0-0! ♕c7 11 h3** *(11 ♘g3 ♘d7 12 ♗d2 ♘f8 13 ♖ae1 ♗d7 14 ♗c4 ♖xe1 15 ♖xe1 ♖e8 16 ♖xe8 ♗xe8 17 a4 ±* Plachetka-Bellon Lopez, Metz 1987)* **11 . . . c5?!** *(11 . . . ♘d7 ±)* **12 dxc5 ♕xc5 13 ♗e3 ♖xe3 14 fxe3 ♕xe3+ 15 ♔h1 ♘d7 16 ♖ad1 ♕e7 17 ♘f4 ♘b6 18 ♖de1 ♕d8 19 ♕d2 ±** Timman-Chernin, Amsterdam 1987.

b) **9 . . . ♔h8!?** This logical response has been neglected in recent years. Unlike 9 . . . g6 or 9 . . . h6, however, it does not weaken the black king position. **10 ♗e3** *(10 ♗xh7 g6 11 ♗xg6 fxg6 12 ♕xg6 is undoubtedly a critical test, though White probably has no more than perpetual check)* **10 . . . ♘d7 11 0-0-0 ♘f8.** If we compare this position to 9 . . . g6 where White responds with h4, or 9 . . . h6 where he follows up the attack with g4, it can be seen that Black's defensive position is much more comfortable. The game Forgács-Duras, St Petersburg 1909 now continued with the dubious pawn sacrifice 12 ♔b1 ♗e6 *(alternatively 12 . . . ♗g4!? 13 ♖d2 ♗h5 14 h4 ♕d7 15 c4 ♕g4 16 g3 ♖ad8 = Mestel-*

Wells, Great Britain (ch) 1987) 13 ♘f4?! *(wiser 13 ♘c1 or 13 c4)* and Black won – see illustrative games for the remainder.

Maybe better for White is **10 0-0 ♕c7 11 ♘g3 g6 12 c4 f5 13 ♗g5 ♗e6 14 ♕d2 ♘d7 15 d5! cxd5 16 cxd5 ♗xd5 17 ♗xf5 ♗c6 18 ♖ad1! ♗xg3** *(18 . . . gxf5 19 ♕xd6 ♕xd6 20 ♖xd6 ♖g8 21 ♗f6+ ♘xf6 22 ♖xf6 ± Jó Horvath)* **19 ♗xd7 ♗xh2+ 20 ♔h1 ♗e5 21 ♗xe8 ♖xe8 22 ♖fe1 ♕c8! ±** J. Horvath-Hodgson, Sochi 1987.

10 h4   ♘d7

a) **10 . . . ♗e6 11 h5** *(11 ♗h6 f5 12 0-0-0 ♘d7 13 ♔b1 ♕a5 14 ♘c1 ♘f6 15 h5!? ♘xh5 16 ♖xh5 gxh5 17 ♖h1 ∞ Chandler-Hodgson, Great Britain (ch) 1988 – 17 . . . f6 ∞; 15 ♘b3 ♕c7 16 c4 ♗f4 17 ♗xf4 ♕xf4 =)* **11 . . . f5 12 hxg6 fxg6 13 ♗h6 ♘d7** *(13 . . . ♕f6!?)* **14 g4!? ♗d5 15 0-0-0! ♗xh1 16 ♖xh1 ♗f8! 17 ♗d2** (Kudrin-King, Bayswater 1988) **17 . . . ♘b6! 18 gxf5 ♕d5 19 ♘g3 ♕xa2 ∞** (Kudrin).

b) **10 . . . c5!?** **11 h5 f5 12 hxg6 hxg6 13 ♗e3** *(13 g4 ♕c7 14 ♗g5 ± was Planinc-Puc, Čačak 1969, better 13 . . . f4! 14 ♗xg6 ♕f6 15 ♗h7+ ♔f8 ∞ Marić)* **13 . . . f4 14 ♗xg6 fxe3?** *(14 . . . ♕f6 ∞)* **15 ♗xf7+ ♔xf7 16 ♖h7+ +−** Zelevinsky-Goldberg, USSR 1961.

11 h5   . . .

Alternatively **11 ♗h6 ♗f8 12 ♗xf8 ♘xf8 13 0-0-0 ±** as in Vogt-Bobzin,

Eger 1987.

11 ...   ♘f8

A2.11: 12 ♗h6
A2.12: 12 hxg6

A2.11

12 ♗h6   **...**

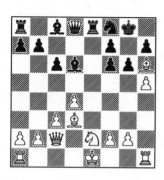

12 ...   ♗e6

For 12 ... ♕c7?! 13 0-0-0 ♗e6 14 c4
♖ad8? see 13 ... ♕c7 (b).

13 0-0-0   **b5**

The pawn thrust seems stronger
than other moves:

a) **13 ...** ♕a5 14 a3 ♕c7 15 hxg6
fxg6 16 ♖h4! ♕f7 17 ♖dh1 f5 18 ♘f4
♗b3 19 ♕d2 ♖e7 20 g4! ♗xf4 21
♗xf4 fxg4 22 ♖xg4 ♗e6 23 ♖gh4 ♗f5
24 ♗d6 ♖d7 25 ♗e5 ± de Firmian–
Odendahl, Philadelphia 1988.

b) **13 ...** *♕c7 14 c4 b6 (14 ... ♖ad8?
15 hxg6 fxg6?! 16 c5! ♗e7 17 ♘f4 ♗f7*

*18 ♗c4! +− Kavalek–Andersson,
Washington DC (m) 1978; 14 ... c5!?
15 d5 ♗d7 16 hxg6 hxg6 17 ♖h4! ±
Byrne, Mednis)* 15 ♕d2! ♖ad8 16 ♖h4
f5 17 ♖hd1 (Huergo–Cabrera, Cuba
1988) 17 ... ♗e7 18 ♗g5 ♗xg5 19
♕xg5 ♕e7 20 ♕g3 ± (Huergo).

14 ♔b1   **...**

14 ♗xf8 ♗xf8 15 hxg6 fxg6 16
♗xg6 hxg6 17 ♕xg6+ ♗g7 18 ♖d3 ∞
(Huergo).

14 ...   ♕c7

White stands slightly better here,
due to the more advanced nature of
his attack (Analysis).

A2.12

12 hxg6   **fxg6**

And here:

a) **13 ♕b3+** ♗e6! 14 ♕xb7 ♗d5 15
♔f1 ♖e7!? *(15 ... a6 16 c4 ♖b8 17
♕xa6 ♖a8 is a draw)* 16 ♕a6 ♕d7 17
♗c4! *(17 c4? ♗xg2+!)* 17 ... ♖ae8 18
♗xd5+ cxd5 19 ♗e3 ♘e6 20 ♕d3
♘g5 21 c4! ♘e4 with chances for both
sides, Szabó–Flohr, Groningen 1946.

b) **13 ♗h6** ♗e6 14 0-0-0 f5 15 ♔b1
b5 16 ♘c1 ♕f6 17 f4 ♗d5 18 ♖h3 ♘e6
∞ Pilnik–Golombek, Amsterdam
1951.

c) **13 ♗d2** ♕e7 14 0-0-0 ♗e6 15
♔b1 b5 16 ♖de1 ♕f7 17 ♘c1 ♖ab8 18
♖h4 ♗d5 19 f3 ♖xe1 20 ♗xe1 f5 ∞
Suetin–Augustin, Sochi 1979.

d) **13 ♔f1!?** ♗e6 14 ♗h6 ♕e7 15 ♖e1 ♕f7 16 b3 ♕c7 17 c4 ♕d7 18 ♘c3 ♗b4! 19 ♖h4 ♗f5 20 ♖xe8 ♖xe8 21 ♗e3 ∞ Gurgenidze–Möhring, Hradec Králové 1977-78 *(21 ♗xf5 ♗xc3!!).*

It would appear that at present Black has satisfactory resources to counter the White attack, though he must clearly proceed with caution.

A2.2

6 . . .   ♗e6

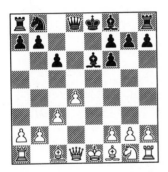

An attempt to hinder White's typical policy of queenside castling.

7 ♗d3   . . .

7 ♗f4 ♗e7 8 ♗d3 0-0 9 ♘e2 c5 10 0-0 ♘c6 11 dxc5 *(11 ♗e3 c4 ∞)* 11 . . . ♗xc5 12 ♕c2 g6 13 ♗h6?! *(13 ♖ad1 ♕e7 14 ♘g3 ♘e5! 15 ♖fe1 − 15 ♗e2 h5! − 15 . . . ♘xd3 16 ♖xd3 ♖ad8 17 ♖xd8 ♖xd8 18 h3 f5 ∓ Stummer–Mirković, Pula 1988)* 13 . . . ♖e8 14

♘f4 ♘e5! 15 ♘xe6 *(15 ♗e4 ♘g4! 16 ♘xe6 ♖xe6 17 ♗f4 ♕e7 18 ♗d3 ♖d8 ∓; 15 ♗b5 ♖e7 16 ♖ad1 ♕b6 17 ♗e2 ♕c6 ∓)* 15 . . . ♖xe6 16 ♗e2 f5 17 ♖ad1 ♕e7 = (∓) Mirković.

7 . . .   ♗d6
8 ♘e2   ♕c7
9 ♕c2   . . .

9 ♘g3 0-0 10 0-0 g6 *(10 . . . ♘d7?! 11 f4 ♖fe8 12 f5 ♗d5 13 ♘h5!? g6 14 ♕g4 ♔h8 15 ♗h6 ± Zapata–Hodgson, Palma de Mallorca 1989)* 11 ♗h6 ♖e8 12 ♘e4!? ± Zapata.

9 . . .   ♘d7
10 c4!   . . .

10 h3 0-0-0 *(10 . . . h6!? 11 . . . 0-0!?)* 11 c4! ♗b4+ 12 ♗d2 ♕a5 13 ♗xb4 ♕xb4+ 14 ♕d2 ♕xd2+ 15 ♔xd2 ± (Markovic).

10 . . .   ♗b4+
11 ♗d2   ♗xd2+
12 ♕xd2   0-0
13 0-0   ♖fe8

14 ♘f4! ♘b6 15 b3 ♖ad8 16 ♖ad1 g6 17 ♗b1 c5 18 d5 ♗c8 19 ♖fe1 *(19 ♘e2 ± Mikhalchisin–Kholmov, Moscow 1989)* 19 . . . ♖xe1+ 20 ♖xe1 ♕d6 21 ♕e3 ± (Mikhalchisin).

A3

6 ♘f3   ♗d6
7 ♗e2   . . .

Others:

a) **7 &c4** 0-0 **8** 0-0 **&g4!** = *ECO (8 ... Ⅱe8? Fischer–Barcza, Stockholm (izt) 1962)*.

b) **7 h3** 0-0 **8 &e2 Ⅱe8 9** 0-0 **⑤d7 10 &e3 ⑤f8 11 ♕d2 ⑤g6 12 c4 f5!** = Sergyán–Varnusz, Hungary 1975.

c) **7 &d3** 0-0 *(7 ... &g4?! before White has castled is dubious due to 8 h3 &h5? – 8 ... ♕e7+! Tartakower – 9 g4 &g6 10 ⑤h4 ⑤d7 11 ⑤f5 &xf5 12 &xf5 g6?! 13 ♕e2+ ♕e7 14 &xd7+! ♔xd7 15 &e3 Ⅱae8 16 d5 ± Pillsbury–Caro, Vienna 1898)* **8** 0-0 **&g4! 9 &e3 ⑤d7 10 c4 c5 11 &c2** *(11 d5 ⑤e5 12 &e2 &xf3!)* **11 ... ♕c7 12 h3 &h5** = Kuijpers–Flohr, Amsterdam 1963.

7 ...   0-0

A very interesting idea is **7 ... ⑤a6!?** as Korchnoi played against Torre in the Buenos Aires Olympiad 1978, the game continuing **8** 0-0 **⑤c7 9 c4** 0-0 **10 &e3 Ⅱe8 11 ♕d2 &f5 12 Ⅱad1 &e4 13 ♕c1 h6 14 ⑤d2 &h7 15 &f3 f5 16 ⑤b3 g5!** *(a brilliant and dynamic interpretation of the Original Caro)* **17 ⑤a5 g4 18 &e2 &b4 19 ⑤xb7 ♕c8 20 ⑤c5 f4 ∓.** White does not have sufficient compensation for his lost bishop.

8 0-0   **Ⅱe8**

Not **8 ... &f5? 9 &e3 ♕c7 10 ♕d2 Ⅱe8 11 c4 c5 12 dxc5 &xc5 13 &xc5 ♕xc5 14 b4! ♕c8 15 ⑤d4 ⑤c6 16 &f3 ⑤e5 17 c5! &d3 18 &e2! ±** Espig–Dietze, East Germany 1971. Instead **8 ... ♕c7 9 c4 Ⅱd8 10 &e3 c5** = is a suggestion of Konstantinopolsky.

**9 &e3   &g4
10 Ⅱe1   ⑤d7
11 ♕d3?!   ...**

Stronger is **11 ⑤h4!.** After the text move Keres–Flohr, AVRO 1938 continued **11 ... ♕c7 12 g3 ⑤f8** *(12 ... f5!)* **13 ⑤d2 ♕d7 14 d5 &xe2 15 Ⅱxe2 ⑤g6 16 dxc6 ♕xc6 17 ♕c4 ♕d7** and Black had equalized.

A4

6 g3   ...

When:

a) **6 ... ♕d5! 7 ⑤f3 &d6 8 &g2** 0-0 **9** 0-0 **♕h5 10 c4 &g4** = Boleslavsky. Black's position is comfortable and White cannot improve with **8 c4? &b4+.**

b) **6 ... &d6 7 &g2** 0-0 **8 ⑤e2 &f5?! 9** 0-0 **Ⅱe8 10 c4 ⑤a6 11 ⑤c3 ♕d7 12 a3 &h3 13 &e3 ±** Rauzer–

Rabinovich, USSR 1933. With this borne in mind, **8 . . . ♖e8!** seems more promising, viz. 9 0-0 ♗g4 10 ♗e3?! *(10 ♖e1!?)* 10 . . . f5! 11 ♕d2 *(11 ♖e1 f4! =)* 11 . . . ♗xe2 12 ♕xd2 f4 13 gxf4 ♗xf4 14 ♕f3 ♗c7 = Dzavlan-Mirkovic, Yugoslavia 1987.

c) **6 . . . ♗e6** 7 ♗g2 ♗d6 8 ♘e2 0-0 9 0-0 ± Boleslavsky — if 7 ♘f3 b6!

d) **6 . . . c5!?** *(a recent idea)* 7 ♘f3 ♗d6 8 ♗e3 ♕c7 9 dxc5 ♗xc5 10 ♗xc5 ♕xc5 11 ♕e2+ ♗e6? *(better 11 . . . ♔f8! 12 ♗g2 ♘c6 13 0-0 g6 = or 12 0-0-0 ♘c6 =)* 12 ♗h3! ± Tal-Lechtinsky, Tallinn 1979.

B

5 ♘g3   . . .

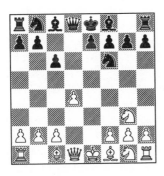

This move avoids the complexities of either 5 . . . exf6 or 5 . . . gxf6, but, as could be expected, is somewhat tamer. Black could now play 5 . . . ♘d7 transposing to the Smyslov System (chapter 1) but he has more effective

ways to equalize:

B1: 5 . . . c5!?
B2: 5 . . . g6
B3: 5 . . . h5!?

Others:

a) **5 . . . e5?!** 6 ♘f3 exd4 7 ♘xd4 *(7 ♕xd4 ♕xd4 8 ♘xd4 ♗c5 9 ♘df5 0-0 10 ♗e3 ♗xe3 = Alekhine-Capablanca, New York 1927)* 7 . . . ♗c5? *(7 . . . ♗e7 8 ♘df5 ♕xd1+ 9 ♔xd1 ♗f8 10 ♗c4 ♗e6 11 ♖e1 ♔d7 12 ♗xe6+ fxe6 13 ♘e3 ± Boleslavsky)* 8 ♕e2+! with advantage to White in Alekhine-Tartakower, Kecskemét 1927 — see illustrative games for further moves.

b) **5 . . . e6** 6 ♘f3 c5 transposes to B1.

c) **5 . . . ♗g4** 6 ♗e2 ♗xe2 7 ♘1xe2 e6 8 ♕d3 ♘bd7 9 0-0 ♗e7 10 c4 0-0 11 b3 ♖e8 12 ♗b2 ♕a5 13 ♕f3 ♖ad8 14 ♖fd1 *(Unzicker-Lein, South Africa 1979)* 14 . . . ♗a3! = Unzicker.

B1

5 . . .   c5!?
6 ♘f3   . . .

On 6 dxc5 ♕a5+ regains the pawn while **6 . . . ♕xd1+** 7 ♔xd1 e6 8 b4 a5 9 c3 ♘a6 etc. has yet to be tried out in practice.

6 . . .   ♘c6

6 . . . e6 is also playable: 7 ♗d3 ♘c6

8 dxc5 ♗xc5 9 a3! 0-0 10 0-0 b6 11 b4
♗e7 12 ♗b2 = Spielmann-Hönlinger,
Vienna 1929.

| 7 ♗e3 | cxd4!? |

7 ... ♘d5 8 ♗e2 e6 9 0-0 ♗e7 10
♗c1 0-0 11 dxc5 ♗xc5 = Tsvetkov-
Sokolsky, Moscow 1947.

| 8 ♘xd4 | ♘xd4 |

Also 8 . . . ♕a5+ 9 c3 ♗d7 =
Boleslavsky.

9 ♗xd4	♗d7
10 c3!?	♗c6
11 ♕b3	e6

12 0-0-0 ♕a5 13 ♗c4 ♗e7 14 ♖he1
0-0 15 ♖e5 *(Rajna-Varnusz, Budapest
1977)* and now 15 ... ♕a4! would have
been equal.

B2

| 5 ... | g6 |

This move has been experimented
with by Larsen.

| 6 ♘f3 | ... |

To be considered is 6 ♗c4!? ♗g7
7 ♘f3 *(7 h3!?)* 0-0 8 0-0 ♗g4 9 c3 ♘bd7
10 ♖e1 *(10 h3 ♗xf3 11 ♕xf3 e5)* 10 ...
♘b6 11 ♗b3 a5 *(Kan-Ragozin, 1939)*
12 a4 ±.

6 ...	♗g7
7 ♗e2	0-0
8 0-0	♕b6!?

Disturbing White's development.

| 9 b3 | ... |

And here:
a) 9 ... ♗g4 10 ♗b2 a5 11 a4 ♘bd7
(11 ... ♘a6!?) 12 h3 ♗xf3 13 ♗xf3
♖ad8 14 ♕e2 *(with his two bishops
White stands slightly better according
to Matanović)* 14 ... ♖fe8 15 ♖fe1
♘f8 16 ♕c4 ♘e6 17 ♖xe6 *("Karpov is
not satisfied with his position" says
Larsen)* 17 ... fxe6 18 ♕xe6+ ♔h8 19
♖e1? *(19 h4)* 19 ... ♕b4! 20 h4 as in
Karpov-Larsen, Tilburg 1979 when
now Larsen gives 20 ... ♖d6! 21 ♕e2
b5 with a clear plus for Black.
b) 9 ... a5 10 a4 ♘a6 11 h3 ♘b4
(11 ... ♕c7!?) 12 ♖e1 ♕c7 13 ♗b2 b6
14 ♕d2 ♗b7 15 c3 ♘bd5 16 c4 ♘b4 17
♗c3 ♖ad8 18 ♖ad1 e6! with equal
chances in Sax-Larsen, Tilburg 1979,
as 19 ♗xb4 axb4 20 ♕xb4 c5 would

give Black good compensation.

B3

5 ...   h5!?

A sharper continuation than the others.

6 h4   ...

6 ♗g5 h4 7 ♗xf6?! hxg3! 8 ♗e5 ♖xh2 9 ♖xh2 ♕a5+! 10 ♕d2 ♕xe5+!? 11 dxe5 gxh2 (Skembris) 12 0-0-0 ∞.

6 ...   e5!?

a) 6 ... ♗g4 7 ♗e2 e6 *(7 ... ♗xe2 8 ♘1xe2 ♘bd7 9 ♕d3 ± Spielmann-Alekhine, Karlsbad 1911)* 8 ♗xg4 *(8 ♘f3!?)* 8 ... ♘xg4 9 ♗f4 ♕b6 10 ♘f3! ± v. Holzhausen-Tartakower, 1926.
b) 6 ... ♕c7 7 ♗c4!? *(7 ♗e2 ♗g4! 8 ♗xg4 ♘xg4 ∓ 9 ♘xh5? ♕a5+)* 7 ... ♗g4 8 ♘1e2 e6 9 f3 ♗d6 ∞ Kupreichik-Skembris, Zenica 1985.

7 ♕e2   ...

Also possible is 7 ♘f3!?

7 ...   ♕xd4
8 ♘f3   ♗b4+!?

8 ... ♕d5 = (Mirkovic).

9 c3   ♗xc3+

10 bxc3   ♕xc3+
11 ♕d2   ♕xa1

was Dmitievic-Mirkovic, Yugoslavia 1988. After 12 ♗c4!? White has plenty of play for the exchange and pawns — Mirkovic assesses this position as unclear.

ILLUSTRATIVE GAMES

8. BLÜMICH-ALEKHINE
Poland 1941

1 e4 c6 2 d4 d5 3 ♘c3 dxe4 4 ♘xe4 ♘f6 5 ♘xf6+ exf6 6 ♗c4 ♗d6 7 ♕e2+ ♗e7 8 ♘f3 ♗g4? (Practice has shown this early bishop move to be hazardous. Here, however, White plays without a considered plan, and this game clearly demonstrates Black's chances against unwary play) 9 c3 ♘d7 10 0-0?! (10 h3! ♗h5 11 g4!) 10 ... ♘b6 11 ♗b3 0-0 12 ♖fe1 ♗d6 13 ♗c2 (?) ♗h5 14 ♕d3 (Relying on his superior pawn formation, White heedlessly goes for mechanical exchanges. 14 b3 followed by 15 ♗b2 and 16 c4 was needed with some advantage) 14 ... ♗g6 15 ♕d1 ♗c7 16 ♗xg6 hxg6 17 ♘d2 (An overcautious plan. The line recommended earlier was still better) 17 ... f5 18 ♘f1 ♕h4! 19 ♕f3 ♖fe8 20 g3 (Weakens the king position. In Kotov's opinion 20 ♗e3 ♘c4 21 b3 ♘xe3 22 ♖xe3 was better) 20 ... ♕h3

21 ♗f4 ♗xf4 22 ♕xf4 ♘d5 23 ♕f3
♘f6! (While White was concentrating
all his efforts on the exchanges, Black
was bringing his knight into an
attacking position) 24 ♖e3 ♖xe3 25
♘xe3 ♖e8 26 ♖d1 ♘e4 27 ♖d3? (An
artificial move, countered with a
pretty combination by the world
champion. 27 d5 was necessary to stay
alive) 27 . . . ♘g5! 28 ♕g2 (28 ♕f4
♕h5! threatening . . . ♕e2 and . . .
♘h3+ and now 29 ♔g2 meets ♖e4!
30 ♕b8+ ♔h7 ∓. 28 ♕d1 f4! 29 ♘g2
fxg3 30 hxg3 ♕f5 offers most resistance) 28 . . . ♕h5! (Alekhine in his
element! 29 . . . ♘f3+ 30 ♔h1 ♘e1 or
29 . . . ♕e2 30 ♖d1 ♖xe3 are
threatened and 29 h4 is answered by
29 . . . ♕e2 30 ♕f1 ♘f3+ 31 ♔h1
♖xe3 32 ♕xe2 ♖xe2 33 ♖xf3 ♖xb2)
29 ♔f1 ♘f3 30 h3 f4! (Preparing the
following combination) 31 gxf4 ♕b5!
32 c4 (32 ♔e2 ♕xd3+!) 32 . . . ♕xc4!
(The point! The queen cannot be cap-
tured because of mate!) 33 ♕xf3
♕xd3+ 34 ♔g2 ♕xd4 35 f5 gxf5 White
resigned.

9. BOGOLYUBOV-ALEKHINE
Salzburg 1942

1 e4 c6 2 d4 d5 3 ♘c3 dxe4 4 ♘xe4
♘f6 5 ♘xf6+ exf6 6 ♗c4 ♗d6 7 ♕e2+
♗e7 8 ♘f3 ♗g4? 9 c3 ♘d7 10 h3! ♗h5
11 g4! ♗g6 12 ♘h4 (The lesson of this
game is that if Black intends playing
♗g4, he would do better to wait till
White castles 'short') 12 . . . ♘b6 13
♗b3 ♘d5 14 ♗d2! (Better than the

hasty 14 f4 f5! 15 ♘xf5 ♗xf5 16 gxf5
0-0) 14 . . . ♕d6? (14 . . . ♕d7 is
superior. A rare sight: Alekhine
trounced in the very opening!) 15
♘f5! ♗xf5 16 gxf5 g6 (Black's kingside looks pitiful. On 16 . . . g5 17 h4!)
17 0-0-0 0-0-0 (17 . . . gxf5 18 ♖de1
and the trebled pawn is not particularly brilliant either) 18 ♕f3 g5 19
♖he1 ♖he8 20 ♖e4 ♗f8 21 ♖xe8!
♖xe8 22 ♕h5! (There is no defence)
22 . . . ♕d7 23 ♕xh7 ♖e4 24 ♕h8 ♕d8
25 ♕h5 ♕d7 26 ♕h8 ♕d8 27 ♖e1
♖xe1+ (27 . . . ♖h4 28 ♕g8) 28 ♗xe1
♔c7 29 ♗d2 ♕e7 30 ♕h5 ♕d7 31 ♕f3
♗h6 32 h4 ♘f4 33 ♗xf4 gxf4 34 ♕h5
♗f8 35 ♗xf7 c5 36 ♗e6 ♕d6 37 ♕f7+
♗e7 38 dxc5 ♕xc5 39 h5 f3 40 h6 ♔b6
41 ♗c4 ♗d6 42 ♗d5! ♕c8 43 ♕e6 ♕f8
44 h7 a5 45 ♗xf3 ♕h6+ 46 ♔c2 Black
resigned.

10. NUNN-ARKELL
London 1987

1 e4 c6 2 d4 d5 3 ♘d2 dxe4 4 ♘xe4
♘f6 5 ♘xf6+ exf6 6 c3 ♗f5?! 7 ♘e2!
♗d6 8 ♘g3 ♗g6? 9 ♗c4 0-0 10 0-0
♖e8?! 11 f4 b5 12 ♗b3 ♗e4 13 ♕h5!
♕d7 (13 . . . g6 14 ♗xf7+! ♔xf7 15
♕xh7+ ♔f8 16 ♘xe4 ♖xe4 17 ♕h8+
♔e7 18 ♕g7+ ♔e6 19 ♕xg6 +−; 13
. . . ♕c7 14 ♖e1 +−) 14 ♘xe4 ♖xe4 15
♗c2 g6 16 ♕h4 ♖e8 17 f5! (17 ♕xf6
♗e7 18 ♕e5 ♗d8 =) 17 . . . ♗e7 (17 . . .
g5 18 ♗xg5 fxg5 19 ♕xg5+ ♔h8 20 f6
♖g8 21 ♕h6 ♖g6 22 ♗xg6 fxg6 23 f7
+−) 18 ♖f3! g5 19 ♕h5 ♗d8 20 ♗xg5
Black resigned (Nunn).

11. KHALIFMAN–SEIRAWAN
Wijk aan Zee 1991

1 e4 c6 2 d4 d5 3 ♘c3 dxe4 4 ♘xe4 ♘f6 5 ♘xf6+ exf6 6 c3 ♗d6 7 ♗d3 0-0 8 ♘e2 ♖e8 9 0-0 ♕c7 10 ♘g3 ♗e6? 11 f4! c5 12 d5! ♗d7 (12 . . . ♗xd5? 13 ♕h5!) 13 c4 ♘a6 14 ♕f3 ♕b6 15 b3 ♗f8 16 ♗b2 ♘c7 17 ♗f5! ♗xf5 18 ♘xf5 ♖ed8 19 ♖ae1 ♘e8 20 ♕h5! ♕a5 21 ♖xe8!! ♖xe8 22 ♘h6+! gxh6 (22 . . . ♔h8 23 ♕xf7!) 23 ♕g4+ Black resigned.

12. KUDRIN–KING
Bayswater 1988

1 e4 c6 2 d4 d5 3 ♘c3 dxe4 4 ♘xe4 ♘f6 5 ♘xf6+ exf6 6 c3 ♗d6 7 ♗d3 0-0 8 ♕c2 ♖e8+ 9 ♘e2 g6 10 h4 ♗e6 11 h5 f5 12 hxg6 fxg6 13 ♗h6 ♘d7?! 14 g4! ♗d5 15 0-0-0! ♗xh1 (15 . . . ♗f8 16 ♗d2 fxg4 17 ♗xg6, or 17 ♖xh7!? ♔xh7 18 ♗xg6+ − Speelman) 16 ♖xh1 ♗f8! 17 ♗d2 (17 . . . gxf5?? ♗xh6+ 18 ♖xh6 ♕g5+) 17 . . . fxg4?

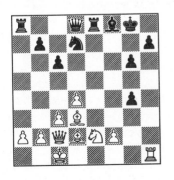

(17 . . . ♘f6 18 ♗c4+ ♔g7 19 gxf5 ±,

so 17 . . . ♘b6! seems best) 18 ♕b3+! ♔g7 19 ♖xh7+! ♔xh7 20 ♕f7+ ♔h8 21 ♘f4 Black resigned (Kudrin).

13. FORGÁCS–DURAŠ
St Petersburg 1909

1 e4 c6 2 d4 d5 3 ♘c3 dxe4 4 ♘xe4 ♘f6 5 ♘xf6+ exf6 6 c3 ♗d6 7 ♗d3 0-0 8 ♕c2 ♖e8+ 9 ♘e2 ♔h8! 10 ♗e3 ♘d7 11 0-0-0 ♘f8 12 ♔b1 ♗e6 13 ♘f4?! (In order to grab the initiative, White sacrifices a pawn, confident that he will have good play on the open g-file) 13 . . . ♗xf4! 14 ♗xf4 ♕d5 15 b3 ♕xg2 16 ♖hg1 ♕f3 17 ♗e3 ♗g4! (Black transfers his bishop to strengthen the kingside and gains time to boot. Characteristically the black pawns hinder the white attack) 18 ♖de1 ♗h5 19 ♖g3 ♕d5 20 f4 (Or 20 ♖eg1 ♗g6 21 f4 ♗xd3 22 ♕xd3 ♕e4 23 ♕xe4 ♖xe4 24 ♖xg7? ♘g6 −+) 20 . . . ♖e7! 21 ♖eg1 ♖ae8 22 c4 (22 ♖xg7 ♗g6) 22 . . . ♕d6 23 ♕f2 g6 24 d5? (Undue optimism which soon ends in disappointment. Although White's pawn sacrifice was incorrect, 24 f5 or ♗e3-c1-b2 in preparation for f5 still gives him good chances) 24 . . . ♘d7 25 ♗d4 ♖e2!! 26 ♗e5 (26 ♗xe2 and ♕a3) 26 . . . ♕xe5 White resigned.

14. TAL–BRONSTEIN
USSR (ch) 1974

1 e4 c6 2 d4 d5 3 ♘d2 dxe4 4 ♘xe4 ♘f6 5 ♘xf6+ exf6 6 ♗c4 ♕e7+!?

7 ♕e2 ♗e6 8 ♗b3! ♘d7 9 ♗f4 ♘b6 10
0-0-0 ♘d5 11 ♗d2 b5!? 12 ♘f3 ♕d7 13
♘e1! ♗e7 14 ♘d3 0-0?! 15 ♗a5!
(Hems Black in) 15 ... ♖fe8 16 ♕d2
♘b6 17 ♘c5 ♗xc5 18 dxc5 ♕xd2+ 19
♖xd2 ♘c4 (Black's defending
prospects are still bright with bishops
of opposite colours) 20 ♗xc4 ♗xc4
(Tal also considered the paradoxical
20 . . . bxc4, after which the
breakthrough is even more difficult
than in the actual game) 21 b3 ♗d5 22
f3 h5 23 ♖hd1 h4 24 h3 ♖ac8 25 ♖d4
♖e2? (This way Black will be forced
to exchange one of his rooks, and the
ever-threatening sacrifice of the
exchange hinders his defence. 25 . . .
g5! still gives reasonable play) 26
♖1d2 ♖xd2 27 ♔xd2 g5 28 ♔d3 ♔f8?
(Overlooking White's next move. 28
. . . ♗e6 leads to passive play, but
White's victory is still in doubt) 29 a4!
a6 30 axb5 axb5 31 ♖xd5! cxd5 32 ♔d4
♔e7 (32 . . . ♖e8 33 c6 ♖e6 34 ♔c5
♔e7 35 ♔b6 +– Tal) 33 ♔xd5 ♔d7 34
b4! ♖e8 (34 . . . ♖c6 35 c4 bxc4 36 b5
+–) 35 c6+ ♔c8 36 c4 ♖e5+ 37 ♔d4

bxc4 38 ♔xc4 ♖e2 39 b5 ♖c2+ 40
♔d5 ♖a2 41 ♗c3! ♖xg2 42 b6 ♖f2 43
b7+ ♔b8 44 ♗xf6 **Black resigned.**

15. ALEKHINE–TARTAKOWER
Kecskemét 1927

1 e4 c6 2 d4 d5 3 ♘c3 dxe4 4 ♘xe4
♘f6 5 ♘g3 e5?! 6 ♘f3 exd4 7 ♘xd4
♗c5? 8 ♕e2+ ♗e7 (8 . . . ♕e7
9 ♕xe7+ ♗xe7 10 ♘df5 ±) 9 ♗e3 c5?
(An unsuccessful bid to prevent
queenside castling. According to
Alekhine 9 . . . 0-0 10 0-0-0 ♕a5 11
♔b1 ♘d5 12 ♕d3 was necessary) 10
♘df5 0-0 11 ♕c4! (Preparing the
development of his f1 bishop by
gaining a tempo) 11 ... ♖e8 (Or 11 ...
b6 12 ♖d1 and ♕h4+ – Alekhine)
12 ♗d3 b6 13 0-0-0 ♗a6 14 ♘h6+!!
gxh6 15 ♗xh7+ ♘xh7 (15 ... ♔h8 16
♕xf7 followed by 17 ♘f5±) 16 ♕g4+
♔h8 17 ♖xd8 ♖xd8 (17 ... ♗xd8 18
♕f3) 18 ♕e4 ♘c6 19 ♕xc6 ♗f8 20
♘f5 ♗c4 21 ♗xh6 ♗d5 22 ♕c7 ♖ac8
23 ♕f4 ♖c6 24 ♗xf8 ♖xf8 25 ♕e5+
♘f6 26 ♘d6! **Black resigned.**

3
Bronstein (Larsen) Variation −
5 . . . gxf6!?

1 e4 c6 2 d4 d5 3 ♘c3 dxe4 4 ♘xe4 ♘f6 5 ♘xf6+ gxf6!?

One of the Caro-Kann's more peculiar variations. Black spoils his king position and may even have problems in the endgame due to his three pawn islands compared to White's queenside majority.

On the other hand, Black has more centre pawns, no development difficulties and the semi-open g-file for his rooks − factors the Danish GM Bent Larsen has uncompromisingly exploited in playing this variation for the win.

Indeed the 5 . . . gxf6 Caro represents one of the most dynamic variations of the whole defence, and seems likely to continue its recent increase in popularity.

White has two basic ideas: to chase Black's bishop after it comes to f5 by ♘g1-e2-g3 and h4, or the more circumspect kingside castling followed up by c4 and d5 or c4-c5 with the possible advance of the b-pawn for good measure.

The various alternatives are arranged in approximate order of importance:

A: 6 ♘e2
B: 6 ♘f3
C: 6 c3
D: 6 ♗e2
E: 6 ♗c4
F: 6 ♕d3
G: 6 ♗e3

Also possible is **6 ♗f4 ♕b6** (see E for 6 . . . ♗f5 7 ♗c4) 7 ♘f3!? ♕xb2 8 ♗d3 ∞ Poulsen−Larsen, Copenhagen 1973. More significant is an idea of the Dutch GM van der Wiel,

59

6 g3. The idea is to stunt Black's pressure on the g-file and direct the bishop against Black's queenside. **6 ... ♕d5** 7 ♘f3 ♘a6 *(7 ... ♗f5 8 c3 ♘d7 9 ♗g2 ♕e4+) 8 c3! (8 ♗g2 ♕e4+ 9 ♗e3 ♘b4 10 ♖c1 ♗f5)* 8 ... ♗g4 *(8 ... e5 9 ♗e3!)* 9 ♗g2 0-0-0 10 h3 ♗f5 11 0-0 ♕d7 12 ♔h2 e6 13 ♘h4 ♗g6 14 b4 ♘c7 15 ♕b3 ♗e7 16 a4 e5 17 dxe5 fxe5 18 ♘xg6 fxg6 19 ♗e3 ♔b8 20 b5 ± van der Wiel–Hofland, Netherlands 1980. Better for Black is **6 ... h5!** 7 ♗g2 *(7 ♘f3 ♗g4 8 ♗g2 h4 9 0-0 ♕d7 10 ♕d3 hxg3 11 fxg3 ♘a6 12 c3 0-0-0 ∞Tseitlin)* 7 ... ♗g4 *(7 ... h4!?)* 8 ♕d3 e6 9 ♗f4 ♗d6 10 ♗xd6 ♕xd6 11 ♘f3 ♘d7 12 ♘h4 *(12 0-0-0 0-0-0 =)* 12 ... e5 13 h3 *(13 d5 ♘c5 14 ♕c4 0-0-0!)* 13 ... ♗e6 14 0-0-0 0-0-0 15 ♕e3 ♘b6 16 dxe5 ♕b4!? *(16 ... ♕xe5 17 ♖xd8+ ♖xd8 18 ♕xe5 fxe5 19 ♖e1 ± Aratovsky–M. Tseitlin, USSR 1988)* 17 a3 *(17 b3? ♘a4! ∓)* 17 ... ♕c4 18 b3 ♕a6 19 ♔b2 ♕b5 20 ♔a2 ♕a5 = (M. Tseitlin).

A

6 ♘e2   ...

And here:

A1: 6 ... h5!?
A2: 6 ... ♗f5
A3: 6 ... ♗g4?!

Or 6 ... ♕b6?! 7 c3! ♗f5 8 ♘g3 ♗g6 9 f4 (normally these positions with f4

give Black counterplay based on the e4 square — this game is an exception) 9 ... f5 10 ♗d3 e6 11 ♕e2 ♗e7 12 ♗e3 ♕a5 Lutikov–Larsen, radio game 1970, and now 13 h4 h5 14 ♘f1 followed by ♘d2-f3 ±/±.

A1

6 ...   h5!?

This secures the bishop's retreat after a later ... ♗f5 and prepares to molest any white knight going to g3.

7 ♕d3   ...

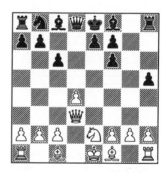

Not of course 7 ♘g3? h4! The text move stops 7 ... ♗f5. Other continuations are:

a) 7 ♘f4 ♗g4 8 ♕d3 e6 9 ♗e3 ♗d6 10 h3 ♗f5 11 ♕d2 ♘d7 12 ♗e2 h4 Garcia–Smyslov, 1964 and now 13 0-0-0 =.

b) 7 ♘c3 ♗g4 8 ♗c2 ♖g8 9 ♗e3 e6 10 h3 ♗xe2 11 ♕xe2 ♕a5 = Kopaev–Bronstein, USSR 1947.

c) 7 ♗f4 ♗f5 8 ♘g3 ♗g6 9 h4 ♘d7
10 ♗e2 e5 11 dxe5 *(11 ♗e3 ♕a5+ 12
c3 0-0-0 ∓ Larsen)* 11 . . . fxe5 12 ♗g5
♕a5+ 13 c3 f6 14 ♗e3 0-0-0 ∓
Baturinsky-Simagin, USSR 1964.

d) 7 **h4** ♗g4 *(. . . ♗f5 will probably
transpose to C2)* 8 ♕d3 *(8 c3 ♘d7
9 ♕b3 ♘b6 10 ♗f4 ♕d7 11 0-0-0 ♗e6
12 ♕c2 a5 13 ♘g3 ♕d5 14 a3 ♕a2 ∓
Yanofsky-Larsen, Dallas 1957)* 8 . . . e5
9 ♗e3 ♘a6 *(9 . . . ♘d7 10 ♘g3 ♕a5+
11 ♕d2 ♕xd2+ 12 ♔xd2 0-0-0 ∓
Zagorovsky-Sokolsky, 1950)* 10 a3?!
♕a5+ 11 ♗d2 ♕b6 12 dxe5 ♘c5
13 ♕e3 0-0-0! 14 b4 ♗h6 15 f4 ♖xd2!
∓ Mikhalchishin-Speelman, Frunze
1979.

7 . . .   **♕a5+**

On 7 . . . h4 8 h3 ±.

8 ♗d2   **♕f5**
9 ♕b3   **♗h6**
10 0-0-0   **. . .**

Or 10 ♗xh6 ♖xh6 11 ♘g3 ♕e6+ =
Larsen.

10 . . .   **♕xf2**
11 ♗xh6   **♖xh6**

12 ♘c3 e6 13 ♗e2 ♕f4+ 14 ♔b1 ♕c7
15 ♘e4 ♕e7 16 ♕e3 ♖h8 17 c4. The
position, from van den Berg-
Pachman, Beverwijk 1965, is unclear
with chances for both sides.

A2

6 . . .   **♗f5**

A natural continuation, developing the bishop on its most obvious
diagonal.

7 ♘g3   **♗g6**
8 h4   **h6**

For the major alternative 8 . . . h5
9 ♗e2 ♘d7 **10 c3** see variation C1.2;
on **10 ♗e3** ♗d6 11 c3 ♗xg3!? 12 fxg3
♘d7 13 0-0 is unclear, although
Milić-Lange, 1951 continued 13 . . .
♕c7?! 14 ♗f4! e5 15 dxe5 ♕b6+
16 ♔h1 fxe5 17 ♗g5! ±.

9 h5   **. . .**

9 c3 c6 10 ♗d3 ♗xd3 11 ♕xd3 ♕a5
12 ♕f3 ♘d7 13 ♘h5 f5 = Ilyin-
Zhenevsky v Kan, USSR 1931.

9 . . .   **♗h7**
10 c3   **e6**

Or:
a) **10 . . . ♕b6** 11 ♗c4 ♘d7 12 a4 a5
13 ♕f3 e6 14 0-0 ♗c2 15 ♗f4 ♗b3 16
♗d3 e5 17 ♗e3 ♗d5 18 ♗e4 ± Flohr-
Horowitz, USSR v USA 1945.

b) **10 . . . ♘d7** 11 ♗d3! ♗xd3 12
♕xd3 ♕c7 13 ♕f3! e6 14 ♗f4 ♕a5 15
0-0 ♕d5 16 ♕e2 ♗d6 17 ♗xd6 ♕xd6
18 ♖ad1 0-0-0 19 c4 ♔b8 20 d5! ±
Hübner-Adorján, Bad Lauterberg (c)
1980.

11	♗e3	♘d7
12	♕d2	♕a5
13	♗e2	0-0-0
14	♗xh6	...

If 14 0-0 e5. The text is Mecking–Larsen, San Antonio 1972 when after 14 . . . ♗xh6 15 ♕xh6 Larsen felt Black did not have quite enough for the pawn although he still considers 15 . . . e5! here to be unclear.

A3

6	...	♗g4?!
7	♕d3!	...

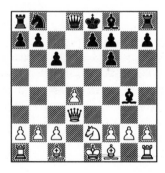

Others:

a) 7 f3 ♗f5 8 ♘g3 ♗g6 9 f4 e6 10 f5? (10 c3 ♗d6 ∓) ♗xf5! 11 ♘xf5 ♕a5+ 12 ♗d2 ♕f5 13 ♗d3 ♕d5 ∓ Euwe–van den Hoek, 1942.

b) 7 c3 ♘d7 8 ♕b3 ♕b6 9 ♕c2 e5 10 ♗e3 0-0-0 11 ♘g3 exd4 12 ♗xd4 ♗c5 ∓ Westerinen–Bronstein, Tallinn 1971.

c) 7 h4 ♗h5 8 g4 ♗g6 9 ♘g3 f5! = Larsen.

7	...	♗h5

On 7 . . . ♘d7?! Larsen suggests 8 ♘g3!?

8	♕b3!	...

On 8 ♘f4 ♗g6 9 ♘xg6 hxg6 Black equalizes after both 10 ♗e3 ♘d7 11 0-0-0 e6 12 ♗e2 ♕a5 = Vuković–Tóth, Yugoslavia (ch) 1957 and 10 ♗d2 ♘d7 11 0-0-0 ♕c7 12 g3 0-0-0 = Bakulin–Shukhanov, USSR 1971.

8	...	♕c8

Also not entirely satisfactory are 8 . . . ♗xe2 9 ♗xe2 ♕c7? 10 ♗h5! ♕a5+ 11 ♗d2 ♕xh5 12 ♕xb7 +− Marić–Tóth, Yugoslavia (ch) 1957 and 8 . . . ♕b6 9 ♕h3! ♗xe2 10 ♗xe2 ♘d7 11 ♗h5! ♗g7 12 0-0 ♘f8 13 ♗e3 ± Marić–Krzisnik, Vukovar 1966.

9	♘f4	♗g6
10	♗c4	e6
11	0-0	♘a6
12	♖e1	♗e7
13	♘xe6!	...

Sacrificing a piece to strand Black's king in the centre. Bednarski–Ermenkov, Varna 1972 continued 13 . . . fxe6 14 ♗xe6 ♕c7 15 ♗h6 ♔d8 when Minev now suggests 16 ♖ad1 ♕b6 17 d5! ±.

B

6 ♘f3   ...

Along with A, one of the most frequent continuations. White generally intends kingside castling, and plays for the break c4 and d5 or c4-c5. Black may now pin the knight if he chooses:

B1: 6 . . . ♗g4
B2: 6 . . . ♗f5

A third possibility is **6 . . . ♖g8!?**, recommended by several British masters and intended to hinder the development of White's king's bishop, which definitely requires experimentation. E.g.: 7 ♕d3?! (attacking the now undefended h-pawn; 7 ♗f4 followed by ♗g3 or 7 g3 comes into consideration) 7 . . . ♕d5! 8 ♕xh7 ♖g6 9 ♗e3 *(9 ♘h4 ♖g4 10 ♗e2 ♖xd4 11 0-0 ♗g4)* 9 . . . ♘d7 10 h4!? ♘b6 11 h5 ♖g4 12 ♕d3 ♗f5 13 ♕b3 ♕xb3 14 cxb3 ♘d5 *(threatening 15 . . . ♘xe3 16*

fxe3 ♗h6 etc.) 15 ♗d2 e6 16 h6 0-0-0 17 0-0-0 ♗h7 18 a3 c5 19 dxc5 ♗xc5 20 ♗e1 ♖h8 21 g3 ♗e4 22 ♗e2 ♔b8 23 ♘d2 ♘c3!! −+ Povah–Basman, London 1977.

B1

6 . . .   **♗g4**
7 ♗e2   ...

Releasing the pin is clearly the most logical response, though others have been tried:

a) **7 g3** e6 8 ♗g2 ♘d7 9 0-0 ♗g7! *(9 . . . ♘b6? 10 ♕d3 ♘d5 11 a3 ♗d6 12 ♖e1 ♘e7 13 b4 a5 14 b5 ♗f5 15 ♕e2 cxb5 16 ♘h4 ♕d7 17 d5! ± Romanovsky–Flohr, USSR 1945)* 10 ♖e1 0-0 11 ♗e3 ♖e8 12 ♕c1 ♘f8 = Konstantinopolsky–Flohr, USSR 1945.

b) **7 ♗c4** ♖g8 8 0-0 e6 9 ♗f4 ♗d6 10 ♗g3 f5 11 ♕d3 ♗xf3 12 ♕xf3 ♗xg3 13 hxg3 ♕xd4 14 ♕b3! ∞ Boleslavsky–Khavin, USSR 1940; Larsen suggests 8 . . . ♕c7!

And here:

B1.1: 7 . . . e6
B1.2: 7 . . . ♕c7

7 . . . ♘a6!? (Larsen) also merits attention.

B1.1

7 . . .   **e6**
8 ♗f4   ...

White has several other choices:
a) **8 ♗e3 ♘d7 9 0-0 ♗d6?!** *(9 ...*
♕c7 is more flexible) **10 c4 f5?** *(10 ...*
♕c7 again) **11 d5!** ± Sokolsky-
Bronstein, USSR (ch) 1944. The
thematic White breakthrough — see
illustrative games for the complete
moves. A little better for Black is *9 ...*
♖g8!? 10 ♔h1 ♕a5 11 c4 0-0-0 12 c5!
e5 *(12 ... ♘xc5?! 13 ♗d2 ♕b6 14 dxc5*
♕xb2 15 ♕a4 ♖xd2 16 ♕xa7 ♖xe2 17
♖fb1! ± M. Tseitlin)* 13 ♕b1! *(13 ♖b1*
exd4 14 b4 ♕xa2 ∞; 13 b4 ♕xb4 14
♖b1 ♕a3 ∞) 13 ... f5! *(13 ... exd4?*
14 b4 ♕c7 15 ♘xd4 ♘e5 16 f3 ± Kr.
Georgiev-Quendro, Thessaloniki (ol)
1988) 14 b4 ♕c7 ∞ (M. Tseitlin).
b) **8 c3 ♘d7 9 ♘h4 ♗xe2 10 ♕xe2**
♕a5 11 0-0 0-0 12 ♗e3 ♖g8 13 a3 f5 14
♘f3 ♕d5 = Yanofsky-Szabó, Dallas
1957.
c) **8 0-0 ♗d6** *(better than 8 ... ♘d7*
9 c4! ♘b6 10 b3 ♗g7!? 11 ♗e3 ♕c7 12
♘h4 ♗xe2 13 ♕xe2 f5?! 14 ♖ad1
0-0-0 15 ♘f3 h5?! 16 a4! ♘d7 17 d5! e5
18 ♘g5 ♘f6 19 d6! +— Matulović-
Dückstein, Le Havre 1977) 9 c4 *(9 h3*
h5!? Larsen) 9 ... ♖g8! 10 ♔h1 ♘d7
(10 ... f5 11 d5 cxd5 12 cxd5 e5 13
♘xe5! ♗xe5 14 ♖e1 ± Matanović-
Szabó, Portorož (izt) 1958; 10 ... ♕c7
11 d5!) 11 d5 ♘c5 12 ♘d4 f5 13 ♗xg4
♖xg4 14 h3 ♕f6 15 ♘f3 ♖xc4 16 dxc6
♘e4 17 cxb7 ♖b8 ∞ Tringov-
Smyslov, Havana 1965.
d) **8 h3** (Recommended by Larsen
in ECO as the strongest continuation)
8 ... ♗h5 9 0-0 ♗d6 *(9 ... ♗g7 10 ♗f4*
0-0 11 c4 ±) 10 ♗e3 ♘d7 11 c4 ♗g6

(11 ... ♕c7!?) 12 d5! exd5 *(12 ... cxd5*
13 cxd5 e5 14 ♕b3 b6 15 ♗b5 ±
Tringov) 13 cxd5 c5 14 ♗h6 ♕a5 15
♘d2 0-0-0 16 ♘c4 ♕c7 17 ♕a4 ±
Tringov-Opočensky, Bratislava 1957.

8 ...   ♗d6

8 ... ♘d7 9 0-0 ♘b6 10 ♗g3 *(10*
♖e1 ♗d6 11 ♗g3 ♗xg3 12 hxg3 ♕d5
13 c3 h5 14 ♕c1 0-0-0 15 a4 ♗xf3 16
♗xf3 ♕g5 = Bronstein-Flohr, USSR
1945) 10 ... h5 11 h3 ♗xf3 12 ♗xf3 h4
13 ♗h2 ♗d6 14 ♗xd6 ♕xd6 15 c3
0-0-0 16 a4 ± Varnusz-Bilek, Hungary
(ch) 1958.

9 ♗g3   ...

On 9 ♕d2 Larsen gives 9 ... ♕c7 10
♗xd6 ♕xd6 11 c4 ♘d7 12 0-0 0-0! 13
♖ad1 ♔h8 ∞.

9 ...   ♕c7
10 0-0   ...

Or 10 ♘d2 ♗f5 11 ♘c4 ♗xg3 12
hxg3 ♘d7 13 ♗d3 ♗xd3 14 ♕xd3
0-0-0 15 0-0-0 ♘e5! = Averbakh-
Simagin, USSR 1946.

10 ...   ♘d7
11 c4   ♗xg3
12 hxg3   0-0-0

Here Martin-Bellon, Spain (ch)
1976 continued 13 ♕a4 ♔b8 14 c5!
f5?! 15 b4! ♘f6 16 b5 with an attack,
but instead **14 ... e5** would have

given even prospects.

B1.2

7 . . .   ♕c7

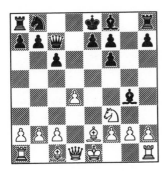

8 h3   . . .

Considered the most promising by
Larsen, though alternatives are
numerous:
  a) **8 c3** ♘d7 9 ♕a4 e6 10 ♗d2 *(10
0-0 ♖g8 11 ♗e3 ♘b6)* 10 . . . ♖g8 11
0-0-0 ♗f5! 12 ♘h4 ♗e4 13 f3 b5! 14
♕b3 ♗d5 ∞ Levenfish-Konstantinopolsky, USSR 1947.
  b) **8 ♘h4** ♗xe2 9 ♕xe2 ♘d7 10 0-0
(10 ♕h5 ♕d6 11 0-0 ♕d5 =) 10 . . . e6
11 c4 0-0-0 *(11 . . . ♘b6 12 g3 h5 13 ♗f4
♕e7 14 ♖fd1 ± Olafsson-Bhend,
Zürich 1959)* 12 g3 *(12 ♘f3 ♖g8 13
♗d2 c5 14 ♗e3 ♕c6 15 g3 ♕e4 16 ♘d2
♕g4 = Hecht-Smyslov, Hamburg 1965)*
12 . . . h5 *(if 12 . . . ♖g8 13 d5!)* 13 d5
♖e8 ∞ Gurgenidze-Savon, USSR
1962.
  c) **8 ♕d2** ♘d7 9 ♕f4 ♕xf4 10 ♗xf4

♘b6 = Arnstein-Semenov, USSR
1962.
  d) **8 0-0** ♘d7 9 c4 ♖g8 *(9 . . . 0-0-0
10 ♕a4 ♔b8 11 ♗e3 ♖g8 Larsen)* 10
d5 *(10 ♗e3 0-0-0 11 ♕a4 e5? 12 ♖fe1!
e4 13 ♘h4 ♗d6 14 g3 ♗h3 15 ♗f1 ± is
Levenfish-Konstantinopolsky, USSR
1949 but better is the earlier game 11 . . .
♔b8! 12 ♖fd1 e6 13 b4 f5 14 d5 c5 ∞
Goldenov-Konstantinopolsky, USSR
1937)* 10 . . . e5 11 ♘h4 *(11 dxc6!?)*
11 . . . ♗xe2 12 ♕xe2 cxd5 13 cxd5
♘b6 14 ♗e3 ♕c4 = Matanović-
Pachman, Vienna 1957.
  e) **8 ♗e3** ♘d7 *(8 . . . e6 9 c4 ♗b4+
10 ♔f1!? Larsen)* 9 c4 *(Also possible
are 9 c3 e6 10 ♘d2 ♗xe2 11 ♕xe2 0-0-0
12 0-0 ♕a5 13 ♔b1 ♗e7 14 ♘b3
♕f5+ 15 ♔a1 ♖hg8 16 g3 ± Prieditis-
R. Larsen, (corr) 1974-76 and 9 h3 ♗f5
10 ♘h4 ♗g6 11 ♗c4 e6 12 ♕e2 0-0-0
13 0-0-0 as in Keres-Konstantinopolsky, USSR (ch) 1952 when now 13 . . .
♘b6! 14 ♘b3 ♘d5 ∞ and 9 ♕d2 0-0-0
10 0-0-0 ♖g8 11 ♗f4 ♕b6 12 ♕d3 ♗e6
13 a3 ∞ Gufeld-Bronstein, USSR
1959)* 9 . . . e6 10 ♘d2 *(10 ♕a4 ♖g8 11
h3 ♗h5! 12 0-0 ♗d6 13 b4 ♗f4 14 ♕b3
0-0-0 15 a4 f5 16 ♖fb1 ♖g7 ∓ Abrosin-
Konstantinopolsky (corr) 1955 or 10
♕b3 0-0-0 11 ♖c1 ♕b6? 12 ♕xb6
axb6 13 ♘d2! ♗xe2 14 ♔xe2 ♗e7 15
♖hd1 ± — better in this line 11 . . . ♗d6!
12 d5 ♘e5 ∞ Voronkov)* 10 . . . ♗xe2 11
♕xe2 f5 12 d5 0-0-0 13 ♗d4 ♖g8 14
dxe6 fxe6 15 0-0-0 e5 ∞ Taimanov-
Flohr, USSR 1948.

8 . . .   ♗h5

On 8 . . . ♗f5 9 c4 ♘d7 10 0-0 ♖g8?
Smyslov–Ratner, USSR 1945 now
continued 11 ♘h4! ♗g6 12 ♘xg6
hxg6 13 d5 ±.

9 0-0   ♘d7

If 9 . . . e6 10 c4 ♘d7 11 d5 and
White's game is better.

10 d5   ♖d8

10 . . . 0-0-0 11 ♕d4 c5 12 ♕a4 and
13 ♗f4 (Larsen).

11 c4   ♘b6
12 ♗e3   ♗xf3
13 ♗xb6   axb6
14 ♗xf3   cxd5

15 cxd5 ♗h6 16 ♕a4+ ♔f8 17 ♖ef1
♗f4 ± Smyslov–Pachman, Amsterdam (izt) 1964. Black's king is not
altogether comfortable, and his
pawns are worse.

It would appear that 6 . . . ♗g4 is
not fully satisfactory for Black, and
perhaps attention will turn to the
possibility discussed next.

B2

6 . . .   ♗f5

Despite his bad experience with
Radulov in this line, Larsen still
admitted a preference for this move
over 6 . . . ♗g4 just discussed.

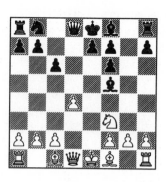

7 ♗d3   . . .

For 7 ♗e2 see D. After 7 ♗c4
instead Black has:

a) 7 . . . e6 8 ♕e2 ♗g7? *(better 8 . . .*
♗e7 9 ♘h4 ♗g6 10 f4 f5 =) 9 ♘h4!
♗g6 10 c3 ♘d7 11 ♗d2 ♘b6 12 ♗b3
♕c7 13 g3 a5!? 14 a3! Formanek–
Čirić, Reggio Emilia 1975-76.

b) 7 . . . ♕c7!? 8 ♗e3 ♘d7 9 ♕d2 e6
10 ♗f4 ♗d6 11 ♗xd6?! ♕xd6 12 0-0-0
0-0-0 13 ♘h4 ♗g6 14 h3 ♘b6 15 ♗b3
♖d7 ∓ Savage–Larsen, Washington
1972.

Interesting is 7 ♗f4 e6 *(7 . . . ♘d7*
8 c3 ♕b6 9 b4 e5 10 ♗g3 0-0-0 11 ♗e2
h5 12 0-0 ♗e4 13 ♘d2 ♗d5 14 ♗xh5!
exd4 15 c4 ♗e6 16 a3 ∓ Karpov–Miles,
Bath 1983) 8 ♗c4 ♘a6! 9 0-0 ♘c7 10
♗g3 ♗d6 11 ♖e1 ♕d7 12 ♘h4 ♗g6
13 c3 0-0-0 = Tal–Larsen, Riga (izt)
1979.

A novelty is 7 g3 ♕d5!? *(7 . . . e6*
8 ♗g2 ♗g7 9 0-0-0-0 10 ♘h4 ♗g6 11 c4
♘d7 12 ♗e3 a5 13 d5 ♘e5 14 ♘xg6
hxg6 16 ♕e2 cxd5 16 cxd5 exd5 17
♖fd1 ♕e7 18 ♖xd5 ♖fd8 19 ♕b5 ±

Gelfand–Nikolic (m) 1991) 8 c3 ♘d7 9
♗g2 ♕c4 10 ♕d2!? a5 11 b3 ♕e6+ 12
♕e2 a4 13 ♗b2 axb3 14 axb3 ♖xa1+
15 ♗xa1 ♕xb3 16 0-0 ∞ O'Donnel–
Marovic, Toronto 1990.

7 . . . **♗g6**

One possible improvement is 7 . . .
♗xd3!? 8 ♕xd3 ♕c7 9 0-0 ♘d7 10 c4
e6 *(10 . . . 0-0-0!?)* 11 d5 0-0-0! 12 dxe6
fxe6 13 ♕e3 ♗c5 with obscure complications where chances seemed
balanced, Fries Nielsen–Pedersen,
Denmark 1979.

8 0-0 **♕c7**

Instead 8 . . . e6 9 c4 ♗d6 10 d5!
♕c7 11 dxe6 fxe6 12 ♖e1 ♗f7 13 ♗f5
e5 14 ♕d3 was ± in Bitman–Rosanov,
USSR 1962 but another possible
improvement suggested by Larsen is
9 . . . ♘a6!? here. Black plans a
possible . . . ♕d7, . . . 0-0-0, and even
. . . ♗h5 and can also at some stage
put the knight on c7, a useful square.

9 c4	**♘d7**
10 d5	**0-0-0**
11 ♗e3	**e5**
12 ♗e2	**♔b8**

13 ♖c1 f5 *(13 . . . c5 14 ♘h4 f5 15 f4 ±)*
14 c5! and now **14 . . . ♘xc5** 15 ♗xc5
gave White a won game in Radulov–
Larsen, Hastings 1972-73 but after **14
. . . cxd5** 15 c6! bxc6 16 ♗b5 Black has
a bad game in any case.

C

6 c3 **. . .**

There was a time when theoreticians attached great significance to
the fact that White's knight is not yet
on f3, wanting to harass Black's
bishop that is about to occupy f5 with
♘g1-e2-g3 and then with h2-h4. But
practical play proved that this scheme
disorganizes White's forces
somewhat and gives him difficulties
in capitalizing on any material
advantage he might gain.

6 . . . **♗f5**

Seldom-played alternatives are:
a) **6 . . . ♕d5** 7 ♗e3?! *(7 ♘f3 ♖g8!?
8 ♗e3 ♘d7 9 g3 ♘b6 10 b3 ♗g4 11
♗g2 e5! 12 dxe5 fxe5 13 h3 ♗h5 14
♕xd5 ♘xd5 15 ♗d2 0-0-0 16 0-0 f6 ∓
Ristić–Pasman, Groningen 1977-78;
7 ♘e2!?)* 7 . . . ♖g8 8 ♘f3 ♘d7 9 ♕b3
♘b6 10 c4?! *(10 ♕xd5)* 10 . . . ♕h5
11 0-0-0 ♗h6 12 ♖e1 ♗e6! ∓

Kagan–Basman, Birmingham 1977.
b) **6 . . . e6** *(6 . . . b6!?* Voronkov)
7 ♘e2 ♘d7 8 ♘g3 ♘b6 9 ♗d3 ♕d5 10
0-0 h5 11 ♗e4 ♕d8 12 ♘xh5 f5 13 ♗f3
♗d6 14 g3 ± Bronstein–Flohr,
Groningen 1946.
c) **6 . . . e5** 7 ♗c4 exd4 8 ♕b3 ♕e7+
9 ♘e2 b5 10 ♗d3 ♗e6 11 ♕c2 ±
Nimzovitch.
d) **6 . . . ♕c7** 7 ♗c4 e6 *(7 . . .*
♗f5 8 ♕f3 ♕d7 9 ♘e2 ♖g8 10 ♘f4
♗g4 11 ♕e4 ♕f5 12 f3 ♕xe4 13 fxe4
e5 14 h3! ± *Bonch-Osmolovsky v*
Konstantinopolsky, USSR 1949) 8 ♕h5!
c5 9 d5 e5 10 ♘e2 ♗d6 11 f4 ±
Kaplan–Rossolimo, Puerto Rico 1967.

C1

7 ♘e2   . . .

The logical continuation to the
previously outlined. Others are:
a) 7 ♗c4 e6 8 ♘e2 h5 *(bad are both*
8 . . . ♗d6? 9 ♘g3 ♗g6 10 ♗h6 and
8 . . . ♗e4? 9 0-0 ♗d5 10 ♗d3 c5 11 c4
♗c6 12 d5! exd5 13 cxd5 ♕xd5 14 ♘f4
±*, however, possible is 8 . . . ♘d7 9 ♘g3*
♗g6 10 0-0 ♕c7 11 a4? 0-0-0 12 ♕e2
h5 ∓ *Pohla-Bronstein, Pärnu 1971;*
11 f4 f5! = is better) 9 ♘g3 ♗g6 *(9 . . .*
♗g4!?) 10 ♕e2 *(10 h4 ♗d6 11 ♗e2*
♕a5 12 b4 ♕c7 13 ♘xh5 ♘d7 ∞
Larsen) 10 . . . ♘d7 11 f4 f5 12 ♘f1 h4
13 ♘d2 ♘f6 14 ♘f3 ♗h5 15 ♗d2 ♗d6
16 0-0 *(16 ♗d3 ♕c7! 17 ♗xf5 ♗xf3 18*
gxf3 0-0-0 19 ♗h3 ♗xf4 ∓ *Ciocaltea-*
Pachman, Moscow 1956) 16 . . . ♕c7 17
♕e1 ♗xf3 *(17 . . . ♗xf4? 18 ♗xf4*

♕xf4 19 ♘xh4 ♕e4 20 ♘xf5! exf5 21
♖xf5! ± *Larsen)* 18 ♖xf3 0-0-0 =
Larsen.
b) **7 ♗d3** ♗g6 8 h4 ♕d5 9 ♗xg6
hxg6 10 ♕f3 ♗g7 11 ♗e3 ♘d7 12
♕xd5 cxd5 with much the better
ending for Black, Nedelković–
Bronstein, Yugoslavia v USSR 1957.
c) **7 ♕b3** ♕c7 8 ♗c4 *(8 ♗f4? ♕xf4*
9 ♕xb7 ♗h6! 10 ♘f3 0-0 11 ♕xa8 ♕c7
12 d5 ♕b6 13 ♗c4 ♗c8 −+ *Fuderer-*
Szabó, Gothenburg 1955) 8 . . . e6 9 ♘f3
♘d7 = Larsen.
d) **7 ♗f4** ♘d7 8 ♗d3 ♗g6 9 ♘e2
♘b6 10 0-0 e6 11 ♗g3 ♗d6 12 b4!?
♕c7 13 a4 ♘d5 14 ♕d2 ♖d8 15 ♖ab1
(15 c4? ♗xd3) 15 . . . 0-0 16 c4 ± Short-
Larsen, Hastings 1988/89.

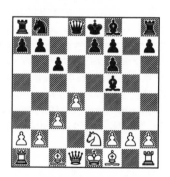

C1.1: 7 . . . h5
C1.2: 7 . . . ♘d7

Similar to C1.2 is **7 . . . e6** 8 ♘g3
♗g6 9 h4 h5 10 ♗e2 ♕a5 11 a3!? *(11*
b4 ♕c7 12 ♘xh5 ♗xh5 13 ♗xh5 a5! ∞
Dorfman) 11 . . . ♘d7 12 b4 ♕c7 13
♗xh5 ♗xh5 14 ♘xh5 0-0-0 15 g3

♕d6! 16 ♘f4 e5 17 ♘g2 exd4 18 cxd4
♘e5! ∞ Petrushin–Dorfman, USSR
1980.

Cl.1

7 . . .   h5
8 ♘f4?!   . . .

White intends to gain tempi for
development by attacking the
h-pawn, but it soon becomes clear
that his pieces lack co-ordination.
Alternatives to occur in practice are:
a) **8 h4** ♘d7 9 ♘g3 ♗g4 *(for 9 . . .
♗g6 see Cl.2)* 10 ♗e2 ♗xe2 11 ♕xe2
♕a5 12 0-0 0-0-0 13 c4 e6 14 a3 *(14
♗f4 ♘b6! 15 ♖fd1 ♗h6 16 ♗xh6
♖xh6 17 ♘e4 ♖g6 18 b4 ♕f5 19 ♘g3
♕g4 ∓ Gudmundsson–Bronstein,
Reykjavik 1974)* 14 . . . ♗d6 *(14 . . .
♕c7!? Larsen)* 15 ♘e4 ♗b8 16 c5 f5 17
b4 ♕a6 18 ♘c3 *(18 ♕xa6 ±)* 18 . . .
♕xe2 19 ♘xe2 Averbakh–Sokolsky,
USSR 1950 and now 19 . . . ♖dg8! 20
♗g5 ♖g6 would have given equality.
b) **8 ♘g3** ♗g4 *(for 8 . . . ♗g6 9 h4 see
Cl.2 again)* 9 f3 *(9 ♗e2 ♗xe2 10 ♕xe2
♕d5 11 0-0 ♘d7 12 ♗e3 ♘b6 =)* 9 . . .
♗e6 10 ♗d3 *(10 ♗f4!?)* 10 . . . ♕c7
(10 . . . h4?! or 10 . . . ♕a5!?) 11 ♘e2
♗h6 12 ♗xh6 ♖xh6 13 ♕d2 ♖h8 14
♘f4 ♕d6 15 0-0 ± Muchnik–
Voronkov, USSR 1957.

8 . . .   h4

8 . . . ♗g4 9 f3 ♗f5 allows 10 ♘xh5
♖xh5 11 g4 ± as in Kaminsky–

Vorotnikov, USSR 1972.

9 ♕f3!?   . . .

Leading to equality is 9 ♗d3 ♗xd3
10 ♕xd3 ♕c7 11 ♗e3 e6 12 0-0-0 ♘d7
13 g3 0-0-0 14 ♘g2 ♕a5 15 ♔b1 hxg3
16 hxg3 ♖xh1 17 ♖xh1 ♕d5 = Fink-
Abrosin, 1959. After the text the game
Bilek–Bronstein, Budapest 1955 continued 9 . . . ♘d7 10 g4? *(Now Black
takes the initiative. 10 ♗d3 was
needed)* 10 . . . hxg3 11 fxg3 *(11 hxg3
♗g4! 12 ♕g2 ♘e5 ∓)* 11 . . . e5!
opening up the position, and Black
won with his superior development −
see illustrative games for the
complete score.

Cl.2

7 . . .   ♘d7
8 ♘g3   ♗g6
9 h4   h5

For 9 . . . h6?! see A2.

10 ♗e2   . . .

Or 10 ♗d3 ♗xd3 11 ♕xd3 ♕a5 =
Pilnik–Bronstein, Gothenburg 1955.

10 . . .   ♕a5!

An improvement on Sokolov–
Szabó, Balatonfüred 1958 where after
10 . . . e5? 11 ♗xh5 ♗xh5 12 ♘xh5
exd4 *(12 . . . ♕a5 13 ♕f3 ±)* White
could have played 13 0-0! ±.

After 10 . . . ♕a5! however, although White can obtain a material advantage, he must overextend his queenside pawns to do so. These are then subject to attack and Black is considered to have good compensation for his pawn deficit.

11 b4   . . .

Very interesting is 11 a4! 0-0-0 *(11 . . . e5 12 b4 ♕d5 13 0-0! exd4 14 cxd4 ♗xb4?! 15 ♗f3 ±; 12 . . . ♕c7!?)* 12 b4 ♕c7 13 a5! e5 *(perhaps 13 . . . a6 instead)* 14 a6 b6 15 0-0 ♗d6 *(15 . . . e4!?)* 16 ♗d3!! ± A. Rodriguez–Pieterse, Dieren 1987.

11 . . .   ♕c7!

The best square: **11 . . . ♕b6?!** 12 ♗e3 ♗h6 13 ♗xh6 ♖xh6 14 0-0 0-0-0 15 c4 ± Liberzon–Christiansen, Hastings 1979-80 or **11 . . . ♕d5** 12 ♗f3 ♕c4 13 ♕b3 ±.

12 ♘xh5   a5!

Another promising idea is 12 . . . e5!? e.g. 13 ♘g3 *(13 dxe5 ♗xh5 14 ♗xh5 ♕xe5+ 15 ♘e2 ♗xb4 ∓)* 13 . . . 0-0-0 14 h5 ♗h7 15 ♕b3 ♘b6 16 dxe5 *(16 b5? c5 17 dxc5 ♗xc5 18 a4?! ♖hg8 ∓ Peters–Seirawan, USA (ch) 1984)* 16 . . . fxe5 17 ♗g5 with an unclear position.

13 ♖h3?!   . . .

Artificial. Better is 13 ♘f4 axb4 14 ♘xg6 fxg6 15 cxb4 e5 **16 ♖b1** 0-0-0 unclear or **16 b5** ♗b4+ 17 ♗d2 ♕d6! = *(Informator)*.

13 . . .   axb4
14 cxb4   e6
15 b5   . . .

There was no other healthy defence of the b-pawn — on 15 ♗d2 ♕b6.

15 . . .   c5!?

Instead 15 . . . ♗xh5 16 ♗xh5 ♕a5+ may be objectively sounder, but Black was trying to complicate in Bellon–Larsen, Las Palmas 1976, the stem game that we have been following. His policy paid off after **16 ♗f4?** as well, as 16 . . . ♗d6! now gave a winning advantage. Necessary was **16 ♘f4!** *(but not 16 dxc5? ♗xh5 17 ♗xh5 ♕e5+ or 16 ♗e3? cxd4 17 ♗xd4 ♗xh5 18 ♗xh5 ♗b4+ 19 ♔f1 ♖xh5!)* with even chances, e.g. 16 . . . cxd4 17 ♘xg6 fxg6 18 ♕xd4 ♗c5!? 19 ♕e4

&f7 20 h5!? gxh5 21 ♗xh5+ &e7 etc. For the full moves of Bellon-Larsen see illustrative games.

It is a feature of this whole sub-variation that White's men are not naturally posted and oversights are more frequent in such situations.

C2

7 ♘f3   . . .

Possibly the best, but what a difference there is compared to positions in **B2** where White has not lost a tempo with c3!

7 . . .   ♕c7

Other possibilities include:

a) 7 . . . e6 8 g3 *(8 ♗f4 ♘d7 9 ♗e2 ♘b6?! 10 0-0 ♘d5 11 ♗g3 ♗h6 12 c4 ♘f4 13 ♗xf4 ♗xf4 14 d5! ± Boleslavsky-Flohr, USSR 1944)* 8 . . . ♕d5 *(8 . . . h5!? 9 ♗g2 ♗e4 10 0-0 ♗e7 11 ♖e1 f5 ∞ Riemersma-Pieterse, Netherlands 1987; 8 . . . ♘d7 9 ♗g2*

♗g7 10 0-0 0-0 11 ♘h4!? — 11 ♗e3 ♘b6 12 ♕c1 ♘d5 ∞ de Firmian-Seirawan, Philadelphia 1987 — 11 . . . ♗g6 12 a4 a5 13 ♗f4 — Adams-Spraggett, Hastings 1989/90 — 13 . . . ♕b6! ̄ₛ) 9 ♗g2 ♕c4 10 ♗e3 *(10 ♘d2 ♕a6! 11 ♘e4 ♘d7 12 g4 ♗g6 13 h4 h5 14 gxh5 ♗xh5 15 ♗f3 ♗xf3 16 ♕xf3 ♗e7 = Grünfeld-Hickl, West Germany 1987)* 10 . . . ♘d7 11 ♘h4 ♗g6 12 ♘xg6 hxg6 13 ♕d2 ♖d8 = A. Rodriguez-Hickl, Dubai (ol) 1986.

b) 7 . . . ♘d7 8 ♗f4 *(8 g3 ♗g7!? — 8 . . . ♕b6!?; 8 . . . ♘b6 9 ♗g2 ♕d7 10 0-0 ♗h3 11 ♗xh3 ♕xh3 12 a4 ♕f5! 13 a5 ♘d5 14 c4 ♘c7 15 ♗f4 0-0-0! ∞ Fedorowicz-D. Roos, France 1990 — 9 ♗g2 e6 10 0-0 0-0 11 ♗e3 ♘b6 12 ♕c1 ♘d5 13 ♗h6 ♗g6 14 ♗xg7 &xg7 15 c4 ♘e7 16 ♕c3 ♕b6 17 ♖d1 a5 ∞ de Firmian-Seirawan, Philadelphia 1987)* 8 . . . ♕b6 9 ♗d3! ♗xd3 10 ♕xd3 ♕xb2 11 0-0 ♕a3! 12 ♖fb1 ♘b6 13 ♗c7 ♗h6 14 ♗xb6 axb6 15 ♖xb6 ♖a7 ± Karpov-Miles, Oslo 1984.

8 g3   . . .

a) 8 ♗c4 e6 9 ♕e2 ♘e7! *(9 . . . ♘d7 10 ♘h4 ♗g6 11 f4 f5 12 ♗xe6 fxe6 13 ♘xg6 hxg6 14 ♕xe6+ ±, or 11 . . . 0-0-0 12 f5! exf5 13 0-0 ♗d6 14 g3 ♖g8 15 ♘g2 ± Boleslavsky)* 10 ♘h4 ♗g6 11 f4 f5! = (Boleslavsky).

b) 8 ♘h4 ♗g6 9 ♕f3 ♘d7 10 g3 e6 11 ♗g2 f5 12 ♗g5 ♗g7 13 0-0 0-0 = Neukirch-Bronstein, Gotha 1957.

8 . . .   e6

8 . . . ♘d7!? 9 ♗g2 0-0-0 10 0-0 e5
(10 . . . e6 11 ♖e1 ♗d6? − 11 . . . ♗g4! −
12 b4 ♗g4 13 ♕a4 ± de Firmian-
Miles, Oslo 1984) 11 ♖e1 ♗d6 12 a4 h5
13 b4 (Ochoa-Vera, Havana 1981) 13
. . . ♗g4! ∞.

9	♗g2	♘d7
10	♗f4	

10 0-0 ♗g4 11 ♖e1 h5! 12 ♗f4 ♗d6
13 ♗xd6 ♕xd6 = Seitai-Skembris,
Kowala 1985.

10	. . .	e5
11	♗e3	0-0-0
12	0-0	♔b8
13	♘h4	♗e6
14	♕c2	♘b6

with slight advantage to White, a
sample game continuation being 15
♖ad1 ♘c4 16 ♗c1 exd4 17 ♗f4 ♗d6
18 ♖xd4 ♗xf4 19 ♖xf4 ♖d2 20 ♕c1
♖hd8 21 ♘f3 ± Durasevic-Hort,
Marianské Lázné 1962.

D

6	♗e2	. . .

White just intends to develop
normally and castle kingside, but
with this order of moves hopes to
avoid the . . . ♗g4 pin.

(see diagram)

6	. . .	♗f5

The only useful waiting move is
6 . . . ♘a6, e.g. 7 ♘f3 *(7 c3 ♘c7 8 ♘f3*
♗g4 9 ♘h4 ♗xe2 10 ♕xe2 ♕d5 =)
7 . . . ♗g4 8 0-0 ♘c7 9 c4 ♕d7 10 ♗e3
(10 ♗f4!?) 10 . . . ♗g7 *(10 . . . h5? 11*
♕b3 b6 12 d5 c5 13 ♖ad1 ♕d6 14
♖fe1 ♗g7 15 ♘h4 ± Matulović-Hort,
Sarajevo 1965) 11 ♘h4?! f5! 12 h3
♗xe2 13 ♕xe2 f4 14 ♗xf4 ♘e6 15
♗e3 ♘xd4 16 ♕h5 0-0-0 =
Jangerberg-Kopilov, USSR 1968. But
the quiet 11 ♕b3 followed by 12 ♖fd1
gives a small plus.

7	♘f3	♕c7

If 7 . . . e6 8 0-0 ♘d7 9 c4 ♗g6?!
(9 . . . ♕c7!?) 10 d5! e5 11 ♘d2 ♕c7 12
♘b3 ♗d6 (Kavalek-Bronstein,
Szombathely 1966) and now 13 dxc6
bxc6 14 ♗e3 ♖d8 15 ♕e1! ± Larsen
or 8 . . . ♗g7 9 c4 *(9 ♖e1 0-0 10 ♗f4*
♕b6 11 ♕c1 ♘d7 12 a4 c5 13 ♗e3 ♕c7
= Ciocaltea-Botwinnik, Hamburg
1965) 9 . . . 0-0 10 ♗e3 ♘d7 11 d5! ±

Ivkov–Donner, Santa Monica 1966.

8 0-0   e6

8 . . . ♘d7 9 c4 0-0-0 **10 ♕a4 ♔b8 11**
♗e3 e6 transposes to further on in the
text. Aside from 10 ♕a4, two other
approaches come to the fore:
a) **10 ♗e3 e6 11 ♕a4 ♔b8 12 b4**
♗d6!? *13 c5?! (13 ♕a5!?, 13 ♔h1!? or
13 ♖fc1!? are better)* 13 . . . ♗f4 14 ♕a5
(14 ♖fc1!?) 14 . . . ♗e4 15 g3 ♖dg8! ∓
Hort–Hodgson, Lugano 1983.
b) **10 d5** e5!? 11 ♗e3 ♔b8 12 ♘h4
♗g6 13 f4?! *(13 ♗g4!?)* 13 . . . cxd5 14
cxd5 *(14 f5 d4!)* 14 . . . ♗c5! 15 ♗xc5
♕xc5+ 16 ♔h1 exf4 17 ♖xf4 ♖he8
18 ♘xg6 hxg6 19 ♗f3 f5! 20 ♖c1 ♕e3
∓ Lubomirov–M. Tseitlin (corr)
1987/88.

9 c4   ♘d7

9 . . . ♗d6 10 d5! c5 11 ♘h4! ♗xh2+
12 ♔h1 ♗g6 13 dxe6 fxe6 14 ♗g4 f5
15 ♗xf5 exf5 16 ♖e1+ ♗e5 17 ♗f4 ±
Matulović–Flesch, Yugoslavia v
Hungary 1964.

10 ♗e3   . . .

With this move White intends to
break through not with d5 but with
c4-c5. **10 d5** immediately gives Black
counter-chances:
a) **10 . . . 0-0-0!** 11 dxc6 *(11 ♗e3 c5
12 b4 ♖g8 13 bxc5 ♗xc5 14 ♘d4 ♗h3
15 g3 ♗xf1 ∓ was an unsound
exchange sacrifice in Spassky–Larsen,*

Buenos Aires 1979) 11 . . . bxc6 12 ♗e3
♗c5 13 ♕c1 ♖hg8 14 ♖d1 ♕b6 =
Kavalek–Larsen, Solingen 1970.
b) **10 . . . ♖g8!?** 11 ♗e3 *(11 ♘d4
♗h3 12 ♗f3 ♘e5 13 ♗f4 ♘xf3+ 14
♕xf3 ♗xg2! Speelman)* 11 . . . ♗e4
*(11 . . . 0-0-0 is now dangerous after
12 ♕a4)* 12 dxe6 fxe6 13 ♕d4 ♖g4 14
♘e1 Timman–Speelman, London
1980 and now 14 . . . c5! 15 ♕d2 ♖g8
gives active play to compensate for
Black's loose position.
The other alternative, **10 ♗d2** *(idea
10 . . . 0-0-0 11 ♕a4 ♔b8 12 ♗a5!?
perhaps)* 10 . . . ♗d6 11 ♔h1 ♖g8 12
c5? ♗e7 13 ♕c1 ♗e4 14 ♗f4 ♕a5 15
♗g3 h5 left Black with all the play in
Kaplan–Larsen, San Antonio 1972.

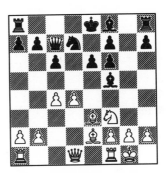

After 10 ♗e3 Black can defend
with **10 . . . ♗e7** which is solid but
passive, or he can try either of:
a) **10 . . . ♗d6** 11 c5! ♗e7 *(11 . . . ♗f4
12 ♘d2! eyes d6)* 12 ♘d2! *(An
important move which prevents the
manœuvre ♗f5-e4-d5 and parries the
attack should Black choose to castle*

kingside. On 12 . . . 0-0-0 instead 13 ♕a4 ♔b8 14 b4! is troublesome — Black cannot get a foothold on d5) 12 . . . 0-0? 13 f4! ♗g6 *(14 g4 was threatened, to win a piece)* 14 f5! with a winning attack in Browne–Bellon, Las Palmas 1977 — see illustrative games.

b) **10 . . . 0-0-0!?** 11 ♕a4 ♔b8 12 b4 *(12 c5!?)* 12 . . . ♖g8 13 ♖fd1 *(13 ♔h1 ♗e4 13 ♘e1 ♘b6 15 ♕b3 e5 ∓ Kavalek–Larsen, Tilburg 1979)* 13 . . . ♗h3?! 14 g3 f5?! 15 ♘g5! ♗h6 16 d5! ± Grószpéter–Pasman, Groningen 1977-78 but clearly this line is capable of improvement. Probably 'unclear' is the correct label of 10 . . . 0-0-0 at this point in time.

E

6 ♗c4   ♗f5

If 6 . . . ♕c7 7 ♕h5! Jamieson–Tal, Nice (ol) 1974.

7 ♘e2   . . .

Instead of the natural text move White also has 7 ♗f4!? ♕b6 *(Larsen also gives 7 . . . e6 8 ♘f3 ♖g8 9 0-0 ♗d6 10 ♗xd6 ♕xd6 11 ♘h4 ♗g6 12 f4 f5! 13 c3 ♘d7 14 ♕e2 0-0-0 =)* 8 ♗b3 a5 9 a4 ♘d7 10 ♘f3 ♕a6!? 11 ♘h4! ♗g6 12 ♕g4! e6 13 ♗c7!? *(13 ♗xe6 fxe6 14 ♕xe6+ ♔d8 15 0-0-0 c5 16 d5 ♕c4 17 ♗c7+ ♔c8 ∓)* 13 . . . f5 14 ♕f4 ♗g7 15 h3?! *(15 0-0-0!)* 15 . . . 0-0 *(15 . . . c5!? 16*

d5 e5 ∞ Tal) 16 0-0-0 ♖ac8 17 g4 c5 = Tal–Larsen, Las Palmas 1977.

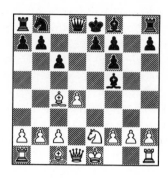

7 . . .   h5

Less attractive possibilities include:

a) **7 . . . ♘d7** 8 ♘g3 *(8 0-0 ♘b6 9 ♗b3 ♕d7 10 c4 ♗g7 11 ♗e3 0-0 12 ♕d2 ± Popovic–Seirawan, Sarajevo 1987; 10 . . . 0-0-0 11 ♗e3 e5 12 a4! ±)* 8 . . . ♗g6 9 h4 h6!? 10 h5 ♗h7 11 ♗d3! ♗xd3 12 ♕xd3 e6?! *(12 . . . ♕c7!?)* 13 ♗f4 ♕a5+ 14 c3 0-0-0 15 0-0 ♘b6 16 c4 ♕a6 17 b3 ± Mateo–Skembris, Prokuplje 1987.

b) **7 . . . e6** 8 0-0 *(8 ♘g3 ♗g6 9 c3 ♘d7 10 h4 h5 11 ♗e2 ♕a5 12 b4 — Unzicker–Miles, West Germany 1985 — 12 . . . ♕c7! ∞, or 9 h4 h5 10 ♗f4 ♗d6 11 ♕d2 ♕c7 12 ♗xd6 ♕xd6 13 0-0-0 ♘d7 14 ♖he1 0-0-0 = Larsen)* 8 . . . ♗d6 *(alternatively 8 . . . h5, or 8 . . . ♘d7)* 9 ♗f4 ♕c7 *(9 . . . h5!?)* 10 ♗xd6 ♕xd6 11 a4 ♘d7 12 a5 *(Sisniega–Grószpéter, New York 1988) 12 . . . a6 ±.*

8 ♗e3 . . .

Others:

a) **8 h4** ♘d7 9 ♗b3 e6 10 ♗f4 a5! 11 a4 ♘b6 12 c4 ♖g8!? 13 ♘g3 *(13 g3)* 13 . . . ♖g4 14 ♘xh5 ♕e7! 15 c5 ♘d7 16 ♗d6 ♕d8 17 ♘g3 ♗xd6 18 cxd6 ♕b6 19 ♘f5 exf5 20 0-0 0-0-0 ∓ Mikhaltchishin-Skembris, Banja Luka 1987.

b) **8** ♘f4 h4 9 c3 e6 10 ♕e2 ♗d6 11 d5 cxd5 12 ♘xd5 ♘d7 13 ♗f4 ♗xf4 14 ♘xf4 ♕c7! ∞ Rigó-Skembris, Rome 1984.

8 . . . ♘d7
9 ♘f4 ♘b6

9 . . . h4?! 10 ♗b3 e6 11 ♕f3 ♕a5+ 12 c3 0-0-0 13 0-0 e5 14 ♘d5 ♗d3 15 ♘xf6 ♗xf1 16 ♖xf1 ♘xf6 17 ♕xf6 ♗d6 18 ♕xf7 ♔b8 19 ♖e1 ♖he8 20 ♕h5 ♖h8 21 ♕g5 ± Hellers-Alber, West Berlin 1988.

10 ♗b3 ♕d7!

∞ (P. Nikolić).

The alternatives seem to have fared less well:

a) **10 . . . a5** 11 a4 ♘d5?! 12 ♘xh5 ♕d7 13 ♘g3 ♘xe3 14 fxe3 ♗g4 15 ♕d3 ♕c7 16 ♕e4! ± Kindermann-Plachetka, Stary Smokovec 1987.

b) **10 . . . ♗g4** 11 f3 ♗f5 12 ♕e2 ♕c7 13 0-0-0 ♗h6! 14 g3 0-0-0 15 ♘g2! *(15 ♗xf7? ♗xf4 16 ♗xf4 e5 wins for Black)* 15 . . . ♗xe3+ 16 ♘xe3 ♗g6 17 ♘g2! ± Popovic-Skembris, Pucarevo 1987.

F

6 ♕d3 . . .

Stopping 6 . . . ♗f5. Black has now:

a) **6 . . .** ♘d7 *(not 6 . . . ♗g4 7 ♘e2 ± Larsen)* 7 ♘e2 ♘b6 8 ♘f4 *(8 ♘g3 h5! 9 h4 ♗g4 10 ♗d2 ♕c7 = Larsen)* 8 . . . e5 9 dxe5 fxe5 10 ♕e4 ♕e7 11 ♘d3 ♗g7 12 ♗d2 ♗e6 13 ♗b4 ♕g5 14 h4 ♕f5 = Marić-Sušić, Vrnjačka Banja 1966.

b) **6 . . . ♕b6** 7 ♗e2 ♗g7? *(7 . . . ♘a6)* 8 ♕g3! ♖g8 9 ♗d3! ± Larsen.

c) **6 . . . ♘a6** 7 ♗d2 ♘c7 *(7 . . . ♕b6? 8 0-0-0 ♗e6 9 a3 0-0-0 10 ♘f3 ♗d5 11 ♗e3 e6 12 c4! ♗xf3 13 gxf3 c5 14 d5 ♗d6 15 f4 f5 16 ♗g2 ± gave White the bishop pair in Bakulin-Konstantinopolsky, USSR 1966. Better is 7 . . . ♗e6!? 8 0-0-0 ♕d6 9 c4 0-0-0 10 ♘e2 h5 11 h4 ♘c7 12 ♕c2 = Lederman-Grünfeld, Israel 1984)* 8 ♘f3 *(8 0-0-0!?)* 8 . . . ♗g4 9 ♗e2 ♕d7 10 ♕b3 ♘b5 11 c3 *(11 c4? ♗xf3 12 cxb5 ♗xg2 13 ♖g1 ♗d5 ∓ Shishov-Zagoriansky, USSR 1953)* 11 . . . ♘d6 12 0-0-0 0-0-0 = Larsen.

G

6 ♗e3 ♗f5

6 . . . ♕b6 7 ♕c1 ♗f5 8 ♘e2 e6 9 ♘g3 ♗g6 10 ♗e2 c5?! 11 dxc5 ♗xc5 12 ♗xc5 ♕xc5 13 ♕f4 ± was Domnitz-Kagan, Netanya 1969; Sokolov suggests **10 . . . h5** 11 h4 ♗d6 ∞.

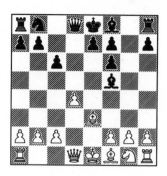

7 ♘e2   ...

Or:

a) 7 ♗d3 ♗xd3 *(7 ... ♗g6 8 ♘e2 ♘a6 9 ♕d2 ♘c7 10 0-0-0 ♘d5 ∞ Larsen)* 8 ♕xd3 ♕a5+ 9 ♗d2 ♕a6 10 ♕b3 ♘d7 11 0-0-0 e6 12 f4? c5 13 ♘f3 c4 14 ♕e3 ♕a2 15 ♗c3 ♘b6 16 ♕e4 ♘d5 ∓ L. Steiner–Sämisch, 1927.

b) 7 ♕d2 e6 8 ♘e2 ♘d7 9 ♘g3 ♗g6 10 ♗e2 ♕c7 (=) 11 0-0? h5! 12 ♖fd1 h4 13 ♘f1 h3 14 g3 0-0-0 15 c4 c5! ∓ Bakulin–Bronstein, USSR 1965.

7 ...   ♘d7

After 7 ... h5 8 h4 ♘d7 9 ♘g3 ♗g6 10 ♗d3 ♗xd3 11 ♕xd3 ♕a5+ 12 c3?! 0-0-0 13 0-0 e6 14 b4 ♕c7 15 b5 cxb5 16 ♕xb5 f5 17 ♘e2 ♗d6 (Clerk–Donner, 1957) R. Schwarz suggests 18 f4 or 18 ♖ab1 ±.

8 ♕d2   ♘b6

8 ... e6!?

9 ♘g3   ♗g6

10 c4 h5 11 h4 e6 12 ♗e2 ♗d6 13 0-0 ♗e7 14 ♖ac1 f5 15 ♗f3 e5 with an unclear position, Matanović–Bronstein, Hastings 1953-54.

ILLUSTRATIVE GAMES

16 BILEK–BRONSTEIN
    Budapest 1955
    1 e4 c6 2 d4 d5 3 ♘c3 dxe4 4 ♘xe4 ♘f6 5 ♘xf6+ gxf6 6 c3 ♗f5 7 ♘e2 h5 8 ♘f4?! h4 9 ♕f3!? ♘d7 10 g4? hxg3 11 fxg3 e5! 12 g4 (White cannot allow the black bishop to occupy the long diagonal, 12 dxe5 fxe5 13 ♘e2 ♗e6) **12 ... ♗h7 13 ♘e2 exd4! 14 cxd4** (14 ♘xd4 ♘e5 15 ♕g2 ♕e7 and then 16 ... 0-0-0) **14 ... ♗b4+ 15 ♔f2** (Forced as on 15 ♗d2 ♗xd2+ 16 ♔xd2 ♘e5 17 ♕e3 − 17 ♕c3 ♗e4 followed by 18 ... ♘f3+ − 17 ... ♕b6 18 b3 0-0-0 −+ R. Schwarz) **15 ... ♕e7 16 ♗g2 0-0-0 17 a3?** (White is unsuspecting. 17 ♗f4 ♘e5! 18 dxe5 ♖d3 19 ♗e3 ♗c5! or 18 ♕g3 ♘d3+ 19 ♔f1 ♖he8 or 18 ♗xe5 fxe5 19 dxe5 ♕xe5 etc. are bad. Schwarz gives 17 ♗e3 as about the best) **17 ... ♗c5!! 18 ♗e3** (18 dxc5 ♘e5! 19 ♕g3 ♖d3 20 ♗e3 − 20 ♕h4 ♕xc5+ 21 ♔e1 ♖hd8 22 ♗f4 ♖d1+leads to checkmate − 20 ... ♘c4 −+ or 18 ♕e3 ♘e5! 19 h3 ♗b6 20 ♖d1 ♕d7 21 ♔f1 ♖he8 −+ is another Schwarz line) **18 ... ♘e5! 19 dxe5 ♖d3 20 ♕xf6 ♕xf6 21 exf6 ♖xe3 22 ♖he1 ♗b6 23 ♗f3** (23 ♔f1 ♗d3 and then 24 ... ♖8e8) **23 ... ♗e4! 24**

♗xe4 ♖xe4+ **White resigned** (On 24 ♔f1 ♖xh2).

17 RODRIGUEZ-PIETERSE
Dieren 1987

1 e4 c6 2 d4 d5 3 ♘d2 dxe4 4 ♘xe4 ♘f6 5 ♘xf6+ gxf6 6 ♘e2 ♗f5 7 ♘g3 ♗g6 8 h4 h5 9 ♗e2 ♘d7 10 c3 ♕a5 11 a4! 0-0-0 12 b4 ♕c7 13 a5 e5!? 14 a6 b6 15 0-0 ♗d6 16 ♗d3! (Intending 17 ♕f3 and ♘f5) **16 ... exd4 17 cxd4 ♗xb4** (17 ... ♗xg3 18 fxg3 ♕xg3 19 ♗xg6! fxg6 — 19 ... ♕xg6 20 ♕f3 ♕c2 21 ♗f4! — 20 ♗f4 ♕g4 21 ♖c1 +—) **18 ♗e3 ♔b8** (18 ... ♘e5 19 ♗xg6 ♘xg6 20 ♕a4 +—) **19 ♖c1 ♗a3!? 20 ♖c2 ♘e5 21 ♗xg6! ♘xg6** (21 ... fxg6? 22 ♕a1 wins) **22 ♕f3! ♖d5** (22 ... ♘h4 23 ♕e4) **23 ♘e4 ♗e7 24 ♖fc1 ♘xh4** (24 ... ♖c8 25 ♘xf6 ♗xf6 26 ♖xc6 wins) **25 ♕h3 ♘g6 26 ♖xc6 ♕d7 27 ♕g3+ ♔a8 28 ♖c7 ♕e6 29 ♖1c6 Black resigned.**

18 BELLON-LARSEN
Las Palmas 1976

1 e4 c6 2 d4 d5 3 ♘c3 dxe4 4 ♘xe4 ♘f6 5 ♘xf6+ gxf6 6 c3 ♗f5 7 ♘e2 ♘d7 8 ♘g3 ♗g6 9 h4 h5 10 ♗e2 ♕a5! 11 b4?! ♕c7! 12 ♘xh5 a5! 13 ♖h3 axb4 14 cxb4 e6 15 b5 c5!? 16 ♗f4? ♗d6! (While White's natural move was bad, this one gives a winning advantage. Black's advantage is not so pronounced after 16 ... ♕a5+ 17 ♗d2 ♕a4) **17 ♗g3?** (Worsens his position decisively. After 17 ♗xd6 ♕xd6 White would have had plenty of problems. According to Larsen 17 b6!

was the most promising) **17 ... cxd4 18 ♕xd4 e5!** (Thanks to the badly-posted h5 knight this wins a piece) **19 b6** (19 ♕d1 ♗xh5 20 ♗xh5 ♕c3+) **19 ... ♕c6 20 ♘xf6+** (20 ♕d1 ♗xh5 21 ♗xh5 ♕c3+ 22 ♔f1 ♖xh5 20 ... ♘xf6 21 ♗xe5 ♗xe5 22 ♕xe5+ ♔f8** (The complications are over. White still has three pawns for his piece, but his forces are in disarray and his king's position is poor. Further material losses and defeat are therefore unavoidable) **23 ♔f1** (23 ♖f3 ♖xh4!) **23 ... ♖xa2! 24 ♖d1** (24 ♖xa2 ♕xc1+ 25 ♗d1 ♕xd1+ 26 ♕e1 ♗d3+) **24 ... ♕xb6 25 ♕f4 ♕b2 26 ♖e3 ♖a1 27 ♕d6+ ♔g7 28 g3 ♘e4 29 ♕f4 ♖xd1+ 30 ♗xd1 ♕d4 31 ♗e2 ♘d2+ 32 ♔e1 ♕xf4 33 gxf4 ♘e4 34 h5 ♗f5 35 ♗d3 ♘d6 36 ♗xf5 ♘xf5 37 ♖b3 ♖e8+ 38 ♔f1 ♖e7 39 ♖b6 ♖d7** and White exceeded the time limit. **0-1.**

19 PETERS-SEIRAWAN
USA (ch) 1984

1 e4 c6 2 d4 d5 3 ♘c3 dxe4 4 ♘xe4 ♘f6 5 ♘xf6+ gxf6 6 c3 ♗f5 7 ♘e2 ♘d7 8 ♘g3 ♗g6 9 h4 h5 10 ♗e2 ♕a5 11 b4?! ♕c7 12 ♘xh5 e5! 13 ♘g3 (13 dxe5 ♗xh5 14 ♗xh5 ♕xe5+ 15 ♗e2 ♗xb4 ∓) **13 ... 0-0-0 14 h5 ♗h7 15 ♕b3 ♘b6 16 b5?** (16 dxe5 fxe5 17 ♗g5 ∞) **16 ... c5 17 dxc5** (17 dxe5? c4! 18 ♕b2 ♘a4!) **17 ... ♗xc5 18 a4?!** (The bishop on c5 is very strong, thus 18 ♗a3!? and 19 ♗xc5 ♕xc5 20 ♕b4 was better) **18 ... ♖hg8 19 a5 ♘d5 20 b6 axb6 21 a6 bxa6 22 ♗xa6+ ♔b8 23**

♗c4 ♘f4 24 ♔f1 (24 ♗xf4 exf4 25
♗d5 ♕e5+ −+; 24 0-0 ♖xg3 25 ♗xf4
exf4 26 ♗d5 ♕e5 −+) 24 ... ♕b7 25
♖h2 b5! 26 ♗e2 (26 ♗xb5 ♗d3+!
wins; as does 26 ♗xf7 ♕xf7!) 26 ...
♘xe2 27 ♘xe2 ♗e4 28 f3 ♗d3 29 ♔e1
(29 h6 ♕xf3+ mates) 29 ... ♗c4 30
♕c2 ♖d3 31 h6 ♕d5 32 h7 ♖d8 33
♗g5 ♗b3 34 ♕xd3 ♕xd3 35 h8=♕
♖xh8 36 ♖xh8+ ♔b7 37 ♗d2 ♗c4 38
♘g3 e4 39 ♖h5 ♗d6 White resigned.

20   BROWNE-BELLON
Las Palmas 1977

1 e4 c6 2 d4 d5 3 ♘c3 dxe4 4 ♘xe4
♘f6 5 ♘xf6+ gxf6 6 ♗e2 ♗f5 7 ♘f3
♕c7 8 0-0 e6 9 c4 ♘d7 10 ♗e3 ♗d6 11
c5! ♗e7 12 ♘d2! 0-0 13 f4! ♗g6 14 f5!
♗xf5 (14 ... exf5 slows down the
attack, but Black's position is still
hopelessly passive) 15 ♖xf5! (After
this Black's king is in a hopeless
position) 15 ... exf5 16 ♗d3 ♖fe8
(The only way to defend h7) 17 ♗xf5
♘f8 18 ♘e4! (The knight is far more
valuable here than the rook) 18 ...
♔h8 19 ♕h5 ♘g6 20 ♖f1 ♖g8 21 ♖f3
♕a5 (Or 21 ... ♖g7 22 ♗h6 ♖g8 23
♖h3 +−) 22 ♕xh7+ Black resigned.

21   SOKOLSKY-BRONSTEIN
USSR (ch) 1944

1 e4 c6 2 d4 d5 3 ♘c3 dxe4 4 ♘xe4
♘f6 5 ♘xf6+ gxf6 6 ♘f3 ♗g4 7 ♗e2
e6 8 ♗e3 ♘d7 9 0-0 ♗d6?! 10 c4 f5?
11 d5! (Perhaps this game is outdated
from the point of view of opening
theory, but the breakthrough is
typical of this version) 11 ... cxd5
12 cxd5 e5 13 ♘d2! ♗xe2 14 ♕xe2
♕e7 15 ♕h5! ♕f6 (If 15 ... f4
16 ♗xf4 exf4 17 ♖fe1 ♘e5 18 ♘f3
♖g8 19 ♘xe5 ♖g5 20 ♕xg5! ♕xg5 21
♘f3+ etc) 16 f4! ♕g6 (16 ...
exf4 17 ♗xf4 ♕d4+ 18 ♔h1 ♗xf4 19
♖ae1+ ♔f8 20 ♘b3 ♕b4 21 ♕xf5 ±)
17 ♕h3 e4 18 ♘c4 ♗c7 19 ♗d4 ♖g8
20 ♘e3 ♗b6 21 ♗xb6 ♕xb6 22 ♖ac1!
(Black is bleeding to death owing
to the insecure position of his king)
22 ... ♘f6 23 ♔h1 ♘g4 24 ♘xg4
♖xg4 25 ♕c3 (25 ♕xh7 ♕xb2) 25 ...
♔f8 26 ♕e5! ♕g6 27 d6 ♖e8 (27 ...
♕e6 28 ♕h8+ ♖g8 29 ♕xh7 ♕g6 30
♕xg6 ♖xg6 31 ♖fd1 ±) 28 ♕h8+
♕g8 29 d7!! Black resigned (29 ...
♕xh8 30 dxe8=♕+ ♔xe8 31 ♖c8+).
The analysis is based on Sokolsky's
notes.

4
Classical Variation — 4 . . . ♗f5

1 e4 c6 2 d4 d5 3 ♘c3 dxe4 4 ♘xe4 ♗f5

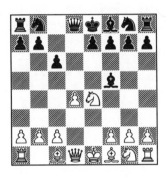

This is the oldest, yet the simplest, way of developing the bishop. It is characterized by the comfortable play Black's pieces get, although by chasing the queen's bishop White does gain time to seize the initiative, or, as frequently occurs, to cramp the black kingside.

It speaks for the solidity of this 4 . . . ♗f5 variation that it remains a tournament visitor even at the very highest levels today.

Transpositions from various move orders are frequent, but undoubtedly the most standard lines are those arising from line A, 6 h4.

5 ♘g3   . . .

Others:

a) **5 ♗d3 ♕xd4 6 ♗e3** (*Trifunović gives the variations 6 ♘f3 ♕d8 7 ♕e2 ♘f6 8 ♗d2 ♗xe4 9 ♗xe4 ♘xe4 10 ♕xe4 e6 11 0-0-0 0-0 or 7 . . . ♗xe4 8 ♗xe4 ♘f6 9 0-0 ♘xe4 10 ♕xe4 e6 11 ♗g5 ♗e7 12 ♖ad1 ♕c7 13 ♖fe1 0-0 14 ♗f4 ♕a5 15 ♗e5, but not 7 . . . e6? 8 ♗f4 ♘d7 9 0-0-0 ♘gf6 10 ♘xf6+ ♕xf6 11 ♗g5 ♕g6 12 ♗xf5 ♕xf5 13 ♕d2 ♕d5 14 ♕f4 ±) 6 . . . ♕d8 7 ♕f3 ♗xe4 8 ♕xe4 ♘f6 9 ♕h4 e6 10 ♘f3 ♘d5 ∓* B. Papp–Varnusz, Budapest 1977.

b) **5 ♕f3** (*harmless for Black*) 5 . . . e6 (*the continuations 5 . . . ♕d5, 5 . . . ♗xe4 and 5 . . . ♗g6 are also good*) 6 ♗e3 ♕a5+ 7 c3 (*7 ♗d2 ♕d5 8 ♗d3 ♕xd4 9 0-0-0 ♘d7 ∓ Felderhof–Euwe, The Hague 1933*) 7 . . . ♗a3!? 8 b4 ♕d5 9 ♗d3 ♗b2 10 ♖b1 ♗xe4 11 ♗xe4 ♗xc3+ 12 ♔f1 ♕xa2 13 ♘e2 ∞ Trifunović.

c) **5 ♘c5!?**

This favourite of Bronstein's results in the following plethora of variations:

5 ... ♕c7 6 ♗d3 ♗xd3 7 ♘xd3 e6 *(7 ... ♘f6 8 ♘f3 e6 9 0-0 ♘bd7 10 c4 ♗e7 11 ♗f4 ♕a5 12 b4 ♕d8 13 ♘c5 ± Kurtenkov-Rasmussen, Plovdiv 1986)* 8 ♗f4 ♕a5+ 9 c3 ♘d7 10 ♘f3 ♘gf6 11 0-0 ♗e7 12 ♖e1 0-0 13 ♗g5 ♕d8 ± Bronstein-Barcza, Budapest 1971.

5 ... e5?! 6 ♘xb7 ♕e7 *(6 ... ♕xd4 7 ♕xd4 exd4 8 ♘f3 ♗xc2 9 ♘xd4 ♗e4 10 f3 ♗d5 11 ♔f2! f6 12 ♗f4 g6 13 ♖e1+ ♗e7 14 ♘e6 ± Bárczay-Grószpéter, Hungary 1976)* 7 ♘a5 exd4+ 8 ♗e2 ♕b4+ **9 ♗d2** ♕xb2 10 ♗d3 ♗xd3 11 cxd3 ♗b4 12 ♘f3 ♗xd2+ 13 ♘xd2 (Klovan-Machulsky, USSR 1978) 13 ... ♕b4! ∓. Better for White is **9 ♕d2!** ♗xc2 10 ♕xb4 ♗xb4+ 11 ♗d2 ∞.

5 ... ♕c8 6 ♘f3 ♘f6 *(6 ... e6? 7 ♘e5 b6 8 ♘cd3 ♘f6 9 g4 ± Peters-Lein, Hastings 1978/79)* 7 ♗d3 ♗g4 8 h3 ♗h5 9 ♗f4 ♘bd7 10 ♘b3 e6 11 c3 ♗e7 12 ♕e2 ♘d5 ∞ Ermenkov-Bagirov, Titovo Uzice 1978.

5 ... ♕b6?! 6 g4! ♗g6 7 f4 e6 8 ♕e2 ♗e7 9 h4 h5 10 f5! exf5 11 g5 ♘d7 12 ♘d3 ♕c7 13 ♘h3 0-0-0 14 ♗f4 ♗d6 15 ♕h2 ♘f8 16 0-0-0 ± Bronstein-Belyavsky, USSR (ch) 1976.

5 ... b6!? 6 ♗b3 *(6 ♘a6?! e6 7 ♕f3 ♘e7 8 ♘xb8 ♕xb8 9 ♗f4 ♕b7 10 c3 ♘d5 11 g4 ♘xf4 12 ♕xf4 ♗g6 13 ♕g3 ♗e7 14 h4 h5 ∓ Timman-Pomar, Orense 1976)* 6 ... e6 *(6 ... ♘f6 7 ♘f3 e6 8 ♗e2 h6 9 ♗d3!? ♗xd3 10 ♕xd3 ♕c7 11 0-0 ♘bd7 12 ♖e1 ♗d6 13 ♘bd2 0-0 14 ♘c4 ♗e7 15 b3 c5 16 ♗b2 ± Larsen-Hübner, Tilburg 1979)* 7 ♘f3

(7 ♗d3!?) 7 ... ♘d7 *(7 ... ♗d6 8 g3 ♘e7 9 ♗g2 h6 10 0-0 0-0 11 ♕e2+ = Bronstein-Petrosian, USSR (ch) 1966)* 8 g3 ♘gf6 9 ♗g2 ♖c8 10 0-0 ♗d6 11 ♕e2 ♕c7 = Schmidt-Birbrager, USSR 1969.

5 ...   ♗g6

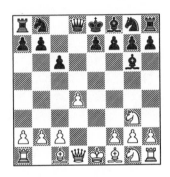

A: **6 h4**
B: **6 ♘f3**
C: **6 ♘h3**
D: **6 ♗c4**
E: **6 ♘1e2**

Or **6 f4** e6 *(6 ... h5 7 ♘f3 h4 8 ♘e2 ♘d7 9 ♘e5 ♘xe5 10 fxe5 e6 11 ♘f4 ♗f5 ∓; if 7 f5? ♗xf5!)* 7 h4 *(7 ♘f3 ♗d6 8 ♗d3 ♘e7 9 0-0 ♘d7 10 ♔h1 ♕c7 11 ♘e5 ♖d8 12 ♕e2 ♗xd3 13 ♘xd3 0-0 14 ♗d2 c5 15 ♘e4 ♘f5 16 dxc5 ♘xc5 ∓ Marshall-Capablanca, New York 1927)* 7 ... h5 *(7 ... h6)* 8 ♘f3 ♘d7 9 ♗c4 ♗e7 10 0-0 ♕c7 *(10 ... ♗xh4? 11 f5! ♗xg3 12 fxg6 fxg6 13 ♕d3 ♘e7 14 ♘g5 ± and **11 ... exf5** 12 ♘xh4 ♕xh4 13 ♘xf5 ♗xf5 14 ♖xf5*

♘gf6 15 ♕e2+ ♔f8 16 ♖f4 ♕g3 17
♖f3 ♕g4 18 ♗f4 ♖e8 19 ♕f2 ±
Ellerman) 11 ♘e2 0-0-0 12 c3 =
Trifunović.

Of the various alternatives White
now has to choose from variation A is
undoubtedly the most frequent. But
transpositional possibilities should
be carefully noted, as there are
several different move orders
possible throughout this main line.

A

6 h4   h6

6 . . . h5 7 ♘h3 e5 8 dxe5 ♕a5+ 9 c3
♘d7 10 e6! ♕e5+ 11 ♗e2 ♕xe6 12
♘f4 ±.

7 ♘f3   . . .

For 7 ♘e2 see variation E. Lines
after 7 ♗d3!? ♗xd3 are examined
shortly — it is dangerous to accept the
pawn sacrifice with 7 . . . ♕xd4?!, viz.:
8 ♘f3 ♕d6 9 ♗xg6 ♕xg6 10 ♕e2 ♕d6
11 0-0 e6 12 ♖d1 ♕c7 13 ♖d4 ♘f6 14
♗f4 ♕a5 15 ♘e5 ± Minić–Vukić,
Yugoslavia 1966 or **10 . . . ♘d7** 11 h5
♕d6 12 ♖h4 e6 13 ♖d4 ♕c7 14 ♗f4
♕a5+ Marić–Sušić, Yugoslavia 1966,
15 ♔f1! ±. White has two other sidelines:

a) **7 f4** e6 8 ♘f3 ♘d7 *(8 . . . ♗d6 9 h5*
♗h7 10 ♗d3 ♗xd3 11 ♕xd3 ♕c7 12
♘e5 ♘f6 13 ♗d2 ♘a6 14 0-0-0 0-0-0
15 ♔b1 c5! = Pedersen–Delander, 1963.

Maybe better is 9 ♘e5!? ♗xe5 10 fxe5
♘e7 11 h5 ♗h7 12 c3 c5?! 13 ♗c4 cxd4
14 0-0! ± Arnason–Adianto, Dubai (ol)
1986) 9 h5 ♗h7 10 ♗d3 ♗xd3 11
♕xd3 ♕c7 12 ♗d2 0-0-0 *(12 . . . ♘gf6*
13 0-0-0 c5 14 ♕e2 0-0-0 15 ♘e5 ±
Kavalek–Saidy, Las Palmas 1973) 13
♕e2 *(13 0-0-0 ♗d6 14 ♘e2 ♘gf6 15*
♔b1 ♔b8 16 ♕b3 ♕b6 17 ♘e5 ♕xb3
= Ciocaltea–Golombek, Moscow 1956)
13 . . . c5! *(13 . . . ♘gf6?! 14 0-0 ♗d6?!*
15 ♘e5 ♖hf8 16 c4 c5 17 ♗e3 ♘b6 18
dxc5! ♗xc5 19 b3 ± Sax–Rodriguez,
Biel 1985) = Hort v Garcia-Palermo,
Reggio Emilia 1984/85.

b) **7 ♘h3** e5 *(7 . . . e6 8 ♘f4 ♗h7*
9 ♗c4 ♘f6 10 0-0 leads to variation F.
Black showed originality in a Porreca-
Bronstein game, Belgrade 1954 with
7 . . . ♗h7!? 8 ♗c4 ♘gf6 9 ♘f4
♘bd7 10 0-0 ♕c7 11 ♖e1 ♗g8!
followed by long castling. However, this
is hardly the simplest solution to
Black's problems) 8 dxe5 ♕a5+ 9 c3 *(9*
♗d2?! ♕xe5+ 10 ♗e2 ♕xb2 11 ♖b1
∞ or 9 ♕d2 ♗b4 10 c3 ♕xe5+ 11 ♗e2
♗c5 12 ♘f4 ♘d7 = Panov) 9 . . .
♕xe5+ 10 ♗e2 ♘f6 *(10 . . . ♘d7 11*
♗f4 ♕e6 12 0-0 0-0-0 13 ♕a4 ± or 10
. . . ♗c5 11 ♗f4 ♕d5 12 ♕xd5 cxd5 13
0-0 ♘e7 14 ♗f3. On 11 . . . ♕e6
Pachman gives 12 0-0 ♘e7 13 ♖e1 0-0
14 b4! ♗b6 15 ♗a6 +–) 11 ♕b3 ♕c7
12 ♗f4 ♕b6 ± Kovács–Lepsényi
(corr) 1963.

7 . . .   ♘d7

Now we have:

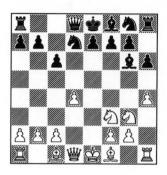

A1: 8 h5
A2: 8 ♗d3

A1

8 h5 ...

White wants to blockade the king-side completely.

8 ... ♗h7
9 ♗d3 ...

White intends to castle queenside and is therefore well advised to exchange the dangerous black bishop. 9 ♗c4 has also been tried on occasion: 9 ... e6 10 ♕e2 ♘gf6 11 ♗b3 *(11 0-0 ♗e7!? 12 ♖e1 ♘d5 13 ♗b3 0-0 14 c4 ±; 11 ... ♗d6! =. Also 11 ♘e5 ♘xe5 12 dxe5 ♘d7 13 ♗f4 ♘b6 14 ♖d1 ♕c7 15 ♗b3 ♘d5 16 ♗c1 0-0-0 17 0-0 ♗e7 = Mnatsakanian-Polyak, USSR 1957 or 13 0-0 ♕c7 14 f4 ♗c5+ 15 ♔h2 ♘b6 16 ♗b3 ♕e7 17 ♕g4 0-0-0 ∓)* 11 ... ♗d6 12 ♘d2 ♕c7 13 ♘de4 ♗f4 14 ♗xf4 *(14 ♕f3? ♗xc1*

15 ♖xc1 0-0-0 16 c3 ♘xe4 17 ♘xe4 e5 ∓ Keller-Barcza, Zürich 1956) 14 ... ♕xf4 15 ♕d2 = Trifunović.

9 ... ♗xd3

In recent years 9 ... ♘gf6?! has also been played occasionally. After 10 ♗xh7 ♘xh7, the following continuations are possible:

a) **11 ♕e2** e6 12 ♗d2 ♗e7 13 0-0-0 ♕b6 14 ♘e5 *(14 ♘f5 exf5 15 ♖he1 ∞ Ljubojević-Larsen, Bugojno 1984)* 14 ... ♖d8 15 ♖he1 0-0 16 ♘g6 ♖fe8 17 ♘xe7+ ♖xe7 18 ♘f5 ♖ee8 19 ♘d6 ♖f8 20 ♗f4 ♘df6 21 ♗e5 ♖d7 22 ♖d3 ± Belyavsky-Larsen, London 1984.

b) **11 ♗f4** e6 12 ♕e2 ♕a5+ 13 ♗d2 ♗b4 14 c3 ♗e7 15 0-0 ♘hf6 16 b4 ♕c7 17 ♖fe1 0-0 18 ♘e5 ± Grünfeld-Murey, Israel 1986.

10 ♕xd3 e6

Both 10 ... ♘gf6 and 10 ... ♕c7 are also common here, though as a rule this only leads to a transposition of moves. We will see the problems unique to the text move order in a moment; here are continuations stemming from the other two moves which do not lead back to the main line:

a) **10 ... ♘gf6**

a1) **11 ♗d2**. This is the main line, though an exception is 11 ... e6 12 0-0-0 ♗e7!? and now **13 ♕e2** 0-0 *(13 ... c5 14 dxc5 − 14 ♖he1!? − 14 ...*

♕c7 15 ♗c3 0-0 16 ♘e4 ♕f4+ 17 ♘fd2 ♘xe4 18 ♕xe4 ♕xe4 19 ♘xe4 ♘xc5 20 ♘xc6 ♗xc5 21 f3 ♖fd8 — *Hjartarson-Korchnoi, Tilburg 1989 — 22 ♖he1 ± Kasparov)* 14 ♘e5 *(14 ♖he1)* 14 . . . c5! 15 dxc5 ♗xc5 16 f4 *(16 ♘xd7 ♕xd7 17 ♗g5 ♘d5 18 c4 hxg5 19 cxd5 ♖ac8 20 ♔b1 exd5 21 h6 g6 22 ♕e5 f6 23 ♕xd5+ ♕xd5 24 ♖xd5 ♖fd8 ∓ van der Wiel-Fette, Lugano 1989)* 16 . . . ♖c8 17 ♔b1 ♕c7 18 ♘xd7 ♕xd7 19 ♘e4 ♘xe4 20 ♕xe4 ♖fd8 21 ♕e2 ♕c6 ∞ *van Mil-Fette, Lugano 1989;* 13 ♘e4 ♘xe4 14 ♕xe4 ♘f6 15 ♕e2 ♕d5 16 c4 ♕e4 17 ♕xe4 *(17 ♖de1 ♕xe2 18 ♖xe2 b5! 19 b3 0-0 20 ♔c2 ♖fc8 ∞ Tischbierek-Lobron, Hanover 1991)* 17 . . . ♘xe4 18 ♗e3 *(18 ♗e1 ♗f6 19 ♘e5 ♖d8 — 19 . . . c5 20 f3! — 20 f3 ♘d6! 21 ♗f2! ♗xe5 22 dxe5 ♘xc4 ∞/± Armas-Tal, West Germany 1990)* 18 . . . f5 *(18 . . . 0-0 19 ♘e5 ♖fd8 20 g4 c5 21 f3 cxd4 22 ♖xd4 ♖xd4 23 ♗xd4 ± Strikovic-Korchnoi, Torcy 1990)* 19 ♘d2 = (Armas).

a2) After **11 ♗f4** the following continuations are possible:

11 . . . ♘d5? 12 ♗d2 e6 13 c4 ♘b4? 14 ♕b3 a5 *(14 . . . ♕b6 15 0-0-0!)* 15 a3 ± Tal-Rodriguez, Las Palmas 1975.

11 . . . ♕a5+ 12 c3 *(After 12 ♗d2 ♕c7 the game transposes into the main variations. Alternatively* **12 b4!?** *♕xb4+ 13 c3 ♕b5 14 c4 ♕a5+ 15 ♗d2 ♕a6 16 0-0 e6 17 ♖fe1 ♗e7 was Velimirović-Hort, Havana 1971,* **18 ♘f5?** *exf5 19 ♖xe7+ ♔xe7 20 ♗b4+ ♔d8 21 ♘e5 ♘e4 ∓; 18 a4!±)* 12 . . . e6 13 a4 c5 14 0-0 ♖c8 *(14 . . . ♗e7*

15 ♖fe1 cxd4 16 b4 ♕a6 17 b5 ♕a5 18 ♘xd4 ± *Vitolins-Arnton, USSR 1978)* 15 ♖fe1 *(15 ♕b5!?)* 15 . . . c4 16 ♕c2 ± see Gaprindashvili-Nikolac, in note to 11 ♗d2.

11 . . . e6 12 0-0-0 ♗e7 and now 13 ♘e5 0-0 *(13 . . . ♘d5!?)* 14 ♕e2 *(14 ♘e4 ♘xe4 15 ♕xe4 ♘xe5 16 ♗xe5 ♕d5! = de Firmian-Korchnoi, Lugano 1989 — for 14 c4 see illustrative game 26 Karpov-Hübner)* 14 . . . ♕a5 15 ♔b1 ♖ad8 16 c4 *(16 ♘g6!?)* 16 . . . ♘xe5 17 dxe5 ♘d7 18 ♖d2 ♗g5 = Belyavsky-Tal, USSR 1981; 13 c4 a5 *(13 . . . b5!? 14 c5! — 14 cxb5 cxb5 15 ♕xb5 0-0 — 14 . . . 0-0 15 ♔b1! a5! 16 ♗c1! a4 17 ♘e2 ♕b8!∞ Ivanchuk-Seirawan, Novi Sad 1990)* 14 ♔b1 a4?! 15 ♘e5 ♘xe5 16 ♗xe5 ♕a5?! 17 ♘e4 0-0-0 18 c5! ♘xe4 19 ♕xe4 ♗f6 *(19 . . . ♖hg8 20 ♖h3!)* 20 ♗xf6 gxf6 21 ♕f4 ± Karpov-Larsen, Amsterdam 1980; or **13 ♔b1** a5 *(13 . . . 0-0 14 ♘e4 ♘xe4 15 ♕xe4 ♘f6 16 ♕e2 ♕d5 17 ♘e5 ♕e4 = Thorsteinsson-Lobron, Reykjavik 1985)* 14 ♘e4 ♘xe4 15 ♕xe4 ♘f6 16 ♕d3 *(16 ♕e2 a4 17 ♘e5 ♕d5 18 g4 a3 ∓ Torre-Karpov, Moscow 1981)* 16 . . . 0-0 17 ♘e5 ♘d5 18 ♗c1 ♗g5 = Wedberg-Christiansen, Reykjavik 1985.

b) **10 . . . ♕c7** 11 ♖h4!? *(11 ♗d2 leads to the main line)* 11 . . . e6 12 ♗f4 ♗d6 13 ♗xd6 ♕xd6 14 ♘e4 ♕e7 15 ♕a3! *(15 0-0-0 ♘gf6 16 ♘xf6+ = Gligorić-Petrosian, Yugoslavia v USSR 1959)* 15 . . . ♕xa3 16 bxa3 ♔e7 17 ♖b1 ♖b8 *(17 . . . b6 18 ♘e5! ♘xe5 19 dxe5 f5 20 ♘c3 ♔f7 21 ♖d4 ♘e7*

Browne–Pomar, Siegen 1970, 22 ♖d7! ♖d8 23 ♖bd1 ♔e8 24 ♖7d6 ± or 20 ♘g3 ♖d8 21 ♖a4 ♖d7 27 ♖d1 ♖xd1+ 23 ♔xd1 a5 24 ♖d4 c5 25 ♖d2 ♔f7 26 ♖d8 ♖h7 Belyavsky–Pomar, Las Palmas 1970, and now 27 ♖b8! ±) 18 ♘c5! ♘xc5 19 dxc5 a5! 20 ♘e5! ♘f6 21 ♖d4! ♖hc8 22 g4 *(22 ♖b3? ♖c7 23 g4! ♖d8! 24 ♖xb7 ♖xd4 25 ♘xc6+ ♔d7 26 ♘xd4 ♖xb7 27 c6+ ♔c7 28 cxb7 ♘xg4 29 ♘c6 ♔xb7 30 ♘xa5 ♔c7 = Bellon–Pomar, Olot 1975)* 22 . . . ♖c7 23 f3! ± Bellon–Pomar, Orense 1976.

11 ♗d2   . . .

Or **11 b3** ♘gf6 12 ♗b2 ♕a5+ 13 ♗c3 *(13 c3 ♗a3 14 0-0-0 ♗xb2+)* 13 . . . ♗b4 14 ♗xb4 ♕xb4+ 15 ♕d2 = Spassky–Karpov, USSR (c) 1974.

The test of Black's move order, however, is in the line **11 ♗f4**. Now after **11 . . . ♕a5+** White can of course transpose back to the main line by **12 ♗d2 ♕c7** *(Not 12 . . . ♕b6? 13 c4 ♘gf6 14 0-0-0 ♕a6 15 ♔b1 ♘d5 16 ♕e2 ♘5b6 17 ♖c1 0-0-0 18 ♖hd1 ♔b8 19 ♘e4 ♔a8 20 g4 ± Gipslis–Fedorov, USSR 1973)* but also possible is **12 c3!?** ♘gf6 13 a4! c5 14 0-0 and now:

a) **14 . . . ♖c8** 15 ♖fe1 c4 16 ♕c2 ♗e7 *(Maybe Black's play can be improved by 16 . . . ♘d5 although White has a promising piece sacrifice with 17 ♗e5 f6 18 ♕g6+ ♔d8 19 ♘e4 etc.)* 17 ♘e5 0-0 18 ♘f5! ♖fe8 19 ♘xg7! ♔xg7 20 ♗xh6+ ♔xh6 21 ♘xf7+ ♔xh5 22 g4+! ♔h4 23 f3 ♘xg4

24 ♖e4 1-0 Gaprindashvili–Nikolac, Wijk aan Zee 1979.

b) **14 . . . ♗e7** 15 ♖fe1 0-0 *(15 . . . ♘d5?! 16 ♗d2 cxd4 17 ♘xd4 0-0 18 c4 ♘b4 19 ♕b3 ♕b6 20 ♘gf5! ± Ermenkov–Gomez, Thessaloniki (ol) 1984)* 16 ♘f5 ♖fe8 17 ♘xh6+!? gxh6 18 ♘e5 ♘xe5 19 dxe5 ♘h7 20 ♗xh6 ♗f8 21 ♗f4 ♔h8 22 ♖e4 ♕c7 23 ♖ae1 ∞ Vitolins–Kliavin, Latvia (ch) 1978.

After 11 ♗f4 also possible is **11 . . . ♗b4+!?** 12 c3 ♗e7 13 0-0-0 ♘gf6 14 ♘e5 *(14 ♔b1 a5 15 ♘e4 ♘xe4 16 ♕xe4 ♘f6 17 ♕d3 ♕d5 18 ♘e5 ♕e4 ∓ Ernst–Larsen, Gausdal 1985)* 14 . . . 0-0 15 c4 c5 16 d5 exd5 17 ♘f5!? ♘xe5 18 ♗xe5 ♘g4 ∞ Andreas–Rodriguez, Palma Soriano 1983.

It should be noted, however, that several top grandmasters continue to play the 10 . . . e6 move order so there may well be improvements to be found.

11 . . .   ♕c7

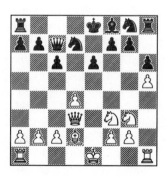

On 11 . . . ♕b6 Milić gives 12 0-0-0 ♘gf6 13 ♘e5 ♗e7 14 ♖he1 ♖d8 15 ♕e2 ±.

A1.1: 12 ♕e2
A1.2: 12 0-0-0

Very interesting is 12 ♔f1!? 0-0-0 13 b4 ♘gf6 14 ♖e1 ♗d6 15 ♕a3 ♔b8 16 c4 ♔a8 17 ♘e2 ♕c8 18 ♘c3 ♖he8 19 ♖h4 ♗b8 ∞ Hector-E. Vladimirov, Gausdal 1990.

A1.1

12 ♕e2   ♘gf6

Here we divide again with:
A1.11: 13 0-0-0
A1.12: 13 c4

A1.11

13 0-0-0   0-0-0

13 . . . c5!? is worth considering — 14 c4!? cxd4 15 ♘xd4 ♗c5 16 ♘b5 ♕c6 17 ♘f5 0-0 18 ♘xh6+!? gxh6 19 ♗xh6 ♖fd8 20 ♖h4 ♗f8 21 ♗xf8 ♘xf8 22 ♕e5 ♖xd1 ∓ Velikov-Bagirov, Wroclaw 1976. Boleslavsky's and other theoreticians' contention that **14 ♖h4** gives White the advantage *(If 14 ♔b1 0-0-0 15 c4 ♗d6 ∞)* after **14 . . . 0-0-0** 15 dxc5 ± is debatable after **14 . . . ♗e7!?** (∓ !?). A novelty here is **14 ♔b1 ♖c8** 15 c4 cxd4 16 ♘xd4 ♗c5 17 ♘b5 *(17 ♗c3)* 17 . . . ♕c6 18 b4! a6 19 bxc5 axb5 20 cxb5

♕xg2 *(20 . . . ♕c5?? 21 ♖c1; 20 . . . ♕c7? 21 ♘f5!)* — Galdunc-Tavadian, USSR 1990 — 21 ♗b4!? ∞/±.

On *13 . . . ♗d6* instead Trifunović gives 14 ♘f5 ♗f4 15 ♘e3! ±.

14 ♘e5!   . . .

This is the essence of White's plan. Whether Black takes the centralized knight or not, he is faced with a difficult, though not insurmountable, problem.

A1.111: 14 . . . ♘xe5
A1.112: 14 . . . ♘b6

A1.111

14 . . .   ♘xe5
15 dxe5   ♘d7

15 . . . ♘d5 16 f4 c5 *(16 . . . ♗e7 17 ♘e4 ♕b6 18 ♖h3 c5 19 ♖f1! ♖he8 20 ♖hf3 ♕c7 21 g4 ♖h8 22 ♗e1! ♖d7 23 ♗g3 ♘b4 24 f5! ± Akopian-Magomedov, Minsk 1990)* 17 c4 ♘b4 18 ♗xb4 ♖xd1+ 19 ♖xd1 cxb4 20 ♘e4 ♗e7 21 ♘d6+ ♔b8 ± Spassky-Botvinnik, USSR 1966.

16 f4   ♗e7
17 ♘e4   . . .

17 ♗e3!? ♕a5 18 ♔b1 ♘c5 19 ♗xc5!? ♕xc5 20 ♘e4 ♕a5 (Shirazi-Hertan, USA 1990) 21 c4!? ± (Hertan).

17 . . .   ♘c5

18 ♘c3   ♖he8

18 . . . f6?! 19 exf6 ♗xf6 20 ♕c4 ♕b6 21 b4! ± Spassky–Petrosian (m) 1966.

19 ♗e3   ♕a5
20 ♔b1   ♘a4

White stands slightly better: 21 ♘xa4 ♕xa4 22 ♕f2 b6 ± Tiller–Grószpéter, Groningen 1977/78.

A1.112

14 . . .   ♘b6
15 ♗a5   . . .

Or 15 ♖h4 when now:
a) 15 . . . ♗d6 16 ♗a5 ♗xe5 17 dxe5 ♖xd1+ 18 ♔xd1 ♘fd7 19 ♖e4 ♖d8+ 20 ♔c1 ♘c5 21 ♖g4! ± Haág–Flesch, Salgótarján 1967 or 16 . . . ♖he8 17 ♘f1! ♗xe5 18 dxe5 ♖xd1+ 19 ♔xd1 ♘fd7 20 ♖e4 ♖d8+ 21 ♔c1 ♘c5 22 ♖g4 ± Gaprindashvili–Pomar, Olot 1975.
b) 15 . . . c5 16 ♗a5 ♗d6 *(16. . . cxd4 17 ♖hxd4 ♗c5 Trifunović)* 17 dxc5 ♗xe5!? *(17 . . . ♗xc5!?)* 18 ♖xd8+ ♖xd8 19 cxb6 axb6 *(19. . . ♗f4+? 20 ♔b1 axb6 21 ♗xb6 ♕xb6 22 ♖xf4 ± Ubilava–Peres, USSR 1974)* 20 ♖c4 bxa5 21 ♖xc7+ ♗xc7 22 ♕f3 *(22 ♕c4!?)* 22 . . . ♖d4 = J. Diaz–Nogueiras, Cuba (ch) 1990.
Instead 15 c3 c5 16 ♔b1 ♗d6 17 f4 cxd4 18 cxd4 ♔b8 *(Boleslavsky)* is harmless for Black.
A very interesting new idea is 15

c4!? ♖xd4 16 ♗e3! ♖xd1+ 17 ♖xd1 ♖g8 18 f4! *(18 ♗f4?! ♘bd7 19 ♕d2 ♗b4! ∓ Hellers–Khalifman, New York 1990)* 18 . . . c5 19 ♕d3! (Zugzwang!) 19 . . . ♗e7 20 ♘xf7 ♖f8 21 ♘e5 ♖d8 22 ♕c2 ♖xd1+ 23 ♔xd1 ♗d6 24 ♘g6 ± Sax–Andersson (m) 1990.

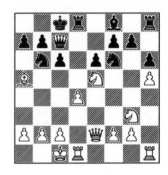

15 . . .   ♖d5!

It is best to get rid of the disagreeable pin as soon as possible. On 15 . . . c5 16 c4 ♔b8 17 dxc5 ♗xc5 18 f4 ♗d4 19 ♔b1 ♗xe5 20 fxe5 ♘fd7 21 ♘e4! ± Runau–Moghadam, Hastings 1971-72.

16 ♗xb6   . . .

Stubbornly maintaining the pin involves a considerable amount of risk because of the possible exchange sacrifice, viz.: 16 b4?! ♖xa5! 17 bxa5 ♗a3+ 18 ♔b1 ♘a4 19 ♖d3 *(19 ♕f3 ♗b4 20 ♖d3 ♕xa5 21 ♘e2 ♘d5 22 ♖h3 f6 23 ♘g6 ♖d8 24 ♘gf4 ♘dc3+ 25 ♘xc3 ♘xc3 ∓ Schepers–*

Tarnai (corr) 1972; if 22 ♕*xf7* ♘*ac3+ 23* ♘*xc3* ♗*xc3 24* ♕*xe6+* ♔*b8 25* ♖*xc3* ♘*xc3+ 26* ♔*b2* ♘*d5 27* ♕*d6+* ♔*a8 28* ♕*c5* ♕*d2 29* ♘*d3* ♖*e8* ∞ *Tarnai)* 19 . . . ♗b2?! *(19 . . .* ♕*xa5!)* 20 ♕d2! c5 21 c3 ♕xa5 ∞ Kosanski-Dely, Yugoslavia 1975.

16 . . .	axb6
17 c4	♖d8

17 . . . ♖a5 is more risky, because if the attack (!?) fails to get off the ground the black rook will be out on a limb: 18 ♔b1 ♗d6 19 f4 ♖d8 20 ♖d2! *(20* ♘*e4* ♘*xe4 21* ♕*xe4* ♔*b8 22 b3 b5 23 c5* ♗*xe5 24 dxe5* ♖*d5 25* ♖*xd5 exd5 26* ♕*b4 =* Jansa-Podgaets, Sombor *1970, or 22 g3?! b5 23 c5* ♗*xe5 24 dxe5?* ♖*a4 25* ♕*e3* ♖*d5 26 b3* ♕*d7* ± *Maeder-Podgaets, Dresden 1969)* 20 . . . b5 *(20 . . . c5 21* ♖*hd1* ±*)* 21 c5 ♗f8 22 ♘e4 ± Trifunović.

18 ♘e4   . . .

Also possible is **18 ♘f3** ♗d6 19 ♘e4 ♘xe4 20 ♕xe4 ♖he8 21 ♔b1 ♔b8 22 ♖d3 ± Hort-Pomar, Las Palmas 1976, but not **18 a3?!** c5 19 dxc5 ♗xc5 20 b4?! ♗xf2 21 ♘xf7 ± Weideman-Grószpéter, Groningen 1976-77.

18 . . .   ♘xe4

18 . . . c5? 19 ♘c3 ♗d6 20 ♘b5 ♕e7 21 dxc5 ♗xc5 22 ♘a7+ ♔c7 23 ♘xf7! +− Tatai-Pomar, Malaga 1968.

19 ♕xe4   ♗d6
20 f4   . . .

20 ♘f3 ♖he8 21 ♔b1 ♕e7 22 ♖he1 ♕f6 23 g3 ♗c7 24 a3 ± Spassky-Pomar, Palma de Mallorca 1968.

The text move was played in Martin-Pomar, Las Vegas 1977 and the end-game reached after 20 . . . f5 21 ♕e3 ♗xe5 22 ♕xe5 ♕xe5 23 dxe5 has become one of the milestones of this variation, White gaining winning chances after **23 . . .** ♖**hg8?** 24 ♖xd8+! ♔xd8 *(24 . . .* ♖*xd8 25* ♖*d1* ±*)* 25 ♖d1+ ♔c7 *(25 . . .* ♔*e7 26* ♖*d3! g5 27 hxg6* ♖*xg6 28 g3* ±*)* 26 ♖d6 g5 27 g3! Nevertheless, Black could have held the position according to the analysis of the Soviet master Korolev: **23 . . . g5!** 24 hxg6 *(24* ♖*xd8+* ♔*xd8 25 fxg5 hxg5 26 h6?* ♗*h7* ∓ *or 24 g3* ♖*hg8 25* ♖*hg1* ♖*d7!)* 24 . . . ♖dg8 25 ♖d3 ♖xg6 26 g3 ♖hg8 27 ♖h3 h5 28 ♔c2 *(28* ♖*f3 h4! 29 gxh4* ♖*g1+ 30* ♔*c2* ♖*8g2+ 31* ♔*b3* ♖*b1)* 28 . . . h4 29 gxh4 ♖h6 30 ♖h2 ♖g4 31 ♖f3 ♖hxh4 =.

A1.12

13 c4   . . .

This has been in fashion since 1974. White delays castling and refrains from committing himself to either side.

(see diagram overleaf)

13 . . .   ♗d6

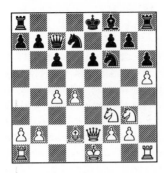

Or 13 . . . 0-0-0 when:
a) **14 ♘e5!? ♘b6** *(14 . . . ♘xe5 15 dxe5 ♘d7 16 ♗c3 ±)* **15 c5!? ♘bd5?!** 16 0-0 ♕e7 17 ♕f3 ♘c7 18 ♗e3 ♕e8 19 b4 ♗e7 20 a4 ± Bach-Teschner, Berlin 1976. *Schach Archiv* came up with the interesting improvement 15 . . . ♗xc5!? 16 dxc5 ♖xd2! 17 ♔xd2 *(17 ♕xd2 ♕xe5+)* 17 . . . ♕xe5 18 ♕xe5 *(18 cxb6 ♕b2+)* 18 . . . ♘c4+ 19 ♔c2 ♘xe5 20 ♖he1 etc., when the opponent's weak points (c5, h5), together with the strong knight position and the pawn advantage, compensate for Black's loss of the exchange.
b) **14 c5!? ♖g8 15 b4! g6!** 16 ♖b1 gxh5 17 ♔f1 ♖g4 18 ♖b3 ♔b8 19 ♘xh5 ♘xh5 20 ♖xh5 ± Hort-Karpov, Portorož–Ljubljana 1975, merits attention.

14 ♘f5   . . .

White's trump card. Now Black has:
a) **14 . . . 0-0-0?** This yields the

initiative — for the continuation see the illustrative game Karpov-Pomar, Nice (ol) 1974.
b) **14 . . . ♗f4!?** The old line which Portisch has rehabilitated. 15 ♗xf4 ♕xf4 16 ♘e3 c5 *(better than 16 . . . ♕c7 17 0-0-0 b5!? 18 cxb5 cxb5+ 19 ♔b1 0-0 20 g4! ♘e4 as in Spassky-Karpov, USSR (c) 1974 when instead of 21 ♖hg1?! Black would have been awkwardly placed after 21 ♘g2!)* 17 ♘d5 ♘xd5 18 cxd5 0-0 19 dxe6 ♖fe8 20 0-0 ♖xe6 21 ♕b5 ♕c7 = Tal-Portisch, Bugojno 1978.
c) **14 . . . 0-0** 15 ♘xd6 ♕xd6. Who stands better is definitely debatable, e.g. **16 ♗c3** *(16 ♖h4? b5 17 ♔f1 bxc4 18 ♕xc4 ♕d5 19 ♕e2 ♕b5 ∓ Lanka-Kasparov, USSR 1977)* 16 . . . b5! 17 cxb5 cxb5 18 ♕xb5 ♘d5 19 ♘e5 ♘xe5 20 dxe5 ♘xc3 21 bxc3 ♕c7 22 ♖h3 ♖fd8 ± Belyavsky-Bagirov, USSR (ch) 1977. **16 0-0-0** is more murky: 16 . . . b5! 17 cxb5 *(In Mnatsakanian-Bagirov, Kirovakan 1978, White played consistently for attack with 17 g4! bxc4 18 g5 hxg5 19 h6 and probably held a slight edge. An interesting question is whether Black can afford to play 17 . . . ♘xg4. After 18 ♖hg1 f5 19 ♘e5!? ♘dxe5 20 dxe5 ♕xe5 21 ♕xe5 ♘xe5 22 ♗c3 ♘g4 23 f3 ♘f6 24 ♖d6 White is very active but should be happy to hold the draw)* 17 . . . cxb5 18 ♔b1 ♖fc8! *(18 . . . ♕d5?! 19 ♘e5! ♘xe5 20 dxe5 ♕e4+ 21 ♕xe4 ♘xe4 22 ♗e3 ± or 19 . . . ♘b6 20 f3 ♘c4 21 ♗c1)* 19 g4?! *(An improvement is 19 ♘e5! ♕c7 20 ♗c1 ♘xe5 21 dxe5*

♘d5 22 ♖d4! — 22 g4 ♕c4! — 22 . . . b4 23 ♖g4 ♔h8 24 ♗xh6!? gxh6 25 ♕d2 ♔h7 26 ♕d3+ ♔h8 27 ♕d2 =) 19 . . . ♕c6! (19 . . . ♘xg4? 20 ♖hg1 f5 21 ♘e5 ♘dxe5 22 dxe5 ♕xe5 23 ♕xe5 ♘xe5 24 ♗c3 ±) 20 ♘e5 ♘xe5 21 dxe5 ♕c2+22 ♔a1 ♘e4 ∓ (Analysis by Yurkov).

A1.2

12 0-0-0   ♘gf6

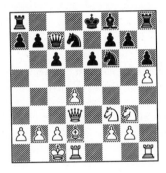

12 . . . 0-0-0 leads either to the main line or to the following possibilities:

a) **13 ♕e2 ♗d6** (13 . . . ♘gf6 is the text) 14 ♘e4 ♗e7 (14 . . . ♗f4!?) 15 c4 ♘gf6 16 ♘c3 ♖he8 17 g3 ♗f8 18 ♔b1 e5!? (18 . . . ♕a5?! 19 ♘e5 ± Spassky-Barcza, Sochi 1966) 19 dxe5 ♘xe5 20 ♗f4 ♖xd1+ 21 ♕xd1 ♘fd7 ∞ Trifunović.

b) **13 c4 ♘gf6** (13 . . . ♗d6!? 14 ♗c3!? Trifunović) 14 ♗c3 ♗d6 15 ♘e4 ♗f4+ 16 ♔c2 ♘e5 17 ♘xe5 ♗xe5 18 ♘c5 ♗d6 19 ♘b3 ± Bronstein-Kotov, Amsterdam 1968.

13 ♘e4   . . .

This, the Ukrainian variation, has become the most popular since White obtained no advantage with 13 ♕e2 in Spassky-Portisch, Tilburg 1978. That game went 13 . . . c5 14 ♖h4 ♗e7 15 dxc5 ♘xc5 16 ♖c4 b5 17 ♖d4 ½-½. Interesting is **13 ♘e5!?** ♘xe5 14 dxe5 ♕xe5 15 ♖he1 ♕c7 (15 . . . ♕d5? 16 ♖xe6+!) 16 ♗c3 (16 ♘f5?! ♘d5 17 c4 0-0-0 18 cxd5 ♖xd5 19 ♘d4 ♗c5 20 ♘xe6 fxe6 ∓ Zhidkov-Podgaets, USSR 1968) 16 . . . ♖d8 (16 . . . ♘d5 17 ♗e5! and 18 c4) 17 ♖xe6+!? fxe6 18 ♕g6+ ♔e7 19 ♘f5+ exf5 20 ♖e1+ ♘e4 21 ♕xf5 ♖d6 22 ♗f6+! ♖xf6 23 ♕xe4+ ♔d7 24 ♕e8+ = Soylu-Öney, Istanbul 1988.

An old idea, but a relatively new continuation is **13 ♔b1** 0-0-0 14 c4 ♔b8!? (14 . . . c5) 15 ♗c3 ♔a8!? 16 ♕e2! ♗d6 (16 . . . c5? 17 ♘e5 ♘xe5 18 dxe5 ±) 17 ♘e5 ♖hf8 18 f4 c5 ∞ Dvoiris-Yudasin, USSR (ch) 1990.

13 . . .   0-0-0

13 . . . ♘xe4 14 ♕xe4 ♘f6 15 ♕e2 0-0-0 16 g3 ♖d5 17 ♗f4 ♗d6 (17 . . . ♕a5 18 ♔b1 ♖b5 19 ♘e5 ±; 18 . . . ♘xh5 19 ♗d2 ♕a6 20 c4 ♘f6 21 ♘e5 ± Trifunović) 18 ♘e5 (18 ♗xd6 ♖xd6 19 ♘e5 ♖hd8 20 c3 c5 = Stein-Korchnoi, Sousse (izt) 1967) 18 . . . ♗xe5 (18 . . . ♘d7 19 ♖he1 ♖d8 20 c4 ♖a5 21 ♔b1 ♘xe5 22 dxe5 ♗b4 23 ♖xd8+ ♔xd8 24 ♖d1+ ♔e8 25 a3 ±

Copié-Vinagre, (corr) 1985/88) 19 ♗xe5 ♕a5 20 ♔b1 ♖hd8 21 g4 ±.

14 g3   . . .

To threaten 15 ♗f4. Another continuation is 14 c4 c5 15 ♘xf6 ♘xf6 *(15 . . . gxf6 16 d5 ♘b6 17 ♗a5 ±)* 16 ♗c3 cxd4 17 ♘xd4 ♕f4+ *(17 . . . a6 = Trifunović)* 18 ♕e3 ♕xe3+ 19 fxe3 ♗c5 20 b4! ♗e7 ∞ Weinstein-Enklaar, Amsterdam 1975.

A1.21: 14 . . . ♘xe4
A1.22: 14 . . . ♘c5!?

A1.21

14 . . .   ♘xe4

Weaker are **14 . . . ♘g4?!** 15 ♕e2 ♘df6 16 ♗f4 ♕a5 17 ♘xf6 gxf6 18 ♘d2 f5 Geller-Petrosian, Moscow 1967, 19 f3 ♘f6 20 ♘b3 ♕b5 21 c4 +− and the more recent attempt of **14 . . . c5** 15 ♗f4 c4 16 ♕e2 ♕c6 17 ♘xf6 gxf6 18 d5! exd5 19 ♘d4 ♕a6 20 ♔b1 ♗d6 21 ♕f3 with advantage to White, Tseshkovsky-Kasparov, USSR (ch) 1978.
14 . . . ♗e7?! is bad. After 15 ♔b1 *(15 ♗f4!? ♕a5 ∞)* 15 . . . c5 16 ♗f4 ♕c6 17 ♘xf6 ♗xf6 18 ♖he1! a6 *(18 . . . ♖he8 19 ♕a3 a6 20 ♗e3! ± Nunn-Portisch, Budapest (c) 1987)* 19 ♕a3! *(19 ♕e3?! cxd4! 20 ♘xd4 ♕b6 21 ♕c3+ ♕c5 22 ♖e3 b6! ∞ Nunn)* 19 . . . c4 *(19 . . . cxd4?! 20 ♘xd4 ♕c5 21 b4! Nunn)* 20 ♕a5! Black has problems

due to the weakness of the dark squares around his king. ± (Nunn).

15 ♕xe4   . . .

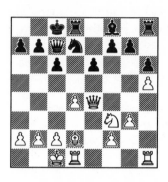

This position can be reached via a number of different move orders.

A1.211: 15 . . . ♗e7
A1.212: 15 . . . ♗d6

A1.211

15 . . .   ♗e7

Others:
a) **15 . . . c5?!** 16 ♗f4 ♗d6 17 ♗xd6 ♕xd6 18 ♘e5 ♘xe5 19 dxe5 ♕a6 *(19 . . . ♕e7 ±)* 20 a3 ♖xd1+ 21 ♖xd1 ± Adorján-Orsó, Hungary (ch) 1977.
b) **15 . . . ♘f6** 16 ♕e2 ♗d6 *(16 . . . c5 17 dxc5 ♗xc5 18 ♖h4 ♔h8? − 18 . . . ♘d5! − 19 ♗f4 ♗d6 20 ♖xd6! ♖xd6 21 ♘e5 ± Tal-Hübner, Montreal 1979)* 17 ♘e5 c5 18 ♖h4 ♗b8 *(18 . . . cxd4?! 19 ♖xd4 ♗xe5? 20 ♖c4; 18 . . . ♗xe5 19 dxe5 ±)* 19 ♘c4 ♔a8 20 ♕f3! *(20*

♗a5?! b6 21 ♗d2 ♕c6 22 dxc5 ♗xc5
♗xc5 23 ♘e5 ♕b7 = *Toskov-*
Skembris, Geneva 1989) 20 . . . ♘d5 21
♗a5 b6 22 ♘xd6 ♖xd6 23 dxc5 ♖c6
24 cxb6 ♖xc2+ *(24 . . . axb6 25 ♗c3!?)*
25 ♔b1 ♕b7 26   ♖f4! ± O'Donnel-
Vranesic, Toronto 1990.

16 ♔b1   ♖he8
17 ♕e2   . . .

Geller–Hort,   Skopje   1968
continued 17 c4 c5 18 ♗f4 ♗d6 19
♘e5 ♘xe5?! *(19 . . . ♖e7! is probably*
preferable) 20 dxe5 and White
ultimately won — see illustrative
games for the complete moves.

17 . . .   ♗f8!?

17 . . . ♗d6 18 ♖he1 ♘f6 *(18 . . .*
♖e7?! 19 c4 c5 20 ♗c3 ♘f6 21 ♘e5
cxd4 Kasparov–Vukić, Skara 1980, 22
♗xd4! ♗xe5 23 ♗xe5 ♖xd1+ 24
♖xd1 ♕c6 25 g4 ♖d7 26 ♖e1! ±
Kasparov) 19 ♘e5 c5 20 dxc5 *(20*
♗c1!? ± Kasparov) 20 . . . ♗xe5 21
♕xe5 ♕xe5 22 ♖xe5 ♖d4 23 ♔c1 ±
Geller–Kasparov, USSR (ch) 1978.

18 ♗c1   ♗d6
19 ♖he1   ♕a5
20 ♘d2 ± . . .

20 . . . ♘f6 21 g4 ♗c7 23 ♘b3?! *(22 c4!)*
22 . . . ♕d5 23 f3 *(23 c4 ♕g2!)* 23 . . .
♗g3?! *(23 . . . b5! 24 a4 ♕c4 =)* 24 ♖g1
♕d6 25 ♘d2 ± Timman–Portisch,
Antwerp (c) 1989 — White has the

slightly better grip on the central
squares.

A1.212

15 . . .   ♗d6

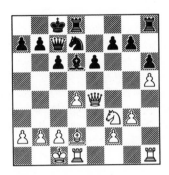

16 c4   c5
17 ♗c3   . . .

Alternatively:
a) 17 ♔b1 ♖he8 *(17 . . . a6 18 d5*
♘f6 19 ♕c2 ±) 18 ♗c3 ♘f6 19 ♕e2
♕c6!? *(19 . . . ♖e7 20 ♘e5 ±*
Gheorghiu–Benkö, Palma de Mallorca
1968) 20 ♖h4! *(20 ♘e5? ♗xe5 21 dxe5*
♘e4 ∓; 20 dxc5 ♗xc5 21 ♘e5 ♕e4+ 22
♕xe4 ♘xe4 23 ♘xf7 ♖xd1+ 24 ♖xd1
♖f8; ∓) 20 . . . ♗c7 21 ♘e5 ♗xe5 22
♕xe5 ♖d7 23 ♖c1 cxd4 24 ♗xd4 b6
(de Firmian–Adianto, San Francisco
1987) 25 ♕f4! ♖ed8 26 ♗xf6 gxf6 27
♕xh6 ♖d1 28 ♕e3 ± (Adianto).
b) 17 ♕e2 ♘f6 18 ♗c3 cxd4 19
♘xd4 a6 20 ♔b1 *(20 ♘b3; 20 ♖d2!?)*
20 . . . ♖d7 21 g4 *(21 ♘b3 ♕c6 =)*
21 . . . ♖hd8 22 ♘b3 ♗f4 23 ♖xd7

♕xd7 24 ♗xf6? gxf6 25 ♔c2 ♕a4! 26 ♕e4 ♗e5 27 ♔b1 ♕b4 28 f4 *(28 g5? ♖d2! 0-1 Renet-Miles, Cannes 1989)* 28 . . . ♗c7 ∓.

c) **17 d5!? ♘f6** *(17 . . . e5 18 ♘h4 ±;* **17 . . . ♖he8** *18 ♗c3 exd5 19 ♕xd5 ♘e5 – 19 . . . ♗e5! = – 20 ♖he1! ±; 20 ♕e4 ♘xf3 21 ♕xf3 f6 ± Alvanov-Miles, Philadelphia 1989;* **17 . . . exd5** *18 ♕xd5 ♘f6 19 ♕f5+ ♕d7 20 ♘h4 ± Tivyakov;* **18 . . . ♘b6!?** *19 ♕f5+ ♔b8 19 ♗a5 g6!? 20 hxg6 fxg6 21 ♕xg6 ♕c6 22 ♕h5 ♕a4 ∞ Solomon-Adianto, Sydney 1991)* 18 ♕c2 exd5 *(18 . . . ♖he8 19 ♗c3! exd5 20 ♗xf6 gxf6 21 ♖xd5 ± Tivyakov)* 19 cxd5 ♖he8 20 ♗c3 ♔b8!? (Tivyakov-Miles, Moscow 1989) 21 ♗xf6 gxf6 22 ♘h4 ± (Tivyakov).

A1.2121: 17 . . . cxd4
A1.2122: 17 . . . ♘f6

A1.2121

17 . . .   cxd4
18 ♗xd4

18 ♘xd4 ♘c5 *(18 . . . ♕xc4?? 19 ♘f5!)* 19 ♕c2 a6 20 ♖he1 ♗e7 21 ♔b1 ♗f6 22 ♘b3 = *(22 f4?! ♖d7 ∓ Hjartarson-Timman, Amsterdam 1989)*.
18 ♕xd4 ♗c5 19 ♕xg7 ♗xf2 ∞.

18 . . .   ♘f6

18 . . . ♕xc4+ 19 ♔b1 ♘f6 *(19 . . . ♘c5? 21 ♕e3 ♔b8 22 ♗xg7 ±)* 20 ♖c1

(20 ♕e3 ♘g4 21 ♕e1 ♔b8 22 ♗xg7 ♖hg8) 20 . . . ♘xe4 21 ♖xc4+ ♔b8 *(21 . . . ♔d7 22 ♗xg7 ♖hg8 23 ♗d4 ±)* 22 ♗xg7 ♖hg8 23 ♖xe4 ♖xg7 24 ♖d1 ± (Hübner).

19 ♕e2   ♕a5
20 ♔b1   ♕f5+!

20 . . . ♗c7?! 21 c5 ♕a4 *(21 . . . ♖d5 22 ♗xf6 ♖xd1+ 23 ♖xd1 gxf6 25 ♕c4 ♖d8 26 ♖c1 ♖d5 ± – Hübner)* 22 b3 ♕c6 23 ♘e5 ♗xe5 24 ♗xe5 Hübner-Hjartarsson, Barcelona 1989; 24 . . . ♖xd1+ ±.

21 ♔a1   ♗c7

21 . . . ♗b8!? ∞ Hellers-Milev, Biel 1989.

22 ♗xa7   ♖xd1+

22 . . . b6?, 23 c5! embarrasses.

23 ♖xd1   ♕xh5

Hübner views this position as unclear, though White seems to have a slight edge due to Black's partially exposed king.

A1.2122

17 . . .   ♘f6

17 ♖he8 18 ♔b1 ♔b8 *(18 . . . ♘f6 19 ♕e2 ♕c6 20 ♖h4 ♗c7 21 ♘e5 ♗xe5 22 ♕xe5 ± de Firmian-Adianto,*

San Francisco 1987) 19 dxc5 ♘xc5 20 ♕c2 f6 21 ♘d4 a6 22 ♖he1 e5 23 ♘f5 ♗f8 (Kruppa–Karpman, USSR 1990) 24 g4!? (±).

18 ♕e2   cxd4
19 ♘xd4   . . .

19 ♗xd4 ♕a5 20 ♔b1 ♕f5+! see A1.2121.

19 . . .   a6
20 ♘f3   ♖d7
21 ♘e5!

White stands slightly better: 21 . . . ♗xe5 22 ♗xe5 ♕a5 23 a3 ♖hd8 24 ♖xd7 ♘xd7 25 ♗c3 ♕g5+ *(25 . . . ♕f5!?)* 26 ♕d2! ± de Firmian–Miles, Biel 1989.

A1.22

14 . . .   ♘c5!?
15 ♘xc5   ♗xc5

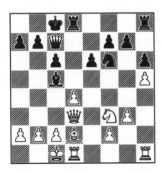

16 ♕e2   . . .

The following are rare replies:

a) **16 ♗f4** *(16 c4 ± is given by Tseshkovsky in* Informator*)* 16 . . . ♗d6 17 ♗e5 ♗xe5 18 ♘xe5 c5 19 ♕c4 ♖d5 20 f4 ♘e4 = Velikov-Podgaets, USSR 1968.

b) **16 c3 ♗d6** 17 ♕e2 ♘d7 18 c4 c5 19 ♗c3 cxd4 20 ♘xd4 a6 21 ♘b3 ♖hg8 22 ♖d2 ♗e7 = Kapengut-Podagets, USSR 1970.

c) **16 ♖h4 ♗d6** 17 ♕e2 ♖d7 18 ♘e5 ♗xe5 19 dxe5 ♘d5 = Suetin-Shamkovich, Tbilisi 1969.

d) **16 ♔b1 ♖he8** *(16 . . . ♗d6 17 c4 c5 18 ♖c1 – 18 ♗c3 a6 and . . . cxd4 = Trifunovic – 18 . . . b6 19 ♕e2 ♕b7 = I. Zaitsev-Petrosian, USSR 1968)* 17 c4 a6! *(17 . . . ♗b6?! 18 b4! ±; 17 . . . ♗d6 18 ♗c3 c5 19 ♕e2 ±)* 18 ♗f4 ♗d6 19 ♗xd6 ♖xd6 20 c5 ♖d5 21 ♘e5 ♘d7!? 22 ♘xf7 ♘xc5 23 ♕g6 ♖f8 24 ♘xh6! (Yudasin-Henkin, Podolsk 1989) 24 . . . ♖f6! 25 ♕c2 ♖xh6 26 dxc5 ♕e5! =.

e) **16 ♕c4 ♗d6** 17 ♕a4 ♔b8 18 ♘e5 ♘d5 19 f4 ♘b6 20 ♕b3 ♗xe5 21 dxe5 ♘d5 (Ljubojević-Karpov, Linares 1981) 22 ♕f3 ♖d7 23 ♕g4 ♖hd8 24 ♕xg7 ♕b6 25 ♕g4 ♘e3 =.

f) **16 c4 ♗d6** *(16 . . . ♗b6 17 ♔b1 c5?! 18 ♗f4 ♕e7 19 d5 ♖he8 20 ♖he1 ♕f8 21 ♘e5 ♗c7 – de Firmian-Miles, Tunis 1985 – 22 ♕a2! ±; 17 ♗c3 ♖he8 = Tal-Miles, Bugojno 1984)* 17 ♗c3 ♔b8 *(17 . . . c5 18 d5 ±)* 18 ♕e2 ♔a8 *(18 . . . c5 19 dxc5 ♗xc5 20 b4 ♗d6 21 c5 ∞ or 20 ♗e5 ♗d6 21 ♖xd6 ♖xd6 22 ♗xd6 ♕xd6 23 ♘e5 ± Karpov)* 19 ♔b1 b5!? 20 cxb5 *(20 d5 cxd5! 21*

♗xf6 gxf6 22 cxd5 ♕c4!? 23 ♕xc4
bxc4 24 dxe6 fxe6 25 ♘d4 ♗c5 26
♘xe6 ♖xd1+ 27 ♖xd1 ♗xf2 28 g4
♖g8 ∞ Karpov) 20 . . . ♖b8 (20 . . .
cxb5!?) 21 bxc6♕xc6 22 ♖c1 ♕d5!=
Sax–Karpov, Haninge 1990.

16 . . .   ♗xd4

16 . . . ♗b6 and now:
a) **17 ♗f4!?** ♕e7 18 c4 ♖he8 19
♕e5 ♗c7 20 ♕xc7+ ♕xc7 21 ♗xc7
♔xc7 22 ♖h4 ± Karpov–Miles,
Amsterdam 1985.
b) **17 ♖h4** ♖d7 18 c4 c5 19 ♗c3 ±.
c) **17 c3** ♕e7 18 ♘e5 ♔b8 (19 f4 c5
20 dxc5 ♗xc5 21 g4 ♕c7 = Geller–
Campora, Bern 1987; 19 ♖h4!?) 19 . . .
♘d7 20 ♘xd7+ ♕xd7 21 ♕e5+ ♗c7
22 ♕xg7 ♕d5 23 ♕f6 ♕xa2 24 ♗xh6
e5 25 ♗e3 exd4 26 cxd4 c5 = Geller–
Campora, Amsterdam 1987.

17 ♗f4   e5

Only move!

18 ♗xe5   . . .

18 ♘xe5 ♖he8!

18 . . .	**♗xe5**
19 ♘xe5	**♖xd1+**
20 ♖xd1	**♖d8**
21 ♖f1!?	**. . .**

21 ♖e1?! ♖d4!

21 . . .   ♕e7

21 . . . ♖d4 22 f4! ♕a5 23 a3 ±.

22 ♖e1   . . .

White stands slightly better: 22 . . .
♕e6 23 b3 ♖d4 24 f3! ♘d7! 25 ♘g4
(25 ♘c4 ±) 25 . . . ♕xe2 26 ♖xe2 ♖d5!
27 ♖e8+ ♔c7 28 f4! ± Kruppa–
Henkin, Minsk 1990.

A2

8 ♗d3   . . .

The old-fashioned way. It commits
White less and is also less ambitious
than 8 h5! which aims at completely
blocking the opposition's kingside.

8 . . .	**♗xd3**
9 ♕xd3	**♕c7**

Black hurries to prevent 10 ♗f4
although 9 . . . ♘gf6 10 ♗f4 ♕a5+ 11
♗d2 ♕c7 also leads to the main
variation. **10 ♗d2** e6 **11 0-0-0** is
illustrative game 25, Lasker–Lee.

Dubious, however, is **9 . . . e6** 10 ♗f4
♘gf6?! 11 0-0-0 ♘d5 12 ♗d2 b5 *(Safe-guarding against 13 c4)* 13 ♔b1 ♗e7
(13 . . . ♗d6 14 ♘e4 ♘7f6 15 ♖hg1
♖b8 16 g4 b4 17 ♘xd6+ ♕xd6 18 g5
♘d7 19 ♖de1 ± Matanović-Wade,
Opatija 1953) 14 ♘h5 ♗f6 15 g4 g6 16
♘xf6+ ♘5xf6 17 g5 ± Suetin-
Kasparian, USSR 1952.

10 ♗d2   . . .

Castling queenside is the logical
follow-up to White's h-pawn advance
on move seven.

10 . . .   ♘gf6

10 . . . e6 is possible, viz. 11 0-0-0
0-0-0 12 ♕b3 ♘gf6 13 ♕a4 ♔b8 14
♗a5 ♘b6 15 ♗xb6 axb6 16 ♘e5 ♗d6
17 ♖he1 b5 18 ♕b3 ♗xe5 19 dxe5 =
Zapata-Miles, Wijk aan Zee 1987.

11 0-0-0   e6
12 c4!?   . . .

The alternative **12 ♖he1** has been
long neglected, but being both a
sound and natural move it is probably
no worse than other tries − see the
illustrative game Lasker-Lee at the
end of this chapter.

Instead **12 ♔b1** is quite frequently
only a transposition of moves with
the text, although it does prevent the
manoeuvre ♗f8-d6-f4, e.g. 12 . . .
0-0-0 13 c4 *(13 ♗c1?! c5 14 ♕e2 c4! 15*
♘e5 ♘b6 16 c3 ♗d6 ∓ Ljubojević-

Miles, Dubai (ol) 1986) 13 . . . ♗d6 14
♘e4 ♘xe4 *(14 . . . ♗f4 15 ♗b4!?)* 15
♕xe4 ♘f6 16 ♕e2 c5 *(16 . . . ♖he8 17*
♗c3 ♕e7 Pilnik-Golombek, Budapest
1952, 18 ♘e5 ±) 17 ♗c3 cxd4 18 ♘xd4
a6 19 ♘f3 ± Trifunović.

12 . . .   0-0-0

12 . . . ♗d6 leads to the exchange of
dark-squared bishops, 13 ♘e4 ♗f4 14
♔b1 ♘xe4 15 ♕xe4 ♗xd2 16 ♖xd2
0-0-0 17 ♖hd1 ♔b8?! 18 g3 ♘f6 19
♕e2 ± Timoschenko-Podgaets, Lvov
1977. The value of **12 . . . b5?!** 13 cxb5
cxb5+ 14 ♔b1 ♕b7 15 ♖he1 ♗e7
16 ♖e1 a6 17 ♘e5 ± Kasparian-
Smyslov, USSR 1947, is doubtful.

13 ♗c3   . . .

Or:

a) 13 ♘e4 ♘g4 14 ♕e2 ♘df6 15
♘xf6 gxf6 16 h5 ♖g8 17 ♔b1 ♗e7 18
♗c1 f5 ∞ Vukčević-Matanović,
Yugoslavia 1958.

b) 13 ♕e2 ♗d6 14 ♘e4 ♗f4 = (!?)
Trifunović.

c)13 ♔b1 c5 14 ♕e2 *(14 ♗e3 is the*
text) 14 . . . ♗d6 *(If 14 . . . a6 15 ♘e5*
♘xe5 16 dxe5 ♘d7 17 f4 ♘b8 18 ♗c3
± Parma-Barcza, Kapfenberg 1970, or
14 . . . cxd4 15 ♘xd4 a6 16 ♘b3 ♗d6 17
c5! ♗xg3 18 ♗a5 ♕e5 19 ♕c2 ♖de8
20 c6 ♘b8 21 cxb7+ ♔xb7 22 fxg3 ±
Parma-Vukić, Yugoslavia 1972) 15
♘e4 ♘xe4 16 ♕xe4 ♘f6 17 ♕e2 a6
(17 . . . cxd4 18 ♘xd4 a6 19 ♗c3 − 19
♘b3!? − ♗c5 20 ♘b3 ♖xd1+ 21 ♖xd1

♖*d8 22* ♖*xd8+* = *Matulović–Kolarov, Havana (ol) 1966)* 18 ♗c3 ♖he8 19 ♖he1 cxd4 20 ♘xd4 ♗c5 = Parma–Ivkov, Yugoslavia 1964.

13 . . .   c5

13 . . . ♗d6 is also a possibility, e.g. 14 ♘e4 ♗f4+ 15 ♔b1 ♘e5 16 ♘xe5 ♗xe5 17 ♕e3 ♘xe4 18 dxe5 *(18 ♕xe4 ♗f6 19 ♖d2 ♖d7 ±)* 18 . . . ♖xd1+ 19 ♖xd1 ♖d8 = Szabó–Barcza, Leningrad 1967.

14 ♔b1   cxd4

Instead 14 . . . ♗d6 15 ♘e4 ♘xe4 16 ♕xe4 ♘f6 17 ♕e2 a6 18 ♘e5 is assessed as equal by Fine.

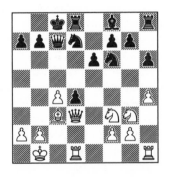

After the text move White now continued with the hapless innovation **15 ♗xd4?!** in the game Pogáts–Portisch, Hungary (ch) 1961 and Black went on to seize the initiative after 15 . . . ♗c5 16 ♕e2 ♗xd4 17 ♖xd4? ♘b8! – see illustrative games.

White can still pose Black more problems with **15 ♘xd4**, e.g. 15 . . . a6 *(15 . . . ♘c5 16 ♕e2 ♘a4 17 ♘b5 ♘xc3+ 18 ♘xc3 ♖d1+ 19 ♖xd1 a6 20 h5 ± Padevsky–Barcza, Kecskemét 1966)* 16 ♘f3 *(The prime goal is to keep control of e5. Other possibilities are* **16 ♘b3** *♘c5 17* ♕*f3 ♗e7 18 ♗a5* ♖*xd1+ 19* ♖*xd1* ♕*e5 20 ♗c3* ♕*c7* = *Spassky–Portisch, 1961, or* **16** ♕*e2* ♗*d6 17 ♘e4 ♗xe4 18* ♕*xe4 ♘c5 19* ♕*c2 ♗e5 20* ♖*he1 ♗f6 21 g3* ♖*d7* = *Unzicker–Porath, Munich (ol) 1958)* 16 . . . ♗c5 17 ♕e2 ♗d6 *(17 . . . ♘g4 18 ♘e4 ♘df6 19 ♘xf6 gxf6 20 ♘d4* ♖ *hg8 21 b4* ♕*e5* = *Sokolov–Sušić, Yugoslavia 1965)* 18 ♘e4 ♗e7 *(18 . . . ♘xe4 19* ♕*xe4 ♘f6 20* ♕*e2* ♕*c6 21* ♖*de1 ♗c7 22 ♘d4 ± Trifunović)* 19 ♘xf6 ♗xf6 20 ♗xf6. Black now suffered some disadvantage after **20 . . . ♘xf6?!** 21 ♘e5! during one of the Spassky v Petrosian 1966 World Championship games. But it was later felt that **20 . . . gxf6** followed by . . . ♘e5 should equalize.

B

6 ♘f3   . . .

A quieter continuation than the classical main line (with 6 h4) that we have just explored.

6 . . .   ♘d7

Care needs to be taken over the

sequence of moves, e.g.:

a) **6 ... e6?** 7 h4! h6 *(7 ... ♘f6 8 h5 ♗e4 9 ♘xe4 ♘xe4 10 ♗d3 ♘f6 11 ♕e2 ±)* 8 ♘e5 ♗h7 9 ♗c4 ♘d7 10 ♕e2 ♘xe5 11 dxe5 ♗e7 12 ♗d2 ♕b6 *(12 ... ♗xc2 13 ♗c3 ♗g6 14 ♖d1 ♕c7 15 h5 ♗h7 16 f4 ± Zavernias-Filipov, USSR 1962)* 13 0-0-0 ±.

b) **6 ... ♘f6?!** 7 h4 h6 *(7 ... ♘h5 8 ♘e2! ♘bd7 9 g4 ♘hf6 10 h5 ♗e4 11 ♘g3 ♕a5+ 12 ♗d2 ♕d5 13 ♗g2 ♗xf3 14 ♕xf3 ♕xd4 15 g5 ♘d5 16 0-0-0 ± Suetin-Ratner, USSR 1951; or 8 ♗c4!? ♘xg3 9 fxg3 e6 10 ♗f4 ♘d7 – 10 ... ♗d6!? – 11 ♕e2 ♗h5?! 12 0-0-0 ♘b6 – 12 ... ♗e7!? ± – 13 d5!! cxd5 14 ♗b5+ ♔e7 15 ♖he1 ± Sznapik-Izeta, Salamanca 1988; 11 ... ♘b6 12 h5! ♗f5 13 ♗b3 ±)* 8 ♘e5 ♗h7 9 ♗c4 e6 10 ♕e2 ♘d5 11 ♗b3 ♘d7 12 ♗d2 ♘7f6 13 0-0-0 Bély-Clarke, Moscow (ol) 1956 gives White good chances.

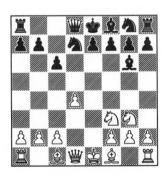

Here White has

B1: 7 ♗d3
B2: 7 ♗c4!?

In response to 7 h4 Black can play 7 ... h6, transposing to the main line in variation A, or he can try 7 ... h5, e.g. **8 ♗d3 ♗xd3 9 ♕xd3 e6 10 ♘e4 ♕a5+ 11 ♗d2 ♕f5 12 0-0-0 0-0-0 13 ♗e3 ♘h6** and Black equalized easily in Karpov-Larsen, Bugojno 1978. An improvement may be **10 ♗d2 ♘gf6 11 0-0-0 ♕c7 12 ♘g5 ±** Kasparov-Sakharov. Perhaps also White can try **8 ♗g5!? ♕b6 9 ♗d3 ♗xd3 10 ♕xd3 ♘gf6 11 0-0-0 e6 12 ♘e5 ♗e7 13 ♖he1 ♘xe5 14 dxe5 ♖d8 15 ♕f3 ♖xd1+ 16 ♖xd1 ♘g4 17 ♘xh5 ±** as in Kapengut-Bikhovsky, USSR 1979.

B1

7 ♗d3   e6

7 ... ♗xd3 prevents the doubling of the pawns, but the slight disadvantage in space remains: 8 ♕xd3 e6 9 0-0 ♘gf6 10 ♗f4 ♗e7 11 ♖fe1 0-0 12 c4 ♖e8 13 ♖ad1 etc. (±). A second alternative is 7 ... ♕a5+?! 8 ♗d2 ♕c7 9 ♗xg6 hxg6 10 ♕e2 e6 11 ♘e4 0-0-0?! 12 g3! c5 13 ♗f4 ♕c6 14 0-0-0 c4 15 ♘c3 ♘h6 16 d5! +– Spassky-Larsen, Bugojno 1978.

8 0-0   ...

An immediate exchange of bishops leads to the same continuation, unless White intends to castle queenside after 8 ♗xg6 hxg6 9 ♕e2 ♘gf6. For instance: 10 ♗d2 ♕c7 11 0-0-0 ♗d6 12 ♔b1 0-0-0 = Fuderer-

Golombek, Belgrade 1952.

8 ...   ⚘gf6

It is perhaps less passive to go for queenside castling. 8 ... ♛c7!? 9 c4 0-0-0 *(9 ... ⚘gf6 10 ♗xg6 hxg6 11 ♛e2 ♗d6 12 ♖d1 0-0 13 ⚘e4 ♗f4 ± Geller-Matulović, USSR v Yugoslavia 1964)* 10 ♗xg6 hxg6 11 ♛a4 ♚b8 12 b4 ⚘h6 13 ♛b3 ⚘f5 14 a4 e5 15 dxe5 ⚘xe5 16 ⚘xe5 ♛xe5 17 ♗b2 ♛c7 ∞ Dückstein-Petrosian, Varna (ol) 1962.

After the text White retains his space advantage, as is usual with the Caro-Kann Defence, but the black position is solid. For **9 c4** now see the illustrative game Spassky-Karpov, Leningrad 1974, which is a good example of these factors. A more recent example, however, is 9 ... ♗d6 10 ♖e1 0-0 11 ♗xg6 hxg6 12 ⚘e4 ⚘xe4 13 ♖xe4 ♖e8 14 ♗g5 ⚘f6 (=) 15 ♖h4!? e5! 16 dxe5 ♗xe5 17 ⚘xe5 ♖xe5 18 ♗e3 c5 19 ♛f3 ♛c8! 20 ♗f4 ♖e8 ∞ van der Wiel-Korchnoi, OHRA 1989. Also possible is **9 ♖e1** ♗e7 10 c4 *(10 ♗g5 ±)* 10 ... 0-0 *(10 ... ♗xd3 11 ♛xd3 0-0 12 ♗d2 ♛c7 13 ♗c3 ♖fe8 14 ♖ad1 ♖ad8 15 ♛e2 c5 16 dxc5 ♗xc5 17 b4 ♗e7 18 ♖c1 ± Unzicker-Golombek, Stockholm 1952)* 11 ♗xg6 hxg6 12 ♗f4 ♖e8 13 ♛c2 c5 14 ♖ad1 cxd4 15 ⚘xd4 ♗b4 16 ♗d2 ♗xd2 17 ♛xd2 a6 18 b4 ± Najdorf-Kotov, Zürich (c) 1953.

B2

7 ♗c4!?   e6
8 0-0   ...

White's somewhat rare seventh move was successful in Kholmov-Kasparov, Daugavpils 1978, after 8 ♛e2 ♛c7 9 0-0 0-0-0 10 c3 ⚘gf6 11 ♖e1 ♗e7 12 a4 ⚘d5 13 a5 a6 14 ♗d2 ♖he8 15 b4 ±. Castling queenside looks like a risky idea for Black.

In two later games Black reached an equal game quite easily by castling kingside:

8 ...   ⚘gf6
9 ♛e2   ...

9 ♗b3 ♗d6 10 ♛e2 ♛c7 11 ♖e1 0-0 12 ⚘e5 c5 13 ⚘xg6 hxg6 14 ♗e3 ♖ad8 15 ♖ad1 ⚘b6 16 dxc5 ♗xc5 17 ♗xc5 ♛xc5 18 ⚘e4 ♛e5 ± Torre-Vukić, Biel 1977.

9 ...   ♗e7

9 ... ♗d6 10 ⚘e5! 0-0? 11 ♗xe6! +−.

10 ♖e1   ...

10 ⚘e5 ⚘xe5 11 dxe5 ⚘d7 12 ♖d1 ♛c7 13 ♗d3 0-0-0 = Panov-Ebralidze, USSR 1937.

10 ...   0-0

10 ... ⚘d5 11 ♗b3 0-0 *(11 ... b5 12*

a4! b4 13 a5 ±) 12 c4 *(12 ♗d2 a5 13 a4*
♖*e8 14* ♖*ad1* ♕*c7 = Puc-Kozomara,*
Yugoslavia 1960) 12 . . . ♘b4 13 a3
♘d3 14 ♖d1 ♘xc1 ± Trifunović.

11 c3   ♕c7

a) **12 ♗d2** ♖ae8 13 ♖d1 ♗c2 14
♖c1 ♗f5 15 ♖cd1 ♗c2 16 ♖c1 ½-½,
Sigurjonsson-Hübner, Munich 1979.

b) **12 ♗g5** (Hübner's attempted
White improvement on the previous
game) 12 . . . h6 13 ♗h4 ♖ad8 14
♖ad1 ♖fe8 15 ♖d2 ♗h7 16 ♘f1 ♘e4
and Black had active play in Hübner-
Portisch, Montreal 1979.

C

6 ♘h3   . . .

And here:
a) **6 . . . ♘f6** 7 ♘f4 e5 8 ♘xg6
(8 dxe5 ♕*a5+ 9 ♗d2* ♕*xe5+ 10 ♗e2*
♕*xb2 11 ♘xg6 hxg6 12* ♖*b1 ±; for*
8 . . . ♕*xd1+ 9* ♔*xd1* ♘*g4 10 ♘xg6 see*
text) 8 . . . hxg6 9 dxe5 ♕xd1+ 10
♔xd1 ♘g4 11 ♘e4 ♘xe5 12 ♗e2 f6
(12 . . . ♗e7 13 ♗e3 0-0 14 g3 ♘bd7 ±)
13 c3 ♘bd7 14 ♗e3 0-0-0 15 ♔e2 ♘b6
Fischer-Foguelman, Buenos Aires
1960. 16 a4 ±.

b) **6 . . . e6** 7 ♘f4 *(7 c3 ♗d6 8 ♗e2*
♘*e7 9 0-0 0-0 10 ♘f4 ♘d7 11 ♘xg6*
♘*xg6 12 ♗d3* ♕*h4 = was a game Bird*
and Blackburne v Bardeleben and
Weiss, 1888!) 7 . . . ♗d6 *(7 . . .* ♕*h4 8*
♗*e2 ♘d7 9 ♗e3 ♗d6 10* ♕*d2* ♕*e7 11*

♘xg6 hxg6 12 ♘e4 ♗c7 13 c4 ±
Novopashin-Furman, USSR 1963 or 8
♕*e2 ♘d7 9 c3 0-0-0 10 ♘xg6 hxg6 11*
♘*e4* ♕*e7 12 ♗g5 ± Ragozin-Flohr,*
Moscow 1935) 8 c3 *(8 ♘xg6 hxg6 9 ♗c4*
♕*c7 10 ♘e3 ∞)* 8 . . . ♘f6 9 h4 ♕c7
10 h5 ♗xf4 11 ♗xf4 ♕xf4 12 hxg6
fxg6 13 ♕d2 ♕xd2+ 14 ♔xd2 ♘bd7
15 ♖e1 ♔f7 16 ♗c4 ♖ae8 ∞
Boleslavsky-Petrosian, Zürich (c)
1953.

D

6 ♗c4   . . .

6 . . .   e6

This is perhaps more exact than
6 . . . ♘d7 7 ♘f3!? *(7 ♘e2 comes*
into consideration, since 7 . . . e5
can then be answered by 8 f4!) 7 . . .
♘f6 8 0-0 e6 transposing into
variation B2.

7 ♘1e2   . . .

7 ♘h3 keeps fewer options open.

7 ...   ♘f6

One of the games we are following is Keres–Golombek from Moscow 1956. Keres's line of play after this move created such a profound psychological effect that even this natural move was given a question mark in the tournament records, and 7 . . . ♗d6 indicated as a better alternative. Yet this is far more perilous because of 8 h4! h6 9 ♘f4 ♗xf4 *(9 . . . ♗h7 10 ♘fh5!)* 10 ♗xf4 ♘f6 11 h5 *(11 ♕d2 ♘bd7 12 0-0-0 ♘d5?! 13 ♖de1 ± Tal–Botvinnik, Moscow 1960; 12 . . . ♘b6!? 13 ♗b3 a5 ∞ Geller)* 11 . . . ♗h7 12 ♕e2 ♘bd7 13 0-0-0 ♘d5 14 ♗d2 ♘7f6 15 ♗d3 ♗xd3 16 ♕xd3 ♕c7 17 ♔b1 0-0-0 18 ♖h4 ♕e7 19 c4 ± Geller–Bagirov, USSR 1959.

8 ♘f4   ...

8 h4 h6 9 ♘f4 ♗h7 10 0-0 ♗d6 transposes to variation E, while a major sideline here is **8 0-0** ♗d6 *(8 . . . ♘bd7!? 9 f4?! ♘b6 10 ♗b3 c5 ∞ Dely–Flórián, Hungary (ch) 1958 or 9 ♗b3 ♘b6 10 ♘f4 ♗d6 11 ♖e1 Westerinen–Pomar, Spain 1970 and now 11 . . . ♕c7 =)* 9 f4 when:

a) **9 . . . ♕c7?!** – White is planning to open the f-file as soon as possible and launch a kingside attack, and with this move Black tries to counter with an indirect attack against h2. How-

ever, now comes 10 f5! *(10 ♔h1 ♘bd7 11 f5 is not bad either)* 10 . . . exf5 11 ♘xf5! when the Keres–Golombek illustrative game, mentioned previously, now continued with the error **11 . . . ♗xh2+?**. The better alternative was **11 . . . ♗xf5** 12 ♖xf5 ♘bd7 13 ♘g3 0-0-0 14 ♕f1 ± Fichtl–Golombek, Munich (ol) 1958.

b) **9 . . . ♘e4** 10 f5 ♗xg3 11 ♘xg3 ♘xg3 12 fxg6 ♘xf1 13 gxf7+ ♔xf7 14 ♕g4 ♖e8 15 ♗h6! ±.

c) **9 . . . ♗f5** 10 ♘xf5 exf5 11 ♘g3 g6 12 ♖e1+ ±.

d) **9 . . . ♕d7!** *(The best way to prevent f5 by White)* 10 ♗d3 *(10 f5?! exf5 11 ♗d3 ♘e4 ∓ or 10 ♔h1 h5 11 f5 exf5 12 ♘f4 ♗xf4 13 ♖xf4 h4 14 ♕e1+ ♔f8 15 ♘e2 h3 16 ♖h4 hxg2+ 17 ♔xg2 ♗h5 ∓ Eolian–Kasparov, USSR 1977)* 10 . . . ♗xd3 11 ♕xd3 g6 = Boleslavsky.

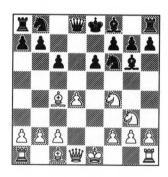

8 ...   ♗d6

8 . . . ♘d5?! 9 ♘xg6 hxg6 10 ♘e4 ♕h4 11 ♕e2 ♗e7 *(11 . . . ♘f6 12 ♘g5*

♛xd4? *13 ♘xf7!)* 12 ♗d2 ♘d7 13 0-0-0 ♘7f6 14 ♘g5 ± Boleslavsky.

9 ♗b3 . . .

Or:

a) **9 c3** ♛c7 10 ♛f3 ♘d5?! *(10 . . . ♘bd7!)* 11 ♘xg6 hxg6 12 ♘e4 ♗e7 13 g3 ♘d7 14 ♗d2 ♘7f6 15 ♘g5 ♗d6 16 0-0-0 0-0-0 17 ♔b1 ♘b6 ± Levitina-Kushnir, Dortmund 1977.

b) **9 ♘xg6** hxg6 10 ♘g5 ♘bd7 11 0-0 ♛a5 Tal-Botvinnik, USSR (m) 1960, 12 ♛d2 =.

c) **9 0-0** ♘d5! 10 ♘gh5 0-0 11 ♗b3 ♘d7 12 ♘xg6 hxg6 13 ♘g3 ♛h4 = Tal-Botvinnik, USSR (m) 1961.

9 . . . **♛c7**

9 . . . ♘d5?! 10 ♘xg6 hxg6 11 ♘e4 ♗e7 12 0-0 ♘d7 13 c4 ♘5f6 14 ♘g5 ♘h7 15 ♘f3 ♛c7 16 g3 c5 *(16 . . . 0-0-0 17 ♛e2 ♖he8 18 ♗f4 ♗d6 19 ♗e3! ±)* 17 d5 e5 18 ♗a4 ± Korchnoi-Petrosian, Stockholm (izt) 1962.

10 ♛f3 **♘bd7**
11 h4?! **. . .**

11 0-0 e5 12 ♘xg6 hxg6 13 ♖e1 0-0-0 14 ♗xf7 exd4 15 ♗xg6 ♘e5 16 ♗f5+ ♔b8 17 ♛d1 g6 18 ♗h3 ♘d5 ∞ Kotov-Antoshin, USSR 1963.

11 . . . **e5!**

An improvement on 11 . . . 0-0-0 12 h5 ♗f5 13 ♘xf5 ♛a5+ 14 c3 ♛xf5

15 ♛xd3 = Keres-Petrosian, Los Angeles 1963.

After the text move the game Rogers-Grószpéter, Groningen 1976-77 continued 12 ♘xg6 *(12 dxe5? ♘xe5 13 ♛e2 0-0-0! 14 h5 ♘eg4 15 hxg6 hxg6 16 ♖xh8 ♖xh8 17 ♛f3 ♘h2 ∓)* 12 . . . hxg6 13 ♗e3 0-0-0 14 0-0-0 *(14 ♗xf7?! exd4 15 ♗xd4 ♘e5 16 ♗e6+ ♔b8 ∞)* 14 . . . exd4 15 ♗xd4 ♘e5! 16 ♛c3?! c5 17 ♗xe5 ♗xe5 18 ♛c4 ♗d4 19 ♛xf7 ♗xf2 20 ♖xd8+ ♖xd8 21 ♛xc7+ ♔xc7 22 ♘f1 ♖d4 ∓.

E

6 ♘1e2 **. . .**

The knight is heading for f4, just as it does in the case of 6 ♘h3, but this is more accurate, since 6 . . . e5? is now an error after 7 dxe5 ♛xd1+ 8 ♔xd1 ♗c5 9 ♘f4! ♗xf2 10 ♘xg6 hxg6 11 ♘e4 ♗d4 12 ♘d6+ ♔e7 13 ♗c4 f6 14 ♘f7 ♖h5 15 c3! ♗b6 16 ♗f4 ♔f8 Prins-Szabó, Venice 1949, 17 g4! ±.

6 . . . **e6**

a) **6 . . . ♘d7** 7 h4 h6 8 ♘f4 ♗h7 9 ♗c4 e5 10 ♘d3! *(In one of the Tal-Botvinnik 1960 match games 10 ♛e2 ♛e7 11 dxe5 ♛xe5 12 ♗e3 ♗c5 = was played)* 10 . . . exd4 11 0-0 ± Tal.

b) **6 . . . ♘f6** 7 ♘f4 e5 8 ♘xg6 hxg6 9 dxe5 ♛xd1+?! *(9 . . . ♛a5+! =)* 10 ♔xd1 ♘g4 11 ♘e4 ♘xe5 12 ♗e2 f6 13 f4!? *(13 ♗f4 and 13 c3 are also worthy*

of consideration) 13 ... ♘f7 14 c3 ♘d7
15 ♔c2 0-0-0 16 ♗d2 ♖e8 17 ♗f3 ♘c5
18 ♖ae1 f5 19 ♘f2 ♗d6 20 ♖xe8+
♖xe8 21 g3 ± Suetin–Perelstein,
Warsaw 1989.

7 h4   h6

7 ... ♘f6?! 8 h5 ♗f5 9 ♘xf5 ♕a5+
10 c3 ♕xf5 11 ♘g3 ♕a5 12 ♗f4 ± Tal–
Bagirov, USSR 1964.

8 ♘f4   ♗h7
9 ♗c4   ♘f6
10 0-0   . . .

This same position could have
developed after 6 ♗c4 e6 7 ♘1e2 ♘f6
8 h4 h6 9 ♘f4 ♗h7 or 6 h4 h6 7 ♘1e2.
Here a Keres–Olafsson game (Bled
1961) went 10 ♕e2 ♗d6 11 c3 *(11 ♗e3
♘bd7? 12 ♘gh5 ♘xh5 13 ♘xh5 ♖g8
= Tal–Botvinnik, USSR 1960)* 11 . . .
♘bd7! 12 ♗xe6! fxe6 13 ♘xe6 ♕e7
14 ♘f5 ♗xf5 15 ♘xg7+ ♔f7 16 ♘xf5
and led to an advantage to White, but
later analysis showed that after **11 . . .
0-0!** Black would have had no
problems.
    An interesting line is **10 ♗b3** ♗d6
11 ♘fh5 0-0!? *(11 . . . ♖g8 12 ♗f4
♗xf4 13 ♘xf4 ♘bd7 14 ♕d2 ♕c7 15
0-0-0 0-0-0 = Ciocaltea–Botvinnik, Tel
Aviv (ol) 1964)* 12 ♗e3 ♘bd7 13
♕e2?! b5!? ∞ Lazzarato–Grószpéter,
Groningen 1977-78.
    Perhaps better is **10 c3** ♗d6 *(10 . . .
♘a6!?)* 11 ♘fh5 0-0 12 ♗g5!? ♗e7
(12 . . . hxg5? 13 hxg5 ♘d5 14 ♗xd5

*exd5 15 ♘f6+! gxf6 16 ♖xh7! ♔xh7 17
♕h5+ ♔g8 18 0-0-0 ♖e8 19 ♘f5 ±
Ravic–Scherba (corr) 1989)* 13 ♗f4 ±.

10 . . .   ♗d6

10 . . . ♘d5? 11 ♕e2! ♘xf4 12 ♗xf4
♕xd4?! 13 ♗xe6! ♕xf4 14 ♗f5+! ♗e7
15 ♗xh7 g6 16 ♖fe1 ♕c7 17 ♗xg6
fxg6 18 ♕e6 ♘a6 19 ♕xg6+ ♔f8 20
♖e3 +− Bárczay–Gy. Honfi,
Budapest 1977.

11 ♘xe6!?   . . .

Whether this is good or bad, it is
the logical result of White's play.

11 . . .   fxe6
12 ♗xe6   . . .

And now:
    a) **12 . . . ♖f8!?** 13 ♖e1 ♖f7 14 ♕f3
♔f8 15 ♗xf7 ♔xf7 16 ♕b3+ ♔f8
17 ♕xb7 ± Bárczay–P. Szilágyi,
Budapest 1965.
    b) **12 . . . ♔e7** 13 ♖e1 ♖e8 14

♗xh6?! *(14 ♗c8+ ♔f8 15 ♖xe8+ and 16 ♗xb7 ±)* 14 ... ♔f8? *(14...gxh6 ∞)* 15 ♘h5! gxh6 16 ♕f3! 1-0 Bárczay–Schneider, Hungary (ch) 1977.

c) 12 ... ♕c7? *(It was later shown that the correct sequence of moves is 12 ... ♘bd7! 13 ♖e1 ♕c7)* 13 ♖e1? *(13 ♘h5! would have taken advantage of Black's faulty move-order and given a powerful attack)* 13 ... ♘d7! *(Just keep calm!)* 14 ♗g8+ ♔f8 15 ♗xh7 ♖xh7 16 ♘f5! with a strong attack in Tal–Botvinnik, Moscow (m) 1960, which, however, Black managed to diffuse starting with 16 ... g6! See illustrative games.

It seems likely that given the correct move-order, the course taken in variation C is the most sensible for Black. The fact that this whole sub-variation with 6 ♘1e2 is quite rare in competition practice probably reinforces this conclusion.

ILLUSTRATIVE GAMES

22 SPASSKY–KARPOV

Candidates Match, Leningrad 1974

1 e4 c6 2 d4 d5 3 ♘c3 dxe4 4 ♘xe4 ♗f5 5 ♘g3 ♗g6 6 ♘f3 ♘d7 7 ♗d3 e6 8 0-0 ♘gf6 9 c4 ♗d6 10 b3 0-0 11 ♗b2 ♕c7 12 ♗xg6 hxg6 13 ♕e2 ♖fe8 (Having no centre pawn, Black has a space disadvantage. The break e6-e5 will not do, and if c6-c5, the b2 bishop's long diagonal would be opened and White would also end up with more material on the queenside.

On the other hand, it is difficult for White to build on his marginal advantage, as his opponent's pieces are solidly posted and show no weaknesses. So there is nothing left but to keep up constant pressure) 14 ♘e4! ♘xe4 15 ♕xe4 ♗e7 (15...e5 16 ♖ad1 ± or 16 c5 ♗f8 17 ♕h4 ±) 16 ♖ad1 ♖ad8 17 ♖fe1 ♕a5!? (Looking for counter-play. 17 ... ♗f6 was also possible) 18 a3 ♕f5 19 ♕e2! (Exchanging the queens brings no advantage, e.g.: 19 ♕xf5 gxf5 20 d5?! ♘c5!) 19 ... g5! (The logical consequence of his stratagem. After 19 ... ♗f6?! 20 h3 the threat is 21 d5! ±) 20 h3 (If 20 d5!? exd5 21 ♘d4 ♕g6 22 cxd5 cxd5 23 ♕b5 ±; best is 21 ... ♕e4! =) 20 ... g4 21 hxg4 ♕xg4 22 d5! (A long impending breakthrough) 22 ... cxd5 23 cxd5 e5! (If 23 ... exd5 24 ♖xd5 ± or 23 ... ♗f6 24 ♗xf6 ♘xf6 25 dxe6 ♕xe6 26 ♕xe6 fxe6 27 ♘g5 ±) 24 d6! (24 ♘xe5 ♕xe2 25 ♖xe2 ♗d6 26 ♖de1 ♘xe5 27 ♗xe5 ♗xa3 = or 24 ♕b5 ♗c5 − threatening ... e4 − 25 ♘xe5 ♘xe5 26 ♗xe5 ♗xf2+ 27 ♔xf2 ♖xe5 −+) 24 ... ♗f6 25 ♘d2?! (25 ♕b5! e4 26 ♘h2 ♕g5 27 ♖d5 ♕g6 28 ♗xf6 ♘xf6 29 ♖g5 ♕h6 ±; 25 ... b6 ±. Counting on the d-pawn and the knight about to move to e4, Spassky hopes to secure an advantage, but it soon transpires that Black has counterplay) 25 ... ♕xe2 (25 ... ♕e6!?) 26 ♖xe2 ♖c8 27 ♘e4? (Unimaginative. The knight, seemingly as strong as a horse, has nothing to attack, while the undermining of the d6 pawn slowly takes shape. 27 ♘c4, with even chances, was better) 27... ♗d8! (The picture is changing — now Black has the more active bishop) 28 g4 f6! (♔g8-f7-e6 is looming) 29 ♔g2 ♔f7 30 ♖c1?! (The more exchanges White forces, the weaker the d6 pawn becomes) 30 ... ♗b6 31 ♖ec2 ♖xc2 32 ♖xc2 ♔e6 33 a4 a5 34 ♗a3 (White has succeeded in buttressing up his advanced pawn, and it seems that he can look forward to the future free of worry and secure in the possession of the c-file) 34 ... ♖b8! (The beginning of a counter-plot on the b-file!) 35 ♖c4 (35 ♘d2!?) 35 ... ♗d4 36 f4 g6 37 ♘g3!? (Threatening 38 f5!) 37 ... exf4 38 ♖xd4 (38 ♘e2 ♗e5 39 ♘xf4 ♗xf4 40 ♖xf4 g5 threatening 41 ... b5 —+) 38 ... fxg3 39 ♔xg3 (39 g5 fxg5 40 ♔xg3 b5 —+) 39 ... ♖c8 40 ♖d3 (40 ♖c4 ♖xc4 41 bxc4 ♘b6 ∓) 40 ... g5! 41 ♗b2 b6 42 ♗d4 (42 ♖c3 ♖xc3 43 ♗xc3 ♔xd6 44 b4! ∞, 42 ... ♖h8! ∓) 42 ... ♖c6 43 ♗c3 ♖c5! (Simplification with 43 ... ♖xd6 44 ♖xd6+ ♔xd6 45 b4! would have been premature and only given drawing chances) 44 ♔g2 ♖c8 45 ♔g3 ♘e5 46 ♗xe5 fxe5 47 b4 (47 ♔f3 ♖f8+ 48 ♔e3 ♖d8 49 b4 ♖xd6 50 ♖b3 ♖d4! 51 bxa5 ♖xg4! 52 ♖xb6+ ♔f5 —+ or 48 ♔e4 ♖f4+ 49 ♔e3 ♔d7 —+ would only have added to Black's task from the point of view of technique) 47 ... e4! (47 ... axb4 48 d7 ♖d8 49 ♖b3 ♖xd7 ±) 48 ♖d4 ♔e5 49 ♖d1 axb4 50 ♖b1 (50 d7 ♖d8 51 ♔f2 b3 52 ♔e3 b2

53 ♖b1 ♖xd7 54 ♖xb2 ♖d4 —+) 50 ... ♖c3+ 51 ♔f2 ♖d3 52 d7 ♖xd7 53 ♖xb4 ♖d6 54 ♔e3 ♖d3+ 55 ♔e2 ♖a3 White resigned.

23   KERES–GOLOMBEK
Moscow 1956

1 e4 c6 2 d4 d5 3 ♘c3 dxe4 4 ♘xe4 ♗f5 5 ♘g3 ♗g6 6 ♗c4 e6 7 ♘1e2 ♘f6 8 0-0 ♗d6 9 f4 ♕c7?! 10 f5! (Mounting an attack involving first a pawn and then an exchange sacrifice) 10 ... exf5 11 ♘xf5! ♗xh2+? (Vital time is lost in rescuing the bishop) 12 ♔h1 0-0 (12 ... ♗xf5 13 ♖xf5 ♗d6 14 ♗h6! ±) 13 g3! ♗xf5 (13 ... ♘g4!? 14 ♖f4 ♗xf5 15 ♖xf5 ♗xg3 16 ♕g1 ♘f2+ 17 ♔g2 ♗h4 ∞, 14 ♕d3! ±) 14 ♖xf5 ♗xg3 15 ♖xf6! (The point of the combination! Its essence is that due to the pin on the g-file White captures two pieces in exchange for his rook. Of course Black's desperate counterplay had to be accurately calculated in advance) 15 ... ♕e7 16 ♕f1 ♕e4+ 17 ♕f3 ♕h4+ 18 ♔g2 ♕h2+ 19 ♔f1 ♕h3+ 20 ♕g2 ♕xg2+ 21 ♔xg2 gxf6 22 ♘xg3 (After considerable 'to-ing and fro-ing' the situation is the same as it would have been after 15 ... gxf6 16 ♕g1. Black's weakened king position makes the winning technique a lot easier) 22 ... ♘d7 23 ♗h6 ♖fe8 24 ♔f3 ♔h8 25 ♘h5! (Black can only avoid the mating net at the cost of material loss) 25 ... ♖g8 26 ♗xf7 ♖g6 27 ♗xg6 hxg6 28 ♘g3 ♖e8 (28 ... g5 29 ♖e1 +—) 29 ♗f4 ♔g7 30 ♘e4 g5 31 ♘d6 ♖e6 32 ♗g3 b6 33 ♖e1 ♖xe1

34 ♗xe1 ♔g6 35 ♘c8 c5 36 dxc5 ♘xc5
37 ♘xa7 f5 38 ♗f2 ♘d7 39 ♗d4 ♔h5
40 ♘c8 ♘f8 41 ♘e7 f4 42 ♘f5 ♘g6 43
♘g7+ ♔h6 44 ♔g4 ♘f8 45 ♘f5+
Black resigned.

24   TAL–BOTVINNIK
World Championship match (9)
1960

1 e4 c6 2 d4 d5 3 ♘c3 dxe4 4 ♘xe4
♗f5 5 ♘g3 ♗g6 6 ♘e2 e6 7 h4 h6
8 ♘f4 ♗h7 9 ♗c4 ♘f6 10 0-0 ♗d6 11
♘xe6!? fxe6 12 ♗xe6 ♕c7? 13 ♖e1?
♘d7! 14 ♗g8+ ♔f8 15 ♗xh7 ♖xh7 16
♘f5! (Tal's attack has reached its
climax and Black must pull out all
stops to repel it) 16 . . . g6! (The best
move! Black sacrifices yet another
pawn, but it shakes off the attack. The
other possibilities, namely 16 . . .
♗h2+ 17 ♔h1 g6 18 ♗xh6+ ♔g8 19
g3 and 18 . . . ♖xh6 19 ♘xh6 ♕f4 20 g3
♕xf2 21 ♖f1 ♕xg3 22 ♘g4 etc., are
weaker) 17 ♗xh6+ ♔g8 18 ♘xd6
♕xd6 (18 . . . ♖xh6 19 ♖e6 ♖xh4 20
♕f3) 19 ♗g5 ♖e7 20 ♕d3 (White
would be struggling for a draw after
20 ♖xe7 ♕xe7 21 h5 ♔g7 22 hxg6
♖h8 or 21 . . . gxh5 22 ♕xh5 ♘xh5 23
♗xe7 ♘f4) 20 . . . ♔g7 21 ♕g3? (We
shall see that White's 'attack' is not
dangerous, but that the pawns
doubled on the g-file prove to be
fatal) 21 . . . ♖xe1+ 22 ♖xe1 ♕xg3 23
fxg3 ♖f8 24 c4 ♘g4 25 d5 cxd5 26 cxd5
♘df6 27 d6 ♖f7 28 ♖c1 ♖d7 29 ♖c7
♔f7 30 ♗xf6 ♘xf6 31 ♔f2 ♔e6 32
♖xd7 ♔xd7 33 ♔f3 ♔xd6 34 ♔f4 ♔e6
35 g4 ♘d5+ 36 ♔e4 (36 ♔g5 ♔f7 37

h5 ♘b4! −+) 36 . . . ♘f6+ 37 ♔f4
♘d5+ 38 ♔e4 ♘b4 39 a3 (39 a4 is
not better either) 39 . . . ♘c6 40 h5
g5! 41 h6 ♔f6 (This was the sealed
move, pondered over by Botvinnik
for 40 minutes. The queenside breakthrough of White's king needed to be
precisely calculated) 42 ♔d5 ♔g6 43
♔e6 (43 ♔d6 ♘a5 44 ♔c7 b5 −+) 43
. . . ♘a5 44 a4 ♘b3 45 ♔d6 a5 46 ♔d5
♔xh6 47 ♔c4 ♘c1 48 ♔b5 ♘d3 49 b3
♘c1 50 ♔xa5 ♘xb3+ 51 ♔b4 ♘c1 52
♔c3 ♔g6 53 ♔c2 ♘e2 54 ♔d3 ♘c1+
55 ♔c2 ♘e2 56 ♔d3 ♘f4+ 57 ♔c4
♔f6 58 g3 ♘e2 **White resigned.**

25   POGÁTS–PORTISCH
Hungary (ch) 1961

1 e4 c6 2 d4 d5 3 ♘c3 dxe4 4 ♘xe4
♗f5 5 ♘g3 ♗g6 6 ♘f3 ♘d7 7 h4 h6
8 ♗d3 ♗xd3 9 ♕xd3 ♕c7 10 ♗d2
♘gf6 11 0-0-0 e6 12 c4!? 0-0-0 13 ♗c3
c5 14 ♔b1 cxd4 15 ♗xd4?! ♗c5 16
♕e2 ♗xd4 17 ♖xd4? (With these
exchanges White is only aiming at a
draw. But the trouble that can be
caused in defending the h4 pawn in
the end-game is characteristic of this
variation. 17 ♘xd4 was needed,
giving equal play) 17 . . . ♘b8! (His
sights are on the weakened d4 square)
18 ♖hd1 ♘c6 19 ♖xd8+ ♖xd8 20
♖xd8+ ♕xd8 21 ♕d2? (Consistent
with the logic of a bad plan. In the
ensuing end-game, Portisch drives
home his advantage with amazing
simplicity. 21 b3 ♘d4 22 ♘xd4 ♕xd4
23 h5 and then 24 ♕e3 would have
resulted in a manageable position)

21 ... ♘g4! 22 ♘e4 ♕xd2 23 ♘fxd2 ♔c7! (This cuts short any possibility of counterplay before the exploration of the king's positional weakness begins in earnest. Instead 23 ... f5?! 24 ♘c5 e5 25 ♘e6 is obscure) **24 ♘f1** (Preparing for f3, but first he frustrates ♘e3; 24 ♔c2 is followed by 24 ... f5! 25 ♘c5 ♘d4+ 26 ♔d3 e5 27 f3 ♘f2+ or 26 ♔c3 e5 27 f3 ♘e3 28 g3 ♘d1+ wins a pawn in both cases) **24 ... ♘d4!** (Defending the e6 pawn so as to threaten f5) **25 f3 ♘e5 26 b3 ♘g6!** (Winning a pawn. This endgame is a good example of the spontaneous spread of weaknesses) **27 h5 ♘f4 28 ♘e3 ♘f5!** (The g-pawn is a more important prize than the h-pawn!) **29 ♘xf5 exf5 30 ♘g3 g6 31 ♔c2 ♘xg2 32 ♔d2 ♔d6 33 hxg6 fxg6 34 ♔e2 ♔e5 35 ♔f2 ♘f4 36 ♔e3 ♘d5+!** (A little combination − 37 cxd5 f4+ −+ − enables Black to loosen up the opponent's queenside with the knight) **37 ♔d2 ♘b4 38 a3 ♘c6 39 ♔e1 ♘d4 White resigned.**

26 LASKER-LEE
London 1899

1 e4 c6 2 d4 d5 3 ♘c3 dxc4 4 ♘xe4 ♗f5 5 ♘g3 ♗g6 6 ♘f3 ♘d7 7 h4 h6 8 ♗d3 ♗xd3 9 ♕xd3 ♘gf6 10 ♗d2 e6 11 0-0-0 ♕c7 (11 ... ♗e7 12 ♘e4 0-0 13 ♔b1 c5 14 dxc5 ♘xc5 15 ♘xf6+ ♗xf6 16 ♕a3 (Larsen-Rasmussen, Esbjerg 1988; 16 ... ♕b6? 17 ♗e3 ♖fc8 18 ♖he1! a5? 19 g4! g6 20 ♘d2! +−) 16 ... ♕c7 17 g4 ±) **12 ♖he1 0-0-0 13 ♕b3** (It is not good to leave the

queen on the rook's file) **13 ... ♗d6!?** (13 ... c5!? 14 ♕a4 ♔b8 − Zapata-Dorfman, Havana 1988 − 15 dxc5 ♘xc5 16 ♗f4 ♗d6 =) **14 ♘e2!?** (Nowadays 14 ♘e4 would be preferred, but preventing the exchange of the black-squared bishops cannot be bad. 14 ♕a4 ♔b8 15 ♗a5 ♘b6 16 ♗xb6 axb6 17 ♘e4 b5 18 ♕b3 ♗f4+ 19 ♔b1 ♘xe4 20 ♖xe4 ♖d5! = Zapata-Adianto, Novi Sad 1990) **14 ... ♘g4?!** (This has but the appearance of being strong, because there is no follow-up to Black's line of play. 14 ... c5, 14 ... ♔b8 or 14 ... ♘e4 gives Black more chance of equalizing) **15 ♖f1 ♘df6** (Black's knights cannot find their proper place) **16 ♕a4 ♔b8 17 c4** (White wins space on the queenside with this. In 1899 this was not yet a matter of course) **17 ... ♕e7?!** (Now Black is playing without a plan. Of course 17 ... e5? was bad because of 18 c5 ♗e7 19 dxe5 ♘xe5 20 ♘xe5 ♕xe5 21 ♗f4 but even a weaker player would continue with 17 ... c5! today) **18 ♘c3 ♕c7 19 g3 ♕c8** (19 ... c5? 20 ♘b5! ±) **20 b4!** (The world champion plays coolly. He is threatening c4-c5 and b4-b5. He need have no fears for his king since Black has no really co-ordinated plan on this wing) **20 ... e5?!** (With the benefit of hindsight this move could be considered a decisive error, if we did not know that to continue with passive play is to court disaster in such positions) **21 dxe5 ♘xe5 22 ♗e3!** (Apart from threatening to capture on a7, this move also makes 23 ♖xd6 possible. The acceptance of the piece offered is fatal: 22 . . . ♘xf3 23 ♕xa7+ ♔c7 24 ♗b6+ ♔d7 25 c5 +−) 22 . . . ♘xc4 23 ♗xa7+ ♔c7 24 ♖d4! b5 (This almost provokes the next sacrifice, but 24 . . . ♕f5 25 ♖xc4 ♕xf3 26 ♗b6+! ♔d7 27 ♖d1! is also hopeless in view of the numerous threats) 25 ♘xb5+! cxb5 26 ♕xb5 (The black king and his knight are both in deep trouble) 26 . . . ♘a3 27 ♕a5+ ♔b7 28 ♗c5 ♗xc5 29 bxc5 ♖xd4 30 ♘xd4 ♕d8 (There was nothing better. White wins back the piece without letting his opponent catch his breath) 31 c6+ ♔c8 32 ♕a8+! ♔c7 33 ♕a7+! ♔d6 34 ♕xa3+ ♔d5 35 ♖d1 ♕b6 36 ♘f3+ ♔e6 37 ♕d6+♔f5 38 ♕d3+ ♔g4 39 ♘e5+ **Black resigned.**

27 KARPOV-HÜBNER
Tilburg 1982
1 e4 c6 2 d4 d5 3 ♘d2 dxe4 4 ♘xe4 ♗f5 5 ♘g3 ♗g6 6 h4 h6 7 ♘f3 ♘d7 8 h5 ♗h7 9 ♗d3 ♗xd3 10 ♕xd3 ♘gf6 11 ♗f4 e6 12 0-0-0 ♗e7 13 ♘e5 0-0 14 c4 c5!? (14 . . . ♕a5!? but not 14 . . . b5?! 15 ♘xc6! bxc4 16 ♕e2 ♕e8 17 d5 ±) 15 d5 (15 ♕e2 or 15 ♕c3 are also possible) 15 . . . ♘xe5 (15 . . . exd5?! 16 ♘f5!) 16 ♗xe5 ♘g4!? 17 ♗xg7!? (A sharp reply! 17 f4 ♘f2 18 ♕c3? ♘xd1 19 ♖xd1 f6! 20 dxe6 ♕b6! 21 ♘f5 ♕xe6 22 ♘xe7+ ♕xe7 23 ♗d6 ♕e4 24 ♗xf8 ♕xf4+! leaves a lot to be desired for White, thus 18 ♕e2!? seems an imrovement on 18 ♕c3?)

17 . . . ♔xg7 (17 . . . ♗g5+!?) 18 ♕e2 (Having the sacrifice of the bishop in mind, White wants to play 19 ♕xg4 or 19 dxe6) 18 . . . ♗g5+ (18 . . . ♘f6 19 dxe6 ♕c7 20 ♘f5+ and 21 g3 ±) 19 ♔b1 ♘f6 20 dxe6 ♕c8 21 e7 ♖e8 22 ♖d6!! (The point of the combination! Black cannot now play 22 . . . ♕e6) 22 . . . ♕g4 (22 . . . ♗f4 23 ♖xf6! ♔xf6 24 ♕f3 +−; 23 . . . ♗xg3 24 ♕f3 ±) 23 ♕e5 ♔g8 24 ♖e1 ♘d7 (24 . . . ♘xh5 25 ♘f5 ♗f4 26 ♕d5! or 25 ♖e4 ♘f4 26 ♘f5 f6 27 ♕xf6 +−) 25 ♖xd7! ♕xd7 26 ♘f5 f6 (26 . . . ♕d3+ 27 ♔a1 ♕d4 − the only move − 28 ♘xd4 ♖xe7 29 ♕xe7 ♗xe7 30 ♘f5 +−) 27 ♕d5+! (White goes into the endgame because the connected pawns will be very strong!) 27 . . . ♕xd5 28 cxd5 ♗f4 29 g3 ♗c7 30 ♔c2! (30 ♘xh6+? ♔h7 31 ♘f5 ♖ad8!) 30 . . . b5 31 ♘xh6+ ♔h7 32 ♘f5 ♖g8 33 d6 ♗a5 34 ♖e6 ♖g5 35 ♖xf6 ♖xh5 36 d7 ♖h2 37 ♘e3 **Black resigns.**

28 KARPOV-POMAR
Nice (ol) 1974
1 e4 c6 2 d4 d5 3 ♘c3 dxe4 4 ♘xe4 ♗f5 5 ♘g3 ♗g6 6 ♘f3 ♘d7 7 h4 h6 8 h5 ♗h7 9 ♗d3 ♗xd3 10 ♕xd3 ♕c7 11 ♗d2 e6 12 ♕e2 ♘gf6 13 c4 ♗d6 14 ♘f5 0-0-0? 15 ♘xd6+ ♕xd6 16 ♗a5! ♖de8 17 ♘e5! (Black is hemmed in. Now 17 . . . ♕xd4? 18 ♘xf7 ♖hg8 19 ♖d1 ♕c5 20 b4! would lose the exchange) 17 . . . ♕e7 18 ♗c3 (Geller recommends 18 0-0 or 18 f4) 18 . . . ♖ed8 19 f4 ♘xe5 20 fxe5 (20 dxe5 ±) 20 . . . ♘h7 21 0-0-0 ♘g5 22 a3! (The

threat of ♗b4-d6 forces the opening of the position, favouring White) **22 ... f5! 23 exf6** (Otherwise the knight entrenches itself on e4) **23 ... gxf6 24 ♖hf1!** (Pressurizing the weak points of e6 and f6) **24 ... ♖he8 25 ♖de1 ♕f7 26 g4 ♖f8 27 ♕c2** (He wants to break through on g6, but d4-d5 is also threatened) **27 ... ♕g8! 28 ♗b4!?** (Geller considered 28 ♕g6!? to be better, although this is not easy to demonstrate after 28 ... ♕xg6 29 hxg6 ♖d7! For example: 30 ♗b4 ♖g8 31 ♖xf6 ♖dg7 or 31 ... ♖xd4!?. Also 30 d5?! exd5 31 ♖xf6 − 31 ♗xf6 ♘e4 − 31 ... ♖g8 or 31 ♖h1 ♖g7 32 ♖xh6 ♖fg8 33 ♖f1 ♘e4 etc.) **28 ... ♖f7 29 ♕g6** (There was no other obvious way. The threat was 29 ... f5 and 30 ... ♘e4) **29 ... ♕xg6 30 hxg6 ♖g7 31 ♖xf6 ♖dg8** (So Black re-establishes material equality, but White's initiative remains formidable in spite of the diminished material) **32 ♖ef1 ♖xg6 33 ♖xg6 ♖xg6 34 ♖f8+ ♔c7?!** (34 ... ♔d7!? gave more chances, though after 35 ♔d2 White controls the game, e.g. 35 ... ♘e4+!? 36 ♔e3 ♖xg4 37 ♖f7+ ♔c8 38 ♖h7 etc. ±) **35 ♗a5+! b6** (On move 16 Black was still able to avoid this weakening) **36 ♗d2 ♘e4 37 ♗f4+ ♔b7 38 ♖f7+ ♔a8** (White is weaving a mating net despite the paucity of material. 38 ... ♔a6? 39 ♗b8!) **39 ♖f8+ ♔b7 40 b4! ♖xg4 41 ♖f7+ ♔a8?!** (41 ... ♔c8 42 ♗e5 c5 43 dxc5 bxc5 44 b5 +−) **42 ♔c2 h5 43 a4! h4 44 ♔d3 ♘g5** (The net is now complete) **45 ♖f8+ ♔b7 46**

♖b8+! ♔a6 47 ♗d2! ♖g3+ 48 ♔c2 Black resigned (48 ... b5 49 cxb5+ cxb5 50 axb5 mate).

29 GELLER–HORT
Skopje, 1968

1 e4 c6 2 d4 d5 3 ♘c3 dxe4 4 ♘xe4 ♗f5 5 ♘g3 ♗g6 6 h4 h6 7 ♘f3 ♘d7 8 h5 ♗h7 9 ♗d3 ♗xd3 10 ♕xd3 ♕c7 11 ♗d2 e6 12 0-0-0 ♘gf6 13 ♘e4 0-0-0 14 g3 ♘xe4 15 ♕xe4 ♗e7 16 ♔b1 ♖he8 17 c4 c5 18 ♗f4 ♗d6 19 ♘e5 ♘xe5?! 20 dxe5 ♗f8 (20 ... ♗e7 also came into consideration, followed by f7-f6, although the e6 pawn would need defending after this) **21 ♗e3 ♖xd1+** (The opening is over. Black has no prospects of active counterplay, so he intends to alleviate his position by exchanges) **22 ♖xd1 ♖d8 23 ♖xd8+ ♕xd8 24 ♔c2 ♕a5 25 a3 ♕a4+ 26 ♔c1 ♔c7?** (Black is unsuspecting. 26 ... ♗e7 was needed to avert the subsequent hemming in that follows and to allow ♗g5! in response to the immediate threats against ♕g4 or ♕f4) **27 ♕f4! ♕d7** (27 ... ♗e7 28 ♕xf7 ♕xc4+ 29 ♔d2 ♕d5+ 30 ♔e1 ♕h1+ 31 ♔e2 ± Geller) **28 b3 ♔d8 29 ♔c2 ♔e8 30 ♕e4!** (Grandmaster Geller gave a very revealing illustration of the plan that White initiated with his moves 7 and 8. It consists of: 1. Blocking Black's kingside. 2. Exchanging redundant pieces. 3. Attacking f4, g4 and f5, possible breakthrough points for White on the kingside) **30 ... ♕c7 31 f4 ♗e7 32 g4 ♗h4 33 f5 ♗g3**

(Black's only chance is to attack the weakened e5 square, but it is too late in the day) **34 fxe6 fxe6 35 ♕g6+ ♔f8 36 ♕xe6 ♗xe5** (Did Black get away with it?) **37 ♔d3!** (The king's penetration through the weakened white squares settles the issue) **37 ... ♗g3 38 ♔e4 ♗h2 39 ♔f5 ♗g3 40 ♗d2** (This is simpler than 40 ♔g6 ♕d6 41 ♕xd6 ♗xd6 42 ♗c1 ♗e5) **40 ... ♗h2 41 ♗c3 ♕f7+**. The game was adjourned here and **Black resigned** without further play as there is no defence against 42 ♕xf7+ ♔xf7 43 ♔e4 and 44 ♔d5.

30 HJARTARSON-TIMMAN
Amsterdam, 1989

1 e4 c6 2 d4 d5 3 ♘d2 dxe4 4 ♘xe4 ♗f5 5 ♘g3 ♗g6 6 h4 h6 7 ♘f3 ♘d7 8 h5 ♗h7 9 ♗d3 ♗xd3 10 ♕xd3 ♘gf6 11 ♗d2 ♕c7 12 0-0-0 e6 13 ♘e4 0-0-0 14 g3 ♘xe4 15 ♕xe4 ♗d6 16 c4 c5 17 ♗c3 cxd4 18 ♘xd4 ♘c5 19 ♕c2 a6 20 ♖he1 ♗e7 21 ♔b1 ♗f6 22 f4?! (White's pawn formation gets very loose — and without seizing the initiative) **22 ... ♖d7! 23 ♘f3?!** (23

♘b3) **23 ... ♖xd1+** (23 ... ♖hd8?! 24 ♖xd7 ♕xd7 25 ♗a5 ∞) **24 ♖xd1 ♖d8!** (Owing to the scattered weaknesses in White's camp, the simplification favours Black) **25 ♖xd8+ ♕xd8 26 ♗xf6** (26 ♘e5 ♘e4! ∓) **26 ... gxf6 27 a3** (27 b4 ♕b6 28 a3 a5 ∓) **27 ... f5 28 ♔a2 f6!** (28 ... ♕d3 29 ♕xd3 ♘xd3 30 ♘g5 ♘f2 31 ♘xf7 ♘e4 32 ♘xh6 ♘xg3 33 ♘g8! ♘xh5 34 ♘e7+ =) **29 b4 ♘e4 30 g4 ♕d6 31 gxf5 ♕xf4 32 ♕g2** (32 ♘d4 e5 −+) **32 ... ♘g5!** (Simplifying into a promising queen ending) **33 ♘xg5 ♕xc4+ 34 ♔b2 fxg5 35 fxe6 ♕xe6 36 ♕c2+ ♔d7 37 ♕h7+ ♔c6** (Due to White's outpost on g6 Black has to play accurately, but his technique does not fail) **38 ♕g6 ♔d6 39 ♕d3+ ♕d5 40 ♕g6+ ♕e6 41 ♕d3+ ♔e7 42 ♕h7+ ♕f7 43 ♕e4+ ♔f8 44 ♕g4 ♕g7 45 ♔c3 ♕d5 46 ♕g3 ♔f6 47 ♕f2+ ♔e6** (Botvinnik refers to Capablanca when he claims that the king should be centralised in positions of this sort and should not be kept in the corner of the board) **48 ♕f8 ♕c6+ 49 ♔b3 ♔e5! 50 ♕g7+ ♔f5 White resigned.**

5
Advance Variation — 3 e5

1 e4 c6 2 d4 d5 3 e5

In this, the advance variation, tension switches from e4 to Black's undermining of the e-pawn. The system is reminiscent of the closed French Defence but with a vital difference. Black's queen's bishop, so often a problem-child in the French, can be immediately developed.

This compensates for Black's slightly lagging kingside development and the fact that the standard ... c5 break, which characterizes the structure, takes two moves in total.

3 e5 had its heyday in the late fifties and sixties, when it was even seen in World Championship games.

Nowadays 3 e5 ♗f5 4 ♘c3 e6 5 g4 ♗g6 6 ♘ge2 is the most fashionable.

Now we examine Black's main continuation in A and a more dubious sideline in B.

A: 3 ... ♗f5
B: 3 ... c5?!

A

3 ...   ♗f5

And White can choose between:

A1: 4 ♘c3
A2: 4 h4
A3: 4 ♘e2
A4: 4 c4
A5: 4 ♗d3
A6: 4 ♗e2

Rarer continuations are:
a) 4 ♘d2 e6 5 ♘gf3 c5?! *(5 ... ♘d7 or 5 ... ♗e7!)* 6 dxc5 ♗xc5 7 ♘b3 ♗b6 8 ♗b5+ ♘d7 9 ♘bd4 ± Polyak-Feldman, 1948.

b) **4 ♘f3 e6 5 ♗d3** *(5 ♗e2 see A6)*
**5... ♘e7 6 0-0 ♘d7 7 c3 ♗xd3 8 ♕xd3
♘g6 9 ♖e1 ♗e7 10 ♗e3 0-0 11 ♘bd2
c5** = Matanović–Milić, Yugoslavia
1955.

c) **4 g4**. Premature, as Black has
either **4... ♗g6 5 h4 h5** *(5... h6 6 h5
♗h7 7 e6 ♘f6 — Filip)* **6 e6 fxe6 7 ♗d3
♗xd3 8 ♕xd3 hxg4 9 ♕g6+ ♔d7 10
♕xg4 ♘f6 11 ♕h3 ♖h5 12 ♘f3!? ♖f5**
∞ Mieses–Speyer, Scheveningen
1923, or **4... ♗d7 5 c4** *(5 b4? a5 6 c3
axb4 7 cxb4 e6 8 ♗d2 ♕b6 ∓
Boleslavsky; 5 ♗e3 h5!? 6 gxh5 ♗f5
7 ♘d2 e6 8 c3 ♕b6 9 b4 ♘d7 10 ♘e2
♗g4 11 ♕c1 ♗xh5 12 ♘g3 ♗g6 13
♘b3 ∞ Apicella–Haik, France, (ch)
1987)* **5... e6 6 ♘c3 ♘e7 7 c5! b6 8 b4
a5 9 ♘a4 ♘c8 10 ♖b1 axb4 11 ♖xb4
bxc5 12 dxc5 ♕c7** ∓ Bronstein–
Petrosian, USSR 1959, or **4... ♗e4
5 f3 ♗g6 6 h4 h5 7 ♗d3** *(7 e6? ♕d6 8
exf7+ ♗xf7 Alekhine)* **7... ♗xd3 8
♕xd3 e6 9 g5 ♘e7** and Black stands
better due to White's over-extended
pawns.

d) **4 c3 e6 5 ♗e3** *(5 ♘e2 c5 6 ♗e3
♘c6 7 f4 ♕b6 ∓ Ilyin-Genevsky; 5 ♗e2
see A6)* **5... ♕b6** *(5... ♘d7 6 ♘d2
♘e7 7 f4 f6 8 ♘gf3 fxe5 9 ♘xe5 ♘xe5
10 fxe5 ♗g6 11 ♕h5 ♕b6 12 b4 ♗e7 13
♗e2 0-0 ∞ Zaichik–Tal, Tbilisi 1986;
5... c5!?)* **6 ♕b3 ♘d7 7 ♘d2 c5**
*(7... a5 8 ♕xb6 ♘xb6 9 a4! ♘e7 10 f4
♘d7 11 ♗e2 ♗g6 12 ♗f2 h5 13 ♘gf3
♘f5 = Gurgenidze–Bagirov, USSR 1981)*
**8 ♕xb6 axb6 9 ♗b5 c4 10 ♘e2 ♘e7 11
0-0 ♘c6 12 b3 ♗a3** ∞ Petrienko–
Sapis, Hradec Králové 1987/88.

A1

4 ♘c3   ...

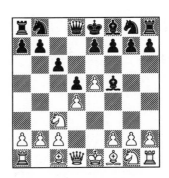

In preparation of g2-g4.

4 ...   e6

Occasional alternatives include:

a) **4... ♕d7 5 ♗e3 h6** *(5... h5
6 ♘f3 ♘h6 7 h3 e6 8 ♗e2 ♗e7 9 ♕d2
b5 10 ♗g5 a5 11 ♖c1 ♕d8 12 a4 b4 13
♘d1 ♘a6 14 0-0 ♗g6 15 ♕f4 ± Nunn–
Hort, Lugano 1987)* **6 h3 e6 7 g4 ♗h7
8 f4 ♗b4 9 ♘e2 ♘e7 10 a3** ± van der
Wiel–Hort, Wijk aan Zee 1986.

b) **4... h6?! 5 g4 ♗h7 6 e6! fxe6
7 ♘f3 ♘f6 8 ♗d3 ♘e4 9 ♕e2 ♘d7 10
♘xe4** ± Nunn–Bellon, Thessalonika
(ol) 1984.

c) **4... ♕b6 5 g4** *(5 ♗d3 ♕xd4?!
6 ♘f3 — 6 ♘ge2!? — 6... ♕g4 7 h3
♕h5 8 0-0 ♗xd3 9 cxd3 ∞; 5... ♗xd3
6 ♕xd3 e6 7 ♘ge2 ♘d7?! — 7... c5, or
7... ♕a6 — 8 0-0 ♘e7 9 a4! c5?! 10 a5!
♕c6 11 dxc5 ± ♗xe5? 12 ♕g3 ♘5g6 13
♘d4! ± Kotronias–King, New York*

*1990) 5 . . . ♗d7 6 ♘a4 (6 ♗g2!? e6
7 ♘ge2 c5 8 dxc5 ♗xc5 9 0-0 ♘e7 10
♖b1!∞ ±) 6 . . . ♕c7 7 ♘c5 (7 ♗e3 e6
8 ♗g2 ♘e7 − 8 . . . ♘a6!? − 9 f4 ♘a6
10 ♘f3 h5 11 h3 ♘g6 12 ♘c3 ♗e7 13
♕e2 ♘h4 14 ♘xh4 ♗xh4+ −
Timman-Kamsky, Tilburg 1990 − 15
♔f1! ♗e7 16 gxh5 0-0-0 17 ♗f3 ±
Kamsky) 7 . . . e6 8 ♘d3!? (8 ♘xd7
♘xd7 9 f4 c5 10 c3 ♘e7 11 ♘f3 h5 −
Velimirovic-Kasparov, Moscow 1982 −
12 gxh5 ♘f5 ∞) 8 . . . c5! (8 . . . h5
9 gxh5 c5 10 dxc5 ♘a6 11 ♘h3! ♘xc5
12 ♘hf4 ♘h6 13 ♖g1 0-0-0 14 ♗h3 −
I. Gurevich-Hodgson, Philadelphia
1990 − 14 . . . d4!∞; 8 . . . ♘a6 9 ♗g2 c5
10 c3 ♘e7 11 ♘e2 ♘c6 12 ♗e3 ±Széll-
Bernei, Budapest 1988) 9 dxc5 ♗b5! 10
f4 ♗xc5 11 ♘f3 ♘e7 12 a4 ♗xd3 13
♗xd3 ♘bc6 14 ♕e2 h5! ∓ Kamsky-
Adams, London 1989.*

d) **4 . . . h5** 5 ♗d3 ♗xd3 6 ♕xd3 e6
7 ♘f3 ♕b6 *(7 ♘h6!?)* 8 0-0 ♕a6?!
(8 . . . ♘e7 is better) 9 ♕d1 ♘e7 *(9 . . .
c5!?)* 10 ♘e2 ♘d7 11 c3 ♘f5 12 ♗g5
♗e7 13 ♘g3! ± Short-Seirawan,
Rotterdam 1989.

5 g4   . . .

5 ♗d3 ♘e7 6 ♘f3 ♘d7 7 0-0 ♗xd3
8 ♕xd3 c5 9 ♖e1 h6 10 ♘e2 ♘c6 11 c3
♕b6 gave equality in Lublinsky-
Simagin, USSR 1944.

5 . . .   ♗g6
6 ♘ge2   . . .

A1.1: 6 . . . ♗b4

A1.2: 6 . . . f6
A1.3: 6 . . . c5
A1.4: 6 . . . ♗e7

A1.1

6 . . .   ♗b4

Other possibilities:
a) **6 . . . h6** 7 h4! c5 8 h5 ♗h7 9 ♗e3
♘c6 10 f4 ± Boleslavsky.
b) **6 . . . ♕h4** 7 ♗e3 ♘h6 8 ♗xh6
gxh6 9 ♘g3 ♗e7 10 f4 f6 11 ♗g2 ±
Blumenfeld-Kasparian, USSR 1931.

7 h4   . . .

7 ♘f4 ♘e7 8 a3 ♗xc3+ 9 bxc3 ♕a5
10 ♗d2 ♘d7 11 h4 ♕a4 12 ♖a2 h6 13
♘xg6 ♘xg6 14 ♗d3 ♘e7 15 ♖b2 b5 ∞
van der Wiel-Hort, Bochum 1981.

7 . . .   ♗e4

Insufficient is **7 . . . h5?!** e.g. 8 ♘f4
♗e4 9 f3 hxg4 10 fxe4 ♖xh4 11 ♖g1
dxe4 12 ♗g2 ± Széll-Varnusz,
(Active Chess) Budapest 1989.
Another possibility is **7 . . . h6**
8 ♗g2 ♘d7 9 h5 ♗h7 10 ♗e3 ♘e7 11
0-0 g6?! 12 ♘g3 ♕c7 13 ♘ce2! 0-0-0?!
14 c3 ♗a5 15 ♗xh6 gxh5 16 ♗g5! ±
Shabalov-Magomedov, Minsk 1990.

8 ♖h3   h5
9 ♘g3   c5

9 . . . ♘d7 10 ♘xh5 g6 11 ♗g5 ♕a5
12 ♘f4 c5 13 a3 ♗xc3+ 14 ♖xc3 ±
Plaskett-Rus, Austria 1981.

10 ♗g5   **♛b6**

10 ... f6 11 ♗d2 ♗xc3 12 bxc3 ♘c6 13 exf6 gxf6 14 ♘xe4 dxe4 15 ♛e2 ♛d7 16 ♛xe4 0-0-0 17 g5 ♘ge7 18 gxf6 ♘f5 19 ♖d3 ± Vasyukov-Razuvayev, USSR 1981.

11 a3

11 ♘xe4?! cxd4 12 ♘d6+ ♗xd6 13 exd6 dxc3 14 ♖xc3 ♘d7 ∓ Day-Vranesic, Canada 1981.

11 ...   **hxg4**
12 axb4   **gxh3**
13 dxc5

± *(ECO)* The sacrifice of the exchange is more than compensated for by the total control that White has in this position.

A1.2

6 ...   **f6**

A1.21: 7 h4
A1.22: 7 ♘f4

A1.21

7 h4   **...**

7 ♗f4 ♘d7 8 ♛d2 h5 *(8 ... ♗f7 9 h4 a6 10 g5 fxe5 11 dxe5 ♘e7 12 h5 c5 13 ♗h3 ♘c6 14 0-0-0 ♘dxe5 15 ♗xe5 ♘xe5 16 g6 hxg6 17 ♘f4 ♘c4 18 ♛e2 ♛g5 19 ♔b1 ♛xf4 20 ♘xd5 ♛d6 21 ♘f6+ +– Hodgson-Crouch, England 1981)* 9 g5 ♗f7 10 ♗h3 fxe5 11 dxe5 ♘e7 12 ♘d4 ♘g6 13 ♗xe6 *(13 ♘xe6 ♗xe6 14 ♗xe6 ♗b4 ∞)* 13 ... ♘dxe5 14 ♗xf7+♘xf7 15 ♘e6 ♛e7 16 0-0-0 ♛xe6 17 ♖he1 ♘fe5 18 ♗xe5 ♘xe5 19 f4 0-0-0 20 ♖xe5 ♛f7 ∓ Mnatsakanian-Tavadian, Erevan 1982.

7 ...   **fxe5**
8 h5   **...**

8 dxe5 ♘d7 9 f4 h5 10 f5 ♘xe5 11 fxg6 ♘f3+ 12 ♔f2 hxg4 13 ♗g2 ♛f6 ∓ Yudasin-Peresipkin, USSR 1982.

8 ...   **♗f7**

8 ... exd4? 9 hxg6! +–; 8 ... ♗e4 9 ♖h3 exd4 10 ♘xe4 dxe4 11 ♛xd4 ♛d5 12 h6 ±.

9 dxe5   **♘d7**
10 f4   **♛b6**

10 ... ♗c5 *(10 ... c5!? and ♘g8-e7-*

c6) 11 ♘d4 ♛b6 12 ♘a4 ♛a5+ 13 c3 ♗xd4 14 ♛xd4 c5 15 ♛d1 ± van der Wiel–Messa, Graz 1981.

11 ♘d4   . . .

11 ♗g2 0-0-0 12 b3 ♘e7 13 ♘a4 ♛c7 14 ♗e3 c5 15 c4! d4 *(15 . . . dxc4?! 16 ♛c1!* ∞ *Timman)* 16 ♗f2 *(16 ♗d2)* 16 . . . g5 17 hxg6 ♗xg6 18 ♘g3 ♘c6 19 0-0 ± van der Wiel–Timman, Amsterdam 1987.

11 . . .	**0-0-0**
12 a3	**c5**
13 ♘f3	**♘e7**

Interesting is 13 . . . ♘h6!?

14 b4!?	**cxb4**
15 axb4	**♛xb4**

15 . . . ♘c6 16 ♘a4 ♛xb4+ 17 ♗d2 ± Marjanovic–Campora, Nice 1985.

16 ♗d2	**♘c6**

16 . . . ♛b6 17 ♖h3! ♘c6 18 ♖b1 ♗b4 19 ♘b5 ±; **18 . . . ♛c7** *(18 . . . ♘b4 19 ♘a2 ±)* 19 ♘b5 ♛b8 20 ♘bd4! ±.

17 ♘g5	**♛e7**

17 . . . ♗g8 18 ♘b5 ♛c5 19 ♖h3 ± with a strong queenside attack.

18 ♘b5	**♔b8**
19 ♘d6 ± (analysis).	

A1.22

7 ♘f4   . . .

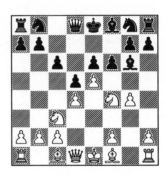

7 . . .	**fxe5**

Also common is 7 . . . ♗f7 8 exf6 *(8 ♘d3 h5 9 gxh5 ♗xh5 10 ♗e2 ♗f7* =*)* 8 . . . gxf6 9 ♛e2 *(9 ♘d3 ♘d7 10 ♛e2 ♛b6 11 ♗e3 0-0-0 12 0-0-0 ♖e8 13 f4 ± Kengis–Timofeyev, USSR 1980)* 9 . . . ♛e7 10 ♘d3 ♘d7 and now:
a) **11 f4** 0-0-0 12 ♗e3?! *(12 h4 ± Lanc–Eperjesi, Zamárdi 1980)* 12 . . . e5!? 13 fxe5 fxe5 14 dxe5 c5 15 ♗f4 c4 16 e6 ♗xe6 17 ♘b5 ♖e8 18 ♘d6+♛xd6! ∓ Vasilyev–Andreyev, USSR 1984.
b) **11 h4** e5! *(11 . . . h6? 12 ♗f4 ♗g7 13 ♖h3! 0-0-0 14 ♖e3 ♖e8 15 0-0-0 e5 16 ♘a4! h5 17 g5 ± Circenic–Stopov, Riga 1982)* 12 dxe5 fxe5 13 ♗g5 ♘gf6 14 0-0-0 ∓ (analysis).

8 ♘xe6

8 dxe5 *(8 ♘xg6 hxg6 9 dxe5 ♗c5 10 ♗f4 ♛b6 ∓ Balashov–Bellon, Karlovy*

Vary 1979) 8 . . . ♗f7 9 ♕e2 *(9 h4 ♘d7 10 ♘d3 h5 11 ♗g5 ♕a5 12 ♗d2 ♕c7 ∞ Kinlay-Freeman, England 1980; 9 ♗g2 ♘d7 10 0-0 ♘xe5 11 ♖e1 ♗d6 12 ♕d4 ♕f6 13 ♘e4?! ♘f3+ 14 ♗xf3 ♕xd4 15 ♘xd6+ ♔f8 16 ♘d3 ♕f6 17 ♘e5 ∓ Petrusin-Spiridonov, Pleven 1985)* and now:

a) **9 . . . c5** 10 ♘cxd5!? exd5 11 e6 ♗g6 12 ♘xg6 *(12 h4?! ♘c6 ∓)* 12 . . . hxg6 13 ♕f3! *(13 ♕b5+ ♘c6 14 ♕xb7 ♘ge7 15 ♗b5 ♕c8 −+ Bottlik)* 13 . . . ♘f6 *(13 . . . ♕c7 14 ♗f4 ♕a5+ 15 b4! ±; 13 . . . ♕e7 14 ♕xd5 ♘c6 15 ♗d3 ♕d6 16 ♗xg6+ ♔d8 17 ♕f3 ∞)* 14 g5 ♕d6 15 gxf6 ♕xe6+ 16 ♗e3 ♘c6 17 0-0-0 d4 18 ♗g5 gxf6 19 ♕xf6 ♕xf6 20 ♗xf6 ♖h7 21 ♗d3 ♗h6+ 22 ♔b1 ♔f7 = Fábry-Kárpáti (corr) 1983.

b) **9 . . . ♘d7** 10 ♗h3 ♕c7 11 g5 *(11 ♘d3 h5 12 ♗g5!? ∞ Lepeskin)* 11 . . . ♕xe5 12 ♘xe6 ♗xe6 13 ♗xe6 ♗d6 *(13 . . . ♕xe2+ 14 ♘xe2 0-0-0 15 ♗f4 ♖e8 16 ♗g4 ♘e7 17 0-0-0 ♘g6 = Efimov-Vdovin, Sochi 1980)* 14 ♗d2 ♘e7 15 0-0-0 ♕xe2 16 ♘xe2 ♘c5 17 ♗g4 0-0 18 ♗e3 ♘g6 = Kapengut-Bagirov, USSR 1981.

	8 ...		♕e7
	9	♘xf8	exd4+
	10	♗e2	

10 ♘e2 ♗e4 11 ♖g1 c5 12 b4 (Széll-Holzapfel, Berlin 1987) 12 . . . b6 ∞.

	10 ...		♕xf8

10 . . . dxc3 11 ♘xg6 hxg6 *(11 . . .*

cxb2 12 ♗xb2 hxg6 13 ♕d3 ♔f7 14 0-0-0 ∞ Széll)* 12 ♕d3 ♘f6 13 ♕xc3 *(13 ♕xg6+ ♕f7 14 ♕d3 ±)* 13 . . . ♘bd7 14 ♗e3 *(14 ♕e3?! ♘e4 15 ♗d2 ♘xd2 16 ♔xd2 ♕xe3+ 17 fxe3 ♖h4 = Minasjan-Karpman, Minsk 1990)* 14 . . . ♘e4 ± Nunn-Andersson, London 1982.

11	♕xd4	♘d7
12	♗f4	♘gf6

12 . . . ♗xc2? 13 ♖c1 ♗g6 14 ♘xd5! cxd5 15 ♗b5 +− Széll-Varnusz (quickplay) Budapest 1989.

13	0-0-0	♕c5
14	♕xc5	♘xc5

∞(±) was Széll-Varnusz (quickplay), Budapest 1989, where White enjoys a slight advantage, resultant from the bishop pair and a more fluid co-ordination of minor pieces.

A1.3

6 ...		c5

The main line.

A1.31: 7 ♗e3
A1.32: 7 h4

A1.31

7 ♗e3   ...

A1.311: 7 ... ♘c6!?
A1.312: 7 ... cxd4

A1.311

7 ...   ♘c6!?
8 dxc5!

8 h4 cxd4 *(8 ... h6 9 ♕d2 c4 10 ♘f4 ♗h7 11 ♘h5 ∞)* 9 ♗xd4 h6 10 ♕d2 ♗b4 11 a3 ♕a5 12 h5 ♗h7 13 ♗g2 ♘ge7 14 ♖c1 ♗xc3 15 ♕xc3 ♖c8 ∓ Lublinsky-Sokolsky, Moscow 1949.

8 ...   ♘xe5?!

8 ... ♕h4!? *(8 ... h5!?)* 9 ♘b5 ♘h6 *(9 ... ♗e4 10 ♘c7+ ♔d7 11 ♘xa8 ♗xh1 12 ♘g3 ♕xh2 13 b4 ♘h6 14 ♕e2 ♗e7 15 b5 ♘xe5 ½-½ van der Wiel-Sosonko, Amsterdam 1982)* 10 h3 *(10 ♘c7+? ♔d7 11 ♘xa8 ♘xg4 12 ♕d2 ♘xe3 13 ♕xe3 ♕b4+ 14 ♕c3 ♗xc5 ∓)* 10 ... ♖c8 *(10 ... ♘xg4? 11 hxg4 ♕xh1 12 ♘g3 ♕h4 13 ♘c7+; 10 ... ♘xe5 11 ♘g3 ♕d8 12 f4 ♘c6 13 f5! exf5 14 ♕e2 ±)* 11 ♘g3 ♘xe5 12 ♘xa7 ♖xc5 *(12 ... ♗xc5!? 13 ♘xc8! ♗xe3 14 ♕e2 ♗f4 15 ♕b5+ ♘d7? 16 ♘b6 0-0 17 ♘xd7 ♗xg3 18 0-0-0 ♗f4+*

19 ♔b1 ♖c8 20 ♗d3 ± Nunn. Here *15 ... ♔d8!? seems an improvement)* 13 c3! f6! *(13 ... ♘c4? 14 ♗xc5 ♗xc5 15 ♕a4+ ♔e7 16 ♗xc4 ♕f6 17 0-0 ♕f3 18 ♗xd5! +— Nunn-Sosonko, Tilburg 1982)* 14 ♕a4+ ♔f7 15 ♗e2 ∞ (Nunn).

9 ♘d4!   ♘f6

Alternatively:

a) 9 ... ♗xc5 10 ♗b5+ ♘d7 11 ♘xe6 fxe6 12 ♗xc5 a6 ± Széll-Varnusz (quickplay), Budapest 1989.

b) 9 ... h5? 10 ♗b5+ ♘d7 11 ♕e2 ♗e7 12 f4 ± Efimov-Machulski, Moscow 1979.

c) 9 ... a6? 10 f4 ♘d7 *(10 ... ♘c4 11 ♗xc4 dxc4 12 f5 exf5 13 gxf5 ♕e7 14 ♔d2 ± van der Wiel-Timman, Wijk aan Zee 1982; 10 ... ♘c6 11 f5 ♘xd4 12 ♕xd4 exf5 13 ♕a4+ ♕d7 14 ♗b5 axb5 15 ♕xa8+ ♕d8 16 ♕xb7 ♕d7 17 c6 +—)* 11 f5 exf5 12 gxf5 ♕h4+ 13 ♗f2 ♕e7+ 14 ♗e2! ♗h5 15 ♘xd5 ♕e4 16 0-0 ♗xe2 17 ♘xe2 0-0-0 18 ♘ec3 ♕xf5 19 b4 ± Eger-Hami (corr) 1985.

d) 9 ... ♘c6 10 ♗b5 ♖c8 *(10 ... ♕c7 11 ♕e2 ♘f6 12 f4 0-0-0 13 ♗xc6 bxc6 14 b4 ± Ovechkin-Rjazancec (corr) 1987; 10 ... ♘e7 11 f4 ♗e4 12 ♘xe4 dxe4 13 ♘xc6 ♘xc6 14 ♕xd8+ ♖xd8 15 ♔e2 h5 16 h3 ± Kengis-Zhuravlev, Riga 1982)* 11 ♕e2 ♘f6 *(11 ... h5!? 12 0-0-0 hxg4 13 ♗f4 ♗e7 14 ♖he1 ♕d7 15 ♗e5 ♘f6 16 ♗xf6 gxf6 17 ♔b1 ♔f8 18 ♕xg4 f5 19 ♕g2 ∞ Sherzer-Bürger, New York 1987)* 12

0-0-0 ♗xc5 13 h4 h5 14 g5 *(14 gxh5?*
♗xh5 15 f3 0-0 16 ♖hg1 ♘xd4 17
♗xd4 ♗xd4 18 ♖xd4 ♕b6 ∓
Kupreichik-Spiridonov, Poland 1981)
14 . . . ♘d7 15 ♘xe6! fxe6 16 ♗xc5
♘xc5 17 ♖xd5 ± Kujf-van den Berg,
Amsterdam 1982.

10 ♗b5+   . . .

10 f4 ♘exg4 11 ♗b5+ ♔e7 12 ♕e2
∞ *(12 ♗g1? ♕c7 13 c6 b6 14 ♕e2 ♕xf4*
∓ *Braga-Timman, Mar del Plata 1982).*

10 . . .   **♘ed7**
11 c6   . . .

11 ♕e2 is 'unclear', according to
Timman.

11 . . .   **bxc6**
12 ♘xc6   **♕c7**
13 f4 ± (Széll).

A1.312

7 . . .   **cxd4**

a) **7 . . . ♕b6** 8 ♕d2 *(8 dxc5*
♗xc5 9 ♗xc5 ♕xc5 10 ♕d4, Nunn-
Seirawan, Wijk aan Zee 1983, 10 . . .
♕a5! ∓) 8 . . . ♕xb2 9 ♖b1 ♕xc2 10
♕xc2 ♗xc2 11 ♖xb7 c4 ∞.
b) **7 . . . ♘d7** 8 h4 cxd4 9 ♗xd4 h6
(9 . . . f6 10 ♘f4 ♗f7 11 exf6 ♘gxf6 12
♕e2 ♕e7 13 g5 ♘e4 14 0-0-0 ♕d6 15
♕e3 ± van der Wiel-Christiansen,
Wijk aan Zee 1981; 11 ♘d3 ±) 10 ♘f4

♗h7 11 ♕e2 ♘e7 12 0-0-0 ♘c6 ∞
(van der Wiel).

8 ♘xd4   **♘c6**

a) 8 . . . ♘e7 9 f4 a6 10 f5 exf5
11 ♕e2 ♘bc6 12 0-0-0 ♘xd4 13 ♖xd4
fxg4 14 ♗g2 ♖c8 15 ♖hd1 ∞
Zijatdinov-Savon, Tashkent 1985.
b) 8 . . . cxd4!? 9 ♘xd4 ♗b4 ∞
(10 h4 h6 see 7 h4 h6 8 ♗e3 cxd4; but
better is 10 . . . h5!).

9 ♗b5   **♖c8**

9 . . . ♘e7 10 f4 a6 11 ♗a4 ♕c7 12
0-0 0-0-0 ∞ van der Wiel-Scheeren,
Netherlands 1982.

10 f4   **♕c7**

10 . . . ♗b4 11 f5 exf5 12 gxf5 ♕h4+
13 ♔d2 ♗h5 14 ♕g1 ♔f8 15 f6! gxf6
16 ♗xc6 bxc6 17 ♘f5! ± Forgács-Wif,
Budapest 1984.

11 0-0   **♗c5**
12 ♔g2   **♗xd4**
13 ♗xd4   **♘e7**
14 ♗c5   **a6**
15 ♗d6   **♕b6**

was Gureili-Muresan, Tbilisi 1982,
with chances for both sides.

A1.32

7 h4   . . .

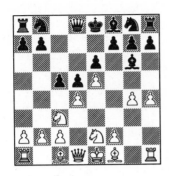

A1.321: 7 . . . h6

A1.322: 7 . . . cxd4

A1.321

7 . . .   h6

Others:

a) **7 . . . ᐸc6** 8 h5 ♗e4 9 ᐸxe4 dxe4
10 c3 cxd4 11 ᐸxd4 *(11 cxd4 f6 =)*
11 . . . ᐸxd4 *(11 . . . ᐸxe5 12 ♕a4+
ᐸd7 13 ♗g2 ±; 11 . . . ♗c5 12 ♗e3
ᐸxd4 13 ♕a4+ ♔f8? 14 cxd4 ±
Kengis–Kivlan, Riga 1929; 13 . . . ᐸc6
14 ♗xc5 ♕d5 15 ♗e3 ♕xe5 16 ♗d4
♕g5 17 ♗a6 ±; 15 . . . 0-0-0 16 ♗g2
ᐸxe5 17 ♕xe4 ±)* 12 cxd4 ♗b4+
(12 . . . a6 13 ♗g2 ♗b4+ 14 ♔f1)
13 ♗d2 ♕a5 14 a3 ♗xd2+ 15 ♕xd2
♕d5 16 ♕b4 ± Sutkus–Kean (corr)
1982-84.

b) **7 . . . f6!?** 8 ᐸf4?! *(8 h5 ♗f7 9 exf6
∞)* 8 . . . ♗f7 9 exf6 cxd4! *(9 . . . gxf6 10
♕e2 ±; 9 . . . ᐸxf6 10 g5 ±)* 10 ♕xd4
(10 ♕e2 ♔d7! ∓ Nunn) 10 . . . gxf6 11
♕a4+ ᐸc6 ∓ Nunn–Cocoza,
Thessalonika (ol) 1984.

c) **7 . . . h5** 8 ᐸf4 ♗h7? *(8 . . . cxd4
9 ᐸxg6 fxg6 10 ᐸb5 ᐸc6 11 ♗d3 ±;
8 . . . ᐸe7 9 ᐸb5! ᐸec6 10 ᐸxg6 fxg6
11 ♗d3 ♔d7 12 c4 ± Babrikovski–
Eichler, Germany 1977)* 9 ᐸxh5
(Possibly 9 gxh5 cxd4 ∞ or even 9 g5!?)
9 . . . cxd4 10 ♕xd4 ᐸc6 11 ♗b5 ᐸe7
(11 . . . ♗xc2!?) 12 ♗h6! ♕d7 *(12 . . .
a6 13 ♗xc6+ ᐸxc6 14 ♕f4 gxh6 15
ᐸf6+ ♔e7 16 ᐸfxd5+!)* 13 ♕f4 0-0-0
14 ♗xg7 ♗xg7 15 ᐸxg7 ᐸg6 16 ♗xc6
♕xc6 17 ♕d4 +– van der Wiel–
Iclicki, Brussels 1985. Better is **8 . . .
ᐸc6!** 9 ᐸxg6 fxg6 10 ᐸe2! *(10 gxh5?
cxd4 11 ᐸb5 ♖xh5; 10 dxc5? ♗xc5; 10
♗e3? cxd4 11 ♗xd4 ᐸh6 12 gxh5?
ᐸf5; 10 ♗b5 cxd4 – 10 . . . ᐸe7!? –
11 ♕xd4 ᐸe7 12 ♕d3 hxg4 13 ♗xc6+
ᐸxc6 14 ♕xg6+ ♔d7 15 ♗f4 ♕e8 16
♕xg4 ♕h5 ∞; 10 ♕d3? cxd4 11 ᐸb5 –
11 ♕xg6+ ♔d7 12 ᐸb5? ᐸxe5 ∓ –
11 . . . hxg4! 12 ♕xg6+ ♔d7 13 ♕xg4
♕b6 14 c3! dxc3 15 ᐸxc3 ᐸh6! 16
♗xh6! ♕xb2 ∓ Timman–Seirawan,
Hilversum (m) 1990)* 10 . . . cxd4! 11
ᐸxd4 ᐸxd4 12 ♕xd4 ᐸe7 ∞
(Seirawan).

8 ♗e3   . . .

8 ᐸf4 ♗h7 9 g5 hxg5 10 hxg5 ♗xc2
∓; **8 h5** ♗h7 9 ♗e3 ᐸc6 **10 f4?!** ♕b6
11 f5 f6! ∓ (Karpov, Zaitsev). **10
dxc5!?** ᐸxe5 11 ᐸxd4 ᐸf6 12 ♗b5+
ᐸd7! 13 ♕e2 *(13 f4? a6! 14 fxe5?!
axb5 15 ᐸdxb5 ᐸxc5! ∓ Yudashin–
Seirawan, Jacksonville 1990)* 13 . . . a6
14 ♗a4 ♗xc5 15 ᐸxe6 fxe6 16 ♗xc5
b5 17 ♗d4 bxa4 18 ♗xe5 ∞

(Seirawan).

8 . . . ♕**b6**

8 . . . ♘c6?! 9 dxc5 *(9 h5 ♗h7 10 dxc5 ♘xe5 11 ♘d4 a6 12 f4 ♘c6 ±)* 9 . . . ♘xe5 10 ♘f4 *(10 ♘d4!? ♘c6 11 ♗b5 ♖c8 12 f4 ± Karpov, Zaitsev;* **10 . . . ♗e7** 11 ♗b5+ ♔f8 12 ♕e2 ♘f6 13 ♖g1 a6 14 ♗a4 ± *Mikhailov-Berkovich, USSR 1981)* and now:
a) **10 . . . d4** 11 ♗b5+ ♔e7 12 ♘xg6+ *(12 ♘fd5+!? exd5 13 ♗xd4 with the idea of ♕e2+!)* 12 . . . fxg6 13 ♗f4 dxc3 14 ♗xe5 cxb2 15 ♕xd8+ ♖xd8 16 ♗xb2 ♘f6 17 f3 ♔f7 =.
b) **10 . . . a6?!** 11 ♗g2 ♘f6 12 ♕e2 ♘fxg4 13 ♗d4 ♗e4 14 ♘xe4! *(14 ♗xe4? ∞ Timman–Karpov, Belfort 1988)* 14 . . . dxe4 15 ♕xe4 ♕a5+ *(15...f5 16 ♕xb7 ♕xd4 17 ♗c6+! +− 15... ♘c6 16 0-0-0 ♘f6 17 ♗xf6 ♕xf6 18 ♕xc6+! +−)* 16 b4! ♕xb4+ 17 c3 ♕c4 18 ♕xb7 ♖d8 19 ♗f1 ♕a4 20 ♗xa6 +− (Timman).
A new idea is **8 . . . cxd4** 9 ♘xd4 ♗b4 10 h5! ♗e4! *(10... ♗h7 11 ♕d2 ♘d7 12 a3 ♗a5 13 b4 ♗b6 14 f4 ± Kotronias–Speelman, New York 1990)* 11 f3 ♗h7 12 ♗d3! ♗xd3 13 ♕xd3 ♘d7 14 0-0-0!? ♗xc3 15 ♕xc3 ♖c8 16 ♕e1 ♘xe5! 17 ♗f4 ♘c6 18 ♘f5! ♔f8! 19 ♗d6+ ♘ge7 ∞ Timman-Seirawan, Hilversum (m) 1990.

9 f4 . . .

a) **9 h5** *(9 ♘f4 ♗h7 10 dxc5 ♗xc5 11 ♗xc5 ♕xc5 12 ♗d3 ♕b4+ ∓ Nunn;*

9 ♘a4 ♕a5+ 10 c3 c4! ∓ Nunn) 9 . . . ♗h7 10 ♕d2 *(10 f4 ♘c6 11 f5 f6 12 fxe6 0-0-0 ∓ Lanc–Lechtinsky, Brno 1975; 10 dxc5 ♗xc5 11 ♗xc5 ♕xc5 12 ♕d4 ♕a5 13 b4 ♕b6 14 ♕xb6 axb6 15 ♘b5 ♔d7 − Oll–Tukmakov, USSR 1986 − 16 c4! ∞)* 10 . . . ♘c6 *(10 . . . ♕xb2?! 11 ♖b1 ♕xc2 12 ♕xc2 ♗xc2 13 ♖xb7 and 14 ♘b5) 11 0-0-0 c4 12 f4 ♕a5 13 f5 b5 14 ♘xd5! b4! (14 . . . ♕xd2+ =; 14 . . . ♕xa2 15 ♘dc3 ♕a1+ 16 ♘b1 ♗b4 ∞) 15 ♘c7+! ♕xc7 16 ♘f4 ∞* (Nunn).
b) **9 ♕d2** ♘c6 10 0-0-0 h5! *(10 . . . ♘b4? 11 ♘f4 ♗xc2 12 ♗b5+ ♔d8 13 dxc5 ♗xc5 14 ♘fxd5 +−; 10 . . . c4 11 f4 ± Karpov, Zaitsev)* 11 dxc5 ♗xc5 12 ♗xc5 ♕xc5 13 ♘f4 ♘ge7 14 ♘xg6?! ♘xg6 15 f4 hxg4 16 h5 ♘ge7 17 ♗e2 ♕a5 ∓ Sokolov–Karpov, Linares (m) 1987.

9 . . . ♘**c6**

9 . . . ♕xb2?! 10 f5 exf5 11 ♖b1 ±.

| **10 f5** | ♗**h7** |
| **11 ♕d2** | **0-0-0** |

In this variation tactical manoeuvres and double-edged situations abound. 11 . . . cxd4 12 ♘xd4 ♗c5 *(12 . . . ♘xe5 13 ♗b5+ ±)* 13 ♘a4 ♘xd4 14 ♗xd4 ♗b4 = Kuindzi and Obechkin.

12 0-0-0	**c4**
13 ♘f4	♕**a6!?**
14 fxe6	**b5**

15 exf7	♘ge7
16 ♘e6	b4

17 ♘c5! *(17 ♘xd8?! ♔xd8! 18 a3 bxc3 − 18 . . . bxa3!? − 19 ♕xc3 ♘c8 20 g5 ♘b6 ∞ Timman–Seirawan, Hilversum (m) 1990)* 17 . . . bxc3 18 ♕xc3 ± (Timman).

A1.322

7 . . .	cxd4
8 ♘xd4	. . .

8 ♕xd4 ♘c6 9 ♕a4 h5 10 ♘f4 ♗h7 11 ♘xh5 a6 ∞ *(ECO)*.

8 . . .	h5

A1.3221: 9 ♗b5+
A1.3222: 9 f4

A1.3221

9 ♗b5+	♘d7
10 ♗g5	♗e7

10 . . . ♕c7 11 ♕e2 ♗b4 12 ♖h3 a6 13 0-0-0 axb5 14 ♘xd5 exd5 15 e6 ♘e5 16 ♕xb5+ ♘c6 17 exf7+ ♗xf7 18 ♘xc6 bxc6 19 ♕xb4 ± Kupreichik–Roizman, Minsk 1979.

11 f4	hxg4
12 ♕xg4	♗xg5

12 . . . a6 13 ♗xd7+ ♕xd7 14 h5 ± Kupreichik–Bagirov, Kirovokan 1978.

13 fxg5	♗h5
14 ♕g3	

14 ♕h3 ♘e7 15 ♔d2 ♖c8 16 ♖ae1 ♕b6 ∓ Hort–Seirawan, Bad Kissingen 1981.

14 . . .	♘e7

14 . . . ♕b6!? is a promising alternative, with dynamic possibilities for both sides ensuing.

15 ♘ce2	♗xe2
16 ♘xe2	♘g6

and the position is complex/unclear, as in Sariego–Rodriguez, Bayamo 1982.

A1.3222

9 f4	. . .

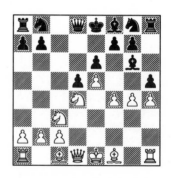

A1.32221: 9 . . . hxg4
A1.32222: 9 . . . ♕d7

A1.32221

9 . . .   hxg4

9 . . . ♗e7!? deserves attention.

10 ♗b5+   ♘d7
11 f5   . . .

11 ♕xg4 ♘h6 12 ♕g2 ♗h5 13 f5 ♘xf5 14 ♘xf5 exf5 15 ♕xd5 a6 16 ♗g5 ♗e7 17 ♗a4 ± Handoko-Adianto, Jakarta 1987.

11 . . .   ♖xh4

11... ♗xf5?! *(11 . . . exf5? 12 e6 fxe6 13 ♘xe6 ♕e7 14 ♕e2 +—)* 12 ♘xf5 exf5 13 ♕xd5 ♕c7 *(13 . . . a6 14 ♗g5 ♘e7 15 ♕xb7 axb5 16 ♘xb5 ±)* 14 ♗f4! ♘e7 *(14... 0-0-0 15 ♕xf7 ± Sax-Vadász, Budapest 1985)* 15 ♕d2 0-0-0 16 e6 ♘e5 17 ♗d7+ ♔b8 18 ♘b5 ♘f3+ 19 ♔d1 +— (Kuindzi and Obechkin).

12 ♖f1

12 ♖g1 *(12 0-0!? ∞)* 12 . . . ♗h5!? *(12... ♖h2? 13 ♗f4 ±; 12 . . . ♗xf5 13 ♘xf5 ♖h5 14 ♘xg7+ ♗xg7 15 ♕xg4 ♖h7 16 ♗d3 ♘xe5 17 ♕a4+ ±; 12... exf5 13 ♘xd5 a6 14 ♗xd7+ ♔xd7 15 c4 ∞; 12... ♖h5 13 fxg6 ♕h4+ 14 ♔f1 ♕h3+ 15 ♖g2 ♕h1+ 16 ♔f2 ♕h4+ = van der Wiel)* 13 fxe6 fxe6 14 ♘xe6 ♕b6 15 ♗xd7+ ♔xd7 16 ♕xd5+ ♗d6 17 ♘d4 ♖e8 18 e6+ ♔c8 ∞ van der Wiel-Speelman, Wijk aan Zee 1983.

12 . . .   exf5

Less remunerative "others" comprise:
a) 12... ♗xf5 *(12 . . . ♗h5? 13 fxe6 fxe6 14 ♖xf8+ +—)* 13 ♘xf5 ♖h5 14 ♘xg7+!? ♗xg7 15 ♕xg4 ♖xe5+ *(15 . . . ♕h4+ 16 ♕xh4 ♖xh4 17 ♖g1 ♖h7 18 ♗d3 ±)* 16 ♔d1 ♗f8 17 ♖g1 ± (Nunn).
b) 12 . . . ♖h2? 13 ♗xd7+ *(13 ♕xg4!? ♗xf5?! 14 ♘xf5 exf5 15 e6! ♕e7 16 ♗xd7+ ♔d8 17 ♕f4 ♖xc2 18 ♕xf5 ♕h4+ 19 ♔d1 +— Nunn-Wells, England 1984; 13 . . . exf5! 14 ♘xf5 ♗xf5 15 ♖xf5 ♕h4+ ±)* 13 . . . ♔xd7 14 ♕xg4 exf5 15 ♘xf5 ♗xf5 16 ♕xf5+ ♔c6 17 ♗g5 ♗e7 18 ♗xe7 ♘xe7 19 ♕f4 *(19 ♕xf7 +—)* 19 . . . ♕h8 20 ♕a4 +— Moor-Mills, USA 1984.

13 ♗f4!   . . .

13 e6?! *(13 ♘xd5? ♖h2! 14 ♗xd7+ ♔xd7 —+)* 13 . . . fxe6 14 ♘xe6 ♕e7 15 ♕e2 ♖h2! 16 ♕e5 *(16 ♕xh2 ♕e6+ and 17 . . . ♗d6)* 16 . . . ♘f6 17 ♗f4 ♖xc2 18 ♘c7+ ♔f7 19 ♕xe7+ ∞ Kotlar-Retter, Israel 1986.

13 . . .   a6
14 e6!?

14 ♗a4 b5 15 ♗b3 ♖h3 16 ♗xd5 ♕h4+ 17 ♔d2 0-0-0 ∞.

14 . . .   axb5
15 ♕e2   ♗e7

(Westerinen–Adianto, Thessalonika (ol) 1988) 16 exf7+ ♗xf7 17 ♘xf5 ♔f8 18 0-0-0 ♖h5 19 ♕xg4 ♖xf5 20 ♕xf5 ♘df6 ∞ (Adianto, Hinting).

A1.32222

9 ...   ♕d7

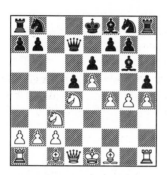

10	f5	exf5
11	gxf5	♗xf5
12	♘xf5	♕xf5
13	♕xd5	♘c6
14	♗h3	...

14 ♘b5? ♗f4+ 15 c3 ♖d8 −+.

14	...	♕xe5+
15	♕xe5+	♘xe5
16	♗f4	♗d6

with a level position, e.g. 17 ♖d1 *(17 0-0-0 ♘d3+ 18 ♖xd3 ♗xf4+ 19 ♔b1 ♘f6 20 ♖e1+ ♔f8 ∞)* 17 ... ♗b8! 18 ♘d5 ♘e7 19 0-0 *(19 ♘xe7 ♔xe7 20 ♗xe5 ♗xe5 21 ♖d7+ ♔f6 22 0-0+ ♔g6 23 ♖fxf7 ♗xb2 =)* 19 ... ♘7g6 =

Korolev–Kastarnov (corr) 1984.

A1.4

6 ...   ♗e7

To delay the h2-h4 attack.

A1.41: 7 ♘f4
A1.42: 7 ♕e3

A1.41

7 ♘f4   ...

Others:

a) 7 ♗g2 ♘d7 8 0-0?! *(8 ♘g3 see b; 8 ♘f4 c5 ∞)* 8 ... h5! 9 ♘f4 hxg4 10 ♘xg6 hxg6 11 ♕xg4 ♘f8 and ♖h4, ♘h6-f5 ∓ (van der Wiel–Miles, Ter Apel 1987).

b) 7 ♘g3 ♘d7 8 ♗g2 f6 9 f4?! *(9 exf6 ♗xf6 ∞)* 9 ... fxe5 10 fxe5 *(10 dxe5 ♗h4 11 ♗e3 ♘e7 12 ♕d2 h5! or 11 0-0 ♕b6+ 12 ♔h1? ♗xg3 13 hxg3 ♘e7 ∓)* 10 ... ♗g5 *(10 ... ♗h4 ∞)* 11 0-0 *(11 ♗xg5? ♕xg5 12 h4 ♕f4!)* 11

. . . ♗xc1 12 ♕xc1 ♕h4 ∓ Széll-
Varnusz (quickplay) Budapest 1989.

7 . . .   c5

For 7 . . . ♗g5!? 8 ♗e3 ♗xf4, see
7 ♗e3 (A1.42).

8 dxc5!?   . . .

8 ♗e3 ♘c6 9 ♗b5 cxd4 10 ♕xd4 a6
11 ♗xc6+ bxc6 12 ♕a4 ♕d7 13 h4 c5
(13 . . . f6 ∞) 14 ♕xd7+ ♔xd7 15 h5!
♗xc2 16 ♖c1 ♗e4 17 ♘xe4 dxe4 18
♗xc5 ♖c8 ∞ Nagy-Varnusz, Szolnok
1989.

8 . . .   d4

8 . . . ♘c6 9 ♗b5 *(9 ♘d3 d4!)* and
then possibly 9 . . . ♗xc5 ∞, or 9 . . . d4
∞.

9 ♘xg6	hxg6
10 ♘e4	♗xc5
11 ♘xc5	♕d5
12 ♘xb7	♕xh1

12 . . . ♕xb7? 13 ♖g1 ♖xh2 14 ♗g5
♘c6 15 ♕f3 ±.

| 13 ♘d6+ | ♔f8 |
| 14 ♕xd4 | . . . |

∞ Nunn-Chandler, Wiesbaden 1981.

A1.42

| 7 ♗e3 | ♘d7 |

7 . . . ♗g5!? 8 ♘f4 ♗xf4 9 ♗xf4 h5!
10 f3 ♘e7 11 ♗d3?! ♗xd3 12 ♕xd3
♘g6! 13 ♗g3 hxg4 14 fxg4 ♕g5! 15
h3? *(15 ♕f3 ♘d7 16 0-0 0-0, and 17 . . .
f6 ∓)* 15 . . . ♕xg4! ∓ Széll-Varnusz
(quickplay) Budapest 1989.

8 ♕d2   . . .

a) 8 ♗g2 ♕b6 9 ♖b1 h5! 10 ♘f4
hxg4 11 ♘xg6 fxg6 12 ♕xg4 ♘f8 ∓
Psakhis-Rogers, Calcutta 1988.
b) 8 ♘f4 b5?! *(8 . . . ♗g5 9 ♕d2
♗xf4 10 ♗xf4 h5! ∓)* 9 ♗g2 ♘f8 10
♘h5 ♗xh5 11 gxh5 ♘d7 12 ♕g4 ±
Sax-Barcza, Budapest 1980.

8 . . .   h5!

8 . . . b5?! 9 ♗g2 h5 10 ♘f4 hxg4 11
♘xg6 fxg6 12 h3 ♕a5 13 ♘e2 ♕xd2+
14 ♔xd2 ± Hjorth-Haig, Dubai (ol)
1986.

9 ♘f4	hxg4
10 ♘xg6	fxg6
11 ♗d3	

11 h3 ♘f8 12 0-0-0 ♕a5 13 a3 b5 14
♘a2 ♕xd2+ 15 ♔xd2 a5 16 ♘c1 ♔f7
17 ♘d3 ♖h4 18 ♗g2 ♘h6 19 hxg4
♖xg4 20 ♗f3 ♖h4 21 ♖xh4 ♗xh4 22
♖h1 ♗e7 = Kamsky-Miles, New
York 1989.

| 11 . . . | ♘f8 |
| 12 0-0-0 | ♖h4 |

12 . . . ♕a5!? 13 ♖dg1 ♖h4! 14 ♗g5

(14 h3 ♘h6 ∞) 14 . . . ♗xg5 15 ♕xg5 ♕d8 16 ♗xg6+ ♔d7 17 ♖xg4 ♕xg5 18 ♖xg5 ♖xd4 19 ♗d3 *(19 ♗f7 ♘h6 20 ♖xg7 ♘f5 ∞)* 19 . . . g6 20 ♗xg6 ♘xg6 21 ♖xg6 ♘e7 = (Dokhoyan).

13	♘e2	♘h6
14	c4	♕d7

14 . . . ♘f5? 15 ♘f4 ± was Minasian-Miles, Moscow 1989.

15	cxd5	cxd5
16	♗g5	♗xg5
17	♕xg5	♕e7
18	♗xg6+	♔d7 ∞

− a position which is fairly contentious, according to Dokhoyan.

A2

4 h4   . . .

Planning to trap the bishop with g2-g4, should Black play 4 . . . e6. Consequently, Black must weaken his kingside slightly.

4 . . .   h5

This is perhaps the simplest, although 4 . . . h6 also gives a perfectly good game. E.g. 5 g4 *(See A3 for 5 ♘e2. On 5 ♗d3 ♗xd3 6 ♕xd3 e6 7 h5, however, Boleslavsky still considers White to hold a slight plus)* 5 . . . ♗d7 *(5 . . . ♗h7 meets 6 e6! fxe6 7 ♗d3 ♗xd3 8 ♕xd3 ♕d6 9 f4 ♘d7 10 ♘f3 0-0 11 ♘e5 ± Gufeld-Spiridonov, Helsinki 1961 or 5 . . . ♗c8 6 ♘c3 ♕b6 7 ♗h3 e6 8 ♘ge2 c5 9 0-0 ♘c6 10 ♗e3 ± Aronin-Bronstein, USSR 1961)* 6 h5 *(Also 6 ♗e3 c5 7 c3 ♘c6 8 a3 a5 9 b3 e6 10 h5 b5! 11 ♘f3 ♕b8 12 ♗g2 c4 13 bxc4 bxc4 ∞ Bronstein-Donner, Budapest 1961 or 6 c3 c5 7 ♗g2 e6 8 ♘e2 ♗b5 9 ♘a3 ♗xe2 10 ♕xe2 cxd4 11 cxd4 ♗xa3 12 bxa3 ♘c6 ∓ Tal-Botvinnik, USSR (m) 1961 and finally 6 c4 e6 7 ♘c3 c5 8 dxc5 ♗xc5 9 cxd5 exd5 ∓ Pachman)* 6 . . . c5 7 c3 e6 8 f4 ♕b6 9 ♘f3 ♘c6 10 ♗h3 *(10 ♘a3 cxd4 11 cxd4 0-0-0 12 ♘c2 ♔b8 13 ♗d3 ♘ge7 = Tal-Pachman, Bled 1961)* 10 . . . 0-0-0 11 0-0 ♔b8 12 ♘a3 cxd4 with even prospects according, once more, to Boleslavsky.

In spite of this we still prefer 4 . . . h5 as the most comfortable variation for Black.

5 c4   . . .

For 5 ♘e2 see variation A3, while 5 ♘c3 c6 6 ♘f3 ♗g4 7 ♗e2 c5 8 ♗e3

♘c6 9 dxc5 ♗xf3 10 ♗xf3 ♘xe5 gave equal chances in Aronin-Smyslov, USSR 1961.

5 . . .   e6

5 . . . dxc4 *(5 . . . ♗xb1 6 ♖xb1 e6 7 c5! b6 8 b4 a5 9 a3 ♘e7 10 ♘f3 axb4 11 axb4 ♘f5 12 ♗d3 ♗e7 13 g3 g6 14 0-0 ♔f8 15 ♗f4 ♔g7 16 ♕e2 ♘d7 17 ♖a1 ± Vasyukov-Skembris, Corfu 1989) 6 ♗xc4 ♗xb1 (6 . . . e6 see 5 . . . e6 6 ♘c3 dxc4) 7 e6!? (7 ♖xb1 e6 ∞) 7 . . . ♗g6 8 ♕b3 ∞* (Vasyukov).

6 ♘c3   ♘d7

a) **6 . . . ♗e7** 7 ♘f3 ♗g4 8 ♗e3 ♘h6 9 cxd5 cxd5 10 ♕b3 ♕d7 ∓ Nunn-Miles, Amsterdam 1985; or **7 cxd5** cxd5 8 ♗g5 ♘c6 9 ♕d2 ♕b6 10 ♗b5 ♗b4 11 ♘ge2 ♘e7 12 a3 ♗xc3 13 ♘xc3 0-0 ∞ Malanyuk-Georgadze, Simferopol 1988.

b) **6 . . . dxc4** 7 ♗xc4 ♘d7 *(7 . . . ♗e7 8 ♘f3 ♗g4 9 ♗g5!? ♘h6 10 ♕d2 ♗xf3 11 gxf3 ♘f5 12 0-0-0 ♘d7 – 12 . . . ♘xh4 13 ♗xh4 ♗xh4 14 ♖dg1 ± – 13 ♗d3! ♘xh4 14 ♗xh4 ♗xh4 15 ♖dg1 ♘f8 16 ♕f4! ± Blatny-Cervenka, Trnava 1987; 9 . . . ♗xf3! 10 gxf3 ♗xg5 11 hxg5 ♕xg5 12 ♘e4 ∞)* 8 ♘ge2 *(8 ♗g5 ♗e7 9 ♕d2 ♘b6 10 ♗b3 ♕d7 11 ♘ge2 ♗b4! 12 a3 ♗a5 13 ♗a2!? ♘d5 14 b4 ♘xc3! 15 ♕xc3 ♗b6 16 ♕g3 ♘e7 ∞ Blatny-Plachetka, Namestovo 1987)* 8 . . . ♗e7! *(8 . . . ♘b6 9 ♗d3! ♘e7 10 ♗g5 ♗xd3 11 ♕xd3 ♕d7 12 0-0 ♘f5 13 ♖ad1 ♗e7*

14 ♘e4! ♗xg5 15 hxg5 0-0-0 16 ♘2g3! ♔b8 17 ♘xf5 exf5 18 ♘c5 ♕c8 19 ♖fe1 ± Oll-Adianto, Sydney 1991) 9 ♘g3 ♗g6 10 ♘ce4 ♘h6! was Chandler-Speelman, England 1985, and now 11 ♗g5! ♗xe4 12 ♘xe4 ♘f5 with a dynamically balanced position.

7 cxd5   . . .

Tal-Averbakh, USSR (ch) 1961 went instead 7 ♘ge2 ♘e7 8 ♘f4 dxc4 9 ♗xc4 ♘g6 10 ♘xh5 ♘dxe5 11 ♗e2 ♘d3+ 12 ♗xd3 ♗xd3 ∓; Filip suggests 8 ♘g3!?

7 . . .   cxd5
8 ♗g5   ♗e7

And now rather than 9 ♘b5? ♕a5+ or 9 ♗xe7 ♘xe7 10 ♘b5 0-0 ∓ *(Boleslavsky)* best is **9 ♕d2 ♗xg5 10 ♕xg5 ♕xg5 11 hxg5 a6** with chances for both sides.

A3

4 ♘e2   . . .

A slightly different method of harassing the black bishop.

4 . . .   e6
5 ♘g3   . . .

Or 5 ♘f4 c5! *(5 . . . h6 6 ♗d3 ♗xd3 7 ♘xd3 ♘d7 8 0-0 c5 9 dxc5 ♘xc5 10 ♘xc5 ♗xc5 11 ♕g4 g6 12 c4 ± Čirić-Hocevar, Yugoslavia (ch) 1960 or 5 . . .*

♗e7 6 ♗d3 ♗xd3 7 ♘xd3 h5 8 ♘d2 ♘d7 9 0-0 g6 10 ♘f3 ♘h6 11 ♗xh6 ♖xh6 12 ♕d2 ♖h7 13 a4 ± *Szabó-Barcza, Hungary 1961)* 6 dxc5 *(6 c3 ♘c6 7 ♗e3 ♕b6 8 ♗d3 ♘h6 9 0-0 ♕xb2 10 dxc5 ♗e7 11 ♘h5 0-0-0 12 ♘xg7 ♗xd3 13 ♕xd3 ♘g4 −+ Ozsváth-Haág, Budapest 1977)* 6 . . . ♗xc5 7 ♗d3 ♘e7 8 0-0 0-0 9 c3 *(9 ♘d2 ♘bc6 10 ♗xf5 ♘xf5 11 ♘f3 ♗b6 12 ♘d3 f6 ∓ Krogius-Ilivitsky, USSR 1957)* 9 . . . ♘d7 10 ♕e2 ♕c7 11 ♖e1 ♖ac8 12 ♘d2 a6 with equality, Ciocaltea-Golombek, Moscow 1956.

5 . . .   ♗g6

Also possible is 5 . . . ♘e7 in order to recapture with the knight on f5 in the event of an exchange, but if White delays then Black has problems with his king's bishop development, viz:

a) **6 ♘xf5?** ♘xf5 7 c3 c5 8 ♕b3? ♕c7 9 ♗b5+ ♘c6 10 0-0 h5 11 ♗e3 a6 12 ♗xc6+ bxc6 ∓ O'Donnel-Larsen, USA 1970.

b) **6 ♗d3** ♗xd3 7 ♕xd3 ♕a5+ 8 c3 ♕a6 9 ♕xa6 ♘xa6 10 ♗e3 ♘f5 11 ♘xf5 exf5 = Simagin-Gufeld, USSR (ch) 1960.

c) **6 c4** ♗g6 7 ♘c3 ♘d7 8 h4 h6 9 h5 ♗h7 10 ♕b3 ♕b6 = Henkin-Flohr, USSR 1960.

d) **6 h4!** (strongest) 6 . . . h6 *(6 . . . c5 7 ♘c3 a6 8 ♗g5 cxd4 9 ♘xf5 exf5 10 ♕xd4 ♘bc6 11 ♕f4 ♕c7 12 0-0-0 ±)* 7 h5 ♗h7 8 ♗d3 ♗xd3 9 ♕xd3 ± Boleslavsky.

6 h4   h5

This is the simplest here as well, but 6 . . . h6 7 h5 ♗h7 8 ♗d3 ♗xd3 is also playable:

a) **9 ♕xd3** c5 *(9 . . . ♕a5+ 10 c3 ♕a6 11 ♕xa6 ♘xa6 12 f4! c5 13 f5 cxd4 14 fxe6 fxe6 15 cxd4 ♗b4+ 16 ♔e2 ♘e7 17 a3 ♗a5 18 ♖f1 ♖c8 19 ♔d3 ± Arutionov-Khalibeili, USSR 1960)* 10 c3 *(10 f4 ♘c6 11 f5?! ♘xd4 ∓ or 10 dxc5 ♘d7 =)* 10 . . . ♕b6 11 0-0 ♘c6 12 ♖d1 *(12 dxc5 ♕c7! 13 f4 ♗xc5! = Pachman)* 12 . . . ♖c8 13 ♘a3 cxd4 14 cxd4 ♗xa3 15 bxa3 ♘a5 = Heidenfeld-Pachman, Madrid 1960.

b) **9 cxd3** ♘d7 *(Better than 9 . . . ♕b6 10 ♗e3! ♕xb2 11 ♘d2 ♗b4 12 0-0 ♗xd2 13 ♖b1 ♕xa2 14 ♗xd2 b6 15 ♗b4 ± Kuzmin-Bordonada, Nice (ol) 1974; 11 . . . ♕b6 12 0-0 ♘e7 13 f4 ♘f5 14 ♘xf5 exf5 15 g4 ± Ashaturian-Hodos, USSR 1969. Sokolov suggests 11 . . . ♕c3!?)* 10 ♘c3 ♕b6 11 ♘ce2 c5 12 dxc5 ♗xc5 13 d4 ♗b4+ 14 ♔f1 ♖c8 15 ♗e3 ♘f8 16 ♖c1 ♘e7 17 ♖xc8+ ♘xc8 = Spassky-Liberzon,

USSR 1960.

7 &d3 ...

Or:

a) 7 &e2 c5! *(7 . . . &e7 8 &xh5 &xh5 9 ♘xh5 g6 10 ♘f4 ♖xh4 11 ♖xh4 &xh4 12 ♕g4 ♘h6 13 ♕h3 ± Pachman)* 8 dxc5 *(8 &xh5 &xh5 9 ♘xh5 g6 10 &g5 &e7 11 &xe7 ♕xe7 12 ♘g3 ♖xh4 ± Brzoska-Veresov, Polanica Żdrój 1958 or 8 ♘xh5 &xh5 9 &xh5 g6 10 &e2 ♖xh4 11 ♖xh4 ♕xh4 12 &e3 ♘c6 13 c3 Espig-Golz, East Germany 1967 and now 13 . . . &h6!±)* 8 . . . &xc5 9 ♘d2 *(9 ♘c3 ♘c6 10 &g5 &e7 11 ♕d2 ♘b4 12 &d3 ♖c8 13 a3 ♘c6 14 &xe7 ♘gxe7 15 f4 a6 16 &e2 ♘a5 17 ♖c1 ♘f5 = Timman-Vukić, Banja Luka 1974; 12 &b5+ &f8 13 &a4 = Vukić)* 9 . . . ♘c6 10 ♘b3 &b6 11 &xh5 ♘xe5 12 &xg6 ♘xg6 13 &g5 ♕d6 14 ♕e2 ♕e5 15 ♕xe5 ♘xe5 16 f3 f6 = Bronstein-Botvinnik, USSR 1966.

b) 7 ♘d2 c5 8 dxc5 ♘c6 *(8. . . &xc5 9 ♘b3 ♕b6 10 ♘xc5 ♕xc5 11 c3 ♘c6 12 &e3 ♕a5 = Spassky-Bronstein, USSR 1961)* 9 ♘f3 &xc5 10 &d3 ♘ge7 11 0-0 &xd3 12 cxd3 ♘g6 ∓ Matulović-Minev, Belgrade 1961.

7 ... &xd3
8 ♕xd3 &e7!?

Also 8 . . . ♕a5+ 9 c3 ♕a6 = Boleslavsky. The text was played in Tompa-Varnusz, Budapest 1967 which continued 9 ♕f3?! g6 10 ♕f4 c5

11 dxc5 &xc5 12 ♘d2 ♘c6 13 ♘f3 ♘h6 14 &e3 &xe3 15 fxe3 ♘g4 16 0-0-0 ♕c7 17 e4 0-0-0! and Black stood better.

A4

4 c4 ...

This had its vogue in the fifties and sixties, and has now reappeared in tournament play. A major objective of 4 c4 is to take possession of the e4 square, at the expense of giving Black d5 for his pieces. The move also offers a pawn sacrifice which Black would be advised to ignore: 4 . . . &xb1? 5 ♖xb1 ♕a5+? 6 &d2 ♕xa2 7 c5! b5 8 ♖a1! ♕xb2 9 ♘e2 b4 10 ♕a4 b3 11 ♘c1 e6 12 &d3 ± (Schwarz).

4 ... e6
5 ♘c3 dxc4

After 5 . . . ♘d7 White can exchange on d5, though Black's position may still be tenable: 6 cxd5 cxd5

7 ♘ge2 *(7 ♘f3 ♘e7 8 ♗g5 a6 9 ♘h4 ♗g6 10 ♗e2 ♕b6 11 ♕d2 ♘c6 12 ♖d1 ♖c8 = Unzicker-Golombek, Munich 1954)* 7 ... ♘e7 8 ♘g3 ♗g6 9 h4 *(9 ♗g5 ♕b6 10 ♕d2 ♘c6 11 ♖d1 h6 = Henkin or 9 ♗d3 ♘c6 10 0-0 ♕h4 11 ♗b5 ♗e7! 12 ♗e3 0-0 13 f4 f5 =Stoltz-Golombek, Amsterdam (ol) 1954)* 9 ... h5 10 ♗g5 a6 11 ♗d3 ♗xd3 12 ♕xd3 ♕b6 13 0-0 ♘c6 14 ♖ad1 ♗e7 = Boleslavsky.

Instead 5 ... ♗b4?! 6 a3! ♗xc3+ 7 bxc3 ♘e7 8 ♗d3 ♘d7 9 ♘e2 0-0 10 ♗g5 was uncomfortable for Black in Conrady-Nei, 1961.

A new idea is 5 ... ♘e7 6 ♘ge2 dxc4 7 ♘g3 ♘d7 8 ♗xc4 ♘b6 9 ♗b3 ♗g6 10 0-0 ♕d7 *(10... ♘f5 11 ♘xf5 ♗xf5 12 g4 ♗g6 13 f4 ♕h4 14 f5 gxf5 15 gxf5 ♗h5 16 ♕d3 0-0-0 17 ♖f4 ♕e1+ 18 ♕e1+ 18 ♕f1 ± Hellers-Rowley, Philadelphia 1990)* 10 ♗e3 ♘bd5 *(10... h5; 10... 0-0-0)* 11 ♕e2 h5 12 ♗g5 h4 13 ♘ge4 ♘f5 14 ♖ad1 ♗e7 16 ♘xd5 cxd5 17 ♘c3 0-0 18 ♕g4 ♗xg5 19 ♕xg5 ♕e7 = J. Benjamin-Christiansen, USA (ch) 1990.

6 ♗xc4   ♘d7
7 ♘ge2   ...

The correct square for the knight, eventually enabling it to control e4 from g3. 7 ♘f3 ♘b6 8 ♗b3 ♘e7 9 0-0 ♘ed5 10 ♕e2 ♗e7 11 ♘e4 0-0 as in Johannes-Porath, Leipzig (ol) 1960 and 9 ... h6 10 ♕e2 ♘ed5 11 ♘e4 ♗e7 12 ♗d2 a5 13 a3 ♘d7 14 ♖ad1 0-0 15 ♗c1 ♕b6 16 ♗c2 ♖fd8 17 ♘g3

♗g6! as in Kotov-Flohr, USSR 1955 both give equality to Black.

7 ...   ♘e7
8 0-0   ♘b6
9 ♗b3   ♕d7

9 ... h6 10 ♘g3 ♗g6 11 ♘ce4 ♘f5? *(11... ♗xe4 is only ±)* 12 ♘f5 ♗xf5 13 ♘g3 ♗g6 14 f4 ♘d5 15 f5 ± Damjanović-Flohr, Balatonfüred 1960, or 9 ... ♘ed5 10 ♘g3 ♗g6 11 ♘ce4 ♗e7 12 h4! h5 13 ♕f3 ♕c7 *(13 ... ♘c7 14 ♖d1 ♘b5 15 ♗g5! ♗xg5 16 ♘xg5 ♘xd4 17 ♕e3 ∞ ±)* 14 ♗g5 0-0-0 15 ♖fe1 *(15 ♘d6+ ♗xd6 16 ♗xd8 ♕xd8 17 exd6 ♕xd6 ±; 17 ... ♕xh4!?)* 15 ... ♔b8 16 a3 ♗xg5! *(16...f6? 17 exf6 gxf6 18 ♘xf6! ± van der Wiel-Peeln, Holland 1990; 16 ... ♖df8 17 ♖ac1 f6 18 exf6 gxf6 19 ♗d2 e5 20 ♘c3! ± van der Wiel)* 17 ♘xg5 ♕e7 18 ♘3e4 f6!? *(18... ♘c7 19 ♘d6 ♘b5!∞)* 19 exf6 gxf6 ∞ van der Wiel-van der Sterren, Lyon 1990.

10 a4   ...

With the intention of meeting 10 ...0-0-0 with 11 a5 ♘bd5 12 ♘a4 ♗g6 13 ♘g3 ±. Instead 10 ♘g3 immediately, 10 ... ♗g6 11 ♗e3 0-0-0 equalizes in Konstantinopolsky's view.

The drawback of the text is that it weakens b4.

10 ...   a5
11 ♘g3   ♗g6

12 ♗c2!   ...

We have been following the illustrative game (number 36) Tal-Golombek, Munich (ol) 1958 which continued 12 ... ♗xc2 13 ♕xc2 ♘ed5 *(13 ... ♕xd4? 14 ♗e3 ♕d8 15 ♕b3 ♘ec8 16 f4 ± Boleslavsky)* 14 ♘ce4 ♘b4 15 ♕e2 ♘6d5 16 f4 g6 17 ♖a3 ♗e7 18 ♗d2, when Black now chooses the dubious exchange of minor pieces with **18 . . . ♘c2?!** 19 ♖d3 ♘db4 20 ♗xb4 ♘xb4. Boleslavsky suggests the improvement **18 . . . b6** followed by transferring the queen to a6, which looks to give an unclear position.

A5

4 ♗d3   ...

Easing the tension rather, but a fashionable move in its day. White intends f2-f4-f5 after exchanging bishops; Black counterbalances this by exerting pressure on the centre pawns. In addition White's queen's bishop, incarcerated by the f2-f4, is often worse off than its counterpart on f8.

4 ...   **♗xd3**

As Black obtains satisfactory counterplay this way there have been few experiments with others such as **4 . . . e6?!** 5 ♗xf5 exf5 6 ♘e2 ♘a6 7 ♘c3 ♘c7 8 ♕d3 g6 9 h4! ± Kokorin-Batnikokov, USSR 1961 or **7 0-0** ♘c7 8 b3 ♘e7 9 ♗a3 ± Vasilshchuk-Bronstein, USSR 1961. **4 . . . ♗g6?** is bad on account of 5 c6!

5 ♕xd3   ...

5 cxd3 e6 6 ♘e2 ♘a6 7 ♗e3 ♘e7 8 0-0 ♕d7 9 a3 ♘f5 10 b4 ♗e7 11 ♘c3 ♘c7 ∓ Radulov-Hort, 1964.

5 ...   **e6**
6 ♘e2   ...

Other continuations:
a) **6 f4** ♕a5+! *(6 ... ♕b6 7 ♘e2! c5 8 c3 ♘c6 9 dxc5! ♗xc5 10 b4 ♗f2+ 11 ♔f1 a5 12 b5 ± Konstantinopolsky)* 7 c3 ♕a6 (This move, introduced by Nimzovitch, often holds the key to this variation for Black) 8 ♕d1 *(8 ♕xa6 ♘xa6 9 ♘f3 c5 10 ♗e3 ♘h6 ∓ Boleslavsky)* 8 . . . c5 9 ♘e2 ♘c6 10 ♘d2 cxd4 11 cxd4 ♕d3 ∓ Boleslavsky.
b) **6 ♘f3** ♕a5+ *(♕b6-a6 is also good)* 7 ♘bd2 *(7 c3 ♕a6)* 7 . . . ♕a6

8 c4 ♘c7 *(8... ♘d7 9 0-0 ♗e7 10 ♘e1
h5 11 cxd5 ♕xd3 12 ♘xd3 cxd5 =
Stoltz-Flohr, Saltsjöbaden (izt) 1948)*
9 0-0 ♘d7 10 b3 ♘f5 11 ♗b2 h5 12 a4
♗e7 13 ♕c3 g5 14 b4 g4 15 ♘e1 dxc4
16 ♘xc4 ♘b6 ∞ Geller-Petrosian,
USSR 1962.

c) 6 ♘c3 ♕b6 *(6... ♘e7 7 ♘ge2
♘d7 8 0-0 a6 9 ♘d1 c5 10 c3 ♖c8 11
♘e3 h5! = Hellers-Ivanchuk, Biel
1989; 6... c5!? 7 dxc5 ♗xc5 8 ♕b5+
♘d7 9 ♕xb7 ♘xe5 or 9... ♖b8
∞)* 7 ♘ge2 **c5!?** is the illustrative
game (number 35) Nimzovitch-
Capablanca, New York 1927 which
was, however, later found to be
perhaps dubious. Thereafter 7 ...
♕a6! 8 ♘f4 ♕xd3 9 ♘xd3 ♘d7 10
♗e3 ♘c7 11 f4 ♘f5 12 ♗f2 h5 13 ♔e2
b6 14 b4 a5 15 a3 was recommended
as a course offering complete
equalization. Yet this is not clear
either: **8 ♕h3!** ♘e7 *(8... c5
9 ♘xd5!)* 9 0-0 ♘d7?! *(9... c5 10 a4!
∞)* 10 a4! *(Casting doubts on the Capablanca manœuvre after half a century)*
10... ♖c8? *(10... b5!?)* 11 ♗e3 c5
12 ♘b5 ± Mokry-Pedersen,
Groningen 1977-78. Perhaps this is
one line of the Advance Variation
which still has good scope for the
White player.

6 ...   ♕b6

Also good is 6... c5 7 c3 ♘c6 8 0-0
♘ge7 9 f4 cxd4 10 cxd4 h5 ∓ as it
was demonstrated in Vestolvan-
Scheltinga, Helsinki (ol) 1952.

7 0-0   ♕a6(!)

There is no question of any
advantage for White here:
a) **8 ♕d1** c5 9 c3?! see illustrative
game Atkins-Capablanca, London
1922.
b) **8 ♕xa6** ♘xa6 9 c3 c5 10 ♗e3 =
*(White captures with the knight after
... cxd4).*

A6

4 ♗e2   ...

The Short System. Today it is very
fashionable. It's possible after 4 ♘f3
or 4 c3.

4 ...   e6
5 c3   ...

5 ♘f3 **c5** 6 0-0 ♘c6 7 ♗e3!? *(7 ♘c3
♗g4 ∓ Konstantinopolsky)* 7... cxd4
8 ♘xd4 ♘xd4 9 ♕xd4 ♘e7 10 ♗b5+
♘c6 11 ♕a4 ♕c7 12 c4 dxc4 13 ♖c1
♗e7 14 ♘d2 0-0 = Vogt-Kasparov,

Baku 1980. Maybe better for White is
6 ♗e3 ♕b6 7 ♘c3 ♘c6 *(7 ... c4 8 b3!
♗b4 9 ♗d2 ♕a5 10 ♘a4 ♗xd2+ 11
♕xd2 ♘c6 12 c3 ♖b8 13 0-0 ♘ge7 14
♘h4 − 14 ♗d1 ± − 14 . . . 0-0
Okhotnik-Sapis, Marianské Lázné
1989, 15 ♘c5! ♖fd8 16 g4 ♗g6 17 f4 b6
18 ♘a4 ±; 7 ... ♕xb2!? 8 ♘b5 ♘a6 9
dxc5 ♗xc2 10 ♕d4 ♕xd4 11 ♘fxd4
♗a4 12 ♘d6+ ♗xd6 13 cxd4 ∞ Sapis)*
8 ♘a4! *(8 0-0 ♕xb2 9 ♘b5 ♖c8 10
dxc5 ♕xc2 ∞)* **8 ... ♕a5+ 9 c3 cxd4 10
♘xd4 ♘xd4 11 ♗xd4 ♘e7 =.**

Or **5 ... ♘d7!? 6 0-0 ♘e7 7 ♘bd2
♗g6 8 c4 ♘f5 9 cxd5 cxd5 10 ♘b3
♖c8 11 ♗d2 ♗e7 12 ♘a5 0-0 13 ♕a4
♘b6** = Nunn-Seirawan, Wijk aan Zee
1991.

5 . . .   c5

The "old" main line. Interesting is
5 ... ♘d7 and **6 . . . ♘e7.** Others:

a) **5 ... ♗e7 6 ♘f3 g5!? 7 0-0 f5
8 ♗e3 ♘d7 9 a4!? g4 10 ♘e1 ♗g5**
(10...f6!?) **11 ♘d3 ♘h6** *(11... ♗xe3
12 fxe3 ♕g5 13 ♘f4 f6 ∞)* **12 ♘d2**
(Short-Kamsky, Tilburg 1990) **12 ...
♕e7** and **. . . 0-0-0 ±.**

b) **5 ... ♘e7!? 6 ♘d2?!** *(6 ♘f3 ♘d7)*
**6 ... c5 7 g4?! ♗g6 8 h4 h6 9 h5 ♗h7 10
♘gf3 ♘ec6 11 a3 ♘d7 12 b4 c4 13
♘f1 b5** ∓ Short-Timman, Praha 1990.

6 ♘f3   . . .

6 a3 c4 7 ♘d2 ♘c6 *(7... ♘e7 8 g4!?
♗g6 9 h4 h6 10 ♘h3)* **8 ♘gf3 ♗e7 9 b3
cxb3 10 ♘xb3 ♘h6 11 a4 0-0 12 a5**

**♖c8 13 0-0 f6 14 ♗xh6 gxh6 15 exf6
♗xf6 16 ♖e1 ♔h8** ∞ Short-Timman,
Hilversum (m) 1989.

6 . . .   ♘c6

**6 ... ♘d7 7 0-0 ♘e7 8 dxc5!? ♘c6
9 ♘d4 ♗xb1 10 ♖xb1 ♗xc5 11 f4 0-0
12 ♔h1 ♖c8 13 ♗e3 a5 14 f5 ♘dxe5
15 fxe6 ♕b6 16 exf7+** ± Xie Jun-
Maric, Belgrade (m) 1991.

7 0-0   ♕b6

a) **7...h6 8 ♗e3! cxd4 9 cxd4 ♘ge7
10 ♘c3 ♘c8 11 ♖c1 a6 12 ♘a4 ♘b6
13 ♘c5 ♗xc5 14 ♖xc5 0-0 15 ♕b3** ±
Short-Seirawan, Manila 1990.

b) **7 ... ♖c8 8 a3 c4 9 ♘bd2 ♘h6 10
b3 cxb3 11 ♕xb3 ♖c7 12 ♗b2 ♗e7 13
c4 0-0 14 ♗c3 f6 15 cxd5 exd5 16
♖ad1 ♔h8** ∞ Short-Hjartarson,
Manila 1990.

8 ♕a4!   c4

8 ... cxd4 9 ♘xd4 and **10 ♗e3 ±;
8... ♘h6!? 9 dxc5 ♗xc5 10 b4 ♗e7 11
♗e3 ♕c7 12 b5 ♕a5 13 ♗d1! ♕xa4 14
♗xa4 ♘a5 15 b6+ ±.**

9 b3!   . . .

a) **9 ♘h4! ♗g6 10 b3** ± (Seirawan).
b) **9 ♘bd2?! ♕a5 10 ♕d1 h6! 11
♖e1 b5** (Short-Seirawan, Tilburg
1990) **12 ♘f1** ∞.

9 . . .   ♕a5

10	♕xa5	♘xa5
11	♘fd2!	♖c8
12	bxc4	dxc4
13	♘a3	♗d3
14	♗xd3	cxd3
15	♘e4	± (Short)

B

3 . . .   c5?!

This rare continuation was chosen by Botvinnik in his 1961 World Championship match with Tal after he had previously experienced some difficulties in the main variation. Usually the positions reached resemble various sidelines of the French Defence where White has an extra tempo in return for concessions such as capturing on c5.

4 dxc5   . . .

For 4 ♘e2 see Short–Lein in the chapter on various continuations.

4 . . .   e6

4 . . . ♘c6 succeeds only if White permits . . . ♗g4 as after 5 ♘f3 ♗g4! 6 ♗b5 ♕a5+ 7 ♘c3 e6 8 ♗e3 ♘e7 *(8 . . . a6 9 ♗xc6+ bxc6 10 a3 ♗xf3 11 ♕xf3 − 11 gxf3?! ♘ge7 12 b4 ♕d8 ∞ − 11 . . . ♗xc5 12 0-0 ♗xe3 13 ♕xe3 ♘e7 14 b4 ♕c7 = Kirov–K. Arkell, Leningrad 1989)* 9 ♗d2 ♕c7 10 ♗e2 a6 11 0-0 ♘g6 ∓ Spassky–Kotov, USSR 1955. Better, according to Keith Arkell, is **9 a3!** a6 10 ♗a4, with the idea of b4. Boleslavsky's suggestion is 5 ♗b5! ♕a5+ *(Interesting is 5 . . . e6 6 ♗e3 ♘e7 7 ♘f3 ♘f5 8 ♗d4!? ♘xd4 9 ♕xd4 ♕a5+! 10 ♘c3 ♕xb5! 11 ♘xb5 ♘xd4 12 ♘bxd4! ♗xc5 13 c3 ±; but wrong is 9 . . . a5? 10 c3 ♗e7 11 0-0 0-0 12 ♗xc6 bxc6 13 b4 ± Blatny– L. Hansen, Baguio City 1987 or 6 b4!? ♕h4 7 c3 ♕e4+ 8 ♘e2 ♕xg2 9 ♘g3! ♕h3 10 ♗g5! g5 11 f3 ♕g2 12 ♘d2 ± Minasjan–Khenkin, Minsk 1990)* 6 ♘c3 e6 7 ♗e3 *(7 ♕d4 ♘e7 8 b4 ♗d7 9 bxa5 ♘xd4 10 ♗xd7+ ♔xd7 11 ♖b1 ∞ Simagin)* 7 . . . ♗d7 8 ♘f3! *(8 ♗xc6 ♗xc6 9 ♘f3 ♗xc5 10 ♗xc5 ♕xc5 11 ♕d4 ± Pachman)* 8 . . . ♘xe5 *(8 . . . ♘ge7 9 a3 ♘g6 10 ♗xc6 ♗xc6 11 ♗d4 ± Boleslavsky)* 9 ♘xe5 ♗xb5 10 ♕h5! g6 11 ♘xg6 ♘f6 12 ♕h4 ♘e4 13 ♘xf8 with decisive advantage.

5 ♕g4!?   . . .

Complicated is 5 ♘c3 ♘c6 6 ♗f4 ♘ge7 7 ♘f3 ♘g6 8 ♗e3!? ♘gxe5 9 ♘xe5 ♘xe5 10 ♕h5!? *(10 ♕d4!?)*

10 . . . ♘c6 11 0-0-0 ♗e7 12 f4 g6 which eventually led to even prospects in Tal–Botvinnik, 4th match game USSR 1961.

The text gives White good chances of the initiative thanks to his aggressively posted pawn on e5. Nevertheless Boleslavsky's recommendation of 5 ♗e3 ♘e7 6 c3 ♘f5 7 ♗d4 ♕c7 8 ♗d3 ♗xc5 9 ♗xc5 ♕xc5 10 ♗xf5 exf5 11 ♘f3 ♘c6 12 0-0 0-0 13 ♘bd2 ± is probably simpler.

5 . . .   ♘c6

Botvinnik comfortably obtained equality in game six after 5 . . . ♘d7! 6 ♘f3?! ♘e7 7 ♗g5 h6 8 ♗xe7 ♕xe7 9 ♘c3 ♕xc5 10 0-0-0 a6 11 ♔b1 ♘b6 12 ♘d4 ♗d7 13 h4 0-0-0. But now (game eight) he was probably afraid of some improvement, e.g. 6 ♗b5! with 6 . . . ♕c7 7 ♘f3 ♕xc5 8 ♘c3 in mind. In his book Schwarz recommends the improvement for Black of 7 . . . ♘e7 8 ♘c3 ♘g6 9 ♕g3 ♗xc5. Our counter-recommendation is 9 0-0 ♗xc5 10 ♖e1 ± (10 ♘xd5?! exd5 11 e6).

6	♘f3	♕c7
7	♗b5	♗d7
8	♗xc6	♕xc6
9	♗e3	♘h6?!

Petrosian considered 9 . . . ♘e7 10 ♘bd2 ♘f5 11 ♘b3 ♘xe3 12 fxe3 the lesser of two evils. The text is Tal–Botvinnik, 8th match game USSR

1961, in which Black submitted to the ugly doubling of his pawns to try and get some scope for his bishop pair – see illustrative games.

ILLUSTRATIVE GAMES

31   NUNN–DLUGY
London 1986

1 e4 c6 2 d4 d5 3 e5 ♗f5 4 ♘c3 h5 5 ♗d3 ♗xd3 6 ♕xd3 e6 7 ♘f3 ♘h6 8 0-0 ♘f5?! (8 . . . ♘d7 was better) **9 ♘e2! ♘d7** (9 . . . ♗e7) **10 ♘g3! ♘h4** (10 . . . ♘xg3 11 fxg3 ♗e7 12 h4 ±; 10 . . . g6 11 ♘xf5 gxf5 – 11 . . . exf5? 12 ♖e1 and e5-e6! – 12 ♗g5 ±) **11 ♘xh4 ♕xh4 12 ♗e3 ♕d8 13 ♖fd1!** (And not 13 f4? g6 14 f5 gxf5 15 ♘xf5 exf5 16 ♕xf5 ♕e7 17 ♗g5 ♕e6 ∓) **13 . . . ♖c8?** (13 . . . ♗e7 ±) **14 b3! c5 15 c4 cxd4** (15 . . . ♘b6 16 dxc5 ♗xc5 17 ♗xc5 ♖xc5 18 ♘e4 +–; 15 . . . h4!? 16 ♘e2! dxc4 17 ♕xc4 cxd4 18 ♕xd4 ♗c5 19 ♕e4 ♗xe3 21 ♕xe3 ± or 16 . . . ♘b6 17 ♖ac1 dxc4 18 bxc4 cxd4 19 ♘xd4 ♗c5 20 ♕e4 ♕e7 21 ♕g4 ±) **16 cxd5!! ♘xe5** (16 . . . exd5 17 ♗xd4 +–; 16 . . . dxe3 17 dxe6 exf2+ 18 ♔f1 ♖c7 – if 18 . . . fxe6 then 19 ♕g6+ ♔e7 20 ♖d6 winning – 19 exf7+ ♔xf7 20 e6+ ♔g8 – 20 . . . ♔xe6 21 ♕f5+ ♔e7 22 ♖e1+! wins – 21 ♕d5! ♗e7 22 exd7+ ♔f8 23 ♘f5) **17 ♕xd4 ♕xd5?** (Less terminal is 17 . . . ♘g4 18 ♕xa7 ±) **18 ♕a4+!** and here **Black resigned**, since after 18 . . . ♕c6 15 ♖ac1! wins, and after 18 . . . b5 19 ♖xd5 is winning.

32   TIMMAN–SEIRAWAN
Hilversum (m) 1990

1 e4 c6 2 d4 d5 3 e5 ♗f5 4 ♘c3 e6 5 g4 ♗g6 6 ♘ge2 c5 7 h4 h5 8 ♘f4 ♘c6! 9 ♘xg6 fxg6 10 ♕d3? cxd4 11 ♘b5 hxg4! 12 ♕xg6+ ♔d7 13 ♕xg4 ♕b6! 14 c3! (14 f4? a6 15 ♘a3 ♘h6 ∓) 14 . . . dxc3 15 ♘xc3 ♘h6! (15 . . . ♕d4!) 16 ♗xh6! ♕xb2! 17 ♗d2! (17 ♖b1 ♕xc3+ 18 ♗d2 ♕xe5+) 17 . . . ♕xa1+ 18 ♔e2 ♕b2? (18 . . . d4! 19 ♗g2 d3+ 20 ♔e3 ♗c5+ 21 ♔e4! ♕b2 22 ♕xg7+ ♘e7 23 ♖b1 − 23 ♔xd3 ♖ad8 − 23 . . . ♕xd2 24 ♖xb7+ ♔c6 25 ♖xe7 ♖xh4+ 26 ♔f3 ♕xf2 mate!) 19 ♗h3! ♖e8 20 ♖b1 ♕c2 21 ♖xb7+ ♔c8 22 ♖b1? (22 ♖b5! g5! 23 h5 ♖h7 24 ♖xd5 ♖c7 ∞) 22 . . . ♗a3! 23 ♖d1 (23 ♕xg7 ♖h7!) 23 . . . ♗b2 24 ♘b5 ♔b8 25 ♘d6 ♘d4+ 26 ♔e3 ♖xh4 27 ♕xh4 ♕xd1 28 ♗g4 ♘c2+ 29 ♔d3 ♘e1+ White resigned (Seirawan).

33   CHANDLER–SPEELMAN
Great Britain (ch) 1985

1 e4 c6 2 d4 d5 3 e5 ♗f5 4 h4 h5 5 c4 dxc4 6 ♗xc4 e6 7 ♘c3 ♘d7 8 ♘ge2!? ♗e7 9 ♘g3 ♗g6 10 ♘ce4 (10 ♗e2!?) 10 . . . ♘h6! 11 ♘g5?! ♕a5+! 12 ♗d2 (12 ♔f1 0-0-0 gives Black a comfortable edge) 12 . . . ♗b4 13 ♘5e4?! (13 a3 ♗xd2+ 14 ♕xd2 ♕xd2+ 15 ♔xd2 0-0-0 16 ♔e3 c5 ∞) 13 . . . ♗xe4 14 ♘xe4 ♘f5 15 ♗c3 ♗xc3+! (After either 15 . . . ♖d8 16 ♕d2! and 15 . . . 0-0-0 16 ♕b3 White has a significant pull) 16 bxc3 ♖d8! (16 . . . 0-0-0? 17 ♕b3 ♘xe5 − 17 . . . ♘xd4?? 18 ♘d6+ − 18 ♗xe6+ fxe6 19 ♕xe6+ ♘d7 20

♕xf5!) 17 ♗d3 (17 0-0 ♘xe5! ∓; 17 ♕c1 ♘b6 − 17 . . . ♘xe5!? − 18 ♘d2 ♘xd4 19 cxd4 ♖xd4 20 ♗e2 0-0 21 ♕c2 ♖fd8 22 0-0-0 ♕xe5 23 ♘f3 ♕f4+ 24 ♖d2 ♖xd2 25 ♘xd2 ♕xf2 ∓) 17 . . . ♘xd4 18 ♘d6+ ♔e7 19 0-0 ♘f3+!! (19 . . . ♕xc3 20 ♖c1 ♕a3 21 f4 ∞) 20 gxf3 (20 ♕xf3 ♘xe5 21 ♘f5+! exf5 22 ♖fe1 ♖he8 ∓; 21 ♕g3 ♖xd6 22 ♕xg7 ♕xc3! wins) 20 . . . ♘xe5 21 ♘xb7 ♕c7!? (21 . . . ♕xc3 22 ♘xd8 ♖xd8 23 ♖c1 ♕xd3 ∓) 22 ♘xd8 ♖xd8 23 f4 ♖xd3 24 ♕xh5 ♘f3+ 25 ♔g2 ♕xf4 26 ♖fd1 (If 26 ♕c5+ then 26 . . . ♔f6!; 26 ♖h1!? is probably best here) 26 . . . ♖xc3! 27 ♖ab1 ♕h2+ 28 ♔f1 ♕h3+ 29 ♔e2 ♖c2+ 30 ♔e3 ♘xh4+ White resigned.

34   ATKINS–CAPABLANCA
London 1922

1 e4 c6 2 d4 d5 3 e5 ♗f5 4 ♗d3 ♗xd3 5 ♕xd3 e6 6 ♘e2 ♕b6 7 0-0 ♕a6 8 ♕d1 c5 9 c3?! (After this seemingly natural move, White has to struggle to equalize. 9 dxc5 ♗xc5 10 b3 followed b7 11 ♗b2 and eventually c2-c4 was better) 9 . . . ♘c6 10 ♘bd2?! (The last chance was 10 ♗e3! cxd4! 11 cxd4 ♘e7 12 ♘bc3 ♘f5 13 ♕d2 = while 10 . . . b6?! 11 f4 ♘b6 12 ♗f2! ♘f5 13 g4! is even favourable) 10 . . . cxd4! (10 . . . ♕d3? 11 ♘f4!) 11 cxd4 ♕d3 12 ♘b3 (Black also gets the initiative after 12 ♘f3. There was hardly any alternative) 12 . . . ♕xd1 13 ♖xd1 ♘ge7?! (A slight inaccuracy. Better is . . . b6! first, as now 14 ♘c5! b6 15 ♘a6! and then ♗d2, b4, a4, etc.

would have given White some play) 14 ♗d2?! a5! (This deprives White of the opportunity given him earlier and heralds the hemming in of the queenside) 15 ♖ac1 b6 16 a4?! (To avert being totally tied down, but this move endangers b4, a weakness for which the possession of h5 gives insufficient compensation. 16 ♗g5! was needed, followed by the capture of the e7 knight − knights are more valuable in closed positions) 16 . . . ♔d7 17 ♘c3 ♘a7 18 ♔f1 ♘ec6 (Thanks to the weakening effect of move 16, this and not f5 is now the natural position for the knight) 19 ♔e2 ♖c8 20 ♗e1 (20 ♗e3 looks more active) 20 . . . ♗e7 21 ♘b1 f5! (The issue cannot be decided solely on the queenside, therefore Black is making preparations for a complete block by means of g5 and h5. If now 22 f4 then 22 . . . h6 and g5 would follow, giving Black a chance to break through on the g-file) 22 exf6 ♗xf6 23 ♗c3 ♘b4! 24 ♗d2 (The intruding knight cannot be exchanged: 24 ♗xb4 axb4 is followed by doubling rooks against the a-pawn or ♘c6-a5-c4) 24 . . . ♘ac6 25 ♗e3 ♘a2! (The black pieces penetrate the weakened queenside) 26 ♖c2 ♖c7! 27 ♘a3 ♖hc8 (threatening 28 . . . ♘xd4+) 28 ♖cd2 ♘a7 29 ♖d3 ♘b4 30 ♖3d2 ♖c6 31 ♖b1 ♗e7! (Preparing the breakthrough combination) 32 ♖a1 ♗d6 33 h3 ♖6c7 (White is so hemmed in that he is even threatened by *zugzwang*) 34 ♖ad1 ♘a2! 35 ♖a1 ♗xa3! (A neat swap yields the c-file to

the world champion) 36 ♖xa2 ♗b4 37 ♖d1 ♖c4! (Threatening 38 . . . ♗e7 followed by ♖b4 and perhaps ♗f6) 38 ♖c1 ♘c6! (Forcing the exchange, after which Black, apart from his space advantage, will have a good knight against the passive bishop. 39 ♔d3 ♖xc1 followed by ♗e7, or 39 ♖aa1 ♗e7 were ineffective against this because of numerous threats) 39 ♖xc4 dxc4 40 ♘d2 ♗xd2! 41 ♔xd2 ♔d6 42 ♔c3 ♔d5 43 ♖a1 g6 44 f3 ♖b8! (Now comes the opening of the b-file) 45 ♖a3 (45 b3 cxb3 46 ♔xb3 ♘xd4+?! 47 ♗xd4 ♔xd4 48 ♖d1+ would still have given White a chance to escape, but 46 . . . ♖c8! 47 ♖d1 ♘e7 is deadly) 45 . . . b5! 46 axb5 ♖xb5 47 ♗f2 ♘b4 48 b3 cxb3 49 ♔xb3 (49 ♖xb3 ♘a2+ 50 ♔b2 ♖xb3+ 51 ♔xb3 ♘c1+ 52 ♔a4 ♘e2 53 ♔xa5 ♘f4! ∓) 49 . . . ♘c6+ 50 ♔c3 ♖b1 51 ♖a4 ♖c1+ 52 ♔d2 ♖c4 53 ♖a1 a4 54 ♖a3 ♘a7 55 ♖a1 ♘b5 56 ♖b1 ♔c6 57 ♔d3 ♖c3+ 58 ♔d2 ♖b3 (Everything is working like clockwork, writes a contemporary reporter) 59 ♖c1+♔b7 60 ♖c2 a3 61 ♗g3 ♘xd4 62 ♖c7+ ♔b6 63 ♖c4 ♔b5! 64 ♖c8 ♘c6 65 ♖a8 ♖b2+ 66 ♔e3 ♖xg2 67 ♗f2 ♘b4! White resigned. An exemplary trouncing!

35   NIMZOVITCH−CAPABLANCA
New York 1927

1 e4 c6 2 d4 d5 3 e5 ♗f5 4 ♗d3 ♗xd3 5 ♕xd3 e6 6 ♘c3 ♕b6 7 ♘ge2 c5!? 8 dxc5 ♗xc5 9 0-0 (9 ♕g3 ♘e7!) 9 . . . ♘e7 10 ♘a4! ♕c6 11 ♘xc5 ♕xc5 12

♗e3 ♕c7 13 f4 ♘f5 14 c3?! (Here analysts later recommended opening up the position by way of 14 ♗f2! h5 15 ♖ac1 ♘c6 16 c4! or 14 ♖ac1! ♘c6 15 ♗f2 h5 16 c4 dxc4 17 ♕xc4 0-0 18 ♖fd1 followed by ♘e2-c3-e4) 14 . . . ♘c6 15 ♖ad1 g6!? (A cunning move tempting a weakness. 15 . . . h5 was also good) 16 g4? (This apparently aggressive move eventually leads to a freezing of White's pawn formation. According to Panov 16 ♗f2 h5 17 ♖d2 — 17 c4? ♘b4 — 18 ♖fc1 and then c3-c4 was needed) 16 . . . ♘xe3 17 ♕xe3 h5! 18 g5 ("This move explains why Black allowed the g2-g4 advance . . . Black acquires a strong square on f5. Moreover, this is not the only pivotal point of the game for White's peasant infantry has generally advanced too far and is therefore weak and full of gaps" — Réti. 18 h3 hxg4 19 hxg4 was no better either because of 19 . . . 0-0-0 and the ensuing threats of g6-g5 and ♖h4 etc.) 18 . . . 0-0 19 ♘d4 ♕b6 20 ♖f2 ♖fc8 21 a3 (A further weakening, but Réti considered it unavoidable sooner or later. Due to his poor pawn formation, White is condemned to passivity) 21 . . . ♖c7 22 ♖d3 ♘a5?! (This knight manœuvre fails to bear the promised fruits, as Black's forces are kept tied down by his opponent's minor tactical opportunities. Although the consequences of this inaccuracy can fortunately be rectified, 22 . . . ♘e7 was more circumspect) 23 ♖e2 ♖e8! (Capablanca is not

prone to the frequent shortcoming of forgetting the opportunities open to his opponent while plotting his own course. 24 f5! was threatened with tactical chances. For instance: 23 . . . ♘c4 24 ♕f2 ♘xa3? 25 f5! exf5 26 e6! etc.) 24 ♔g2 ♘c6! ("Capablanca finds the right plan, and forgoes the seemingly obvious move ♘c4. Let the rooks have that square to attack e4 and f4 and let us get rid of the knight on d4 which is preventing this . . ." — Réti. Here White should have played 25 ♘xc6 ♕xc6 26 ♖d4 while 26 ♕xa7? was out of bounds because of 26 . . . b6) 25 ♖ed2 ♖ec8 26 ♖e2 ♘e7 27 ♖ed2 ♖c4 28 ♕h3 ♔g7 29 ♖f2 a5! ("The continuation of Black's plan is a5-a4 followed by ♘c6-a5-b3. With the threat of ♘b3-c5-e4, White would be obliged to exchange the knights, putting even more wind into Black's sail. The next move, instead of which ♖fd2 was again called for, gives Capablanca the opportunity to summarily exchange the knights." — Réti) 30 ♖e2 ♘f5! ("This crafty move just would not have done against 30 ♖fd2! because of 31 ♘xf5+ gxf5 32 ♕xh5! ♖h8 33 ♕f3 ♖h4 and then 34 ♖d4!" — Réti. The opening of the fourth rank to the black rooks is now unavoidable, because of 31 ♖ed2 ♘xd4 32 ♖xd4 ♖xd4 33 cxd4 ♕b5! followed by 34 . . . ♖c1 to which there is no answer) 31 ♘xf5+ gxf5 32 ♕f3 ♔g6 33 ♖ed2 ♖e4! 34 ♖d4 ♖c4 35 ♕f2 ♕b5 36 ♔g3 (After 36 ♖xc4 ♕xc4 37 ♖d4 ♕b3! the queen end-

game is hopeless in the long run)
36 ... ♖cxd4 37 cxd4 (37 ♖xd4 ♖e2)
37 ... ♕c4 38 ♔g2 b5! ("The defence
of the d4 and f4 pawns and of the
second rank ties down the white
queen and rook so much that they
cannot even move. We will see that
this gives Capablanca the opportunity
to decide the game by a *zugzwang*.
But to get there, the b-pawn is also
needed" — Réti) **39 ♔g1 b4 40 axb4
axb4 41 ♔g2 ♕c1** ("The first
zugzwang. The queen and the rook
cannot move, as can be readily seen,
and h2-h4 would weaken White's
position even further. Black's best
answer would be b4-b3, followed
either by ♖e1 or even by ♕e1. For
this reason White must move his
king, with the result that Black's
queen penetrates to h1" — Réti)
42 ♔g3 ♕h1! 43 ♖d3 (43 ♖e2 ♖xe2
44 ♕xe2 ♕g1+ or 43 ♕f3 h4+ etc.
−+) **43 ... ♖e1 44 ♖f3 ♖d1** (White is
in *zugzwang* again. 45 ♔h3 is answered by 45 ... ♖d2! while 45 ♖b3 is
equally decisively followed by 45 ...
♕e4 46 ♖xb4 ♖d3+ 47 ♔h4 ♖f3)
45 b3 ♖c1! 46 ♖e3 (46 h3 ♖g1+47
♔h4 ♖g4 mate!) **46 ... ♖f1! White
resigned.** 47 ♕e2 is followed by 47 ...
♕g1+ 48 ♔h3 ♖e1!!

36   TAL-GOLOMBEK
Munich Olympiad 1958

**1 e4 c6 2 d4 d5 3 e5 ♗f5 4 c4 e6
5 ♘c3 dxc4 6 ♗xc4 ♘d7 7 ♘ge2 ♘e7
8 0-0 ♘b6 9 ♗b3 ♕d7 10 a4 a5 11 ♘g3
♗g6 12 ♗c2! ♗xc2 13 ♕xc2 ♘ed5 14**

♘ce4 ♘b4 **15 ♕e2 ♘6d5 16 f4 g6 17
♖a3 ♗e7 18 ♗d2 ♘c2?!** (The
exchange can only benefit White)
19 ♖d3 ♘db4 20 ♗xb4 ♘xb4 21 ♖3d1
(The rook danced a spectacular waltz
while an important enemy piece was
exchanged) **21 ... ♖d8?** (It is a pity to
eliminate the chance of queenside
castling. 21 . . . ♕d5 was more
flexible) **22 ♔h1 h5?!** (Black is very
optimistic. 22 . . . ♘d5 was more
cautious) **23 ♘f6+! ♗xf6 24 exf6 ♔f8**
(25 f5! was threatened. Castling kingside is also hazardous) **25 ♘e4 h4 26
♘c5 ♕c8 27 f5!** (It's starting!) **27 ...
gxf5?! 28 ♕e3! b6 29 ♕g5! ♖h7** (29 ...
♖g8 30 ♕h6+ ♔e8 31 ♕h7 ♖f8 32
♘xe6! or 31 ... ♔f8 32 ♘xe6+ ♕xe6
33 ♕h6+ ♔e8 34 ♖fe1) **30 ♖f4! bxc5
31 ♖xh4 ♖xh4 32 ♕g7+ ♔e8 33
♕g8+ ♔d7 34 ♕xf7+ ♔d6 35 ♕e7+
Black resigned.**

37   TAL-BOTVINNIK
World Championship Match (8)
1961

**1 e4 c6 2 d4 d5 3 e5 c5?! 4 dxc5 e6
5 ♕g4!? ♘c6?! 6 ♘f3 ♕c7 7 ♗b5 ♗d7
8 ♗xc6 ♕xc6 9 ♗e3 ♘h6?! 10 ♗xh6!**
gxh6 **11 ♘bd2 ♕xc5 12 c4!** (Grandmaster Flohr recalls that none of the
analysts in the press room expected
this move since it was generally
accepted that the opening up of the
position favoured the side possessing
a pair of bishops. But Tal plays
without any preconceived notions,
relying on an examination of the
actual opportunities provided by the

position) **12 ... 0-0-0** (12 ... dxc4 13 0-0 ♗c6 14 ♖ac1 ± Flohr) **13 0-0 ♔b8 14 ♖fd1!** (In order to prevent the queen from capturing on d5 in the event of an exchange) **14 ... ♕b6** (14 ... ♗e7!? Flohr) **15 ♕h4!** (A versatile move! The queen controls several important squares from here, also threatens 16 b4!) **15 . . . a5?!** (Botvinnik fends off this threat, but in doing so makes White's play on the queenside easier. 15 ... ♗c5 was also bad, because of 16 cxd5 exd5 17 ♘b3. According to Grandmaster Flohr, 15 ... ♖c8 or 15 ... ♖g8 gave the most realistic chances) **16 ♖ac1 ♖g8 17 ♘b3! a4** (17 ... dxc4 18 ♖xc4 and Black succumbs on the d-file) **18 c5 ♕c7 19 ♘bd4 ♖c8** (19 ... ♗xc5 20 b4 axb3 21 ♘xb3 b6 22 a4! ±) **20 b4** (Now, as if to placate the adherents of

classical principles, Tal gives a magnificent demonstration of the supremacy of the knights over the bishops in closed positions!) **20 ... axb3 21 axb3 ♕d8 22 ♕xd8!** (Tal, the great tactician, exchanges queens this time with barely a second thought. White gains excellent attacking opportunities in the position that develops, in spite of the diminished material) **22 ... ♖xd8 23 b4 ♖g4 24 b5 ♖c8 25 c6 ♗e8 26 ♖c2!** (There are various threats from the doubled rooks. They eagerly await Black's attempt to break out) **26 ... ♗g7 27 ♖a1! ♗xe5 28 ♘xe5 ♖xd4 29 ♘d7+!** (29 ... ♔c7 30 b6+ ♔d8 31 cxb7 and if 29 ... ♗xd7 then 30 cxd7 ♖d8 31 ♖c8+! ♖xc8 32 ♖a8+ decides) **Black resigned.**

6
Exchange Variation: 4 ♗d3 and Others

1 e4 c6 2 d4 d5 3 exd5 cxd5 4 ♗d3

Although once relatively frequent, less has been seen of this variation over recent years. Play usually leads to a variety of the Queen's Gambit Declined with colours reversed, and an extra tempo for White.

After 4 ♗d3 (4 c4 is dealt with in the next chapter) the struggle revolves around the satisfactory development of Black's queen's bishop. Sometimes he even resorts to . . . g6 and . . . ♗f5. However, both main continuations (5 . . . ♘f6 and 5 . . . g6) give good prospects of equality and it is perhaps understandable that the popularity of this safe but unambitious system has waned recently. First we examine fourth move alternatives for White, all being rather harmless since they allow the c8 bishop to develop:

a) 4 c3 ♗f5! *(4 . . . ♘c6 5 ♗f4?! ♗f5 6 ♘f3 e6 7 ♕b3 ♕c8 8 ♘bd2 ♘f6 9 ♗e2 ♗e7 10 0-0 ♘e4 = Larsen-Spassky, San Juan 1969)* 5 ♘f3 ♘f6 6 ♗b5+ ♘bd7 7 ♘h4 ♗g6 8 ♗f4 e6 9 ♘d2 ♘h5 10 ♘xg6 = Fischer-Hort, Vinkovci 1968.

b) 4 ♘c3 ♗f5! 5 ♘f3 ♘c6 6 ♗b5 e6 7 ♘e5 ♕c7 8 g4 ♗g6 9 h4 f6 10 ♘xg6 hxg6 ∞ Botvinnik. This position can also develop via the 2 ♘c3 d5 3 ♘f3 ♗g4 4 h3 ♗h5 variation!

c) 4 ♘f3 ♗g4 5 ♗d3 ♘c6 6 c3 e6 7 ♕b3 ♕d7 8 ♘bd2 = Spielmann-Stahlberg, (m) 1933.

4 ...   ♘c6

On 4 . . . ♘f6 5 c3 ♗g4 correct is 6 ♕b3! *(6 ♕a4+ ♘bd7!? 7 ♘e2 ♗h5 8 ♘f4 ♗g6 9 ♘xg6 hxg6 10 ♗f4 e6 11 ♘bd2 ♗e7 12 h3 ♘h5! 13 ♗h2 g5! =*

Tompa–Vadász, Budapest 1977) 6 . . . ♕b6 7 ♗f4! *(Better than 7 ♘e2 e6 8 ♗f4 ♘bd7 9 ♘d2 ♗h5 = Mecking–Hort, Manila 1976 or 7 f3 ♗h5 8 ♘e2 ♗g6! 9 ♘f4 Széll–Varnusz, Budapest 1977 when now 9 . . . ♗xd3 10 ♘xd3 e6 =)* 7 . . . e6 8 ♘a3! ±.

5 c3   . . .

Here we have:

A: 5 . . . ♘f6
B: 5 . . . g6!?
C: 5 . . . ♕c7

Weaker is 5 . . . e5?! 6 dxe5 ♘xe5 7 ♕e2 ♕e7 8 ♗b5+ ± Botvinnik – Black has no compensation for the isolated d-pawn.

A

5 . . .   ♘f6

The main variation, after which the Queen's Gambit position (1 d4 d5 2 c4 e6 3 cxd5 exd5 4 ♘c3 c6 5 ♘f3) with colours reversed and an extra tempo has emerged.

6 ♗f4!   . . .

6 ♘e2 and 6 ♘f3 are met by 6 . . . ♗g4! and the waiting move 6 h3?! by 6 . . . e5! e.g. 7 dxe5 ♘xe5 8 ♘f3 *(8 ♕e2 ♕e7 9 ♗b5+ ♗d7 10 ♗xd7+ ♘fxd7 11 ♔f1 ∓ Honfi–Portisch,*

Hungary 1962) 8 . . . ♗d6 9 0-0 0-0 10 ♘xe5 ♗xe5 11 ♘d2 ♗c7 = Botvinnik.

6 ♗g5 gets nowhere either: 6 . . . ♘e4 *(6 . . . ♘g4?! 7 f3! ♗h5 8 ♘e2 e6 9 ♘d2 ♗g6 10 ♘f1 ♗xd3 11 ♕xd3 ± P. Atanasov–Spiridonov, Bulgaria (ch) 1977; 7 ♕b3 ♕d7 8 ♘e2 e6 9 ♘g3 ♘h5 10 f3 ♘xg3 11 hxg3 ♗f5 12 ♗xf5 exf5 = van den Bosch–Capablanca, Budapest 1929, or in this line 7 . . . ♕b6 8 ♘d2 e6 9 ♘gf3 ♗d6 10 0-0 h6 11 ♕xb6 axb6 12 ♗e3 0-0 13 ♖fe1 ± Ragozin–Petrosian, USSR 1949)* 7 ♗xe4 dxe4 8 d5 ♘e5 9 ♕a4+ b5 10 ♕xe4 f6 ∞ or 10 ♕xb5+? ♗d7 11 ♕e2 ♘d3+ Botvinnik, but clearest seems 9 . . . ♕d7 10 ♕xe4 ♕f5 ∓ Fischer.

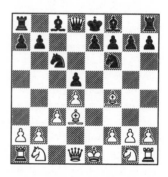

Now Black must make a decision:

A1: 6 . . . g6
A2: 6 . . . ♗g4

The move 6 . . . e6 is unsatisfactory as Black's queen's bishop is shut out of play.

A1

6 ...   g6

With this move Black postpones the problem of his c8 bishop. A frequent motif is to leave this piece at home altogether and later begin a kingside initiative with . . . ♘h5 and then . . . f5. At present White can maintain a slight edge, however.

7 ♘f3   ...

On 7 ♘e2 the curious (but logical) 7 . . . ♗f5! to exchange White's good bishop is possible: 8 ♗xf5 gxf5 9 ♘d2 e6 10 ♗g5 ♗e7 11 ♗xf6 ♗xf6 12 f4 ♗h4+ 13 g3 ♗e7 14 ♘f3 0-0 ∞ Vasiliev–Khalibeili, USSR 1964.

7 ...   ♗g7
8 ♘bd2   ...

Or:
a) **8 0-0** 0-0 *(8 . . . ♗g4 9 ♘bd2 ±)* 9 ♖e1! *(9 h3 ♗f5! 10 ♗xf5 gxf5 11 ♕d3?! ♘e4! 12 ♖e1 e6 13 ♘bd2 ♖c8 14 ♘f1 a6 15 a4 was Gavrilakis–Varnusz, Athens 1976 and now 16 . . . ♘e7! = or 10 ♖e1 ♕b6! 11 ♗xf5 gxf5! 12 ♕b3 e6 Kholmov–Tseshkovsky, Sochi 1974 and here 13 ♕xb6 =)* 9 . . . ♗g4?! *(Better 9 . . . ♗f5!)* 10 h3 ♗xf3 11 ♕xf3 ♕b6?! 12 ♘a3! ♖ac8 13 ♖e2 a6!? 14 ♗g5! ♖fd8 15 ♕f4 ± Tompa–Varnusz, Budapest 1977.
b) **8 h3** This transposes to Lasker–Tartakower, Moravska Ostrava 1923

in which Black tried to maintain a knight on e4 with 8 . . . ♘e4?! *(8 . . . ♗f5 or first 8 . . . 0-0 and then ♗f5 is correct)* 9 ♘bd2 f5? 10 0-0 0-0 11 ♘e5! ♘xe5 12 ♗xe5 ♗xe5 13 dxe5 when the difference between White's 'good' and Black's 'bad' bishop was pronounced — see illustrative games for the continuation.

8 ...   ♘h5

8 . . . 0-0 9 h3 ♘h5?! *(Once again 9 . . . ♗f5!)* 10 ♗h2 f5 11 0-0 f4 12 ♖e1 ♕d6 13 ♖e2 ♘g3 14 fxg3 hxg3 15 ♗xg3 ♕xg3 16 ♕b3! e6 17 ♖ae1 a6 18 ♕b6 ± Geller–Benkö, Curaçao (c) 1962.

9 ♗e3   0-0

Also falling slightly short of equality are 9 . . . f5 10 ♘b3 f4 11 ♗d2 0-0 12 0-0 ♗g4 13 ♗e2 ♕d6 14 ♘c1 ♘f6 15 ♘d3 ♘e4 16 ♖e1 ± Hennings–A. Zaitsev, Debrecen 1970 and 9 . . . ♕c7 10 0-0 0-0 11 ♖e1 f5 12 ♘b3 f4 13 ♗d2 ± Bronstein–Dominguez, Las Palmas 1972.

10 0-0   f5
11 ♘b3   ♕d6
12 ♖e1   ...

12 ♗b5 f4 13 ♗d2 ♗g4 14 h3 ♗xf3 15 ♕xf3 ♔h8 16 ♘c5? ♘e5! ∞ Saveraide–Ivánka, Tbilisi 1976.

12 ...   f4

13 ♗d2   ♗g4

Here Fischer–Czerniak, Netanya 1968 led to a small plus for Black after 14 ♗e2 ♖ae8 15 ♘c1?! ♗xf3! 16 ♗xf3 e5! Better, however, is 15 ♘e5! with a slight edge for White.

A2

6 ...   ♗g4
7 ♕b3!   ...

The critical move, attempting to immediately exploit the bishop's absence from the queen's wing. Harmless are 7 f3 ♗h5 8 ♘e2 e6 9 ♘d2 ♗d6 = Botvinnik, 7 ♘e2 ♕d7 8 ♕b3 ♗h5 9 0-0 ♗g6 = Botvinnik and 7 ♘f3 ♕b6 8 ♕b3 ♗xf3 9 gxf3 e6 10 ♘d2 ♘d7 = as in Milner-Barry v Flohr, Hastings 1934-35.

7 ...   ♘a5!

The sharpest move and perhaps the best. The alternatives (apart from

7 ... ♕b6?! 8 ♘a3!) are:

a) 7 ... ♕d7 8 ♘d2 e6 9 ♘gf3 ♗xf3 10 ♘xf3 a6 *(10 ... ♗e7 11 ♘e5 ♕c8 12 h3 0-0? 13 ♕c2 ±; 12 ... ♘d7 ±)* 11 0-0!? *(11 h3)* 11 ... ♘h5 12 ♘e5! ♘xe5 13 ♗xe5 ♗e7 14 ♕d1 ♘f6 15 ♕e2 0-0 16 ♖ae1 ± Quinteros-Benkö, Sao Paulo 1977.

b) 7 ... ♕c8!? *(Similar to the 7 ... ♕d7 line except that now the black queen is not molested by ♘e5)* 8 ♘d2 ♗h5! *(8 ... e6 9 ♘gf3 ♗e7 10 ♘e5 ♘xe5 11 ♗xe5 0-0 12 ♕c2 ♗f5 13 ♗xf5 exf5 14 ♕b3 ♕c6 Nezhmetdinov-Shamkovich, USSR 1970 and now 15 a4 ±)* 9 ♘gf3 ♗g6 10 ♗xg6 hxg6 11 ♘e5 e6 12 0-0 ♘h5! 13 ♗e3 ♗d6 14 ♖fe1 ♕c7 15 ♘df3 ♘f6 16 h3 0-0 17 ♗f4 ♘e4 18 ♘xc6 *(18 ♗h2 may be better here)* 18 ... ♗xf4 *(18 ... bxc6 seems stronger)* 19 ♘ce5 g5!? 20 ♘d3 (L. A. Schneider-Ornstein, Sweden (ch) 1988) to be followed by 20 ... ♖fe8 and 21 ... f6 ∞ (Ornstein).

8 ♕a4+   ♗d7
9 ♕c2   ♕b6

The point of White's queen manœuvre was to force back the queen's bishop, so now Black sets about exchanging it on b5. Instead 9 ... a6 10 ♘f3 b5 11 ♘bd2 g6 12 0-0 ♗g7 13 ♖fe1 0-0 14 b4 ± Botvinnik or 9 ... e6 10 ♘f3 ♕b6 11 0-0 ♗d6?! 12 ♗e5! ♕c7 13 ♖e1 ♘c4 14 ♗xc4 dxc4 15 ♘bd2 b5 16 ♘e4 ± Timman-Pomar, Las Palmas 1977 both favour White. A new idea is 9 ... ♖c8!? e.g. 10 ♘d2 a6!

11 a4 ♗g4 12 ♘gf3 e6 13 ♘e5 ♗d6 14 ♗g5 ♗h5 15 f4 h6 16 ♗h4 g5 17 ♗g3 ♘g4 18 ♘df3 ♖g8 ∞ J. Benjamin-Duric, New York 1988.

10 ♘f3   e6

On the immediate 10 ... ♗b5 unpleasant is 11 ♗xb5+ ♕xb5 12 ♘a3, e.g. 12 ... ♕b6 13 ♕a4+ ♘c6 14 0-0 e6 15 ♘b5 ♖c8 16 ♘d6+ ♗xd6 17 ♗xd6 ♘e7 18 ♗a3 ♕a5 19 ♕b3 b5 20 ♖ad1 and Black will experience difficulty castling, Romanovsky-Konstaninopolsky, USSR 1945.

The text, however, offers good prospects for equality:

a) **11 0-0 ♗b5!** 12 ♘bd2 ♗xd3 13 ♕xd3 ♖c8 = Maróczy-Capablanca, Lake Hopatcong 1926 (illustrative game number 38).

b) **11 a4!?** Fischer's innovation to prevent the equalizing trade of bishops. The drawback is that b3 is weakened. Now Fischer-Petrosian, USSR v Rest of the World 1970, continued **11 ... ♖c8?** *(Also bad is 11 ... ♘b3 12 ♖a2 ♖c8 13 0-0 ±)* 12 ♘bd2 ♘c6 13 ♕b1 with advantage to White – see illustrative games for the continuation. Best is **11 ... ♕b3!** reaching a double-edged position after 12 ♕e2 *(12 ♘bd2 ♕xc2 =)* 12 ... ♘c4! *(Not 12 ... ♗xa4 13 ♖xa4)* 13 ♗c1! *(13 ♗xc4 dxc4! 14 ♘e5 ♗xa4! 15 ♘d2?! ♕xb2 16 ♖xa4? ♕c1 17 ♕d1 ♕xd1+ 18 ♔xd1 ♘d5!! wins for Black)*. Here White threatens to win with 14 a5 and 15 ♘bd2 but several

counters are possible for Black: **13 ... a5, 13 ... ♗c6** or even the pawn sacrifice with **13 ... ♗d6!?** 14 a5 ♘e4! 15 ♗xe4 dxe4 16 ♕xe4 ♗c6.

All in all a complicated position in which Black's chances appear no worse.

B

5 ...   g6!?

An interesting continuation. Of course Black may sometimes transpose back into A1 with ... ♘f6, but he also has the possibility of developing his knight on h6, and perhaps following up with f7-f6 and e7-e5.

6 ♘f3   ...

Instead 6 ♗f4 ♗g7 7 h3? f6! 8 ♘e2 e5 9 dxe5 fxe5 10 ♗h2 ♘ge7 ∓ Barry-Grószpéter, Innsbruck 1977 is a good example of Black's aggressive possibilities.

6 ...   &g7

6 . . . *&g4 7 ♕b3! (7 h3?! &xf3*
8 ♕xf3 &g7 9 0-0 e6 10 ♘d2 ♘f6 11
♕e2 ♕d6 12 ♘f3 ♘d7 13 ♖e1 ∞
Mozhionzik–Bronstein, USSR 1969)
7 . . . *&xf3 8 ♕xb7 ♕c8 9 ♕xc8 ♖xc8*
10 gxf3 ♘xd4 11 *&e3 ♘xf3+ (11 . . .*
♘c6 12 &h5 ± Rossolimo–Bronstein,
Monte Carlo 1969 12 ♔e2 ♘e5 ±
Botvinnik.

7 0-0   ...

Or:
a) 7 *&f4* ♘h6 8 ♘bd2 0-0 9 0-0 f6?!
10 c4! ± Mecking–Ciocaltea, Vršac
1971 but see the similar line Hort–
Bellon below!
b) 7 **h3** ♘h6 8 *&f4* 0-0 9 ♕d2 ♘f5
10 0-0 f6 11 ♖e1 ♖e8 12 c4!? ♘cxd4
13 ♘xd4 ♘xd4 14 cxd5 ∞ Tseitlin–
Savon, USSR 1970.

7 ...   ♘h6
8 ♖e1   0-0

And here:
a) **9 a4** ♘f5 *(Perhaps 9 . . . ♔h8!?*
10 b4 a6 planning . . . f6 etc.) 10 *&f4*
♖e8 11 ♘bd2 f6 12 *&b5!* g5!? 13 *&g3*
♘xg3 14 hxg3 e5 15 c4! a6 16 cxd5
axb5 17 dxc6 g4 18 ♘h4 ± Khalikian–
Machulsky, USSR 1977.
b) **9 &f4** transposes to Hort–
Bellon, Montilla 1978, which was
reached via a slightly different move-
order. That game resulted in a superb
victory for the Spanish grandmaster,

and should encourage any prospect-
ive adherents of 5 . . . g6!?: 9 . . . ♔h8!?
10 ♘bd2 f6 11 b4 a6 12 a4 e5! 13 *&xh6*
(13 dxe5 fxe5 14 &xe5 ♘xe5 15 ♘xe5
♕c7! planning . . . ♕xc3 ∓) 13 . . .
&xh6 14 b5 *(14 dxe5 fxe5 15 ♘xe5*
♘xe5 16 ♖xe5 &g7 ∓) 14 . . . axb5 15
axb5 ♖xa1 16 ♕xa1 e4 17 bxc6 exd3
18 cxb7 *&xb7* 19 ♘b3 *&c8* 20 ♖d1?!
(20 ♕d1!? &f5 21 ♘c5 ♕a5 ∓
Ciocaltea) 20 . . . *&g4* 21 h3 *(21 ♖xd3*
&f5 22 ♖d1 &c2 −+) 21 . . . *&xf3* 22
gxf3 ♕d7 23 ♖xd3 ♖b8! 24 ♘d2? *(24*
♘c5) 24 . . . ♕f5 25 ♕f1 *&d2* 0-1.

C

5 ...   ♕c7

A waiting move as well as preventing *&f4*.

6 ♘e2!   ...

Renewing the *&f4* threat. Less
testing are **6 h3** ♘f6 7 ♘f3 g6 8 0-0

♗f5 Tolush–Flohr, USSR 1944 and **6 f4?!** ♘f6 **7** ♘f3 ♗g4 **8** 0-0 ♘e4 ∓ Botvinnik.

6 . . .   **e6?!**

Navarovsky gives 6 . . . ♗g4! 7 f3 ♗h5 8 ♘f4 *(8 ♗f4 ♕d7 =)* 8 . . . ♘f6!? unclear, when 9 g4?! ♗g6 10 g5 ♘h5 11 ♘xd5 ♕a5 ∓ though this variation has yet to be seen in practical play.

7 ♗f4   **♗d6**
8 ♗xd6   **♕xd6**

9 ♘d2 e5 (Otherwise the c8 bishop will be hemmed in. This way, however, the d-pawn is isolated) 10 dxe5 ♘xe5 11 ♗b5+ ♗d7 12 ♗xd7+ ♕xd7 13 0-0 ± Botvinnik.

ILLUSTRATIVE GAMES

38 MARÓCZY–CAPABLANCA
Lake Hopatcong 1926

1 e4 c6 2 d4 d5 3 exd5 cxd5 4 ♗d3 ♘c6 **5 c3** ♘f6 **6** ♗f4 ♗g4 **7** ♕b3 ♘a5 **8** ♕a4+ ♗d7 **9** ♕c2 ♕b6 **10** ♘f3 e6 **11** 0-0 ♗b5! **12** ♘bd2 ♗xd3 **13** ♕xd3 ♖c8 (13 . . . ♕xb2? 14 ♖ab1 ♕a3 15 ♕b5+ etc.) **14** ♖ab1 ♗e7 **15 h3** 0-0 **16** ♖fe1 ♘c4 **17** ♘xc4 ♖xc4! (Black accepts the loss of tempo in order to maintain his play in the c-file. After 17 . . . dxc4 the knight takes control of d5, but there is nevertheless not much life left in the position) **18** ♘e5

♖4c8 **19** ♗g5 (Maróczy, already past his peak, plays against the World Champion with the aim of only drawing. 19 ♖e2 followed by ♖f1, ♗h2 and perhaps f2-f4-f5 keeps up the tension) **19 . . .** ♕d8 (Loss of the exchange was threatened) **20** ♗xf6! gxf6! (20 . . . ♗xf6! 21 f4! and the knight would have to be taken sooner or later. Following the recapture fxe5 White's major pieces would menace on the kingside) **21** ♘g4 ♔h8 (In exchange for his disrupted pawn formation, Black has achieved counterplay on the g-file) **22 f4** f5 (f5! by White was threatened) **23** ♘e5 ♗d6 **24** ♕f3 (If White is in any case only playing for a draw, 24 ♕e3 is more to the point, enabling the queen to capture later on e5) **24 . . .** ♗xe5 **25** ♖xe5 ♖g8 **26** ♖e2?! (Now the initiative slides in Black's favour. 26 ♔h2! ♕h4 27 ♖g1 followed by 28 g3 and 29 g4! was necessary, giving even chances) **26 . . .** ♕h4 **27** ♔h2 ♖g6 **28 g3** ♕f6 **29** ♖g1 ♔g7! (Capablanca goes all out to unbalance the drawish position. His last move has prepared the advance of the h-pawn, viz.: 30 ♖g2 h5! 31 ♕xh5? ♖h8 32 ♕f3 ♖xh3+!. White could still play g3-g4, although the continuation chosen is also satisfactory) **30** ♕d3 a6 **31** ♖c1 h5 **32 h4** ♔h6 **33 c4!?** (White begins counterplay at last, although the preparatory 33 b3 would have been useful) **33 . . . dxc4 34** ♖xc4 ♖xg3!!? (A witty sacrifice! Against optimal defence it leads to a draw, but the pressure could not be escalated any further. Thus 34 . . . ♖cg8 35 ♖g2 ♖d8 36 ♖d2 ♖d7 37 ♖c8 etc.) **35 ♕xg3?** (In time-trouble, Maróczy overlooks the problem-like draw 35 ♔xg3 ♖g8+ 36 ♔h3 — 36 ♔h2? ♕xh4+ 37 ♕h3 ♕xf4+ 38 ♔h1 ♖g3! or 36 ♔f2? ♕xh4+ 37 ♔f1 ♕h1+ 38 ♔f2 ♖g2+ or 36 ♔f3 ♕xh4 etc. — 36 . . . ♖g4 37 ♔h2? ♕xh4+ 38 ♕h3! and it transpires that the seemingly active g4 rook is actually in the way. 38 . . . ♕f6 39 ♕e3 ♕h4+ etc.) **35 . . . ♖xc4 36 ♖d2 ♕g6 37 ♕g5+** (White apparently pinned his hopes on this move, but the World Champion conducts the rook endgame with clockwork precision) **37 . . . ♕xg5 38 hxg5+ ♔g6 39 ♔g3 ♖c6!** (The rook's most active square is d6, where it ties down its counterpart) **40 ♔f3 ♖d6 41 ♔g3** (41 ♔e3 h4! 42 ♔f3 ♔h5! 43 ♖d3 h3! 44 ♔g3 h2! 45 ♔xh2 ♔g4 —+; if 44 ♖d2 ♔h4) **41 . . . f6! 42 gxf6 ♔xf6 43 ♔f3** (43 ♔h4 ♖d8! and 44 . . . ♖g8! is threatened) **43 . . . h4! 44 ♖h2 ♖xd4 45 ♖xh4 b5!** (For 45 . . . ♖d2? the reply is 46 ♖h6+!) **46 ♖h6+ ♔e7 47 ♖h7+ ♔d6 48 ♖a7 ♖a4 49 a3 ♔d5 White resigned.**

39 FISCHER-PETROSIAN

Rest of the World v USSR, 1970
1 e4 c6 2 d4 d5 3 exd5 cxd5 4 ♗d3 ♘c6 5 c3 ♘f6 6 ♗f4 ♗g4 7 ♕b3 ♘a5 8 ♕a4+ ♗d7 9 ♕c2 e6 10 ♘f3 ♕b6 11 a4!? ♖c8? 12 ♘bd2 ♘c6 13 ♕b1 ♘h5?! (13 . . . g6 Fischer) **14 ♗e3 h6** (14 . . . f5? 15 g4! fxg4 16 ♘g5! ♗d6 17

♗xh7+ — Fischer) **15 ♘e5 ♘f6** (Petrosian only realized at the last minute that his plan of 15 . . . ♘xe5 fails to 16 dxe5 ♗c5 17 a5! against which interesting but insufficient is the piece sacrifice 17 . . . ♕c7 18 g4 ♗xe3 19 fxe3 ♕xe5 20 gxh5 ♕xe3+21 ♗e2 ♗b5 22 ♕d1 followed by ♘d2-f1-g3. Fischer in his notes looked at 18 ♘f3) **16 h3 ♗d6 17 0-0 ♔f8?** (17 . . . a5 18 ♔h1 0-0 19 g4 ♖fd8 20 ♖g1 ♗e8 21 g5 hxg5 22 ♗xg5 ♔f8 23 f4! ± Kholmov, or 17 . . . 0-0 18 f4! ♘xe5 19 a5! ± were the lesser evils) **18 f4 ♗e8 19 ♗f2! ♕c7** (19 . . . g6 20 f5! gxf5 21 ♗xf5 exf5 22 ♕xf5 ♕d8 23 ♗h4! ±) **20 ♗h4 ♘g8 21 f5! ♘xe5 22 dxe5 ♗xe5 23 fxe6 ♗f6 24 exf7 ♗xf7 25 ♘f3 ♗xh4** (25 . . . g5 26 ♗f2 ♔g7 27 ♗d4 ±. Black's king is exposed, his kingside is undeveloped and the pawn on d5 is weak. He has no compensation) **26 ♘xh4 ♘f6 27 ♘g6+ ♗xg6 28 ♗xg6 ♔e7!** (Fischer goes so far as to provide this move with double exclamation marks. The king wants to slip through to the other side) **29 ♕f5 ♔d8 30 ♖ae1 ♕c5+ 31 ♔h1 ♖f8?** (31 . . . ♖c6 32 ♕e5?! ♕d6 offers more resistance) **32 ♕e5!** (Robs the king of c7 and threatens 33 b4) **32 . . . ♖c7** (32 . . . ♕c7 33 ♕xd5+ ♘xd5 34 ♖xf8+ ♔d7 35 ♗f5+) **33 b4 ♕c6 34 c4! dxc4 35 ♗f5! ♖ff7 36 ♖d1+ ♖fd7** (36 . . . ♘d7 37 ♖fe1!) **37 ♗xd7 ♖xd7 38 ♕b8+ ♔e7** (38 . . . ♕c8 39 ♖xd7+ ♘xd7 40 ♕xc8+ ♔xc8 41 ♖f4!) **39 ♖de1+ Black resigned** (39 . . . ♔f7 40 ♕e8+ and mate!)

40   LASKER–TARTAKOWER

Moravska Ostrava 1923

1 e4 c6 2 d4 d5 3 exd5 cxd5 4 ♗d3 ♘c6 5 c3 ♘f6 6 ♗f4 g6 7 h3 ♗g7 8 ♘f3 ♘e4?! 9 ♘bd2 f5? 10 0-0 0-0 11 ♘e5! ♘xe5 12 ♗xe5 ♗xe5 13 dxe5 ♘xd2 (On 13 ... ♕c7 14 ♘f3 and 15 ♕e2 the threat is 16 ♘d4!) **14 ♕xd2 f4!?** (Risky, but the passive 14 . . . e6 involves even greater danger because of ♖fd1, ♖ac1 and then c4! opening the file) **15 ♖ad1!** (Lasker braves the threat of f4-f3) **15 ... ♕c7?!** (Or 15 ... f3? 16 ♗e4! fxg2 17 ♕xd5+ ♔g7 18 ♔xg2! ♕b6 19 ♖d2 ±. Tartakower considered 15 ... ♗e6! 16 ♗c2 ♕d7 17 ♗b3 ♖ad8 18 f3 ♖f5 19 ♕d4 ♔g7 ± to be the strongest) **16 ♖fe1 e6?** (16 . . . f3 17 ♗f1 e6 was the last slim chance of stirring things up. Now the ex-World Champion demonstrates his advantage very instructively) **17 ♖c1!** (Threatening to open the position) **17 . . . ♕d8 18 ♗e2!** (Preparing a concerted assault on d5 and b7 and at the same time removing the threat of f4-f3 once and for all)

18 . . . ♕a5 (18 . . . ♕c7!?) **19 b4! ♕c7 20 c4!** (20 ♕d4 ♕b6! or 20 ♗f3 b5! would still have allowed stubborn resistance) **20 . . . ♕xe5 21 cxd5 ♕d6** (21 . . . ♕xd5 22 ♕xd5 exd5 23 ♗f3 ♗f5 24 ♗xd5+ ♔h8 25 ♗xb7 ±; 22 ♕b2!? Tartakower) **22 ♗f3 ♖d8 23 ♕d4!** (Hampering Black's natural development. On 23 . . . exd5? 24 ♗xd5+! ♕xd5 25 ♖e8+!) **23 . . . ♗d7 24 ♕c5!** (This move once again proves the age-old truth: when the position offers a simple way to win, don't start chasing unnecessary complications) **24 . . . ♕xc5 25 bxc5 ♖ac8 26 c6!** (Far more powerful than 26 dxe6 ♗c6) **26 . . . bxc6 27 dxc6 ♗e8 28 c7 ♖d7** (28 . . . ♖d6 29 ♗b7) **29 ♖xe6 ♗f7 30 ♖ec6 ♗d5** (31 ♗g4 was threatened, and on 30 . . . h5 then 31 ♖6c5 and 32 ♗b7) **31 ♗xd5 ♖xd5 32 ♖a6** (32 ♖b1 ♖e5 33 ♖b8 ♖ee8 Tartakower) **32 . . . ♔f7 33 ♖xa7 ♔e7 34 ♖a4! g5 35 ♖ac4 ♔d7 36 ♖c5 ♖xc5 37 ♖xc5 ♖xc7 38 ♖xc7+ ♔xc7 39 ♔f1 ♔d6 40 ♔e2 ♔d5 41 a4 ♔d4 42 ♔f3 Black resigned.**

7
Panov Attack — Including 5 . . . g6

1 e4 c6 2 d4 d5 3 exd5 cxd5 4 c4

This is the so-called Panov Variation. It is one of the most aggressive lines against the Caro-Kann, and regarded by many as the critical test of the defence. It is also perhaps the most "hybrid" of variations, not only of the Caro-Kann, but of all opening theory, since it can branch off into the most diverse openings (Scandinavian, Grünfeld, Nimzo-Indian, Sicilian Defence, English Opening). However, it is most frequently reminiscent of the Queen's Gambit.

4 c4 was played by Leonhardt as long ago as the last century, but it was Alekhine and Botvinnik who, by elaborating on Panov's groundwork, eventually developed it into a true system. Indeed the variation is also commonly known as the Panov-Botvinnik Attack.

In this chapter we examine early deviations as well as the major line of 5 . . . g6. The most popular defences of 5 . . . ♘c6 and 5 . . . e6 are dealt with in the following two chapters.

4 . . . ♘f6

The most natural answer and the most common in practice: . . . dxc4 or . . . e6 can be played later, so Black avoids committing himself immediately.

4 . . . e5?! is doubtful — 5 dxe5 d4 6 ♘f3 ♘c6 7 ♗d3 ♕a5+ *(7 . . . ♘xe5? 8 ♕e2!)* 8 ♗d2 ♕c5 9 0-0 ♗g4 10 ♖e1 +— Bogdanović–Puc, Yugoslavia 1952.

The only deviation of any real significance here is **4 . . . ♘c6!?** after which White can transpose to lines examined in the next chapter by way of 5 ♘f3 ♗g4 6 ♘c3 ♘f6, while the continuation 5 ♘c3 e5! gives Black acceptable play according to Schwarz: 6 cxd5! *(6 ♘xd5 ♘xd4 7 ♘f3 ♘xf3+ 8 ♕xf3 ♗e6 = or 6 dxe5 d4 7 ♘d5 ♗e6 8 ♕b3 ♘ge7 9 ♘xe7 ♗xe7 10 f4 ♗b4+ −+) 6 . . . ♘xd4 7 f4 f6 8 ♘f3 ±* etc.

Stronger, however, is **5 cxd5!** ♕xd5 6 ♘f3 transposing to a minor variation of the Sicilian Defence that favours White (1 e4 c5 2 c3 d5 3 exd5 ♕xd5 4 d4 ♘c6 5 ♘f3 cxd4?! 6 cxd4).

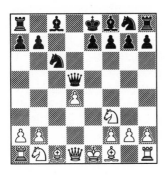

E.g.:

a) **6 . . . e5** 7 ♘c3 ♗b4 8 ♗d2 *(8 ♕d2 ♗xc3 9 bxc3 exd4 10 cxd4 ♘ge7 ∞ Rosentalis-Witkowski, Poland 1985)* 8 . . . ♗xc3 9 ♗xc3 e4 *(9 . . . exd4?! 10 ♘xd4 ♘xd4 11 ♕xd4)* 10 ♘e5 ♘xe5 11 dxe5 ♘e7 12 ♗e2! *(Also good is 12 ♕e2! 0-0 13 ♖d1! ± Ubilava-Zaichik, USSR 1976; rather laboured is 12 ♕a4+?! ♗d7 13 ♕a3 ♕e6! 14 ♕b4 0-0! ∞)* 12 . . . 0-0 13 0-0 ♗d7 14 ♕c1! *(Threatening 15 ♖d1 and 16 ♖d6)* ± Grószpéter-Baart, Groningen 1976-77.

b) **6 . . . ♗g4** 7 ♘c3!? (Rather startling at first glance, but more forcing than 7 ♗e2 e6 8 ♘c3 ♕a5 *[8 . . . ♕d7 9 0-0 ♘f6 10 ♘e5! ♗xe5 11 ♘xd7 ♗xd1 12 ♘xf6+ gxf6 13 ♖xd1 0-0-0 14 ♗e3 ♗b4 15 d5! ♗xc3 16 dxc6 ♗xb2 17 cxb7+ ♔b8 18 ♖ab1 ♗e5 19 g3 ♗c7 20 ♖dc1 ± Boleslavsky]* 9 0-0 *[9 h3 ♗h5 10 a3 ♘f6 11 ♕b3 ± Rosentalis-Kishinev, USSR 1984, or 9 d5!? 0-0-0?! 10 ♘d2 ♗xe2 11 ♕xe2 exd5 12 0-0 ± N. Ristic-Sorm, Seefeld 1987, 9 . . . exd5 10 ♘d4 ♗d7 11 ♘b3 ± N. Ristic]* 9 . . . ♘f6 10 h3! ♗h5 11 a3 ♗e7 12 ♗e3 0-0 13 b4 ♕d8 when instead of either **14 b5?!** ♘a5 15 ♕a4 ♗xf3! 16 ♗xf3 ♖c8! ∓ Gupton-Kuindzhi, Moscow 1976, or **16 g4?!** ♗g6 15 b5 ♘a5 16 ♕a4 b6 17 ♖fc1 ♘d5 = Pisetski-Gupton, Moscow 1977, White can maintain some initiative with **14 ♕b3! ±**) 7 . . . ♗xf3 8 gxf3 ♕xd4 9 ♕xd4! ♘xd4 10 ♘b5! ♘c2+ *(10 . . . e5 11 ♘c7+ ♔d7 12 ♘xa8 ♗b4+ 13 ♔d1 ±)* 11 ♔d1 ♘xa1 12 ♘c7+ ♔d8 13 ♘xa8 e5 14 ♗e3 b6 15 ♗a6 ± or if **10 . . . 0-0-0** 11 ♘xd4 ♖xd4 12 ♗e3 ♖d7 *(12 . . . ♖b4 13 ♗c5! ♖h4 − if 13 . . . ♖xb2 14 ♗h3+! − 14 ♗xa7 ±)* 13 ♗b5 ♔c7 14 ♗xa7 e6 15 ♗a6 ± Hennings-Bindrich, East Germany 1969.

c) **6 . . . e6** 7 ♘c3 ♕d6 8 ♗c4 ♘f6 9 0-0 ♗e7 10 ♘b5! *(10 ♗g5 0-0 11 ♕d2?! − 11 ♖e1!? − 11 . . . a6 12 ♖ad1 b5 13 ♗d3 ♗b7 14 ♖fe1 ♘b4 ∓ Blatny-Dlugy, Sharjah 1985)* 10 . . . ♕d8 11 ♗f4 0-0 12 ♗c7! ♕d7 13 ♘e5 ♘xe5 14 dxe5 ± Nun-Hába,

Czechoslovakia (ch) 1986.

5 ♘c3   . . .

5 c5!? **g6** *(5 . . . b6 6 b4 e6 7 ♗e3 bxc5 8 dxc5 a5 9 ♕a4+ ♘fd7 10 ♘d2 ♗b7 11 ♘b3 axb4 12 ♕xb4 ♕c7 ∞; Minić gives 5 . . . e5! 6 dxe5 ♘e4) 6 ♘c3 ♗g7 7 ♗b5+ ♘c6 8 ♘ge2 0-0 9 0-0* Mariotti–Savon, Venice 1974, *9 . . . ♗d7 ∞.*

This position after 5 ♘c3 is the basic starting-point of the Panov. The most frequent continuations are now **5 . . . ♘c6** and **5 . . . e6** and are analysed in subsequent chapters.

Before continuing with the text, let us consider a fourth alternative, namely **5 . . . ♗e6**, e.g. 6 ♘ge2! dxc4 7 ♘f4 ♗c8 *(7 . . . ♗g4!? 8 f3 ♗d7?! 9 ♗xc4 e6 10 d5 e5 11 ♘d3 ♗d6 12 ♗g5 ♕b6 13 ♕e2 ± Sveshnikov– Kotrionas, Moscow 1987; better is 12 . . . ♗f5! 13 ♘f2 ♘bd7 14 ♗d3 ♗xd3 15 ♕d3 ♕b6! =)* 8 ♗xc4 e6 9 d5 e5 10 0-0!? ± Hebden–And. Martin,

Great Britain 1985.

5 . . .   g6

The bishop's development on the flank is logical, but a bit slow. In most instances Black has to sacrifice his d5 pawn, at least temporarily, in order to complete his development.

A: 6 cxd5
B: 6 ♕b3

A couple of rarer variants are:
a) 6 ♘f3 ♗g7 7 ♕b3 *(7 c5? ♘c6 8 ♗b5 0-0 9 0-0 ♗g4 10 ♗e3 ♘e4 ∓ Bogatirchuk–Levenfish, USSR 1935 or 7 cxd5 ♘bd7!? 8 ♗c4 0-0 9 0-0 ♘b6 10 ♗b3 ♘fxd5 11 ♗g5 h6 12 ♗e6 ♗e3 13 ♘e4 ♘c7 14 ♘c5 ♗d5 15 ♘e5 e6 = Platonov–Lazarev, USSR 1969; 7 . . . ♘xd5!?)* 7 . . . dxc4 8 ♗xc4 0-0 9 ♘e5 e6 10 ♗e3 ♘c6 11 ♘xc6 bxc6 12 0-0 ♕c7 13 h3 ♘d5 14 ♖ac1 ♖b8 15 ♕c2 ♘xe3 16 fxe3 c5! ∓ Pogáts–Szabó, Budapest 1961.

b) 6 ♗g5 ♗g7! 7 ♘f3 *(7 ♗xf6 ♗xf6 8 ♘xd5 ♗g7 9 ♘f3 ♘c6 =)* 7 . . . ♘e4 *(7 . . . 0-0!? 8 ♗xf6 ♗xf6 9 ♘xd5?! ♗g7 10 ♘e3 ♘c6! 11 d5 ♕a5+ 12 ♘d2 ♗xb2! 13 ♖b1 ♗c3 14 dxc6 ♖d8 15 ♘d5 ♗xd2+ 16 ♕xd2 ♕xd2+ 17 ♔xd2 bxc6 18 ♗d3 cxd5 19 c5 ♖d7 20 c6 ♖c7 21 ♖hc1 ♔f8 ∓ Knaak–H. Grünberg, East Germany (ch) 1989; 12 ♕d2 ♗xb2! 13 ♕xa5 ♘xa5 14 ♖d1 ♗c3+ 15 ♘d2 b6 ∓ or 9 cxd5 ♗g4 10 ♗e2 ♕b6! 11 ♕d2 ♗xf3 12 ♗xf3 ♗xd4 ∓ 12 . . . ♕xd4 = − 13 ♘a4 ♕f6*

14 ℤd1 ♗e5 15 ♘c5 ♕b6 16 ♘xb7
♕xb7 17 d6 ♘c6 18 ℤc1 ♗xd6 — 18 . . .
♗xb2 19 ℤxc6 ♕b5 20 ♕d5! = — 19
♗xc6 ♕b6 20 0-0 ℤfd8 21 ♕e2 ℤac8
22 ♗a4 ♕d4 = I. Sokolov-Nunn,
Haifa 1989) 8 cxd5 ♘xg5 9 ♘xg5 0-0
10 ♗c4 *(10 ♕d2 ♘d7 11 ♗c4 a6 12 a4*
♕b6 13 ♘f3 ♕b4 14 ♗e2 ♘b6 15 a5
♘c4 16 ♗xc4 ♕xc4 ∓ Enevoldsen-
Karaklajić, Berverwijk 1967) 10 . . . e5
11 ♘f3 exd4 12 ♘xd4 ♕h4 13 ♘ce2
♗g4 = Bessenay-Marić, France 1971.

A

6 cxd5   **♗g7**

6 . . . ♘xd5 can also be considered,
with the following possibilities:

a) **7 ♕b3 ♘b6** 8 ♗b5+ *(8 d5?! ♗g7*
9 ♗e3 0-0 10 ℤd1 ♘a6 11 ♘f3 ♕d6!
12 a3?! — 12 ♗e2! — 12 . . . ♘c5 13 ♕b5
♘ca4! 14 ♘e4 ♕d7 15 ♕b3?! ♘xb2 16
♗b5 ♕g4 ∓ Barle-Adorjan, Reykjavik
1988; or 10 . . . ♗d7 11 ♘f3 ♘a6 12
♘b5 ♘c7! ∓ Palac-Skembris, Genoa
1989) 8 . . . ♗d7 *(8 . . . ♘8d7 9 a4 a5*
10 h4 ♗g7 11 h5 0-0 12 hxg6 hxg6 13
♘ge2 e5 14 ♘e4 ± Velimirović-Vukić,
Yugoslavia 1970) 9 a4 *(9 ♘f3 ♗g7 10*
♘e5 0-0 11 ♘xd7 ♘8xd7 12 ♗e3 ♘f6
13 0-0 ♘fd5 = Botvinnik) 9 . . . ♘c6
(9 . . . ♗g7 10 a5 ♘c8 11 ♘f3 0-0 12
♗xd7 ♕xd7 13 0-0 ± Ljubojević-Tal,
Manila 1976) 10 ♘f3 ♘a5! 11 ♕b4
♘c6 12 ♕b3 ♘a5 13 ♕a2 ♗xb5 14
axb5 ♘ac4 15 0-0 ♗g7 16 ℤe1 0-0 17
♗g5 ℤe8 ∞ Velimirović-Gipslis,

Amsterdam 1976, or **10 . . . ♗e6** 11 d5
♘xd5 12 ♘d4 ♘c7 13 ♘xe6 ♘xe6 14
0-0 ♘ed4 15 ♗xc6+ bxc6 16 ♕c4
♗g7 17 ♗e3 0-0 = de Jong-Peelen,
Wijk aan Zee 1990. Playable is 7 . . .
♘xc3 8 ♗c4 e6 9 bxc3 ♘c6 10 ♘f3
♗g7 11 ♗a3 ♗f8 12 0-0 *(12 ♗xf8!?*
♔xf8 13 0-0 ♔g7 14 ♗b5 ♗d7 15 ♕b2
♘a5 16 ♗e2! ℤc8 17 ℤac1 ± Agapov;
16 c4?! *♗xb5 17 d5+ ♕f6 18 ♕xb5 b6*
= Kochiev-Agapov, USSR 1987) 12 . . .
♘a5! *(12 . . . ♗xa3? 13 ♕xa3 ♕e7 14*
♕c1 ± Tal-Pohla, USSR 1972) 13
♗b5+ ♗d7 14 ♕a4 ♗xa3 15 ♗xd7+
♕xd7 16 ♕xa3 ♘c4 17 ♕b4 ℤc8 18
♘e5 a5! = (Agapov).

b) *7 ♗c4 ♘b6 (7 . . . ♘xc3 8 ♕b3*
leads to the variation just examined)
8 ♗b3 ♗g7 9 ♘f3 *(9 ♘ge2 0-0 10 0-0*
♗f5 11 d5 ♘a6 12 ♗e3 ♘c8 =
Bisguier-Larsen, Palma de Mallorca
1971) 9 . . . ♘c6 *(9 . . . 0-0 10 0-0 ♗g4 11*
d5 ♘8d7 12 h3 ♗xf3 13 ♕xf3 ♘c5 14
ℤd1 a5?! 15 ♗c2 ♘c4 16 ♕e2 ♘d6 17
♗e3 ℤc8 18 ♗d4 ± Jansa-Gaprin-
dashvili, Yugoslavia 1976) 10 d5!? *(10*
a4 ♘xd4 11 ♘xd4 ♕xd4 12 ♕xd4
♗xd4 13 a5 ♘d7 14 ♘d5 ♗e5 15 0-0 ∞
Botvinnik, 10 ♗e3 Minić) 10 . . . ♘a5!?
(10 . . . ♘b4?!) 11 0-0 0-0 12 ℤe1
Jansa-Gerusel, Leipzig 1975, and now
12 . . . ♘xb3! 13 axb3 ♗xc3! 14 bxc3
♕xd5 15 ♕xd5 ♘xd5 16 c4 ♘b4 17
ℤxe7 ♘c6 18 ℤc7 ℤd8 ±.

c) **7 ♗b5+ ♗d7** 8 ♕b3?! *(8 ♗c4! ±*
8 . . . ♘b6 9 ♘f3 ♗g7 = Degenhardt-
Delander, West Germany 1967.

          7 ♗b5+   **. . .**

Or 7 ♗c4 0-0 (7 ... ♘bd7 8 d6! exd6 9 ♕e2+ ♕e7 10 ♗f4 ± *Epstein-Zagorovska, USSR 1977*) 8 ♘ge2 ♘bd7 9 ♘f4 ♘b6 (9 ... ♘e8 10 0-0 ♘d6 11 ♗b3 ♘b6 12 ♗e3 ♗d7 *Padevski-Bilek, Nice (ol) 1974, when best is now 13 ♘d3 ±, or 9 ... a6 10 a4 b5?! 11 axb5 ♘b6 12 ♗e2 a5 13 ♗f3 ♗b7 14 d6! ♗xf3 15 ♕xf3 ♕xd6 16 0-0 e6 17 ♖d1 ♖fb8 18 d5 ± Tseitlin-Reshko, USSR 1975*) 10 ♗b3 ♗f5 (10 ... ♗g4?! 11 f3 ♗f5 12 g4! ♗c8 13 h4! ♘e8 14 a4 ♘d6 15 ♕d3 ± *Marjanović-Vukić, Belgrade 1977*) 11 0-0 ♘c8 (11 ... ♕d7 12 ♖e1 a5 13 a4 ♖fd8 14 h4 h5 15 ♕e2 ± Szabó-Kostro, Luhačovice 1971*) 12 ♖e1 ♘d6 13 h3 ♖c8 14 ♗d2 ♘fe4 15 ♘xe4 ♘xe4 Tseitlin-Rytov, USSR 1972, 16 ♗e3 ± Botvinnik.

7 ...   ♘bd7

We have now transposed into a position that can be reached via the 1 e4 c6 2 c4 d5 move order. 7 ... ♗d7 is met by 8 ♗c4 ±.

8 d6   ...

This is more or less forced, as otherwise Black plays ... 0-0, ... ♘b6 and ... ♘xd5 with a good game.

8 ...   0-0

Or **8 ... e6?!** 9 d5 e5 10 ♘f3 0-0 11 0-0 **a6** 12 ♗a4 b5 13 ♗b3 ♕b6 14 ♘g5! ♘c5 (*14 ... ♗b7? 15 ♗e3 ♕d8?! 16 ♘e6 ± Janosević-Vadász, Yugoslavia 1977*) 15 ♗e3 ♕xd6 16 ♗xc5 ♕xc5 17 ♘ge4 ♘xe4 18 ♘xe4 ♕d4 ± (*Janošević*) or **11 ... ♘e8?!** 12 ♖e1! ♘xd6 13 ♗xd7 ♗xd7 14 ♘xe5 ♗f5 15 ♗f4 ± Sax-Orsó, Hungary (ch) 1977.

However, a very important improvement was found for Black after **8 ... exd6!?** 9 ♕e2+ (*9 ♗f4 ♕e7+ 10 ♕e2 amounts to the same thing*) 9 ... ♕e7 10 ♗f4 ♕xe2+ 11 ♘gxe2 and now instead of **11 ... d5?!** 12 ♗d6 as in Jansa-Grószpéter, Budapest 1978, best is **11 ... ♔e7!** = as in Nunn-Stean, Hastings 1979-80, which continued 12 0-0 ♘b6 13 ♖fe1 ♗e6 14 ♖ad1 a6 15 d5! (*Sparking off a tactical sequence which ultimately leads to a draw*) 15 ... ♘fxd5 16 ♘xd5+ ♘xd5 17 ♗c4 ♘xf4 18 ♘xf4 ♗e5 19 ♘xe6 fxe6 20 f4 ♗xf4 21 ♖xe6+ ♔d7 22 g3 ♖ac8 23 ♗b3 ♖c1 24 ♖exd6+ ½-½.

9 dxe7   ♕xe7+
10 ♘ge2   ...

10 ♗e2!?

10 . . .   **a6**

11 ♗xd7   **. . .**

11 ♗d3 b5 12 0-0 ♗b7 13 ♗g5 *(13 a3 ♖fe8 14 ♗g5 ∞ Minić–Bronstein, Vinkovci 1970)* 13 . . . ♘b6 14 ♕d2 ♖fe8 15 ♘g3 ♕d7 16 ♘ce2 ♘e4 17 ♗xe4 ♗xe4 18 b3 ∞ Bronstein–Gurgenidze, USSR 1972.

11 . . .   **♕xd7!**

11 . . . ♗xd7? 12 ♗g5! h6 13 ♗f4 ♕b6 14 ♗e5 ♖fd8 15 0-0 ♗c6 16 ♕d2 ± Sveshnikov–Gipslis, USSR 1975.

12 0-0   **. . .**

White has an extra pawn, but hits on great difficulties trying to exploit it. In a Stean–Bronstein game, England 1975, the players agreed to a draw after 12 . . . b5 13 ♗f4?! ♗b7 14 ♗e5 ♖ad8 15 ♕b3.

B

6 ♕b3   **. . .**

Tantamount to winning a pawn, as neither **6 . . . dxc4** 7 ♗xc4 e6 8 d5 exd5 9 ♘xd5 ♘xd5 10 ♗xd5 ♕e7+ 11 ♗e3 ♗g7 12 ♘f3 0-0 13 0-0 ♘c6 14 ♖fe1 ± (Boleslavsky) nor **6 . . . ♘c6** 7 cxd5 ♘a5 8 ♕a4+ ♗d7 9 ♗b5 a6 10 ♗xd7+ ♘xd7 11 ♘ge2 b5 12 ♕d1 ♘f6 13 ♘f4 ♗g7 14 0-0 are really playable.

6 . . .   **♗g7**

7 cxd5   **0-0**

An interesting game: 7 . . . ♘bd7 8 ♗e2 ♘b6 9 ♗f3 ♗g4 10 ♗xg4 ♘xg4 11 ♘ge2 ♕d7 12 0-0 0-0 13 h3 *(13 ♗f4!? ♖fd8 14 h3 ♘f6 15 d6 ±)* 13 . . . ♘f6 14 ♘f4 ♖fd8 15 ♖e1 ♘fxd5 16 ♘fxd5 ♘xd5 17 ♘xd5 ♕xd5 18 ♖xe7 ♕xb3 19 axb3 ♗xd4 20 ♖xb7 ♖ac8! ∞ Kosten–Berg, Budapest 1989.

The starting position of variation B. White has won a pawn but is lagging behind in development. Black may stalk the d5 pawn with . . . ♘b8-d7-b6 or ♘b8-a6-c7, but if White continues to delay his development he can also try e7-e6!? aiming at opening up the position. The counter-sacrifice of the pawn by means of d5-d6, which often leads to a space advantage for White, is a fairly common resource.

B1: 8 ♘ge2
B2: 8 g3!
B3: 8 ♗e2

Other possibilities are:

a) **8 ♗f4 ♘bd7** *(8 . . . e6 9 d6?! ♘h5!
10 ♗e5 f6 11 ♗g3 ♘xg3 12 hxg3 ♕xd6
13 ♘f3 ♘c6 14 ♖d1 ♕b4 15 ♕c2 f5! ∓
Botvinnik and Estrin, or 9 dxe6 ♖e8!
10 0-0-0 ♗xe6 11 ♕xb7! ♘d5 12
♘ge2! − not 12 ♕xa8 ♘xc3 13 bxc3
♕a5 ∞)9 g3? (For 9 ♗e2 see variation
C. 9 d6 is dubious due to 9 . . . exd6 10
♗xd6 ♖e8+ ∓) 9 . . . ♘b6 10 ♗g2 e6!*
11 dxe6 ♗xe6 12 ♕d1 ♘fd5 ∓
Botvinnik and Estrin.

b) **8 ♗g5 ♕a5 9 ♗xf6 exf6 10 0-0-0
♘d7 11 ♔b1 ♘b6 12 ♗d3 ♗g4 13
♖c1 ♗h6 14 ♖c2 ♖ad8 15 h3 ♖fe8 16
♘ge2 ♗xe2** = Vasyukov–Bronstein,
Kislovodsk 1968.

c) **8 ♗d3 ♘a6 9 ♘ge2 ♘c7 10 ♘f4
b6 11 0-0 ♗b7 12 ♗c4 ♕d6** =
Botvinnik.

d) **8 ♗c4 ♘bd7 9 ♘ge2 ♘b6 10 0-0
♘xc4 11 ♕xc4 b6 12 ♗g5 ♗b7 13 ♘f4
♕d7** = Alekhine–Euwe, Bern 1932.

B1

8 ♘ge2   ♖e8

Preparing to open the e-file.

9 g3   . . .

White's best chances perhaps lie
with **9 ♗g5!** against which 9 . . . e6?! 10
dxe6 ♗xe6 11 d5! *(11 ♕xb7?! ♘bd7
12 0-0-0 ♕a5 13 ♕b5 ♕xb5 14 ♘xb5
♗xa2 = Boleslavsky)* 11 . . . ♗f5 *(11 . . .
♗xd5? 12 ♗f6 +−; 11 . . . ♗g4!?)*
12 0-0-0 ♘a6 13 ♘d4 ± *(Schach*

Archiv) is suspect. **9 . . . ♘a6** or **9 . . .
♘bd7** are probably better.

**9 . . .   e6
10 dxe6   . . .**

Or 10 ♗g2 exd5 11 ♗e3 =. The text
is a line by Botvinnik, which he continues 10 . . . ♗xe6 11 ♕xb7 ♘bd7 12
♗g2 ♖b8 13 ♕a6 *(13 ♕xa7 ♗c4 14
♗f3 ♘d5 15 ♘xd5 ♖xe2+ 16 ♗xe2
♗xd5 ∓)* 13 . . . ♘b6 14 b3 ♘fd5 15 0-0
♘xc3 16 ♘xc3 ♕xd4 *(17 ♗f4! ♕xc3
18 ♗xb8 ♖xb8 19 ♕xa7)* with even
prospects.

B2

8 g3!   ♘bd7

Black can also try to exploit his
development advantage through the
sacrifice **8 . . . e6!?**, e.g. 9 dxe6 *(9 ♗g2
♘xd5 10 ♘ge2 ♘c6 =)* 9 . . . ♘c6 10
exf7+ ♔h8 11 ♘ge2 ♕e7 12 ♗e3 ♘g4
13 ♔d2 *(13 ♘d5 ♕xf7 ∓)* 13 . . . ♗e6
14 d5 ♗xf7 15 ♗h3 ♘ge5 16 ♖ad1
Gheorghiu–Johanssen, Havana (ol)
1966, 16 . . . ♘a5 ∞.

Less good is **8 . . . ♘a6?!** 9 ♗g2
♕b6 10 ♕xb6 axb6 11 ♘ge2 ♘b4 12
0-0 ♖d8 13 d6 e6!? *(13 . . . exd6 14 ♗g5
♖e8 15 a3 ♘c6 16 ♖fe1 ♗g4 17 ♗xf6
♗xf6 18 ♘d5 ± Tal–Botvinnik, USSR
1966; 13 . . . ♖xd6 14 ♗f4 ♖d7 15
♖fd1 ♘bd5 16 ♗e5 ± Spassky–
Petrosian, USSR (m) 1966)* 14 a3 ♘bd5
*(14 . . . ♘d3 15 ♗g5! h6 16 ♗xf6 ♗xf6
17 ♖ab1 +−; 14 . . . ♘c6 15 ♗f4 ♘h5*

16 d5! ±) 15 ♘xd5 ♘xd5 16 ♗xd5
exd5 17 ♗f4 h6 *(17 . . . ♗h3?! 18 ♖fe1*
h6 19 ♘c3! g5 20 ♗e5!! ± Novik-
Dzuban, USSR 1989; 19 . . . ♗xd4 20
♘xd5 ♗xb2 21 ♖ab1 ♗xa3 22 ♘xb6
±) 18 h4 f6 19 ♖fe1 g5 20 hxg5 hxg5 21
♗d2 ♖xd6 22 ♗b4 ♖d8 23 ♘c3 ±
(Novik).

9 ♗g2   ♘b6

9 . . . ♘e8 10 ♘ge2 ♘d6 11 ♗f4 ±
Makarichev-Tseitlin, USSR 1974.

10 ♘ge2   ♗f5

and now:
  a) **11 0-0** ♕d7 12 ♖e1 *(12 a4 ♗h3*
13 ♗xh3 ♕xh3 14 ♘f4 = Botvinnik)
12 . . . ♖fd8 *(12 . . . h6 13 a4 ♖ad8 14*
d6 ♕xd6 15 ♘b5 ♕d7 16 ♘xa7 ±
Fuchs-Bronstein, Berlin 1968) 13 d6!
exd6 14 a4! ♗e6! *(14 . . . d5? 15 a5 ♘c8*
16 ♗g5 ♘e7 17 ♘f4 ♗e6 18 ♘a4! +—
Novik-Dzanaridze, Berlin 1989) 15
♕b5 ♗c4 16 ♕xd7 ♖xd7 17 a5
(Novik-Sapix, Katowice 1990) 17 . . .
♘bd5! 18 a6 ♖b8! ∞.
  b) **11 ♘f6** h6 *(11 . . . a5?! 12 0-0 g5 13*
♘fe2 h6 14 ♖e1 ♖c8 15 h3 ±
Matanović-Vukić, Yugoslavia (ch)
1967) 12 0-0 g5 13 ♘fe2 ♕d7 14 f4 g4
15 a4 etc., giving chances to both
players (Botvinnik).

B3

8 ♗e2   . . .

Perhaps the most natural move in
this position. White postpones the
decision as to which one of his men
should be developed to f3 until the
game unfolds.

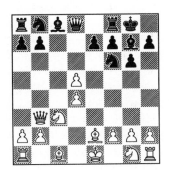

8 . . .   ♘bd7

Black is trying to win back the d5
pawn. Several other attempts have
been made with the same purpose in
mind:
  a) **8 . . . a5?!** 9 ♗f3 ♘a6 10 ♘ge2?
(10 a3 ±) 10 . . . ♘b4 11 0-0 ♗f5 12
♗g5 ♗c2 13 ♕a3 h6 14 ♗e3 ♖c8
15 ♖ac1 b6 16 h3 g5 ∞ Bellon-
Bronstein, Hastings 1975-76.
  b) **8 . . . ♘a6** and now:
  — 9 ♗g5 ♕b6 10 ♕xb6 axb6 **11 a3**
♖d8 12 ♗xf6 ♗xf6 13 ♖d ♗f5 14
♗c4 ♖ac8 15 ♗b3 b5 ∞ Fischer-
Yanofsky, Netanya 1968; **11 d6!?** exd6
12 ♘f3 ♘b4 13 0-0 ♗e6 14 ♘b5 ♘e4
15 ♗e7 ♖fc8 16 ♘xd6 ♘xd6 17 ♗xd6
♘c2 18 ♖ad1 ♖xa2 19 d5 ♗f5 =
Wahls-L. Hansen, Hastings 1987-88.
  — 9 ♗f4 ♕b6 *(9 . . . ♕a5!?)* 10 ♕xb6

axb6 11 ♖c1! ♘b4 12 d6 ♖e8 *(12 ...*
♘xa2 13 ♘xa2 ♖xa2 14 dxe7 ♖e8 15
♗d6 ♖xb2 16 ♗f3 ±) 13 dxe7 ♖xe7
14 ♗e5 (Inkiov-Hodgson, Palma de
Mallorca 1989) 14 ... ♘fd5!? 15 ♘xd5
♘xd5 16 ♘f3 ♗xe5 17 dxe5 ♘f4 ∞.
 − **9 ♗f3 ♕b6** 10 ♕xb6 axb6 11
♘ge2 *(11 ♗f4 ♘b4 15 ♔d2 ♗f5 ∞*
Botvinnik) 11 ... ♘b4 12 0-0 ♖d8 13
d6! ♖xd6 14 ♗f4 ♖d7 15 ♖fd1 ♘bd5
16 ♗e5 ♖d8 17 ♘f4 *(17 ♘xd5!?)* 17
... ♘xf4 18 ♗xf4 ♗g4 19 ♗xb7!
♗xd1 20 ♗xa8 ♗g4 21 ♗b7 ♖xd4 22
♗e3 ♖d7 23 ♗a6 ♖d6 24 ♖c1 ±
Wahls-Adorjan, Altensteig 1989.
    c) **8 ...** ♘e8 9 ♘f3 ♘d6 10 ♗f4 ♗g4
11 ♖d1 ♗xf3 12 ♗xf3 ♘d7 13 0-0
♘b6 14 ♖fe1 ± Vasyukov-Doda,
Belgrade 1964.
    d) **8 ...** b6 9 ♗f3 ♗b7 **10** ♘ge2 ♕d7
(10 ... ♘a6 11 0-0 ♕d7 12 ♗g5 ♖fd8
13 ♖fe ♘xd5 14 ♗xd5 ♗xd5 15 ♕a3
± Zinn-Brummer, East Germany 1964)
11 ♗f4 ♖d8 12 ♖c1 ♘a6 13 ♕a3 ♗f8
14 b4 ± Boleslavsky, or **10 ♗f4** ♕d7
11 ♘ge2 ♖d8 12 ♖c1! ♘a6 13 ♕a3!
♗f8 14 ♗e5! *(14 b4 − Boleslavsky −*
14 ... ♘c7! 15 ♗xc7 − 15 d6 ♘e6!
∓; 15 0-0 ♘cxd5 ∓ − 15 ... ♕xc7
16 ♘e4 ♕d7 17 ♘xf6+ exf6 18 ♕b2
♕b5! ∓) 14 ... ♘e8 *(14 ... e6 15*
dxe6 ♕xe6 16 ♗xb7 ♗xa3 17 bxa3!)
15 0-0 ♘ac7 16 ♗xc7 ♕xc7 17 ♘e4
♕b8 18 ♘2c3! *(18 ♘4c3! ♘f6! 19 ♕b3*
♖d7 ∞ Kruszynski-L. Hansen, Lyngby
1989) 18 . . . ♘d6! ± (Kruszynski).
Alternatively White can play **9 ♗g5**
♗b7 10 ♗xf6 exf6 11 ♗f3 ♘a6 12
♘ge2 ♕d6 13 0-0 ♖fd8 14 ♖ad1 f5

(14 ... ♘c7 15 ♘e4 ♕d7 16 d6 ±) 15
♖fe1 ♘c7 16 ♘c1! ♖d7 *(16 . . .*
♘xd5?? 17 ♘xd5 ♗xd5 18 ♗xd5
♕xd5 19 ♖e8+! wins) 17 ♘d3
(Kosten-Berg, Naestved 1988) 17 . . .
♘xd5! 18 ♘e5 ♘xc3 19 ♕xc3 ±.

9 ♗f3   . . .

9 ♘h3 ♘b6 10 ♘f4 ♗g4! 11 ♗xg4
♘xg4 12 h3 ♘f6 13 0-0 ♕d7 =
Botvinnik.

9 . . .   ♘b6
10 ♘ge2   . . .

It is worth considering developing
the bishop first:
    a) **10 ♗f4** (A Grünfeld Defence has
evolved by transposition − 1 d4 ♘f6 2
c4 g6 3 ♘c3 d5 4 ♗f4 ♗g7 5 e3 0-0
6 ♕b3 c5 7 cxd5 cxd4 8 exd4 ♘bd7
9 ♗e2 ♘b6 10 ♗f3) 10 ... ♗g4 *(10 ...*
♗f5 11 ♖d1! − thwarts the manœuvre
♗f5-d3-c4 − 11 ... ♕d7 12 h3 h5 13
♗e5! ♖df8 14 ♗xf6 exf6 ± Levenfish-
Botvinnik, USSR (m) 1937 or 10 ... e6
11 d6! ♘fd7 − 11 ... ♘e8?! 12 ♕b5! −
12 ♘ge2 e5 13 dxe5 ♘xe5 14 ♗xe5
♗xe5 15 ♖d1 ± Kluger-Benkö,
Budapest 1954, or 11 ... ♗d7 12 ♗e5
♘bd5 13 ♘ge2 ♗c6 14 ♘xd5 ♘xd5 15
0-0 ♕g5! − 15 ... ♗xe5 16 dxe5 ♕g5
17 ♗xd5 ♗xd5 18 ♕g3 ♕d2 19 ♘f4
♕xb2 20 ♘h5 ± − 16 ♗g3 ♖fd8 17
♘c3 ♘xc3 18 bxc3 ♗f8 19 c4 ♗xd6 10
d5 ± Sveshnikov-Gipslis, USSR 1988)
11 ♗xg4 ♘xg4 12 ♘f3 ♘f6 13 d6!
exd6 14 0-0 ♘h5 15 ♗g5 ♕d7 Šajtar-

Lilienthal, Prague 1946, 16 a4! ±.
b) **10 ♗g5** and now:
b1) **10 . . . ♗g4** 11 ♗xf6 ♗xf3 12 ♘xf3 ♗xf6 *(12 . . . exf6 13 0-0 ♕d7 14 ♖ac1 ±)* 13 a4 ♕c7 14 0-0 ♖fd8 15 a5 ♕c4 16 ♖a3 ± Botvinnik.
b2) **10 . . . ♗f5** 11 ♖d1 ♕c8 *(11 . . . ♕d7 12 h3 h5 13 ♘ge2 ♘c8!? – 13 . . . ♖ad8?! 14 d6! ± – 14 0-0 ♘d6 15 ♘g3 ♖ac8 16 ♖fe1 ♖fe8 17 ♗f4! b6 ± Mainka-Fries Nielsen, West Germany 1989/90, or 11 . . . a5 12 a4 – 12 ♘ge2 a4 13 ♕b5 ♘e8 14 ♘g3 ♘d6 15 ♕e2 ♖e8 16 0-0 ♖c8 17 ♗f4 a3 18 ♖fe1 axb2 19 ♕xb2 ♘bc4 20 ♕b4 ♕d7 21 h3 ± King-Campora, Bern 1988 – 12 . . . ♖c8 13 ♘ge2 ♖c4 14 ♕a2 ♕d7 15 b3 ♖c7 16 ♗xf6 ♗xf6 17 ♕d2 ± Zinn-Spiridonov, Cracow 1964 or finally 11 . . . ♘e8 12 ♘ge2 ♘d6 13 0-0 ±)* 12 h3 ♕c4 13 ♕xc4 ♘xc4 14 g4 ♗d7 *(14 . . . ♗c2? 15 ♖d2!)* 15 ♗c1 ± Botvinnik.
b3) **10 . . . a5** 11 ♗xf6 exf6 12 ♘ge2 ♗f5 13 ♕d1 *(13 ♕b5? ♘c8 14 0-0 ♘d6 15 ♕b3 ♗d3 16 ♖fd1 ♗c4 17 ♕c2 f5 ∓ Bagirov-Gurgenidze, USSR 1969)* 13 . . . ♘c4 14 b3 ♘b2 15 ♕d2 ♘d3+ 16 ♔f1 ♘b4 17 a3 ♘a6 18 h3 ± Grabczewsky-A. Zaitsev, Albena 1970.

10 . . .   ♗g4

This was played in Hort-Gipslis, Prague 1974 when White maintained a slight plus after 11 ♗xg4 ♘xg4 12 a4 – see the illustrative game for the continuation.

Instead of the text, other possibilities are **10 . . . a5?!** 11 ♗f4 ♗f5 12 ♖d1 ♖c8 13 0-0 ♖c4 14 ♕b5 ± Pietzsch-Spiridonov, Sofia 1967 or **10 . . . ♗f5!?** 11 0-0 *(11 ♘f4 g5 12 ♘h5 ♘xh5 13 ♗xh5 e6 14 g4 ♗g6 15 dxe6 ♕xd4 ± – if 12 ♘fe2 g4 13 ♘g3 ♗g6 14 ♗e2 ♘bxd5 15 ♕xb7 ♖b8 16 ♕xa7 ♘b4 ∞. Alternatively 11 ♗g5 a5 12 0-0 ♗d3 13 d6 exd6 14 ♗xb7 ♖b8 15 ♗f3 is given as unclear by Botvinnik)* **11 . . . a5** 12 a4 *(12 ♗f4 ♗d3 13 d6! exd6 14 ♕d1 ♗a6 15 b3 h6 16 h3 ♘h7 17 g3! ♖c8 18 ♗g2 ♖e8 19 ♖e1 ♘f6 20 ♖c1 ± Dolmatov-Adams, Hastings 1989/90)* 12 . . . ♕d6 *(12 . . . ♖c8 13 ♗g5 ♖c4 14 ♕a2 ♕d7 15 b3 ♖c7 16 ♗xf6 ♗xf6 17 ♕d2 ±Gipslis)* 13 ♘b5 ♕d7 14 d6 exd6 15 ♗f4 ♗e6 16 ♕d1 ♘e8 17 d5 ♗g4 ± van Barle-Gaprindashvili, Amsterdam 1976. Alternatively, finally, **11 . . . ♕d7** 12 a4 ♗d3 13 d6! ♗c4 14 ♕b4 ♗xe2 15 ♘xe2 ♘bd5 16 ♕a3 exd6 17 ♕b3 ± Milos-Christiansen, Szirák (izt) 1987.

ILLUSTRATIVE GAMES

41   NOVIK-DZJUBAN
     USSR 1989
     1 e4 c6 2 d4 d5 3 exd5 cxd5 4 c4 ♘f6 5 ♘c3 g6 6 ♕b3 ♗g7 7 cxd5 0-0 8 ♘ge2 ♘a6 9 g3 ♕b6 10 ♕xb6 axb6 11 ♗g2 ♘b4 12 0-0 ♖d8 13 d6! e6!? 14 a3 ♘bd5 15 ♘xd5 ♘xd5 16 ♗xd5 exd5 17 ♗f4 ♗h3?! 18 ♖fe1 h6 19 ♘c3! g5 20 ♗e5!! f6 21 ♘xd5 fxe5 22 dxe5 ♖a5! 23 ♖ad1 ♗e6 24 ♘e7+! ♔f7 25 f4 gxf4

26 gxf4 ♗f8 27 f5 ♗b3 (27 . . . ♗xe7 28
fxe6+ ♔xe6 29 dxe7 ♖g8+ 30 ♔f2
♔xe7 31 ♖e3 ±) 28 ♖d3! (28 e6+?
♔f6 29 ♖d3 ♗xe7 30 dxe7 ♖g8+)
28 . . . ♗xe7 (28 . . . ♗c4 29 e6+! +−)
29 ♖xb3 ♗xd6 30 exd6 ♖xd6 31 ♖e6!
♖d2 32 ♖exb6 ♖xf5 33 ♖xb7+ ♔f8
34 ♖c3 ♖d8 35 ♔g2 ♔g8 36 b4 h5 37
a4 h4 38 a5 ♖f6 39 ♔h3 **Black
resigned.**

42   KOSTEN–BERG
      Naestved 1988
      1 e4 c6 2 d4 d5 3 exd5 cxd5 4 c4 ♘f6
5 ♘c3 g6 6 ♕b3 ♗g7 7 cxd5 0-0 8 ♗e2
b6 9 ♗g5 ♗b7 10 ♗xf6 exf6 11 ♗f3
♘a6 12 ♘ge2 ♕d6 13 0-0 ♖fd8 14
♖ad1 f5 15 ♖fe1 ♘c7 16 ♘c1! ♖d7 17
♘d3 ♗xd4?! 18 ♘b4 (Highlighting
the weakness of the c5 square) 18 . . .
♗xc3?! (18 . . . ♗f6 was better) 19
♕xc3 ♘a6 20 ♘c6 ♖c8 21 ♕e3 ♖a8
22 b4! ♘xb4? 23 ♘e7+ ♔g7 24 ♕c3+
♔h6 (24 . . . f6 25 ♖e6 ♘xd5 26 ♖xd6
wins) 25 ♘xf5+! (An elegant finish)
25 . . . gxf5 26 ♖e6+! **Black resigned**
(26 . . . fxe6 27 ♕f6 mate!).

43   HORT–GIPSLIS
      Prague 1974
      1 e4 d5 2 cxd5 ♘f6 3 c4 c6 4 ♘c3
cxd5 5 d4 g6 6 ♕b3 ♗g7 7 cxd5 0-0
8 ♗e2 ♘bd7 9 ♗f3 ♘b6 10 ♘ge2 ♗g4
11 ♗xg4 ♘xg4 12 a4 ♘f6 (12 . . . a5 13
0-0 ♕d6 14 ♗f4 ♕b4 15 ♕d1 ♖fd8 −
15 . . . ♘f6 16 d6 exd6 17 ♘b5! − 16
♗c7! ♖d7 17 d6 exd6 18 ♗xb6 ♕xb6
19 ♘d5 ± J. Polgár–Skembris, Corfu
1990) 13 ♘f4 (He is trying to defend

the d5 pawn. 13 a5!? ♘bxd5 14 ♕xb7
±) 13 . . . ♕d7 (13 . . . g5?! 14 ♘fe2 h6
15 h4; 13 . . . a5!? Hort) 14 a5 ♘c8 15
0-0 ♘d6 16 ♖e1 (White has kept his
pawn advantage and limited the
opponent's forces to a narrow area.
Nevertheless, it is difficult for him to
increase his advantage) 16 . . . ♖fe8?!
(In a Hort–Hennings game, East
Germany 1972, 16 . . . ♘f5 17 ♖a4!
also favoured White. According to
Hort, the doubling of the rooks was
needed on the c-file, but even then
the rook manœuvre introduced in
this game maintains White's advantage) 17 h3 ♖ad8 18 ♖a4! (A subtle
manœuvre. The rook is attacking the
b-file at the same time as defending
the d4 pawn) 18 . . . ♘f5 19 ♖b4 g5?
(Mistakenly believing that 20 ♖xb7?
♘xd4 would follow, Black fatally
compromises his position. Hort said
that 19 . . . ♕c7 20 ♖xb7 ♕xa5 21 ♖b4
held the position) 20 ♘fe2! ♘xd5 21
♖xb7 ♕c6 (21 . . . ♕e6 22 ♗d2 ±) 22
♕b5! ♕e6 23 ♘xd5 ♕xd5 (23 . . .
♖xd5?? 24 ♕xe8+ ±, 23 . . . ♘xd4 24
♘c7 ♕e4 25 ♕xg5! ±) 24 ♕xd5 ♖xd5
25 ♖xa7 ♘xd4 26 ♘c3! (Hort does the
technical bit superbly!) 26 . . . ♖c5 27
a6 ♘c6? 28 ♖c7! ♖a8 (28 . . . ♗e5 29
♖xc6!) 29 ♗e3 ♖c4 30 ♘d5 ♖xa6 31
♘xe7+ ♔f8 32 ♘f5 ♖a8 33 ♗xg5
♘e5 34 ♖b7 ♘g6 35 ♖xf7+! 1-0.

44   BARLE–ADORJAN
      Reykjavik 1988
      1 e4 c6 2 d4 d5 3 exd5 cxd5 4 c4 ♘f6
5 ♘c3 g6 6 cxd5 ♘xd5 7 ♕b3 ♘b6

8 d5?! ♗g7 9 ♗e3 0-0 10 ♖d1 ♘a6 11 ♘f3 ♕d6 12 a3?! ♘c5 13 ♕b5 ♘ca4! (13 . . . ♗xc3+ 14 bxc3 ♘e4 15 ♕b3 ♗d7 16 ♖d4! ∞) **14 ♘e4 ♕d7 15 ♕b3!?** (15 ♕a5 ♘xb2! ∓; 15 ♕b4 ♕f5!! 16 ♗xb6 axb6 17 b3 ♘b2 18 ♖d2 ♖xa3!! ∓) **15 . . . ♘xb2 16 ♗b5 ♕g4 17 ♘g3 ♘xd1 18 h3** (18 ♕xd1? ♗c3+ 19 ♔f1 ♗d7 −+) **18... ♘xe3 19 hxg4 ♘xg2+! 20 ♔f1 ♘f4 21 ♘g5 h6 22 d6 exd6 23 ♘5e4 ♗xg4 24 ♖h4 ♗e6?!** (24 . . . h5! −+) **25 ♕f3 ♘fd5**

26 ♘xd6 ♘c3! 27 ♘ge4? (27 ♔g1 is preferable) **27 . . . ♖ad8?!** (27 . . . ♘xb5 28 ♘xb5 ♗c4+ 29 ♔g1 ♗xb5 30 ♘f6+ ♗xf6 31 ♕xf6 ♘d7 32 ♕b2 ♗c6 33 ♖xh6 f6 34 ♖xg6+ ♔f7 winning) **28 ♘f6+ ♗xf6 29 ♕xf6 ♖xd6 30 ♕xc3 ♖c8 31 ♕b2 h5 32 ♗e2 ♖c5 33 a4? ♗d7 34 ♖d4 ♘xa4 35 ♕d2 ♖xd4 36 ♕xd4 ♗c6 37 ♕d8+ ♔h7 38 f3 ♖f5 39 ♔f2 ♘c3 40 ♗d3 ♖xf3+ 41 ♔e1 a5 42 ♔d2 ♘e4+ White resigned.**

8
Panov Attack − 5 . . . ♘c6

1 e4 c6 2 d4 d5 3 exd5 cxd5 4 c4 ♘f6 5 ♘c3 ♘c6

This old continuation has recently come into fashion again. In variation A we examine a line which includes the end-game made famous by the Fischer–Euwe encounter at Leipzig 1960. The assessment at present is that White can continue to maintain a slight plus, although this may not prove enough to win. However, in variation A2 the Black deviation of 9 . . . ♘b6!? still offers great scope for both sides.

Variation B is on the whole sharper and again, although White may thread his way to a slight initiative, Black has a wide choice of resources.

A: 6 ♘f3
B: 6 ♗g5

A

6 ♘f3 . . .

Somewhat more solid than 6 ♗g5, but if both players are so disposed, there need be no lack of complications here either.

6 . . . ♗g4

This is the best strategically, although it has the tactical shortcoming of weakening b7. Alternatives are:

a) **6 . . . e6?!** 7 c5! ♘e4 *(7 . . . ♗e7 8 ♗b5! 0-0 9 0-0 ♘e4 10 ♗xc6 ♘xc3 11 bxc3 bxc6 12 ♕a4 ± Foltys–Opočensky, 1941)* 8 ♗b5! ♘xc3 9 bxc3 ♗d7 *(9 . . . ♕a5 10 ♕b3 ♗d7 11 0-0 ♕c7 Koch–Arlamovsky, 1951, 12 g3! ±)* 10 0-0 ♗e7 11 ♗f4 *(11 ♖e1 0-0 12 ♗f4 ♗f6 13 ♗d3 ± Gereben–Tipary, Budapest 1952)* 11 . . . b6?! 12 ♕a4 ♖c8 13 c4 ± Dubinin–Bergraser (corr) 1962.

b) **6 . . . g6** is interesting. 7 cxd5
(7 ♗g5 ♘e4? 8 cxd5 ♘xc3 9 bxc3
♕xd5 10 ♕b3 ± Botvinnik − for 7 . . .
♗e6! see variation B. On 7 ♕b3?!
instead 7 . . . ♘a5! gives Black the
initiative) 7 . . . ♘xd5 8 ♕b3 ♘xc3
9 ♗c4 ♘d5! 10 ♗xd5 e6 11 ♗xc6+
bxc6 12 0-0 ♕d5 13 ♕a4 ♕b5 14 ♕c2
♗g7 15 ♗f4 0-0 16 ♖ac1 ♗a6
± Nunn−Dzindzihashvili, Hastings
1977-78.

c) **6 . . . ♗e6** and now 7 c5 *(7 ♗g5*
g6!? 8 ♗xf6 exf6 9 ♗e2 ♗g7 10 0-0 0-0
11 ♕d2 − 11 c5 f5 12 ♕d2 ♕f6 13
♖fd1 f4 ∞ − 11 . . . dxc4! 12 d5 ♘e5 13
♘xe5 fxe5 = Speelman−Korchnoi,
Reykjavik 1988; 7 . . . ♘e4!? 8 ♘xe4
dxe4 9 d5 exf3 10 dxe6 ♕a5+ 11 ♕d2
♕e5+ 12 ♗e3 ♕xe6 13 gxf3 g6 =
Anand or 7 cxd5 ♗xd5 8 ♘xd5 ♕xd5
9 ♗e2 e6 =; 9 . . . g6 =) 7 . . . g6
(7 . . . ♗g4 8 ♗b5 ±; 7 . . . a6 8 h3 ±
Anand) 8 ♗b5 ♗g7 9 ♘e5 ♗d7
10 ♗xc6 bxc6 11 0-0 0-0 12 ♖e1 ♗e8!
13 h3 ♔h8!? *(13 . . . ♕c8 14 ♕a4 ±)*
14 ♗f4 ♘g8 15 b4 f6 *(If 15 . . . a5!? then*
16 a3 and ♘a4-b6 ±) 16 ♘f3 ♕d7 17
a4 a6 18 ♗h2 g5 19 ♕e2 h5 was
unclear in Anand-Miles, Wijk aan
Zee 1989. A new variation is **7 ♕b3**
♘a5?! (7 . . . dxc4! 8 ♗xc4 − 8 ♕xb7?!
♖c8 ∓ − 8 . . . ♗xc4 9 ♕xc4 e6 =)
8 ♕b5+ ♗d7 9 cxd5!? ♗xb5 10
♗xb5+ ♘d7 11 ♘e5 ♕c7 12 ♗xd7+
♔d8 13 ♗h3 ♔e8 14 0-0!? ♖d8
15 ♖e1 ∞ Rantanen-Vladimirov,
Helsinki 1990.

7 cxd5 . . .

With a view to attacking b7. Less
testing are 7 ♗e3?! e6 8 h3 ♗xf3
9 ♕xf3 ♕b6 10 0-0-0 ♗b4 11 c5 ♕a5
12 ♘b5 0-0 13 ♔b1 ♘e4 14 ♕f4 a6 ∓
Larsen-Trifunović, Belgrade 1964 or
7 ♗e2 e6! *(7 . . . dxc4? 8 d5 ♗xf3*
9 ♗xf3 ♘e5 10 0-0 ♕d7 11 ♕e2
♘xf3+ 12 ♕xf3 0-0-0 13 b3! ±
Mikenas-Flohr, Folkestone 1933) 8 c5
♘e4 9 h3 ♗xf3 10 ♗xf3 ♘xc3 11 bxc3
♗e7 = Botvinnik.

7 . . . **♘xd5**
8 ♕b3! **. . .**

8 ♗b5 was the vogue of the thirties.
8 . . . ♖c8 *(8 . . . ♕a5!? 9 ♕b3 ♗xf3*
10 gxf3 ♘xc3 11 bxc3 e6 12 d5 a6! − 12
. . . exd5? 13 0-0! ± Alekhine-Winter,
London 1932 − 13 dxc6 axb5 14 cxb7
♖b8 15 ♖b1 ♖xb7 16 a4 b4 17 ♗d2
♕e5+ 18 ♔f1 ♕d6! = Keene-Roth,
Aarhus 1976 or 11 ♗xc6+ bxc6 12
♕b7? ♘d5+ 13 ♗d2 ♕b6 14 ♕xa8+
♔d7 ∓ Nimzovitch-Alekhine, Bled
1931) 9 h3 ♗xf3! *(9 . . . ♗h5 10 0-0 e6*
11 ♖e1 ♗e7 12 ♖e5! ± Khasin-

Bagirov, USSR (ch) 1961) 10 ♕xf3 e6
11 0-0 a6 *(11 ... ♗e7 12 ♘xd5 ♕xd5
13 ♕xd5 exd5 14 ♗e3 ♗d6 15 ♖ac1
♔d7 16 ♖c3 = Kestler-Holzapfel,
West Germany 1989/90)* 12 ♗xc6+
♖xc6 13 ♘xd5 ♕xd5 14 ♕xd5 exd5
15 ♖e1+ ♖e6! = Jokšić-Vukić,
Yugoslavia (ch) 1976.

8 ...	♗xf3
9 gxf3	...

Black has a relatively tame end-
game or a double-edged line in which
he may have to sacrifice several
pieces.

A1: 9 ... e6
A2: 9 ... ♘b6

Bad are **9 ... ♘xc3?** 10 ♕xb7!
♘xd4 11 bxc3 +− and **9 ... ♘xd4?** 10
♗b5+! +−.

A1

9 ...	e6
10 ♕xb7	♘xd4
11 ♗b5+	♘xb5
12 ♕c6+	♔e7
13 ♕xb5	...

Not 13 ♘xb5? ♖b8! 14 ♘d4 ♕d7
15 ♗e3 ♖xb2 16 ♕c4 f6 17 ♖d1 ♔f7
18 ♘b3 ♗e7 19 0-0 ♖c8 −+
Zhuravlev-Stetsko, USSR 1971.

(see diagram)

13 ...	♕d7!

The famous stem game Fischer-
Euwe, Leipzig (ol) 1960 continued 13
... ♘xc3(?!) 14 bxc3 *(14 ♕b4+ ♔e8 15
♕xc3 ♖c8 16 ♕b3 ♖b8 17 ♕a4+ ♕d7
= Velimirović-Augustin, Moscow 1977)*
14 ... ♕d7 15 ♖b1!, a recommendation of Benkö. The weaknesses of
White's pawn formation (five isolated
pawns!) are counterbalanced by
Black being unable to develop his
kingside. For the continuation of this
game and further analysis see
illustrative games.

Black can also try **14 ... ♕d5** in this
line. 15 ♖b1 *(15 ♕xd5 exd5 16 ♖b1
♔e6 ± or 15 ♕e2 f6 16 0-0 ♔f7 17 ♖d1
♕c6 18 ♕e4 ♕xe4 19 fxe4 ♗c5 20
♖d7+ ♔g6 ∓ Shardarov-Bagirov,
USSR 1964)* 15 ... ♖d8 16 ♗e3 ♕xb5
17 ♖xb5 ± Cortlever-Karaklajić,
Wijk aan Zee 1972.

14 ♘xd5+	...

14 ♕a5 is an idea, when after 14 ...

♘xc3 we have:

a) **15 bxc3** f6 16 ♖b1 ♔f7 17 ♕a6 ♗c7 18 ♖b7 ♕d5 19 ♗a3 ♖he8 20 0-0 ♕xf3 21 ♖fb1 ♖ad8 22 ♕xa7 ♕g4+ 23 ♔f1 ♕h3+ 24 ♔g1 ½-½ Gaprindashvili-Chiburdanidze, USSR (m) 1978.

b) **15 ♕xc3** f6 16 ♗e3 ♔f7 17 0-0 ♗e7 18 ♖ac1 ♕d5! 19 ♖fd1 *(19 ♕c6 ♕xa2)* 19 . . . ♕xf3 20 ♖d7! ♕g4+ 21 ♔f1 ♖hd8 22 ♖c7 ♔f8! *(22 . . . ♖d1+ 23 ♖xd1 ♕xd1+ 24 ♕e1 ±) 23 ♗xa7 ♖d5! 24 ♕g3 ♖d1+ (On 24 . . . ♕b4!? Gufeld gives 25 ♗e3 ∞ or 25 ♖xe7!? ♖g5! 26 ♖cc7 ♖xg3 27 ♖f7+ ♔e8 28 hxg3 ♖c8!!)* 25 ♖xd1 ♕xd1+ 26 ♔g2 ♕d5+ 27 ♕f3 ♕g5+ = Tseitlin-Kasparov, USSR 1978.

14 . . .   ♕xd5

14 . . . exd5 is riskier: **15 ♕e2+** *(15 ♕b4+ ♔e8 16 ♕d4 ± is Fischer's suggestion)* **15 . . . ♔f6!?** 16 h4! *(16 0-0 ♗d6 17 ♖d1 ♕h3 18 ♗g5+ ♔g6 19 ♕d3+ f5 20 f4 ♕xd3 21 ♖xd3 h6 22 ♖xd5 was Benkö-Addison, San Francisco 1961, and now 22 . . . ♗a3!=)* 16 . . . ♖e8 *(If 16 . . . ♗b4+ 17 ♔f1)* 17 ♗g5+! ♔g6 18 ♗e3 d4 *(18 . . . ♗b4+ 19 ♔f1 f6! 20 ♕d3+ ♔f7 21 ♖d1 ♖e5 22 f4 ♖f5 ∞)* 19 ♖d1 ± or **15 . . . ♕e6** 16 ♗e3 f6 17 ♖c1 ± Panov-Sergeev, Moscow 1930. Also strong is **15 ♕b3!?** ♔f6 16 h4 ♖e8+?! *(16 . . . h6 was better)* 17 ♔f1 g6 18 ♗g5+ ♔g7 19 ♖d1 d4 20 ♕c4 f6 21 ♖xd4 ♕b7 22 ♗xf6+!! ♔xf6 23 ♖f4+♔g7 24 h5! h6 25 hxg6 ♖e7 26 ♕d4+1-0 Zvoinitski-

Gody, USSR 1989.

15 ♕xd5   . . .

15 ♕b4+ is followed by ♔e8 16 ♕a4+ ♕d7.

15 . . .   exd5

White's edge in development gives him a slight advantage in this endgame. Nevertheless a draw is the usual outcome due to the weaknesses of his pawn formation and the reduction of material.

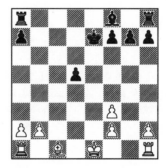

A1.1: 16 ♗e3
A1.2: 16 0-0

A1.1

16 ♗e3   . . .

16 ♗f4!? ♔f6 *(16 . . . ♔e6 17 0-0-0 ♗b4 18 a3 ♖ac8+ 19 ♔b1 ♗a5 20 b4 ♗b6 21 ♖he1+ ♔f5 22 ♗g3 d4 ±)* 17 0-0-0 ♖d8 *(17 . . . ♗c5!?)* 18 ♖hg1!

(18 ♖he1 ♗d6 19 ♖d4 g5 20 ♗d2 ♗xh2 ∞ S. Polgár-de Jong, Wijk aan Zee 1990) 18 ... ♖d7 19 ♗e3 ♖g8 20 ♖g4! ♔e6 21 ♖e1 h5 22 ♖a4 ♔f5 23 ♖xa7 ± Kindermann-Lobron, Bern 1990.

16 ...   ♔e6
17 0-0-0   ...

a) 17 ♖c1 ♗b4+ *(17 ... ♗d6 =)* 18 ♔e2 ♖hc8 = Suetin-Lilienthal, USSR 1981.

b) 17 ♖g1 ♗d6 18 ♖xg7 *(18 ♗d4 ♗xh2)* 18 ... ♗e5 19 ♖g4 ♗xb2 20 ♖b1 ♖hb8 21 ♔f1 ♗e5 ∞ Rogers-Adams, London 1988.

c) **17 0-0** ♗b4 *(17 ... ♗e7 18 ♖fe1 ♗f6 19 ♖ad1 ±)* 18 ♗d4 ♖hc8 19 ♖ac1 ♖c4 = (van der Sterren).

d) **17 ♔e2** ♗d6 18 ♖ac1 ♖hc8 19 h3 ♗e5 20 ♖xc8 ♖xc8 21 ♖c1 ♖xc1 22 ♗xc1 d4! = Tringov-Marovic, Plovdiv 1973.

17 ...   ♗b4

17 ... ♖c8+ 18 ♔b1 ♗c5 19 ♖he1 ♔d6 *(19 ... ♗xe3? 20 ♖xe3+ ♔d6 21 ♖a3 ±)* 20 ♖d3 *(20 ♗f4+ ♔c6 21 ♖e2 ♖hd8 22 ♖c1 ♔d7 23 ♖e5 ♗xf2 24 ♖xd5+ ♔e6 25 ♖e5+ ♔f6 = J. Polgár-de Jong, Wijk aan Zee 1990)* 20 ... ♖hd8 21 ♗g5 *(21 a3 =, ±)* 21 ... f6 22 ♗f4+ ♔c6 23 ♖c1 ♔b7 = Rogulj-Vukic, Bjelovar 1979.

18 ♔b1   ...

18 a3 ♖hc8+ 19 ♔b1 ♗c5 20 ♖he1 ♗xe3 = Vaganjan-Dreev, Odessa 1989.

18 ...   ♖hd8
19 ♖d3   ♖d7

19 ... a6 20 ♖b3 *(20 ♖hd1!?)* 20 ... ♖ab8 21 ♗a7 ♖b5 22 ♗d4 f6 23 h3 ♗d6 24 ♖xb5 axb5 25 ♖c1 ♔f5 26 ♖c6 ± Sokolov-Spraggett (m) 1988.

20 ♖c1   ♖b8

The position is even: 21 ♖c6+ ♔f5 22 ♖a6 ♖bb7 23 a3 ♗e7 24 b4 ♗d8! 25 ♔c2 ♗b6, Rogulj-Bellon Lopez, Bucharest 1979.

A1.2

16 0-0   ♔e6
17 ♖e1+   ...

17 ♗e3 ♗b4 18 ♖ac1 ♖hd8 19 ♖fd1 ♖d7 20 ♖c6+ ♖d6 21 ♖c7 ♖a6 22 a3 ♗d6 23 ♖b7 ♖b8 = Ruxton-M. Lago, Tunja 1989.

17 ...   ♔f5
18 ♖d1   ...

18 ♗e3 ♗e7 19 ♖ac1 ♗f6 20 ♖c5 ♖hd8 21 b4 ♔g6! = Smejkal-Filip, Czechoslovakia 1969.

18 ...   ♖d8
19 ♗e3   ♖d7
20 ♖ac1   ♗e7

21 ♖d4

21 ♖c4 ♗f6 22 ♖f4+ ♔g6 23 ♖g4+ ♔f5 = Kuzmin-Svchenko, USSR 1989.

21 . . .   g5!

21 . . . ♗f6?! 22 ♖f4+ ♔e5 23 ♖a4 d4 24 ♖a5+! ♔e6 *(24 . . . ♖d5? 25 ♗xd4+!)* 25 ♗f4 ♖b7 26 b3 ♖d8 27 ♔f1! d3 28 ♖e1+ ♔d7 29 ♖e4! ± Belyavsky-Wells, London 1985.

22 ♖c6   . . .

22 ♖a4 ♗f6 *(22 . . . ♖b8)* 23 b4!? d4 24 ♖a5+ ♔g6 25 ♗d2 ♖e8 26 ♔f1 d3?! *(26 . . . ♖e6 ∞)* 27 ♖a6! ± Archipov-Filipenko, Belgrade 1989.

22	. . .	♖hd8
23	♔f1	♗f6
24	♖b4	d4
25	♖b5+	♖d5!

25 . . . ♗e5?! 26 ♗xg5! ♔xg5 27 ♖xe5+ ♔f4 28 ♖cc5 ♔xf3 29 ♖f5+ ♔e4 *(29 . . . ♔g4? 30 f3+ ♔h3 31 ♖h5 mate!)* 30 ♔e2 +− Brunner-Adorjan, Luzern 1989.

26	♖cc5	♖xc5
27	♖xc5+	♔g6

28 ♗d2 d3 29 b4 ♖d7 ∞ (Gufeld).

A2

9 . . .   ♘b6!?

Black is taking greater risks than in the 9 . . . e6 variation, but he also has more opportunities.

10 ♗e3!?   . . .

Thorough study ought to be given to 10 d5!? ♘d4 and the continuations:

a) **11 ♕d1!?** e5 *(11 . . . ♘f5?! 12 ♗b5+ ♘d7 13 0-0 ♘d6 14 ♗a4 a6)* 12 dxe6 fxe6 *(12 . . . ♕f6 13 ♗b5+! ♘xb5 14 ♘xb5 ♗b4+ 15 ♔f1 0-0 16 ♕d4 fxe6 and now not 17 ♕xb4?? ♕xf3 but 17 ♕xf6 ♖xf6 18 ♗e3 ♘c4 19 ♔e2 = as in Puhm-Kozma, Milan 1974)* 13 ♗e3 ♗c5 14 ♗g2! *(14 b4 ♕f6! 15 bxc5 ♘xf3+ 16 ♔e2 0-0 17 cxb6 ♖ad8! 18 ♕c1 ♕f5 19 ♕b1 ♕h5! 20 ♕b2 ♕g4 21 ♕b3 ♘d4+ ∓ Hermlin-Pishkin (corr) 1976; or 18 ♗g2! ♖xd1 19 ♖hxd1 axb6 20 ♖ac1 ♘xh2 ∞; or 14 . . . 0-0 15 bxc5 ♘xf3+ 16 ♔e2 ♕f6 17 cxb6 ♖ad8 18 ♕c2! ♘d4+ 19 ♗xd4*

♕xd4 20 ♘e4 − 20 ♔e1 ♖xf2! − 20...
♕xa1 21 ♗g2 ♕e5 − L. Hansen-Kuijf,
Graested 1990 − 22 bxa7 ♕b5+ 23
♔e3! ∞ − Kuijf) 14 ... 0-0 15 0-0 e5 16
♘e4 ♘d7 17 ♘xc5 ♘xc5 18 f4 ±
Romero Holmes-Boersma, Amsterdam 1987.

b) 11 ♗b5+ ♘d7 (11 ... ♘xb5 12
♘xb5 a6 13 ♘c3 threatening 14 ♗e3)
12 ♕a4 ♘xb5 (12 ... ♘xf3+?! 13 ♔e2
♘fe5 14 ♗f4 ∞) 13 ♕xb5 g6 (13 ... e5?
14 dxe6 fxe6 15 ♗e3 ♕c7 16 ♖c1 a6
17 ♕b3 ± Alburt-Dorfman, USSR (ch)
1975) 14 ♗g5 h6 15 ♗h4 ♗g7 16 d6!
g5 17 ♗g3 (17 dxe7 ♗xc3+ 18 bxc3
♕xe7+ 19 ♔f1 0-0-0 ∓) 17 ... 0-0 18 h4
♖c8 ∞, as analysed by Balashov and
Kozlov.

10 ...	e6

There is nothing better, as 10 ...
♘xd4? fails to 11 ♗xd4 ♕xd4 12
♗b5+ and 10 ... g6 to 11 d5 ♘e5 12
♗b5+ ♘d7 13 ♗d4 +−.

11 0-0-0!?	...

11 ♖g1 first was also a possibility,
e.g. 11 ... g6 (11 ... ♗b4!? 12 ♗b5
♘d5 13 ♖xg7 ♕b6 14 ♔f1 ♘xc3 15
♗xc6+ ♕xc6 16 bxc3 ♗f8 17 ♖g5
♗e7 18 ♖b5 ♕xf3 19 ♖xb7 0-0
∞ Ehlvest-Kasparov, USSR 1977; or
12 0-0-0 ♗xc3 13 bxc3 − Jansa-Kraut,
West Germany 1988 − 13 ... 0-0! 14
♗h6 g6 15 ♗xf8 ♕xf8 ∞) 12 0-0-0
♗g7 13 d5 ♘xd5 14 ♘xd5 (14
♕xb7?!) 14 ... exd5 15 ♗c5!? ♕c7 16

♖xd5 (16 ♖e1+ ♔d8 ∞) 16 ... ♗d4 ∞
Fatalibekova-Kushnir, USSR (m) 1977.

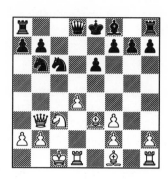

The position in the diagram may
be the critical one for this 9 ... ♘b6
variation. Here 11 ... ♗b4 is bad
because of 12 ♗b5! ♕e7 13 ♖he1.
11... ♖c8? 12 ♔b1 ♕c7 13 ♘b5! ♕b8
14 ♘xa7 +− was played in the
original game in this line, Sisniega-
Grószpéter, Innsbruck 1977. The
correct line is 11 ... ♗e7! 12 d5 exd5
(12 ... ♘xd5 13 ♕xb7 ♕c8 14 ♗a6
+−) 13 ♗xb6 (A little better here is
13 ♘xd5! ♘xd5 14 ♖xd5 ♕c7 15 ♔b1
0-0 16 f4! ♘b4! 17 ♖d4! − 17 ♖e5?!
♗d6 18 ♖g5 ♗xf4 19 ♖g4 ♗xe3 20
fxe3 ♘c6 ∓ Stein-Finegold, Dortmund
1990 − 17 ... ♘c6 18 ♖d1 ♗f6 19 ♗g2
♖fd8 20 ♗e4 ± Anand-Károlyi,
Frunze 1987) 13 ... ♕xb6 (13 ... axb6!?
14 ♘xd5 0-0! 15 ♘f6+ ♗xf6 16
♖xd8 ♖fxd8 is a queen sacrifice suggested by Keene − Black can probably
hold the position. If 15 ♘xb6? ♘d4!
tips the scales in favour of Black. For
15 ♖g1 ♗f6 16 ♖g4 ♖a5? − 16 ...

♕d6! ± — *see illustrative game 46, Short-Miles, Great Britain (ch) 1984) 14* ♕xb6 axb6 *15* ♘xd5 0-0 = *(16* ♘xe7+♘xe7 17 ♖d7? ♖ac8+ *and 18 . . .* ♖fd8!).

B

6 ♗g5 . . .

This is Botvinnik's move, sometimes more popular than 6 ♘f3. The bishop move creates various threats, but does leave the kingside undeveloped — which can give tactical chances to the opponent.

B1: 6 . . . e6
B2: 6 . . . dxc4
B3: 6 . . . ♕a5!?
B4: 6 . . . ♕b6?!
B5: 6 . . . ♗e6

A sixth, rather dubious alternative is **6 . . . ♗g4?! 7 ♗e2!** *(stronger than 7 f3 ♗e6 which is an improved version*

of variation B5 for Black) **7 . . . ♗xe2 8** ♘gxe2 dxc4 *(8 . . . e6 9 cxd5 exd5 10* ♕b3!) **9 d5** ♘e5 **10 0-0 h6** *(10 . . . g6 11 d6! exd6 12* ♗xf6 ♕xf6 *13* ♘d5 ♕d8 *14* ♕a4+ *wins for White. On 10 . . . e6, instead of 11* ♕d4?! *h6 12* ♕xe5 hxg5 *13 dxe6* ♗d6 *14* ♕b5+ ♔f8 *—+ Mortensen-Birnboim, Haifa 1976, best is 11* ♗xf6 *when Black has a poor choice of either 11 . . . gxf6 12* ♕a4+ ♕d7 *13* ♘b5! ♖c8 *14 dxe6 fxe6 15* ♖ad1 +— *or 11 . . .* ♕xf6 *12* ♕a4+ ♘d7 *13* ♖ad1 ± *Pachman)* **11 ♗f4** ♘g6 **12** ♕a4+ ♕d7 **13** ♕xc4 ♖c8 **14** ♕b3 e5 **15 dxe6** ± Tal–Bronstein, USSR (ch) 1971.

B1

6 . . . e6
7 ♘f3 . . .

To be considered is **7 c5!** immediately, e.g. **7 . . . ♗e7 8 ♗b5 0-0 9 ♗xc6 bxc6 10 ♘f3 ♘e4** *(10 . . . ♗a6 is bad because of 11 ♘e5 followed by 12* ♕a4) **11 ♗xe7 ♕xe7 12 0-0 ♘xc3**. The position is even in Botvinnik's view, while Boleslavsky thinks that the knight is more valuable here than the passive bishop, and that White therefore has a small but lasting advantage.

7 . . . ♗e7

For **7 . . . dxc4(?!)** see the illustrative game Botvinnik–Euwe, Hastings 1934-35. But as we shall see there is little reason to fear the c4-c5 variation in this line, and it should be noted that by capturing immediately here Black is a tempo down on the Alekhine–Richter game which is analysed in the note after White's next move.

8 c5   . . .

For **8 &d3?! dxc4** 9 &xc4 0-0 10 0-0 **b6!** see the illustrative game Alekhine–Richter, where White has a tempo disadvantage on certain lines of the Queen's Gambit. Others: **10 . . . a6** 11 a3 b5 12 &a2 &b7 13 ♕d3 b4 14 ♘a4 ♕a5 15 &xf6 gxf6 16 &b3 ♕h5 17 ♖fc1 ♕g6 18 ♕xg6+ hxg6 19 ♘c5 bxa3 20 ♖xa3 ∞/± Mortensen–Berg, Kerteminde 1991, or **8 . . . 0-0** 9 0-0 ♘b4 10 &e2 dxc4 11 &xc4 &d7 12 a3 ♘bd5 13 ♕d3 ♘xc3 14 bxc3 ♖c8 15 ♘e5 ♘g4!? 16 ♘xg4 &xg5 17 f4 &f6 18 &b3 g6 19 c4 &g7 20 ♘e5 ∞/± Fedorowicz–Seirawan, Wijk aan Zee 1991. Instead **8 ♖c1** 0-0 9 c5 ♘e4 10 &xe7 ♕xe7 11 &b5 transposes to a later note in the text.

8 . . .   0-0

If 8 . . . ♘e4 9 &xe7 ♕xe7 10 ♕c2! f5? 11 &b5! &d7 12 &xc6! and the possession of e5 gives White a strategically winning advantage as in Szabó–Honfi, Hungary (ch) 1950. However, the improvement 10 . . . ♘g5! 11 ♘xg5 ♕xg5 12 ♖d1 e5 restricts White to a very small advantage.

9 &b5!   . . .

The aim is to gain control of e5 by attacking the knight. 9 ♖c1 ♘e4 10 &xe7 ♕xe7 transposes to the illustrative game Botvinnik-Konstantinopolsky, analysed in the next chapter.

9 . . .   ♘e4!

9 . . . &d7? 10 0-0 ♘e8 11 &xe7 ♕xe7 12 ♖b1 ± Schwarz.

10 &xe7   . . .

Not 10 ♘xe4 dxe4 11 &xc6 bxc6 12 &xe7 ♕xe7 13 ♘e5 &a6! 14 ♕g4 ♕b7 15 0-0-0 ♖ab8 ∓ Letelier-Pfeiffer, 1950. But after the text Black also has chances of obtaining a good game:

a) **10 . . . ♘xe7** 11 ♖c1 *(11 ♕c2 ♘g6 12 0-0 ♘g5 13 ♘xg5 ♕xg2 14 ♖fd1 ♘h4 15 &f1 f5 16 ♖d3 f4 17 ♕d2 e5! ∓ Teschner–Dalbert, 1942)* 11 . . . b6! *(Not 11 . . . ♘g6? 12 0-0 &d7 13 &d3 f5 14* *b4* ± *Botvinnik-Kmoch, Leningrad 1934 or 11 . . . ♘xc3 12 ♖xc3 b6 13 c6 ♕d6 14 0-0 f6 as in Averbakh-Füstér, Moscow v Budapest 1948, and now 15 ♕e2! a6 16 ♗d3 ♘xc6 17 ♗xh7+ wins according to Euwe)* 12 ♘xe4! *(12 b4? a5 13 a3 axb4 13 axb4 bxc5 15 dxc5 ♘xc3 16 ♖xc3 ♖b8* ∓ *Schwarz; 12 c6!?)* 12 . . . dxe4 13 ♘e5 bxc5 14 ♖xc5 ♕a5+ *(We cannot agree with Botvinnik, according to whom 14 . . . f5 gives a perceptible advantage to Black)* 15 ♕d2 ♕xd2+ *(15 . . . ♕xa2!?)* 16 ♔xd2 ♖d8 17 ♘c6 ± Pachman.

b) **10 . . . ♕xe7** 11 ♕c2 *(11 ♖c1 ♗d4 12 0-0 f6 13 ♖e1 a6 14 ♗xc6 ♗xc6 15 b4 a5 ∞ or 11 ♕c1!? f6 12 0-0 ♗d7 13 ♖e1 ♘xc3 = Schwarz)* 11 . . . ♘g5 12 ♘xg5 ♕xg5 13 ♗xc6 bxc6 *(13 . . . ♕xg2?! 14 ♗xd5 exd5 15 0-0-0 ±)* 14 0-0 e5! 15 f4! *(15 dxe5 ♕xe5 16 ♖fe1 ♕f6 17 ♖ad1 ♖b8 18 ♕d2 ♗g4 19 f3 ♗e6 20 b3 ♕e7 21 ♕e3 ♖fe8 = Keres-Alekhine, AVRO 1938)* 15 . . . exf4 16 ♕d2 ♖b8 17 b3 etc. White has only a minimal advantage *(17 . . . ♗d7! 18 ♖xf4 Pachman).*

B2

6 . . .   dxc4

Abandoning the centre so early like this cedes the initiative to White, but exploiting this is of course far from a trivial task.

7 d5   . . .

A practical test is needed for Alekhine's recommendation of 7 ♗xc4! e.g. 7 . . . ♕xd4? *(Also 7 . . . ♘xd4?! 8 ♘f3! ♘xf3+ 9 ♕xf3 ±. Black's best course is probably to switch to another variation with 7 . . . e6 8 ♘f3 ♗e7)* 8 ♕xd4 ♘xd4 9 0-0-0 e5 10 f4 ♗c5 11 fxe5 ♘g4 12 ♘f3! ♘c6 13 ♖he1 h6 14 ♘e4 ± Paerulek-Lundguis (corr) 1970.

B2.1: 7 . . . ♘e5?!
B2.2: 7 . . . ♘a5!?

B2.1

7 . . .	♘e5?!
8 ♕d4	♘d3+
9 ♗xd3	cxd3
10 ♘f3!	. . .

Instead 10 ♗xf6 exf6 11 ♕xd3 ♗d6 12 ♘ge2 0-0 13 0-0 ♖e8 14 ♖ad1 ♗g4 15 ♖d2 a6 = was played in the first game of the 1933 Botvinnik-Flohr match.

After the text Black has tried:

a) **10 . . . g6?!** 11 ♗xf6 exf6 12 0-0 ± Botvinnik-Flohr (m) 1933.

b) **10 . . . e6?!** 11 0-0-0 ♗e7 *(11 . . . exd5 12 ♖he1+ ♗e6 13 ♗xf6 gxf6 14 ♘xd5 or 13 . . . ♕xf6 14 ♕a4+)* 12 ♖he1! 0-0 13 ♖xd3 ♕a5 14 d6 ♗d8 15 ♘e5 ♘d7 *(15 . . . ♗d7 16 ♖h3 ± Keres-Laurentius (corr) 1934)* 16 ♗e7! ♖e8 17 ♖g3 ± Janošević-Ivanović, Yugoslavia 1974.

c) **10 . . . ♗f5** 11 0-0 h6 12 ♗xf6 gxf6 13 ♕f4 ± Bobotsov-O'Kelly,

Zevenaar 1961.

d) **10 ... h6** 11 ♗xf6 *(11 ♗f4 g5 12 ♗e5 ♗g7 13 ♕xd3 ∓ Botvinnik)* 11 ... exf6 *(11 ... gxf6 12 0-0 ♗g7 13 ♕xd3 0-0 14 ♘d4 ±)* 12 0-0 *(12 0-0-0 ♗d6 13 ♖he1+ ± Botvinnik)* 12 ... ♗e7 13 ♘e4 ♕b6 14 ♕xd3 ± Znosko-Borovsky–Reilly 1934.

B2.2

7 ...   ♘a5!?

Röpert's idea has been revived afer more than three decades.

8 b4   ...

8 ♘f3 e6 9 ♗xf6 gxf6 10 ♗xc4 ♘xc4 11 ♕a4+ ♗d7 12 ♕xc4 ♖c8 13 ♕h4 f5 14 dxe6 ♗xe6 ∞ Hebden–Orr, London 1988.

8 ...   cxb3
9 axb3   ♗d7!

a) **9 ... ♕b6** 10 ♗b5+ ♗d7 11 ♗xf6 exf6 12 ♗xd7+ ♔xd7 13 ♕g4+ ♔d8 White gains a strong attack for the material. Botvinnik judges the position even.

b) **9 ... b6** 10 b4 ♘b7 11 ♗b5+ ♗d7 12 ♘f3 White keeps Black under strong pressure. The exact evaluation of the position still needs the test of competition practice.

10 b4   ♖c8
11 ♘b5   ...

11 ♘a4!? ♘c4 *(11 ... ♘e4!? is an interesting alternative)* 12 ♘c5 ♕b6 ∞ (Tischbierek).

11 ...   ♘c4
12 ♘xa7   ...

12 ♗xf6?! ♗xb5 13 ♗c3 ♘d6 14 ♕b3 ♗xf1 15 ♔xf1 ♘e4 ∓ Fehér-Röpert, Budapest 1988.

12 ...   e6!
13 ♕b3   ...

a) **13 ♘xc8 ♗xb4+ 14 ♔e2 ♗b5! 15 ♔f3 ♘e5+ −+.**

b) **13 ♖b1!? ♘a3 14 ♘xc8 ♘xb1 15 ♕xb1 ♕xc8 =** *(Perhaps 15 ... exd5)* Röpert.

13 ...   ♕b6!
14 ♘xc8   ...

After 14 ♗xc4, 14 ... ♕xb4+! is strong.

14 ...   ♗xb4+
15 ♔e2   ...

15 ♔d1? ♕d4+ 16 ♔c2 ♘d2! −+.

15 ...   ♕c5
16 ♗xf6!   ...

a) **16 ♖b1?! ♘xd5 17 ♔f3 ♘e5+ 18 ♔g3 ♕xc8 ∓ Sveshnikov–Röpert, Budapest 1988.**

b) **16 ♘a7 ♘e4** *(16 ... 0-0!? is also worthy of consideration)* 17 ♗e3 ♘xe3

18 fxe3 exd5 ∞ (Röpert).

16 . . .   **gxf6**
17 ♖a8!   **. . .**

a) 17 ♘a7? exd5 18 ♘c6 ♗xc6 19
♖a8+ ♔d7 20 ♖xh8 ♕e7+ −+.

b) 17 ♖b1 ♗b5! 18 ♔d1 ♕xf2 19
♘f3 *(19 ♘d6+♔e7 20 ♘xc4 ♕xf1+21
♔c2 ♕xg2+ 22 ♔c1 ♕f1+ 23 ♔c2
♕xc4+ 24 ♕xc4 ♗xc4 25 ♖xb4 ♗xd5
−+)* 19 . . . ♘e3+ 20 ♕xe3 *(20 ♔c1?
♗a3+!)* 20 . . . ♗a4+! 21 ♕b3 ♗xb3+
22 ♖xb3 ♗c5 ∓ (Röpert).

17 . . .   **0-0**
18 ♘e7+   **♕xe7**
19 ♕g3+   **. . .**

19 ♖xf8+ ♔xf8 20 d6 ♕xd6 21
♕xc4 ♕e5+ 22 ♔f3 ♗c6+ 23 ♔g4
h5+ 24 ♔h3 ♕f5+ 25 ♔g3 ♕g5+ 26
♔h3 ♗e1! 27 ♘f3 *(27 f3 ♗b5 −+)*
27 . . . ♕f5+ 28 ♔g3 ♕g6+ 29 ♔h3
♗e4 −+ (Röpert).

19 . . .   **♔h8**
20 ♖xf8+   **♕xf8**
21 ♕h4   **exd5**

According to Röpert this position
is equal, although Black could have
tried the enterprising 21 . . . ♕c5!?
after which the possibilities are
complex.

B3

6 . . .   **♕a5!?**

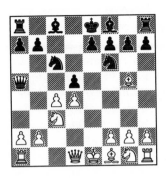

An active, sharp continuation. It
has the slight drawback that in one of
the variations White is immediately
able to force a draw.

7 ♕d2   **. . .**

For 7 ♘f3 ♗g4 *(7 . . . ♘e4 8 cxd5 ±
Durašević)* 8 ♕b3!? *(8 ♗xf6!?)* 8 . . .
0-0-0 see Martin-Bellon in
illustrative games. A second
alternative is 7 ♗xf6 exf6 8 cxd5 ♗b4!
*(One of the standard moves of this
variation)* 9 ♕d2! *(9 dxc6 ♗xc3+ 10
bxc3 ♕xc3+ 11 ♔e2 0-0 12 f3 ♖e8+ 13
♔f2 ♕e3+ 14 ♔g3 ♕g5+15 ♔f2 =)* 9
. . . ♘e7 *(9 . . . ♗xc3 10 bxc3 ♕xd5 11
♘f3 0-0 12 ♗e2 ♗g4?! 13 0-0 ♘e5!? 14
♘xe5 ♗xe2 15 ♕xe2 fxe5 16 dxe5
♖fe8 17 ♖fe1 ♕c5! ± Jansa-Bellon,
Cirella di Diamante 1976-77; 11 . . .
♗h3!? 12 gxh3! ♕xf3 13 ♕e3+ ♕xe3
14 fxe3 0-0 15 ♗d3 ♖ac8 ± Estrin-
Onat, Albena 1974)* 10 ♗b5+ ♕xb5!
*(10 . . . ♔d8! 11 ♘ge2! ♘xd5 12 ♗c4
♗e6 13 ♗xd5 ♗xd5 14 0-0 ♗c4 15
♖fe1 ± Jansa-Vukić, Belgrade 1977;*

10 . . . ♔f8!?) 11 ♘xb5 ♗xd2+ 12 ♔xd2 ♘xd5 13 ♘e2 ± Jansa. A third alternative is **7 ♗d2 ♕d8** *(7 . . . dxc4 8 ♗xc4 e6 9 d5 exd5 10 ♘xd5 ♕d8 11 ♕e2+ ♗e6 12 ♘f4 ♘d4 13 ♘xe6 fxe6 14 ♕d3 ♕b6 15 ♘e2 0-0-0 16 0-0 e5 ± Bronstein-Bagirov, Tallinn 1981; or 9 ♘f3 ♗e7 10 ♘d5 ♕d8 11 ♘xe7♘xe7! 12 0-0 ♗d7 13 ♗g5 ♗c6 14 ♖e1 h6 15 ♗h4 ♗d5 16 ♗b5+ ♔f8 17 ♗g3 ♘e4 = Tal-Marovic, Malaga 1981)* 8 ♘f3 ♗g4 9 cxd5 ♘xd5 10 ♗b5 ♖c8 11 h3 ♗xf3 12 ♕xf3 e6 13 ♘xd5 ♕xd5 14 ♕xd5 exd5 15 0-0 ♗e7 16 ♖fe1 ♔d8 17 ♖ed1 ♔c7 = Hebden-Garcia Palermo, Malmö 1987/88.

After the text move of 7 ♕d2 Black has the following alternatives:

a) **7 . . . dxc4** 8 ♗xc4 c5 9 d5 ♘d4 10 f4! ♗d6 *(10 . . . ♗f5 11 fxe5 ♘c2+ 12 ♔f1 ♘xa1 13 exf6 ± Keres)* 11 ♘ge2 ♘f5?! *(11 . . . ♘xe2 12 ♕xe2 0-0 13 ♗xf6! gxf6 14 0-0 ± Keres)* 12 ♗b5+ ♗d7 13 ♗xf6 gxf6 14 ♗xd7+ ♔xd7 Keres-Czerniak, Buenos Aires (ol) 1939, and now 15 ♕d3! ±.

b) **7 . . . e5?!** 8 ♗xf6 *(8 dxe5 ♘e4! 9 ♘xe4 ♗b4 10 ♘c3 d4 ∓) 8 . . . gxf6 9 ♘f3! (9 ♘xd5?! ♕xd2+ 10 ♔xd2 ♗h6+ 11 ♔d1! − 11 ♖e1 ♘xd4 −+ − 11 . . . 0-0! 12 ♘xf6+ ♔g7 13 dxe5 ♘xe5 14 ♘d5 ♖fd8 15 ♔e1 b5! 16 ♘c7? ♗e6 17 ♘xe6+ fxe6 18 cxb5 ♖d2 19 ♘f3 ♘xf3+ 20 gxf3 ♖ad8 − Šajtar-Pachman, Lomnic 1944; 16 b3 bxc4 17 bxc4 ♗e6 = is an improvement, while 17 ♘xa8 ♗d2+ 18 ♔d1 ♗g5+ 19 ♔e1 ♗d2+ draws) 9 . . . ♗f5!? (9 . . . ♗g4 10 ♘xd5 ♗xf3 11 ♕xa5 ±)* 10 cxd5 exd4 11 ♘xd4 ♘xd4 12 ♕xd4 0-0-0 13 ♕xf6 ♗g4 14f3 *(14 ♕xh8!? ♖e8+ 15 ♗e2 ♗xe2 16 ♕d4! ± Pachman)* 14 . . . ♗e7! 15 ♕d4! ± Eslon-Bellon, Wijk aan Zee 1977.

c) **7 . . . ♗e6!?** 8 c5 ♘e4 9 ♘xe4 dxe4 10 ♕xa5 ♘xa5 11 ♗b5+ ♘c6 12 ♘e2 0-0-0 13 ♗e3 ♘b4 14 0-0 a6 15 ♗a4 ♗c4 16 ♖fe1 ♘d3 ∞ Lerner-Sveshnikov, Leningrad 1976.

d) **7 . . . ♗f5** 8 ♗xf6 *(8 cxd5 ♘xd5 9 ♗c4 ♘xc3 10 bxc3 ♗e4!? 11 ♘f3 ♗xf3?! 12 gxf3 e5?! 13 0-0! ± Keres)* 8 . . . exf6 9 cxd5 ♘b4 10 ♗b5+ ♔d8 11 ♖c1 *(11 ♔f1 ♘xd5 ∓) 11 . . . ♖c8 12 ♘ge2 a6! (12 . . . ♕xb5?? 13 ♘xb5 ♖xc1+ 14 ♘xc1) 13 a3! ♘xd5 14 ♘xd5 ♖xc1+ 15 ♘xc1 ♕xb5 ∞.

B4

6 . . .   ♕b6?!

Very sharp. This move has been considered incorrect on more than one occasion, yet has still to be conclusively discredited.

7 cxd5   . . .

Schwarz gives 7 ♗xf6 ♕xb2 8 ♘xd5 exf6 9 ♕e2+ ♕xe2+ 10 ♘xe2 ±.

7 . . .   ♘xd4 (!)

Rather better than 7 . . . ♕xb2? 8 ♖c1! ♘b4 9 ♘a4! ♕xa2 10 ♗c4 ♗g4 11 ♘f3 ♗xf3 12 gxf3 1-0,

Botvinnik-Spielmann, Moscow 1935
or **7 . . . ♘xd5?** 8 ♘xd5 ♕a5+ 9 ♘c3
♕xg5 10 ♘f3 ♕a5 11 d5! ♘d8 12
♗b5+ ± Muffang-Grob, 1953.

8 ♗e3   . . .

If **8 ♖c1** e5 =, **8 ♘f3** ♘xf3+ 9 ♕xf3
♗d7 ± Botvinnik or **8 ♘ge2** ♘f5 *(8...*
♘xe2 9 ♗xe2 ♕xb2? 10 ♘b5 ♘e4 11
♖b1 +−) 9 ♕d2 *(9 ♘g3 ∞)* 9 . . . h6 10
♗f4 *(10 ♗xf6 exf6 11 ♘g3 ♗d6 =*
Polugayevsky-Bagirov, USSR 1969)
10 . . . g5 11 ♗e5 ♘g4 12 ♗d4 ±.

8 . . .	**e5**
9 dxe6	**♗c5**
10 exf7+	**. . .**

Not 10 ♕a4+ ♔e7 **11 b4?!** ♗xb4 12
♘e2 ♖d8 13 ♖c1 ♗xe6 14 a3 ♗c5 ∓
Estrin-Bagirov, USSR 1958; Euwe
gives **11 0-0-0** ∞.

10 . . .	**♔e7**

10 . . . ♔xf7? 11 ♗c4+ and 12 ♘ge2
±.

11 ♗c4   . . .

11 ♗d3?! ♖d8 12 ♖c1 ♗g4! 13
♕d2 ♖ac8 14 h3 ♗f5 15 ♗xf5 ♘xf5
16 ♗xc5+ ♖xc5 ∓ Schubert-Pasman,
Groningen 1977-78.

11 . . .   ♗g4

The pawn is poisoned − **11 . . .**

♕xb2? 12 ♘ge2! ♘c2+ 13 ♕xc2
♕xa1+ 14 ♗c1 b5 15 ♗b3 ♗b7 16 0-0
♖he8 17 ♗f4 ± Dely-Sallay,
Budapest 1964. Also bad is **11 . . . ♖d8**
12 ♘f3 ♕xb2 13 0-0! ♕xc3 14 ♖c1
♕b2 15 ♖e1+ ♔f8 16 ♘xd4 ♗xd4 *(16*
. . . ♖xd4 17 ♕h5! ♘xh5 18 ♗xd4
♕xf2+ 19 ♗xf2 ♗xf2+ 20 ♔xf2) 17
♕d3! ± Romanov-Flerov (corr) 1963;
12 . . . ♗g4 13 ♗xd4 ♖xd4 14 ♕e2+
♔f8 15 ♗b3 a5 16 0-0 a4 17 ♗d1! ±
Boleslavsky.

12 ♕c1   . . .

Zhdanov gives **12 ♕xg4!? ♘c2+!**
13 ♔f1 *(13 ♔d1 ♖ad8+ ∓)* 13 . . .
♘xg4! 14 ♘d5+ ♔f8 15 ♘xb6
♘gxe3+ 16 fxe3 ♗xb6 17 ♖c1 ♘xe3+
18 ♔e2 ♖c8 19 b3 ♘xc4 ∓ or
12 f3?! ♗e6! 13 ♗xe6 ♕xe6 14 ♔f2
♖ad8 15 ♘ge2 ♕xe3!? 16 ♔xe3
♘e6+! ∓.

12 . . .	**♗f5**
13 ♗xd4	**♗xd4**
14 ♕d2	**♖hc8**

This was played in Schardtner-
Sallay, Budapest 1969. Now Botvinnik
suggests 15 ♗d3 ♗e6 16 ♘f3 ±.

B5

6 . . .	**♗e6**

Flohr's move. Undeservedly neglected?

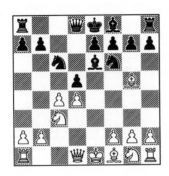

7 ♗xf6   . . .

a) 7 ♘f3 is not very promising: **7 . . .
♘e4!** 8 ♘xe4 dxe4 9 d5 exf3 10 dxe6
♕a5+ 11 ♗d2 ♕e5+ 12 ♗e3 ♕xe6 =
Estrin-Flohr, Vilnius 1960; **7 . . . g6**
8 ♗e2?! ♗g7 9 0-0 0-0 10 cxd5 *(10 c5
♘e4!)* 10 . . . ♘xd5 11 ♕d2 ♖c8 12
♗h6?! ♘xc3 = Lublinsky-Flohr,
USSR (ch) 1949.

b) 7 ♘ge2 dxc4 8 ♘f4 ♘xd4 *(8 . . .
♕xd4!? 9 ♘xe6?! ♕e5+ 10 ♕e2 fxe6
∓; 9 ♕xd4 ♘xd4 10 0-0-0 ∞)* 9 ♘xe6
♘xe6 10 ♗xc4 a6! *(10 . . . ♘xg5? 11
♕a4+! ♘d7 12 0-0-0 a6 13 ♖xd7!
♕xd7 14 ♗b5 axb5 15 ♕xa8+ ♕d8 16
♕xb7 f6 17 ♖d1 ♕a5 18 f4 ♘e6 19 f5
♘d8 20 ♕d7+ ♔f7 21 ♕d5+! e6 − 21
. . . ♔e8 22 ♘xb5! − Mortensen-Fetta,
Malmö 1987 − 22 ♕d7+! ♗e7 23 ♘xb5
±)* 11 ♕b3 ±.

c) 7 g3 ♕a5!? 8 ♗g2 ♘e4!? 9 ♗xe4
dxe4 10 d5 0-0-0 11 ♗d2 ♘b4 12 ♘xe4
♗f5 13 ♕b1 ♕b6 14 ♘e2 e6 15 ♗e3
♕a6! ∞ Tal-Hodgson, Sochi 1986.

d) 7 ♕d2!? g6 8 g3 ♘a5 9 ♗xf6 exf6
10 c5 h5 11 ♗g2 ♗h6 12 ♕c2 0-0 13

♘ge2 ♖e8 14 0-0 ♗f5 ± Sveshnikov-
M. Tseitlin, Sochi 1985.

B5.1: 7 . . . exf6
B5.2: 7 . . . gxf6!?

B5.1

7 . . .   exf6
8 c5   . . .

8 ♘f3 g6 9 c5 ♗h6!? *(9 . . . ♗g7 10
h3 0-0 11 ♗b5 ±; 9 . . . ♗e7 10 ♗b5 0-0
11 0-0 f5 12 ♕d2 ♗f6 13 ♗xc6 bxc6 14
b4 ± Botvinnik)* 10 ♗b5 0-0 11 ♗xc6
bxc6 12 h3 ♖b8 13 b3 ♖e8 14 0-0 ±
(analysis).

8 . . .   a6!

a) **8 . . . ♗e7** 9 ♗b5 0-0 10 ♘ge2
♕c7 11 0-0 f5 12 ♕c2 ♗f6 13 ♗xc6
bxc6 14 b4! ± Botvinnik-Flohr, USSR
(m) 1933.

b) **8 . . . g6** 9 ♘f3 ♗g7 10 h3 0-0 11
♗b5 ± I. Zaitsev-Shamkovich, USSR
1967.

9 ♘ge2	b6!
10 b4	♗e7
11 ♕a4?	b5
12 ♕b3	a5!

This was played in Yurtayev-
Dreyev, USSR 1988, where Black now
had a slight edge.

B5.2

| 7 . . . | gxf6!? |
| 8 c5 | . . . |

Alternatively:

a) 8 ♞f3 ♛d7 *(8 . . . ♛a5 9 a3!?)* 9 c5 ♝g4! 10 ♝e2 ♝xf3 11 ♝xf3 e6 12 0-0 ♝g7 13 ♝e2 *(13 ♞e2!? ∓)* 13 . . .a6! 14 ♛a4 0-0 15 ♜fd1 f5 16 ♜d3 ♛c7 17 ♜ad1 b6 ∓ Sax–Miles, Wijk aan Zee 1989.

b) 8 ♛d2 ♛a5 9 c5 0-0-0! 10 ♝b5 ♜g8 11 f4 ♝h6! 12 ♛f2 ♞b4 ∓ Miles–Yusupov, Tunis (izt) 1985.

| 8 . . . | ♛d7! |

8 . . . ♝g7 9 ♝b5 0-0 10 ♞ge2 ♝g4 11 f3 ♝f5 12 ♛b3 e6 13 ♜d1 ♝g6 14 0-0 ♛a5 15 ♞f4 a6?! *(15 . . . ♝h6!? is an improvement)* 16 ♝xc6 bxc6 17 ♛b6 ♛xb6 18 cxb6 ± Chiburdanidze–Hodgson, Hastings 1986/87.

9 ♝b5	♜g8!?
10 g3	0-0-0
11 ♛h5?!	. . .

11 ♞ge2 ♝g4 12 ♛a4 ∞.

11 . . .	♝g4!
12 ♛xh7	♛e6+
13 ♔f1	∞/∓

13 . . . ♞xd4! *(13 . . . ♜g6? 14 ♜e1!)* 14 ♛xg8! *(14 ♜e1 ♛f5 15 ♛xg8? ♝h3+ 16 ♞xh3 ♛xh3+ 17 ♔g1 ♞f3 mate!)* 14 . . . ♝h6! 15 ♝e8! *(15 ♛h7*

♝h3+ *16 ♞xh3 ♛xh3+ 17 ♔e1 ♝d2+! winning)* 15 . . . ♝h3+ 16 ♞xh3 ♛xh3+ 17 ♔e1 ♞c2+ 18 ♔e2 ♞d4+ 19 ♔e1 ♞c2+ ∞/∓ Mainka–Miles, Bad Wörishofen 1989.

ILLUSTRATIVE GAMES

45 FISCHER–EUWE
     Leipzig Olympiad 1960
     1 e4 c6 2 d4 d5 3 exd5 cxd5 4 c4 ♞f6 5 ♞c3 ♞c6 6 ♞f3 ♝g4 7 cxd5 ♞xd5 8 ♛b3 ♝xf3 9 gxf3 e6 10 ♛xb7 ♞xd4 11 ♝b5+ ♞xb5 12 ♛c6+ ♔e7 13 ♛xb5 ♞xc3 14 bxc3 ♛d7? 15 ♜b1! ♜d8?! (Fischer reckoned that after 15 . . . ♛xb5 16 ♜xb5 ♔d6! 17 ♜b7 f6 18 ♔e2 ♔c6 19 ♜f7 a5 20 ♝e3 Black's problems are less serious, while after 15 . . . ♜c8 16 ♝e3 ♛xb5 17 ♜xb5 ♜xc3 18 ♜b7+ ♔e8 19 ♔d2 ♜a3 20 ♜c1! also favoured White in Saltsman–Yakchin, USSR 1974) 16 ♝e3 ♛xb5 17 ♜xb5 ♜d7 18 ♔e2! (18 ♜a5 is unnecessary, since the a-pawn will not run away) 18 . . . f6 19 ♜d1! (Eliminating Black's one and only developed piece) 19 . . . ♜xd1 20 ♔xd1 ♔d7 21 ♜b8! (With this move White's strategy has reaped winning dividends. Fischer has handled the problem-like middle game like a virtuoso. If 21 ♝xa7?! had been played, Black would have been allowed counterplay with 21 . . . ♝d6 22 ♜b7 ♔c6 23 ♜xg7 ♝xh2) 21 . . . ♔c6 22 ♝xa7 g5 23 a4 ♝g7 24 ♜b6+

(24 ♖xh8 ♗xh8 ±) 24 ... ♔d5 25 ♖b7
♗f8 26 ♖b8 ♗g7 27 ♖b5+ ♔c6 28
♖b6+ ♔d5 29 a5 f5 (29 ... ♖a8 30
♖b7 ♗f8 31 ♖xh7 ♗c5 32 ♗b6! ±)
30 ♗b8! ♖c8 31 a6 ♖xc3 32 ♖b5+
♔c4 (On 32 ... ♔c6 33 ♖a5 ♗d4 34
♔e2! +—; but not 34 ♗e5? ♖c5!)
33 ♖b7 ♗d4 34 ♖c7+ ♔d3 35 ♖xc3+
♔xc3 36 ♗e5! Black resigned.

44   SHORT-MILES
Great Britain (ch) 1984
**1 e4 c6 2 d4 d5 3 exd5 cxd5 4 c4 ♘f6
5 ♘c3 ♘c6 6 ♘f3 ♗g4 7 cxd5 ♘xd5
8 ♕b3 ♗xf3 9 gxf3 ♘b6!? 10 ♗e3!? e6
11 0-0-0!?** ♗e7 12 d5 exd5 13 ♗xb6
axb6 14 ♘xd5 0-0 15 ♖g1! ♗f6 16
♖g4 ♖a5? 17 ♔b1 ♖c5 (17 ... ♕d6
18 ♘xb6 ♕xh2? 19 ♘d7 winning)
18 ♘xb6 ♘d4 19 ♕b4 ♖c6 20 ♘c4
♕d7 21 ♖e4 ♖fc8? (21 ... ♕f5?! 22
♘e3 ♕xf3 23 ♖exd4 ±; 21 ... ♖d8
seems best) 22 a3 (22 ♘b6! ♘e2 23
♕f8+!!) 22 ... ♖d8 23 ♘a5! ♖e6
(23 ... ♖c7 24 ♘b3 ±; 23 ... ♖d6
24 ♘xb7 wins) 24 ♗h3 ♕c7 25
♖exd4! ♖xd4 26 ♖xd4 ♗xd4 27
♗xe6 fxe6 28 ♕xb7! ♕e5 (28 ... ♕xa5
29 ♕c8+ ♔f7 30 ♕d7+ wins the
bishop back) 29 ♘c6 ♕e1+ 30 ♔a2
♗f6 (30 ... ♗xf2 31 ♘d8 h6 32 ♕f7+
♔h8 33 ♘xe6 ♕e5 34 ♘f8 +—) 31
♕b3 h5 32 ♕c2 ♕h1 33 a4 ♕xf3 34 a5
♕d5+ 35 ♔a3 ♕d6+ 36 b4 ♕xh2 37
a6 ♕h3+ 38 ♔a4 ♕f1 39 a7 ♕a6+ 40
♔b3 h4 41 ♕c4 ♕a1 42 ♕xe6+ ♔h7
43 ♕e4+ g6 44 ♘e5! ♕d1+ 45 ♔c4
♕f1+ 46 ♘d3 Black resigned.

47   SVESHNIKOV-RÖPERT
Budapest 1988
**1 e4 c6 2 d4 d5 3 exd5 cxd5 4 c4 ♘f6
5 ♘c3 ♘c6 6 ♗g5 dxc4!? 7 d5 ♘a5 8 b4
cxb3 9 axb3 ♗d7! 10 b4 ♖c8 11 ♘b5
♘c4 12 ♘xa7 e6! 13 ♕b3 ♕b6! 14
♘xc8 ♗xb4+ 15 ♔e2 ♕c5 16 ♖b1?**
♘xd5 17 ♔f3 (17 ♗e7 ♘f4+ 18 ♔f3
♘d2+ 19 ♔g3 ♘h5+ 20 ♔h3 e5+ 21
g4 ♕xf2 —+) 17 ... ♘e5+ 18 ♔g3
♕xc8 19 f4? (19 ♘f3 ♘c6! 20 h4 h6 21
♗d2 ♕c7+ 22 ♔h3 g5 ∓) 19 ... ♘c6
20 ♘f3 h6 21 ♗h4 ♕b8! 22 ♕c4
(22 ♔f2!? is probably stronger here)
22 ... g5 23 ♗xg5 hxg5 24 ♘xg5 ♘xf4
25 ♔f2 ♕a7+ 26 ♔g3 ♕e3+ 27 ♘f3
White resigned.

48   MARTIN-BELLON
Las Palmas 1977
**1 e4 c6 2 d4 d5 3 exd5 cxd5 4 c4 ♘f6
5 ♘c3 ♘c6 6 ♗g5 ♕a5!? 7 ♘f3 ♗g4
8 ♕b3!? 0-0-0 (8 ... ♕b4?** 9 cxd5
♕xb3 10 axb3 ♘b4 11 ♖a4 ±
Durašević) **9 ♗xf6 gxf6 10 cxd5 ♘b4
11 ♗c4?!** (11 ♘d2 with the threat of
♘c4-e3 was better — if 11 ... ♘xd5 12
♘xd5 followed by 13 ♖c1 Durašević)
11 ... ♔b8 12 a3? (Too slow. 12 ♘d2
♗h6 13 ♘de4 or 12 ... e6 13 0-0 exd5
14 ♗e2 was needed) **12 ... e6! 13 dxe6
fxe6 14 0-0?** (He castles right into the
line of the attack! 14 ♘d2 ♘c6 was
better) **14 ... ♗xf3! 15 axb4 ♖g8! 16
g3 ♕h5 17 ♖fc1** (White is forced to
fend off the threat of 18 ... ♕h3. On
17 ♗xe6 comes 17 ... ♖xd4 18 ♘b5
♖xb4 19 ♕c3 ♖xg3+!! 20 fxg3 ♗c5+
21 ♖f2 ♖xb5 ∓ Durašević) **17 ...**

♖xd4 18 ♘b5 (18 ♗f1 ♖d2 19 ♘d1 ♖xg3+!) 18 . . . ♖d2 19 ♕e3 ♖xg3+!! (A pretty combination to open the file!) 20 fxg3 ♕xh2+ 21 ♔f1 ♕h1+ 22 ♕g1 ♗g2+ 23 ♔e1 ♕xg1+ 24 ♔xd2 ♗h6+ White resigned.

49   BOTVINNIK−EUWE
Hastings 1934-35.

1 c4 c6 2 e4 d5 3 exd5 cxd5 4 d4 ♘f6 5 ♘c3 ♘c6 6 ♗g5 e6 7 ♘f3 dxc4?! 8 ♗xc4 ♗e7 9 0-0 0-0 10 ♖c1?! (The rook has little business on the c-file. The line taken in the following game ought to have been followed) **10 . . . a6** (10 . . . b6, as in the Nimzo-Indian, is also good) **11 ♗d3 h6** (11 . . . ♘b4 12 ♗b1 b5 13 a3 ♘bd5 14 ♕d3 g6 15 ♗h6 ♖e8 16 ♘e5 ± or 11 . . . b5!? 12 ♘xb5 axb5 13 ♖xc6 ♖xa2 14 ♕b3 ♗d7! ∞ Euwe) **12 ♗e3?!** (This passes the initiative to Black − better is 12 ♗h4 maintaining the tension. E.g. 12 . . . ♘b4 13 ♗b1 b5 14 a3 ♘bd5 15 ♕c2 ∞ Euwe) **12 . . . b5 13 ♗b1 ♘b4!** (The knight intends to proceed to d5. The concession of e5 is of no great consequence, since no attack can develop on the f-file owing to Black's counterplay) **14 ♘e5 ♗b7 15 ♕d2 ♖e8 16 f4?** (White cannot develop the intended attack because of his weakness on the long diagonal. After 16 f3! the theoretical weakness of the isolated d4 pawn is counterbalanced by White's spatial advantage) **16 . . . ♘bd5 17 ♘xd5** (17 ♗f2 ♘xc3 18 bxc3 ♘e4 19 ♕d3 ♕d5 20 ♖fe1 f5 ∓ Euwe) **17 . . . ♕xd5 18 f5 ♗d6!** (Action in the

centre, just in time!) **19 fxe6** (19 ♗f4 was not playable because of the possibility of 19 . . . exf5 20 ♗xf5 ♗xe5!) **19 . . . ♖xe6 20 ♗f5** (If 20 ♘d3?? ♖xe3! −+ or 20 ♘f3 ♘g4! 21 ♗f2 ♗xh2+! −+ or 20 ♗f4 ♗xe5 21 dxe5 ♕xd2 ∓ Euwe) **20 . . . ♖e7 21 ♗h3 ♗xe5 22 dxe5 ♕xe5 23 ♗f4** (23 ♗d4 ♖d8 24 ♗xe5 ♖xd2 25 ♗c3 ♖de2 ∓ Euwe) **23 . . . ♕d5 24 ♕xd5** (24 ♗xh6 gxh6 25 ♕xh6 ♖e2! −+) **24 . . . ♘xd5 25 ♗d2 ♖ae8 26 b3 ♖e2 27 ♖f2 ♘f6** (28 . . . ♖xf2 and 29 . . . ♘e4+ is threatened) **28 ♗a5 ♖xf2 29 ♔xf2 ♘e4+ 30 ♔f1 ♘g5 31 ♗d7** (31 ♗g4!?) **31 . . . ♖e7 32 ♗f5** (32 ♖c7 ♗e4 and then ♗d3 ∓ is threatened) **32 . . . ♖e5 33 ♗b1 ♗e4!** (Dr Euwe plays the still difficult end-game with great vigour. His winning chances improve after taking off one of the bishops) **34 ♗xe4 ♘xe4 35 ♖c6** (35 ♖c8+ ♔h7 36 ♗e1 may be more stubborn) **35 . . . ♖f5+ 36 ♔e1 ♖f2!** (The result of thorough thinking: Black acquires a considerable material advantage, but the resulting white passed pawn looks dangerous because of the bishop's support) **37 a4 ♖xg2 38 ♖xa6 bxa4 39 bxa4 ♖xh2 40 ♖a8+ ♔h7 41 ♗b6 ♖a2 42 a5 h5 43 a6 h4 44 a7 h3 45 ♗g1 ♘f6 46 ♔d1** (The Dutch master and subsequent World Champion has handled the end-game extremely accurately: the duel of the passed pawns was won by Black because after 46 ♖d8 ♖xa7 47 ♗xa7 h2 wins) **46 . . . ♘g4 47 ♖e8 h2?!** (47 . . . ♘f2+! 48 ♔e1 ♘d3+ 49 ♔d1 ♖xa7! −+

Botvinnik) 48 ♗xh2 ♖xa7 49 ♗b8
♖a8 50 ♖d8 ♘e5 51 ♗c7 ♖xd8 52
♗xd8 ♔g6 53 ♔e2 ♔f5 54 ♔e3 ♔g4
55 ♗c7 ♘f3 56 ♔f2 f5 **White resigned.**

50 ALEKHINE–RICHTER
Munich 1942

**1 e4 c6 2 d4 d5 3 exd5 cxd5 4 c4 ♘f6
5 ♘c3 ♘c6 6 ♗g5 e6 7 ♘f3 ♗e7
8 ♗d3?! dxc4 9 ♗xc4 0-0 10 0-0 b6! 11
a3 ♗b7 12 ♕d3** (White intends to
open an attack with ♖ad1 followed by
♗e4-a2-b1. Similar positions could
also arise from the 5 . . .e6 6 ♘f3 ♗b4
variation) **12 . . . ♘d5?** (Black tries to
release the tension in the centre too
fast. 12 . . . ♖c8 first and then . . . ♖e8
was stronger) **13 ♗xd5! ♗xg5** (13 . . .
exd5 14 ♗xe7 ♘xe7 15 ♖fe1 ±
Alekhine) **14 ♗e4 f5** (According to
the World Champion, 14 . . . g6 15
♕b5 ♗f6 16 ♗xc6 a6 17 ♕c4! ♖ac8
18 ♘e5 ♗xe5 19 dxe5 ♖xc6 20 ♕f4
♖c7 21 ♖ad1 or 14 . . . h6 15 ♖ad1 f5
16 ♘xg5 ♕xg5 − 16 . . . hxg5 17 ♗xc6
♗xc6 18 ♖fe1 − 17 ♗f3 both favour
White) **15 ♘xg5 ♕xg5 16 ♗f3 ♔h8?**
(Alekhine thought that Black could
have set a pretty trap here: 16 . . .
♖ad8 17 ♕c4 ♔h8 18 ♗xc6 ♖c8 19
♕xe6 ♖xc6 20 ♕d7 ♕xg2+! but the
simple 17 ♕e3 is more favourable for
White) **17 ♖fe1!** (17 ♕c4? ♘e5!)

17 . . . ♖ad8 (The d-pawn is hanging,
and e6-e5 is also threatened) **18 ♕f1!**
("The concept behind this move is to
prompt Black into taking on d4 with
his rook, which makes the attacking
move 19 ♕b5 feasible. This was not
possible immediately because of 18
. . . ♘xd4. But, should Black forego
the capture, White would play 19
♖ad1" − Alekhine) **18 . . . ♖xd4 19
♕b5! ♖d6?!** (19 . . . ♘d8 20 ♗xb7
♘xb7 21 ♖xe6 ♘c5 22 ♖e8 was the
lesser evil) **20 ♘e4 ♕g6 21 ♘xd6!** (He
sacrifices his queen, but gets a lot in
compensation. 21 ♗h5 ♕xh5? 22
♘xd6 ♘d4 23 ♕d3 ♘xf3+ 24 gxf3
♗xf3 25 ♖e3 ± or 21 . . . ♖d5! 22
♕xd5 exd5 23 ♗xg6 fxe6 24 ♗h5 ♘e5
as given by Alekhine) **21 . . . ♘d4 22
♗xb7 ♘xb5 23 ♘xb5 ♕f6 24 ♘c3 e5
25 ♖ad1 e4 26 ♖d7! h5** (26 . . . ♖d8+
27 ♘d5 ♕g5 28 ♖xd8 ♕xd8 29 ♖c1 +
−) **27 h3 h4** (27 . . . ♖d8 28 ♘d5 ♕g5
29 h4 ♕xh4 30 ♘e7 +−) **28 ♖ed1
♔h7 29 ♗a6 ♖f7 30 ♖7d6 ♕g5 31
♖6d5 ♕f4 32 ♘e2 ♕g5 33 ♘d4 ♖f6
34 ♗e2! ♔h6** (34 . . . ♖g6 35 ♗g4!)
**35 ♘c2 ♖f7 36 ♘e3 g6 37 ♗c4 ♕f4 38
♖d6 ♖c7 39 b3 ♔h7 40 a4 ♕e5
41 ♖e6 ♕c3 42 ♘d5 ♕c2 43 ♖f1 ♖g7
44 f3! exf3 45 ♖xf3 ♔h6** (45 . . . ♕c1+
46 ♔h2 ♕g5 47 ♘f4 and ♗c4-b5-e8)
46 ♘e3 Black resigned.

9
Panov Attack — 5 ... e6

1 e4 c6 2 d4 d5 3 exd5 cxd5 4 c4 ♘f6 5 ♘c3 e6

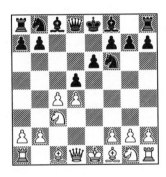

This is still seen as the most modern continuation, in spite of the recent renaissance of 5 . . . ♘c6. Black can develop his king's bishop to b4 or e7, and in the latter case it is useful that the queen's knight is not yet developed.

Play from the . . . ♗b4 line will frequently transpose into a variation of the Nimzo-Indian Defence — one that is also quite fashionable from the Nimzo move order at present. From the . . . ♗e7 lines the most likely transposition is to the standard isolated queen's pawn position which can arise from the Semi-Tarrasch, c3

Sicilian and many other openings.

    6 ♘f3   ...

The most natural continuation. For **6 cxd5?!** ♘xd5 7 ♗d3 ♗b4! see variation B, while **6 c5?!** leads in practice to the lines discussed in variation A2.

A: 6 . . . ♗e7
B: 6 . . . ♗b4

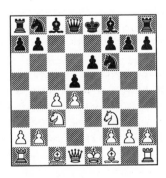

For the situation arising after 6 . . . dxc4?! compare the illustrative game Botvinnik–Euwe, chapter 8.

A

6 ...   ♗e7

Now White can try a Queen's Gambit-like handling of the position, as in A1, or something close to the original Panov idea as in A2.

A1: 7 cxd5
A2: 7 c5

Others:

a) 7 ♗g5?! 0-0 8 ♖c1!? ♘c6 *(8 ... dxc4!?)* 9 c5 ♘e4 10 ♗xe7 ♕xe7 11 ♗e2 *(For 11 ♗b5 see A2)* 11 ... ♗d7 *(11 ... ♘xc3 12 ♖xc3 e5 13 ♘xe5 ♘xe5 14 ♖e3 ± Fine)* 12 a3 f5? 13 ♗b5! was played in Botvinnik-Konstantinopolsky, see illustrative games.

b) 7 ♗d3?! dxc4 8 ♗xc4 0-0 9 0-0 ♘d7 loses a tempo *(9 ... ♘c6 is also good — see the illustrative game Alekhine-Richter in the previous chapter).* After 10 ♕e2 *(10 ♗f4 a6 11 ♖c1 b5 12 ♗d3 ♗b7 13 ♘e5 ♘b6 14 ♖e1 ♖c8 ∓ Schuwalow-Alekhine, 1941)* 10 ... ♘b6 *(10 ... a6 11 ♗g5 b5 12 ♗b3 ♘b6 13 ♖ad1 ♗b7 14 ♖fe1 ♘bd5 15 ♘e5?! ♘xc3! 16 bxc3 ♗d5 ± Gerstenfeld-Konstantinopolsky, USSR 1940)* 11 ♗b3 ♘bd5 12 ♖e1 b6 13 ♘e5 ♗b7 Black had equality in List-Kotov, England v USSR 1946.

c) 7 a3?! 0-0 8 c5 ♘e4! 9 ♕c2 f5 10 ♗e2 ♘c6 11 ♗b5 ♗f6 12 ♗xc6 bxc6 13 0-0 g5! = Keres-Konstantinopolsky, USSR (ch) 1948.

d) 7 ♗f4 ♘c6 *(7 ... dxc4 8 ♗xc4 0-0 9 0-0 ♘c6 10 ♖c1 a6 = Ljubojević-Smyslov, Petropolis (izt) 1973)* 8 a3 0-0 9 ♖c1 ♘e4 10 ♗d3 ♘xc3 11 ♖xc3 dxc4 12 ♖xc4 ♕a5+ 13 ♗d2 ♕d5 = Keres-Tal, USSR (ch) 1957.

A1

7 cxd5   ♘xd5

A passive, though playable, continuation is 7 ... exd5?! followed by:

a) 8 ♗b5+ ♗d7 *(8 ... ♘c6?!9 ♘e5 ♗d7 10 0-0 0-0 11 ♖e1 ♖c8 12 ♗g5 — also 12 ♗f4 ± — 12 ... ♗e6?! 13 ♗xc6 bxc6 14 ♘a4! h6 15 ♗xf6 ♗xf6 16 ♘c5 ± Velimirović-Benkö, Vrnjacka Banja 1976 or 14 ... c5 15 dxc5 ♗xc5 16 ♘xc5 ♖xc5 17 ♕d4 ± Pachman-Szabó, Leipzig 1960. White can also play 9 0-0 0-0 10 ♘e5 ♕b6 — 10 ... ♗d7 ± — 11 ♗g5 ♘d8! 12 ♕d3?! — 12 ♗d3! ± Adams — 12 ... ♘e6 13 ♗e3! ♖d8 14 f4 ♘c7 15 ♗a4 ♕xb2 — 15 ... ♕a6? 16 ♕xa6 ♘xa6 17 f5 ♔f8 18 ♗b3 ♘c7 19 g4! ± Adams-Larsen, Cannes 1989; 16 ♖ab1 ♕a3 17 ♗c2 g6 18 ♖b3 ♕d6 19 f5 ± (Adams). Instead 8 ... ♘bd7 9 0-0 0-0 10 ♖e1 a6 11 ♗d3 ♖e8 12 ♕b3 ♘f8 13 ♗g5 is also rather lacklustre according to Schwarz)* 9 ♕a4 *(9 ♗xd7+ ♘bxd7 10 0-0 0-0 11 ♕b3 ♘b6 12 ♗g5 ♖e8 13 ♖fe1 ± Botvinnik; 9 ♕b3 ± Botvinnik)* 9 ... 0-0 10 ♘e5! ♗e6 11 0-0 ♘e4 12 ♖e1 ♘d6 13 ♗d3 ♕b6 14 ♕c2 ±± Fuchs-Golz, East Germany 1961.

b) 8 ♗d3 0-0 *(8 ... ♗g4 9 h3 ♗xf3*

10 ♕xf3 ♘c6 *11* ♗e3 ±; *9 . . .* ♗h5
10 ♕a4+ ♘bd7 *11* ♘e5 ±) 9 h3!? ♘c6
10 0-0 ♗e6 *(10 . . . h6 11* ♗f4! ♗e6 −
11 . . . ♗d6 *12* ♗e5 ± − *12* ♖e1 ♖c8 *13*
♕d2 ♖e8 *14* ♖ad1 ♗b4?! − *14 . . .* ♗f8
− *15 a3!* ♗b8 *16* ♗b1 ♘d7 − *Anand-*
Ravi, India (ch) 1988 − *17* ♖e2! ♘b6
18 ♖de1 ± *Anand)* 11 ♗e3 *(11* ♘e5?!
♘xd4 *12* ♗xh7+ ♘xh7 *13* ♕xd4 =;
11 ♖e1 ♖c8 *12* ♗f4 ♘h5 *13* ♗h2 g6 *14*
♕d2 ♖e8 *15* ♖ad1 ♗f8 *16* ♗f1 a6 *17*
♘e5 b5 *18* ♘xc6 ♖xc6 *19* ♗e5 ±
Salov-Nogueiras, Barcelona 1989; or
11 . . . ♕c8 *12* ♗g5 h6 *13* ♗h4 ♘h5 *14*
♗xe7 ♘xe7 *15* ♖c1 ♕d8 *16* ♕d2 ♖c8
± *Dolmatov-Shamkovich, Amsterdam*
1979) 11 . . . ♘d7? *(11 . . .* ♕c8!? *12* ♘e5
♗f5 *13* ♘xc6 bxc6 *14* ♖c1 ±) *12* ♘e2!
♕b6 *13* ♘f4 ♖ac8 *14* ♕b1! h6 *15*
♗h7+! ♔h8 *16* ♗f5 ± Vaganyan–van
der Wiel, Rotterdam 1989.

A1.1: 8 ♗d3
A1.2: 8 ♗c4

Fashion oscillates between these
two moves, the first aiming for kingside play and the second for pressure
on d5. Alekhine's continuation of
8 ♗b5+ is less dangerous, since the
exchange of the white-squared
bishop is not particularly advantageous, viz: 8 . . . ♘c6! *(8 . . .* ♗d7?!
9 ♗xd7+ ♘xd7 *10* ♘xd5 exd5 *11* ♕b3
♘b6 *12* 0-0 0-0 *13* ♗f4 ♗d6 *14* ♗xd6
♕xd6 *15* ♖fe1 ♖ac8 *16* ♖ac1 *h6?*
17 ♘e5 ± *Alekhine-Eliskases, Buenos*
Aires (ol) 1939; 16 . . . f6! 17 g3 ±)
9 ♘e5 *(9* ♕a4? *0-0!* 10 ♗xc6 ♘b6! 11

♕a5 bxc6 *12* 0-0 ♘d5 ∓ *Pachman-*
Kotov, Prague 1946) 9 . . . ♗d7 *(9 . . .*
♘xc3 *10* bxc3 ♕d5 ∓ *Schwarz)*
10 ♗xc6 bxc6 ∓ Pachman.

A1.1

8 ♗d3   **♘c6**

8 . . . 0-0 9 0-0 b6!? 10 ♘xd5 exd5 11
♘e5 ♗a6!? 12 ♗xa6 ♘xa6 13 ♕a4
♕c8? *(13 . . .* ♘c7! ±) 14 ♗f4 ♕b7 15
♕c6! ± Larsen-Pomar, Centelles
1978.

9 0-0   **0-0**

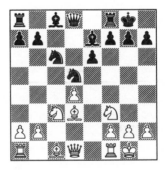

This standard isolated queen's
pawn position can arise from many
different openings, the most frequent
being the Semi-Tarrasch (1 d4 d5 2 c4
e6 3 ♘c3 ♘f6 4 ♘f3 c5 5 cxd5 ♘xd5
6 e3 cxd4 7 cxd4 ♘c6 8 ♗d3 ♗e7 9 0-0
0-0).

10 ♖e1   **. . .**

This move is more frequent and probably better than 10 ♕e2 because c2 is often the best square for the queen, e.g.: 10 . . . ♘db4 *(10 . . . ♘f6 11 ♖d1 ♘b4 12 ♗c4 b6 13 ♘e5 ♗b7 14 ♗g5?! ♘bd5 15 ♖ac1 h6 16 ♗d2 ♖c8 17 ♗b3 a6 = Najdorf-Horowitz, 1948 or 10 . . . ♘cb4 11 ♗b1 b6 12 ♘xd5 ♕xd5 13 ♗e4 ♗a6 14 ♕e3 ♕b5 = Saborido-Portisch, Torremolinos 1961)* 11 ♗e4 ♘xd4 *(11 . . . b6 12 ♗b1! ± Larsen-Robatsch, Beverwijk 1967)* 12 ♘xd4 ♕xd4 13 ♗e3 ♕e5 14 f4 ♕b8 *(14 . . . ♕a5 15 a3 ♘d5 16 ♗xd5 exd5 17 b4 ± Bobekov-Bondarevsky, USSR 1961)* 15 ♖ad1 f5 16 ♗f3 ♘c6 17 ♕c4 ♔h8 ∞ Udovčić-O'Kelly, Havana 1964.

Also to be considered is 10 ♗c2 ♘cb4 11 ♗b1 b6! 12 a3 ♘xc3 13 bxc3 ♘d5 14 ♕d3 ♘f6 = Parma. Interesting is 10 a3:

a) 10 . . . ♘f6 *(10 . . . ♗d7 11 ♕c2 g6 12 ♗h6 ♖e8 13 ♗e4 ± Korchnoi-Bisguier, Budapest 1961, or 11 ♘xd5 exd5 12 ♕b3 ♗g4 13 ♕xb7 ♘a5 =)* 11 ♗g5 *(11 ♗e3 b6 12 ♕e2 ♗b7 13 ♖fd1 ♕b8 14 h3 ± Podgaets-Zhuravlev, USSR 1971, or 11 ♗c2 b6 12 ♕d3 ♗b7 13 ♗g5 g6 14 ♖fe1 ♖e8 15 h4 ± Reshevsky-Fischer, Los Angeles 1961; 14 ♖ad1 ♘d5 15 ♗h6 ♖e8 16 ♖fe1 Larsen-Najdorf, Palma de Mallorca 1969, 16 . . . ♖c8 ∞)* 11 . . . b6 12 ♕e2 ♗b7 13 ♖ad1 ♖e8 14 ♖fe1 g6 15 ♗c4 ♘d5 16 ♗xd5! ♗xg5 *(16 . . . exd5 17 ♗xe7 ♖xe7 18 ♕d2 ±)* 17 ♗e4 ♗f6 18 ♘e5 ± Korchnoi-Tal, Moscow 1968.

b) 10 . . . ♗f6 11 ♗e4 *(11 ♕c2 h6 12 ♖d1 ♕b6 13 ♗c4 ♖d8 14 ♘e2 ♗d7 15 ♕e4 ♘ce7 16 ♗d3 − Smyslov-Ribli (c) 1983 − 16 . . . ♗b5!=)* 11 . . . ♘ce7?! 12 ♘e5 *(12 ♕d3 h6!? 13 ♘e5 ♘xc3 14 ♕xc3 ♘f5 − 14 . . . ♕d6!? is an interesting alternative − 15 ♗e3 − Karpov-Timman, Moscow 1981 − 15 . . . ♘xe3 ±; 12 ♕c2 g6 13 ♘e5 b6 14 ♗h6 ♗g7 15 ♘xd5 exd5 ± Portisch-Ribli, Budapest 1981)* 12 . . . g6 13 ♗h6 ♗g7 14 ♗xg7 ♔xg7 15 ♖c1! b6 16 ♘xd5 ♘xd5 17 ♗xd5! ♕xd5 18 ♖c7 ± Smyslov-Ribli, London (c) 1983. Better is 11 . . . ♕d6! 12 ♕d3 h6 13 ♖e1 *(13 ♖d1!?)* 13 . . . ♖d8 14 ♗xd5!? exd5 15 ♘b5 ♕d7! *(15 . . . ♕b8 16 g3 ♗g4 17 ♗f4 ♕c8 18 ♘e5 ±)* 16 ♗f4 *(16 ♘e5 ♗xe5 17 dxe5 a6! 18 ♘d4 ♘xd4 19 ♕xd4 ♕g4 =)* 16 . . . ♕g4! = I. Ivanov-Dlugy, Las Vegas 1989.

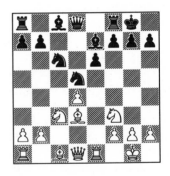

After the text we have:

A1.11: 10 . . . ♗f6
A1.12: 10 . . . ♘f6?!
A1.13: 10 . . . ♘cb4?!

Others are:

a) **10 . . . ♗d7** 11 a3 *(11 ♗c2 ♗f6 12*
♕*d3 g6 13 ♗b3 ♗c8 14 ♗h6 ♗g7 15*
♗*xg7 ♔xg7 16 h4 ♕a5 17 ♘e4 ♕c7 18*
♖*ac1* ± *Larsen-Pomar, Costa Brava
1976 or 11 ♘xd5 exd5 12 ♘e5 ♗f6
13 ♗e3 ♗xe5 14 dxe5 ♘xe5 15 ♗xh7+*
± *Portisch-Pomar, Siegen (ol) 1970)*
11 . . . ♖c8 *(11 . . . a6 12 ♕e2?!* ♖*c8
13* ♕*e4 f5 = Bronstein-Flohr, Saltsjöbaden (izt) 1948; 12 ♕c2! ±)* 12 ♗c2
♘xc3 13 bxc3 ♘a5 14 ♕d3 g6 15 ♗h6
♖e8 16 ♘e5 ♗c6 17 ♕g3 ♗f8 18
♗xf8 ♖xf8 19 ♕f4 ± Gheorghiu-
Letzelter, Vraca 1975.

b) **10 . . . ♕d6** *(Preparing . . .* ♖*d8 or
. . . ♗d7)* 11 ♕c2 *(11 a3 ♗d7 12 ♗c2*
♖*fd8 13* ♕*d3 g6 14 h4 ♗e8 15 ♗h6
♘xc3 16 bxc3 ♖ac8 17 h5 ♕d5 18 hxg6
hxg6 19* ♖*e3 ♗f6* ± *Balashov-
Shamkovich, 1972, or 12* ♕*c2 h6 13*
♖*e4* ♖*fd8 14* ♗*d2* ± *Jokšić-
Commons, Plovdiv 1975, or 11 . . .* ♖*d8
12* ♕*c2 h6 13 ♗e3 ♗d7 − 13 . . .*
♘*xe3!?* − *14 ♘xd5 ♕xd5 15 ♗h7+*
♔*h8 16 ♗e4 ♕h5 17 ♖ad1 ♖ac8 18*
♕*e2 ♗e8 19 b4 ± Mortensen-Larsen
(m) 1989)* 11 . . . g6 12 ♘e4 ♕c7 13 a3
♗d7 14 ♕d2! ± Velimirović-
Rukavina, Yugoslavia (ch) 1975.

c) **10 . . . ♘xc3** 11 bxc3 b6 12 ♕c2 g6
13 ♗h6 ♖e8 **14 h4** ♗f8 15 ♕d2 ♗b7
16 h5 ♖c8 17 hxg6 hxg6 18 ♖ad1 ±
Barle-Čirić, Krk 1976; **14 ♗e4** ♗b7 15
♕d2 ♕c7 16 h4 ♗f6 17 ♖ad1 ♖ad8?!
(17 . . . ♘e7?) 18 ♗g5 ♗e7 19 ♗xe7
♕xe7 20 h5 ± Honfi-Čirić, Yugoslavia 1976.

d) **10 . . . a6?!** 11 ♗e4 ♘f6 12 ♗xc6

bxc6 13 ♘a4 ± Parma.

A1.11

10 . . .   ♗**f6**
11 ♗e4   **. . .**

The aim is to hinder Black's development. 11 a3?! ♘xc3 12 bxc3 b6 =
Parma.

11 . . .   ♘**ce7**

White stands well after **11 . . . h6** 12
♗b1! ♘ce7 13 ♕d3 ♘g6 14 ♘e5 ±
Ivkov-Pomar, Malaga 1969 or **11 . . .**
♘**de7** 12 ♕d3 *(12 ♗e3 ♕a5 13 ♘d2*
♖*d8 14 ♘b3 ♕c7 15 ♕h5 g6 16 ♕f3 ±
Smyslov-Bisguier, Leipzig 1960)* **12 . . .**
♘**g6?!** 13 ♗e3 ♕d6 14 ♖ac1 ♖d8 15
♖ed1 ♗d7 16 d5 ± Krashilnikov-
Goldenov, USSR 1968, although
maybe Black can improve his game
after **12 . . . g6!?** 13 ♗h6 ♗g7 14 ♗xg7
♔xg7 15 ♖ad1 f6 16 ♕c4 ♗d7 *(16 . . .
♕b6 17 d5 exd5 18 ♘xd5 ♘xd5 19
♗xd5 ♔h8 20 ♕h4 ±)* 17 d5! exd5 18
♘xd5 ♗e6 19 ♕b5 ♗xd5 20 ♗xd5
♕c7 *(20 . . . ♕b6?! 21 ♕xb6 axb6 22
♘d4 ♔h8 23 ♗b3 ±)* 21 ♗b3 (±)
Korolev-Razvaliaev, USSR 1988.
Thirdly Black has **11 . . . ♘xc3** 12 bxc3
♗d7 13 ♗a3 ♖e8 14 ♕b1 ±
Averbakh-Durašević, USSR v Yugo-
slavia 1959. A final alternative is **11 . . .**
♕**d6** 12 ♗g5!? *(12 ♘b5?!* ♕*b8 13 g3
♗d7 14 ♘c3 ♘ce7 15 ♗xd5 ♘xd5 16
♘xd5 exd5 17 ♗g5 ♗xg5 18 ♘xg5
♕d8* ∓ *Beliavsky-Portisch, Reggio
Emilia 1987, or 12 a3 ♗d7 13 ♘b5?!*

♕b8 14 ♘g5 ♗xg5 15 ♗xg5 ♘ce7 16 ♘c3 ♗c6 17 ♕h5 ♘g6 18 ♖ad1 ∞ *Mortensen–Hansen, Graestved 1990)* 12 ... ♗xg5 13 ♘xg5 ♘f6 *(13 ... h6 14 ♘f3 ♗d7? – 14 ... ♘f6! improves – 15 ♗xd5! exd5 16 ♘e5 ± Gheorghiu-Petursson, USA 1979)* 14 d5!? exd5 15 ♘xd5 ♘xe4 16 ♘xe4 ♕h6! 17 ♕c1 ♕xc1 *(17 ... ♕g6!?)* 18 ♖axc1 ♗e6 *(18 ... ♗f5 19 ♘c5 ±)* 19 ♘c7 ♖ad8 20 ♘xe6 fxe6 21 f3 ± Alonso–Barroso, Matanzas 1988.

12 ♘e5   ...

Or 12 ♕c2 *(12 ♕b3 b6 13 ♗g5 ♗b7 14 ♖ad1 ♕b8 = Bobotsov–Bertok, Zagreb 1964; 12 ... ♕b6?! 13 ♕xb6 axb6 14 ♗g5 ♖d8 15 ♖ed1 h6 16 ♗xf6 ♘xf6 17 ♗c2 ♗d7 18 ♘e5 ♗e8 19 ♗b3 ± Chiburdanidze-Ioseliani (m) 1988; or 12 ♗g5 ♗xg5 13 ♘xg5 h6 14 ♘f3 b6 15 ♕b3 ♗b7 = Taimanov-Osnos, Budapest 1965 or 12 ♕d3 g6 13 ♗h6 ♗g7 14 ♗xg7 ♔xg7 15 ♗xd5 ♘xd5 16 ♘xd5 ♕xd5 17 ♖e5 ♕d6 18 ♖ae1 ♗d7 19 ♘g5 ♗c6 20 d5 Darga-O'Kelly, Madrid 1966, 20 ... ♗xd5 ∞ Schwarz; 12 ... h6 13 ♘e5 – 13 h4 ♗d7 14 a3 ♗c6 ∞ – 13 ... ♘xc3 14 ♕xc3 ♘f5 15 ♗e3 ♘xe3 16 fxe3 ♖b8 17 ♖ad1 ♗d7 18 ♗b1 ♗e8 19 ♘g4 ♗g5 20 e4 h5 21 ♘f2 ± Chiburdanidze-Ioseliani (m) 1988)* 12 ... g6 *(12 ... ♘g6 13 ♕b3 ± Portisch–Pomar, Malaga 1964)* 13 ♗h6 *(13 ♕b3 ♕b6 =)* 13 ... ♗g7 14 ♗g5 *(14 ♗xg7 ♔xg7 15 ♕b3 ♘f6 =)* 14 ... f6 15 ♗d2 ♗d7 16 ♕b3 ♗c6 17 ♗xd5 exd5 18 ♘e4 ♖f7

etc. White has some space advantage, but Black's position is perfectly sound, Spassky–Petrosian, Moscow (m) 1966.

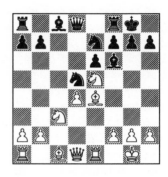

12 ...   g6

12 ... ♗d7 13 ♕d3 g6 14 ♗h6 ♗g7 15 ♗xg7 ♔xg7 16 ♘xd5 exd5 *(16 ... ♘xd5 17 ♗xd5 exd5 18 ♕b3 ± Gligorić-Eliskases, Buenos Aires 1960)* 17 ♗f3 ♗e6 18 ♕b3 ± Šmejkal-Kupka, Luhačovice 1969, or 12 ... ♘c6 13 ♕d3 h6 14 ♗xd5 ♘b4 15 ♕g3 ♗h4 16 ♕f3 exd5 17 ♖e2 ♗e6 18 a3 ♘c6 18 ♘xc6 bxc6 20 ♘a4 ± Smyslov-Ivanchuk, USSR (ch) 1988, or 12 ... ♘f5?! 13 ♘g4! ♘xd4 14 ♕d3 ♘xc3 15 ♗xh7+ ♔h8 16 bxc3 ± Pich-M. Tseitlin, Minsk 1990.

13 ♗h6   ♗g7
14 ♗xg7   ...

There is no time to prevent the exchange of the light-squared bishops after 14 ♕d2 ♘f6! because the d-pawn is hanging *(15 ♗f3 ♗xh6! 16 ♕xh6 ♕xd4)*. What can follow is 15 ♖ad1 ♘xe4 16 ♖xe4 b6 *(16 . . . ♘f5? 17 ♗xg7 ♔xg7 18 d5! ± Smyslov-Padevsky, Moscow 1963)* 17 ♖h4 ♘f5 18 ♗xg7 ♔xg7 19 ♖h3 ♗b7 = Liberzon-Podgaets, USSR (ch) 1968-69.

14 . . .   ♔xg7
15 ♗f3

White's spatial advantage provides plenty of compensation for the isolated centre pawn.

Other possibilities include: **15 ♕f3** *(15 ♕b3 ♘f6 16 ♖ad1 ∓)* 15 . . . ♘f6 *(15 . . . ♕b6 16 ♖ad1!? ♕xb2 17 ♗xd5 ♘xd5 18 ♘xd5 exd5 19 ♕xd5 ♗e6 ∞)* 16 ♗xb7 ♗xb7 17 ♕xb7 a5! ∞ Nunn-Campora, Biel 1983.

A1.12

10 . . .   ♘f6?!

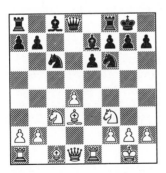

There was a time when this was considered to be the strongest.

11 a3!   . . .

White sets about preparing the attacking formation of his bishop on c2 and queen on d3. Other methods are 11 ♗g5 b6 *(11 . . . ♘b4 12 ♗b1 b6 13 ♘e5 ♗b7 14 ♖e3 g6 15 ♖g3 ± Keene-Miles, Hastings 1975-76; 11 . . . a6!?)* and now:

a) **12 a3 ♗b7 13 ♗c2** *(13 ♗b1 ♖c8 14 ♕d3 g6 15 ♗a2 ♘g4 ∞ Neamtu-Korchnoi, Bucharest 1966)* 13 . . . ♖c8 *(13 . . . ♗a6 14 ♕d2 ♖c8 15 ♕f4 ♖e8 16 ♖ad1 ± Szabó-Unzicker, Amsterdam (ol) 1954)* 14 ♖c1 *(14 ♕d3 g6 15 ♖ad1 ♘d5 16 ♗h6 ♖e8 17 ♗a4 ♗f6 18 ♘e4 ♗g7 19 ♗g5 ± Sax-Haág, Budapest 1976 or 15 . . . ♖e8 16 ♗a4 a6 17 ♗xc6 ♖c6 18 ♘e5 ♖c7 ∞ Bilek-Kholmov, Kecskemét 1962)* 14 . . . ♖e8 15 ♕d3 g6 16 ♗h6 *(In the text line White can occupy h6 in one move)* 16 . . . ♕d6 17 h3 ♗f8 18 ♗g5 ♗g7 ∞ Hort-Muhin, Luhačovice 1973.

b) **12 ♕e2 ♗b7 13 ♖ad1 ♘b4 14 ♗b1 ♖c8 15 ♘e5 ♘bd5** *(15 . . . ♘fd5 16 ♗d2 ♘f6? 17 ♕e3 ♘fd5 18 ♕h3 f5 19 a3 ♘a6 20 ♗a2 ± Petrosian-Najdorf, Moscow 1967; 16 . . . ♘xc3! 17 bxc3 ♘d5 ± Parma)* 16 ♕d3 *(16 ♖d3? ♗a6 17 ♘xd5 exd5 18 ♗xf6 ♗xf6 19 ♖h3 ♗xe2 20 ♗xh7+ ♔h8 21 ♗d3+ ♗h4 −+ Parma)* 16 . . . ♘xc3 *(16 . . . g6 17 ♗h6 ♖e8 18 ♕h3 ± Kottnauer-Donner, Netherlands 1967)* 17 bxc3 ♕d5 18 ♕h3 ♖xc3 19 f3 h6 20 ♗xf6 ♗xf6 21 ♗e4 ♕xe4 22 ♖xe4

♗xe4 23 ♘d7 ± Polugaevsky–Khasin, USSR 1961.

11 ...   b6

11 ... a6 12 ♗c2 ♕c7 13 ♕d3 ♖d8 14 ♗g5 g6 15 ♖ad1 ± Fuchs–Hartmann, East Germany 1964; **12 ... b5!?**

A1.121: 12 ♗c2
A1.122: 12 ♗g5

A1.121

12 ♗c2   ...

Others:
a) **12 ♗f4 ♗b7 13 ♖c1 ♖c8 14 h3** a6 ∞ Vasyukov–Dolmatov, Frunze 1983.

b) **12 ♗e3 ♗b7 13 ♖c1** *(13 ♕c2 ♖c8 14 ♖ad1 ♘a5 ∞)* 13 ... ♖c8 14 ♗b1 ♖c7 15 ♕d3 ♖d7 16 ♕c2 g6 17 ♗a2 ♘g4 = Uhlmann–Karpov, Leningrad 1973.

c) **12 ♘e5 ♗b7 13 ♗a6 ♕c8 14** ♗xb7 ♕xb7 15 ♘xc6 ♕xc6 16 d5 ♕c4 17 ♕e2 ♕xe2 18 ♖xe2 ♗c5 ∞ Ribli–Kavalek, Tilburg 1980.

A1.1211: 12 ... ♗b7
A1.1212: 12 ... ♗a6!

A1.1211

12 ...   ♗b7
13 ♕d3   ...

The battery is ready to fire! It should be noted that a similar position can develop from the 6 ... ♗b4 variation as well, but with a tempo advantage for Black, his rook already being on c8 or e8. Even then, however, Black's game is not entirely trouble-free.

13 ...   ♖c8?

It was imperative to play 13 ... g6, when after 14 ♗h6! White has a tempo advantage compared to the note after White's 11th move in this line, since his bishop reaches h6 in one move.

Instead of **14 ♗g5?!** (see the illustrative game Smyslov–Karpov) it is now known that **14 d5!** is extremely strong, viz.: **14 ... exd5 15 ♗g5 g6 16** ♖xe7! ♕xe7 17 ♘xd5 ♘xd5 18 ♗xe7 ♘6xe7 ± or **14 ... ♘a5 15 ♗g5 ♖xc3!?** *(15 ... g6? 16 d6!)* 16 bxc3 ±.

A1.1212

12 ...   ♗a6!
13 b4?!   ♖c8!

13 ... ♗c4?! 14 b5! *(14 ♘e5 ♘xe5 15 dxe5 ♕xd1 = Gheorghiu–Henley, Indonesia 1983)* 14 ... ♘a5 15 ♘e5 ♖c8 16 ♖e3 g6 17 ♖h3 ♗d5 (Buturin–Savon, Lemberg 1981) 18 ♗h6 ♖e8 19 ♕d2 ±.

14 ♘e4   ...

14 ♗b2?! *(14 b5?! ♘a5 15 bxa6*

♖xc3 ∓) 14 . . . ♗c4 ∓ Lanka-Ostenstad, Trnava 1989.

14 . . .   **♘xe4**
15 ♗xe4   **♗f6 =.**

A1.122

12 ♗g5   **. . .**

Or 11 ♗g5 b6 12 a3.

12 . . .   **♗b7**
13 ♗c2   **. . .**

13 ♗b1 ♖c8 14 ♕d3 g6 15 ♗a2 ♖e8 *(15 . . . ♘g4!?)* 16 ♖ad1 ♘d5 17 ♗h6 *(17 h4 ♘xc3 18 bxc3 ♘a5 ∞)* 17 . . . ♘xc3 18 bxc3 ♗f8 ∞ Suba-Velikov, Luzern 1982.

13 . . .   **♖c8**

a) **13 . . . ♗a6** 14 ♕d2 ♖c8 15 ♕f4 ± Szabó-Unzicker, Amsterdam 1954.

b) **13 . . . ♖e8** 14 ♕d3 g6 15 ♖ad1 *(15 h4 ± Reshevsky-Fischer (m) 1961)* 15 . . . ♘d5 16 ♗h6 *(16 h4 ±)* 16 . . . ♘xc3 17 bxc3 ♕d5 18 c4 ♕h5 19 ♗c1 ± Larsen-Najdorf, Palma de Mallorca 1969.

14 ♕d3   **g6**
15 ♖ad1   **♘d5**

15 . . . ♖e8 16 h4 a6 17 ♗b3 ♘a5 18 ♗a2 b5 19 ♘e5 ± Kavalek-Larsen, Solingen 1970.

16 ♗h6   **♖e8**
17 ♗a4   **a6**

17 . . . ♗f8?! 18 ♗g5 ♗e7 19 h4 a6 20 ♘d5 exd5 21 ♗xc6 ♖xc6 22 ♗xe7 ♖xe7 23 h5 ± Mortensen-Ostenstad, Espo Zonal 1989.

18 ♘xd5   **♕xd5**
19 ♕e3   **♗f6**
20 ♗b3   **♕d7**

20 . . . ♕h5 21 d5 ♘d8 22 d6 ± Smyslov-Karpov, USSR (ch) 1971.

21 d5

21 . . . exd5 22 ♕xb6 ± Belyavsky-Karpov, USSR 1986.

A1.13

10 . . .   **♘cb4?!**

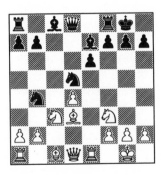

This is another defensive attempt. If correctly played the knights plant themselves on d5 and f6, defending the kingside and blockading d5. The drawback is that e5 is conceded to the opponent.

11 ♗b1   ...

Harmless for Black is 11 ♗f1 b6 12 a3 ♘c6 13 ♗d3 ♗b7 14 ♕c2 g6 15 ♘xd5 ♕xd5 16 ♗e4 ♕d7 ∞ as in Bobotsov-Padevsky, Varna 1965, while 11 ♗e4 ♘f6 12 ♗b1 etc. loses a tempo.

After the text Black can try:

a) 11 ... ♗d7? (Contradicts Black's basic idea, as he will soon have to exchange on c3 – mobilizing White's centre pawns) 12 a3! ♘xc3 13 bxc3 ♘d5 14 ♕d3 ± – see the illustrative game Portisch-Bagirov.

b) 11 ... ♕c7 12 ♘e5! ♘xc3 13 bxc3 ♕xc3 14 ♖e3! ♕xa1 15 ♖b3 ♕xb1 16 ♖xb1 ♘d5 17 ♕g4 ♖d8 18 ♖b3 ± Gipslis-Khalibeili, USSR 1961.

c) 11 ... b6 12 a3 (12 ♘e5 ♗b7 13 a3 ♘xc3 14 bxc3 ♘d5 15 ♕f3 ♖b8 16 ♕h3 ± Muratov-Yurkov, USSR 1967) 12 ... ♘xc3 13 bxc3 ♘d5 14 c4 (14 ♕d3 ♘f6 15 ♘g5 g6 16 ♕h3 ± Szabó-Pogáts, Kecskemét 1962, or 15 ♗g5 g6 16 ♘e5 ♗b7 17 ♗h6 ♖e8 18 ♕h3 ♕c8 19 ♗a2 ± Adams-Seirawan, Wijk aan Zee 1991; 14 ... g6 15 ♘e5 ♗g5! ∞ Kotov-Steiner, Groningen 1946) 14 ... ♘f6 15 ♘e5 ♗b7 16 ♗g5 g6 17 ♗c2 ± Belov-Sokolov, USSR 1964.

d) 11 ... ♘f6 12 a3 (12 ♘e5 ♘bd5 13 ♕d3 g6 14 ♕f3! ± Bednarski-Kostro, Poland 1969; better is 13 ...

♗d7!. Alternatively 12 ♗g5 ♗d7 13 ♘e5 ♗c6?! 14 ♖e3 g6 15 ♖g3 ♘d7 ±, but better here is 13 ... ♖c8! 14 ♖e3 g6 15 ♗h6 ♖e8 16 ♖g3 ♗c6 ∞ Filip-Pogáts, Budapest 1961) 12 ... ♘bd5 13 ♘e5 (13 ♕d3 g6 14 ♗a2 ± Mason-Burn, Hastings 1895!) 13 ... ♗d7 14 ♕d3 ♗c6 15 ♕h3 ♖e8 16 ♗g5 g6 17 ♗a2 ♘h5 18 ♗h6 ♗f8 ± (18 ... ♗g5?! 19 ♗xg5 ♕xg5 20 ♘xd5 exd5 21 ♕f3 ± Polugayevsky-Šahović, 1969).

A1.2

8 ♗c4   ...

Exerting pressure on d5. One of the features of this variation is that White will exchange on d5 at a given moment, in order to bring about a favourably symmetrical position.

8 ...   ♘c6
9 0-0   0-0
10 ♖e1   ...

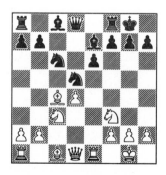

This position originally developed

from the Tarrasch Defence delayed. Other continuations at White's disposal are:

a) **10 ♕e2 ♘b6!** 11 ♖d1 *(The difference from ♖e1 is that the bishop cannot be moved because of the hanging d4 pawn)* 11 . . . ♘xc4 =.

b) **10 ♗e3 a6** 11 ♗d3 ♘cb4 12 ♗b1 b5 13 ♘e4 ♗b7 14 ♗d2 ♕b6 ∞ Botvinnik-Ravinsky, USSR (ch) 1944.

c) **10 ♗xd5 exd5** 11 ♕b3 ♗g4! 12 ♘xd5 *(12 ♕xb7 ♘b4 13 ♘e5 ♖b8 14 ♕xa7 ♖a8 =)* 12 . . . ♗xf3 13 ♘xe7+ ♕xe7 14 ♕xf3 ♘xd4 = Parma.

Black should answer other continuations with 10 . . . ♘xc3 and 11 . . . b6.

10 . . . ♘xc3

a) **10 . . . b6?!** (Falling in with White's plan) 11 ♘xd5! exd5 12 ♗b5 with advantage to White − see the Botvinnik-Alekhine illustrative game.

b) **10 . . . ♗f6** 11 ♘e4 b6 12 a3 ♗b7 13 ♕d3 ♖c8 14 ♘fg5 ♗xg5 15 ♗xg5 f6! 16 ♗d2 ♕d7 17 ♖ac1 ♘ce7 18 ♗a2 ♖fe8 19 h4!? ♔h8 20 ♗b1 g6 21 ♕h3 ♘f5 ∞ P. Nikolić-Ribli, Portoroz 1985.

c) **10 . . . ♕d6** 11 ♘e4 ♕d7 12 ♗g5 ♖d8 13 ♖c1 ± Stein-Tal, Pärnu 1971.

d) **10 . . . a6** 11 ♗b3 *(11 ♗xd5 exd5 12 ♕b3 ♗g4 13 ♕xd5 ♗xf3 = Osnos-Krogius, USSR 1965 or 11 a3 b5 12 ♗d3 ♗b7 13 ♘xd5 ♕xd5 14 ♗e4 ♕d7 = Najdorf-Fischer, Buenos Aires 1970 or 11 a4 b6 12 ♗d2 ♘db4 13 ♗e3 ♗b7 14*

♖c1 ♖c8 ∞ Pachman-Bisguier, Bled 1961 or 11 ♗d3 ♘cb4 − 11 . . . ♘f6!? − 12 ♗b1 b5 13 ♘e4 ♘f6 14 a3 ♘bd5 15 ♘c5 ♕b6 16 ♕c2 a5 ∞ Botvinnik-Makogonov, USSR 1943)* 11 . . . ♘xc3 12 bxc3 b5 13 ♗c2!? *(13 ♕d3 ♖a7 14 ♗c2 g6 15 ♗h6 ♖e8 16 ♕e3 ♖d7 17 h4 ± Sokolov-Karpov, Linares (m) 1987)* 13 . . . ♗b7 14 h4 ♗f6 *(14 . . . ♗xh4 15 ♘xh4 ♕xh4 16 ♖e3 ±)* 15 ♘g5 g6 16 ♕g4 ± Sokolov-Kharitonov, USSR 1990.

Capturing on c3, as with the text move, is generally better here than in the 8 ♗d3 variation as White's bishop is now forced to lose time in transferring to the b1-h7 diagonal in order to make way for the c-pawn.

11 bxc3 b6

Fianchettoing the bishop is a logical decision, since **11 . . . ♕c7** 12 ♗d3 ♗d7 13 ♕e2 ♗f6 14 ♗g5 (Lublinsky-Kamishov, USSR 1945) and **11 . . . ♗d7** 12 ♗d3 ♖c8 13 ♕e2 ♗f6 14 ♕e4 (Eliskases-Sapre, Leipzig (ol) 1960) favour White. **11 . . . ♗f6** 12 ♕e2 b6 13 ♗a3 ♗e7 ± Kluger-Lengyel, Budapest 1953 was also a possibility.

12 ♗d3   ♗b7
13 ♕c2   . . .

13 ♕e2 ♖c8 14 ♕e4 g6 15 ♗h6 ♖e8 16 ♖e3! ± Suba-Faragó, Budapest 1976 is rather interesting, or perhaps stronger is **13 h4!?** ♗f6 *(13 . . .*

♗*xh4 14* ♘*xh4* ♕*xh4 15* ♖*e3* ±*; 13 . . .*
♘*a5 14* ♘*g5* ♗*xg5 15* ♗*xg5* ♕*d5 16*
♕*g4 f5 17* ♕*g3* ♖*ac8 18* ♗*f1* ♕*d7 19*
h5 ±*)* 14 ♘g5 g6 15 ♕g4 h5 16 ♕g3
♘e7 17 ♗a3 ± Hansen–Kir.
Georgiev, Kiliava 1984.

13 . . .   g6

13 . . . h6? 14 ♕e2! ±. After the text
move we have:
a) **14 ♕d2?!** ♗f6 15 h4 ♖c8! 16 h5?
♘xd4!! won in Paulsson–Faragó,
Gausdal 1976 – see illustrative games.
b) **14 ♗h6!** *(14 h4!?* ♗*xh4* ∞*)* 14 . . .
♖e8 15 ♕d2! ♖c8 *(15 . . .* ♗*f6 16* ♕*f4*
♗*g7 17* ♖*ad1* ♕*f6 18* ♕*e3* ♗*xh6 19*
♕*xh6* ♖*ac8* ∞ *Neukirch–Fuchs, Sofia
1957)* 16 h4 *(16* ♖*ac1* ♗*f6 17* ♕*f4*
♗*g7! 18* ♗*xg7* ♔*xg7 19* ♘*g5* ♕*c7*
∞ *Pachman–Kozma, Czechoslovakia
1959; 16 . . .* ♕*c7? 17 h4!* ± *Portisch–
O'Kelly, Spain 1964; 16 . . .* ♖*c7!?)*
16 . . . ♘a5 *(16 . . .* ♗*f6 17* ♗*g5 h5 18*
♕*f4* ♗*xg5 19* ♘*xg5* ♕*c7* ∞ *Lein–
Platonov, USSR 1971)* 17 ♘g5 *(17 h5*
♗*xf3* =*)* 17 . . . ♗f8 18 ♗xf8 ♖xf8 19
h5 ♘c4 20 ♕f4!? *(20* ♗*xc4* ♖*xc4 21
hxg6 hxg6 22* ♕*f4* ♕*d5!* ∞ *Najdorf–
Tal, Rest of the World v the USSR
1970)* 20 . . . h6 21 ♘e4! g5 22 ♕c1!
(22 ♘*f6+?* ♔*g7* ∓*; 22* ♕*g3?* ♕*c7 23*
♕*f3 f5!* ∓*)* 22 . . . ♔g7 23 f4 g4 =
Langeweg–Faragó, Amsterdam 1976.

A2

7 c5   . . .

Nowadays this is less frequent than
the Queen's Gambit-like handling of
the position, as examined in A1.
Some hold that the c4-c5 advance is
not overly advantageous for White in
the absence of a black knight on c6.
Nevertheless, Black's defence has to
be managed very accurately, since
half-hearted play would lead to his
queenside being swamped.

7 . . .   0-0

Before Black embarks on any
action on the queenside (b7-b6) or in
the centre (e6-e5), it is advisable to
tuck the king away safely. For
instance: 7 . . . b6 8 b4 a5 9 ♘a4 ♘bd7
(9 . . . ♘*fd7 10* ♗*b5 0-0 11 a3?! axb4
12 axb4 e5!* ∞ *Botvinnik; 11* ♗*f4! bxc5
12 bxc5* ♗*a6 13* ♗*xa6* ± *Euwe–
Kramer (m) 1941)* 10 ♗f4! 0-0 11 ♗d3!
axb4?! *(11 . . . bxc5 12 bxc5* ♘*e5* ∓*)*
12 c6 ♘h5 13 ♗g3! ♘xg3 14 ♗xh7+
♔xh7 15 hxg3+ ♔g8 16 cxd7 ♗a6!
17 ♘e5 ± Alesnia–Symkin, USSR
1973.

8 ♗d3 ...

a) **8 b4** ♘e4 **9 ♕c2** ♘c6 *(9 . . . f5 10 ♗d3 ♗f6 11 ♖b1 g5 12 0-0 g4 13 ♘e5 ♗xe5 14 dxe5 ♘c6 15 f3 ± Estrin-Ilivitsky, USSR 1964)* 10 a3 e5 ∓ Botvinnik. The text move is aimed at preventing 8 . . . ♘e4.

b) **8 ♗g5?!** (Renders Black's development easier) 8 . . . ♘e4 *(8 . . . b6!? 9 b4 a5 10 a3 ♘e4! 11 ♗xe7 ♕xe7 12 ♘a4 axb4 13 axb4 bxc5 14 bxc5 ♕a7! 15 ♗d3 ♕a5+ 16 ♘d2 ♗d7 17 ♗c2 ♗b5 ∓ Kan-Makogonov, USSR (ch) 1939)* 9 ♗xe7 ♕xe7 10 ♕c2 f5 *(10 . . . ♘g5 11 ♗e2 ♘c6 12 ♕d2?! ♘xf3+ 13 ♗xf3 ♕h4 14 ♖d1 e5 15 dxe5 d4 ∓ Eising-Mohrlock, 1961. 12 0-0-0! was a possibility)* 11 ♗e2 *(The illustrative game Troianescu-Flórián instructively shows why 11 ♗b5? immediately is not good)* 11 . . . ♘c6 12 ♗b5! ♘d8 13 ♘e5 ♘f7 14 ♘xf7 ♖xf7 15 0-0 ♕h4 16 f3 ♘f6 17 ♕f2 ♕h6 18 ♖ae1 a6 ∞ Geller-Aronin, USSR 1956.

8 . . .   **b6**
9 b4   **a5!?**

The main variation; others are:

a) **9 . . . bxc5** 10 bxc5 ♘c6 11 0-0 ♗d7 12 h3 ♘e8 13 ♗f4 ♗f6 14 ♗b5 ♘c7 Fischer-Ivkov, Buenos Aires 1960, and now 15 ♗xc6 ♗xc6 16 ♕d3 etc. leads to a slight plus for White.

b) **9 . . . ♗d7?!** *(The idea is to enable 11 . . . ♗xa4 to be played after 10 . . . a5 11 ♘a4, but it is very slow)* 10 ♗e3! *(To answer 10 . . . a5 with 11 b5!)* 10 . . .

♘g4! 11 0-0 a5? *(A venture that only leads to the weakening of the queenside. 11 . . . bxc5 12 bxc5 ♘xe3 13 fxe3 ♘c6 was playable)* 12 ♘a4! and Black's scheme has been refuted — see illustrative game Botvinnik-Golombek.

10 ♘a4!   ...

And now:

A2.1: 10 . . . ♘fd7!?
A2.2: 10 . . . ♘bd7!?

A2.1

10 . . .   **♘fd7!?**
11 h4   ...

a) **11 b5** bxc5 12 dxc5 e5! *(12 . . . ♘xc5? 13 ♘xc5 ♗xc5 14 ♗xh7+ etc. +−)* 13 c6 e4 14 cxd7 ♘xd7 15 0-0 exf3 16 ♕xf3 ♘e5 17 ♕g3 ♘xd3 18 ♕xd3 d4! = Sokolsky-Simagin (corr) 1966.

b) **11 ♕c2** ♘c6 12 b5 ♘b4 13 ♗xh7+ ♔h8 14 ♕b1 bxc5 **15 dxc5** ∞

Neustadt-Chernishev, USSR 1959 or
15 a3!? c4 16 axb4 axb4 17 ♗c2 b3 18
♗xb3 cxb3 ± Liberzon-Opočensky,
Leipzig 1965.

11 . . .   f5?

The threat was 12 ♘xb6 ♘xb6 13
♗xh7+! e.g.; **11 . . . axb4?!** 12 ♘xb6
♘xb6 13 ♗xh7+ ♔h8 14 cxb6 ♘d7 15
♗c2 ♗a6 16 ♘e5 ♔g8 17 ♘c6 ♕c8 18
b7 ♗xb7 19 ♘xe7 ± Shkurovich-
Khasin (corr) 1968.
Another possibility is **11 . . . h6!**
12 ♖h3!? *(12 ♗xh6?! gxh6 13 ♕d2
♔g7 14 ♖h3 ♖h8 15 ♕f4 ∞)* **12 . . . e5**
*(Dubious is 12 . . . axb4 13 ♗xh6 ♖e8
14 ♖g3 ♗f6 15 ♘g5 gxh6 16 ♘h7+ ±
Botvinnik)* 13 ♗xh6 ♗f6 *(13 . . . e4?!)*
14 ♗e3 e4! *(And not 14 . . . exd4? 15
♗h7+ ♔h8 16 ♘g5 g6 17 ♗xg6 fxg6 18
h5 ♗xg5 19 hxg6+ ♔g8 20 ♖h8+ ♔g7
21 ♖h7+ ♔g8 22 ♕h5 ♘f6 23 ♗xd4
♕e8+ 24 ♔f1 ♗a6+ 25 ♔g1 +−
Botvinnik)* 15 ♘g5 g6 16 ♗b5 ±
Botvinnik. Better for Black is **12 . . .
♗f6!** 13 ♖g3 e5! 14 ♗xh6 e4 15 ♘g5
exd3 16 ♕xd3 ♖e8+ 17 ♔d2 *(17 ♔f1
♘f8 18 ♘xb6 axb4!)* 17 . . . ♘f8 18
♘xb6   axb4   ∓   Blatny-Adams,
Oakham 1990.

12 ♘g5   ♕e8
13 ♗b5!   . . .

13 ♔f1 axb4 14 ♘xe6 ♘xc5 15
♘axc5 bxc5 16 ♘xf8 c4 17 ♘xh7 cxd3
18 ♘g5 ♗a6 19 ♔g1 ♘c6 20 ♕f3 ∞
Karlsson-Mahlin (corr) 1970.

13 . . .   ♗a6
14 ♗xa6   . . .

Stronger than 14 ♘xb6?! ♗xb5 ∞
as after 14 . . . ♘xa6, 15 b5 ♘c7 16 c6
♗b4+ 17 ♔f1 ♘f6 18 ♕e2 is ±,
Shkurovich-Khasin (corr) 1973.

A2.2

10 . . .   ♘bd7!?

A continuation involving a piece
sacrifice.

11 ♗f4   . . .

11 a3 axb4 12 axb4 bxc5 13 bxc5 e5
14 ♘xe5 *(14 dxe5 ♘xc5 15 exf6
♘xd3+ 16 ♕xd3 ♗xf6 17 ♘d4 ♕e8+
18 ♗e3 ♖xa4 ∓)* 14 . . . ♗xc5 15 0-0
♘xe5 16 dxe5 ♘e4 = Botvinnik.

11 . . .   ♘h5

11 . . . axb4 12 c6 ♘c5! 13 dxc5
*(13 c7? ♘xd3+ 14 ♕xd3 ♕e8 15 ♘xb6
♖a3! ∓ etc.)* 13 . . . bxc5 14 0-0 *(14 c7?!
♕e8 15 ♘b2 ♘h5! 16 ♗g3 f6 17 ♕c2
g6 18 ♘h4 ♘g7 ∓ Pachman, is more
dangerous for White)* 14 . . . ♕a5 15
♘b2 ♗a6 ∞ Botvinnik.

12 ♗d2   . . .

12 ♗g3 f5 13 ♘e5 ♘xg3 14 ♘c6
♕e8 15 ♘xe7+ ♕xe7 16 hxg3 axb4 17
c6 ♘f6 18 ♘xb6 ♖a3 ∓.

12 . . .   **axb4**
13 c6   **. . .**

with an unclear position, Simagin–
A. Zaitsev (corr) 1966.

B

6 . . .   ♗b4

A resilient continuation which is
not only reminiscent of the Nimzo-
Indian Defence, but does in fact
overlap with the Indian system in a
number of variations.

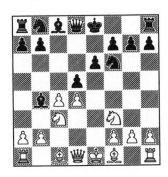

B1

7 ♗d3   **. . .**

This is generally considered best,
but there are several other continuations:

a) **7 a3** ♗xc3+ **8 bxc3 dxc4 9** ♗xc4
♕c7 = (See the Nimzo-Indian

Defence).

b) **7 ♗g5 ♕a5 8 ♗xf6?!** ♗xc3+
9 bxc3 ♕xc3+ 10 ♘d2 gxf6 11 cxd5
0-0 12 ♕g4+ ♚h8 13 ♖b1 exd5 14
♕h4 ♘d7 ∓ Novoselski–Filip,
Kragujevac 1977. Better **8 ♗d2** =.

c) **7 ♕b3 ♘c6 8 ♗g5 dxc4** *(8 . . . 0-0*
9 ♖d1 dxc4 10 ♗xc4 ♗xc3+ 11 bxc3
♘a5 12 ♕b4 ♕c7 13 ♗xf6 ♘xc4! 14
♗e7 ♖e8 ∞ Dely–Portisch, Budapest
1961) **9** ♗xc4 ♗e7 **10** ♗b5 ♗d7 **11** 0-0
0-0 12 ♗d3 ♖c8 **13** ♖ad1 *(13 ♕xb7?*
♘b4! ∓) **13 . . . h6 14** ♗c1 ♕b6 **15**
♕xb6 axb6 **16** ♘e5 ♖fd8 **17** ♘xd7
♖xd7 = Matanović–Petrosian, Bled
1961.

d) **7 ♕a4+ ♘c6 8 ♘e5 ♕a5 9 ♕xa5**
♗xa5 **10** ♘xc6 bxc6 **11 cxd5 cxd5 12**
♗d3 ♖b8 **13** ♖b1 ♗xc3+ **14 bxc3**
♖xb1 **15** ♗xb1 ♗a6 ∓ Karaklajić–
Larsen, Manila 1975.

e) **7 ♗d2 0-0 8** ♖c1 b6 **9 cxd5** ♗xc3
10 bxc3 ♕xd5 11 c4 ♕d6 12 ♗e2 ♗b7
13 0-0 ♘bd7 14 ♕b3 ♖fe8 15 ♖fd1 h6
16 h3 ♕c7 17 ♕e3 = Hort–Ribli,
Manila 1976.

7 . . .   **dxc4**
8 ♗xc4   **0-0**

8 . . . ♕c7 is interesting:
a) **9 ♕b3 ♘c6 10 0-0 ♗xc3!** **11 bxc3**
(11 ♕xc3 0-0 =) **11 . . . ♘a5 12 ♗b5+**
♗d7 **13** ♗xd7+ ♕xd7 **14 ♕b4 ♘c6 =**
(van der Wiel).

b) **9 ♕e2!** 0-0 *(9 . . . a6!)* **10 0-0**
♘bd7 *(10 . . . ♗xc3 11 bxc3 ♘bd7 12*
♗a3 ♖d8 13 ♖ac1 ±) **11 ♘b5! ♕c6**
(on 11 . . . ♕b8, 12 g3 is strong) **12 a3**

(12 ♘e5?! ♕e4 13 a3 ♗e7 ± Karpov-van der Wiel, Thessaloniki (ol) 1988) 12 . . . ♗a5 (12 . . . ♗e7 13 ♗g5 ±) 13 ♘e5 ± (van der Wiel).

9 0-0   . . .

9 . . .   b6

A fashionable variant of the Nimzo-Indian has developed (1 d4 ♘f6 2 c4 e6 3 ♘c3 ♗b4 4 e3 0-0 5 ♘f3 d5 6 ♗d3 c5 7 0-0 dxc4 8 ♗xc4). More experience is needed of **9 . . . ♗xc3** 10 bxc3 ♕c7 11 ♘e5!? ♘c6 12 ♘xc6 ♕xc6 13 ♕b3 ± Simagin-Zukhovitsky, USSR 1967.

On the other hand, **9 . . . a6** merits serious attention. Black threatens b7-b5 and perhaps gets more space than is the case with 9 . . . b6. However, he does lose tempi (in most cases White's bishop gets to d3 anyhow) and later a2-a4 is possible for White. Only the future will tell. Some variations:

a) **10 ♕e2** b5 11 ♗d3 ♗b7 12 a4

bxa4 13 ♖xa4 a5 14 ♗g5 h6 15 ♗h4 ♗e7 16 ♖e1 ♘bd7 = Gligorić-Durašević, Yugoslavia 1961.

b) **10 ♗g5** b5 *(10 . . . ♘bd7 11 a4 ♘b6 12 ♗b3 ♗e7 13 ♖e1 ♘fd5 14 ♗xe7 ♕xe7 15 ♕d3 ± Taimanov-Korchnoi, Buenos Aires 1960 or 10 . . . h6 11 ♗h4 b5 12 ♗b3 ♗e7 13 ♕e2 ♘bd7 ±)* 11 ♗d3 *(11 ♗b3 ♗b7 12 ♕d3 ♘bd7 13 ♖ad1 ♗xc3 14 bxc3 ♕c7 15 ♖c1 ♘g4 16 ♗h4 ♗xf3 17 ♗g3 ♘ge5 = Panno-Petrosian, Gothenburg 1955; 15 ♖fe1 ♖ac8 16 ♖c1 ♗d5 = Taimanov-Durašević, USSR v Yugoslavia 1958)* 11 . . . ♗b7 12 ♕e2 *(12 ♖c1 ♗e7 13 ♕e2 ♘bd7 14 ♖fd1 ♖c8 15 ♘e5 ♘b6 16 ♗c2 ♘bd5 = Furman-Bannik, USSR 1949 or 12 a4 bxa4 13 ♖xa4 ♗e7 14 ♕e2 ♗c6 15 ♖aa1 a5 = Lengyel-Korchnoi, Moscow 1971)* 12 . . . ♘bd7 13 ♖fd1 ♗e7 14 ♘e5 ♘d5 15 ♗xe7 *(15 ♗d2? ♘xc3 16 bxc3 ♘xe5 ∓ Sigurjonsson-Larsen, Geneva 1972)* 15 . . . ♕xe7 16 ♘xd5 ♗xd5 17 ♗e4 = Larsen.

c) **10 a4 ♕a5?** *(10 . . . ♘c6 11 ♗f4 ± Ivkov; 10 . . . ♘bd7 11 ♗d3 ± Parma; 10 . . . b6!?)* 11 ♗g5 ♘d5 12 ♘e4 ♘d7 13 ♕e2 ♖e8 14 ♖fc1 ♘f8 15 ♘c5! ± Spassky-Petrosian, USSR 1975.

d) **10 a3 ♗xc3** 11 ♗xc3 b5 12 ♗d3 ♗b7 13 a4 ♕d5 14 axb5 *(14 ♕e2 ♖c8 15 ♗d2 ♘e4 16 ♗xe4 ♕xe4 17 ♕xe4 ♗xe4 18 axb5 axb5 19 ♖xa8 ♗xa8 20 ♖b1 ♗c6 21 ♘e5 ♗e8 = Ulybin-Kharitonov, USSR (ch) 1988)* 14 . . . axb5 15 ♖xa8 ♗xa8 16 ♕e2 ♖c8 17 ♗d2 ♘e4 18 ♗xe4 ♕xe4 19 ♕xe4 ♗xe4 20 ♘e5 ♘c6 = Goldin-

Kharitonov, Moscow 1989.

After the text we have a flexible position in which it is difficult to demonstrate White's advantage.

B1.1: 10 ♖e1
B1.2: 10 ♗g5
B1.3: 10 ♕e2

Or:

a) 10 ♗d3 ♘c6 11 ♗g5 ♗b7 12 ♗e4 ♗e7 13 ♗xf6 ♗xf6 14 ♕a4 a6 15 ♖fd1 b5 16 ♕c2 g6 17 a3 ♖c8 = Portisch-Gheorghiu, Montana-Crans 1976.

b) 10 ♗f4 ♗b7 11 ♕e2 ♗xc3 12 bxc3 ♘d5 13 ♗d2 ♕c7 (Gulko-Sosonko, Biel (izt) 1976) 14 ♗d3 ♘xc3 15 ♗xc3 ♕xc3 16 ♖fc1 ♕a5 17 ♖c7 ∞ Ivkov.

c) 10 ♕b3 ♗xc3 11 bxc3 ♗b7 12 ♘e5 ♕c7 13 ♗a3 ♖e8 14 ♗b5 ♘c6 15 ♗xc6 ♗xc6 16 c4 ♗b7 = Larsen-Petrosian, Las Palmas 1975.

Yugoslavia 1975, Black secured satisfactory play after 13 ♗b1 ♖c8 14 ♕d3 ♖e8 15 ♗g5 g6 16 ♗a2 ♘d5 17 ♗h6 ♘xc3 18 bxc3 ♗f6 19 ♖ad1 ♘e7 20 ♘e5 ♘f5 21 ♗f4 ♗g5.

13 . . .   ♖e8
14 ♕d3   g6

14 . . . ♖c8?! 15 d5! exd5 16 ♗g5 ♘e4 *(16 . . . g6? 17 ♖xe7!)* 17 ♘xe4 dxe4 18 ♕xe4 g6 19 ♕h4 h5 *(19 . . . ♕c7 20 ♗b3! h5 21 ♕e4 ♔g7 22 ♗xf7! +– Petrosian-Balashov, USSR (ch) 1974)* 20 ♖ad1!? *(20 ♗b3!?)* 20 . . . ♕c7 21 ♗xg6! fxg6 Portisch-Karpov, Milan 1975, 22 ♖e6! ± Flórián.

The text was played in Polugayevsky-Furman, USSR (ch) 1975 which continued 15 ♗f4 ♖c8 16 ♖ad1 ♘a5 17 ♘e5 *(17 ♗a4!?)* 17 . . . ♘d5 18 ♗d2 ♘xc3 19 ♗xc3 ♗f6 with slightly better chances for White.

B1.1

10 ♖e1   ♗b7
11 ♗d3   ♘c6
12 a3   ♗e7
13 ♗c2   . . .

Once again this characteristic manœuvre, keeping the queenside play alive (♗a4) as well as the kingside attack (♕d3). Compared to line A1.12 and the illustrative game Smyslov-Karpov, Black has a tempo advantage here. Instead in Gligorić-Furman,

B1.2

10 ♗g5   ♗b7

11 ♖c1   . . .

Here:

a) 11 ♘e5 ♗xc3 *(11...♗e7 12 ♕e2 h6 ± 13 ♘xf7!? ♖xf7 14 ♕xe6 ♕f8 ∞ Faragó-Dely, Szolnok 1975 or 11... ♘c6!? 12 ♗xf6!? ♕xf6! 13 ♘d7 ♕h4 14 ♘xf8 ♖xf8 15 ♘e2 ♖d8 16 ♕b3 ∞ Faragó-Rigó, Hungary (ch) 1976)* 12 bxc3 ♕c7! 13 ♖e1 ♘bd7?! *(13... ♘c6!)* 14 ♘xd7 ♘xd7 15 ♗d3 ♖e8 16 ♖e3 e5 17 ♕h5 e4 18 ♖ae1 ± Portisch-Rigó, Hungary (ch) 1976.

b) 11 ♖e1 ♘bd7 12 ♗d3 ♗xc3 *(12 ... ♖c8 13 ♖c1 ♖e8 14 ♕e2 ♗xc3 15 bxc3 ♕c7 16 c4 ♕c6 17 h3 ♖cd8 18 ♖cd1 ♘f8 19 ♕e5 ♘6d7 20 ♕g3! ± Gligorić-Portisch, Lugano (ol) 1968)* 13 bxc3 ♕c7 14 c4 ♕d6 15 ♘e5 ♘xe5 16 dxe5 ♕c6 17 ♗f1 ♘e4 = Gligorić-Unzicker, Milan 1975.

c) 11 ♕d3 ♘bd7 12 ♖ad1 ♗xc3 13 bxc3 ♕c7 14 ♗b3 ♗e4! ∓ Gheorghiu-Ostojić, Cleveland 1975.

d) 11 ♕e2 ♗xc3! *(11 ... ♘c6?! 12 ♖ad1 ♘a5 13 ♗d3 ♗e7 14 ♘e5 ±; 11 ... ♘bd7?! 12 ♖ac1 ♖c8 13 ♘e5 ♕c7!? 14 ♗b5 ♕d6 15 ♖fd1 ♗xc3 16 bxc3 ♕d5 17 f4 ± Belyavsky-Karpov, USSR (ch) 1973 or 13... h6 14 ♘xd7! ♕xd7 15 ♗xf6 gxf6 16 d5 exd5 17 ♗d3! ± Keres)* 12 bxc3 ♘bd7 13 ♗d3 *(13 ♗h4 ♖c8 14 ♖ac1 ♗xf3 15 gxf3 ♖e8 16 ♗b5 ♖e7 17 c4 ♘f8 18 ♗a6 ♖c6 = Kuzmin-Polugayevsky, Sochi 1976 or 13 ♘e5!? ♕c7 14 ♘xd7 ♘xd7 − ♕xd7? 15 ♗xf6 gxf6 16 d5!! ♗xd5 17 ♖ad1 ± Vaiser-Polugayevsky, Sochi 1988 − 15 ♖ac1 ♖fe8 − 15 ...*

♖ac8 16 ♗d3 ♕c6 17 f3 ♕d6 ± Knaak-Vaiser, Szirák 1985 − 16 ♖fe1 ♕c6 17 f3 ♖ec8 18 ♗d3 ♕d6 19 ♕f2 h6 20 ♗d2 ♖e8 21 ♕h4 ♖ad8 ± Dokhojan-Rogers, Wijk aan Zee 1989)* 13 ... ♕c7 14 c4 ♘g4 15 ♗e4 ♗xe4 16 ♕xe4 ♘gf6 17 ♕d3 *(17 ♕e2 ♖ac8 18 ♖ac1 ♕b7 19 ♕b2 ♕a6 20 ♕b3 ♖c6 ∓ Belyavsky-Karpov, USSR 1975)* 17 ... h6 18 ♗xf6 ♘xf6 19 a4 ♖ac8 20 ♖fc1 ♖fd8 = Petrosian-Karpov, Milan 1975.

11 ...	♘c6
12 a3	♗e7
13 ♕d3	♘d5

13 ... ♖c8 14 ♖fd1 ♘d5! 15 ♗xd5 ♗xg5 16 ♘xg5 ♕xg5 17 ♗e4 h6 18 ♕e3 ♖fd8 = Portisch-Karpov, Milan 1975.

14 ♗xd5	exd5
15 ♗xe7	♘xe7
16 ♖fe1	♖c8

White stands slightly better: 17 h4 h6 18 h5! ♖c7 19 ♘b5 ♖xc1 20 ♖xc1 ♗a6 21 a4 ♗xb5 22 ♕xb5 ± Ivanchuk-Karpov, Linares 1991.

B1.3

10 ♕e2   . . .

The position developed originally from the Nimzo-Indian move order, favoured by Karpov.

10 . . .   **♗b7**

Here the most frequent try, 11 ♗g5, was discussed in the previous variation, B1.2. Other interesting possibilities are:

a) **11 a3** ♗xc3 12 bxc3 ♕c7 13 ♘e5 ♘bd7 14 ♗d3?! *(14 ♘xd7 ♕xd7 = Ivkov)* 14 . . . ♖ac8 *(14 . . . ♘xe5 15 dxe5 ♕c6 16 f3 ♘d7 ∓ Euwe)* 15 f4 ♕xc3 16 ♗b2 ♕b3! *(16 . . . ♕c7? 17 f5 ♕d6 18 ♖f4 ± Szabó-Filip, Portorož 1958)* 17 ♗c4 ♖xc4! 18 ♘xc4 ♗a6 19 ♖ac1 ♖ac8 20 ♕e3 ♕a2 ∓ Donner-Unzicker, 1959.

b) **11 ♖d1** ♘bd7 12 ♘e5 *(12 ♗d2 [12 ♗d3 ♖c8 13 ♖d2 ♗e7 14 ♖ac1 ♘d5 =] 12 . . . ♖c8 13 ♗a6?! ♗xa6 14 ♕xa6 ♗xc3! 15 bxc3 ♖c7! = Taimanov-Karpov — see illustrative games for a fuller explanation of both sides' strategy)* 12 . . . ♖c8 13 ♗g5 ♗xc3! 14 bxc3 *(14 ♘xd7? ♕xd7 15 ♗xf6 gxf6 16 bxc3 ♕c6 ∓)* 14 . . . ♕c7 15 ♘xd7 ♘xd7 16 ♗b5 h6! *(16 . . . ♗d5 17 ♕g4! f5 18 ♕h3 h6 19 c4! ♗xg2! 20 ♕xg2 hxg5 21 ♕xg5 ♖f6 22 ♖d3 ♘f8 ± Skembris-Belyavsky, Haifa 1989)* 17 ♗e7 ♖fe8 18 ♗h4 a6! 19 ♗g3 ♕d8 20 ♗xa6 ♗xa6 21 ♕xa6 ♖xc3 22 ♖ab1 ♕a8 = Illescas-Magem, Terrassa 1990.

B2

7 cxd5   **. . .**

B2.1: 7 . . . exd5
B2.2: 7 . . . ♘xd5

B2.1

7 . . .   **exd5**

8 ♗b5+   **. . .**

Others:

a) **8 ♕a4+** ♘c6 9 ♗b5 0-0 *(9 . . . ♗d7 10 0-0 ♕a5 ∞)* 10 0-0 *(10 ♗xc6?! ♗xc3+ 11 bxc3 bxc6 12 ♕xc6 ♕a5 ∞)* 10 . . . ♕a5 11 ♗d2 ♕xa4 12 ♗xa4 ♗f5 = Peresypin-Bagirov, USSR 1977.

b) **8 ♗d3** 0-0 9 0-0 ♗g4 10 ♗g5 ♗xc3 11 bxc3 ♘bd7 12 ♕d2! ♕c7! *(12 . . . ♗xf3 13 gxf3 ♖c8 14 ♔h1 ♖c6 15 ♖g1 ± Benjamin-Douven, Wijk aan Zee 1989)* 13 ♘h4 ♘e4 14 ♗xe4 dxe4 15 h3 ♗h5 16 ♘f5 ♗g6 17 ♗f4 ♕a5 ∞ Brenninkmeijer-Kuijf, Groningen 1989.

8 . . .	♗d7
9 ♕e2+	♘e4
10 0-0	♗xc3
11 bxc3	0-0
12 ♗d3	. . .

12 ♗xd7? ♘xd7 13 c4 ♖e8 14 ♕b2 dxc4 15 ♕xb7 ♘b6 ∓ Tatai–Larsen, Las Palmas 1977.

12 ...   ♗f5

12... ♖e8!? 13 ♘e5 ♘c6 14 ♘xf7! *(14 ♗xe4 dxe4 15 ♕xe4 ♘xe5 16 dxe5 ♗c6 ∞)* 14... ♕f6 15 ♘e5 ♘xe5 16 dxe5 ♖xe5 ± Sveshnikov–Vyzmanavin, Moscow 1990.

13 ♕b2!   ...

13 ♗xe4?! ♗xe4 14 ♘e5 f6 15 ♘g4 ♘c6 16 ♘e3 ♕a5 17 ♗b2 ♖ae8 18 ♖fe1 ♖e6 ∓ Sveshnikov–Tal, USSR (ch) 1977.

13 ...	♕c8
14 ♗f4	♘d7
15 ♘h4	♗e6
16 c4	♘b6
17 ♖ac1	...

was Sveshnikov–Kalinichev, USSR 1988, where White had a slight advantage – due to possession of the bishop pair, and better co-ordination of pieces.

B2.2

7 ...   ♘xd5

B2.21: 8 ♕c2
B2.22: 8 ♗d2

(see diagram)

B2.21

8 ♕c2   ...

8 ♕b3 ♘c6 9 ♗d3 0-0 10 0-0 ♗e7 11 a3 ♗f6 12 ♖d1 h6 13 ♗b1 ♘ce7 14 ♕c2 ♘g6 15 ♘e5 ♗xe5 16 dxe5 b6 ∞ Mortensen–van der Sterren, Kerteminde 1991.

| 8 ... | ♘c6 |
| 9 ♗d3 | ... |

Alternatives include:

a) 9 ♗c4 ♘b6 10 ♗b5 0-0 11 ♗e3 ♗d7 12 ♗d3 h6 13 0-0 ♖c8 14 ♗h7+ ♔h8 15 ♗e4 ♘c4 16 ♖ad1 f5 17 ♗d3 ♘6a5 = Timman–van der Wiel, Tilburg 1988.

b) 9 ♗e2 0-0 10 0-0 ♗e7 *(10 ... ♖e8!? 11 ♖d1 ♗f8 12 ♗g5 ♕a5 13 ♘e4 ♗d7 14 a3 ♖ac8 15 ♕d3 ♕c7 16 ♖ac1 ♘f4 ∞ Wolf–Speelman, New York 1990)* 11 ♖d1 ♕d6 *(11...b6!? 12 ♘xd5 ♕xd5 13 ♗d3 ♘b4! or 11 ... ♗d7!? Benjamin)* 12 ♗g5! ± *(12 ... ♘xc3?! 13 bxc3 b6 14 ♕e4! ♗b7 15*

♗d3 g6 16 ♕h4 ± *Benjamin–Miles,
USA (ch) 1988).*

9 . . .   **♗a5**

Very interesting is 9 . . . ♘xc3!? 10
bxc3 ♘xd4 11 ♘xd4 ♕xd4 12 0-0!?
♕xc3 13 ♗b5+ ♔f8 *(13 . . . ♔e7)* 14
♕e4 ♗d6 15 ♖b1 ∞ Pirrot–Schulz,
West Germany 1989/90.

10 a3   **. . .**

10 0-0?! ♘db4! *(10 . . . ♘cb4? 11
♗b5+ ♗d7 12 ♕a4 ±)* 11 ♕e2 ♘xd3
12 ♕xd3 h6! 13 ♖d1 0-0 14 ♕e4
♗xc3! 15 bxc3 ♕d5 16 ♕d3! ♖d8! 17
♗f4! = *(17 ♖b1? ♕xa2 18 ♗f4 ♕a3!
19 ♖e1 b6 20 ♘e5 ♘xe5 21 ♗xe5 ♗b7
22 ♖e3 ♕f8 23 ♖be1 f6 24 ♗g3 e5 ∓
Plaskett–Smagin, Belgrade 1988; 17 c4
♕h5 18 ♗b2 e5 19 d5 ♗g4! ∓ Smagin).*

10 . . .   **♘xc3!?**
11 bxc3   **♘xd4**
12 ♘xd4   **♕xd4**
13 ♗b5+!?   **. . .**

13 0-0? ♕e5! 14 ♗e3 ♗b6!
(Kindermann–Speelman,   Plovdiv
1983) 15 ♗d4 ∓.

13 . . .   **♔e7!?**
14 0-0   **♕xc3**
15 ♕e4!   **f6**

15 . . . f5?! 16 ♕e2 and ♗b2 ∞.

16 ♗f4!?   **. . .**

16 ♗e3 (Rogers–Effert, Altensteig
1988) 18 . . . a6! ∞.

16 . . .   **e5**
17 ♖fd1!   **f5**
18 ♗g5!   **. . .**

White's chances are promising.

B2.22

8 ♗d2   **. . .**

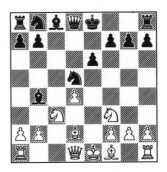

8 . . .   **♘c6**

The old variation is **8 . . . 0-0** 9 ♗d3
♗e7 *(9 . . . ♘f6 10 0-0 ♗xc3 11 bxc3 b6
12 ♕e2 ♗b7 13 ♘e5 ♘c6 = Padevsky–
Barcza 1964 or 10 . . . ♗d7?! 11 ♕e2
♗c6 12 ♖ad1 ♘bd7 13 ♘e5 ♘b6 14
♗g5 ♗e7 15 ♕e3 g6 16 ♗h6 ♖e8 17
♖fe1 ± Zude–Lutz, West Germany
1989/90)* 10 0-0 ♘c6 11 ♖e1 *(11 a3
♗f6 12 ♕c2 g6 13 ♗h6 ∞ Banas–
Eperjesi, Budapest 1976)* 11 . . . ♗f6 12
♘xd5 exd5 13 h3 ♕b6 14 ♗c3 ♗e6 =

Varnusz–Eperjesi, Budapest 1976.

9 ♗d3   0-0

9 ... ♗e7 10 a3 *(10 0-0 0-0 11 a3 ♗f6 12 ♕c2 h6 13 ♖ad1 ♗d7 14 ♘xd5 exd5 15 ♕b3 ♗g4 16 ♗b1 h5 17 h3 ♗xf3 18 ♕xf3 g6 19 ♗c3 ♗g7 20 ♗a2 ♕b6 ± Korolev–Kastarnov (corr) 1988)* 10 ... ♗f6 11 0-0! ♗xd4?! *(11 ... 0-0 is preferable)* 12 ♘xd4 ♘xd4 13 ♘xd5 ♕xd5 *(13 ... exd5!? 14 ♖e1+ ♘e6 15 ♕h5 with initiative)* 14 ♕g4! ± Vaiser–Sveshnikov, Moscow 1989.

10 0-0   ♘f6

10 ... ♗e7 11 a3 *(11 ♘xd5 exd5 12 h3 ♗f6 13 ♗c3 ♕b6 14 ♕d2 ♖e8 15 ♖fe1 ♗d7 16 ♗c2 h6 17 ♕d3 g6 18 ♗b3 ♗f5 = Smyslov–Magem, Barcelona 1990)* 11 ... ♗f6 12 ♕e2 ♘xd4 13 ♘xd4 ♗xd4 14 ♗xh7+ ♔xh7 15 ♕e4+ ♔g8 16 ♕xd4 ♘xc3 17 ♕xc3 ♗d7 18 ♕g3 ♗a4 19 ♗b4 ♖e8 20 ♖fe1 f6 21 ♖e3 ± Hübner–Campora, Biel 1987.

11 a3   ...

11 ♗g5 ♗e7 12 ♖c1 ♗d7!? *(12 ... b6?! 13 ♗xf6 ♗xf6 14 ♘e4 ♗b7 15 ♘xf6+ ♕xf6 16 ♗e4 ♖ac8 17 ♗c3 ± Duric–Tarjan, Vrsac 1983)* 13 ♖e1 ±.

11 ...   ♗e7
12 ♗e3   b6
13 ♖e1   ...

13 ♗c2 ♗a6 14 ♖e1 ♘a5 ∞.

13 ...   ♗b7
14 ♗c2   ♖c8

Here White has a very slight advantage. Deviant possibilities include 14 ... ♕d6!?; 14 ... a6 (±); 14 ... ♘a5?! 15 ♘e5 ♖c8 16 ♕d3 (Dlugy-Oll, Moscow 1989) 16 ... ♘c6! ±.

ILLUSTRATIVE GAMES

51 VAGANYAN–VAN DER WIEL
Rotterdam 1989

1 c4 c6 2 e4 d5 3 exd5 cxd5 4 d4 ♘f6 5 ♘c3 e6 6 ♘f3 ♗e7 7 cxd5 exd5 8 ♗d3 0-0 9 h3 ♘c6 10 0-0 ♗e6 11 ♗e3!? ♘d7? 12 ♘e2! ♕b6 13 ♘f4 ♖ac8 (13 ... ♕xb2 14 ♖b1 ♕xa2 15 ♘xe6 fxe6 16 ♖xb7 ♖ad8 17 ♘g5! ♗xg5 18 ♗xg5 ♘f6 19 ♗xf6! ♖xf6 20 ♕g4 g6 21 ♕h4 +−) **14 ♕b1! h6** (14 ... g6? 15 ♘xe6 fxe6 16 ♗xg6!) **15 ♗h7+! ♔h8 16 ♗f5 ♗xf5 17 ♕xf5 ♘f6 18 ♘xd5 ♘xd5 19 ♕xd5 ♗f6** (19 ... ♕xb2 20 ♖ab1 ♕a3 21 ♖xb7 +−) **20 ♖ad1** (20 ♖fd1?! ♕xb2! 21 ♖ab1 ♕e2) **20 ... ♘e7** (20 ... ♕xb2 21 ♖b1 ♕a3 22 ♖xb7 ±; 20 ... ♖cd8!? may be more apposite) **21 ♕h5 ♖c2 22 d5 ♕a6** (22 ... ♕d6? 23 ♗xh6! gxh6 24 ♕xh6+ ♔g8 25 ♘g5 wins) **23 d6 ♘g8** (23 ... ♘g6 24 ♗xh6 gxh6 25 ♕f5) **24 d7! ♕xa2 25 ♖fe1!** (25 ♗g5 ♕a5!; 25 ♗d4 ♕e6! 26 ♖fe1 ♕xd7 27 ♗xf6 ♘xf6 =) **25 ... ♖d8 26 ♗g5!** (26 ♗xh6? g6 embarrasses) **26 ... ♖c7**

(26 . . . ♕a5 27 ♗xf6! ♕xh5 28 ♗xd8
♕c5 29 ♗h4) 27 ♘e5! ♔h7 28 ♗xf6
♘xf6 29 ♕f5+ ♔h8 30 ♖d6! Black
resigned.

52   BOTVINNIK-GOLOMBEK
Moscow 1956

1 e4 c6 2 d4 d5 3 exd5 cxd5 4 c4 ♘f6
5 ♘c3 e6 6 ♘f3 ♗e7 7 c5 0-0 8 ♗d3 b6
9 b4 ♗d7?! 10 ♗e3 ♘g4 11 0-0 a5? 12
♘a4! bxc5 (Black's scheme has been
refuted, because after 12 . . . ♗xa4 13
♕xa4 ♘d7 14 ♕c2 there is the double
threat of 15 ♗xh7+ and 15 c6!) 13
bxc5 ♗xa4 14 ♕xa4 ♘xe3 15 fxe3
♘a6 16 ♖ab1! (Invasion along the
open file now begins!) 16 . . . ♗g5 17
♖fe1 (It is not economical to counter
the bishop's attack with the rook, but
this is by now the only feature of the
position which favours Black) 17 . . .
♗h6 (17 . . . ♘b4 18 ♗b5 followed by
a2-a3 ±) 18 ♖b7 ♕c8 19 ♗xa6! (This
is the simplest approach. White's
heavy pieces will soon break in along
the b-file and then across the seventh
rank. 19 c6 ♘b4 20 ♗b5 ♖b8! 21
♖xb8 ♕xb8 22 ♕xa5 ♘c2 etc. was
worse) 19 . . . ♖xa6 20 ♕d7! f6 (This is
about the best in view of the threat of
21 ♘e5!. Instead 20 . . . ♕xd7 21 ♖xd7
f6 − 21 . . . ♖b8 22 ♘e5 f6 23 ♘f3! −
22 ♖b7 ♖f7 23 ♖b8+ ♖f8 24 ♖xf8+
♔xf8 25 ♔f2 ♔e7 26 ♖b1 ♖a7 27 a4
♔d7 28 ♖b6 was also poor according
to Botvinnik) 21 ♕xc8 ♖xc8 22 ♔f2
♖aa8?! (22 . . . e5!?) 23 ♖eb1 e5 24
♖d7 (The d-pawn is already doomed
because of the threat of doubled

rooks. Still, Black cannot be faulted
for his last move; there was nothing
better) 24 . . . exd4 25 exd4 ♖d8 26
♖1b7 ♖ac8 (26 . . . ♖xd7 27 ♖xd7
♖b8 28 c6 +−) 27 ♘h4! (28 ♘f5 is
threatened, and this forces the
exchange) 27 . . . ♖xd7 28 ♖xd7 g6 29
g3 (The capture of the pawn is not
urgent and the knight is sent to f4
first) 29 . . . f5 (Changing the plan) 30
♘f3 ♗g7 31 ♖xd5 ♖c7 32 ♘g5 ♗f6 33
h4 h6 34 ♘f3 ♔f7 35 ♘e5+ ♔g7 36
♔e3 g5 37 hxg5 ♗xg5+ 38 ♔f3 a4 (38
. . . ♗f6 39 ♔f4) 39 ♖d7+ ♖xd7 40
♘xd7 ♔f7 41 d5 ♔e7 42 ♘b6 a3 43
♘c4 ♔d7 (43 . . . ♗c1 44 c6) 44 ♘xa3
♗e7 45 c6+ Black resigned.

53   BLATNY-ADAMS
Oakham 1990

1 e4 d5 2 exd5 ♘f6 3 c4 c6 4 d4 cxd5
5 ♘c3 e6 6 ♘f3 ♗e7 7 c5 0-0 8 ♗d3 b6
9 b4 a5 10 ♘a4 ♘fd7 11 h4 h6 12 ♖h3
♗f6 13 ♖g3 e5! 14 ♗xh6 e4 15 ♘g5
exd3 16 ♕xd3 ♖e8+ 17 ♔d2 ♘f8 18
♘xb6 axb4! 19 ♘xf7 (19 ♘xa8 ♕a5 or
19 . . . ♘c6 is the critical position)
19 . . . ♔xf7 20 ♕f3 g6 21 ♘xa8 (21
♗g5 ♖a3 22 ♕f4 ♘c6) 21 . . . ♘c6 22
♗e3 ♗f5 23 h5 (23 ♘b6 ♗e4 24 ♕f4
♘e6 −+) 23 . . . ♗e4 24 ♕f4 ♕xa8 25
♖h3 g5 26 ♕c7+ ♖e7 27 ♕d6 ♖d7 28
♕h2 ♕a3 29 ♖d1 ♕b2+ 30 ♔e1
♘xd4 31 ♗xd4 ♗xd4 32 ♖b3 White
resigned.

54   TROIANESCU-FLÓRIÁN
Bucharest 1949

1 e4 c6 2 d4 d5 3 exd5 cxd5 4 c4 ♘f6

5 ♘c3 e6 6 ♘f3 ♗e7 7 c5 0-0 8 ♗g5?!
♘e4 9 ♗xe7 ♕xe7 10 ♕c2 f5 11 ♗b5?
(Had the knight already been on c6,
this would have been an excellent
move, in that it would have secured
e5 for White. As it is, Black gains
chances on the kingside) 11 ... ♗d7
12 ♗xd7 ♘xd7 13 0-0 g5! (Heralding
the attack characteristic of this pawn
structure) 14 ♖fe1 (14 ♖ae1!) 14 ...
g4 15 ♘d2 ♕h4! 16 ♘f1 ♖f6! (The
clouds are gathering on White's kingside and there is no counterplay in
sight) 17 ♖e2 ♘g5 18 ♕d3 f4 19 ♖d2
f3 20 ♘e3 (20 g3 ♕h3 21 ♘e3 ♖h6 ∓)
20 ... ♖h6 21 h3 ♘xh3+! – A murder-
ous sacrifice that can neither be accepted (22 gxh3 ♕xh3) nor repulsed
(22 ♔f1 ♘f4), so **White resigned.**

55   BOTVINNIK–
KONSTANTINOPOLSKY
Sverdlovsk 1943

1 e4 c6 2 d4 d5 3 exd5 cxd5 4 c4 ♘f6
5 ♘c3 e6 6 ♘f3 ♗e7 7 ♗g5?! 0-0
8 ♖c1!? ♘c6 9 c5 ♘e4 10 ♗xe7 ♕xe7
11 ♗e2 ♗d7 12 a3 f5? (This weakens
e5. Botvinnik, by not developing his
bishop to b5, has obviously thrown
Black off his guard) 13 ♗b5!
(Alekhine defined the essence of
chess talent as flexibility) 13 ... ♘g5
14 ♗xc6 ♘xf3+ 15 ♕xf3 bxc6 16 ♕f4!
♖ae8 17 0-0! (He is not afraid of
Black's attempt to escape. 17 ♕e5
♕f6 18 ♕xf6 gxf6 or 18 f4 ♕xe5 etc.
would have given Black more
chances) 17 ... e5 18 ♕xe5 ♕xe5 19
dxe5 ♖xe5 20 f4! ♖e7 (20 ... ♖e3 21

♔f2 d4 22 ♖fd1 ±) 21 ♖fe1 ♖fe8 22
♖xe7 ♖xe7 23 ♔f2 ♔f7 24 ♖d1! (The
dominating feature of the position is
the superiority of the active knight
over the opposing bishop, which is
locked in behind his own pawns. This
superiority is enhanced by the pre-
ponderance of White's pawns on the
queenside. This is one of the chief
objectives of the c4-c5 variants of the
Panov Attack as exemplified by
several master-games, but the logical
consistency shown by the future
World Champion in exploiting his
advantage, in the teeth of dour
resistance, is exceptional. Against the
obvious 24 ♖e1 for instance 24 ...
♖xe1! 25 ♔xe1 d4! 26 ♔e2 ♔e6
and the pawn sacrifice gives Black
counterchances) 24 ... ♖e8?! (Black
intends to deploy his rook on the
queenside, but this counterplay is
pure self-delusion. 24 ... ♗c8! 25
♘e2 ♖e4 26 g3 ♖c4 27 b4 a5 etc. was
much more stubborn) 25 ♖d2! h6 26
♖e2! (This is something altogether
different! If the rooks are exchanged,
White would reach d4, and the good
knight wins against the bad bishop) 26
... ♖b8 27 ♔e3 ♖b3 28 ♔d4 ♔f6 29
♘a2 ♖b8 (29 ... a5 would be followed
by 30 ♘c1 ♖b8 31 b3 and then b3-b4)
30 b4 g5 (Black desperately wants to
open a file for his rook. 30 ... a5? 31
bxa5 ♖a8 32 ♘c3 ♖xa5 33 a4 ± Fine)
31 g3 gxf4 32 gxf4 a6 33 ♘c3 (♖b2 and
a3-a4 is threatened as well as b3-b4)
33 ... ♖g8 34 a4 ♖g4 35 ♖f2 (Black's
rook is more active, but other factors

ensure a decisive advantage for White) **35 . . . ♗e6** (35 . . . ♗e8 36 b5 axb5 37 axb5 cxb5 38 ♘xd5+ ♔e6 39 ♖e2+ ♔f7 40 ♖xe8 ♔xe8 41 ♘f6+ ♔e7 42 ♘xg4 fxg4 43 f5 h5 44 c6 is no better) **36 b5!** (A typical breakthrough) **36 . . . axb5 37 axb5 cxb5 38 ♘xb5 ♖g1 39 ♘c3! ♔f7 40 ♖b2 ♖f1 41 ♘e2!** (Accurate to the end! 41 ♔e5 ♖e1+ 42 ♔d6 d4! ∞) **41 . . . ♖e1** (41 . . . ♔f6 42 c6 ♖f2 43 c7 ♖xh2 44 ♖b6! ±) **42 ♔e5! d4** (42 . . . ♔e7 43 c6 d4 44 ♖b7+ ♔d8 45 ♔d6 ♖xe2 46 ♖b8+ ♗c8 47 c7+ ± Fine) **43 ♔xd4 ♔g6 44 ♘c3** (44 ♔e5?? ♗c4) **44 . . . ♔h5 45 ♖e2 ♖xe2 46 ♘xe2 ♔g4 47 ♔e5 ♗c8 48 ♘d4 h5 49 ♘xf5! ♗d7** (49 . . . ♗xf5 50 h3+! ±) **50 ♘g7 ♗a4 51 f5 ♔g5 52 ♘e6+ Black resigned.**

56 BOTVINNIK−ALEKHINE
AVRO Tournament 1938

1 e4 c6 2 d4 d5 3 exd5 cxd5 4 c4 ♘f6 5 ♘c3 e6 6 ♘f3 ♗e7 7 cxd5 ♘xd5 8 ♗c4 ♘c6 9 0-0 0-0 10 ♖e1 b6?! 11 ♘xd5! exd5 12 ♗b5 ♗d7?! (This leads to simplification, after which White's development advantage will make itself felt. 12 . . . ♘a5 was better, while 12 . . . ♗b7 13 ♕a4 ♖c8 14 ♗f4 also results in a difficult game) **13 ♕a4! ♘b8** (A bitter necessity for the great tactician, but 13 . . . ♖c8 14 ♗d2! − 14 ♗xc6? ♗xc6 15 ♕xa7 ♗b4! and 16 . . . ♖a8 − 14 . . . a6 15 ♗xc6 ♗xc6 16 ♕xa6 ±) **14 ♗f4 ♗xb5 15 ♕xb5 a6 16 ♕a4 ♗d6 17 ♗xd6 ♕xd6 18 ♖ac1 ♖a7** (He has got to develop somehow) **19 ♕c2!** (This paralyses

the opponent's forces) **19 . . . ♖e7** (Enables White to simplify towards a favourable end-game; 19 . . . f6 20 ♕f5! ±) **20 ♖xe7 ♕xe7 21 ♕c7! ♕xc7 22 ♖xc7 f6?!** (The World Champion has successfully avoided immediate collapse because 23 ♖b7 ♖c8 24 ♔f1 b5 would still be defendable, and otherwise 23 . . . ♖f7 is threatened. Possession of the c-file is nonetheless a trump in White's hand, even though he needs to play with absolute precision) **23 ♔f1 ♖f7 24 ♖c8+ ♖f8 25 ♖c3!** (It becomes clear that Black has no useful development move, because after 25 . . . ♖e8 or ♔f7 or ♘d7 26 ♖c7 would follow. Pawn moves on the other hand are structurally weakening) **25 . . . g5 26 ♘e1** (♘c2-e3 is threatened) **26 . . . h5** (Black is planning to respond to 27 ♘c2 with 27 . . . ♔f7 28 ♖c7+ ♔e6 29 ♖h7 ♘d7. The same could not be done after 26 . . . h6 because of 27 ♘c2 ♔f7 28 ♘e3 ♔e6 29 g4!) **27 h4!** (This move creates weaknesses in Black's pawn position. The main threat is 28 hxg5 fxg5 29 ♘f3 g4 30 ♘e5 and Black is totally wrapped up, but if 27 . . . ♔f7 the ensuing 28 ♘f3! g4 29 ♘e1 ♔e6 30 ♘d3 ♔f5 31 g3 ♔e4 32 ♘f4 ± is even stronger) **27 . . . ♘d7** (27 . . . gxh4 28 ♘f3) **28 ♖c7 ♖f7 29 ♘f3! g4 30 ♘e1 f5 31 ♘d3 f4 32 f3** (32 ♘b4 would have won a pawn, but this is even better) **32 . . . gxf3 33 gxf3 a5 34 a4 ♔f8 35 ♖c6 ♔e7 36 ♔f2 ♖f5 37 b3 ♔d8 38 ♔e2 ♘b8 39 ♖g6** (39 ♖xb6 ♔c7 and 40 . . . ♘c6) **39 . . . ♔c7 40 ♘e5 ♘a6 41

🖹g7+ ♔c8 42 ♘c6 🖹f6 43 ♘e7+ ♔b8 44 ♘xd5 🖹d6 45 🖹g5 ♘b4 46 ♘xb4 axb4 47 🖹xh5 🖹c6 (47 ... 🖹xd4 48 🖹f5 ♔b7 49 🖹f6 ♔c7 50 h5) 48 🖹b5 ♔c7 49 🖹xb4 🖹h6 50 🖹b5 (50 ♔d3 🖹e6!) 50 ... 🖹xh4 51 ♔d3 **Black resigned.**

57 PAULSSON–FARAGÓ
Gausdal 1976

1 e4 c6 2 d4 d5 3 exd5 cxd5 4 c4 ♘f6 5 ♘c3 e6 6 ♘f3 ♗e7 7 cxd5 ♘xd5 8 ♗c4 ♘c6 9 0-0 0-0 10 🖹e1 ♘xc3 11 bxc3 b6 12 ♗d3 ♗b7 13 ♕c2 g6 14 ♕d2?! ♗f6 15 h4 🖹c8! 16 h5? ♘xd4!! (Black manœuvres his forces into a favourable position on the long diagonal with a brilliant double sacrifice. White's queenside attack came too early, as he had not yet succeeded in blocking the centre) 17 ♘xd4 (17 cxd4 ♗xf3 18 gxf3 ♗xd4 19 ♗a3 − 19 🖹b1 ♗c3 ∓ − 19 ... ♗c3!! 20 ♕e3 ♗xa1 21 🖹xa1 − 21 ♗xf8 ♗c3! 22 h6 ♗xe1 23 ♕e5 ♗c3 ± − 21 ... 🖹c3 ∓; 20 ♕e2! ♕g5+ 21 ♔f1 ♕xh5 ∓ Ermenkov) 17 ... 🖹xc3!! 18 ♕xc3 ♗xd4 19 ♕c2 (19 ♕d2 ♗xa1 20 ♗a3 ♕d5! ∓) 19 ... ♗xa1 20 ♗a3 ♕g5 21 ♗e4 🖹c8 22 ♕e2 ♗xe4 23 ♕xe4 ♗g7 24 ♕b7 ♕d8 25 hxg6 hxg6 26 ♕xa7 ♕d2 27 🖹e3 ♕d1+ 28 ♔h2 ♕h5+ 29 ♔g1 (29 🖹h3 ♗e5+! 30 g3 ♗xg3+!) 29 ... ♗e5 30 g3 🖹d8 31 🖹e1 ♗d4 32 ♕b7? (An oversight, but in an already lost position) 32 ... ♕a5 **White resigned.**

58 PORTISCH–BAGIROV
Beverwijk 1965

1 c4 c6 2 e4 d5 3 exd5 cxd5 4 d4 ♘f6 5 ♘c3 e6 6 ♘f3 ♗e7 7 cxd5 ♘xd5 8 ♗d3 ♘c6 9 0-0 0-0 10 🖹e1 ♘cb4?! 11 ♗b1 ♗d7? 12 a3! ♘xc3 (Black takes aim at White's hanging pawns, but 12 ... ♘c6 13 ♘xd5 or 13 ♗a2 would have given him very passive play anyhow) 13 bxc3 ♘d5 14 ♕d3 ♘f6 15 ♘e5 🖹c8 16 🖹a2! (The threatened doubling of rooks on the e-file is directed against e6 and f7, but it also makes the eventual breakthrough d4-d5 possible) 16 ... 🖹e8 17 🖹ae2 g6 (Sooner or later this weakening is inevitable) 18 ♗a2! (The bishop has a bright future on the a2-g8 diagonal) 18 ... 🖹c7 19 ♗h6! (The mating net is in the making! 20 ♘xf7! ♔xf7 21 🖹xe6! is threatened) 19 ... ♗f8 20 ♗g5! ♗g7? (This seemingly reinforces the threatened wing, but it forgets about the breakthrough d4-d5) 21 d5! ♕c8 21 ... exd5 22 ♗xf6! would cost a piece) 22 ♕f3! (This interferes with Black's plans on the e-file, because if 22 ... 🖹xc3 then 23 ♕f4! wins) 22 ... ♘xd5 23 ♕xf7+ ♔h8 24 ♘xg6+! (A simple and effective file opening sacrifice) 24 ... hxg6 25 🖹e4! **Black resigned.**

59 SMYSLOV–KARPOV
USSR Championship 1971

1 e4 c6 2 d4 d5 3 exd5 cxd5 4 c4 ♘f6 5 ♘c3 e6 6 ♘f3 ♗e7 7 cxd5 ♘xd5 8 ♗d3 ♘c6 9 0-0 0-0 10 🖹e1 ♘f6?! 11 a3! b6 12 ♗c2! ♗b7 13 ♕d3 🖹c8? 14

♗g5?! g6 15 ♖ad1 ♘d5 16 ♗h6 ♖e8 17 ♗a4! (Black is endangered on both sides) 17 . . . a6?! (He is making preparations for 18 . . . b5 but in so doing weakens b6. If 17 . . . ♘xc3 18 bxc3 ♗xa3 19 c4 ♗f8 20 ♕e3 or 20 ♗g5 White finishes up with a tremendous pressure for the pawn) 18 ♘xd5! ♕xd5 (Black is unsuspecting. 18 . . . exd5 would have been more circumspect) 19 ♕e3! (The point of White's scheme. 20 ♗b3 is threatened, followed by 21 d5!, with threats to the b6 pawn and the e-file) 19 . . . ♗f6?! (He is losing the ground from under his feet. The alternative 19 . . . ♕h5 20 d5! exd5 21 ♕xb6 would have offered more resistance, although even so Black's position would be rather miserable) 20 ♗b3 ♕h5 21 d5! (19 . . . ♗f6 was to no avail, Black cannot capture on d5 because of the mating threat on the eighth rank. The advance of the d-pawn refutes the text move) 21 . . . ♘d8 22 d6 ♖c5 (22 . . . ♗xf3 23 d7!) 23 d7 ♖e7?! (22 . . . ♖f8 and a sacrifice of the exchange gave relatively more) 24 ♕f4 (Gains a tempo for the breakthrough) 24 . . . ♗g7 25 ♕b8 ♕xh6 26 ♕xd8+ ♗f8 27 ♖e3! (Smyslov plays magnificently right through the game: the threat of ♕xf8+! will not run away, therefore he first prevents the dislocation of his pawn position) 27 . . . ♗c6 28 ♕xf8+! ♕xf8 29 d8=♕ **Black resigned.**

60 BELYAVSKY-PORTISCH
Reggio Emilia 1986/87

1 e4 c6 2 c4 d5 3 exd5 cxd5 4 cxd5 ♘f6 5 ♘c3 ♘xd5 6 ♘f3 e6 7 d4 ♗e7 8 ♗d3 ♘c6 9 0-0 0-0 10 ♖e1 ♗f6 11 ♗e4 ♕d6!? (An improvement in this position) 12 ♘b5? (Too early!) 12 . . . ♕b8 13 g3 (With the idea of 14 ♗xd5 exd5 15 ♗f4) 13 . . . ♗d7 14 ♘c3 (The attack is over) 14 . . . ♘ce7 15 ♗xd5 (15 ♘e5 ♗xe5 16 dxe5 ♗c6 17 ♕h5 f5! =) 15 . . . ♘xd5 16 ♘xd5 exd5 17 ♗g5 ♗xg5 18 ♘xg5 ♕d8 19 ♘f3 ♕b6 20 ♕d2?! (20 ♖e3 ♗g4 or 20 ♕b3 ♕xb3 21 axb3 ♗g4 are equal, or only a little better for Black) 20 . . . ♖fe8 21 ♘e5 ♗h3! (Black has a chance to attack White's king) 22 ♖e3? f6 23 ♖b3 (23 ♘f3 ♖xe3 24 fxe3 ∓) 23 . . . ♕a6! 24 ♘d3 g5!! (Not a nice move, but a very strong one. Portisch prevents White from occupying f4) 25 f3 (25 ♖a3 ♕e6 26 ♖e1 ♕g4 ∓; 25 ♘c5 ♕e2 26 ♕xe2 ♖xe2 27 ♘xb7 ♖ae8 28 ♖e3 ♖8xe3 29 fxe3 ♖xb2 ∓) 25 . . . ♖e7! 26 ♘f2 (26 g4 ♖ae8 27 ♘f2 ♖e2 28 ♕d1 ♕d6 with the idea of 29 . . . ♖xf2!) 26 . . . ♖e2! 27 ♕b4 ♖c8! **White resigned** (If 28 ♖c3, then 28 ♖ce8! wins; alternatively 28 ♕xb7 ♕e6 29 ♕b4 ♖xf2! 30 ♔xf2 ♖c2+ 31 ♔g1 ♕e2 32 ♕b8+ ♗c8 mates).

61 TAIMANOV-KARPOV
Moscow 1973

1 e4 c6 2 d4 d5 3 exd5 cxd5 4 c4 ♘f6 5 ♘c3 e6 6 ♘f3 ♗b4 7 ♗d3 dxc4 8 ♗xc4 0-0 9 0-0 b6 10 ♕e2 ♗b7 11 ♖d1?! ♘bd7 12 ♗d2 ♖c8 13 ♗a6?!

(In positions like this the exchange is not advantageous for White owing to his isolated pawn. He should instead concentrate on attack or keeping up the pressure. In any event there can be no question of advantage after 11 ♖d1) 13 ... ♗xa6 14 ♕xa6 ♗xc3! 15 bxc3 ♖c7! (With this Black equalizes. In the following White fails to recognize his opponent's subtle plan, and pins his hopes on a queenside initiative by means of c3-c4) 16 ♖ac1?! (16 ♗f4!=) 16 ... ♕c8 17 ♕a4 (Continuing the plan which began on move 13; 18 c4! threatens) 17 ... ♖c4! (A profound pawn sacrifice, in consequence of which Black immobilizes the pawns on c3 and d4, taking a grip on the game with this and the steady pressure on a2) 18 ♕xa7 ♕c6 19 ♕a3 ♖fc8 20 h3 h6 21 ♖b1 ♖a4 22 ♕b3 ♘d5 (We are witnessing a long positional manœuvre, where White is surrounded and has to wait patiently until he sees what his opponent intends. Taimanov solves this task well for a long time) 23 ♖dc1 ♖c4 24 ♖b2 (Exchanging the queens would have substantially altered the character of the position; 24 ♕b5 ♕xb5 25 ♖xb5 ♖a8 followed by f6-f5, e6-e5 and the king's march to the centre gives ample compensation for the loss of the pawn) 24 ... f6!? (Lodging his claim for the full point. White would happily have given his bad pawn away as after 24 ... ♘xc3 25 ♗xc3 ♖xc3 26 ♖xc3 chances are even) 25 ♖e1 ♔f7 26

♕d1 ♘f8 27 ♖b3 ♘g6 28 ♕b1 ♖a8 29 ♖e4 (29 ♕d3!? ♖xa2?! 30 ♖xe6! would have given counter-chances, but Black does not have to take the pawn) 29 ... ♖ca4 30 ♖b2 ♘f8 31 ♕d3 ♖c4 32 ♖e1 ♖a3 (32 ... ♘g6 33 ♖xe6!) 33 ♕b1 ♘g6 34 ♖c1?! (Returning the pawn is long overdue but it comes at an awkward moment. After 34 ♕d3! ♘xc3?? would lose because of 35 ♖b3!) 34 ... ♘xc3! 35 ♕d3 ♘e2+! 36 ♕xe2 ♖xc1+! 37 ♗xc1 ♕xc1+ 38 ♔h2?! The game is still very drawish after 38 ♘e1) 38 ... ♖xf3! (Considering the opponent's serious time-trouble, 38 ... ♘f4?! 39 ♕d2 gives excellent chances) 39 gxf3 ♘h4! and **White exceeded the time limit.** On 40 ♖xb6? ♕c7+ ∓, or 40 ♔g3 ♕g5+ ∓, or 40 ♖b3 ♕g5 41 ♕f1 ♕f4+ 42 ♔g1 ♘xf3+ ∓ etc. 40 d5! recommended by Gufeld, would still have given White some hope.

62   BENJAMIN–MILES
   USA Championship 1988
   1 e4 c6 2 d4 d5 3 exd5 cxd5 4 c4 ♘f6 5 ♘c3 e6 6 ♘f3 ♗b4 7 cxd5 ♘xd5 8 ♕c2 ♘c6 9 ♗e2 0-0 10 0-0 ♗e7 11 ♖d1 ♕d6 12 ♗g5! ♘xc3?! 13 bxc3 b6 14 ♕e4! ♗b7 15 ♗d3 g6 (15 ... f5 16 ♕e3 ±) 16 ♕h4 ♖fe8 17 ♖e1 ♖ac8 18 ♖e3 ♘d8 19 ♗b5 ♗c6 20 ♗a6 ♖a8? (20 ... ♖c7 is more active) 21 ♘e5 ♕d5 22 ♗f1 ♗xg5 23 ♕xg5 ♖c8 24 ♗c4 (24 ♖h3 ♖c7 25 ♕h6 f6 26 ♘xg6 ♖g7 27 ♘f4 +−) 24 ... ♕a5 (24 ... ♕d6 25 ♘g4; 24 ... f6 25 ♗xd5 fxg5 26 ♘xc6 +−) 25 ♖h3 ♖c7 26

♕h4 h5 27 g4! ♔g7 28 gxh5 ♖h8 29 ♕g5 (29 ♖g3! ♗b7 30 ♘xg6 fxg6 31 ♖xg6+♔h7 32 ♖h6+! ♔xh6 33 ♕f6+ ♔xh5 34 ♗e2+ mates) 29 ... ♗b7 30 ♖g3 ♖h6? 31 ♕xd8 ♖xc4 32 ♘xc4 ♕xh5 33 h3 ♕e2 34 ♕c7 ♕e4 35 ♕e5+ ♕xe5 36 ♘xe5 ♖h4 37 a4 ♖e4 38 ♖e3 ♖f4 39 a5 **Black resigned.**

10
1 e4 c6 2 d4 d5 Various

1 e4 c6 2 d4 d5

A: 3 ♘c3
B: 3 f3

3 ♘d2 has significance in itself, as it has tended to become a frequent path to the main variations after 3 . . . dxe4 4 ♘xe4. Its point is perhaps to avoid the in any case dubious **3 . . . b5?!** and in the event of 3 . . . g6 White has the opportunity of playing c2-c3, viz: **3 . . . g6** 4 ♗d3 *(4 ♘f3?! ♗g4 5 e5 e6 6 ♗e2 h5 7 ♘b3 ♗e7 8 0-0 ♘d7 9 a4 ♔f8 10 ♗d2 ♘h6 11 a5 ♘f5 ∞ Reshevsky-Ivanović, Skopje 1976 or 4 . . . ♗g7 5 h3 ♘h6?! 6 ♗e2 f6 7 0-0 ♘f7 8 ♖e1 0-0 9 c4! dxe4 10 ♘xe4 ♘d7*

11 c5 b6 12 ♗c4 ± Campora-Ioseliani, Biel 1990) 4 . . . ♗g7 5 c3 dxe4 *(5 . . . ♘h6 6 ♘gf3 0-0 7 0-0 f6 8 ♖e1 ♘f7 9 ♗c2! ♘a6 10 ♘f1 e5 11 dxe5 fxe5 12 h4! ± Darga-Ciocaltea, West Germany v Romania 1971, or 6 h4!? ♘d7! 7 ♘e2 ♘f6 8 ♘g3 dxe4 9 ♘dxe4 ♘xe4 10 ♘xe4 ♘f5 11 h5 ♘d6 12 ♘c5 b6 13 ♘e4 − Bareyev-Schneider, Naestved 1988 − 13 . . . ♗f5! 14 h6 ♗f8 15 ♘xd6+ ♕xd6 16 ♗xf5 gxf5 ∞) 6 ♘xe4 ♗f5 7 ♘c5 b6 8 ♘b3 ♗xd3 9 ♕xd3 ♘f6 10 ♘f3 0-0 11 0-0 ♕c7 12 ♖e1 ♖e8 13 ♘e5 ♘bd7 14 ♗f4 ±* Geller-Botvinnik, USSR 1967.

A

3 ♘c3   g6

The bizarre **3 . . . b5** ought to be examined here: 4 ♗d3! *(4 e5 e6 5 a3 a5 6 ♘ce2 ♗a6 7 ♘f4 b4 8 ♗xa6 ♘xa6 9 axb4 axb4 10 ♘f3 ♗e7 11 h4 h5 12 ♘g5 ♗xg5 13 hxg5 g6 14 g4 h4 15 ♗e3 ± Zaitsev-Gurgenidze, USSR 1968 or 4 a3 dxe4 5 ♘xe4 ♗f5 6 ♗d3!*

♗xe4?! 7 ♗xe4 ♘f6 8 ♗d3 **e6?!** 9 ♘f3
♗e7 10 ♕e2 ♘bd7 11 0-0 0-0 12 ♖e1
♖e8 13 ♘e5 ± *Tal-Gurgenidze, USSR
1968; better in this line is* **8 . . . ♕xd4**
9 ♘f3 ♕d5 10 0-0 ∞) 4 . . . dxe4 5 ♗xe4
(5 ♘xe4 ♕xd4 6 ♘f3 is also good) 5 . . .
♘f6 6 ♗f3 b4 7 ♘a4 ♗a6 8 ♘e2 ♗b5
9 ♘c5 ♘bd7 10 ♘d3 e6 11 0-0 ♘d5 12
♖e1 ♕f6 13 a3! bxa3 14 b3! ♗xd3 15
♕xd3 a2 16 ♗xd5! cxd5 17 ♘f4 ±
*Kupreichik-Bellon, Wijk aan Zee
1977.*

The gambit variation **3 . . . dxe4 4 f3**
lacks any substance: 4 . . . exf3 *(4 . . .
e3!?; 4 . . . e5 5 dxe5 ♕xd1+ 6 ♘xd1
exf3 ∓ Filip)* 5 ♘xf3 ♗f5 6 ♗c4 *(6 ♘e5
♘d7 7 ♕f3 e6 ∓)* 6 . . . e6 7 0-0 ♗e7
8 ♘e5 ♗g6 9 ♕f3 ♘f6 ∓ Gunderam.

Finally a continuation similar to,
but even more passive than, the main
variation is **3 . . . dxe4 4 ♘xe4** g6 5 ♘f3
♗g7 6 ♗c4 ♘f6 7 ♘xf6+ ♗xf6 *(7 . . .
exf6 8 0-0 0-0 9 ♖e1 ♗g4 10 c3 ±
Jansa-Sitiriche, Tel Aviv (ol) 1964)* 8 c3
*(8 ♗h6? ♕a5+! 9 c3 ♕h5 10 ♕d2
♗h3! 11 ♘e5 ♗xe5 ∓ Ageichenko-
Bunatian, USSR 1964)* 8 . . . 0-0 *(8 . . .*

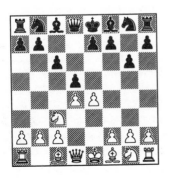

♗g7!?)* 9 ♗h6 ♗g7 *(9 . . . ♖e8 10 ♘g5
e6 11 h4 ±, analysis by Filip)* 10 ♕d2
♘d7 11 h4 ♘f6 12 h5 ± *Sherwin-
Denker, New York 1968.*

4 ♘f3   . . .

The simplest strategy. After the
exchange of the e4 pawn, White
finishes up with an advantage in space
because of the passive g7 bishop.
Other continuations from competition practice are **4 e5** *(4 ♗e3 ♗g7
5 ♕d2 ♘f6 6 e5 ♘g4 7 ♗f4 f6 8 exf6
♘xf6 9 0-0-0 0-0 10 f3 ♘bd7 11 h4
♘h5 12 ♗h2 e5! 13 g4?! exd4! ∓
Teufel-Czerniak, Biel 1975; **4 f4** dxe4
5 ♘xe4 ♗f5 — 5 . . . ♘f6!? 6 ♘xf6+exf6
7 ♗c4 ♗d6 ∞ — 6 ♘g3 ♘f6?! 7 ♘xf5
gxf5 8 ♘f3 e6∞/±)* 4 . . . ♗g7 *(4 . . . h5 5
f4 ♘h6 6 ♘f3 ♗g4 7 ♗e3 ♘f5 8 ♗f2 e6
9 ♗e2 ♗e7 ∓ Velimirovic-Ciocaltea,
Budapest 1973; 5 ♗e2 ♘h6 6 ♘f3 — 6
h3 ♘f5 7 ♘f3 ± — 6 . . . ♗g4 7 ♗g5
♕a5 8 h3 ♗xf3 9 ♗xf3 ♘f5 10 g4 hxg4
11 hxg4 ♖xh1+12 ♗xh1 ♘g7 13 ♕f3
♘e6 14 ♗e3 ♘d7 = Sax-Kosanski,
Osijek 1978)* 5 f4 *(5 h3 ♘h6 6 ♘f3 f6! 7
♗f4 0-0 8 ♕d2 ♘f7 9 0-0-0 —
Czerniak-Hernando, Biel 1975 — 9 . . .
♘a6! 10 g4 ♘c7 ∞)* and now:
a) **5 . . . ♘h6**
a1) **6 h3** b6! 7 ♘f3 ♘f5 8 ♘e2 h5
9 g3 ♗a6 10 ♖g1 e6 11 g4 ♘h4 12 ♘g5
♕e7 ∓ *Ehlvest-Titov, Minsk 1986.*

a2) **6 ♗e2** f6! 7 ♘f3 ♗g4 8 ♗e3
0-0 9 0-0 ♘f5 10 ♗f2 ♗xf3 11 ♗xf3
fxe5 12 dxe5 e6 = *Sveshnikov-
Yurtayev, USSR 1983.*

a3) **6 ♘f3 ♗g4** *(6 ... 0-0 7 ♗e3 ♗g4 8 ♗e2 f6 9 0-0 **fxe5** 10 fxe5 ♗xf3 11 ♗xf3 e6 12 ♘e2 ♘f5 13 ♗f2 ♕e7 14 c3 ♘d7 15 a4 c5 16 a5 ± Anand-Kantsler, Frunze 1987 or 9 ... ♘f5!? 10 ♗f2 ♗xf3 11 ♗xf3 fxe5 12 dxe5 e6 13 ♘e2 ♘d7 14 ♗g4 ♕e7 15 ♘d4 ♘xd4 16 ♕xd4 − Sveshnikov-Stanciu, Bucharest 1975 − 16 ... c5! ∞)* 7 h3 ♗xf3 8 ♕xf3 ♕b6 *(8 ... f6?! 9 g4 fxe5 10 fxe5 e6 11 h4 ♖f8 12 ♕h3 ♕b6 13 ♘e2 ± Lanka-Yuferov, Sochi 1978; 8 ... ♘f5?! 9 ♘e2 ♕b6 10 c3 e6 11 g4 ♘e7 12 ♘g3 f5 − Kupreichik-Sveshnikov, USSR 1974 − 13 exf6! ♗xf6 14 ♗d3 ±)* 9 ♘e2 f6 10 g4 fxe5 11 dxe5 ♘a6 12 ♗g2 0-0-0 13 ♗e3 d4 14 ♗f2 ±.

b) **5 ... h5 6 ♘f3** *(6 ♗e3 ♘h6 7 ♘f3 ♗g4 8 ♗e2 ♘d7 9 ♕d2 e6 10 g3 ♗f8 11 h3 ♗xf3 12 ♗xf3 ♘f5 13 ♗f2 **b5?!** 14 ♔f1 ♕a5 15 ♔g2 ♘b6 16 g4 ♘c4 17 ♕e1 hxg4 18 hxg4 ♖xh1 19 ♔xh1 ♘g7 20 a4! ± Marjanović-Trois, Zemun 1983 or 13 ... **h4!?** 14 g4 ♘g3 15 ♖g1 ♕b6! 16 0-0-0 ♕a6 17 ♕d3 ♕xd3 18 ♖xd3 c5! 19 ♘b5 c4 20 ♖dd1 ♖c8+ = Arnason-Christiansen, Reykjavik 1986; 7 **h3** ♘f5?! − 7 ... b6 and ♗a6 = Filip − 8 ♗f2 b5 9 ♗d3 e6 − 9 ... b4! 10 ♘ce2 ♗a6 11 ♘f3 ♗xd3 12 cxd3! ± Lepeshkin − 10 ♘f3 h4 11 0-0 ♗f8 12 ♕e1 ♗e7 13 ♘d1 a5 14 ♘e3 ♘d7 15 c3 a4 16 ♖c1 ♘b6 17 ♘g4± Honfi-Stanciu, Bucharest 1975)* 6 ... ♘h6 *(6 ... ♗g4 7 h3 ♗xf3 8 ♕xf3 e6 9 **g3** ♕b6 10 ♕f2 ♘e7 11 ♗d3 ♘d7 12 ♘e2 − 12 ♗d2 ♘f5 13 ♗xf5 gxf5 14 0-0-0 ± Fischer − 12 ... 0-0-0 13 c3 f6 14 b3 ♘f5* 15 ♖g1 c5 16 ♗xf5 gxf5 17 ♗e3 ♕a6 18 ♔f1 cxd4 = Fischer-Petrosian, Belgrade 1970; 9 ♗e3 h4 10 ♗d3 ♘e7 11 0-0 ♘d7 12 ♘e2 ♘f5 13 ♗f2 a5 14 b3 a4 15 c4 axb3 16 axb3 ♘b6 17 c5 ♘d7 ± Sokolov-Lerner, USSR 1983) 7 ♗e3 ♗g4 *(7 ... **b5** 8 ♗d3 a5 9 ♘e2 ♘a6 10 a3 ♗f5 11 ♘g3 ♗xd3 12 ♕xd3 e6 =; 7 ... **♕b6** 8 ♘a4 ♕a5+ 9 c3 ♗g4 10 ♘c5 ♘d7 11 ♘b3 ♕c7 12 h3 ♘f5 13 ♗f2 ♗xf3 14 ♕xf3 h4 15 ♗d3 e6 = Peters-Kavalek 1984 or 8 ... **♕c7** 9 ♗f2 ♗f5 10 h3 ♘d7 11 ♕d2 b5 12 ♘c3 a5 13 ♗e2 a4 14 0-0 0-0 15 ♘h4 ♘b6 16 b3 ± Mestel-Murshed, Great Britain (ch) 1988)* and now:

b1) **8 h3** *(8 ♗d3 ♘f5 9 ♗f2 e6 10 h3 ♗xf3 11 ♕xf3 ♘h4 12 ♕g3 ♘f5 13 ♕f3 ♘h4 14 ♗xh4 ♕xh4+ 15 g3 ± Anand-Blatny, Baguio City 1987)* 8 ... ♗xf3 *(8 ... ♘f5 9 ♗f2 ♗xf3 10 ♕xf3 h4 11 ♗d3 e6 12 0-0 ♘e7 13 ♘e2 ± Gagarin-Lubimov, USSR 1985)* 9 ♕xf3 h4 *(9 ... ♕b6 10 ♖b1 ♘f5 11 ♗f2 ♘xd4 12 ♕d3 ± Sokolov)* 10 ♗d3 e6 11 0-0 ♗f8 12 ♘e2 ♘d7 13 b3 ♘f5 14 ♗f2 ± Sokolov-Sere, Thessalonika (ol) 1984.

b2) **8 ♗e2** e6 9 ♕d3 *(9 ♕d2 ♘f5 10 ♗f2 ♗f8 11 ♘d1 ♘d7 12 ♘e3 ♗e7 13 ♘xf5 ♗xf5 14 0-0 ♔f8 15 b3 b5 16 c4 bxc4 17 bxc4 ♔g7 18 c5 ± Malanyuk-Glanez, USSR 1985; for 9 ... **♘d7!** 10 g3 ♘f5 11 ♗f2 ♗f8 12 h3 see 6 ♗e3 ♘h6 7 ♘f3 ♗g4 8 ♗e2 ♘d7)* 9 ... ♘f5 10 ♗f2 ♕a5 10 ... ♘d7 11 g3 ♗f8 12 h3 ♗xf3 13 ♗xf3 c5 was Aseyev-Titov, Kostroma 1985) 11 0-0 ♘h6 12 g3 *(12 ♘g5? ♗xe2 13 ♘xe2*

♘d7 ∓) 12 ... ♘d7 13 ♔g2 0-0-0 14
♘d1!? *(14 h3 ♗xf3 15 ♗xf3 ♗f8!)* 14
... h4! 15 ♘xh4 ♘xh4+ 16 gxh4 ♗f5
17 ♕e3 ♗xc2 ∓ Chernin-Ivanov,
New York 1988.

4 ...   ♗g7

To be considered is 4 ... ♗g4, e.g.:
5 ♗e3!? ♕b6 6 ♕d2 ♗xf3 *(6... ♘f6 7
e5 ♘e4 8 ♘xe4 dxe4 9 ♘g5 ♕xb2 10
♖c1 ♕xa2 11 ♘xe4 ⯑ Vogt)* 7 gxf3 e6
8 h4? Vogt-Ivanović, Naleczow 1979,
and now Vogt gives 8 ... ♕xb2 9 ♖b1
♕a3 10 h5 *(If 10 ♖xb7 ♗b4−+)* 10 ...
gxh5; alternatively 5 h3 ♗xf3 6 ♕xf3
e6 7 ♗f4 ♘d7 8 0-0-0 ♘gf6 9 exd5
(9 e5!?) 9 ... ♘xd5 10 ♘xd5 cxd5 11
♕b3 ♕b6 12 ♗b5 ♗d6 13 ♗xd7+
♖xd7 14 ♕f3 ± Ljubojevic-Epishin,
Reggio Emilia 1991.

5 h3   ...

5 ♗e2 ♗g4 6 0-0!? dxe4 7 ♘xe4
♗xf3?! 8 ♗xf3 ♕xd4 9 ♕e2 ♘d7 10
♖d1 ♕e5 11 ♗d2! ♕c7 12 ♘d6+!
♔f8 13 ♗f4 e5 ∞ Treybal-Prybl,
Czechoslovakia 1976 or 5 ♗f4 ♗g4 6
exd5! cxd5 7 ♘b5 **♘a6?** 8 h3 ♗xf3 9
♕xf3 ♘f6 10 ♗d3 0-0 11 c3 ♘e8 12
0-0 e6 13 ♕g3 ± Krinić-Notaroe, Krk
1976; better is **7 ... ♔f8!** 8 h3 ♗xf3 9
♕xf3 ♘c6 10 c3 ♖c8 11 ♗d3 a6 12
♘a3 ♘f6 13 0-0 h5 14 ♘c2 h4! =
Budde-Pachman, Berlin 1983.

A1

5 ...   dxe4

Instead **5 ... ♘h6!?** is much more
risky: 6 ♗e2 *(6 g4!? dxe4 7 ♘xe4 f5
8 ♘eg5! fxg4 9 hxg4 ♗xg4 10 ♗c4! ±;
6 ... f6 7 g5 ♘f7 8 gxf6 exf6 9 exd5!
cxd5 10 ♕e2+! ± Tseitlin or 6 ♗f4
dxe4 7 ♘xe4 ♘f5 8 c3 0-0 9 ♗d3 b6 10
0-0 ♗b7 11 ♖e1 ± Ničevski-Notaros,
Yugoslavia 1973; 6 ... f6 7 exd5! cxd5
8 ♘b5 − 8 ♗xb8!? ♖xb8 9 ♗b5+ ♔f7!
10 ♕e2 e6 11 g4 a6 12 ♗d3 ♕d6 13 g5
± Barlov-Gaprindashvili, Palma de
Mallorca 1989 − 8 ... 0-0 − 8 ... ♘a6 9
c4 0-0 10 cxd5 ♕xd5 11 ♘c3 ♕f7
Grünfeld-Gaprindshvili, Palma de
Mallorca 1989 12 ♗e2 ± − 9 c4 g5?! 10
♗c7! ♕d7 11 ♗h2 Velimirovic-
Ciocaltea, Reykjavik 1976; 6 ... ♕b6
7 ♕d2 dxe4 8 ♘a4 ♕d8 9 ♗xh6 ♗xh6
10 ♕xh6 exf3 11 0-0-0 ± Zhuravlev-
Tseitlin, USSR 1972 or finally 6 e5 f6
7 ♗f4 0-0 8 ♕d2 ♘f7 9 0-0-0 b6 10
♖e1 a5 11 ♗d3 ± Tseitlin-Bukhman,
USSR 1967)* 6 ... 0-0 7 0-0 f6!? 8 ♖e1
♘f7 9 ♗f1 b6 10 b3 *(10 exd5 cxd5 11
♗f4)* 10 ... e6 11 a4 ♖e8 12 ♗a3 a6 ±
Honfi-Clemens, Solingen 1974.

6 ♘xe4   ♘d7

Or:

a) 6 ... ♘f6?! 7 ♘xf6+ exf6 (7 ...
♗xf6? 8 ♗c4 ♗f5 9 0-0 ♘d7 10 ♖e1
♘b6 11 ♗b3 h5 12 ♘e5 ± Najdorf-
Rossetto, Argentina 1973)8 ♗d3 0-0
9 0-0 ♘d7 10 ♗f4 ♖e8 11 ♕d2 ♘f8 12
♖fe1 ♘e6 13 ♗h6 Panchenko-
Gofstein, USSR 1976, 13 ... ♕d6 ±.
b) 6 ... ♗f5 7 ♘g3 ♘f6 (7 ... ♘d7
8 ♗c4 ♘gf6 9 ♕e2 e6 10 ♗b3±
Johansson-Botvinnik, Varna (ol)
1962) 8♘xf5 gxf5 9 ♗d3 e6 10 ♕e2 c5
(10 ... 0-0? 11 g4!) 11 dxc5 (11 ♗xf5 ±)
11 ... ♕a5+ Šahović-Botvinnik,
Belgrade 1969, 12 c3 ♕xc5 13 ♗e3 ±.

7 ♗c4   ...

7 ♗d3 ♘gf6 8 ♘xf6+ (8 ♕e2 ♘xe4
9 ♕xe4 ♘f6 = Bellon-Larsen,
Torremolinos 1978; 8 0-0 ♘xe4 9 ♗xe4
0-0 10 ♗g5 ♖e8 — 10 ... h6 see A2 —
11 c3 ♕b6 12 ♕d2 ♘f8 13 ♖ad1 ♗e6
14 b3 ♗d5 15 ♖fe1 f6 16 ♗h6 ♖ad8 17
♗xg7 ♔xg7 18 c4 ♗f7 19 h4 e5 = de
Firmian-Seirawan, Wijk aan Zee 1986)
8 ... ♘xf6 9 0-0 0-0 10 c4!? (10 ♖e1
♕d6!? 11 ♗g5! c5 12 ♕e2 e6 13 dxc5
♕xc5 14 ♗e3 ♕c7 15 ♗d4 b6 16 a4 ±
Kottnauer-Hübner, Hastings 1968/69)
10 ... c5 11 dxc5 ♘d7 12 ♗e3 ♗xb2 13
♖b1 ♗g7 14 ♗e4 ♕c7 15 c6 bxc6 16
♕a4 ♘b8 = Velimirovic-Duric,
Yugoslavia (ch) 1988.

7 ...   ♘gf6
8 ♘xf6+   ...

8 ♕e2 ♘xe4 9 ♕xe4 ♘b6 10 ♗b3
a5 11 a4 ♗f5 12 ♕h4 ♕d7 Keres-
Donner, Amsterdam 1971, 13 ♗h6! ±
(13 ... ♗xh6? 14 ♗xf7+ +—).

8 ...   ♘xf6
9 0-0   0-0
10 ♖e1   ♗f5

10 ... b6 11 ♗g5 ♗b7 12 ♕e2 e6
13 ♘e5 ♕d6 14 ♗b3 h6 15 ♗h4
± Ghizdavu-Spiridonov, Bucharest
1971, or 10 ... a5?! 11 ♘e5! e6 12 ♗b3
♘d7 13 ♗f4 ± Korostensky-
Pachman, Sekunda 1989.

11 ♗b3   ...

11 ♘e5 ♗e4 12 ♗g5 ♗d5 13 ♗d3
♗e6 14 c3 ♘d7 15 ♘f3 ± Tal-
Kolarov, Kapfenberg 1970.

11 ...   ♕d6
12 ♕e2   ♖ae8
13 c3   ♘d5
14 ♘e5   ...

Black's position is lack-lustre. In a
Balashov-Petrosian   game   (USSR
(ch) 1976) 14 ... ♕d8 15 ♗d2 ♔h8 was
played, and according to Balashov
16 c4! ♘f6 17 ♗c3 ♘d7 18 ♘f3 would
now have given a lasting advantage to
White.

A2

5 ...   ♘f6

6 e5   . . .

Quite often, the move 6 ♗d3 is played: 6 . . . dxe4 7 ♘xe4 ♘xe4 8 ♗xe4 0-0 *(8 . . . ♗f5 9 ♗xf5 ♕a5+ 10 c3 ♕xf5 11 0-0 ♘d7 12 ♖e1 e6 13 ♕b3 b6 14 ♕a3 ± Lobron-Grünfeld, Lucerne 1979)* 9 0-0 ♘d7 and now:

a) **10 ♖e1** c5 11 c3 cxd4 12 ♘xd4 *(12 cxd4 ♘f6 13 ♗c2 b6 =)* 12 . . . ♘c5 13 ♗c2 e5 14 ♘b3 ♕c7 15 ♘xc5 ♕xc5 16 ♗b3 ± Gipslis-Zaichik, USSR 1977.

b) **10 c3** c5 11 ♗g5 h6 12 ♗f4 cxd4 13 cxd4 ♘f6 14 ♗c2 ♗e6 15 ♕d2 ♗d5 = Kudrin-Dzhindzhihashvili, USA (ch) 1984.

c) **10 ♗g5** h6 *(10 . . . ♖e8 see A1)* 11 ♗e3 ♕c7 *(11 . . . c5 12 dxc5 ♕c7 13 ♕e2 ♖b8 — 13 . . . ♘xc5 14 ♕c4 ♘e6 15 ♕xc7 ♘xc7 16 c3 ± — 14 ♕b5 ♘f6 15 ♗b3 — Chandler-Christiansen, Thessaloniki (ol) 1984 — 15 . . . ♘d5!∞)* 12 ♕c1 ♔h7 13 ♗f4 ♕a5 14 c3 ♘f6 15 ♗c2 ♗f5 16 ♖e1! ♗xc2 17 ♕xc2 e6 18 ♗e5 ♖fd8 19 a4 (Barlov-Dzhindzhihashvili, New York 1987) 19 . . . ♖d7! ±.

6 . . .   ♘e4
7 ♘xe4   . . .

7 ♗d3 ♘xc3 8 bxc3 c5 and now:

a) **9 dxc5** 0-0! *(9 . . . ♕a5 10 0-0 0-0 11 ♗e3 ♘d7 12 c4 ± Gheorghiu-Cardoso, Torremolinos 1974; 10 . . . ♕xc5 11 ♖b1!?)* 10 ♗e3 ♘d7 11 ♗d4 ♕c7 12 0-0?! *(12 ♕e2 =)* 12 . . . ♘xe5 13 ♘xe5 ♗xe5 14 ♕e2 ♗h2+! 15 ♔h1 e5! 16 ♗e3 (Chandler-Gufeld, Hastings 1986/87) 16 . . . ♗f4 ∓.

b) **9 0-0** c4 10 ♗e2 ♕a5 11 ♕d2! *(11 ♗d2?! f6! = Popovic-Ehlvest, Vrsac 1987)* 11 . . . ♕a4 *(If 11 . . . f6, then 12 a4! and ♗a3)* 12 ♘h4! ♘c6 13 f4 f5 14 g4 ± Bohosian-Spiridonov, Bulgaria (ch) 1975.

7 . . .   dxe4
8 ♘g5   c5
9 ♗c4!   . . .

Others:

a) **9 e6** ♗xe6 10 ♘xe6 fxe6 11 dxc5 ♕xd1+ *(11 . . . ♕a5+!?)* 12 ♔xd1 0-0 ± Timoshchenko-Machulsky, USSR 1974.

b) **9 dxc5** ♕a5+! 10 ♗d2 ♕xc5 11 ♗c3 ♘c6 12 ♘xe4 ♕b6 13 ♗c4 0-0 14 0-0 ♗xe5 15 ♗xe5 ♘xe5 16 ♗b3 ♗e6 = Dvoretsky-Silberstein, USSR 1973.

9 . . .   0-0
10 c3!?   . . .

10 e6 f6 11 ♘xe4 b5! 12 ♗e2 *(12 ♗xb5? ♕a5+ 13 ♘c3 cxd4 with*

advantage to Black) 12 ... cxd4 13 ♗f3 ♘c6 14 0-0 ♕b6 = Spassky-Tseshkovsky, USSR 1974.

10 ...	cxd4
11 cxd4	♘c6

11 ... b5?! 12 ♗b3 ♗b7 13 h4! ♗d5 *(13 ... h6 14 h5! hxg5 15 hxg6 wins; 13 ... ♘c6 14 ♗e3 ♕a5+ 15 ♔f1 ♖ad8 16 h5! ♘xe5 17 ♘xh7! +—)* 14 h5 ♗xb3 15 axb3 ♕d5 *(15 ... ♕c8!?)* 16 hxg6 hxg6 17 ♕g4! ♖d8 *(17 ... ♕xd4 18 ♖h8+!! mating)* 18 e6 +— Chudinovsky-Nogovitsin, USSR 1988.

12 ♗e3	♘a5

12 ... ♕a5+?! 13 ♔f1! is good for White.

13 ♗b3	...

13 ♗e2?! ♕d5 14 ♕c2 ♗f5 15 g4 ♖ac8 with reasonable chances for both sides.

13 ...	♘xb3
14 ♕xb3	...

The critical position:
a) 14 ... ♕a5+ 15 ♗d2 ♕a6 16 ♕e3! ±.
b) 14 ... h6 15 ♘xe4 ♗e6 16 ♕a3 ♗d5 17 f3 *(17 ♕d3 ♕b6!?)* 17 ... f6 18 exf6 exf6 19 0-0 ♖e8 ∞.
c) 14 ... b6 15 ♘xe4 ♗e6! 16 ♕a3 ♗d5 17 f3 f6 ∞.

B

3 f3	...

White bolsters his centre pawn and prepares a complicated and sharp line involving a pawn sacrifice.

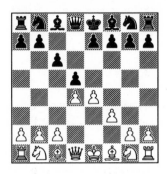

B1: 3 ... g6
B2: 3 ... e6

After **3 ... ♘f6** White can switch to the French Defence via 4 e5 ♘fd7 5 f4 e6, but could also play 4 ♘c3 dxe4 *(4 ... e6!?)* 5 fxe4 e5 6 ♘f3 exd4 7 ♘xd4 *(7 ... ♗g4 8 ♕d3 ♘a6? 9 ♘xc6! ± Ozsváth-Popov, Bulgaria 1971; 8 ... ♘bd7 ∞)*.

Instead **3 ... dxe4** is an interesting continuation. 4 fxe4 e5!? 5 ♘f3 ♗e6! *(5 ... exd4 6 ♗c4 ♗e7 7 e5! ♕a5+ 8 c3 dxc3 9 ♘xc3 ♗g4 10 ♕b3 ♗xf3 11 ♗xf7+ ♔f8 12 0-0 Ozsváth-M. Kovács, Budapest 1963 or 5 ... ♗g4 6 ♗c4 ♗h5?! 7 g4! ♗g6 8 ♘xe5 ♘d7 9 ♘xg6 hxg6 10 0-0 ± Ozsváth-Scholl, Budapest 1969)* 6 c3 ♘f6 7 ♗d3 ♘bd7

8 0-0 ♗d6 9 ♘bd2 *(9 ♔h1 ♕e7! 10 ♗e3 ♗c7 11 ♘bd2 0-0 12 ♗g5 h6 13 ♗h4 ♖ae8! 14 ♕e1 ♕d8! ∓ Ozsváth-Barcza, Budapest 1969)* 9 . . . 0-0 10 ♕e1 ♖e8 11 ♗c4 b5 12 ♗xe6 ♖xe6 13 ♔h1 ∞ Ozsváth-Flesch, Budapest 1967.

B1

    3 . . .   **g6**
    4 ♘c3   **. . .**

White can play e5 now or on his next move. Black can retaliate with . . . h5 and . . . ♘h6, with a tempo advantage compared with variation A (the f-pawn gets to f4 in two moves), but he can also try . . . c5 and . . . f6.

    4 . . .   **♗g7**
    5 ♗e3   **dxe4**

5 . . . ♕b6 6 ♕d2! ♕xb2 7 ♖b1 ♕a3 8 exd5 ♘f6 9 dxc6 bxc6 10 ♗c4 0-0 11 ♘ge2 ♘bd7 12 ♗b3 ♗a6 13 0-0 e5 14 ♖fd1 ± Hodgson–Fuller, Novi Sad 1990.

    6 fxe4   **♘f6**
    7 ♘f3   **. . .**

7 ♗e2!? ♕a5!? 8 ♗f3 ♘bd7 9 ♘ge2 e5 10 0-0 exd4 11 ♘xd4 ♘e5 12 ♘b3 ♕c7 13 ♗f4 0-0 14 ♗e2 ♕e7 15 h3 ± Ozsváth–Csom, Budapest 1968.

    7 . . .   **0-0!?**

Or 7 . . . ♘g4?! 8 ♗f4?! e5! 9 dxe5 ♕xd1+ 10 ♖xd1 ♘bd7 11 e6! fxe6 12 ♗c4 ♘de5 13 ♘xe5 ♗xe5 14 ♗g5? 0-0 15 ♗e7? ♖e8 16 ♗c5 Ozsváth-Flesch, Budapest 1967 and now 16 . . . ♗xh2 is very strong. 7 . . . b5 8 ♗d3 0-0 9 h3 ♗b7 10 ♕d2 ♘a6 11 a3 ± Hazai-Vadász, Budapest 1976.

    8 ♗d3   **. . .**

a) **8 h3!?** ♘h5!? *(8 . . . b5?! 9 ♗d3 ♘bd7 10 0-0 a6 11 ♕e1 ♗b7 12 ♕h4 c5 13 d5 c4 14 ♗e2 e6 15 dxe6 fxe6 16 ♘g5 ± Ozsváth-Haág, Budapest 1967)* 9 ♗d3 *(9 ♗c4?! b5 10 ♗b3?! ♘g3! 11 ♖g11 b4 ∓)* 9 . . . ♘g3 10 ♖g1 f5 ∞.

b) **8 ♗e2** ♘g4 9 ♗f4 e5! 10 dxe5 ♕b6 11 ♕d4 ♕xd4 12 ♘xd4 ♘xe5 13 0-0-0 ♘bd7 14 ♖d2 ♘c5 15 ♖hd1 ♖e8 ∓ Horváth-Varnusz, Budapest 1991.

    8 . . .   **♘g4!**
    9 ♕e2   **. . .**

9 ♗g1 e5! 10 d5 cxd5 11 ♘xd5 ♘c6 12 h3 ♘f6 13 ♗c5 ♖e8 14 ♘c3 ♕a5 15 ♗e3 ♘b4 ∓ Ozsváth-Varnusz, Budapest 1968.

    9 . . .   **♘xe3**
    10 ♕xe3   **♕b6**
    11 0-0-0   **e5**
    12 ♗c4   **♗g4**

Black has a comfortable game, Dr Nagy-Varnusz, Budapest 1974.

B2

3 ...	e6
4 ♗e3	...

Or:

a) 4 ♘d2 dxe4 5 ♘xe4 ♘f6 6 ♗g5 ♘bd7 7 ♕d2 ♗e7 8 ♘xf6+ ♗xf6 = Jimenez-Barcza, Havana 1963.

b) 4 ♘c3 ♗b4 *(4... ♘f6 5 e5 ♘fd7 6 f4 e6 leads to the French Defence, and 5 ♗e3 to variations examined shortly. Alternatively 5 ♗g5 h6 6 ♗h4 ♕b6 7 a3 c5 8 ♘ge2 ♘c6 9 dxc5 ♗xc5 10 ♘a4 ♕a5+ 11 ♘ec3 ♗e7 12 ♗xf6 ♗xf6 13 exd5 ♘d4 ∞ was Smyslov-Botvinnik, USSR (m) 1958) 5 ♗e3 (5 ♗d3 dxe4 6 ♗xe4 = Kasparov-Sakharov, USSR 1979, or 5 ♗f4 ♘f6 6 ♕d3 b6 7 ♘ge2 ♗a6 8 ♕e3 0-0 9 0-0-0 ♘bd7 10 h3 ♖c8 11 a3 ♗xc3 12 ♘xc3 ♗xf1 13 ♖hxf1 b5 14 ♗d6 ♖e8 15 e5 ± Murey-Saidy, New York 1989 or 9 ... ♗e7 10 g4!? b5 − 10 ... dxe4 11 fxe4 ♘xg4 12 ♕f3 ♘f6 13 ♖g1 ∞ − 11 ♘g3 b4 12 ♘ce2 ♗c4 ∞ T Wall-Hodgson, Great Britain (ch) 1990) 5 ... dxe4 6 a3 ♗xc3+ 7 bxc3 ♕a5 8 ♗d2 =* Tartakower-Flohr, Kemeri 1937.

4 ...	dxe4?

Four pawn moves in order to win one pawn is mortally dangerous in the opening. 4 ... ♕b6?! 5 ♘d2 ♘d7 6 ♗d3 c5 7 c3 c4?! 8 ♗c2 ♕xb2 9 ♘e2 ♕a3 10 0-0 ♘b6 11 exd5 exd5 12 ♖fe1 ♗d7 13 ♘f1 0-0-0 14 ♗c1! ♕a5 15 a4 was also risky, because White gains

the initiative in exchange for the pawn as happened in Smyslov-Makogonov, USSR 1944.

Maybe **4 ... ♘f6!** is best: 5 ♘c3 ♕b6 *(5 ... dxe4 6 fxe4 ♗b4 7 ♗d3 ♘xe4!? 8 ♘ge2 ♘f6 9 0-0 e5 10 ♗g5 ♗e7 11 ♕e1 ♘g4 12 ♗xe7 ♕xe7 13 ♕g3 exd4 14 ♘e4 0-0 15 h3 ♘h6 16 ♘xd4 f5 17 ♘d6 ± Ozsváth-Barcza, Budapest 1968 or 5 ... ♗b4 6 e5 ♘g8 7 f4 h5 8 ♘f3 ♘h6 9 ♗d3 g6 10 0-0 b6 ± Ozsváth-Tipary, Budapest 1965)* 6 ♖b1?! *(6 a3!? Ozsváth)* 6 ... c5 7 exd5 exd5 8 ♗b5+ ♘c6 = Filip.

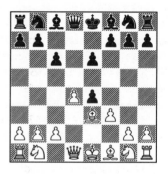

5 ♘d2!	...

Not 5 fxe4? ♕h4+!

5 ...	exf3?!

This opens the way for the ultra-rapid development of White's pieces, made additionally dangerous by the open f-file.

6 ♘gxf3	♘f6

7 ♘c4 ...

Instead 7 ♘e5 ♘bd7 8 ♕f3 ♗d6! ∓ *(planning 9 ♘dc4? ♘xe5 10 dxe5 ♗xe5 −+)* Mariasin-Sakharov, USSR 1979.

The text move was successful in the illustrative game Smyslov-Gereben which follows.

ILLUSTRATIVE GAMES

63 CHUDINOVSKY-NOGOVITSIN
USSR 1988

1 e4 c6 2 d4 d5 3 ♘c3 g6 4 ♘f3 ♗g7 5 h3 ♘f6 6 e5 ♘e4 7 ♘xe4 dxe4 8 ♘g5 c5 9 ♗c4 0-0 10 c3 cxd4 11 cxd4 b5?! 12 ♗b3 ♗b7 13 h4 ♗d5 14 h5 ♗xb3 15 axb3 ♕d5 16 hxg6 hxg6 17 ♕g4! ♖d8 18 e6 f5 (18 . . . f6 19 ♕h4 ♕xd4 − 19 . . . ♕f5 20 g4 − 20 ♕h7+ ♔f8 21 ♗e3 ♗b4+ 22 ♔f1 ♕xb3 23 g3 +−; 18 . . . fxe6 19 ♕h4 ♕f5 20 ♕h7+ ♔f8 21 ♖h4 e5 22 g4 ♕f6 23 dxe5 +−) 19 ♖h8+!! (A devastating riposte!) 19 . . . ♗xh8 20 ♕h4 ♗g7 21 ♕h7+ ♔f8 22 ♕xg6 ♔g8 23 ♗e3 ♕xb3 24 ♕h7+ ♔f8 25 ♕xf5+ ♔g8 26 ♕h7+ ♔f8 27 ♕g6 ♔g8 28 ♖c1! (With the idea of 29 ♖c5!) 28 . . . ♘a6 29 ♖c3

♕xb2 30 ♗d2 ♕a1+ 31 ♔e2 ♕xc3 32 ♗xc3 ♖dc8 33 ♗d2 ♖c2 34 ♕f7+ ♔h8 35 ♕xe7 ♘c7 36 ♕d7 b4 37 e7 b3 38 ♕h3+ **Black resigned.**

64 SMYSLOV-GEREBEN
Moscow–Budapest 1949

1 e4 c6 2 d4 d5 3 f3 e6 4 ♗e3 dxe4? 5 ♘d2! exf3?! 6 ♘gxf3 ♘f6 7 ♘c4 ♘d5?! 8 ♗d2 ♗e7 9 ♗d3 ♗h4+? (Losing time again) 10 g3 ♗f6 11 ♕e2 a5 (Black expects queenside castling) 12 a3 0-0 13 h4! (There is no need to castle long. 14 ♗xh7+ is threatened, therefore Black is forced to make way for his knight to return to f6) 13 . . . ♗e7 14 ♘g5 ♘f6 15 ♘e5 b5 (Black still expects White to castle queenside, but in any case, what else can he do? 15 . . . ♕xd4 16 ♗c3 is even worse) 16 ♖f1! h6 17 ♖xf6!! gxf6 (17 . . . ♗xf6 18 ♗h7+! ♔h8 19 ♘xf7+ would lose the queen, while 17 . . . hxg5 18 ♕h5 g6 19 ♗xg6 fxg6 20 ♖xg6 is mate!) 18 ♕h5 fxg5 19 ♕xh6 f5 20 ♕g6+ ♔h8 21 hxg5! (Opening the h-file. The threat is 22 ♔e2 or 22 0-0-0, and 21 . . . ♕e8 would be answered by 22 ♕h6+ ♔g8 23 g6) 21 . . . ♗xa3 22 ♔e2! ♕d5 23 ♘f3 (Fatal blocking of the file!) **Black resigned.**

11
Two Knights Variation
1 e4 c6 2 ♘c3 d5 3 ♘f3

The advantage of the Two Knights variation is that White delays the decision regarding his d-pawn, and the position is therefore more flexible. Its drawback is that the Caro-Kann bishop can develop comfortably without Black having to commit himself in the centre.

This variation had its heyday from about 1940 up to the sixties. Competition practice showed, however, that Black had good chances of equalization with the variation 3 ... ♗g4 4 h3 ♗xf3 and when 4 ... ♗h5 also turned out to be perfectly playable, the Two Knights variation

considerably dropped in popularity.

Of the three divergences below, variation A is clearly the most logical and popular. But also worthy of attention is C, which aims to transpose into either the exf6 lines of chapter 2 or the gxf6 lines of chapter 3.

A: 3 ... ♗g4
B: 3 ... ♘f6
C: 3 ... dxe4

Instead 3 ... d4 is dubious: 4 ♘e2 c5 *(4 ... d3?! 5 cxd3 ♕xd3 6 ♘c3)* 5 ♘g3 *(5 c3!? dxc3! 6 bxc3 ♘c6 7 ♘g3 g6!? 8 ♗b5 ♗d7 9 0-0 ♗g7 10 d4 cxd4 11 cxd4 Lisitsin–Budo, USSR 1949 and now 11 ... a6 ∞)* 5 ... ♘c6 6 ♗c4 e5 7 d3 ♗e7 8 0-0 ♘f6 9 ♘h4! 0-0 *(9 ... ♘xe4 10 ♘xe4 ♗xh4 11 ♘xc5 or 11 ♕h5 ±)* 10 a4 ♘xe4 11 ♘xe4 ♗xh4 12 f4! exf4 13 ♗xf4 ♗e7 14 ♕h5 ♗e6 15 ♖f3 ± Keres–Tartakower, Paris 1954.

A

3 ...   ♗g4

218

4 h3　　　...

There are no other strong continuations. 4 d4 e6 or 4 exd5 are colourless.

A1: 4 ... $\hat{\underline{\mathbb{Q}}}$xf3
A2: 4 ... $\hat{\underline{\mathbb{Q}}}$h5!?

A1

4 ...　　　$\hat{\underline{\mathbb{Q}}}$xf3

5 ♕xf3　　　...

The following clearly cannot be taken too seriously although it did actually occur in a world championship game! — 5 gxf3 e6 6 d4 ♘d7 7 $\hat{\underline{\mathbb{Q}}}$f4 *(7 $\hat{\underline{\mathbb{Q}}}$e3)* 7 ... $\hat{\underline{\mathbb{Q}}}$b4 8 h4 ♘gf6 9 e5 *(9 a3! $\hat{\underline{\mathbb{Q}}}$xc3+ 10 bxc3 dxe4 11 fxe4 ♘xe4 12 ♕f3 ♕a5 13 ♖h3 ∓ Trifunović)* 9 ... ♘h5 10 $\hat{\underline{\mathbb{Q}}}$g5 ♕a5 11 $\hat{\underline{\mathbb{Q}}}$d2 ♕b6 12 a3 $\hat{\underline{\mathbb{Q}}}$e7 13 $\hat{\underline{\mathbb{Q}}}$e3 g6 ∓ Tal-Botvinnik, (m) 1960.

Here we have:

A1.1: 5 ... ♘f6
A1.2: 5 ... e6

A1.1

5 ...　　　♘f6

This is probably more accurate than 5 ... e6. Now White can choose between:

A1.11: 6 d3
A1.12: 6 d4

Or:
a) **6 g4?!** ♘xe4 7 ♘xe4 dxe4 8 ♕xe4 ♘d7 9 $\hat{\underline{\mathbb{Q}}}$g2 *(9 c4 ♘c5 10 ♕e3 ♘e6 11 b3 ♘d4 12 $\hat{\underline{\mathbb{Q}}}$d3 g6 13 $\hat{\underline{\mathbb{Q}}}$b2 $\hat{\underline{\mathbb{Q}}}$g7 14 $\hat{\underline{\mathbb{Q}}}$c3 ♕d6 ∓ Shaposhnikov–Simagin, USSR 1965)* 9 ... e6 10 d4 $\hat{\underline{\mathbb{Q}}}$d6 = Trifunović.

b) **6 g3** ♘xe4 7 ♘xe4 dxe4 8 ♕xe4 ♕d5 9 ♕xd5 cxd5 10 $\hat{\underline{\mathbb{Q}}}$g2 e6 11 c4 ♘c6 12 cxd5 ♘b4 = Boleslavsky.

c) **6 e5** (too early) ♘fd7 7 ♕g3 *(7 e6 fxe6 8 d4 e5! 9 dxe5 ♘xe5 10 ♕g3 ♘f7 11 $\hat{\underline{\mathbb{Q}}}$d3 e5 12 0-0 ♘d7 13 ♖e1 ♕f6 −+ Vasyukov–Petrosian, USSR 1954)* 7 ... e6 8 $\hat{\underline{\mathbb{Q}}}$e2 *(8 f4 c5 9 f5?! ♘c6 10 $\hat{\underline{\mathbb{Q}}}$b5 ♕c7 ∓)* 8 ... c5 *(8 ... ♕c7 9 f4 a6 10 b4?! c5 11 b5 c4 12 ♖b1 d4 13 ♘e4 axb5 14 0-0 ♖xa2 ∓ Spassky–Reshko, USSR 1961)* 9 f4 ♘c6 10 b3 ♘d4 ∓.

A1.11

6 d3　　　...

The most popular continuation,

shunning the simplifications Black threatened on e4.

6 ...   e6

And here:

A1.111: 7 g3
A1.112: 7 a3

Others are:

a) 7 ♗d2 ♗d4! *(7 ... ♘bd7 8 g4 ♗b4 9 a3 ♗a5 10 g5 ± Trifunović)* 8 a3 ♗d6 9 g4? d4 10 ♘e2 ♕b6 ± Zuckerman-Marović, Malaga 1968.

b) 7 g4!? ♗b4 8 ♗d2 *(8 g5?! ♕a5! 9 ♗d2 d4 10 gxf6 dxc3 11 bxc3 ♗xc3 12 ♖d1 gxf6 13 ♕xf6 ♗xd2+ 14 ♖xd2 ♖g8 ∓ Boleslavsky)* 8 ... ♕a5 *(8 ... d4 9 ♘b1 ♗xd2+ 10 ♘xd2 ♕a5 11 h4 ♘a6 12 a3 h6 13 0-0-0 0-0-0 14 ♖g1 ± Muratov-Gutop, Moscow 1976)* 9 a3?! d4 10 ♘b1 ♗xd2+ 11 ♘xd2 h5! ∓ Boleslavsky.

c) 7 ♗e2 ♘bd7 8 ♕g3 g6 9 h4?! *(White first forces a weakness in the Black camp − 8 ... g6 − and then immediately launches into the attack. But all these actions over-commit him: the attack is repelled and g4 is weak later. 9 0-0 ♗g7 10 ♗f4 ♕b6 11 ♖ab1 0-0 = was steadier, as in Smyslov-Botvinnik, Moscow (m) 1958)* 9 ... h5 10 0-0 ♕b6 *(10 ... ♘h7 was also possible: 11 exd5 exd5! 12 ♖e1 ♗e7 13 ♗h6 ♘hf8)* 11 ♖b1 ♗h6!*. A subtle positional move, characteristic of Petrosian − for the complete moves see the illustrative game Gurgenidze-Petrosian.

A1.111

7 g3   ...

A natural move, but 7 a3 (see A1.112) was later thought to be better in view of Black's subsequent counterplay.

7 ...   ♗b4

The most aggressive continuation, but Black could also try 7 ... g6, 7 ... ♗e7 or 7 ... ♘bd7 8 ♗g2 ♗c5 9 0-0 0-0 10 ♕e2 ♗d4! 11 ♔h2 ♗xc3 12 bxc3 dxe4 13 dxe4 ♕a5 = Smyslov-Flohr, USSR (ch) 1950.

8 ♗d2   d4
9 ♘b1   ♕b6!

This frustrates White's development with the threat against b2. Instead the game Fischer-Petrosian, Yugoslavia (c) 1959 continued 9 ...

♗xd2+ 10 ♘xd2 e5! 11 ♗g2 c5 12 0-0 ♘c6 13 ♕e2 ♕e7 14 f4 0-0-0 15 a3?! *(15 ♘c4!)* 15 . . . ♘e8! 16 b4 cxb4 18 ♘c4 f6! 18 fxe5 fxe5 19 axb4 ♘c7 20 ♘a5 ♘b5 21 ♘xc6 bxc6 and Black had the better prospects as the white bishop is passive.

10 b3   . . .

Fischer played this move twice against the late Estonian grandmaster Keres during the Yugoslav Candidates' Tournament of 1959, and came to grief on both occasions due to the weakness of c2 and c3. The analysts tried unsuccessfully to improve the variation with 10 c3, e.g. 10 . . . ♗c5 *(Not 10 . . . ♗a3? 11 ♘xa3 ♕xb2 12 ♖b1! ♕xa3 13 cxd4 ♕xa2 14 ♕d1 when White has compensation for the pawn − Euwe)* 11 ♗c1 ♘d7 12 ♕e2 *(12 ♗g2? ♘e5 13 ♕e2 dxc3 14 bxc3 ♗xf2+! or 12 ♘d2?! ♘e5 13 ♕e2 0-0-0 14 c4 g5 ∓)* 12 . . . 0-0-0 13 e5 *(13 ♗g2 dxc3 14 bxc3 ♘e5 15 d4 ♗xd4 16 cxd4 ♕xd4 17 ♗b2 ♕xb2!)* 13 . . . ♘d5 14

♗g2 *(14 c4 ♘b4 15 a3 ♘xd3+ 16 ♕xd3 ♘xe5 17 ♕e2 d3 18 ♕xe5 ♗xf2+ 19 ♔d2 ♗d4 20 ♕f4 g5 ∓ Boleslavsky)* 14 . . . ♕c7 15 f4 f6! = Boleslavsky.

After 10 b3 the two games continued differently:

a) **10 . . . a5** 11 a3 ♗e7 12 ♗g2 a4 13 b4 ♘bd7 14 0-0 c5 and after 15 ♖a2? 0-0 16 bxc5 ♗xc5 17 ♕e2 e5 18 f4 ♖fc8 19 h4 ♖c6 20 ♗h3 ♕c7 Black acquired an advantage, Fischer−Keres, Bled/Zagreb/Portorož (c) 1959.

b) **10 . . . ♘bd7** 11 ♗g2 a5 12 a3 ♗xd2+ 13 ♘xd2 ♕c5! − taking a long look at the weakness of the queenside. For the remainder of this splendid second Fischer−Keres clash from the Yugoslav Candidates' Tournament, 1959, see illustrative game number 68.

A1.112

7 a3   . . .

First White prevents the uncomfortable 8 . . . ♗b4.

7 . . .   ♗e7

Other tries have been:

a) **7 . . . ♘bd7** 8 g4 g6 *(8 . . . ♗d6 9 g5 ♘g8 10 h4 ♘e7 11 h5 ♕b6 12 ♗h3 ±* Fischer−Kagan, Netanya 1968) 9 h4 h5 10 g5 ♘g4 11 ♗h3 ±.

b) **7 . . . ♕a5** 8 ♗d2 ♕b6 9 0-0-0 d4 10 ♘e2 a5 11 g4 ♗c5 12 g5 ♘fd7 13 h4

♕b5 14 ♘c3! dxc3 15 ♗xc3 ♕b6 16 ♗xc7 ♖g8 17 ♗c3 ♗d4 ∞ Muchnik-Khalibeili, USSR 1958.

c) 7 . . . ♗c5 8 ♗e2 *(8 g4 0-0 9 h4 ♘bd7 10 g5 ♘e8 11 ♗h3 ∞ Trifunović)* 8 . . . 0-0 9 0-0 ♘bd7 10 ♕g3 ♗d4 11 ♗h6 ♘e8 12 ♗g5 ♘df6 13 ♗f3 ♕d6 14 ♗f4 ♕c5 = Fischer-Larsen, Zürich 1959.

8 g4!?   . . .

8 g3 0-0 9 ♗g2 ♘e8! 10 0-0 f5 11 ♕e2 ♘c7 12 ♗d2 ♘d7 13 ♖ae1 ♗f6 = Boleslavsky-Bagirov, USSR 1959.

8 . . .   ♘fd7

8 . . . dxe4 9 dxe4 ♘fd7 10 ♗e3 ♗g5 11 0-0-0 ♗xe3+ 12 ♕xe3 ±, analysis by Trifunović.

9 d4   ♕b6!

Better than 9 . . . ♗g5? 10 ♗e3 ♗xe3 11 fxe3 ± or 9 . . . ♘f8? 10 ♗e3 ♘g6 11 ♕g3! − see the illustrative game Smyslov-Botvinnik. After 9 . . . ♕b6, however, Black can equalize by 10 ♕d3 e5 11 exd5 exd4 12 ♘e2 0-0 13 ♗g2 ♘f6 14 dxc6 ♘xc6 15 0-0 ♖ad8.

A1.12

6 d4   dxe4
7 ♕e3!   . . .

In contrast to the 5 . . . e6 variation, the pawn sacrifice is bad here:

7 ♘xe4? ♕xd4 8 ♗d3 ♘bd7! 9 ♗e3 ♕d5 10 ♖d1 e6 11 0-0 ♗e7 12 ♘xf6+ ♘xf6 13 ♕g3 ♗d6 14 ♕h4 ♕e5 15 g3 ♗c5 ∓ Dubinin-Ilivitsky, USSR 1957.

White loses time with the text move, but trusts in the latent power of his pair of bishops.

7 . . .   ♘bd7

If 7 . . . ♘d5 8 ♕xe4 ♘xc3 9 bxc3 ♘d7 10 ♖b1 ♕c8 11 c4 e6 12 ♗d3 ♗e7 13 0-0 is ± according to Boleslavsky, but 7 . . . ♕a5 is interesting; 8 ♗d2 ♕f5 9 0-0-0 e6 10 f3! exf3 11 g4 ♕a5 12 ♗c4 Messing-Nemet, Yugoslavia 1967. Also possible is 7 . . . e6 8 ♘xe4 ♘xe4 9 ♕xe4 ♘d7 10 c3 *(Alternatively 10 ♗e2)* 10 . . . ♘f6 11 ♕f3 ♗e7 *(11 . . . ♕d5 is worthy of consideration)* 12 ♗d3 *(12 ♗c4 ♘d5!?)* 12 . . . 0-0 13 0-0 ♕b6 14 ♗g5 ♖fd8 15 ♖fe1 ♖d5! 16 ♗h4 ♖ad8 17 ♗c4 ♖5d7 ∞ Ghinda-Watson, Thessalonika (ol) 1988.

8 ♘xe4   ♘xe4
9 ♕xe4   ♘f6
10 ♕d3   ♕d5

Or 10 . . . e6 11 ♗e2 ♗e7 12 0-0 0-0-0 ± Boleslavsky.

11 c4   ♕e4+

Interesting is 11 . . . ♕d6 12 ♗e2 e5!? 13 d5!? when instead of 13 . . . e4?! 14 ♕c2 ♗e7 15 dxc6 ♕xc6 16 0-0 0-0 17 ♗e3 ± Fischer-Keres, Bled

1961, Black could perhaps accept the pawn by **13 ... cxd5** 14 cxd5 ♕xd5 15 ♕xd5 ♘xd5 16 ♗b5+ ♔e7 17 0-0 ∞.

12 ♕xe4   ♘xe4
13 d5!

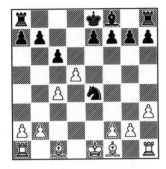

White has some initiative on the strength of his bishop pair.

A1.2

5 ...   e6
6 d4!?   ...

Theorists used to consider 5 ... ♘f6 for Black to be indisputably more accurate, holding that the d4-pawn sacrifice, which is possible here, was dubious in the case of ♘f6. Opinions today, however, are by no means so unequivocal in this matter. Alternatives are harmless:

a) **6 a3** *(For 6 d3 ♘f6 see A1.11)* 6 ... dxe4 7 ♘xe4 ♘f6 8 ♘c3 ♘d5 9 ♗e2 ♘d7 10 0-0 ♕f6 = Karpov-Pomar, Madrid 1973.

b) **6 ♗e2** ♘f6 *(6 ... d4 7 ♘b1 ♘f6 8 d3 c5 9 ♕g3 ♘c6 10 0-0 h5 – 10 ... ♗e7!? 11 ♕xg7 ♖g8 12 ♕h6 ♕c7 ∞ Minic, Sindik – 11 f4 h4 12 ♕f2 ♘h5 13 ♗xh5 ♖xh5 14 ♘d2 – Short Seirawan, Barcelona 1989 – 14 ... ♗e7 ±)* 7 0-0 ♘bd7 8 d4 dxe4 9 ♘xe4 ♘xe4 10 ♕xe4 ♘f6 11 ♕d3 ♕c7 12 c4 ♗e7 13 ♗d2 0-0 = Milić-Clarke, Moscow 1956.

c) **6 g3** ♘f6 7 ♗g2 dxe4 8 ♘xe4 ♘xe4 9 ♕xe4 ♕d5 10 d4 ♘d7 11 0-0 ♕xe4 12 ♗xe4 ♘f6 = Lutikov-Ilivitsky, USSR 1957.

6 ...   ♘f6

The pawn sacrifice can also be accepted immediately by **6 ... dxe4** 7 ♘xe4 ♕xd4 *(7 ... ♘f6 8 ♗d3 ♘bd7 9 c3 ♘xe4 10 ♕xe4 ♘f6 11 ♕e2 ♕d5 12 0-0 ♕h5 13 ♕xh5 ♘xh5 14 ♗e3 ± Boleslavsky-Bronstein, USSR 1951)* 8 ♗d3 *(8 c3 ♕d5!? 9 ♗f4 f5 10 ♘g5 ∞ Trifunović)* 8 ... ♘d7 *(8 ... ♘f6 leads back to the text)* 9 ♗e3 *(9 ♗f4!?)* 9 ... ♕d5 10 0-0 ♘gf6 *(10 ... ♕a2!?)* 11 ♔b1 when the position is unclear according to Trifunović. Bad, however, are **6 ... ♕b6** 7 ♗d3 ♕xd4 8 exd5 exd5 9 ♗f4 ♘d7 10 0-0-0 as in Keres-Flohr, Budapest 1950 and **6 ... ♗b4** 7 e5 *(7 ♕g3!?)* 7 ... c5 8 a3 ♕a5 9 axb4! ♕xa1 10 ♗xb5+ ± Ciocaltea-Soós, Romania 1952.

7 ♗d3   dxe4

7 ... ♗e7? 8 e5 ♘fd7 9 ♕g3 g6

(9 ... ♗f8 10 ♘e2 c5 11 c3 ♘c6 12 0-0 cxd4 13 cxd4 ♕b6 14 ♗e3 ± Bronstein-Makogonov, USSR 1947) 10 h4 ♕b6 11 ♘e2 c5 12 h5 ♖g8 *(12 ... c4 13 hxg6!)* 13 c3 ♘c6 14 ♕e3 0-0-0 15 h6 ± Bronstein-Makogonov, USSR 1951.

7 ... ♕b6 8 0-0 ♕xd4 9 ♗e3 ♕b4 10 exd5 exd5 *(10 ... cxd5 11 ♘b5 ±; 10 ... ♘xd5 11 ♘xd5 cxd5 12 c4 ±)* 11 ♖fe1 ♗e7 12 ♗f4 ♔f8 13 ♕g3 ♘bd7 14 ♖xe7+!! ♔xe7 – Balashov-Lechtynski, Trnava 1988 – 15 ♖e1+ ♔d8 16 ♗d6 ±.

8	♘xe4	♕xd4
9	♗e3!?	...

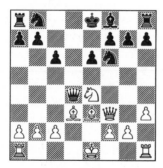

While Boleslavsky regards this offer of a second pawn to be definitely good for White, Trifunović in the *Encyclopaedia* judges the variations to give equal chances. Instead 9 c3 ♕d8 10 0-0 ♗e7 11 ♖d1 ♘bd7 12 ♕g3 ♘xe4 13 ♗xe4 g6 14 ♗f4 is unclear, Korchnoi–Spassky, USSR 1959.

9 ...		♕d8

Clearly requiring some tests in practical play are 9 ... ♗b4+ 10 ♔e2 ♕d8 11 ♖hd1 ♘xe4 12 ♕xe4 and 9 ... ♕xb2 10 0-0 ♘xe4 11 ♕xe4 ♕f6 12 ♖ab1; in each case White has compensation for the sacrificed material. The text move of 9 ... ♕d8 was played in the illustrative game Boleslavsky-Flohr, USSR (ch) 1950 when instead of **10 0-0-0?!** as played, Boleslavsky gives **10 ♘xf6+ ♕xf6 11 ♕g3** threatening 12 ♕c7.

A2

4 ...		♗h5!?

A move which was for years considered an error and which, in view of the stronger lines found in recent years, has been said to call the soundness of the Two Knights system into question.

5 exd5		...

This initiates a sharp line, but it is

one which commits White. If his attack fails to penetrate, his pawn position may prove to be weak. 5 d4 is cautious but harmless, 5 . . . e6 *(5 . . . ♘f6!?)* 6 exd5 *(6 ♗e2 ♘f6 7 e5 ♘fd7 8 0-0 ♗e7 9 ♘h2 ♗g6 10 f4 f6 11 ♗g4 f5 12 ♗f3 ♘b6 = Solontiev-Volovich, USSR 1961)* 6 . . . exd5 7 ♗e2 ♗xf3!? 8 ♗xf3 ♗d6 9 0-0 ♘e7 10 ♖e1 0-0 11 ♗g5 h6 12 ♗h4 ♕d7 = Bárczay-Varnusz, Budapest 1975.

5 . . .	cxd5
6 g4	♗g6
7 ♗b5+	. . .

For years this was considered strong, but now that Black's resources appear to be at least adequate, attention may divert to a new idea tried out in Ghinda-Chandler, West Germany 1981, of 7 d4 ♘c6 8 ♘e5!? e6 9 h4 f6 10 h5! fxe5 11 hxg6 h6 12 dxe5 with highly obscure complications.

7 . . .	♘c6
8 ♘e5	. . .

8 d4 e6 9 ♘e5 ♘e7 10 h4 f6 11 ♘xg6 hxg6 12 ♗e3 ♖c8 13 ♗d3 ♘b4 14 ♗f1 ♔f7 15 a3 ♘bc6 16 ♗d3 Keres-Filip, Buenos Aires 1964; 16 . . . e5! =.

8 . . .	♖c8!

8 . . . **♕d6** proves inadequate after 9 d4 *(Planning 10 ♗f4)* 9 . . . f6 10 ♘xg6 hxg6 11 ♕d3! 0-0-0 *(11 . . . ♔f7? 12 ♘xd5!)* 12 ♗xc6 ♕xc6 13 ♕xg6 e5 14 ♕d3! *(14 ♗d2 e4! 15 ♕f5+ ♔b8 16 0-0-0 ± Boleslavsky)* 14 . . . ♗b4 15 ♗d2 e4 16 ♕b5 ♗c3 17 ♕xc6+ bxc6 ± Keres-Bondarevsky, USSR 1941.

Also **8** . . . **♕c7** is suspect: 9 d4 e6 10 ♕e2 ♘f6 11 h4 ♗b4 12 h5 ♗e4 13 f3 0-0 14 ♗xc6 bxc6 15 g5! c5 16 ♗e3 ♗xf3 17 ♘xf3 ♘e4 18 0-0 ♘xc3 19 bxc3 ♗xc3 20 ♖ad1 ♖ab8 21 ♖f2 ♖b2 22 h6 +− Suetin-Veresov, USSR 1955.

9 d4	. . .

Intended to counter the liberating manœuvre f7-f6, which cannot be played now because of 10 ♘xg6 hxg6 11 ♕d3! ♔f7 12 ♘xd5!

9 . . .	e6
10 ♕e2	. . .

This again prevents f6, and renews the attempt to trap the bishop on g6. 10 h4 is harmless: 10 . . . f6! 11 ♘xg6 *(11 h5 ♗xc2 12 ♘xc6 bxc6 13 ♕xc2 cxb5 14 ♕e2 b4 15 ♕xe6+ ♕e7 16 ♕xe7+ ♘xe7 = Moses-Kelbeck, Harrachov 1967)* 11 . . . hxg6 12 ♗e3 *(12 ♗d3!? f5!? 13 gxf5 gxf5 was Mestel-Rogers, Groningen 1976-77 or 12 ♕d3 ♔f7 13 h5 gxh5 14 gxh5 ♘ge7 15 ♗e3 ♘f5 ∓ Fischer-Smyslov, Yugoslavia (c) 1959)* 12 . . . ♗b4 13 ♔f1 ♗xc3 14 bxc3 ♘e7 15 ♕e2 a6 16 ♗d3 ♘a5 = Liberzon-Smyslov, USSR (ch) 1960.

10 ...   ♗b4

Black has to play very accurately if he wants to counter the threat of h4-h5. Less good are **10 ... ♗d6** 11 ♘xg6 hxg6 12 ♘xd5 ♗b8 13 ♘c3 ♕xd4 14 ♗e3 ♕b4 15 0-0-0 ± Gurgenidze-Liberzon, USSR 1960 or **10 ... ♗e7** 11 ♗f4 ♔f8 12 ♘xc6 bxc6 13 ♗a6 ± Klovan-Tabrosian, USSR 1959.

11 h4   ...

Poor is 11 a3?! ♗xc3+ 12 bxc3 ♘e7 13 h4 ♕a5 14 ♖h3 a6 15 ♗xc6+ ♘xc6 16 ♘xc6 ♖xc6 17 ♖b1 b5 18 h5 ♗e4 19 ♖b3 h6 20 ♖g3 f6 ∓ Zilin-Bagirov, USSR 1962.

11 ...   ♘e7

Black sacrifices a piece, but if it is taken White's weaknesses and under-development may show. Of the alternatives, bad is **11 ... ♕b6?** 12 0-0! ♘e7 *(12 ... ♕xd4 13 ♖d1 +−; 12 ... a6 13 ♗xc6+ bxc6 14 h5 ♗e4 15 ♘xe4*

dxe4 16 c3 ♗e7 17 f3! exf3 18 ♖xf3 +− Klovan-Tsirtsenis, USSR 1960 or 12 ... ♘f6 13 ♘a4! ♕a5 14 h5 ♗e4 15 f3 a6 16 ♗xc6+ bxc6 17 b3 ♗c3 18 ♘xc3 ♕xc3 19 ♗e3 ♕xc2 20 ♕xa6 0-0 21 ♖ac1 +− Boleslavsky) 13 h5 ♗c4 14 ♘e4 dxe4 15 c3 ♗d6 16 ♘c4 ♕d8 17 ♘xd6+ ♕xd6 18 ♕xe4 ± Trifunović.

However, Trifunović and Minev do consider **11 ... ♗xc3+** 12 bxc3 ♕a5 to be playable, with the following variations:

a) **13 0-0** ♕xc3 14 ♗xc6+ *(14 ♗e3 ♘e7 15 h5 ♗e4 16 f3 ♗xc2 17 ♖ac1 0-0 ∓)* 14 ... bxc6 15 ♕a6 ♘e7 16 ♗a3 ♕xd4 17 ♗xe7 ♔xe7 18 ♕a3+ *(18 ♕b7+ ♔d6 ∓)* 18 ... c5 19 ♕xa7+ ♔f8 20 ♕d7 ♖e8 ∓.

b) **13 ♖h3** ♘e7 14 h5 ♗e4 15 ♗d2 h6 16 c4 ♕d8 ∓.

c) **13 ♗d2** ♘e7 14 c4 *(14 h5 ♗c2 15 ♖c1 ♗e4! 16 f3 f6 17 ♘xc6 bxc6 18 ♗a6 ♗xf3 ∓)* 14 ... ♕a3 15 h5 *(15 cxd5 exd5 16 c3 0-0 17 h5 ♗e4 18 f3 ♘xe5 19 fxe4 ♘f3+ 20 ♕xf3 ♕b2 21 0-0 ♕xd2 ∓)* 15 ... ♗xc2 16 0-0-0 0-0 17 ♘xc6 ♘xc6 18 ♗xc6 ♖xc6 ∓.

d) **13 ♗b2!** ♘e7 14 h5 ♗e4 15 f3 f6 16 fxe4 *(16 ♘xc6 bxc6 17 ♗a6 ♖b8 18 0-0-0 ♗xf3 19 ♕xf3 ♕xa6 20 h6 gxh6 21 ♕xf6 ♖f8 22 ♕xe6 ♕xa2 ∓ or 17 ♗xc6+ ♖xc6 18 fxe4 0-0 19 exd5 ♘xd5 20 0-0 ♖b8 ∓)* 16 ... fxe5 17 0-0 ∞.

12 h5   ♗e4
13 f3   ...

13 0-0 0-0 14 ♗xc6 leads us back to

the text, while **14 ♘xe4? ♘xd4** is bad. Black played less accurately in Romanishin–Bagirov, USSR 1974 with **13 . . . ♗xc3** 14 bxc3 a6? 15 ♘xc6 ♘xc6 16 ♗xc6+ ♖xc6 17 f3 ♖xc3 18 fxe4 when, in contrast to the main continuation, Black is still uncastled.

     13 . . .   **0-0**

A2.1

     14 ♗xc6   . . .

On 14 fxe4? ♘xd4! is very strong.

     14 . . .   **♘xc6**
     15 ♘xc6   **♖xc6**

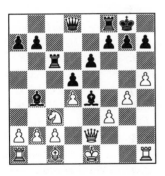

The critical stage of this variation. Even with the most accurate play White can only achieve a position where both players have equal chances:

   a) **16 fxe4? ♖xc3** −+.

   b) **16 ♗d2 ♗xc2** 17 ♖c1 ♗a4 18 b3 ♛c7 ∓.

   c) **16 ♗e3 ♖xc3!** 17 bxc3 ♗xc3+ 18 ♔f2 ♗xa1 19 ♖xa1 ♛h4+ 20 ♔g2?! ♛xg4+! −+.

   d) **16 ♔f1 f5!** 17 fxe4 fxe4+ 18 ♔g2 ♗xc3 19 bxc3 ♖xc3 planning . . . ♖8f3 −+.

   e) **16 ♔d1 ♛f6** 17 fxe4 ♛xd4+ 18 ♛d3 *(18 ♛d2 ♗xc3 19 bxc3 ♛e4 −+ or 18 ♗d2 dxe4 19 ♘xe4 ♛xb2 ∓)* 18 . . . ♗xc3 *(18 . . . ♛e5!?)* 19 bxc3 ♛e5! ∞ ∓!?

   f) **16 0-0!** ♗xc3 17 bxc3 ♖xc3 18 ♗d2! *(18 fxe4? ♖g3+ 19 ♔f2 ♛h4 ∓)* 18 . . . ♖xc2 19 fxe4 dxe4 20 ♖fc1 ♖b2 ∞ *(20 . . . ♛xd4+? 21 ♗e3 ♖xe2 22 ♗xd4 ±)* 21 ♖ab1?! *(21 ♖cb1 ♖c2 22 ♖c1 =)* 21 . . . ♖xa2 22 ♖xb7? ♛xd4+ 23 ♗e3 ♛d5 24 ♛b5 ♛d6 −+ (analysed by Navarovsky).

A2.2

     14 ♘xc6   **♘xc6**

     15 ♗e3!   . . .

15 fxe4? ♘xd4 16 ♛d3 dxe4 ∓.

15 ...	♕f6!
16 fxe4	♘xd4
17 ♗xd4	♕xd4
18 ♖d1	...

18 ♕d3 ♕e5 19 0-0-0 ♗xc3 20 bxc3 dxe4 −+ (Byrne and Mednis).

18 ...	♗xc3+
19 bxc3	♕xc3+
20 ♔f1	...

20 ♖d2 dxe4 21 0-0 ♖c5 22 ♗d7 ♖g5 23 ♖fd1 ♕h3 0-1 Grefe-Commons, USA 1975.

20 ...	dxe4
21 ♕xe4	...

21 ♖h2? ♕e5 22 ♖f2 ♖c3! 23 ♖e1 ♖h3! 24 ♔g1 ♕g3+ 25 ♖g2 ♕h4 −+ Sikora-Varnusz, Zamárdi 1979.

21 .	.	.f5!

21 ... ♕xc2? 22 ♕xc2 ♖xc2 23 ♖d7 ♖xa2 24 ♖xb7 ♖c8 25 ♗e2 h6 26 ♖h3 ± Sikora-Gralka, Leszczny 1985.

22 ♕xe6+	♔h8
23 ♔g2!	

23 ♗d3? ♕d4! ∓ van der Wiel-Timman, Amsterdam 1986.

23 ...	♕xc2+
24 ♕e2	fxg4
25 ♖c1	♕f5

26 ♗d3	♖ce8

With equal chances (Sikora-Stohl, Trnava 1989).

B

3 ...	♘f6

This old line is no longer used, as Black's knight loses time without compensation.

4 e5	♘e4

After 4 ... ♘fd7, at the very best, an unfavourable French-type position comes about:

a) 5 d4 e6 6 ♘e2! c5 7 c3 ♘c6 8 g3 b5 (8 ... cxd4 9 cxd4 ♗b4+ 10 ♘c3 f6 11 exf6 ♕xf6 12 ♗g2 0-0 13 0-0 ± Soloviev-Chistyakov, USSR 1961) 9 ♗g2 ♕b6 10 0-0 a5 11 ♘f4 ± Boleslavsky.

b) 5 e6 fxe6 6 d4 e5 (6 ... g6 7 h4! ♘f6 8 h5! ♘xh5 9 ♖xh5! gxh5 10 ♘e5 ± Boleslavsky) 7 dxe5! e6 8 ♗f4! ♗e7 (8 ... c5 9 ♘g5 ± Boleslavsky) 9 ♘g5! ♗xg5 10 ♕h5+ g6 11 ♕xg5 ♕xg5 12 ♗xg5 0-0 13 f4 ± Boleslavsky.

| 5 ♘e2! | ... |

Avoiding the exchange in order to seize the centre later, afer chasing the knight away. Of little importance are 5 ♗e2 ♘xc3 6 dxc3 ♗g4 = and 5 ♘xe4

dxe4 6 ♘g5 ♕d5 7 d3 exd3 8 ♗xd3 =.
5 ♘b1 is slightly more acceptable:
5... ♗f5 6 d3 ♘c5 7 ♗e3 e6 8 ♘bd2
♗e7 9 ♗e2 0-0 10 0-0 ♘cd7 11 c4
(11 d4 c5? 12 c4! cxd4 13 ♘xd4 ♘xe5
14 ♕b3 dxc4 15 ♕xb7 ±) 11 ... ♘a6
(11 ... dxc4! 12 dxc4 c5 ±) 12 a3 ♘c7
13 b4 ± Trifunović.

5 ...	♕b6

White can turn 5 ... ♗g4 to
advantage in several ways: **6 h3!** ♗xf3
7 gxf3 ♘c5 *(7 ... ♘g5 8 ♘f4! ♘e6*
9 ♘xe6 fxe6 10 d4 g6 11 h4 ± Flohr)
8 d4 ♘ca6 9 h4! e6 10 h5 ± Flohr or
6 ♘fg1 *(6 d4 e6 7 h3 ♗xf3 8 gxf3 ♘g5*
9 ♘f4 ± Boleslavsky) 6 ... ♘c5 7 f3
♗d7 8 d4 ♘ca6 9 c3 e6 ± Savitsky-
Veresov, USSR (ch) 1937.

In the event of any other quiet
moves from Black, White forces the
knight to retreat by 6 d3.

6 d4	c5
7 dxc5	♕xc5?!

Here the queen will be subjected to
further molesting. Perhaps the pawn
sacrifice was better, namely 7 ...
♘xc5 **8 ♕xd5?** ♘c6 9 ♘ed4 ♕a5+
and Black has counterplay. Boleslavsky's opinion, however, is that the
positional **8 ♘f4** e6 9 ♗e2 ♗e7 10 0-0
0-0 11 c4 dxc4 12 ♗xc4 ♘c6 13 ♕e2
gives White the advantage.

8 ♘ed4	♘c6
9 ♗b5	...

And here:

a) **9... ♗d7** 10 0-0!? ♘xe5 *(10... e6*
11 ♗e3 ♕b4 12 c4 dxc4 13 ♕c2 ♘c5 14
a3 ♕a5 15 ♗xc4 ± Boleslavsky)
11 ♘xe5 ♗xb5 12 ♘xb5 ♕xb5
13 ♖e1 ♘f6 14 ♗g5 e6 15 c4 *(The*
better developed side needs to open a
file!) 15 ... ♕a5 *(15 ... dxc4 16 ♗xf6*
gxf6 17 a4 ♕d5 18 ♕xd5 exd5 19
♘g6+ etc. Boleslavsky) 16 ♗xf6 gxf6
17 ♘xf7! ♔xf7 18 ♕h5+ ♔e7 9 cxd5
e5 20 f4 ♕xd5 21 fxe5 f5 22 e6
Nezhmetdinov-Kamishov, USSR
1950. Although White broke through
here, however, an improvement for
Black amidst the great complications
is conceivable.

b) **9... a6?!** (This is definitely bad)
10 ♗xc6+ bxc6 11 0-0 ♕b6 *(Prevent-*
ing 12 ♗e3. The threat is 12 ... c5 and
13 ... e6 with a comfortable game) 12
e6! fxe6 *(12 ... f6 13 c4! c5 14 ♕a4+)*
13 ♗f4 and White succeeded in
exploiting Black's busted pawn
formation in Fischer-Olafsson,
Yugoslavia (c) 1959 – see illustrative
games.

C

3 ...	dxe4
4 ♘xe4	...

Now:

a) **4 ... ♘f6 5 ♘xf6+** generally leads to variations examined in chapters two and three *(5 ♘g3 h5 6 h3!? h4 7 ♘e2 ♗f5 8 d4 e6 9 c3 ♗e7 10 ♘f4 ♘bd7 11 ♗d3 ♗xd3 12 ♘xd3 ± Balashov–T. Fischer, West Berlin 1988).* A few rare exceptions are **5 ... exf6** 6 ♗c4 ♗d6 7 ♕e2+!? ♕e7 8 ♕xe7+ ♔xe7 9 0-0 ♗e6 10 ♖e1 *(10 ♗b3 ♗xb3 11 axb3 ♘a6! = is Keres–Flohr, Moscow 1951)* 10 ... ♔d7 11 ♗e2!? *(11 ♗f1 ♗d5)* 11 ... a5?! *(11 ... ♖e8 planning 12 ... ♗d5 ∞)* 12 d4 a4 13 ♗e3 ♘a6 14 c3 ♘c7 15 c4 ± Klovan–Vistanetskis, USSR 1964, and **5 ... gxf6** 6 g3 *(6 b3 ♖g8 7 ♗b2 ♗h6 8 ♕e2 ♗g4 9 0-0-0 ♘d7 = Penrose–Larsen, Hastings 1956)* 6 ... ♗g4 7 ♗g2 ♕d7 *(7 ... e6 8 b3 ♘d7 9 ♗b2 ♗g7 10 h3 ♗h5 11 ♕e2 ± Keres–Pachman, Moscow 1967 or 7 ... h5!? 8*

h3 ♗e6 9 b3 ♘d7!? 10 ♗b2 ♗d5 11 ♕e2 ♕a5 12 h4 0-0-0 13 c4 ♗xf3 14 ♗xf3 e6 15 a3 ♘e5 16 ♗e4! ♖d7! ∞ *Ghinda–Skembris, Athens 1988)* 8 h3 *(8 0-0 ♗h3 9 b3 ♘a6 10 ♗b2 ♗xg2 11 ♔xg2 0-0-0 12 ♖e1 h5 13 ♕e2 ♘c7 = Rauser–Budo, USSR 1937)* 8 ... ♗e6 9 b3 ♘a6 10 ♗b2 0-0-0 11 ♕e2 ♗h6 = Rauser–Konstantinopolsky, USSR 1937.

b) **4 ... ♗g4 5 h3 ♗xf3** can also develop from the main variation. After 6 ♕xf3 White ends up with the two bishops and some space advantage, although Black's position is not easily penetrated. But Black can choose a more subtle continuation in **5 ... ♗h5?!? 6 ♘g3 ♗xf3!** *(6 ... ♗g6 7 h4 h6 8 ♘e5 ♗h7 9 ♕h5 g6 10 ♕f3 ♘f6 11 ♕b3 ♕d5 12 ♕xb7 +− Lasker–Muller, Zürich 1934)* 7 ♕xf3 ♘f6 8 ♗c4 *(8 ♗e2 e6 9 0-0 ♗d6 10 b4 ♕c7 11 ♖b1 ♘d7 12 d4 0-0 13 c4 ♖fe8 14 c5 ♗f8 15 ♗c4 e5 = Taimanov–A. Zaitsev, USSR 1969)* 8 ... e6 9 0-0 *(9 c3 ♗d6 10 d4 0-0 11 ♗g5 ♘bd7 12 0-0 ♕a5 13 h4 ± Boleslavsky–Panov, USSR 1943)* 9 ... ♘bd7 10 ♖e1 ♕c7 11 d4 0-0-0 12 a4 c5 13 a5 a6 as in Zaitsev–Bronstein, Moscow 1968 when Filip now suggests 14 ♗f4! ♗d6 15 ♗xd6 ♕xd6 16 dxc5 ♕xc5 17 ♗f1 ±.

c) **4 ... ♘d7** *(4 ... ♗f5 5 ♘g3 ♗g4 6 h3 transposes to b above)* 5 ♗c4 *(5 ♕e2 ♘df6 6 d3 ♘xe4 7 dxe4 ♗g4 8 h3 ♗h5 9 ♗d2 ♕c7 10 0-0-0 0-0-0 ∞ Smyslov–Flohr, USSR 1947)* 5 ... e6 *(For 5 ... ♘gf6 6 ♘ge5 see chapter 1)*

6 0-0 ♘gf6 7 d3! *(The variation's flexibility is evident here)* 7 ... ♗e7 8 ♗f4 *(8 ♕e2 ♘xe4 9 dxe4 b5! 10 ♗b3 ♘c5 11 ♖d1?! ♕c7 12 ♗d2 a5 13 c4 ♘xb3 14 axb3 b4 ∞ Tolush-Kasparian, USSR 1939)* 8 ... ♘c5 9 ♘xf6+ ♗xf6 10 d4 ♘d7 11 ♕e2 0-0 12 ♖ad1 ± Schwarz.

ILLUSTRATIVE GAMES

65 FISCHER–OLAFSSON
Candidates' Tournament,
Yugoslavia 1959

1 e4 c6 2 ♘c3 d5 3 ♘f3 ♘f6 4 e5 ♘e4 5 ♘e2! ♕b6 6 d4 c5 7 dxc5 ♕xc5?! 8 ♘ed4 ♘c6 9 ♗b5 a6?! (The Icelandic grandmaster would like to establish a strong centre after easing the tension, but he does not succeed) 10 ♗xc6+ bxc6 11 0-0 ♕b6 12 e6! fxe6 13 ♗f4 (Blocks Black's pawns. 13 ♘e5 was also good) 13 ... g6 14 ♗e5 ♘f6 15 ♘g5! ♗h6! (15 ... c5? was not playable because of 16 ♘dxe6! ♗xe6 17 ♗xf6 exf6 18 ♘xe6 ♕xe6? 19 ♖e1) 16 ♘dxe6 ♗xg5 17 ♘xg5 0-0 (Olafsson has warded off the main threats, but flounders because of his disrupted pawn position. The young Fischer proceeds to probe Black's positional weaknesses with relentless logic. His prime objective is to increase pressure on e7, which Black can only defend at the expense of his pieces being condemned to passivity) 18 ♕d2 ♗f5 19 ♖ae1! ♖ad8 20 ♗c3 ♖d7 21 ♘e6 ♗xe6 22 ♖xe6 d4

(Seems logical, but it is not only the d-pawn, but also the one on c6, that is exposed in the long run. There was hardly anything better, however) 23 ♗b4 ♘d5 24 ♗a3 ♖f7 25 g3 ♘c7 (There is no hope of counterplay) 26 ♖e5 ♘d5 27 ♕d3! (A bright future is awaiting the queen on c4) 27 ... ♘f6 28 ♕c4 ♘g4 29 ♖e6 (As long as Black tried to defend his e-pawn, he inevitably upset his position still further. Now his pieces just stand by passively, unable to rescue the c-pawn. Taking on e7 was weaker because of the hanging b2 pawn) 29 ... ♕b5 30 ♕xb5 axb5 31 ♖xc6 ♘e5 32 ♖c8+ ♔g7 33 ♗b4 (To prevent 33 ... ♘c4) 33 ... ♘f3+ 34 ♔g2 e5 35 ♖d1 g5 (Not 35 ... e4 36 ♖e8!. But now only one more move, 36 ... g4, is needed and Black's position improves. The subsequent exchange, however, puts paid to this) 36 ♗f8+ ♖xf8 (36 ... ♔g6 37 ♖c6+!) 37 ♖xf8 ♔xf8 38 ♔xf3 ♔f7 39 c3 ♔e6 40 cxd4 exd4 41 ♔e4 ♖f7 42 f3 Black resigned.

66 BOLESLAVSKY–FLOHR
USSR Championship 1950

1 e4 c6 2 ♘f3 d5 3 ♘c3 ♗g4 4 h3 ♗xf3 5 ♕xf3 e6 6 d4!? ♘f6 7 ♗d3 dxe4 8 ♘xe4 ♕xd4 9 ♗e3!? ♕d8 10 0-0-0?! ♘bd7 11 ♗c4 ♕a5 12 ♗d2 ♕b6?! (12 ... ♕a4! was more active: 13 ♘xf6+ ♘xf6 14 ♗b3 ♕e4 15 ♕g3 0-0-0 ∞) 13 ♖he1 ♘xe4? (This accelerates White's attack. 13 ... ♗e7 14 g4 0-0 ±) 14 ♖xe4 ♘f6 (14 ... ♘c5 15 ♖e2 ♗e7 16 ♗c3 0-0 17 ♕g3 g6 18

♕e5 ±) **15 ♗xe6!! fxe6 16 ♖xe6+ ♗e7**
(On 16 . . . ♔f7 17 ♖xf6+! gxf6 18
♕h5+ wins, e.g. 18 . . . ♔e7 19 ♖e1+
♔d6 20 ♗f4+♔d7 21 ♕f7+, or 18 . . .
♔g7 19 ♗h6+♔g8 20 ♕g4+ ♔f7 21
♖d7+ ♗e7 22 ♕g7+, or 18 . . . ♔g8 19
♕g4+ ♔f7 − 19 . . . ♗g7 20 ♕e6+ ♔f8
21 ♗f4 − 20 ♕c4+ ♔g7 − 20 . . . ♔g6
21 ♕e4+! ♔f7 22 ♗a5 ♗h6+ 23 ♔b1
♖ad8 24 ♕c4+ ♔g7 25 ♕g4+ − 21
♗e3 ♕b4 22 ♖d7+ ♔g6 23 ♕f7+ ♔f5
24 c3 ♕b5 25 g4+ Boleslavsky) **17
♖de1 ♘d5** (17 . . . 0-0 18 ♖xe7 ♘d5 19
♖xg7+! ♔xg7 20 ♗c3+ ♘xc3 21
♖e7+ ♔h6 22 ♕c3 ±) **18 ♗g5 0-0-0
19 ♗xe7 ♘xe7 20 ♖xe7 ♖hf8 21
♕g4+ ♔b8 22 ♕xg7 ♕xf2** (22 . . .
♖xf2 23 ♖e8) **23 b3!** (23 ♖xb7+??
♔a8 24 ♖be7 ♕d2+) **23 . . . ♖g8 24
♕xh7 ♖xg2 25 ♖xb7+ ♔a8 26 ♖be7
♕c5 27 h4 a5 28 ♖e8 ♕d4 29 ♔b1
♖d2 30 ♖xd8+ ♕xd8 31 ♕e4 ♕f6 32
h5 Black resigned.**

67 GURGENIDZE–PETROSIAN
USSR Team Championship 1961

**1 e4 c6 2 ♘c3 d5 3 ♘f3 ♗g4 4 h3
♗xf3 5 ♕xf3 ♘f6 6 d3 e6 7 ♗e2 ♘bd7
8 ♕g3 g6 9 h4?! h5 10 0-0 ♕b6 11 ♖b1
♗h6! 12 ♗g5?!** (12 ♗xh6 ♖xh6 13
♕f4 followed by e5 and d4 was better)
12 . . . ♗xg5 13 hxg5?! (After 13 ♕xg5
♕d4!, although Black is active,
White's pawn position is more
resilient) **13 . . . ♘h7 14 exd5 exd5!**
(The natural 14 . . . cxd5 is answered
by 15 d4! and the threat of 16 ♘b5!
would upset Black's plans, whereas
the opening of the e-file works for

him now) **15 ♔h1 0-0-0 16 f4** (This
weakens e3 without getting an attack
with f4-f5. But the queen had to be
relieved of the humiliating function
of guarding the g5 pawn) **16 . . . ♖de8
17 ♕f2!** (Wanting to take the sting out
of an attack starting with . . . ♖e3)
17 . . . ♕xf2 18 ♖xf2 ♘hf8! (With an
eye on e3) **19 ♗f3** (19 f5? ♘e5 and 20
. . . ♘g4!) **19 . . . ♘e6 20 ♘e2 f6!** (The
start of the kingside attack!) **21 gxf6
♘xf6 22 b4?** (Misjudging the
developing attack; 22 ♖2f1 was
needed) **22 . . . ♘g4 23 ♖2f1** (It
becomes clear now why 22 ♖2f1
would have been better, for after 23
♗xg4 hxg4+ 24 ♔g1 ♘g7 25 ♘g3 ♘f5
26 ♘xf5 gxf5 the move 27 ♔f2 would
have held the position) **23 . . . ♘e3!**
(Petrosian first pushes back the
opponent's pieces and then launches
a queenless attack against the king's
position) **24 ♖fc1 g5 25 fxg5 ♘xg5 26
♘d4 h4!** (Not only White's king but
also his bishop are threatened by the
impending 27 . . . h3! viz. 27 ♔g1 h3 28
g3 h2+ 29 ♔h1 ♖ef8 ∓, or 27 ♖e1 h3
28 ♔g1 ♖h4 29 c3 − 29 ♔f2 hxg2 30
♖xe3 ♘h3+ 31 ♔xg2 ♖g8+ 32 ♗g4+
♖gxg4+ 33 ♖g3 ♖xd4 ∓ − 29 . . . hxg2
30 ♗xg2 ♘h3+ 31 ♗xh3 ♖xh3 etc.
In the face of Black's violent attack,
Gurgenidze attempts to break out but
in so doing hastens his defeat) **27 ♘f5
♘xf3!** (Avoiding the pitfall 27 . . .
♘xf5 28 ♗g4 ♖hf8 29 ♖f1 ♖e5 30 d4
♔b8 31 dxe5 ♘g3+ 32 ♔g1) **28 ♘d6+
♔b8 29 ♘xe8 ♘d2 30 ♖e1 ♘xc2!**
(A rare sight − both white rooks are

hanging in mid-air!) 31 ♘d6 ♘xb1 32 ♖xb1 ♖f8! (Fences in the knight and puts an end to the struggle) 33 b5 ♔c7 **White resigned.**

68   FISCHER–KERES
Candidates' Tournament
Yugoslavia 1959

1 e4 c6 2 ♘c3 d5 3 ♘f3 ♗g4 4 h3 ♗xf3 5 ♕xf3 ♘f6 6 d3 e6 7 g3 ♗b4 8 ♗d2 d4 9 ♘b1 ♕b6! 10 b3 ♘bd7 11 ♗g2 a5 12 a3 ♗xd2+ 13 ♘xd2 ♕c5! 14 ♕d1 h5! 15 ♘f3 (According to Boleslavsky, after 15 h4 ♘g4 16 0-0 ♘de5 Black's splendidly positioned knights cannot be chased away without a weakening of e3) 15 . . . ♕c3+ 16 ♔e2 ♕c5 17 ♕d2 ♘e5 18 b4 (White is hoping for counterplay on the b-file. 18 ♘xe5 ♕xe5 19 f4 was better, though the threat of h5-h4 is also uncomfortable here) 18 . . . ♘xf3 19 ♗xf3 ♕e5 20 ♕f4 ♘d7 21 ♕xe5 ♘xe5 (In the interests of the safety of his centrally positioned king and pinning his hopes on the attack developing on the b-file, Fischer forces the exchange of queens. But Keres proves in a very instructive manner that b7 can be economically defended by the king and that the power of the strong knight against the passive bishop, hemmed in by his own pawns, is enhanced by the successive exchanges) 22 bxa5 ♔d7! 23 ♖hb1 ♔c7 24 ♖b4 ♖xa5! 25 ♗g2? (Not 25 ♖xd4? of course, because of 25 . . . c5!. White does not sense the danger lurking on the black squares,

otherwise he would have played 25 h4! and perhaps, after moving the bishop to h3, f2-f4) 25 . . . g5! 26 f4 (This hastens the end, but something had to be done about the threat of h5-h4) 26 . . . gxf4 27 gxf4 ♘g6 28 ♔f3 (28 ♖xd4 ♘xf4+ 29 ♔f3 e5 30 ♖b4 ♖g8 ∓) 28 . . . ♖g8 29 ♗f1 e5 30 fxe5 ♘xe5+ 31 ♔e2 c5 32 ♖b3 b6 33 ♖ab1 ♖g6 (Also 33 . . . ♖a6) 34 h4 (Otherwise Black would have moved there) 34 . . . ♖a6 35 ♗h3 ♖g3 (Keres's single-minded devotion to pursuing his chosen objective, the probing of White's kingside weaknesses, is a wonder to behold. The fruit is now ripe and White's first pawn drops off without the pressure exerted by Black's pieces slackening in the slightest) 36 ♗f1 (36 ♗f5 ♖g2+) 36 . . . ♖g4 37 ♗h3 ♖xh4 38 ♖h1 ♖a8! 39 ♖3b1 ♖g8 40 ♖bf1 ♖g3 41 ♗f5 ♖g2+ 42 ♔d1 ♖4h2 43 ♖xh2 ♖xh2 44 ♖g1 c4! (This makes the knight position even better!) 45 dxc4 ♘xc4 46 ♖g7 ♔d6! 47 ♖xf7 ♘e3+ 48 ♔c1 ♖xc2+ 49 ♔b1 ♖h2 50 ♖d7+ ♔e5 51 ♖e7+ ♔f4 52 ♖d7 ♘d1! (Excellent! 53 ♖xd4 is answered by ♘c3+ and mate or the rook is lost) 53 ♔c1 ♘c3 54 ♗h7 h4 55 ♖f7+ ♔e3 0-1.

69   SMYSLOV–BOTVINNIK
World Championship Match
(19) 1958

1 e4 c6 2 ♘c3 d5 3 ♘f3 ♗g4 4 h3 ♗xf3 5 ♕xf3 ♘f6 6 d3 e6 7 a3 ♗e7 8 g4!? ♘fd7 9 d4 ♘f8? 10 ♗e3 ♘g6 11

♕g3! (This, with the threat of g5 and h4, forces Black's hand and puts the bishop out of the game) 11 ... ♗h4 (If 11 ... ♗g5 12 ♗xg5 ♕xg5 13 ♕c7) 12 ♕h2 ♘d7 13 0-0-0 ♕b8? (The queen has no future here, because her intended later foray to g3 will be prevented by White. 13 ... 0-0 was better) 14 f4 dxe4 15 ♘xe4 ♘f6 16 ♘xf6+ ♗xf6 (16 ... gxf6 17 ♔b1 followed by c2-c4) 17 ♕f2! (Preparing the later breakthrough. 17 g5 would have ceded an outpost for Black's knight on f5) 17 ... ♗h4 18 ♕f3 ♘e7 19 ♗d3 g6? (This move fatally weakens the kingside; best was 19 ... ♕d6! 20 g5 ♘d5 21 ♗d2 0-0-0 22 ♖hf1 h6 23 ♕g4 ±) 20 f5! exf5 (20 ... ♕g3 21 ♕xg3 ♗xg3 22 fxe6 fxe6 23 ♗h6 0-0-0 24 ♖hf1 +−) 21 ♗f4! (21 gxf5? ♕g3!) 21 ... ♕d8 22 gxf5 ♕d5 23 ♕g4 ♗f6 (23 ... ♗f2 24 f6 ♘f5 25 ♕e2+) 24 ♖he1 h5 25 ♕g3 h4 (25 ... 0-0 26 fxg6 fxg6 27 ♖xe7 ±, 25 ... 0-0-0 26 ♗b8 ♕a5 27 fxg6 fxg6 28 ♖e6 ±) 26 ♕g4 gxf5 (26 ... 0-0-0 27 ♖xe7 ♗xe7 28 f6+) 27 ♗xf5 ♔f8 28 ♗e4 ♕a2 29 c3 ♖ad8 30 ♖ef1! ♘d5 31 ♗d2 ♖d6 (31 ... ♗g7 32 ♖xf7+ ♔xf7 33 ♕g6+ ♔f8 34 ♖f1+) 32 ♕c8+ ♔e7 33 ♕xb7+ (33 ♖de1 was also good) 33 ... ♖d7 34 ♖de1! ♕a1+ 35 ♗b1+ **Black resigned** (On 35 ... ♔d6 36 ♖xf6+! ♘xf6 37 ♗f4+ ♔d5 38 ♕b3

mate! Panov remarks: "The final position is conceived in the spirit of the Calabrian school!").

70　GHINDA–SKEMBRIS
Athens 1988

1 e4 c6 2 ♘c3 d5 3 ♘f3 dxe4 4 ♘xe4 ♘f6 5 ♘xf6+ gxf6 6 g3 ♗g4 7 ♗g2 h5!? 8 h3 ♗e6 9 b3 ♘d7!? 10 ♗b2 ♗d5 11 ♕e2 (11 c4? ♗xf3 12 ♗xf3 h4 ∓) 11 ... ♕a5! 12 h4 0-0-0 13 c4 ♗xf3 14 ♗xf3 e6 15 a3 (If 15 0-0?, then 15 ... ♗d6 and ... ♖dg8 ∓) 15 ... ♘e5 16 ♗e4! ♖d7! 17 b4 ♕d8 18 d4 (18 0-0-0 ♗h6! ∞) 18 ... ♗h6! 19 0-0 (19 dxe5 ♖d2 20 ♕f3 ♖xb2 21 ♕xf6 ♕d2+ 22 ♔f1 ♗g7 ∓; 21 exf6 ♗d2+ 22 ♔f1 ♖h6 ∓) 19 ... ♘g4 20 d5 ♖g8! 21 ♖fd1 (21 dxc6? ♖d2 22 cxb7+ ♔b8 −+; 21 ♗c1 ∞) 21 ... ♕c7! 22 dxc6?! (22 ♗d4 ♔b8 23 dxc6 ♖xd4 24 ♖xd4 ♗e3! ∓; 22 ♔f1!? f5 ∞) 22 ... ♖xd1+ 23 ♖xd1 ♗e3! 24 ♔f1?! (24 fxe3?! ♕xg3+ 25 ♕g2 ♕xe3+ 26 ♔f1 ♘h2+!! ∓; 25 ♗g2 ♕h2+ 26 ♔f1 ♘xe3+ 27 ♕xe3 ♕xg2+ ∓; 24 cxb7+! ♔b8 25 fxe3 ♕xg3+ 26 ♕g2 ♕xe3+ 27 ♔f1 e5!∓) 24 ... ♗xf2! (24 ... ♘xf2 25 ♕xe3 ♘xd1 26 ♕xa7 ∞) 25 cxb7+ ♔b8 26 ♖d3 ♗xg3 27 ♕d2 ♗f4 28 ♕e1 ♗e3! 29 ♖xe3 ♕f4+ 30 ♗f3 ♘xe3+ 31 ♔e2 ♘xc4 32 ♗a1 **White resigned.**

12
King's Indian Set-up — 2 d3

1 e4 c6 2 d3

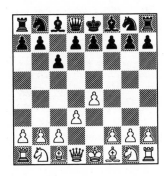

With his restrained second move, White keeps open the possibility of a variety of pawn structures. Consequently the system is characterized by a great degree of flexibility. Generally, after completion of development, White will seek space in the centre by means of d3-d4 and this often leads to a sudden sharpening of the position.

Black's responses include seizing the centre for himself with e7-e5 as in variation A, where Razuvaev's continued adoption of 4 . . . ♗d6 should be noted.

Alternatively 3 . . . g6 as in C may prove a solid defensive system. But both B and D should be viewed with suspicion.

2 ...   d5

The most natural. Others are **2 ... g6** 3 f4!? ♗g7 4 ♘f3 d5 5 ♘bd2 ♘f6?! 6 e5 ♘g4 7 ♘b3 ♘a6 10 a4 ± Kurajica–Csom, Budapest 1976 and **2 ... e5** and then:

a) 3 g3 ♘f6 4 ♗g2 d5 5 ♘d2 ♗d6 transposing to variation A2.

b) 3 ♘f3 d6 4 d4 ♘f6 5 ♘c3 ♘bd7 6 ♗c4 *(6 g3 ♗e7 7 ♗g2!?)* 6 . . . ♗e7 with a Philidor's Defence where Black has an extra tempo, though this may not be of much significance here. Black's game might be better after **3 . . . ♘f6!?** and now **4 g3 d6 5 ♗g2 g6** *(5 . . . ♗e7 6 0-0 0-0 7 ♖e1 ♘bd7 8 d4 ♖e8 9 c4 exd4?! — 9 . . . a6 = Speelman — 10 ♘xd4 ♘e5 11 ♘a3! ♕b6 12 ♖e3! ♗g4 13 f3 ∞ d5?! 14 cxd5! cxd5 15 fxg4! ♗c5 16 ♘ac2 ♘fxg4 17 ♖b3 ♕f6 18 h3! ± Ljubojević–Speelman, Barcelona 1989)* 6 0-0 ♗g7 7 a4 *(7 ♖e1 0-0 8 d4?! ♕c7 9 h3?! ♘bd7 10 c4 a6!*

11 ♘c3 b5 12 dxe5 dxe5 13 ♕c2 ♖e8 14 ♗e3 ♗f8 15 a3 ♗b7 16 ♘d2 ♖ac8 17 ♖ac1 a5 ∓ Ljubojević–Karpov, Brussels 1988) 7 ... a5 (7 ... 0-0?! 8 a5!) 8 ♘c3 (8 ♘bd2 0-0 9 ♘c4 ± Hjartarsson) 8 ... 0-0 9 h3 h6 10 ♗e3 d5!? (10 ... ♘bd7 11 ♘d2! ±; 10 ... ♗e6!? is an interesting possibility) 11 exd5 ♘xd5! 12 ♗d2 ♗e6 13 ♕c1 ♔h7 14 ♖e1 ♘d7 = Ljubojević–Hjartarson, Rotterdam 1989, or 4 ♗e2 d6 5 0-0 ♘bd7 6 ♖e1 g6 7 a4 (7 ♗f1 ♗g7 8 d4 0-0 9 dxe5 ♘xe5 10 ♘xe5 dxe5 11 ♕f3 ♗e6 12 ♘d2 ♕c7 13 ♕c3 ♘d7 14 a4 ♖fe8 15 a5 ♖ab8 16 ♘c4 b5 = Ljubojevic–Khalifman, Manila 1990) 7 ... ♗g7 8 ♘c3?! (8 a5!?) 8 ... 0-0 9 d4?! exd4 10 ♘xd4 ♖e8 11 ♗f1?! (11 ♗f3 ♘e5 12 ♗e2 =) 11 ... ♘c5 12 f3 d5! 13 e5 ♘h5! 14 g4? (14 f4 f6 15 e6!? f5! 16 ♘xf5 gxf5 17 ♕xh5 ♗xe6 18 ♗e3 d4! 19 ♖ad1 ♗d7 ∓ Ivanchuk) 14 ... ♖xe5 15 ♖xe5 ♗xe5 16 gxh5 ♕h4 17 f4 ♕g4+! −+ Ljubojevic–Ivanchuk, Linares 1990.

c) 3 f4 d5 (3 ... exf4 4 ♗xf4 possibly favours White due to the open f-file) 4 ♘f3 dxe4 5 ♘xe5 (All more like a Vienna Opening than the Caro-Kann) 5 ... ♕h4+ 6 g3 ♕e7 7 d4 ♘h6 8 ♗c4 (8 ♘c3!?) 8 ... ♗e6 9 d5?! cxd5 10 ♗xd5 f6 11 ♘c4 ♘c6 12 ♘e3 ♖d8 13 c4 ♕f7 14 ♘c3 ♗c5 15 ♘xe4 ♗d4! ∞ Tal–Bronstein, Moscow 1966.

d) 3 ♘d2 ♘f6 4 ♘gf3 d6 5 g3 g6 6 ♗g2 ♗g7 7 0-0 0-0 8 a4 ♘bd7 9 a5 ♖e8 10 b4 ♖b8 (Alternatively 10 ... d5) 11 ♗b2 b5 12 axb6 axb6 13 ♖a7 ♗b7 (Possibly 13 ... ♖b7) 14 c4 (14

♘c4 ♕c7 15 ♕e2 d5!) 14 ... ♕c7 15 ♕b3 ♖a8 16 ♖xa8 ♗xa8 17 ♖a1 d5 18 cxd5 cxd5 19 ♘g5! ± Ljubojević–Karpov, Amsterdam 1988.

3 ♘d2   ...

Black can now choose between:

A: 3 ... e5
B: 3 ... dxe4
C: 3 ... g6
D: 3 ... ♘f6

Three rarer continuations are:
a) 3 ... ♘a6 4 ♘gf3 ♗g4 5 h3 ♗h5 6 exd5! cxd5 7 d4 ♘c7 8 c4 ± Konstantinopolsky.

b) 3 ... ♘d7 4 ♘gf3 ♕c7 (4 ... e6 5 b3 dxe4 6 dxe4 ♘gf6 7 ♗b2 ♗e7 8 e5 ♘d5 9 c4 ♘5b6 10 ♗e2 0-0 ± Čirić–Šumić, Yugoslavia 1975) 5 exd5 (5 g3 dxe4 6 dxe4 e5 7 ♗g2 ♗c5 8 0-0 ♘e7 9 b3 ♘g6 10 ♗b2 ± Olafsson–Eliskases, 1960) 5 ... cxd5 6 d4! g6 7 ♗d3 ♗g7 8 0-0 e6 9 ♖e1 ♘e7 10 ♘f1 ♘c6 11 c3 0-0 12 ♗g5! e5 13 ♘e3!

♘b6 *(13 . . . exd4 14 ♘xd5 ♕d6 15 ♘e7+ etc. or 13 . . . e4? 14 ♘xd5! ♕d6 15 ♗xe4 f5 16 ♗c2 +—)* 14 dxe5 ♘xe5 15 ♗f4 f6 16 a4 ± Fischer-Marović, Rovinj-Zagreb 1970.

c) **3 . . . e6** does not comply with the spirit of the Defence. After 4 f4 c5 5 ♘gf3 ♘c6 6 g3 White stands better.

A

3 . . .   e5

The most natural response, occupying the centre.

4 ♘gf3   . . .

Here:

A1: 4 . . . ♘d7
A2: 4 . . . ♗d6

Instead Rogoff–Pomar, Olot 1971 went 4 . . . ♗g4 5 c3 *(5 h3!?)* 5 . . . ♘d7 6 ♗e2 ♘gf6 7 0-0 ♗d6?! which could have been countered by 8 exd5! cxd5 9 ♘xe5! ♘xe5 10 d4 ±.

A1

4 . . .   ♘d7
5 d4   . . .

This immediate counter-attack in the centre is more active than **5 g3** ♘gf6 6 ♗g2 ♗d6 *(6 . . . dxe4 7 dxe4 ♗e7 8 0-0 0-0 9 b3?! ♕c7 10 ♗b2 ♖e8 11 a4*

b6 12 ♘c4 ♗f8 = Platonov–A. Zaitsev, USSR (ch) 1969; 9 c3! is better) 7 0-0 0-0 8 exd5 cxd5 9 ♖e1 ♖e8 10 ♘f1 h6 11 ♗d2 a5 12 ♘e3 ♘b6 = Stein-Barcza, Tallinn 1971, or **5 ♕e2!?** dxe4 6 ♘xe4 ♗e7 7 ♗d2 ♘gf6 8 ♗c3 ♘d5!? 9 ♘xe5 ♘xc3 10 ♘xc3 ♘xe5 11 ♕xe5 0-0 12 ♗e2 ♖e8 13 ♕h5 ♗f6 14 0-0 g6 15 ♕f3 ♗e6 16 ♖fe1 ♗d4 17 ♕f4 ♕b6 18 ♗f1 ± Ljubojević-Christiansen, Szirak (izt) 1987.

5 . . .   dxe4

Clearly inferior are **5 . . . ♘gf6?** 6 exd5 ± (Konstantinopolsky and Veits) and **5 . . . exd4?** 6 exd5 c5? *(6 . . . cxd5 was called for although after 7 ♘xd4 Black has no compensation for his IQP)* 7 ♘c4! ♘df6 8 ♕e2+ ♕e7 9 ♘d6+ ♔d7 *(9 . . . ♔d8 10 ♘e5!)* 10 ♘xf7! +—.

6 ♘xe4   exd4

If 6 . . . ♘gf6 then 7 ♘xf6+ ♕xf6 8 ♗g5.

7 ♗c4   . . .

Or 7 ♕xd4 ♘gf6 8 ♗g5 ♗e7 9 0-0-0 0-0 10 ♘d6 ± Tal-Smyslov, Yugoslavia (c) 1959.

7 . . .   ♘df6
8 ♘eg5   . . .

8 ♘fg5 also proved effective in Kupreichik-Kapengut, USSR 1968

after 8 ... &e6? 9 &xe6 fxe6 10 &g5
♕a5+ 11 &f1 &d5 12 ♕e2 &e7 13
&d2 &e3+ 14 &xe3 dxe3 15 &xe6
♕e5 16 f4 ±.

8 ...	&h6
9 0-0	&e7
10 &xd4	0-0
11 c3	♕c7!

Better than 11 ... &f5? 12 &ge6!
± as in Ljubojević–Marović, Yugoslavia (ch) 1972. After the text,
12 g3 &g4 leaves Black with only a
small disadvantage according to
Konstantinopolsky and Veits.

A2

4 ...   &d6

5 g3   ...

After **5 d4!?** exd4 6 exd5! *(6 &xd4
&f6 =)* Black should continue not **6
... &f6?!** 7 dxc6 &xc6 8 &e2! 0-0 9 0-0

&c7 10 &b3 &b6 11 &g5 ± as in
Popović–Grószpéter, Innsbruck 1977
but **6 ... cxd5** where Black has an
extra tempo compared to the lines of
the French Tarrasch.
   Interesting is **5 ♕e2 &f6!** *(5 ...
♕e7 6 g3 &f6 7 &g2 0-0 8 0-0 dxe4 9
dxe4 &bd7 10 &c4 &c7 11 b3 b5 12
&a3 b4 13 &b2 ± Ljubojević–Bouaziz,
Szirák (izt) 1987)* 6 g3 *(6 exd5?! cxd5 7
&xe5 0-0 ∓)* 6 ... 0-0 7 &g2 ♖e8 8 0-0
&bd7 9 b3 *(9 c3 a5 ∓ Henkin)* 9 ... a5!
10 a3 (Akopian–Henkin, USSR 1988)
10 ... ♕c7 11 &b2 &c5 ∓ (Henkin).

5 ...   &f6

   Or 5 ... &e7 6 &g2 0-0 7 0-0 and
now:
   a) 7 ... **f5** 8 exd5 cxd5 9 c4! &bc6
10 cxd5 &xd5 11 ♕b3 &c7 12 &xe5!
&e6 13 &xc6 bxc6 14 ♕a4 ± Savon-
Pomar, Wijk aan Zee 1972.
   b) 7 ... **f6** 8 d4! &g4 9 c4 exd4
10 cxd5 cxd5 11 exd5 &d7 12 &b3
&b6 13 ♕xd4 ± Stein–De Lange,
Havana (ol) 1966.
   c) 7 ... &d7 8 ♖e1 f5 9 exf5 &xf5
10 b3?! *(10 c4! ±)* 10 ... ♕f6 11 &b2
&h6 12 c4 &f7 13 cxd5 cxd5 14 ♕e2
&b6 −+ Timman–Pomar, Wijk aan
Zee 1972.

6 &g2	0-0
7 0-0	...

   The waiting move 7 c3 was to be
considered, as then Black would have
to think twice about playing &g4.

7 ...   ♗g4

A later deviation by Razuvaev on this stem game should be seriously examined: 7 ... ♖e8!? 8 ♖e1 *(8 c3; 8 ♘h4!?)* **8 ... ♘bd7** 9 a4 a5 10 b3 ♘f8 11 ♗b2 ♘g6 12 ♖e2 *(Minić and Sindik in Informator 29 give this an ?! and recommend 12 d4 ♗g4 13 h3 ±)* 12 ... ♕c7 13 d4 ♗g4 14 ♕e1?! *(14 h3 ♗xf3 15 ♗xf3 =)* 14 ... ♗b4! with advantage to Black in Planinc-Razuvaev, Polanica Zdrój 1979. Alternatively Black can play **8 ... ♗g4** 9 h3 ♗h5 10 ♘f1 ♘bd7 *(10 ... ♘a6!? 11 g4 ♗g6 12 ♘g3 dxe4 13 dxe4 ♘c7 and ♘e6-f4 ∞ − Seirawan)* 11 g4 ♗g6 12 ♘g3 dxe4 13 dxe4 ♗c5 14 ♘d2! ♘f8 15 g5 ♘6d7 16 h4 h6! ∞ Ljubojević-Seirawan, Rotterdam 1989.

8 h3   ♗h5
9 g4!?   ...

An aggressive move which, however, fails to live up to expectations. Instead **9 c3** followed by ♕c2 and ♖e1 would have put Black's set-up to the real test; less effective are:

a) **9 ♖e1** ♘bd7 10 g4?! ♗g6 11 ♘h4 h6 12 ♘f1 dxe4 13 dxe4 ♘c5 14 ♘g3 ♗c7?! 15 ♘4f5 ♘e6 16 b3?! ♗a5! ∓ Halász-Varnusz, Budapest 1977.

b) **9 ♕e1** *(In Sax-Grószpéter, Hungary 1978 White played 9 ♕e2 but later had to return to e1)* 9 ... ♘bd7 10 ♘h4 ♖e8 11 ♘b3 ♖c8 12 a4 ♘c5 13 ♘xc5 ♗xc5 14 ♗g5 ♗g6 15 ♖d1 dxe4

= Dolmatov-Grószpéter, Groningen 1977-78.

9 ...   ♗g6
10 ♘h4!   ♘bd7!

Instead 10 ... ♘xe4 11 dxe4 ♕xh4 12 exd5 cxd5 13 c4! ♘c6 14 cxd5 and 15 ♘f3 favours White.

11 ♘xg6   hxg6

And now the game Pripis-Razuvaev, Moscow 1977 continued 12 g5? ♘h5 and Black subsequently mounted a decisive attack against the weakened white kingside. An improvement is **12 exd5** when 12 ... cxd5 13 c4! ± or 12 ... ♘xd5 13 ♘e4 ∞.

B

3 ...   dxe4
4 dxe4   e5

Unsatisfactory is 4 ... ♘f6?! 5 ♘gf3 ♗g4 6 h3 ♗h5? *(Also very bad is 6 ... ♗xf3 7 ♕xf3 ♘bd7 8 ♗e2 e6? when 9 0-0 ♕c7 10 a4 ♖d8 11 ♘c4! b5 12 axb5 cxb5 13 ♗f4 ♕c6 14 ♘a5 ♕b6 15 c4 ± ocurred in Hort-Pomar, Wijk aan Zee 1972. Correct in his line was 8 ... e5 with a defensible position)* 7 e5 ♘d5 8 e6! ± Stein-Birbrager, USSR 1966 (see illustrative games).

5 ♘gf3   ♗c5

5 ... ♕c7 6 ♘c4 ♘d7 7 a4 ♘gf6
8 ♗d3 ♗c5 9 0-0 0-0 10 ♗g5 gives
White a large plus according to Veits
and Konstantinopolsky.

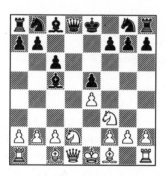

The text move has been univer-
sally regarded as an effective
response by various sources, but an
analysis by Keene throws doubt on its
soundness. We have:

a) **6 ♗e2 ♕e7 7** 0-0 ♘f6 8 c3 a5 9 b3
0-0 unclear, Sax–Markland, Nice (ol)
1974.

b) **6 ♗c4 ♘f6?** *(6 ... ♕e7 7 0-0 ♘f6
=)* 7 ♘xe5 ♗xf2+ 8 ♔e2! ♗e6 9 ♗xe6
fxe6 10 ♘dc4 ♕xd1+ 11 ♖xd1 ♗c5
12 ♗e3 ♘xe4 13 ♔f3 ♗xe3 14 ♔xe4
♗c5 15 ♖hf1 ± Boleslavsky.

c) **6 ♗d3 ♘f6 7 ♕e2 ♘bd7 8 ♘c4
♕c7** = Karner–Korchmar, USSR
1968.

d) **6 c3!** ♘f6 *(On 6 ... ♕c7 7 ♘c4 f6
— 7 ... ♘d7 8 ♗e3 ♗xe3 9 ♘d6+ ♔e7
10 ♘f5+ — 8 ♗e3 ♗xe3 9 ♘d6+ ♔e7,
8 ♘xc8+ ♕xc8 9 fxe3 +— or 6 ... ♕e7
7 ♘c4 ♘d7 8 b4! b5 9 ♘e3 ♗xe3 or
6 ... ♕b6 7 ♘c4! ♗xf2+ ♔e2 +—)* 7 b4

♗b6 8 ♘xe5 ♕e7 9 ♘ec4 ♘xe4 10
♘xe4 ♕xe4+ 11 ♗e3! 0-0 12 ♘xb6
axb6 13 ♕d3! *(13 ♕d6? ♖xa2!)* ±
Konstantinopolsky and Veits.

However, Keene's idea — which he
suddenly spotted during a game
against Hug as Black in Rome 1979 —
may make all these examples redundant. It runs **6 ♘xe5 ♗xf2+** (∓ *ECO*)
7 ♔xf2 ♕d4+ 8 ♔e1 ♕xe5 9 ♘c4!
(9 ♘f3 ♕xe4+ 10 ♔f2 ♘f6 11 ♗d3 ∞)
9 ... ♕xe4+ 10 ♗e2 *(Mariotti suggests
10 ♔f2!?)* **10 ... ♕e6** *(10 ... ♕xg2 11
♘d6+ ♔f8 12 ♖f1 ♗e6 — what else? —
13 ♘xf7!! ♗xf7 14 ♕d8 mate is a line
of Keene's)* **11 ♘d6+♔e7** *(11 ... ♔f8
12 ♖f1 ♘f6 — 12 ... f6 13 ♘xc8 ♕xc8
14 ♕d6+ ♘e7 15 ♗h6 +— — 13 ♘xc8
♕xc8 14 ♕d6 ♔g8 15 ♖xf6 gxf6 16
♗h6 winning)* **12 ♘xc8+♕xc8 13 ♕d4**
± (Keene). Although White has lost
the right to castle the activity of his
queen and bishops on the open board
gives him a dominating position.

C

3 ...   g6

One of the most frequent Black
set-ups, delaying e7-e5 for a time.
Here:

C1: 4 ♘gf3
C2: 4 g3

A third possibility is **4 f4!?** ♗g7
5 ♘gf3 ♘f6?! 6 ♕e2 ♕b6?! 7 e5 ♘g4

8 ♘b3 h5 9 h3 ♘h6 10 ♗e3 ♕b7 11 ♗f2 a5 12 a4 b6 13 ♘bd4 ♘f5 as in Sax-Eperjesi, Hungary (ch) 1977 when White had a slight advantage due to Black's inaccurate play.

C1

4 ♘gf3   ♗g7

Now:

C1.1: 5 g3
C1.2: 5 ♗e2

An idea adopted by Ljubojević (though he was later to switch to 5 ♗e2) is 5 c3, e.g.: 5 . . . e5 6 a4!? *(6 ♗e2 ♘e7 7 h4?! h6 8 h5 g5 9 d4! exd4 10 ♘xd4 0-0 11 0-0 c5! ∓ Ljubojević-Hort, Madrid 1973)* 6 . . . ♘e7 7 a5!? (No routine piece development for the Yugoslav) 7 . . . 0-0 8 ♗e2 h6 9 0-0 f5 10 b3 and now, rather than the bizarre 10 . . . ♔h7 11 ♗a3 ♖g8 12 ♖e1 g5?! 13 exf5 ♗xf5 14 ♘f1 ♘d7 15 ♘g3 ♗g6 16 a6 b6 17 d4! with

difficulties for Black in Ljubojević-Savon, Petropolis (izt) 1973, best is 10 . . . ♗e6 11 ♗a3 ♖f7 etc. Variation C1.2 is probably more logical as after a queenside fianchetto the diagonal remains open.

C1.1

5 g3   e5

5 . . . ♘f6 transposes to C2 while 5 . . . dxe4 6 dxe4 b6 is interesting, viz: 7 ♗c4?! ♘f6 8 0-0 0-0 9 ♖e1 ♕c7 10 c3 e5 11 a4 a5 12 b3 ♖d8 13 ♕c2 h6 = Nezhmetdinov-A. Zaitsev, USSR 1967 or 7 ♕e2! ♗a6 8 c4 *(9 e5 is threatened)* 8 . . . c5 *(8 . . . e5 9 b4!)* 9 a3 *(9 e5!? ♘c6 10 a3 ♕c7 11 ♗g2 ♖d8 12 e6 ∞)* 9 . . . ♘c6 10 ♖b1 ∞. The sideline can be avoided by 4 g3.

6 ♗g2   ♘e7

6 . . . ♘h6 7 0-0 0-0 8 exd5! cxd5 9 c4 ♘c6 10 cxd5 ♕xd5 11 ♘c4 ♕e6 12 ♗xh6! ♗xh6 13 ♘fxe5! ♘xe5 14 ♖e1 f6 15 f4 ± Ribli-Barcza, Budapest 1971.

7 0-0   0-0

(see diagram)

8 b4!   . . .

Coupling the queenside fianchetto with space acquisition. Other tries:
a) 8 ♖e1 d4 *(8 . . . ♘d7 9 b4 a5 ∞)*

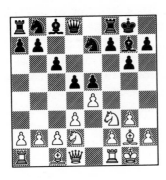

9 a4 a5! *(9 . . . c5? 10 ♘c4 ♘bc6 11 c3 ♗e6 12 cxd4 ♗xc4 13 dxc4 exd4 14 e5 ± Fischer-Hübner, Palma de Mallorca (izt) 1970)* 10 ♘c4 b5 11 ♘a3 ♗a6 = Hübner.

b) **8 ♕e2 ♕c7 9 a4** *(9 c3 dxe4 10 ♘xe4 — 10 dxe4 h6 11 ♘c4 ♗e6 = — 10 . . . ♗g4! 11 h3 ♗xf3 12 ♕xf3 ♘d7 Lombardy-Vukić, and now 13 h4! ± Vukić)* 9 . . . a5 10 b3 ♘a6? 11 ♗a3 d4 12 ♘c4 ♘b4 13 ♘h4! ♗e6 14 f4 exf4 15 gxf4 f5 16 ♗h3 ♖ae8 17 ♕d2 ± Korsin-Konstantinopolsky, Moscow 1966.

c) **8 c3 ♘d7** *(8 . . . ♕c7 9 ♖e1 ♘d7 10 ♕c2 f5 ∞ Gufeld-Lazarev, Kiev 1963)* 9 b4 b6 10 ♗b2 ♗b7 11 ♖e1 ♖e8 = Stein-Hort, Los Angeles 1968.

d) **8 a4 ♖e8** *(Also 8 . . . h6 9 ♖e1 ♕c7!? — 9 . . . d4!? — 10 c3 dxe4 — 10 . . . ♖d8!? — 11 dxe4 ♗e6 12 ♕e2 ♖d8 13 b3! ± Tompa-Varnusz, Budapest 1977 or 8 . . . a5!? 9 c3 dxe4 10 dxe4 ♕c7 11 ♘c4 ♖d8 12 ♕b3?! b5!? ∞ Hazai-Esperjesi, Hungary (ch) 1977)* 9 ♖e1 d4? 10 b4! f6?! 11 c3 dxc3 12 ♕b3+ ♔h8 13 ♕xc3 ♗e6 14 d4 ± Hazai-

Bárczay, Zalaegerszeg 1977.

e) **8 b3 d4?!** 9 a4 ♘a6 10 ♗a3 c5 11 ♘c4 ♘c6 12 ♘e1 ♘ab4 13 f4 exf4 14 gxf4 f5 15 e5 ± Kochiev-Smyslov, USSR 1977.

8 . . .   a5!

Black must immediately counter the White expansion — weaker are **8 . . . dxe4** 9 dxe4 ♕c7 10 ♗b2 ♗g4 11 h3 ♗xf3 12 ♕xf3 ♘d7 13 ♖fd1 ♖fd8 14 ♗f1 ♘f6 15 ♗c4 ♘c8 16 a4 ± Smyslov-Bouwmeester, Leipzig (ol) 1960, and **8 . . . ♘d7** 9 ♗b2 ♕c7 *(9 . . . b6 10 d4! ±)* 10 ♖e1 d4 11 c3! dxc3 12 ♗xc3 ± Stein-Golombek, Kecskemét 1968.

9 bxa5   . . .

C1.11: 9 . . . ♖xa5
C1.12: 9 . . . ♕xa5

C1.11

9 . . .   ♖xa5
10 ♗b2   ♕c7
11 a4   . . .

Instead **11 ♕e2** d4?! 12 c3 dxc3 13 ♗xc3 ♖a4 14 ♘c4 b5 15 ♕c2 ♗e6 16 ♘cxe5! f6 17 ♘c4 gave White a large plus in Stein-Wade, Tallinn 1969 while also promising is **11 ♖e1** d4 12 ♘c4 ♖a6 13 c3.

The text, 11 a4, was played in Stein-Cobo, Havana 1968 when after 11 . . . h6 12 ♖e1 d4 13 c3 c5 14 ♖c1 dxc3 15 ♗xc3 ♖a6 White should have played 16 d4! ±.

C1.12

9 . . .   ♕xa5

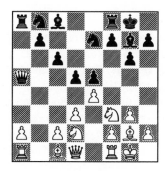

10 ♗b2   d4

10 . . . ♕c7 11 ♕e2 d4 12 c3 c5 13 cxd4 cxd4 *(13 . . . exd4 14 ♖fc1 ♕b6 15 ♘c4 ♕a7 ±)* 14 a4 ♘bc6 15 ♗a3 ♖d8 *(15 . . . ♖xa4 16 ♗d6 ♕a5 17 ♘c4 ♕a6 18 ♖xa4 ♕xa4 19 ♕b2 ± Trapl)* 16 ♖fb1 ♘a5 *(16 . . . ♖xa4? 17 ♗d6 ♕a5 18 ♗c7! wins)* 17 ♖b5 ♘ec6 18 ♗c5! ± Trapl-Javelle (corr) 1987.

11 a4   . . .

Deviants include:
a) 11 ♘c4 ♕c7 12 a4 *(12 c3 b5!? 13 ♘cxe5 ♗xe5 14 ♘xe5 ♕xe5 15 cxd4 ♕h5!? 16 ♕d2 with complex possibilities)* 12 . . . c5 13 ♘fd2 ♗h6 14 c3 ♘ec6 = Hartoch-Bukic, Banja Luka 1974.

b) 11 ♕c1?! ♘d7 12 ♘b3 *(12 c3 ♘c5!?)* 12 . . . ♕a4! ∓ Short-Miles, Wijk aan Zee 1987.

11 . . .   ♕c7
12 c3   dxc3
13 ♗xc3   c5

13 . . . ♖d8 14 ♕b1! ±.

14 ♘c4   ♘ec6
15 ♕b3   . . .

± Ermolinsky-Tukmakov, Sverdlovsk 1987 — White exerts a slight pressure on the queenside.

C1.2

5 ♗e2   . . .

Ljubojević's favourite move.

5 . . .   e5

5 . . . ♘gf6 6 0-0 0-0 7 ♖e1 c5!? 8 c3 ♘c6 9 ♗f1 ♕c7 10 a3 ♖d8 11 ♕c2 b6 ± Adorján-Eperjesi, Hungary (ch) 1977.

6 0-0   ♘e7
7 b4!   . . .

Once again a good move in these types of position.

7 . . .   a5!

It is important to play this before

White gets in ♗b2. Ljubojević–Pfleger, Manila 1975 went instead 7 ... 0-0?! 8 ♗b2 ♘d7 9 ♖e1 a5 10 a3 ♕c7 11 ♗f1 b6 12 d4! and White had achieved his objectives.

8 bxa5   ♖xa5?

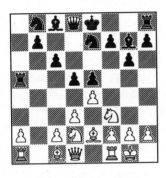

Black wants to avoid the loss of tempi, but ironically this incurs even more serious time-wasting. According to Sokolov 8 ... ♕xa5 9 ♗b2 ♕c7 is needed as it prevents an early d3-d4 by White.

After the text White quickly achieved this break in Ljubojević–Čirić, Yugoslavia 1975 by 9 ♗b2 ♕c7 10 ♘b3 ♖a8 11 d4! with a favourable opening up of the position — see illustrative game number 72.

C2

4 g3	♗g7
5 ♗g2	dxe4
6 dxe4	♘f6

6 ... e5 7 ♘gf3 ♗e6 8 0-0 ♘h6 *(8 ... ♕c7 9 ♘g5)* 9 ♕e2!0-0 10 ♘c4 f6 11 b3 b5!? *(11 ... ♘f7 12 ♗a3 ♖e8 13 ♖fd1 ±)* 12 ♘e3 ♘d7 13 h4! ♕c7 14 h5 ± Gufeld–Smyslov, USSR 1975.

7 ♘gf3	0-0
8 0-0	♘a6

Not 8 ... ♘bd7? 9 e5! ♘d5 10 e6! fxe6 11 ♘g5 ♘c5 12 ♕e2 e5 13 ♘c4 ♕c7 14 ♖e1 ± Stein–Berger, Amsterdam (izt) 1964.

The text is Stein–Portisch, Moscow 1967 which continued 9 e5 ♘d5 10 ♘b3 ♗g4 11 ♕e2 ♕c8 12 ♖e1 ♘ac7 13 ♗d2 f6 14 exf6 ♗xf6 15 c3 and although Black has comfortable posts for his pieces White's chances are somewhat better.

D

3 ...	♘f6

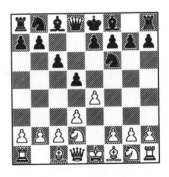

4 ♘gf3	♗g4

4 ... e6 contradicts the spirit of the Defence: 5 g3 b6 6 ♕e2 ♗e7 7 ♗g2 0-0 8 0-0 ♗b7 9 ♖e1 ♖e8 10 e5! ♘fd7 11 ♘f1 c5 12 h4! with a standard position in White's favour, Ignatiev-Hodos, USSR 1960.

5 e5   ...

Or 5 h3 when:
a) 5 ... ♗xf3 6 ♕xf3 e6 7 g3 ♘a6 8 ♗g2 ♗b4 9 c3 ♗e7 10 0-0 0-0 11 e5! ♘d7 12 ♕e2 ♘c7 13 ♘f3 a5 14 h4! b5 15 h5 ± Smyslov-Khalibieli, USSR 1968.
b) 5 ... ♗h5(?!) 6 ♕e2 ♕c7?! *(Still ... ♗xf3. After the text the bishop gets shut out of the action)* 7 g4! ♗g6 8 ♗g2 e6 9 0-0 ♗e7 10 ♘h4! ± Sax-Vadász, Budapest 1977 — see illustrative games.

5 ...   ♘fd7?!

5 ... ♘g8 would at least prevent White's next, an idea of Bronstein.

6 e6!   ♗xe6

Or 6 ...fxe6 7 h3 ♗h5 8 g4 ♗f7 9 ♘g5 ♗g8 10 d4 e5 11 dxe5 ♘xe5 12 f4 e6 13 ♕e2 ♘bd7 14 ♘b3 ± Mashlovsky-Birbrager, USSR 1973.

7 ♘d4   ♘f6
8 ♘xe6   fxe6

9 g3 c5 10 ♗h3 e6 11 ♘f3 ♗d6 12 ♘g5 with the more favourable prospects for White, Bronstein-Vorotnikov,

USSR 1970. It would appear that, due to the harassment White can inflict on the knight, 3 . . . ♘f6 is an unsatisfactory continuation for Black.

ILLUSTRATIVE GAMES

71   STEIN-BIRBRAGER
USSR Team Championship 1966
1 e4 c6 2 d3 d5 3 ♘d2 dxe4 4 dxe4 ♘f6?!5 ♘gf3 ♗g4 6 h3 ♗h5? 7 e5 ♘d5 8 e6! f6 (8 . . . fxe6 was perhaps the lesser of two evils) **9 g4 ♗g6 10 ♘d4!** (A strong move which paralyses Black's position and prepares for the subsequent complications) **10 ... ♘c7** (Development is difficult while the e-pawn is on the board, so Black strives to eliminate it at any cost. 10 . . . ♘f4 is answered by 11 ♘c4 or 11 ♘2f3) **11 c3 ♕d5** (Black's trump card) **12 ♕b3! ♕xh1 13 ♕xb7 ♔d8** (Mate was threatened) **14 ♘2f3 ♗d3 15 ♗f4!** (Stein plays in the spirit of the Romantic school. Of the two kings, Black's is in graver danger, because the white monarch can flee to the centre. Material advantage plays no role here) **15 . . . ♕xf1+ 16 ♔d2 ♕xf2+ 17 ♔xd3 ♘xe6** (On 17 . . . ♘8a6 18 ♗xc7+ ♘xc7 19 ♘xc6+ ♔e8 20 ♘cd4! ♔d8 21 ♖d1! is safest, with the threat 22 ♘b5!) **18 ♘xe6+ ♔e8 19 ♕c8+ ♔f7 20 ♘fg5+ Black resigned.**

72   LJUBOJEVIĆ–ČIRIĆ
Yugoslavia 1975

1 e4 c6 2 d3 d5 3 ᐧd2 g6 4 ᐧgf3 ᨕg7 5 ᨕe2 e5 6 0-0 ᐧe7 7 b4! a5! 8 bxa5 ᖴxa5 9 ᨕb2 ᘻc7 10 ᐧb3 ᖴa8 11 d4! dxe4 (11 . . . exd4 12 ᨕxd4 is no better) 12 ᐧxe5 0-0 13 ᘻd2 (Thanks to his dominating knight outpost, White stands better. The dislodging of this e5 knight causes Black to weaken himself) 13 . . . f6 14 ᐧc4 ᐧd5 15 f3! exf3 16 ᨕxf3 b6?! (16 . . . ᐧb6!?) 17 ᨕa3! ᖴd8 18 ᖴfe1 ᨕa6 19 ᐧe3 ᨕb7 20 ᐧxd5?! (The beginning of a bold and combinative simplification, in the course of which White even accepts a nasty pin thanks to a hidden trump card. Black subsequently gets tangled up in the complications – justifying White's tactics, but objectively 20 ᨕb2! with advantage to White would have been simpler) 20 . . . cxd5 21 ᨕe7!? ᖴe8 22 ᘻe2 ᐧc6? (22 . . . ᘻd7! 23 ᘻe6+ ᘻxe6 24 ᖴxe6 ᘜf7? would have fallen into the trap: 25 ᖴxb6! ᖴxe7 26 ᖴxb7! ᖴxb7 27 ᨕxd5+, but 24 . . . ᐧd7! and Black has no troubles – 25 ᖴae1?! ᘜf7 26 a3? ᨕf8!) 23 ᘻe6+! (23 ᨕxd5+ ᘜh8 24 ᘻc4 ᖴxe7 25 ᖴxe7 ᘻxe7 26 ᨕxc6 ᖴc8 ∞) 23 . . . ᘜh8 24 ᨕd6! ᘻd8 25 ᘻf7 ᖴxe1+ 26 ᖴxe1 ᘻxd6 27 ᘻxb7 ᖴb8 28 ᘻf7 ᖴf8 29 ᖴe6! ᘻb4 30 ᖴe8! (White handles the still rather complicated game magnificently) 30 . . . ᐧe5 (30 . . . ᐧxd4? 31 ᨕxd5 ᐧe2+ 32 ᘜf2 +–) 31 ᖴxf8+ ᨕxf8 32 ᘻxf6+ ᨕg7 33 ᘻd8+ ᨕf8 34 c3! ᐧxf3+ 35 ᘜf2! ᘻa3 36 ᘜxf3 ᘜg7

37 ᘻc7+ ᘜg8 38 ᘻxb6 ᘻxa2 39 ᘻe6+ ᘜg7 40 ᘻe5+! ᘜh6 41 ᘻf4+ ᘜg7 42 ᘻe5+ ᘜh6 43 ᘻf6! ᨕa3 44 ᐧc5! ᨕxc5 45 dxc5 ᘻa8 46 c6 ᘻe8 47 ᘻf4+ ᘜg7 48 ᘻd4+ ᘜh6 49 ᘻe3+ **Black resigned.**

73   SAX–VADÁSZ
Budapest 1977

1 e4 c6 2 d3 d5 3 ᐧd2 ᐧf6 4 ᐧgf3 ᨕg4 5 h3 ᨕh5?! 6 ᘻe2! ᘻc7?! 7 g4! ᨕg6 8 ᨕg2 e6 9 0-0 ᨕe7 10 ᐧh4! dxe4 (10 . . . ᐧxe4? 11 ᐧxg6 ᐧxd2 12 ᐧxe7 ᐧxf1 13 ᐧf5 +–) 11 dxe4 ᐧbd7? (For better or worse 11 . . . e5 was necessary. With the text, Black only protects himself against the threat of . . . f5, hoping for: 12 f4 ᨕxe4! 13 ᐧxe4 ᐧxe4 14 ᨕxe4 ᨕxh4 15 g5 h5) 12 ᐧf5! exf5 13 exf5 ᨕxf5 14 gxf5 ᐧb6 (Hoping that the knight can occupy an outpost on d5. Perhaps 14 . . . ᘜf8!? puts up more resistance, although even this is not all that attractive) 15 ᖴe1 ᐧbd5 16 ᐧb3 b5 17 a4 b4 18 c4! bxc3 19 bxc3 0-0 (The knight's position is untenable. 19 . . . ᐧxc3 20 ᨕxc6+!) 20 c4 ᨕb4 21 cxd5 ᨕxe1 22 ᘻc4!?! ("Sax's perspective is inaccessible to ordinary mortals! He does not take the hard-won bishop on e1, but covets the 'worthless' c6 pawn, giving the exchange for it" – Haág. The truth is that 22 ᘻxe1 cxd5 causes only small discomfort to Black, while now the c-pawn becomes the trump in White's hand) 22 . . . ᘻe5 23 dxc6 ᘻc3 24 ᘻxc3 ᨕxc3 25 ᖴb1 ᨕe5 26 ᐧc5 (White has judged the con-

sequences of his sacrifice correctly: Black is unable to marshal his forces around the c-pawn. E.g. 26 . . . ♖ab8 27 ♖b7! or 26 . . . ♘e8 27 ♘d7) 26 . . . ♗d4 27 ♘a6 ♖ac8 28 c7 ♗b6 29 ♗f4 ♖fe8 30 ♗b7 g5 31 fxg6 hxg6 32 ♗xc8 ♖xc8 33 ♖b5 ♔f8 34 a5 Black resigned.

74 LJUBOJEVIĆ–KARPOV
Brussels 1988

1 e4 c6 2 d3 e5 3 ♘f3 ♘f6 4 g3 d6 5 ♗g2 g6 6 0-0 ♗g7 7 ♖e1 0-0 8 d4?! ♕c7 9 h3 ♘bd7 10 c4 (10 a4 d5! ∓) 10 . . . a6! 11 ♘c3 b5 12 dxe5 dxe5 13 ♕c2 ♖e8 14 ♗e3 ♗f8 15 a3 ♗b7 (15 . . . ♘c5?! 16 b4 ♘e6 17 c5+) 16 ♘d2 (16 b4?! a5 ∓) 16 . . . ♖ac8 17 ♖ac1 (17 ♗f1 ♘c5 18 b4 ♘e6 19 ♘b3 c5 20 ♘d5 ♘xd5 21 cxd5 ♘d4 22 ♗xd4 cxd4 23 ♕xc3 ♖xc7 24 ♖ac1 ∞; 17 . . . ♕b8! ∓ is stronger) 17 . . . a5 18 cxb5 cxb5 19 ♕b1 b4! 20 ♘d5 ♕b8 21 ♘xf6+ ♘xf6 22 a4? (22 axb4 ♗xb4 23 ♖xc8 ♖xc8 24 ♖c1 ♖d8 ∓; 24 . . . ♖xc1+ 25 ♕xc1 ♕a8 ∓) 22 . . . ♕a8 23 ♖xc8 ♖xc8 24 ♖c1 ♗a6! (24 . . . ♖xc1+?! 25 ♕xc1 ♘xe4 26 ♘xe4 ♗xe4 27 ♗xe4 ♕xe4 28 ♕c8 ∞) 25 ♖xc8 ♕xc8 26 ♗g5 (26 ♗f1?! ♗xf1 27 ♕xf1 ♕c2 ∓) 26 . . . ♘d7 27 ♗f1 ♗xf1 28 ♕xf1 ♘c5 29 b3 (29 ♕b5 ♕xh3 30 ♕xa5 ♕g4 is good for Black) 29 . . . ♕e6 30 ♕b5 ♘xb3 31 ♘xb3 ♕xb3 32

♕xe5 (32 ♕e8 ♕e6) 32 . . . ♕xa4 33 ♗e3 ♕d1+ 34 ♔g2 ♕d6 35 ♕xa5 b3 36 ♕b5 ♕b4 37 ♕e5 b2 38 ♗d4 ♕xd4 39 ♕xd4 b1=♕ 40 h4 ♕b4 41 ♕e5 ♕c5 42 ♕b2 h5 43 ♕e2 ♕d4 44 ♕c2 ♗c5 45 ♕e2 ♕c3 46 ♔f1 ♗d4 47 ♔g2 ♕b2 48 ♕f3 ♕d2 49 ♔f1 ♔g7 50 ♔g1 ♕c1+ 51 ♔g2 ♕e1 52 ♕f4 ♕e2 53 ♔g1 ♕g4! White resigned.

75 LJUBOJEVIĆ–KARPOV
Amsterdam 1988

1 e4 c6 2 d3 e5 3 ♘d2 ♘f6 4 ♘gf3 d6 5 g3 g6 6 ♗g2 ♗g7 7 0-0 0-0 8 a4 ♘bd7 9 a5 ♖e8 10 b4 ♖b8 11 ♗b2 b5 12 axb6 axb6 13 ♖a7 ♗b7 14 c4 ♕c7 15 ♕b3 ♖a8 16 ♖xa8 ♗xa8 (16 . . . ♖xa8 17 d4 ±) 17 ♖a1 d5 (17 . . . ♗b7 improves) 18 cxd5 cxd5 19 ♘g5! ♕d6 (19 . . . h6? 20 ♘xf7! ♔xf7 21 exd5 ♕d6 22 ♘c4 +−) 20 exd5 ♗xd5 21 ♘c4 ♕c6 (21 . . . ♗xc4 22 ♕xc4 ±; 21 . . . ♕f8 22 ♗xd5 ♘xd5 23 ♘xf7! ♕xb4 24 ♕xb4 ♘xb4 25 ♖a7 ±; 21 . . . ♕e7 22 ♗xd5 ♘xd5 23 ♖a7! ♕xg5 24 ♖xd7 ±) 22 ♘e3!! ♗xb3 (The only move) 23 ♗xc6 h6 (23 . . . ♖c8 24 ♗b5 h6 25 ♖a3 ♗c2 26 ♘e4 ±) 24 ♖a3! hxg5 25 ♖xb3 ♗f8 26 ♔g2 ♖e6 27 ♗b5 ♔g7 28 h3 ♗e7 29 ♗c3 (With the idea of ♖b3-a3-a7) 29 . . . ♗d6 30 ♖a3 ♗b8 31 ♖a8 ♖e7 32 ♗d2! e4 33 d4 ♗c7 34 ♖c8 ♘f8 35 ♗c3 ♘8h7 36 ♗c6 ♘f8 37 b5! Black resigned.

13
1 e4 c6 Various

1 e4 c6

Here we examine several off-beat and fairly rarely-used continuations.

A: 2 ♘c3 d5 3 ♕f3
B: 2 c4

The alternatives are as follows:

a) **2 ♘e2 d5** *(Aiming for a Caro-Kann type of game. 2 ... e5 is also good)* 3 e5 c5 4 d4 ♘c6 5 c3 ♗f5 *(5 ... ♗g4 6 f3 ♗d7 7 e6 ♗xe6 8 dxc5 ♘f6 9 b4 g6 10 ♗f4 ♗g7 11 ♘d4 0-0 12 ♘xc6 bxc6 13 ♗e5 ♗h6 14 ♗d3 ♘d7 ∓ Barendregt-Botvinnik, Amsterdam 1966 or 5 ... cxd4 6 cxd4 ♗f5 7 ♘bc3 e6 8 a3 ♘ge7 9 ♘g3 ♗g6 10 h4 h6 11 h5 ♗h7 12 ♗e3 ♘c8 ∓ Nezhmetdinov-Ilivitsky, USSR 1963 and 5 ... e6 6 ♘d2 ♘e7 7 ♘f3 cxd4 8 ♘exd4?! ♘g6 9 ♘xc6 bxc6 10 ♗d3 ♕c7 11 ♕e2 f6!∓ Bronstein-Petrosian, USSR (ch) 1960)* 6 ♘g3 ♗g6 7 dxc5 *(7 ♗e3!?)* 7 ... e6 8 ♗e3 ♘xe5 9 f4 ♘c6 10 ♗d3 ♗xd3 11 ♕xd3 ♘f6 12 ♘bd2 ♗e7 13 0-0 Rossetto-Bronstein, Amsterdam (izt) 1964, 13 ... a5! ∓.

b) **2 ♘f3 d5 3 e5 ♗g4** *(3 ... c5 4 b4?! cxb4 5 a3 bxa3 6 ♘xa3 ♘c6 7 ♗e2*

♗g4 8 d4 e6 9 0-0 ♘ge7 10 c3 ♘f5 11 ♕d3 ♗e7 ∓ Milner-Barry-Golombek, England 1955)* 4 d4 e6 5 c3 ♘d7 6 ♘bd2 c5 7 dxc5 ♗xc5 8 ♕a4 ♗xf3 9 ♘xf3 ♘e7 10 ♗f4 *(10 ♕g4!? ♘g6 11 ♗b5 0-0 12 ♗xd7 ♕xd7 13 0-0 ♗b6 14 h4! ♖ac8 ∞ Tolush-Konstantinopolsky, USSR 1939)* 10 ... 0-0 11 ♗d3 ♘g6 12 ♗g3 ♗e7 13 ♗c2 ♕c7 14 ♕d4 ♕b6 ∞ Tolush-Goglidze, USSR 1939.

c) **2 b3 d5** *(2 ... e5 3 ♗b2 d6 4 d4 ♘f6 5 ♘d2 exd4 6 ♗xd4 d5!? 7 e5 ♘e4 8 ♘xe4 dxe4 9 ♕d2 ♗a3 10 ♘e2 ♗f5 11 ♘g3 ♗g6 12 ♗e2 0-0 13 h4 h6 14 ♖d1 ♕e7 ∓ Vasyukov-Furman, USSR 1964; 7 exd5!?)* 3 ♗b2 dxe4 4 ♘e2 *(4 ♘c3 ♘f6 5 ♘ge2 ♗f5 6 ♘g3 e6 7 ♕e2 ♗b4 8 0-0-0 ♕e7 = Sackes-Goldberg, USSR 1961 or 5 ... ♕c7 6 ♘g3 ♕f4 7 ♕e2 ♗g4 8 ♕e3 ♕xe3+ 9 fxe3 e5 10 ♗e2 ♗xe2 11 ♔xe2 Vasyukov-Čirić, 1964)* 4 ... ♗f5 5 ♘g3 ♗g6 6 h4 h6 7 ♘c3 ♘f6 8 h5 ♗h7 9 ♕e2 e6 10 0-0-0 ♘bd7 11 ♘gxe4 Bokudzhava-Kholmov, USSR 1967, 11 ... ♕a5! 12 ♔b1 ♗e7 13 g3 0-0 14 ♗g2 ♘d5 = Filip.

d) **2 e5 d5 3 exd6 e6 4 b3 ♗xd6**

248

5 ♗b2 ♘f6 6 ♘a3 b5 7 c4 a6 8 g3 0-0 9 ♗g2 ♕e7 10 ♘c2 van Geet-Hort, Beverwijk 1968, 10 . . . e5! ∓ Filip.

e) **2 f4** d5 3 e5 ♗f5 4 d4?! (It is not logical to go over into the closed variation) 4 . . . e6 5 ♘f3 c5 6 c3 ♘c6 7 ♗d3 ♘h6 ∓ Krauss-Konecke, 1952.

A

2 ♘c3	d5
3 ♕f3	. . .

Bringing the queen into play in such an early stage of the game is not without its dangers for Black, but neither is it a truly convincing move.

3 . . .   **dxe4**

The simplest. More complicated is 3 . . . ♘f6 4 e5 ♘fd7 *(4 . . . d4 5 exf6 dxc3 6 fxg7 cxd2+ 7 ♗xd2 ♗xg7 8 0-0-0 ♕b6 9 ♗c3 ± Schwarz)* 5 ♕g3 *(5 d4 e6 6 ♕g3 c5 7 ♘b5 cxd4 8 ♘f3 a6 9 ♘bxd4 ♘c6 10 ♗d3 ♕c7 11 ♘xc6*

bxc6 12 0-0 ♘c5 13 b4 ♘xd3 14 cxd3 ± Schmidt-Delander, Berlin 1970; 8 . . . ♘b6 ∞; 6 . . . a6!?) 5 . . . e6 6 ♘f3 a6 7 ♗e2 c5 8 0-0 ♘c6 9 ♖e1 ♘d4 10 ♗d1 ♘f5 ∞ Smyslov-Flohr, Budapest 1950.

Instead **3 . . . d4** is dubious: 4 ♗c4 ♘f6 5 e5 dxc3 6 exf6 cxd2+ *(6 . . . cxb2 7 ♗xf7+ ♔d7 8 ♗xb2 exf6 9 ♘e2 ♔c7 10 0-0 ± Shanov-Trudov, USSR 1964)* 7 ♗xd2 exf6 8 0-0-0 ±.

4 ♘xe4	♘d7

If anyone is particularly taken with the variations covered in chapters two or three he can choose the continuations 4 . . . ♘f6 5 ♘xf6+ gxf6 or 5 . . . exf6.

5 b3	. . .

5 d4 ♘gf6 6 ♗d3?! *(6 ♗c4!)* 6 . . . ♘xe4 7 ♕xe4 ♘f6 8 ♕h4 ♗f5 9 ♗xf5 ♕a5+ 10 c3 ♕xf5 11 ♘e2 Lehmann-Romi, 1953, 11 . . . ♕b5 = but simpler is **5 . . . ♘df6!** 6 c3 ♘xe4 7 ♕xe4 ♘f6 8 ♕c2 ♗g4 9 ♘e2 e6 10 ♘g3 ♕d5 = Lutikov-Petrosian, USSR 1960.

5 . . .	♘df6

5 . . . ♘gf6 6 ♘g3 e6! *(6 . . . g6 7 ♗b2 ♗g7 8 h4 ♕c7 9 0-0-0 0-0 10 ♖e1 c5 11 h5 a5 12 hxg6 hxg6 13 ♘e4 ♖e8 14 ♘g3 ± Lombardy-Brinck-Claussen, Cracow 1964)* 7 ♗b2 ♕a5 =.

6 ♘xf6+	♘xf6

7 ♗b2   ♗g4

The game Csom–Navarovsky, Kecskemét 1969 now continued 8 ♕g3 e6 9 ♗e2 ♗f5 10 ♗d1 ♗g6 11 ♘f3 ♗d6 12 ♕h4 ♗e7 =.

B

2 c4   . . .

Actually this is quite a common move, but the game frequently transposes to the Panov Variation, and it rarely has much character of its own. Here we divide with:

B1: 2 . . . e5
B2: 2 . . . d5

A third possibility is 2 . . . e6 3 ♘c3 *(3 ♘f3 d5 4 exd5 exd5 5 cxd5 cxd5 6 ♗b5+ ♘c6 7 0-0 ♗d6 8 d4 ♘e7 9 ♘bd2?! ♗g4 = Levenfish–Nimzovitch, 1912 or 3 d4 d5 4 cxd5 exd5 – after 4 . . . cxd5 5 e5 a variation of the 3 e5 version*

of the French Defence, favouring White, develops — 5 e5?! ♘a6 6 ♘c3 ♘c7 7 ♘ge2 ♘e7 8 ♘f4 ♘f5 9 ♗e3 ♘e6 10 ♘xe6 ♗xe6 11 ♗d3 ♘xe3 12 fxe3 ♕h4+ 13 g3 ♕g5 ∓ Tal–Bisguier, Bled 1961; 5 exd5! cxd5 ±) 3 . . . d5 4 cxd5 exd5 5 exd5 cxd5 6 ♘f3 ♘f6 7 ♗b5+ ♘c6 (7 . . . ♗b7 8 ♕b3 ♗xb5 9 ♕xb5+ ♕d7 10 ♘e5 ± Suetin) 8 0-0 ♗e7 9 ♘e5 ♗d7 10 d4 0-0 11 ♗g5 (11 ♗f4 ±) 11 . . . ♘xe5 12 dxe5 ♘e4 13 ♗xe7 ♘xc3 14 ♗xd8 ♘xd1 15 ♗xd7 ♖fxd8 16 e6 ± Hübner–Petrosian, Seville (c) 1971.

B1

2 . . .   e5
3 d4   . . .

3 ♘f3 and now:
a) 3 . . . ♘f6?! *(For 3 . . . d6 4 d4 ♗g4 see 3 d4 d6 4 ♘f3 ♗g4)* 4 ♘xe5 d6 5 ♘f3 ♘xe4 6 ♘c3! ♘g5? 7 d4 ♗e7 8 ♘xg5 ♗xg5 9 ♕e2+! ♗e7 10 ♗g5 ± F. Garcia-Gil, Cala d'Or 1986 or 4 ♘c3 ♗b4 5 ♘xe5 0-0 6 ♗e2 d6 7 ♘d3!? ♗xc3 8 dxc3 ♘xe4 9 0-0 ♖e8 10 f3 ♘f6 11 ♗g5 (Vaganian–Nogueiras, USSR 1987) 11 . . . ♗f5! ±.
b) 3 . . . ♕a5 4 ♘c3 ♗b4 5 ♕c2 ♘f6 6 ♗e2 0-0 7 0-0 d5?! 8 cxd5 cxd5 9 exd5?! *(9 ♘xe5 d4? 10 ♘c4 ♕d8 11 ♘b1 ±)* 9 . . . ♘bd7 10 d4 exd4 11 ♘xd4 ♘xd5 = Hardicsay–Hector, Budapest 1989.

3 ♘c3 ♗c5 4 ♘f3 ♕f6 5 ♗e2 h6 6 0-0 ♘e7 7 d3 d6 8 ♗e3 ♗d4 9 ♗xd4 exd4 10 ♘b1 ♘g6 11 ♘bd2 ♘f4 =

Berg–Hector, Kerteminde 1991.

3 ...   d6

3 ... ♗b4+ 4 ♗d2 *(4 ♘c3!?)* 4 ...
♗xd2+ 5 ♕xd2 d6 6 ♘c3 ♘f6! *(6 ...
♘f6 7 f4 − 7 0-0-0 ♕e7 8 f4 exf4 9 ♕xf4
0-0 10 ♗d3 ♘bd7 11 ♘f3 ± Nei–Böök,
Tallinn 1969; 7 ... ♘bd7!? − 7 ... 0-0
8 ♘f3 cxd4 9 ♕xd4 c5 10 ♕d2 ♘c6 11
0-0-0 ± Tal–Nei, Pärnu 1971)* 7 ♘ge2
(7 0-0-0!?) 7 ... ♘e7 8 0-0-0 0-0 9 f4!?
♗g4 (=) 10 f5?! *(10 ♔b1?! exf4 11 h3
♗h5 12 ♖e1 ♗xe2 13 ♗xe2 c5 14 e5!?
dxe5 15 dxe5 ♕h6 16 ♗f3 ♘bc6 17
♗d5 ♖ad8 ∓ West–Miles, Sydney
1991)* 10 ... ♘c8! 11 dxe5?! *(11 d5
♘d7 =)* 11 ... dxe5 12 h3 ♗xe2 13
♗xe2 ♘a6 14 g4 ♕e7 15 g5 f6 16 ♖hg1
♘b6 ∓ Sax–Miles, Lugano 1989.

4 ♘f3!?   ...

4 ♘c3 *(4 d5)* 4 ... ♗e7 5 ♗e2 ♗g5!
6 ♗xg5 ♕xg5 7 dxe5 dxe5 8 ♘f3 ♕e7
9 h3 ♘d7 10 ♕d2 ♘8f6 11 g4? ♘c5! 12
♕e3 ♘fd7 13 h4 ♘e6 14 0-0-0 ♘f4 ∓
Morvay–Varnusz, Budapest 1991.

4 ...   ♗g4!

4 ... ♘bd7 leads to the Old Indian
Defence.

5 dxe5   ...

5 ♗e2 ♗xf3! *(5 ... ♘d7 6 ♘c3
♘gf6 7 0-0 ♗e7 8 ♗e3 0-0 9 ♘d2!
♗xe2 10 ♕xe2 ♕a5 11 g4! ± Mikenas–*

Flohr, 1938) 6 ♗xf3 ♗e7 7 0-0 ♘d7
(7 ... ♗g5) 8 ♘c3 Szabó–Navarovszky,
Budapest 1965, 8 ... ♗g5! =.

5 ...   ♗xf3
6 gxf3!   ...

6 ♕xf3?! dxe5 7 ♘c3 ♘f6 *(7 ...
♗c5 8 ♕g3 ♕f6 =Barcza)* 8 ♕g3
♘bd7 9 ♗e2 ♕c7 10 0-0 ♘c5 11 f4?!
♘cxe4! 12 ♘xe4 ♘xe4 13 ♕f3 ♗c5+
14 ♔h1 f5 ∓ Flórián–Barcza, Hungary
(ch) 1958.

6 ...   dxe5
7 ♕xd8+   ♔xd8
8 ♗h3!   ...

A dynamic equilibrium has developed. White's active bishops compensate for his structural weaknesses
(Kinzel–Barcza, Budapest 1961).
Instead 8 f4? is weaker: **8 ... ♘f6!**
9 fxe5?! ♘xe4 10 ♗g2 ♘c5 11 ♔e2
♘bd7 12 f4 ♔e7 13 ♗e3 ♖e8! 14 ♖d1
g5! ∓ Paoli–Barcza, Vienna 1961, or
8 ... f6!? 9 ♗h3 ♕c7 10 ♘c3 ♘a6 11
♗e3 ♖d8 12 ♔e2 ♗c5 13 ♖ag1 g6 14
fxe5 ♗xe3 15 ♔xe3 fxe5 16 ♖g5 ♖e8
= Seirawan–Nikolic, Tilburg 1990.

B2

2 ...   d5
3 exd5   ...

3 cxd5 cxd5 4 e5?! ♘c6 5 d4 ♗f5
6 ♗d3 ♗xd3 7 ♕xd3 e6 8 ♘f3 ♘ge7
9 0-0 ♘f5 10 ♘c3 ♗e7 11 a3 h5 =

Bogolyubov-Pfeiffer, 1952.

3 ...   cxd5
4 cxd5   ...

White's idea is to disturb the development of the black pieces while his opponent is winning back the pawn. Instead 4 d4 leads to the Panov Variation.

B2.1: 4 ... ♘f6
B2.2: 4 ... ♛xd5

B2.1

4 ...   ♘f6

Instead 4 ... a6 5 ♘c3 ♘f6 6 ♛a4+ ♘bd7 7 g3 g6 8 ♗g2 ♗g7 9 d4 0-0 10 ♘ge2 results in the position (unfavourable for Black) discussed in chapter 7.

B2.11: 5 ♛a4+
B2.12: 5 ♗b5+
B2.13: 5 ♘c3

B2.11

5 ♛a4+   ♘bd7

5 ... ♗d7 6 ♛b3 ♘a6 (6 ... ♛b6?! 7 ♗c4 ♘a6 8 ♘c3 ♘b4 9 ♘f3 ♛c5 10 0-0 ± F. Garcia) 7 d4 ♛b6 8 ♗c4 ♖c8 9 ♘c3 (9 ♘e2?! ♛b4+ 10 ♘d2 b5 11 a3 bxc4 ∓ Szabó-Sliva, Poland 1957) 9 ... ♘b4 10 ♗e2 ∞ (Filip).

6 ♘c3   g6
7 ♘f3!

Others:
a) 7 g4?! ♗g7 8 g5 ♘h5 9 d4 0-0 10 ♗e3 ♘b6 11 ♛a5 e6 12 dxe6 ♗xe6 ∓ Adamski-Lilienthal, Baku 1964.
b) 7 h4?! ♗g7 8 h5 ♘xh5 9 g4 ♘f6 10 g5 ♘g8 11 d4 ♔f8 12 ♗e3 ♘b6 13 ♛b3 ♗f5 ∓ Littleton-Filip, Praia da Rocha 1969.
c) 7 d6 exd6 8 ♘f3 ♗g7 9 ♗e2 0-0 10 d4 ♘b6 11 ♛d1 ♘bd5 12 0-0 h6 13 ♘xd5 ♘xd5 14 ♛b3 ♘e7 = Matulović-Udovčić, Yugoslavia (ch) 1963.
d) 7 g3 ♗g7 8 ♗g2 0-0 9 ♘ge2 ♘b6 *(9 ... e6!? 10 ♘f4 ♘b6 11 ♛b3 exd5 ∓ Musatov-Korchmar, USSR 1968, 10 d6 =)* 10 ♛b3 a5 11 ♘f4 a4 12 ♛b5 ♗d7 13 ♛b4 ♖e8 14 0-0 ♗f8 15 ♛d4 ♗f5 16 ♛e5 ♗g7 ∞ Suetin-Gurgenidze, Kislovodsk 1972.

7 ...   ♗g7

7 ... a6 8 ♗b5 ♖b8 9 ♗xd7+ ♗xd7 10 ♛b3 b5 11 d3! ♗g7 12 0-0±.

8 ♕b3 0-0

8 ... a6 (8 ... ♘b6) 9 a4 ♘b6 10 a5
♘bxd5 11 ♗c4 e6 12 0-0 0-0 13 d3
*(13 d4 b5 14 ♗xd5 ♘xd5 15 ♘xd5
♕xd5 16 ♕xd5 exd5 =)* 13 ... b5 14
axb6 ♘xb6 15 ♗e3 ♘fd7 *(15 ... ♘xc4
16 dxc4 ♕c7 17 ♗b6 ±)* 16 ♗xe6 fxe6
17 ♘g5 ♖e8 18 ♘xe6 ♖xe6 19
♕xe6+ ♔h8 ± F. Garcia-Andruet,
Las Palmas 1987.

9 ♗c4 ♘b6

9 ... a6 10 a4 ♕a5!? *(10 ... ♘c5 11
♕a3 ♕c7 12 0-0 ♗g4 13 d4 ♘cd7 14
♗e2 ±)* 11 ♖a3 ♘b6 ∞ (F. Garcia).

10 d3 ♘e8

10 ... ♗g4 11 ♘e5 ♗f5 12 0-0 ♖c8
13 ♖e1 ♕c7? 14 ♗f4! ♘h5? 15 ♘xg6
♘xf4 16 ♘xe7+ ♔h8 17 ♘xf5 ± (F.
Garcia).

11 h3!?

± (Fernandez Garcia-Jadoul, Pau
1988) — White retains his extra pawn,
but the brittleness of the central
white square complex gives Black
play for the pawn.

B2.12

5 ♗b5+ ...

See diagram.

5 ... ♘bd7

5 ... ♗d7 6 ♗c4 and now:
a) **6 ... b5?!** 7 ♕b3 ♘a6?! 8 d4 ♘c7
9 ♘f3 ♘cxd5 10 ♘e5 e6 11 0-0 ♖c8 ±
Thomas-Golombek, England 1949.

b) **6 ... ♕c7 7 d3** *(7 ♕e2?? /
7 ♕b3??, 7 ... b5! ∓; 7 ♕b3?! ♘xd5!
8 ♘c3 ♘xc3 9 bxc3 ♘c6 10 ♘f3 g6 =
Filip)* 7 ... b5 8 ♗b3 ♘a6 *(8 ... g6
9 ♘f3 ♗g7 10 0-0 0-0 11 ♖e1 ♗g4 12
h3 ♗xf3 13 ♕xf3 ♘a6 14 ♘c3 ♕d7 15
d6! ♕xd6 16 ♘xb5 ± Nunn-Iclicki,
Brussels 1985; 8 ... a5 9 a3 ♘a6 10
♘c3 g6 11 ♘f3 ♗g7 12 0-0 0-0 13 ♖e1
b4 ± Gseinov-Vdovin, USSR 1980)* 9
♘f3 ♘c5 10 0-0 (M. Garcia-Plachetka,
Kecskemét 1983) 10 ... a5! ∞.

6 ♘c3 a6

6 ... g6?! 7 d4 a6 8 ♗xd7+ ♕xd7
9 ♘f3 ♗g7 10 ♘e5 ♕d8 11 0-0 0-0 12
♕b3 ± Fernandez-Bass, Barcelona
1990.

7 ♕a4 ...

Alternative deviants:

a) 7 ♗c4 *(7 ♗a4?! b5 8 ♗c2 ♘b6 regains the pawn immediately)* 7 ... b5 8 ♗b3 ♗b7 9 ♘f3 b4 10 ♘a4 ♗xd5 11 d4 e6 12 ♗f4 ♗xb3 13 axb3 ♘d5 14 ♗g3 ♗e7 15 0-0 0-0 16 ♕e2 ♕c8 = Hodgson–G. Palermo, Brussels 1985.

b) 7 ♗xd7+?! ♕xd7 8 ♕b3 ♕g4! 9 ♘ge2 b5 10 0-0 e6 11 d4 ♗d6 = Varnusz–Flesch, Hungary (ch) 1963.

7 ...   ♖b8!

7 ... g6!? 8 ♘f3 (8 d4?! ♗g7 9 ♗e2 0-0 10 ♗f3 b5 11 ♕b3 ♘b6! 12 ♗g5 ♗b7 13 ♗xf6 ♗xf6 14 ♘ge2 ♕d7 15 0-0 ♖ad8 16 a4 ♘xa4! ∓ Korchnoi–Sveshnikov, Torcy 1990) 8 ... ♗g7 9 0-0 0-0 10 ♗xd7 ♗xd7 (10 ... ♕xd7 11 ♕xd7 ♗xd7 12 ♖e1 ♖fe8 13 d4 ♖ad8 14 ♗g5 ♗f5 15 ♗xf6 ♗xf6 16 ♘e5 ± Tringov–Pfleger, Moscow 1977) 11 ♕b3 b5 (11 ... ♕c7 12 d4 ♖ad8 13 ♗g5 h6 14 ♗h4 ♗c8 15 ♖fe1 ± Evdokimov–Gorenstein (corr) 1962) 12 d4 ♕a5 13 ♘e5 ♖ac8 14 ♗g5 ♖fd8 15 d6 ♗e6 16 d5 ♘xd5 17 ♘xd5 ♗xe5 18 ♘xe7+ ♔g7 19 ♕e3 ± Speelman–Kuijf, Beersheva 1987.

8 ♗xd7+   ♗xd7
9 ♕f4   e6!?

a) 9 ... g6? 10 ♘f3 ♗g7 11 0-0 0-0 12 d4 ♗f5 13 ♕h4! ♘xd5 14 ♗h6 ± (Kasparov).

b) 9 ... b5 10 a3 ♖d6 11 ♘f3 e6 12 ♘e5 exd5 13 ♘xd5 ♖e6 14 d4 ♗d6 15 ♘e3! ♕c7 16 ♗d2 ♗xe5 17 dxe5

♕xe5 18 ♕xe5 ♖xe5 19 ♗c3 ± Miles–Torre, Biel 1989.

10 ♘f3   exd5
11 0-0   ♗e6
12 d4   ♗d6
13 ♕h4   ♖c8
14 ♘g5   0-0 ±

15 ♘xe6 fxe6 16 ♕h3 ½:½ Chandler–Speelman, Hastings 1987/88.

B2.13

5 ♘c3   ...

5 ...   ♘xd5

5 ... g6!? 6 ♕b3 ♗g7 7 g3 b6!? 8 ♗g2 ♗b7 9 ♘ge2 e6 10 ♘f4 (10 0-0 exd5 11 ♘f4 0-0 12 ♘fxd5 ♘xd5 13 ♗xd5 ♗xd5 14 ♕xd5 ♕xd5 15 ♘xd5 ♘c6 ∞) 10 ... exd5!? (10 ... e5? 11 ♘fe2 0-0 12 0-0 ♘a6 13 d4 exd4 14 ♘xd4 ♘c5 15 ♕c4 ♖c8 16 ♘c6 ♕d7 17 ♕h4! ± Tal–Sveshnikov, Moscow 1990) 11 ♘fxd5 ♘xd5 12 ♘xd5 (12

♗xd5? ♕e7+) 12 ... 0-0 13 0-0 ♘c6 ∞
(Sveshnikov).

| 6 | ♘f3 | ... |

6 ♗c4 ♘b6 7 ♗b3 ♘c6 (7 ... g6
8 ♕f3 e6 9 ♘ge2 ♗g7 10 d4 ♘c6 11 0-0
0-0 12 ♖d1 ♘a5 13 ♗c2 ♗d7 14 ♗f4
♗c6 15 ♕g3 ♗d5 – Chiburdanidze-
S. Arkell – 16 ♖ac1 ♕d7 =) 8 ♘f3 ♗f5
9 d4 e6 10 0-0 ♗e7 11 ♗e3 0-0 12 h3?!
(12 d5! =) 12 ... ♗f6 13 ♕e2 ♘a5 14
♖fd1 ♘xb3 15 axb3 ♘d5 ∓ Honfi-
Varnusz, Hungary (ch) 1966.

| 6 ... | ♘c6 |

Others:
a) 6 ... e6 7 d4 ♘c6 8 ♗d3 ♗b4
9 0-0!? (9 ♗d2 or 9 ♕c2 see chapter 9)
9 ... ♘xc3 10 bxc3 ♗xc3 11 ♖b1 ♗b4
12 d5!? ♕xd5 13 ♕e2 ♗e7 14 ♗e4
♕d6 15 ♖d1 ♕c7 16 ♕c4 0-0 17 ♗f4
∞ Romero-Yudasin, Pamplona 1991.
b) 6 ... g6?! 7 ♕b3! ♘b6 8 ♗b5+
♗d7 9 ♘e5 e6 10 ♘e4 ♗e7 11 d4
♗xb5 12 ♕xb5+ ♘8d7 13 ♗h6 ±
Illescas-Kamsky, Manila 1990.
c) 6 ... ♘xc3! 7 bxc3 g6 8 h4?!
(8 d4!) 8 ... ♗g7! 9 h5 ♘c6 10 ♖b1
♕c7 11 ♗a3?! (11 d4) 11 ... ♗f5 ∓
Sokolov-Karpov, Linares (c) 1987.

| 7 ♗b5?! | ... |

7 d4! ♗g4 8 ♕b3 see chapter 8, or
7 ... e6 see chapter 9.

| 7 ... | e6 |

8	0-0	♗e7
9	d4	0-0
10	♖e1	...

The chances are equal: 10 ... ♗d7
11 ♘d5 exd5 12 ♗f4 ♗g4 13 ♗xc6
bxc6 14 ♖c1 ♖e8= Keres-Filip,
Moscow 1967.

B2.2

| 4 ... | ♕xd5 |
| 5 ♘c3 | ... |

| 5 ... | ♕d6!? |

Others:
a) After 5 ... ♕d8 6 d4 e6 White
can transpose into the variations examined in chapter 9. Also promising
is 7 ♗f4 ♘f6 8 ♘f3 ♘c6 9 ♗c4 ♗e7
10 0-0 0-0 11 a3 b6 12 b4 ♗b7 13 d5
exd5 14 ♘xd5 ♘xd5 15 ♗xd5 ♖c8 16
♖c1 ♔h8 17 ♕b3 ± Keres-Radovici,
Leipzig 1960.
b) 5 ... ♕a5 6 ♗c4 ♘f6 7 ♘f3 e6
8 0-0 ♗e7 9 d4 0-0 10 ♕e2 ♘c6 11 ♗f4

♗d7 12 ♖fd1 ± L. Steiner-Carls, 1928.

**6 d4   ♘f6
7 ♘ge2   . . .**

7 ♗c4 e6 8 ♘f3 ♘c6 9 0-0 ♗e7 10 ♘b5 ♕d8 11 ♗f4 = Makarichev-Speelman, Hastings 1979-80.

**7 . . .   e6
8 g3   ♗d7
9 ♗f4   ♕b6**

9 . . . ♕c6?! 10 d5! exd5 *(10 . . . ♘xd5 11 ♗g2 ±)* 11 ♗g2 ♗e6 12 0-0 ♕d7 13 ♗g5 ♗e7 14 ♘f4 ♘c6 15 ♗xf6 ♗xf6 16 ♘cxd5 ± A. Rodriguez-Dlugy, Athens 1984.

**10 ♗g2   ♗c6
11 d5!?   exd5**

11 . . . ♘xd5?! 12 ♗xd5! *(12 ♘xd5 ♗b4+! 13 ♘ec3 ♗xd5 14 ♗xd5 ♗xc3+ 15 bxc3 exd5 16 0-0 0-0 = Short-Dlugy, London 1986)* 12 . . . ♗xd5 *(12 . . . exd5 seems stronger)* 13 ♘xd5 exd5 14 0-0 ♗c5 15 ♘c3 ± Sax-Bass, Seville 1987.

**12 0-0   ♗b4
13 ♘xd5   . . .**

13 ♗g5 ♘bd7 14 ♘xd5 ♘xd5 15 ♗xd5 0-0 = Mestel-Dlugy, London 1986.

13 . . .   ♘xd5

**14 ♗xd5   0-0
15 ♗e3   ♕a5**

15 . . . ♗c5!? = F. Garcia.

16 ♘f4   ♗xd5

16. . . ♖d8? 17 ♗xf7+! ♔xf7 18 ♕b3+ ♔e7 19 a3 ♗d6 *(19 . . . ♗d2 20 ♕e6+ ♔f8 21 b4 +−)* 20 ♖fe1 ♔d7 21 ♖ad1 +−.

**17 ♕xd5   ♘c6
18 a3   ♕xd5
19 ♘xd5   ♗d6
20 ♖fd1!**

20 ♖ac1 ♖fd8 21 ♖fd1 ♗e5 22 b4 ♗b2 23 ♖b1 *(23 ♖c2 ♗xa3 24 ♖cd2 ♔h8 ∞)* 23 . . . ♗xa3 24 ♖d3 ♘e5! = F. Garcia-Hába, Thessalonika (ol) 1988.

**20 . . .   ♖fd8
21 b4**

± (Fernandez Garcia) − White dominates both in the centre and on the queenside.

ILLUSTRATIVE GAMES

76 SOKOLOV-KARPOV
Candidates' Match, Linares 1987
1 e4 c6 2 c4 d5 3 exd5 cxd5 4 cxd5 ♘f6 5 ♘c3 ♘xd5 6 ♘f3 ♘xc3 7 bxc3 g6 8 h4?! ♗g7! (8 . . . h6?! 9 ♕a4+ ♘d7 10 ♕d4 e5 11 ♕d5 ±) **9 h5 ♘c6 10 ♖b1**

♕c7 11 ♗a3?! ♗f5 12 ♖b5 a6 13 ♖c5 ♕d7 14 ♕b3 0-0 15 hxg6 hxg6 16 ♗c4 ♗f6! (16 ... b5? 17 ♗d5 ♘a5 18 ♕b4 ♘b7 19 ♘g5! ♘xc5 20 ♖h8+!!) 17 d4 b5! 18 ♗d5 ♘a5 19 ♕d1 ♘b7! 20 ♘e5 (20 ♕d2 ♘xc5 21 ♕h6 ♘d3+ 22 ♔f1 g5! wins) 20 ...♗xe5 21 dxe5 ♘xc5 22 ♕d4 ♘d3+ 23 ♔f1 ♕a7! 24 ♗xe7 (24 ♕h4 ♕xf2+) 24 ... ♕xd4 25 cxd4 ♘f4 **White resigned.**

77 KERES-RADOVICI
Leipzig 1960

1 e4 c6 2 c4 d5 3 exd5 cxd5 4 cxd5 ♕xd5 5 ♘c3 ♕d8?! 6 d4 e6 7 ♗f4 ♘f6 8 ♘f3 (8 ♗xb8?! ♖xb8 9 ♕a4+ ♗d7 10 ♕xa7 ♖a8 11 ♕xb7 ♖b8 ∞) 8 ... ♘c6 9 ♗c4 ♗e7 10 0-0 0-0-0 11 a3! b6 12 b4! ♗b7 13 d5!? (13 ♕d3 ♖c8 14 ♖ac1 ±) 13 ... exd5 14 ♘xd5 ♘xd5 15 ♗xd5 ♖c8 (15 ... ♘a5 16 ♗xb7 ♘xb7 17 ♕a4! ±) 16 ♖c1 ♔h8?! (16 ... ♗f6! 17 ♗d6 ♖e8 18 b5 ♘a5 19 ♗xb7 ♘xb7 29 ♗b4 ±) 17 ♕b3 ♘d4!? 18 ♖xc8 ♘xf3+ 19 ♕xf3 ♗xc8 20 ♖d1 ♕d7 21 h3! (21 ♗xf7 ♕f5 22 ♗d6 ♕xf3 23 gxf3 ♖xf7 24 ♗xe7 h6 =) 21 ... a5!? 22 ♗c4 ♕a7 (22 ... ♕a4 23 ♖e1! ±; 22 ... ♕f5 23 ♕e3 ♗e6 24 ♗d3 ±) 23 ♗d6 axb4 24 axb4 h6 25 ♕e4! ♗xd6 26 ♖xd6 ♔g8 27 ♕d4 ♕c7 28 ♖g6! **Black resigned.**

List of Illustrative Games

1. Efseev-Flohr, Odessa 1949
2. Tal-Vasyukov. USSR (ch) Tallinn 1965
3. Jansa-Kholmov, Budapest 1976
4. Tal-Petrosian, USSR (ch) Moscow 1973
5. Tal-Speelman, Subotica (izt) 1987
6. Simagin-Smyslov, Moscow 1963
7. Nunn-Tal, Brussels 1988
8. Blümich-Alekhine, Poland 1941
9. Bogolyubov-Alekhine, Salzburg 1942
10. Nunn-Arkell, London 1987
11. Khalifman-Seirawan, Wijk aan Zee 1991
12. Kudrin-King, Bayswater 1988
13. Forgacs-Duras, St. Petersburg 1909
14. Tal-Bronstein, USSR (ch) Leningrad 1974
15. Alekhine-Tartakower, Kecskemét 1927
16. Bilek-Bronstein, Budapest 1955
17. Am. Rodriguez-Pieterse, Dieren 1987
18. Bellon-Larsen, Las Palmas 1976
19. Peters-Seirawan, USA (ch) 1984
20. Browne-Bellon, Las Palmas 1977
21. Sokolsky-Bronstein, USSR (ch) 1944
22. Spassky-Karpov, Candidates' Match (6), Leningrad 1974
23. Keres-Golombek, Moscow 1956
24. Tal-Botvinnik, World Championship Match (9), Moscow 1960
25. Pogats-Portisch, Hungary (ch) 1961
26. Lasker-Lee, London 1899
27. Karpov-Hübner, Tilburg 1982
28. Karpov-Pomar, Nice (ol) 1974